Writing and Reading Across the Curriculum

TWELFTH EDITION

Laurence Behrens
University of California Santa Barbara

Leonard J. Rosen
Bentley University

PEARSON

Boston Columbus Indianapolis New York San Francisco Upper Saddle River
Amsterdam Cape Town Dubai London Madrid Milan Munich Paris Montréal Toronto
Delhi Mexico City São Paulo Sydney Hong Kong Seoul Singapore Taipei Tokyo

Why Do You Need This New Edition?

If you're wondering why you should buy this twelfth edition of *Writing and Reading Across the Curriculum*, here are 9 good reasons!

1. Over 60 brand-new readings span the disciplines and help stimulate your writing by offering new, engaging perspectives on all themes covered in the anthology.

2. To help you make the transition from the instruction of Part I to the anthology chapters in Part III, the twelfth edition offers a brand-new section of "Brief Takes"—three short chapters on "tiger moms," artificial intelligence (AI), and "Cinderella." A series of step-by-step exercises in these brief chapters prompts you to work on the kinds of academic writing discussed in the rhetoric chapters of Part I, giving you the confidence to proceed to the more complex readings and writing assignments in the full-length anthology chapters of Part III.

   a. The readings on AI introduce the so-called "singularity"—the point at which computer intelligence will outstrip human intelligence and usher in a new era.

   b. The chapter on "tiger moms" plunges you into the controversy surrounding the op-ed and the book by a mother who (in what she deemed the interest of her children) denied them playdates so that they could study relentlessly and master musical instruments.

3. The new anthology chapter "The Pursuit of Happiness" introduces you to the controversial new social science of positive psychology, an effort to study and teach behaviors that boost our sense of well-being.

4. The new anthology chapter "Have You Heard This? The Latest on Rumor" takes a close look at several fascinating rumors of recent decades and provides you with a number of approaches to analyzing these and other rumors—so that you can examine why they began, how they spread, and how they might be stopped.

5. This new edition offers a completely revised and reorganized chapter on analysis that gives you a thorough grounding in both the process of and rhetorical strategies for writing analyses. The chapter includes a new, excellent student example, "The Case of the Missing Kidney: An Analysis of Rumor." You can pursue the current, fascinating topic of rumor creation and spread more fully in Chapter 11.

6. The twelfth edition includes two new model papers: one, an analysis of a rumor about kidneys surgically extracted from drugged international travelers; the other, an explanatory synthesis on space elevators, a plan to raise objects to Earth orbit along a nanotube tether.

7. Roughly half of the anthology selections are new to the twelfth edition, with two returning chapters from the eleventh undergoing major revision. Nearly seventy percent of the reading selections for the chapter "The Changing Landscape of Work in the Twenty-First Century" are new to this edition. Also, roughly half of the readings in "Green Power" are new to this edition. Both chapters have been substantially reorganized into clusters of topical readings.

8. The remaining content chapters, "Obedience to Authority" and "New and Improved: Six Decades of Advertising," have also been updated, with two new reading selections in "Obedience" and several new print ads and TV commercials in "Advertising."

9. *VIDEO LINKS* allow readers to more fully explore aspects of the subject matter through videos readily available on YouTube and other sites. You will be directed to engaging interviews, dramatizations, animations, documentaries, news features, clips from feature films and TV shows, music, and more—all of which should deepen your understanding and enjoyment of the subject at hand.

PEARSON

To: Keiko and Charlotte

Senior Acquisitions Editor: Brad Potthoff
Project Manager: Paul Augustine Smith
Senior Marketing Manager: Sandra McGuire
Senior Supplements Editor: Donna Campion
Executive Digital Producer: Stefanie A. Snajder
Digital Manager: Janell Lantana
Digital Editor: Sara Gordus
Production Manager: Savoula Amanatidis
Project Coordination, Text Design, and Electronic Page Makeup: Integra
Cover Design Manager: Wendy Ann Fredericks
Cover Designer: Nancy Danahy
Photo Researcher: Jorgensen Fernandez
Senior Manufacturing Buyer: Roy L. Pickering, Jr.
Printer and Binder: Edwards Brothers Malloy
Cover Printer: Lehigh-Phoenix Color Corporation–Hagerstown

For permission to use copyrighted material, grateful acknowledgment is made to the copyright holders on pp. 673–676, which are hereby made part of this c opyright page.

Library of Congress Cataloging-in-Publication Data
Behrens, Laurence.
    Writing and reading across the curriculum/Laurence Behrens, Leonard J. Rosen.—12th ed.
        p. cm.
    Includes index.
    ISBN-13: 978-0-205-88543-5
    ISBN-10: 0-205-88543-8
        1. College readers.   2. Interdisciplinary approach in education—Problems, exercises, etc.
3. English language—Rhetoric—Problems, exercises, etc.   4. Academic writing—Problems,
exercises, etc. I. Rosen, Leonard J. II. Title.
    PE1417.B396 2012
    808′.0427—dc23

                                                                                    2012018286

10 9 8 7 6 5 4 3 2—EBM —15 14 13 12

www.pearsonhighered.com

Student Edition
ISBN-10:   0-205-88543-8
ISBN-13: 978-0-205-88543-5
A La Carte Edition
ISBN-10:   0-321-82887-9
ISBN-13: 978-0-321-82887-3

Detailed Contents

Chapter 2 Critical Reading and Critique   48

Chapter 6 Analysis   178

Part ▉▉ II ▉▉   Brief Takes   201

Chapter 7   Artificial Intelligence   203

For almost one hundred years, people have dreamed of intelligent robots—humanoid machines that clean our homes, serve our food, and generally relieve us of life's tedium. What had been a dream of science fiction writers such as Isaac Asimov (I, Robot, 1950) and directors such as Ridley Scott (Blade Runner, 1982) is now becoming a distinct possibility. Soon, writes futurist Raymond Kurzweil, we will see the "singularity": the point at which computers will become "not just intelligent but more intelligent than humans." At that point, "humanity—our bodies, our minds, our civilization—will be completely and irreversibly transformed."

Chapter 8   Fairy Tales: A Closer Look at "Cinderella"   226

More than seven hundred variants of this classic fairy tale exist in Europe, Africa, Asia, and North and South America. How could one simple story have spread so widely? Has "Cinderella" sprouted up everywhere independently—a phenomenon that suggests some universal quality of the human imagination? Or perhaps the tale has migrated with storytellers across continents, oceans, and centuries, changing form and successfully adapting to different cultures in the course of its far-ranging journey? In this chapter, we offer five of the multitudinous versions of "Cinderella"—some known to you, others that you'll find altogether strange.

Chapter 9 The Roar of the Tiger Mom   **258**

"Here are some things my daughters, Sophia and Louisa, were never allowed to do," announces Yale law school professor Amy Chua in an op-ed titled "Why Chinese Mothers Are Superior." Among her list of prohibitions: having a playdate, watching TV, playing computer games, and getting any grade less than A. Chua's piece provoked a deluge of responses from readers and professional commentators, some outraged, some cheering her on. Here is a sampling of some of those responses, part of what became a national debate over the best way to raise children to become successful adults.

Part ▍▍▍ An Anthology of Readings   287

Chapter 10 The Changing Landscape of Work in the Twenty-First Century   289

Chapter 11   Have You Heard This? The Latest on Rumor   340

Chapter 12 The Pursuit of Happiness   408

Is solar power the energy of the future? It is certainly changing the landscape. As Los Angeles Times reporter Marla Dickerson reports, "Rows of gigantic mirrors covering an area bigger than two football fields have sprouted alongside almond groves near California 99." But can solar energy provide the quantities of energy that are needed to significantly reduce our dependence upon fossil fuels? And can it compete in the marketplace without extensive government support? Such questions are considered by the authors of the three selections in this cluster.

The residents of an island off the coast of Denmark generate all of the electrical energy they need for their homes and farms from wind power. How viable a model is the island of Samsø for the United States? Two analysts discuss the practicalities of wind turbines for large-scale energy generation.

During most of the twentieth century, the gasoline-powered internal combustion engine reigned supreme. That situation is rapidly changing. The success of hybrids such as the Toyota Prius, the advent of plug-in hybrids such as the Chevrolet Volt and all-electric Nissan Leaf, and improvements in battery technology may signal the end of the internal combustion era. In this cluster, two experts in energy issues discuss the prospects for the electric car.

Chapter 14   New and Improved: Six Decades of Advertising   548

"[A]n advertising message contains something primary and primitive, an emotional appeal, that in effect is the thin edge of the wedge, trying to find its way into a mind." Advertisements are designed to appeal to the "unfulfilled urges and motives swirling in the bottom half of our minds."

Chapter 15   Obedience to Authority   619

Preface for Instructors

When *Writing and Reading Across the Curriculum* was first published in 1982, it was—viewed from one angle—an experiment. We hoped to prove our hypothesis that both students and teachers would respond favorably to a composition reader organized by the kinds of specific topics that were typically studied in general education courses.

The response was both immediate and enthusiastic. Instructors found the topics in that first edition of *WRAC* both interesting and teachable, and students appreciated the links that such topics suggested to the courses they were taking concurrently in the humanities, the social sciences, and the sciences. Readers also told us how practical they found our "summary, synthesis, and critique" approach to writing college-level papers. Instructors, and students as well, welcomed the addition of "analysis" to our coverage in Part I of the ninth edition.

In developing each successive edition of *WRAC*, we have been guided by the same principle: to retain the essential multidisciplinary character of the text, while providing ample new topics and individual readings to keep it fresh and timely. Some topics have proven particularly enduring—our "Cinderella" and "Obedience" chapters have been fixtures of *WRAC* since the first edition. But we take care to make sure that at least half of the book is completely new every time, both by extensively revising existing chapters and by creating new ones. While we have retained an emphasis on summary, critique, synthesis, and analysis, we continue to develop content on such issues as the process of writing and argumentation that addresses the issues and interests of today's classrooms.

WHAT'S NEW IN THIS EDITION?

Students will benefit from a variety of new content and features, including:

- A Pearson e-Text version of WRAC, available in MyCompLab.
- New student model papers in the "Critique," "Explanatory Synthesis," and "Analysis" chapters.
- A completely revised and reorganized "Analysis" chapter.
- Over sixty-five new readings throughout the book.
- Search-term referrals throughout to relevant online text and video sources.
- A new Part II, "Brief Takes," consists of three mini-anthology practice chapters, featuring step-by-step exercises to help students transition from the rhetorical instruction of Part I to the more complex readings and writing assignments in the full-length anthology chapters of Part III.
- A new anthology chapter, "The Pursuit of Happiness," introducing students to the social science of positive psychology.

- A new anthology chapter, "Have You Heard This? The Latest on Rumor," featuring numerous examples of rumors old and new, together with theories about how and why rumors originate and spread.
- Major revisions to two returning chapters, "The Changing Landscape of Work in the Twenty-First Century" (nearly seventy percent new readings) and "Green Power" (roughly half new readings).
- An updated "Advertising" chapter with several new print ads and TV commercials.
- A new section of "Video Links": referrals to online videos related to the subject matter of textual sources for virtually every chapter in the book.

Additional details on these new features are presented below.

WRAC IN THE DIGITAL AGE

The present edition marks a landmark development: for the first time, *Writing and Reading Across the Curriculum* is available in both print and digital versions. On a computer, iPad, or other tablet device, you can access the contents of this volume as an eBook. As you've no doubt already discovered, increased portability and easier searchability are only two of the significant advantages offered by digital books. But whether paper or virtual, WRAC increasingly draws upon online text and video resources to supplement the anthology materials already provided with the basic text. To access such resources, you will be directed to a Web site or to a search engine such as Google or Bing and asked to enter a particular set of search terms. And of course, by adjusting the search terms—by making them more or less restrictive or by slightly varying the key terms—you gain access to an almost inexhaustible set of resources on the subject of the chapter. These resources will allow you to find related materials, conduct additional research, and enhance your understanding of the subject matter.

STRUCTURE

Like its predecessors, the twelfth edition of *Writing and Reading Across the Curriculum* is divided into a rhetoric and an anthology of readings. With this edition, however, the anthology of readings is further subdivided into two parts, the first of these serving as a kind of bridge between the rhetoric and the anthology. (See "Part II: New Feature: Brief Takes," p. xxiv.) Part I introduces the strategies of summary, critique, synthesis, and analysis. We take students step-by-step through the process of writing papers based on source material, explaining and demonstrating how summaries, critiques, syntheses, and analyses can be generated from the kinds of readings students will encounter later in the book—and throughout their academic careers. Parts II and III consist of nine subject chapters drawn from both academic and professional disciplines. Each subject is not only interesting in its own right, but is also representative of the kinds of topics typically studied during the course of an undergraduate education. We also believe that students and teachers will discover connections among the thematic chapters of this edition that further enhance opportunities for writing, discussion, and inquiry.

CONTINUED FOCUS ON ARGUMENTATION

Part I of *Writing and Reading Across the Curriculum* is designed to prepare students for college-level assignments across the disciplines. The twelfth edition continues the previous edition's strengthened emphasis on the writing process, and on argument in particular. In treating argument, we emphasize the following:

- **The Elements of Argument: Claim, Support, Assumption.** This section adapts the Toulmin approach to argument to the kinds of readings that students will encounter in Parts II and III of the text.
- **The Three Appeals of Argument:** *Logos, Ethos, Pathos.* This discussion may be used to analyze and develop arguments in the readings that students will encounter in Parts II and III of the book.
- **Developing and Organizing the Support for Your Arguments.** This section helps students to mine source materials for facts, expert opinions, and examples that will support their arguments.
- **Annotated Student Argument Paper.** A sample student paper highlights and discusses argumentative strategies that a student writer uses in drafting and developing a paper.

PART I: NEW APPARATUS, TOPICS, READINGS, AND STUDENT PAPERS

Chapter 2: Critical Reading and Critique

Chapter 2 features a new model critique based on Charles Krauthammer's "The Moon We Left Behind," an argument against the cancellation of the manned lunar program.

Chapter 3: Thesis, Introduction, Conclusion

Chapter 3 has been reorganized so that it now begins with a discussion of theses, followed by discussions of introductions and conclusions.

Chapter 4: Explanatory Synthesis

Chapter 4 features a new model explanatory synthesis on the space elevator, a plan (considered feasible by NASA) to lift objects to earth orbit along a thin nanotube ribbon. The synthesis builds on several articles in the chapter itself (as well as on other sources) and explains the physics of the space elevator, obstacles to building the structure, and possible consequences—positive and negative.

Chapter 5: Argument Synthesis

The model argument synthesis in Chapter 5 has been revised to show a current example—airport security pat-downs—of how the issue of individual privacy versus public safety will follow students off campus, into the wider world.

Chapter 6: Analysis

Chapter 6, on analysis, has been almost completely reorganized and rewritten. The new model analysis in this chapter applies a classic theory of rumor propagation to a particular rumor that some years ago went "viral" on the Internet and raised fears of travelers in foreign lands being drugged and surgically deprived of their kidneys. Note: The subject of this model analysis—rumor—is the basis of a new full-length subject chapter in the anthology section in Part III.

PART II: NEW FEATURE: BRIEF TAKES

Chapter 7: Artificial Intelligence

Chapter 8: Fairy Tales: A Closer Look at "Cinderella"

Chapter 9: The Roar of the Tiger Mom

In this edition, we are delighted to offer an entirely new feature to *Writing and Reading Across the Curriculum*: a series of "brief takes" designed to allow students to test their skills at summary, critique, synthesis, and analysis before immersing themselves in the full-length chapters of the anthology. As a transition from the rhetoric of Part I to the anthology section of Part III, "Brief Takes" offers three mini-chapters on subjects of interest, including the latest developments in artificial intelligence and a look at the recent and intensely heated debate over "tiger moms" (that is, parents heavily invested in their child's academic and other achievements). A scaled-down version of our perennial favorite, "Cinderella," rounds out the first set of "Brief Takes." Each of these mini-chapters consists of between five to seven readings, fewer than in our standard chapters, and is accompanied by a set of sequential writing exercises distinct from those in the chapters of Part III. Together, the introduction, readings, and writing exercises of each "brief take" chapter run no more than twenty-five to thirty pages, about a third the length of the typical Part III chapter. We see working on one or more of these brief takes as a kind of "warm-up" exercise for the more intensive intellectual activities involved in tackling the full-length chapters.

PART III: NEW THEMATIC CHAPTERS

As in earlier editions, the anthology section of *Writing and Reading Across the Curriculum* provides students with opportunities to practice the skills of summary, synthesis, critique, and analysis that they have learned in Part I. In addition to the three new "Brief Takes" chapters, we have prepared two new thematic chapters for Part III of the twelfth edition of *WRAC*.

Chapter 11: Have You Heard This? The Latest on Rumor

Almost everyone deplores rumors, yet almost everyone has helped start or spread them sometime in their lives. Our new chapter on rumors includes multiple perspectives on this uniquely and universally human phenomenon. The chapter is concerned with how rumors operate: how they start, mutate, and spread; how they help us make sense of the world; why we believe them; how we attempt to counteract them. This chapter builds on the model student analysis in Chapter 6, which examines how the notorious missing-kidney rumor follows some of the basic rules of rumor propagation and adaptation to different locales.

Chapter 12: The Pursuit of Happiness

"Everyone thinks they know something about what happiness is," writes one philosopher in this new anthology chapter, but "very few people manage to convince anyone else that they are right." And yet for thousands of years we have tried to do just that. Most recently, efforts to define this most fundamental of human attributes has moved from the province of philosophers, religious thinkers, and poets to the laboratories of psychologists. In "The Pursuit of Happiness," we introduce students to the young social science of *positive psychology*. Building on the pioneering work of Abraham Maslow (1908–1970), scholars such as Martin Seligman, Mihaly Csikszentmihalyi, and Daniel Gilbert hope to complement psychology's traditional focus on mental *dis*order by investigating conditions that "lead to well-being … [and] positive individuals." Their efforts to understand happiness—and some rather heated challenges to their efforts—provide the focus of this chapter.

PART III: REVISED THEMATIC CHAPTERS

Four anthology chapters are carried over from the eleventh edition. Many of the reading selections for each, however, are new to this edition.

Chapter 10: The Changing Landscape of Work in the Twenty-First Century

Retained from the eleventh edition, "The Changing Landscape of Work in the Twenty-First Century" continues to offer students a wealth of information and informed opinion on how the workplace they are about to enter already differs markedly from the workplaces of their parents and grandparents. Emphasizing the promise and perils of the new economy, this chapter continues to draw from a number of disciplines: economics, sociology, public policy, business, and investigative journalism. Students will consider questions on the changing nature of work, the role of technology in these changes, and the security of jobs they intend to pursue upon graduation. Because the data on employment and the trends emerging from this data are in constant flux, we have revised extensively to keep pace with these changes.

Chapter 13: Green Power

A growing body of evidence points to a global climate crisis caused by massive levels of carbon dioxide and other greenhouse gases that are being ceaselessly spewed into the atmosphere by the burning of coal and oil. Reducing our dependence upon these fossil fuels involves developing renewable sources of clean energy that can power our cars, our homes, our businesses, and our public buildings. In this chapter, students will consider the views of scientists, environmentalists, businesspeople, members of a government task force, and reporters about the nature of the problem and about ways of addressing it. This chapter has been re-organized and includes seven new readings, including a cluster on the viability of nuclear power in the wake of the nuclear accident at Fukushima after the 2011 earthquake and tsunami.

Chapter 14: New and Improved: Six Decades of Advertising

The centerpiece of this chapter continues to be a set of two portfolios of memorable advertising: twenty-two full-page print ads and twenty-one TV commercials. The print ads, which have appeared in popular American magazines since the mid-1940s, promote cigarettes, liquor and beer, automobiles, and beauty and cleaning products. The section on TV commercials refers students to historical and current gems of the genre viewable on YouTube. New examples of ads in each category are included in this edition. Like genetic markers, print advertisements and TV commercials are key indicators of our consumerism, our changing cultural values, and our less variable human psychology. Students will find this material both entertaining and well suited for practicing and honing their skills of analysis.

Chapter 15: Obedience to Authority

The "Obedience" chapter builds on the profoundly disturbing Milgram obedience experiments and, in this edition, directs students to dramatic online videos documenting the famous mock-prison experiment at Stanford University. We also add a selection on situational ethics by journalist Jonah Lehrer and an op-ed by *New York Times* columnist David Brooks, who explores how those who hold positions of authority depend on informed followers.

NEW FEATURE: VIDEO LINKS

Video Links for most chapters appear in a separate section at the end of the text. They allow readers to more fully explore aspects of the subject matter through videos readily available on YouTube and other sites. Students will be directed to engaging interviews, dramatizations, animations, documentaries, news features, clips from feature films and TV shows, music, and more—all of which should deepen their understanding and enjoyment of the subject at hand.

RESOURCES FOR TEACHERS AND STUDENTS

The *Instructor's Manual* for the twelfth edition of *Writing and Reading Across the Curriculum* provides sample syllabi and course calendars, chapter summaries, classroom ideas for writing assignments, introductions to each set of readings, and answers to review questions. ISBN: 0-321-83859-9.

The Web site *MyCompLab* integrates the market-leading instruction, multimedia tutorials, and exercises for writing, grammar, and research that users have come to identify with the program, along with a new online composing space and new assessment tools. The result is a revolutionary application that offers a seamless and flexible teaching and learning environment built specifically for writers. Created by faculty and students across the country, the new MyCompLab provides help for writers in the context of their writing, with: instructor and peer commenting functionality; proven tutorials and exercises for writing, grammar, and research; an e-portfolio; an assignment-builder; a bibliography tool; tutoring services; and a gradebook and course management organization created specifically for writing classes. Visit www. mycomplab.com, <www.mycomplab.com/> for information.

An eBook version of *Writing and Reading Across the Curriculum* is also available in MyCompLab. This online version integrates the many resources of MyCompLab, such as extra help with composing, researching, and documenting sources, thereby creating an enriched, interactive learning experience for writing students.

ACKNOWLEDGMENTS

We have benefited over the years from the suggestions and insights of many teachers—and students—across the country. We would especially like to thank these reviewers of the twelfth edition: David Bordelon, Ocean County College; Michelle LaFrance, University of Massachusetts Dartmouth; Meg Matheny, Jefferson Community and Technical College, Southwest; Catherine Olson, Lone Star College-Tomall; Scott Vander Ploeg, Madisonville Community College; Jeff Pruchnic, Wayne State University; and Ellen Sorg, Owens Community College.

We would also like to thank the following reviewers for their help in the preparation of past editions: Angela Adams, Loyola University Chicago; James Allen, College of DuPage; Fabián Álvarez, Western Kentucky University; Chris Anson, North Carolina State University; Phillip Arrington, Eastern Michigan University; Anne Bailey, Southeastern Louisiana University; Carolyn Baker, San Antonio College; Bob Brannan, Johnson County Community College; Joy Bashore, Central Virginia Community College; Nancy Blattner, Southeast Missouri State University; Mary Bly, University of California, Davis; Laurel Bollinger, University of Alabama in Huntsville; Paul Buczkowski, Eastern Michigan University; Jennifer Bullis, Whatcom Community College; Paige Byam, Northern Kentucky University; Susan Callendar, Sinclair Community College; Anne Carr, Southeast Community College; Jeff Carroll, University of Hawaii; Joseph Rocky Colavito, Northwestern State University; Michael Colonneses, Methodist College; James A. Cornette, Christopher Newport University; Timothy Corrigan, Temple University; Kathryn J. Dawson, Ball State University; Cathy Powers Dice, University of Memphis; Kathleen Dooley, Tidewater Community College; Judith Eastman, Orange Coast College; David Elias, Eastern Kentucky University; Susan Boyd English, Kirkwood Community College; Kathy Evertz, University of Wyoming; Kathy Ford, Lake Land College; University of Wyoming; Wanda Fries, Somerset Community College; Bill Gholson, Southern Oregon University; Karen Gordon, Elgin Community College; Deborah Gutschera, College of DuPage; Lila M. Harper, Central Washington University; M. Todd Harper, University of Louisville; Kip Harvigsen, Ricks College; Michael Hogan,

Southeast Missouri State University; Sandra M. Jensen, Lane Community College; Anita Johnson, Whatcom Community College; Mark Jones, University of Florida; Daven M. Kari, Vanguard University; Jane Kaufman, University of Akron; Kerrie Kawasaki-Hull, Ohlone College; Rodney Keller, Ricks College; Walt Klarner, Johnson County Community College; Jeffery Klausman, Whatcom Community College; Alison Kuehner, Ohlone College; William B. Lalicker, West Chester University; Dawn Leonard, Charleston Southern University; Lindsay Lewan, Arapahoe Community College; Clifford L. Lewis, U Mass Lowell; Signee Lynch, Whatcom Community College; Jolie Martin; San Francisco State University; Krista L. May, Texas A&M University; Stella Nesanovich, McNeese State University; Kathy Mendt, Front Range Community College–Larimer Campus; RoseAnn Morgan, Middlesex County College; David Moton, Bakersfield College; Roark Mulligan, Christopher Newport University; Joan Mullin, University of Toledo; Susie Paul, Auburn University at Montgomery; Thomas Pfau, Bellevue Community College; Aaron Race, Southern Illinois University–Carbondale; Nancy Redmond, Long Beach City College; Deborah Reese, University of Texas at Arlington; Alison Reynolds, University of Florida; Priscilla Riggle, Bowling Green State University; Jeanette Riley, University of New Mexico; Robert Rongner, Whatcom Community College; Sarah C. Ross, Southeastern Louisiana University; Deborah L. Ruth, Owensboro Community & Technical College; Amy Rybak, Bowling Green State University; Raul Sanchez, University of Utah; Rebecca Shapiro, Westminster College; Mary Sheldon, Washburn University; Horacio Sierra, University of Florida; Philip Sipiora, University of Southern Florida; Joyce Smoot, Virginia Tech; Bonnie A. Spears, Chaffey College; Bonnie Startt, Tidewater Community College; R. E. Stratton, University of Alaska–Fairbanks; Katherine M. Thomas, Southeast Community College; Victor Villanueva, Washington State University; Deron Walker, California Baptist University; Jackie Wheeler, Arizona State University; Pat Stephens Williams, Southern Illinois University at Carbondale; Kristin Woolever, Northeastern University; Angela Adams, Loyola University Chicago; Fabián Álvarez, Western Kentucky University; Laurel Bollinger, University of Alabama in Huntsville; David Elias, Eastern Kentucky University; Wanda Fries, Somerset Community College; Kerrie Kawasaki-Hull, Ohlone College; Kathy Mendt, Front Range Community College, Larimer Campus; RoseAnn Morgan, Middlesex County College; Alison Reynolds, University of Florida; Deborah L. Ruth, Owensboro Community & Technical College; and Mary R. Seel, Broome Community College.

We gratefully acknowledge the work of Michael Behrens, who made significant contributions to the "Argument Synthesis" chapter.

The authors also wish to thank Robert Krut, of the University of California, Santa Barbara Writing Program, for his invaluable contributions to the new "Rumor" chapter and to the revised "Green Power" and "Advertising" chapters.

Finally, special thanks to Brad Pothoff, Suzanne Phelps Chambers, Paul Smith, Lisa Yakmalian, Jorgensen Fernandez, and Martha Beyerlein for helping shepherd the manuscript through the editorial and production process. And our continued gratitude to Joe Opiela, longtime friend, supporter, and publisher.

LAURENCE BEHRENS
LEONARD J. ROSEN

A Note to the Student

Your sociology professor asks you to write a paper on attitudes toward the homeless population of an urban area near your campus. You are expected to consult books, articles, Web sites, and other online sources on the subject, and you are also encouraged to conduct surveys and interviews.

Your professor is making a number of assumptions about your capabilities. Among them:

- that you can research and assess the value of relevant sources;
- that you can comprehend college-level material, both print and digital;
- that you can use theories and principles learned from one set of sources as tools to investigate other sources (or events, people, places, or things);
- that you can synthesize separate but related sources;
- that you can intelligently respond to such material.

In fact, these same assumptions underlie practically all college writing assignments. Your professors will expect you to demonstrate that you can read and understand not only textbooks, but also critical articles and books, primary sources, Internet sources, online academic databases, and other material related to a particular subject of study. An example: For a paper on the changing nature of the workforce in the twenty-first century, you would probably look to articles and Internet sources for the latest information. Using an online database, you might find articles in such journals as *The Green Labor Journal, The Economic Journal*, and *The Journal of Labor Research*, as well in as leading newspapers and magazines. A Web search might lead you to the Occupational Employment Statistics homepage (http://www.bls.gov/oes/), which is published online by the Bureau of Labor Statistics. You'd be expected to assess the relevance of such sources to your topic and to draw from them the information and ideas you need. It's even possible that the final product of your research and reading wouldn't be a conventional paper at all, but rather a Web site that alerts fellow students to job categories that experts think are expanding or disappearing.

You might, for a different class, be assigned a research paper on the films of director Wes Anderson. To get started, you might consult your film studies textbook, biographical sources on Anderson, and anthologies of criticism. Instructor and peer feedback on a first draft might lead you to articles in both popular magazines (such as *Time*) and scholarly journals (such as *Literature/Film Quarterly*); you might also consult relevant Web sites (such as the "Internet Movie Database," http://us.imdb.com).

These two example assignments are very different, of course, but the skills you need to work with them are the same. You must be able to research relevant sources. You must be able to read and comprehend these sources. You must be able to perceive the relationships among several pieces of source material. And you must be able to apply your own critical judgments to these various materials.

Writing and Reading Across the Curriculum provides you with the opportunity to practice the essential college-level skills we have just outlined and the forms of writing associated with them, namely:

- the *summary*
- the *critique*
- the *synthesis*
- the *analysis*

Each chapter of Parts II and III of this text represents a subject from a particular area of the academic curriculum: Sociology, Economics, Psychology, Business, Public Policy, Computer Science, Folklore, and Philosophy. These chapters—dealing with such topics as rumor, the pursuit of happiness, obedience to authority, and advertising—illustrate the types of material you will study in your other courses.

Questions following the readings will allow you to practice typical college writing assignments. "Review Questions" help you recall key points of content. "Discussion and Writing Suggestions" ask you for personal, sometimes imaginative, responses to the readings. "Synthesis Activities" allow you to practice assignments of the type that are covered in detail in Part I of this book. For instance, you may be asked to *summarize* the Milgram experiment and the reactions to it, or to *compare and contrast* a controlled experiment with a real-life (or fictional) situation. Finally, "Research Activities" ask you to go beyond the readings in this text in order to conduct your own independent research on these subjects.

In this book, you'll find articles and essays written by literary critics, sociologists, psychologists, lawyers, folklorists, political scientists, journalists, and specialists from other fields. Our aim is that you become familiar with the various subjects and styles of academic writing and that you come to appreciate the interrelatedness of knowledge. Happiness can be studied by philosophers, psychologists, sociologists, economists, geographers, religious thinkers, and poets. Human activity and human behavior are classified into separate subjects only for convenience. The novel you read in your literature course may be able to shed some light upon an assigned article for your economics course—and vice versa.

We hope, therefore, that your writing course will serve as a kind of bridge to your other courses and that, as a result of this work, you will become more skillful at perceiving relationships among diverse topics. Because it involves such critical and widely applicable skills, your writing course may well turn out to be one of the most valuable—and one of the most interesting—of your academic career.

LAURENCE BEHRENS
LEONARD J. ROSEN

P art

I

How to Write Summaries, Critiques, Syntheses, and Analyses

1

Summary, Paraphrase, and Quotation

After completing this chapter, you will be able to:

LO 1.1   Explain what a summary is.

LO 1.2   Describe how prior knowledge and frame of reference can affect the objectivity of a summary.

LO 1.3   Identify the situations in which a summary would be useful.

LO 1.4   Apply systematic strategies as you read in order to prepare a summary.

LO 1.5   Write summaries of varying lengths by reading critically, dividing a passage into stages of thought, writing a thesis, and drafting.

LO 1.6   Determine the appropriate length for your summary.

LO 1.7   Write a summary of visual presentations, including charts, graphs, and tables.

LO 1.8   Write a paraphrase to clarify difficult or confusing source material.

LO 1.9   Know how to use both direct and indirect quotations and to integrate them into your writing.

LO 1.10 Avoid plagiarism by citing sources and using your own words and sentence structure.

WHAT IS A SUMMARY?

The best way to demonstrate that you understand the information and the ideas in any piece of writing is to compose an accurate and clearly written summary of that piece. By a *summary* we mean a *brief restatement, in your own words, of the content of a passage* (a group of paragraphs, a chapter, an article, a book). This restatement should focus on the *central idea* of the passage. The briefest of summaries (one or two sentences) will do no more than this. A longer, more complete summary will indicate, in condensed form, the main points in the passage that support or explain the central idea. It will reflect the order in which these points are presented and the emphasis given to them. It may even include some important examples from the passage. But it will not include minor details. It will not repeat points simply for the purpose of emphasis. And it will not contain any of your own opinions or conclusions. A good summary, therefore, has three central qualities: *brevity*, *completeness*, and *objectivity*.

CAN A SUMMARY BE OBJECTIVE?

Objectivity could be difficult to achieve in a summary. By definition, writing a summary requires you to select some aspects of the original and leave out others. Since deciding what to select and what to leave out calls for your personal judgment, your summary really is a work of interpretation. And, certainly, your interpretation of a passage may differ from another person's.

One factor affecting the nature and quality of your interpretation is your *prior knowledge* of the subject. For example, if you're attempting to summarize an anthropological article and you're a novice in that field, then your summary of the article will likely differ from that of your professor, who has spent twenty years studying this particular area and whose judgment about what is more or less significant is undoubtedly more reliable than your own. By the same token, your personal or professional *frame of reference* may also affect your interpretation. A union representative and a management representative attempting to summarize the latest management offer would probably come up with two very different accounts. Still, we believe that in most cases it's possible to produce a reasonably objective summary of a passage if you make a conscious, good-faith effort to be unbiased and to prevent your own feelings on the subject from coloring your account of the author's text.

USING THE SUMMARY

In some quarters, the summary has a bad reputation—and with reason. Summaries are often provided by writers as substitutes for analyses. As students, many of us have summarized books that we were supposed to *review critically*. All the same, the summary does have a place in respectable college work. First, writing a summary is an excellent way to understand what you read. This in itself is an important goal of academic study. If you don't understand your source material, chances are you won't be able to refer to it usefully in a paper. Summaries help you understand what you read because they force you to put the text into your own words. Practice with writing summaries also develops your general writing habits, because a good summary, like any other piece of good writing, is clear, coherent, and accurate.

Second, summaries are useful to your readers. Let's say you're writing a paper about the McCarthy era in the United States, and in part of that paper

WHERE DO WE FIND WRITTEN SUMMARIES?

Here are just a few of the types of writing that involve summary:

Academic Writing

- **Critique papers** summarize material in order to critique it.
- **Synthesis papers** summarize to show relationships between sources.
- **Analysis papers** summarize theoretical perspectives before applying them.
- **Research papers:** Note-taking and reporting research require summary.
- **Literature reviews:** Overviews of work are presented in brief summaries.
- **Argument papers** summarize evidence and opposing arguments.
- **Essay exams** demonstrate understanding of course materials through summary.

Workplace Writing

- **Policy briefs** condense complex public policy.
- **Business plans** summarize costs, relevant environmental impacts, and other important matters.
- **Memos, letters, and reports** summarize procedures, meetings, product assessments, expenditures, and more.
- **Medical charts** record patient data in summarized form.
- **Legal briefs** summarize relevant facts and arguments of cases.

you want to discuss Arthur Miller's *The Crucible* as a dramatic treatment of the subject. A summary of the plot would be helpful to a reader who hasn't seen or read—or who doesn't remember—the play. Or perhaps you're writing a paper about the politics of recent American military interventions. If your reader isn't likely to be familiar with American actions in Kosovo and Afghanistan, it would be a good idea to summarize these events at some early point in the paper. In many cases (an exam, for instance), you can use a summary to demonstrate your knowledge of what your professor already knows; when writing a paper, you can use a summary to inform your professor about some relatively unfamiliar source.

Third, summaries are required frequently in college-level writing. For example, on a psychology midterm, you may be asked to explain Carl Jung's theory of the collective unconscious and to show how it differs from Sigmund Freud's theory of the personal unconscious. You may have read about Jung's theory in your textbook or in a supplementary article, or your instructor may have outlined it in her lecture. You can best demonstrate your understanding of it by summarizing it. Then you'll proceed to contrast it with Freud's theory—which, of course, you must also summarize.

THE READING PROCESS

It may seem to you that being able to tell (or retell) in summary form exactly what a passage says is a skill that ought to be taken for granted in anyone who can read at high school level. Unfortunately, this is not so: For all kinds of reasons, people don't always read carefully. In fact, it's probably safe to say that usually they don't. Either they read so inattentively that they skip over words, phrases, or even whole sentences, or, if they do see the words in front of them, they see them without registering their significance.

When a reader fails to pick up the meaning and implications of a sentence or two, usually there's no real harm done. (An exception: You could lose credit on an exam or paper because you failed to read or to realize the significance of a crucial direction by your instructor.) But over longer stretches—the paragraph, the section, the article, or the chapter—inattentive or haphazard reading interferes with your goals as a reader: to perceive the shape of the argument, to grasp the central idea, to determine the main points that compose it, to relate the parts of the whole, and to note key examples. This kind of reading takes a lot more energy and determination than casual reading. But in the long run it's an energy-saving method because it enables you to retain the content of the material and to draw upon that content in your own responses. In other words, it allows you to develop an accurate and coherent written discussion that goes beyond summary.

CRITICAL READING FOR SUMMARY

- *Examine the context.* Note the credentials, occupation, and publications of the author. Identify the source in which the piece originally appeared. This information helps illuminate the author's perspective on the topic he or she is addressing.
- *Note the title and subtitle.* Some titles are straightforward; the meanings of others become clearer as you read. In either case, titles typically identify the topic being addressed and often reveal the author's attitude toward that topic.
- *Identify the main point.* Whether a piece of writing contains a thesis statement in the first few paragraphs or builds its main point without stating it up front, look at the entire piece to arrive at an understanding of the overall point being made.
- *Identify the subordinate points.* Notice the smaller subpoints that make up the main point, and make sure you understand how they relate to the main point. If a particular subpoint doesn't clearly relate to the main point you've identified, you may need to modify your understanding of the main point.
- *Break the reading into sections.* Notice which paragraphs make up a piece's introduction, body, and conclusion. Break up the body paragraphs into sections that address the writer's various subpoints.
- *Distinguish between points, examples, and counterarguments.* Critical reading requires careful attention to what a writer is *doing* as well as

what he or she is *saying.* When a writer quotes someone else, or relays an example of something, ask yourself why this is being done. What point is the example supporting? Is another source being quoted as support for a point or as a counterargument that the writer sets out to address?

- *Watch for transitions within and between paragraphs.* In order to follow the logic of a piece of writing, as well as to distinguish between points, examples, and counterarguments, pay attention to the transitional words and phrases writers use. Transitions function like road signs, preparing the reader for what's next.
- *Read actively and recursively.* Don't treat reading as a passive, linear progression through a text. Instead, read as though you are engaged in a dialogue with the writer: Ask questions of the text as you read, make notes in the margin, underline key ideas in pencil, put question or exclamation marks next to passages that confuse or excite you. Go back to earlier points once you finish a reading, stop during your reading to recap what's come so far, and move back and forth through a text.

HOW TO WRITE SUMMARIES

Every article you read will present its own challenge as you work to summarize it. As you'll discover, saying in a few words what has taken someone else a great many can be difficult. But like any other skill, the ability to summarize improves with practice. Here are a few pointers to get you started. They represent possible stages, or steps, in the process of writing a summary. These pointers are not meant to be ironclad rules; rather, they are designed to encourage habits of thinking that will allow you to vary your technique as the situation demands.

GUIDELINES FOR WRITING SUMMARIES

- *Read the passage carefully.* Determine its structure. Identify the author's purpose in writing. (This will help you distinguish between more important and less important information.) Make a note in the margin when you get confused or when you think something is important; highlight or underline points sparingly, if at all.
- *Reread.* This time divide the passage into sections or stages of thought. The author's use of paragraphing will often be a useful guide. *Label*, on the passage itself, each section or stage of thought. *Underline* key ideas and terms. Write notes in the margin.
- *Write one-sentence summaries*, on a separate sheet of paper, of each stage of thought.
- *Write a thesis—a one- or two-sentence summary of the entire passage.* The thesis should express the central idea of the passage as you have

(continued)

determined it from the preceding steps. You may find it useful to follow the approach of most newspaper stories—naming the *what, who, why, where, when,* and *how* of the matter. For persuasive passages, summarize in a sentence the author's conclusion. For descriptive passages, indicate the subject of the description and its key feature(s). *Note:* In some cases, *a suitable thesis statement may already be in the original passage.* If so, you may want to quote it directly in your summary.

- *Write the first draft of your summary* by (1) combining the thesis with your list of one-sentence summaries or (2) combining the thesis with one-sentence summaries *plus* significant details from the passage. In either case, eliminate repetition and less important information. Disregard minor details or generalize them (e.g., Bill Clinton and George W. Bush might be generalized as "recent presidents"). Use as few words as possible to convey the main ideas.

- *Check your summary against the original passage,* and make whatever adjustments are necessary for accuracy and completeness.

- *Revise your summary,* inserting transitional words and phrases where necessary to ensure coherence. Check for style. *Avoid a series of short, choppy sentences.* Combine sentences for a smooth, logical flow of ideas. Check for grammatical correctness, punctuation, and spelling.

DEMONSTRATION: SUMMARY

To demonstrate these points at work, let's go through the process of summarizing a passage of expository material—that is, writing that is meant to inform and/or persuade. Read the following selection carefully. Try to identify its parts and understand how they work together to create an overall statement.

WILL YOUR JOB BE EXPORTED?

Alan S. Blinder

Alan S. Blinder is the Gordon S. Rentschler Memorial Professor of Economics at Princeton University. He has served as vice chairman of the Federal Reserve Board and was a member of President Clinton's original Council of Economic Advisers.

The great conservative political philosopher Edmund Burke, who probably would not have been a reader of *The American Prospect,* once observed, "You can never plan the future by the past."* But when it comes to preparing the American workforce for the jobs of the future, we may be doing just that.

---

*Edmund Burke (1729–1797) was a conservative British statesman, philosopher, and author. *The American Prospect,* in which "Will Your Job Be Exported?" first appeared in the November 2006 issue, describes itself as "an authoritative magazine of liberal ideas."

For about a quarter-century, demand for labor appears to have shifted toward the college-educated and away from high school graduates and dropouts. This shift, most economists believe, is the primary (though not the sole) reason for rising income inequality, and there is no end in sight. Economists refer to this phenomenon by an antiseptic name: skill-biased technical progress. In plain English, it means that the labor market has turned ferociously against the low skilled and the uneducated.

In a progressive society, such a worrisome social phenomenon might elicit some strong policy responses, such as more compensatory education, stepped-up efforts at retraining, reinforcement (rather than shredding) of the social safety net, and so on. You don't fight the market's valuation of skills; you try to mitigate its more deleterious effects. We did a bit of this in the United States in the 1990s, by raising the minimum wage and expanding the Earned Income Tax Credit.* Combined with tight labor markets, these measures improved things for the average worker. But in this decade, little or no mitigation has been attempted. Social Darwinism has come roaring back.†

With one big exception: We have expended considerable efforts to keep more young people in school longer (e.g., reducing high-school dropouts and sending more kids to college) and to improve the quality of schooling (e.g., via charter schools and No Child Left Behind‡). Success in these domains may have been modest, but not for lack of trying. You don't have to remind Americans that education is important; the need for educational reform is etched into the public consciousness. Indeed, many people view education as the silver bullet. On hearing the question "How do we best prepare the American workforce of the future?" many Americans react reflexively with: "Get more kids to study science and math, and send more of them to college."

5   Which brings me to the future. As I argued in a recent article in *Foreign Affairs* magazine, the greatest problem for the next generation of American workers may not be lack of education, but rather "offshoring"—the movement of jobs overseas, especially to countries with much lower wages, such as India and China. Manufacturing jobs have been migrating overseas for decades. But the new wave of offshoring, of *service* jobs, is something different.

Traditionally, we think of service jobs as being largely immune to foreign competition. After all, you can't get your hair cut by a barber or your broken

---

*The Earned Income Tax Credit, an antipoverty measure enacted by Congress in 1975 and revised in the 1980s and 1990s, provides a credit against federal income taxes for any filer who claims a dependent child.

†Social Darwinism, a largely discredited philosophy dating from the Victorian era and espoused by Herbert Spenser, asserts that Charles Darwin's observations on natural selection apply to human societies. Social Darwinists argue that the poor are less fit to survive than the wealthy and should, through a natural process of adaptation, be allowed to die out.

‡Charter schools are public schools with specialized missions to operate outside of regulations that some feel restrict creativity and performance in traditional school settings. The No Child Left Behind Act of 2001 (NCLB) mandates standards-based education for all schools receiving federal funding. Both the charter schools movement and NCLB can be understood as efforts to improve public education.

arm set by a doctor in a distant land. But stunning advances in communication technology, plus the emergence of a vast new labor pool in Asia and Eastern Europe, are changing that picture radically, subjecting millions of presumed-safe domestic service jobs to foreign competition. And it is not necessary actually to move jobs to low-wage countries in order to restrain wage increases; the mere threat of offshoring can put a damper on wages.

Service-sector offshoring is a minor phenomenon so far, Lou Dobbs notwithstanding; probably well under 1 percent of U.S. service jobs have been outsourced.* But I believe that service-sector offshoring will eventually exceed manufacturing-sector offshoring by a hefty margin—for three main reasons. The first is simple arithmetic: There are vastly more service jobs than manufacturing jobs in the United States (and in other rich countries). Second, the technological advances that have made service-sector offshoring possible will continue and accelerate, so the range of services that can be moved offshore will increase ineluctably. Third, the number of (e.g., Indian and Chinese) workers capable of performing service jobs offshore seems certain to grow, perhaps exponentially.

I do not mean to paint a bleak picture here. Ever since Adam Smith and David Ricardo, economists have explained and extolled the gains in living standards that derive from international trade.† Those arguments are just as valid for trade in services as for trade in goods. There really *are* net gains to the United States from expanding service-sector trade with India, China, and the rest. The offshoring problem is not about the adverse nature of what economists call the economy's eventual equilibrium. Rather, it is about the so-called transition—the ride from here to there. That ride, which could take a generation or more, may be bumpy. And during the long adjustment period, many U.S. wages could face downward pressure.

Thus far, only American manufacturing workers and a few low-end service workers (e.g., call-center operators) have been competing, at least potentially, with millions of people in faraway lands eager to work for what seems a pittance by U.S. standards. But offshoring is no longer limited to low-end service jobs. Computer code can be written overseas and e-mailed back to the United States. So can your tax return and lots of legal work, provided you do not insist on face-to-face contact with the accountant or lawyer. In writing and editing this article, I communicated with the editors and staff of *The American Prospect* only by telephone and e-mail. Why couldn't they (or I, for that matter) have been in India? The possibilities are, if not endless, at least vast.

10   What distinguishes the jobs that cannot be offshored from the ones that can? The crucial distinction is not—and this is the central point of this essay—the required levels of skill and education. These attributes have been critical to

---

*Lou Dobbs, a conservative columnist and former political commentator for CNN, is well known for his anti-immigration views.

†Adam Smith (1723–1790), Scottish author of *An Inquiry into the Nature and Causes of the Wealth of Nations* (1776), established the foundations of modern economics. David Ricardo (1772–1823) was a British businessman, statesman, and economist who founded the classical school of economics and is best known for his studies of monetary policy.

labor-market success in the past, but may be less so in the future. Instead, the new critical distinction may be that some services either require personal delivery (e.g., driving a taxi and brain surgery) or are seriously degraded when delivered electronically (e.g., college teaching—at least, I hope!), while other jobs (e.g., call centers and keyboard data entry) are not. Call the first category personal services and the second category impersonal services. With this terminology, I have three main points to make about preparing our workforce for the brave, new world of the future.

First, we need to think about, plan, and redesign our educational system with the crucial distinction between personal service jobs and impersonal service jobs in mind. Many of the impersonal service jobs will migrate offshore, but the personal service jobs will stay here.

Second, the line that divides personal services from impersonal services will move in only one direction over time, as technological progress makes it possible to deliver an ever-increasing array of services electronically.

Third, the novel distinction between personal and impersonal jobs is quite different from, and appears essentially unrelated to, the traditional distinction between jobs that do and do not require high levels of education.

For example, it is easy to offshore working in a call center, typing transcripts, writing computer code, and reading X-rays. The first two require little education; the last two require quite a lot. On the other hand, it is either impossible or very difficult to offshore janitorial services, fast-food restaurant service, college teaching, and open-heart surgery. Again, the first two occupations require little or no education, while the last two require a great deal. There seems to be little or no correlation between educational requirements (the old concern) and how "offshorable" jobs are (the new one).

15   If so, the implications could be startling. A generation from now, civil engineers (who must be physically present) may be in greater demand in the United States than computer engineers (who don't). Similarly, there might be more divorce lawyers (not offshorable) than tax lawyers (partly offshorable). More imaginatively, electricians might earn more than computer programmers. I am not predicting any of this; lots of things influence relative demands and supplies for different types of labor. But it all seems within the realm of the possible as technology continues to enhance the offshorability of even highly skilled occupations. What does seem highly likely is that the relative demand for labor in the United States will shift away from impersonal services and toward personal services, and this shift will look quite different from the familiar story of skill-biased technical progress. So Burke's warning is worth heeding.

I am *not* suggesting that education will become a handicap in the job market of the future. On the contrary, to the extent that education raises productivity and that better-educated workers are more adaptable and/or more creative, a wage premium for higher education should remain. Thus, it still makes sense to send more of America's youth to college. But, over the next generation, the kind of education our young people receive may prove to be more important than how much education they receive. In that sense, a college degree may lose its exalted "silver bullet" status.

Looking back over the past 25 years, "stay in school longer" was excellent advice for success in the labor market. But looking forward over the next 25 years, more subtle occupational advice may be needed. "Prepare yourself for a high-end personal service occupation that is not offshorable" is a more nuanced message than "stay in school." But it may prove to be more useful. And many non-offshorable jobs—such as carpenters, electricians, and plumbers—do not require college education.

The hard question is how to make this more subtle advice concrete and actionable. The children entering America's educational system today, at age 5, will emerge into a very different labor market when they leave it. Given gestation periods of 13 to 17 years and more, educators and policy-makers need to be thinking now about the kinds of training and skills that will best prepare these children for their future working lives. Specifically, it is essential to educate America's youth for the jobs that will actually be available in America 20 to 30 years from now, not for the jobs that will have moved offshore.

Some of the personal service jobs that will remain in the United States will be very high-end (doctors), others will be less glamorous though well paid (plumbers), and some will be "dead end" (janitor). We need to think long and hard about the types of skills that best prepare people to deliver high-end personal services, and how to teach those skills in our elementary and high schools. I am not an education specialist, but it strikes me that, for example, the central thrust of No Child Left Behind is pushing the nation in exactly the wrong direction. I am all for accountability. But the nation's school system will not build the creative, flexible, people-oriented workforce we will need in the future by drilling kids incessantly with rote preparation for standardized tests in the vain hope that they will perform as well as memory chips.

20   Starting in the elementary schools, we need to develop our youngsters' imaginations and people skills as well as their "reading, writing, and 'rithmetic." Remember that kindergarten grade for "works and plays well with others"? It may become increasingly important in a world of personally delivered services. Such training probably needs to be continued and made more sophisticated in the secondary schools, where, for example, good communications skills need to be developed.

More vocational education is probably also in order. After all, nurses, carpenters, and plumbers are already scarce, and we'll likely need more of them in the future. Much vocational training now takes place in community colleges; and they, too, need to adapt their curricula to the job market of the future.

While it is probably still true that we should send more kids to college and increase the number who study science, math, and engineering, we need to focus on training more college students for the high-end jobs that are unlikely to move offshore, and on developing a creative workforce that will keep America incubating and developing new processes, new products, and entirely new industries. Offshoring is, after all, mostly about following and copying. America needs to lead and innovate instead, just as we have in the past.

Educational reform is not the whole story, of course. I suggested at the outset, for example, that we needed to repair our tattered social safety net and turn it into a retraining trampoline that bounces displaced workers back into productive employment. But many low-end personal service jobs cannot be turned into more attractive jobs simply by more training—think about janitors, fast-food workers, and nurse's aides, for example. Running a tight labor market would help such workers, as would a higher minimum wage, an expanded Earned Income Tax Credit, universal health insurance, and the like.

Moving up the skill ladder, employment is concentrated in the public or quasi-public sector in a number of service occupations. Teachers and health-care workers are two prominent examples. In such cases, government policy can influence wages and working conditions directly by upgrading the structure and pay of such jobs—developing more professional early-childhood teachers and fewer casual daycare workers for example—as long as the taxpayer is willing to foot the bill. Similarly, some service jobs such as registered nurses are in short supply mainly because we are not training enough qualified personnel. Here, too, public policy can help by widening the pipeline to allow more workers through. So there are a variety of policy levers that might do some good—if we are willing to pull them.

25   But all that said, education is still the right place to start. Indeed, it is much more than that because the educational system affects the entire population and because no other institution is nearly as important when it comes to preparing our youth for the world of work. As the first industrial revolution took hold, America radically transformed (and democratized) its educational system to meet the new demands of an industrial society. We may need to do something like that again. There is a great deal at stake here. If we get this one wrong, the next generation will pay dearly. But if we get it (close to) right, the gains from trade promise coming generations a prosperous future.

The somewhat inchoate challenge posed here—preparing more young Americans for personal service jobs—brings to mind one of my favorite Churchill quotations: "You can always count on Americans to do the right thing—after they've tried everything else." It is time to start trying.

Read, Reread, Highlight

Let's consider our recommended pointers for writing a summary.

As you reread the passage, note in the margins of the essay important points, shifts in thought, and questions you may have. Consider the essay's significance as a whole and its stages of thought. What does it say? How is it organized? How does each part of the passage fit into the whole? What do all these points add up to?

Here is how several paragraphs from the middle of Blinder's article might look after you have marked the main ideas by highlighting and by marginal notations.

Service-sector offshoring is a minor phenomenon so far, Lou Dobbs notwithstanding; probably well under 1 percent of U.S. service jobs have been outsourced. But I believe that service-sector offshoring will

Offshored service jobs will eclipse lost manufacturing jobs — 3 reasons

eventually exceed manufacturing-sector offshoring by a hefty margin—for three main reasons. The first is simple arithmetic: There are vastly more service jobs than manufacturing jobs in the United States (and in other rich countries). Second, the technological advances that have made service-sector offshoring possible will continue and accelerate, so the range of services that can be moved offshore will increase ineluctably. Third, the number of (e.g., Indian and Chinese) workers capable of performing service jobs offshore seems certain to grow, perhaps exponentially.

I do not mean to paint a bleak picture here. Ever since Adam Smith and David Ricardo, economists have explained and extolled the gains in living standards that derive from international trade. Those arguments are just as valid for trade in services as for trade in goods. There really are net gains to the United States from expanding service-sector trade with India, China, and the rest. The offshoring problem is not about the adverse nature of what economists call the economy's eventual equilibrium. Rather, it is about the so-called transition—the ride from here to there. That ride, which could take a generation or more, may be bumpy. And during the long adjustment period, many U.S. wages could face downward pressure.

Long-term economy will be ok. Short-to-middle term will be "bumpy"

Thus far, only American manufacturing workers and a few low-end service workers (e.g., call-center operators) have been competing, at least potentially, with millions of people in faraway lands eager to work for what seems a pittance by U.S. standards. But offshoring is no longer limited to low-end service jobs. Computer code can be written overseas and e-mailed back to the United States. So can your tax return and lots of legal work, provided you do not insist on face-to-face contact with the accountant or lawyer. In writing and editing this article, I communicated with the editors and staff of *The American Prospect* only by telephone and e-mail. Why couldn't they (or I, for that matter) have been in India? The possibilities are, if not endless, at least vast.

High-end jobs to be lost

What distinguishes the jobs that cannot be offshored from the ones that can? The crucial distinction is not—and this is the central point of this essay—the required levels of skill and education. These attributes have been critical to labor-market success in the past, but may be less so in the future. Instead, the new critical distinction may be that some services either require personal delivery (e.g., driving a taxi and brain surgery) or are seriously degraded when delivered electronically (e.g., college teaching—at least, I hope!), while other jobs (e.g., call centers and keyboard data entry) are not. Call the first category personal services and the second category impersonal services. With this terminology, I have three main points to make about preparing our workforce for the brave, new world of the future.

B's main point: Key distinction: Personal service jobs stay; impersonal jobs go

3 points re: prep of future workforce

First, we need to think about, plan, and redesign our educational system with the crucial distinction between personal service jobs and impersonal service jobs in mind. Many of the impersonal service jobs will migrate offshore, but the personal service jobs will stay here.

Movement: impersonal → personal

Second, the line that divides personal services from impersonal services will move in only one direction over time, as technological progress makes it possible to deliver an ever-increasing array of services electronically.

Level of ed. not related to future job security

Third, the novel distinction between personal and impersonal jobs is quite different from, and appears essentially unrelated to, the traditional distinction between jobs that do and do not require high levels of education.

Divide into Stages of Thought

When a selection doesn't contain sections with thematic headings, as is the case with "Will Your Job Be Exported?", how do you determine where one stage of thought ends and the next one begins? Assuming that what you have read is coherent and unified, this should not be difficult. (When a selection is unified, all of its parts pertain to the main subject; when a selection is coherent, the parts follow one another in logical order.) Look particularly for transitional sentences at the beginning of paragraphs. Such sentences generally work in one or both of two ways: (1) They summarize what has come before; (2) they set the stage for what is to follow.

Look at the sentences that open paragraphs 5 and 10: "Which brings me to the future" and "What distinguishes the jobs that cannot be offshored from the ones that can?" In both cases, Blinder makes a clear announcement. Grammatically speaking, "Which brings me to the future" is a fragment, not a sentence. Experienced writers will use fragments on occasion to good effect, as in this case. The fragment clearly has the sense of a complete thought: The pronoun "which" refers readers to the content of the preceding paragraphs, asking them to summarize that content and then, with the predicate "brings me to the future," to move forward into the next part of the article. Similarly, the question "What distinguishes the jobs that cannot be offshored from the ones that can?" implicitly asks readers to recall an important distinction just made (the definitions of offshorable and non-offshorable jobs) and then clearly moves readers forward to new, related content. As you can see, the openings of paragraphs 5 and 10 announce new sections in the article.

Each section of an article generally takes several paragraphs to develop. Between paragraphs, and almost certainly between sections of an article, you will usually find transitions that help you understand what you have just read and what you are about to read. For articles that have no subheadings, try writing your own section headings in the margins as you take notes. Blinder's article can be divided into five sections.

Section 1: *Recent past: education of workers important*—For twenty-five years, the labor market has rewarded workers with higher levels of education (paragraphs 1–4).

Section 2: *Future: ed level won't always matter—workers in service sector will lose jobs offshore*—Once thought immune to outsourcing, even highly trained service workers will lose jobs to overseas competition (paragraphs 5–9).

Section 3: *Which service jobs at highest risk?* <u>Personal</u> service workers are safe; <u>impersonal</u> service workers, both highly educated and not, will see jobs offshored (paragraphs 10–15).

Section 4: *Educating the future workforce*—Emphasizing the <u>kind</u>, not amount, of education will help to prepare workers for jobs of the future (paragraphs 16–22).

Section 5: *Needed policy reforms*—Government can improve conditions for low-end service workers and expand opportunities for higher-end service workers; start with education (paragraphs 23–26).

Write a Brief Summary of Each Stage of Thought

The purpose of this step is to wean yourself from the language of the original passage, so that you are not tied to it when writing the summary. Here are brief summaries, one for each stage of thought in "Will Your Job Be Exported?":

Section 1: Recent past: education of workers important (paragraphs 1–4).

> For the past twenty-five years, the greater a worker's skill or level of education, the better and more stable the job.

Section 2: Future: ed level won't always matter—workers in service sector will lose jobs offshore (paragraphs 5–9).

> Advances in technology have brought to the service sector the same pressures that forced so many manufacturing jobs offshore to China and India. The rate of offshoring in the service sector will accelerate and "eventually exceed" job losses in manufacturing, says Blinder, and jobs requiring both relatively little education (such as call-center staffing) and extensive education (such as software development) will be lost to workers overseas.

Section 3: Which service jobs at highest risk? (paragraphs 10–15).

> While "personal services" workers (such as barbers and surgeons) will be relatively safe from offshoring because their work requires close physical proximity to customers, "impersonal services" workers (such as call-center operators and radiologists), regardless of their skill or education, will be at risk because their work can be completed remotely without loss of quality and then delivered via phone or computer. Blinder believes that "the relative demand for labor in the United States will [probably] shift away from impersonal services and toward personal services."

Section 4: Educating the future workforce (paragraphs 16–22).

> Blinder advises young people to plan for "a high-end personal service occupation that is not offshorable." He also urges educators to prepare the future workforce by anticipating the needs of a personal services economy and redesigning classroom instruction and vocational training accordingly.

Section 5: Needed policy reforms (paragraphs 23–26).

> Blinder urges the government to develop policies that will improve wages and conditions for low-wage personal service workers (such as janitors); to encourage more low-wage workers (such as daycare providers) to retrain and take on better jobs; and to increase opportunities for professional and vocational training in high-demand areas (such as nursing and carpentry).

Write a Thesis: A Brief Summary of the Entire Passage

The thesis is the most general statement of a summary (or any other type of academic writing). It is the statement that announces the paper's subject and the claim that you or—in the case of a summary—another author will be making about that subject. Every paragraph of a paper illuminates the thesis by providing supporting detail or explanation. The relationship of these paragraphs to the thesis is analogous to the relationship of the sentences within a paragraph to the topic sentence. Both the thesis and the topic sentences are general statements (the thesis being the more general) that are followed by systematically arranged details.

To ensure clarity for the reader, *the first sentence of your summary should begin with the author's thesis, regardless of where it appears in the article itself.* An author may locate her thesis at the beginning of her work, in which case the thesis operates as a general principle from which details of the presentation follow. This is called a *deductive* organization: thesis first, supporting details second. Alternatively, an author may locate his thesis at the end of the work, in which case the author begins with specific details and builds toward a more general conclusion, or thesis. This is called an *inductive* organization. And, as you might expect, an author might locate the thesis anywhere between beginning and end, at whatever point it seems best positioned.*

A thesis consists of a subject and an assertion about that subject. How can we go about fashioning an adequate thesis for a summary of Blinder's article? Probably no two versions of Blinder's thesis statement would be worded identically, but it is fair to say that any reasonable thesis will indicate that Blinder's subject is the future loss to offshoring of American jobs in the service sector— that part of the economy that delivers services to consumers, from low end (e.g., janitorial services) to high end (e.g., neurosurgery). How does Blinder view the situation? How secure will service jobs be if Blinder's distinction between personal and impersonal services is valid? Looking back over our section summaries,

---

*Blinder positions his thesis midway through his five-section article. He opens the selection by discussing the role of education in the labor market during the past twenty-five years (Section 1, pars. 1–4). He continues by summarizing an earlier article on the ways in which service jobs are following manufacturing jobs offshore (Section 2, pars. 5–9). He then presents a two-sentence thesis in answer to the question that opens paragraph 10: "What distinguishes the jobs that cannot be offshored from the ones that can?" The remainder of the article either develops this thesis (Section 3, pars. 10–15) or follows its implications for education (Section 4, pars. 16–22) and public policy (Section 5, pars. 23–26).

we find that Blinder insists on three points: (1) that education and skill matter less than they once did in determining job quality and security; (2) that the distinction between personal and impersonal services will increasingly determine which jobs remain and which are offshored; and (3) that the distinction between personal and impersonal has implications for the future of both education and public policy.

Does Blinder make a statement anywhere in this passage that pulls all this together? Examine paragraph 10 and you will find his thesis—two sentences that answer his question about which jobs will and will not be sent offshore: "The crucial distinction is not—and this is the central point of this essay—the required levels of skill and education…. Instead, the new critical distinction may be that some services either require personal delivery (e.g., driving a taxi and brain surgery) or are seriously degraded when delivered electronically (e.g., college teaching—at least, I hope!), while other jobs (e.g., call centers and keyboard data entry) are not."

You may have learned that a thesis statement must be expressed in a single sentence. We would offer a slight rewording of this generally sound advice and say that a thesis statement must be *expressible* in a single sentence. For reasons of emphasis or style, a writer might choose to distribute a thesis across two or more sentences. Certainly, the sense of Blinder's thesis can take the form of a single statement: "The critical distinction is X, not Y." For reasons largely of emphasis, he divides his thesis into two sentences—in fact, separating these sentences with another sentence that explains the first part of the thesis: "These attributes [that is, skill and education] have been critical to labor-market success in the past, but may be less so in the future."

Here is a one-sentence version of Blinder's two-sentence thesis:

> The quality and security of future jobs in America's service sector will be determined by how "offshorable" those jobs are.

Notice that the statement anticipates a summary of the *entire* article: both the discussion leading up to Blinder's thesis and his discussion after. To clarify for our readers the fact that this idea is Blinder's and not ours, we might qualify the thesis as follows:

> In "Will Your Job Be Exported?" economist Alan S. Blinder argues that the quality and security of future jobs in America's service sector will be determined by how "offshorable" those jobs are.

The first sentence of a summary is crucially important, for it orients readers by letting them know what to expect in the coming paragraphs. In the example above, the sentence refers directly to an article, its author, and the thesis for the upcoming summary. The author and title reference could also be indicated in the summary's title (if this were a freestanding summary), in which case their mention could be dropped from the thesis statement. And lest you become frustrated too quickly with how much effort it takes to come up with this crucial sentence, keep in mind that writing an acceptable thesis for a summary takes time. In this case, it took three drafts, roughly ten minutes, to compose a thesis and another few minutes of fine-tuning after a draft of the entire summary was completed. The thesis needed revision because the first draft was vague; the second draft was improved but too specific on a secondary point; the third draft was more complete but too general on a key point:

> **Draft 1:** We must begin now to train young people for high-quality personal service jobs.
>
> *(Vague. The question of why we should begin training isn't clear, nor is the phrase "high-quality personal service jobs." Define this term or make it more general.)*
>
> **Draft 2:** Alan S. Blinder argues that, unlike in the past, the quality and security of future American jobs will not be determined by skill level or education, but rather by how "offshorable" those jobs are.
>
> *(Better, but the reference to "skill level or education" is secondary to Blinder's main point about offshorable jobs.)*
>
> **Draft 3:** In "Will Your Job Be Exported?" economist Alan S. Blinder argues that the quality and security of future jobs will be determined by how "offshorable" those jobs are.
>
> *(Close—but not "all" jobs. Blinder specifies which types of jobs are "offshorable.")*
>
> **Final Draft:** In "Will Your Job Be Exported?" economist Alan S. Blinder argues that the quality and security of future jobs in America's service sector will be determined by how "offshorable" those jobs are.

Write the First Draft of the Summary

Let's consider two possible summaries of Blinder's article: (1) a short summary, combining a thesis with brief section summaries, and (2) a longer summary, combining thesis, brief section summaries, and some carefully chosen details. Again, keep in mind that you are reading final versions; each of the following summaries is the result of at least two full drafts. Highlighting indicates transitions added to smooth the flow of the summary.

Summary 1: Combine Thesis Sentence with Brief Section Summaries

> In "Will Your Job Be Exported?" economist Alan S. Blinder argues that the quality and security of future jobs in America's service sector will be determined by how "offshorable" those jobs are. For the past twenty-five years, the greater a worker's skill or level of education, the better and more stable the job. No longer. Advances in technology have brought to the service sector the same pressures that forced so many manufacturing jobs offshore to China and India. The rate of offshoring in the service sector will accelerate, and jobs requiring both relatively little education (such as call-center staffing) and extensive education (such as software development) will increasingly be lost to workers overseas.

These losses will "eventually exceed" losses in manufacturing, but not all services jobs are equally at risk. While "personal services" workers (such as barbers and surgeons) will be relatively safe from offshoring because their work requires close physical proximity to customers, "impersonal services" workers (such as call-center operators and radiologists), regardless of their skill or education, will be at risk because their work can be completed remotely without loss of quality and then delivered via phone or computer. "[T]he relative demand for labor in the United States will [probably] shift away from impersonal services and toward personal services."

Blinder recommends three courses of action: He advises young people to plan for "a high-end personal service occupation that is not offshorable." He urges educators to prepare the future workforce by anticipating the needs of a personal services economy and redesigning classroom instruction and vocational training accordingly. Finally, he urges the government to adopt policies that will improve existing personal services jobs by increasing wages for low-wage workers; retraining workers to take on better jobs; and increasing opportunities in high-demand, well-paid areas such as nursing and carpentry. Ultimately, Blinder wants America to prepare a new generation to "lead and innovate" in an economy that will continue exporting jobs that require "following and copying."

The Strategy of the Shorter Summary

This short summary consists essentially of a restatement of Blinder's thesis plus the section summaries, modified or expanded a little for stylistic purposes. You'll recall that Blinder locates his thesis midway through the article, in paragraph 10. But note that this model summary *begins* with a restatement of his thesis. Notice also the relative weight given to the section summaries within the model. Blinder's main point, his "critical distinction" between personal and impersonal services jobs, is summarized in paragraph 2 of the model. The other paragraphs combine summaries of relatively less important (that is, supporting or explanatory) material. Paragraph 1 combines summaries of the article's Sections 1 and 2; paragraph 3 combines summaries of Sections 4 and 5.

Between the thesis and the section summaries, notice the insertion of three (highlighted) transitions. The first—a fragment (*No longer*)—bridges the first paragraph's summaries of Sections 1 and 2 of Blinder's article. The second transition links a point Blinder makes in his Section 2 (*Losses in the service sector will "eventually exceed" losses in manufacturing*) with an introduction to the key point he will make in Section 3 (*Not all service jobs are equally at risk*). The third transition (*Blinder recommends three courses of action*) bridges the summary of Blinder's Section 3 to summaries of Sections 4 and 5. Each transition, then, links sections of the whole: Each casts the reader back to recall points just made; each casts the reader forward by announcing related points about to be made. Our model ends with a summary of Blinder's motivation for writing, the sense of which is implied by the section summaries but nowhere made explicit.

Summary 2: Combine Thesis Sentence, Section Summaries, and Carefully Chosen Details

The thesis and brief section summaries could also be used as the outline for a more detailed summary. However, most of the details in the passage won't be necessary in a summary. It isn't necessary even in a longer summary of this passage to discuss all of Blinder's examples of jobs that are more or less likely to be sent offshore. It would be appropriate, though, to mention one example of such a job; to review his reasons for thinking "that service-sector offshoring will eventually exceed manufacturing-sector offshoring by a hefty margin"; and to expand on his point that a college education in itself will no longer ensure job security.

None of these details appeared in the first summary; but in a longer summary, a few carefully selected details might be desirable for clarity. How do you decide which details to include? First, working with Blinder's point that one's job type (personal services vs. impersonal services) will matter more for future job quality and security than did the once highly regarded "silver bullet" of education, you may want to cite some of the most persuasive evidence supporting this idea. For example, you could explore why some highly paid physicians, such as radiologists, might find themselves competing for jobs with lower-paid physicians overseas. Further, your expanded summary might reflect the relative weight Blinder gives to education (seven paragraphs, the longest of the article's five sections).

You won't always know which details to include and which to exclude. Developing good judgment in comprehending and summarizing texts is largely a matter of reading skill and prior knowledge (see p. 4). Consider the analogy of the seasoned mechanic who can pinpoint an engine problem by simply listening to a characteristic sound that to a less experienced person is just noise. Or consider the chess player who can plot three separate winning strategies from a board position that to a novice looks like a hopeless jumble. In the same way, the more practiced a reader you are, the more knowledgeable you will become about the subject and the better able you will be to make critical distinctions between elements of greater and lesser importance. In the meantime, read as carefully as you can and use your own best judgment as to how to present your material.

Here's one version of a completed summary with carefully chosen details. Note that we have highlighted phrases and sentences added to the original, briefer summary.

> In "Will Your Job Be Exported?" economist Alan S. Blinder argues that the quality and security of future jobs in America's service sector will be determined by how "offshorable" those jobs are. For the past twenty-five years, the greater a worker's skill or level of education, the better and more stable the job. Americans have long regarded education as the "silver bullet" that could propel motivated people to better jobs and a better life. No longer. Advances in technology have brought to the service sector the same pressures that forced so many manufacturing jobs offshore to China and India. The rate of offshoring in the service sector will accelerate, says Blinder, and jobs requiring both relatively little education (such as call-center staffing) and extensive education (such as software development) will increasingly be lost to workers overseas.

Blinder expects that job losses in the service sector will "eventually exceed" losses in manufacturing, for three reasons. Developed countries have more service jobs than manufacturing jobs; as technology speeds communications, more service jobs will be offshorable; and the numbers of qualified offshore workers is increasing. Service jobs lost to foreign competition may cause a "bumpy" period as the global economy sorts out what work gets done where, by whom. In time, as the global economy finds its "eventual equilibrium," offshoring will benefit the United States; but the consequences in the meantime may be painful for many.

That pain will not be shared equally by all service workers, however. While "personal service" workers (such as barbers and surgeons) will be relatively safe from offshoring because their work requires close physical proximity to customers, "impersonal service" workers (such as audio transcribers and radiologists), regardless of their skill or education, will be at risk because their work can be completed remotely without loss of quality and then delivered via phone or computer. In the coming decades, says Blinder, "the relative demand for labor in the United States will [probably] shift away from impersonal services and toward personal services." This shift will be influenced by the desire to keep good jobs in the United States while exporting jobs that require "following and copying." Highly trained computer coders will face the same pressures of outsourcing as relatively untrained call-center attendants. A tax attorney whose work requires no face-to-face interaction with clients may see her work migrate overseas, while a divorce attorney, who must interact with clients on a case-by-case basis, may face no such competition. Same educations, different outcomes: What determines their fates in a global economy is the nature of their work (that is, personal vs. impersonal), not their level of education.

Based on this analysis, Blinder recommends three courses of action: First, he advises young people to plan for "a high-end personal service occupation that is not offshorable." Many good jobs, such as carpentry and plumbing, will not require a college degree. Next, Blinder urges educators to prepare the future workforce by anticipating the needs of a personal services economy and redesigning classroom instruction and vocational training accordingly. These efforts should begin in elementary school and develop imagination and interpersonal skills rather than capacities for rote memorization. Finally, Blinder urges the government to develop policies that will improve wages and conditions for low-wage personal services workers (such as janitors); to encourage more low-wage workers (such as daycare providers) to retrain and take on better service jobs; and to increase opportunities for professional and vocational training for workers in high-demand services areas (such as nurses and electricians). Ultimately, Blinder wants America to prepare a new generation of workers who will "lead and innovate . . . just as we have in the past."

The Strategy of the Longer Summary

Compared to the first, briefer summary, this effort (70 percent longer than the first) includes Blinder's reasons for suggesting that job losses in the services sector will exceed losses in manufacturing. It emphasizes Blinder's point that job type (personal vs. impersonal services), not a worker's education level, will ensure job security. It includes Blinder's point that offshoring in the service sector is part of a larger global economy seeking "equilibrium." And it offers more on Blinder's thoughts concerning the education of future workers.

The final two of our suggested steps for writing summaries are (1) to check your summary against the original passage, making sure that you have included all the important ideas, and (2) to revise so that the summary reads smoothly and coherently. The structure of this summary generally reflects the structure of the original article—with one significant departure, as noted earlier. Blinder uses a modified inductive approach, stating his thesis midway through the article. The summary, however, states the thesis immediately, then proceeds deductively to develop that thesis.

HOW LONG SHOULD A SUMMARY BE?

The length of a summary depends both on the length of the original passage and on the use to which the summary will be put. If you are summarizing an entire article, a good rule of thumb is that your summary should be no longer than one-fourth the length of the original passage. Of course, if you were summarizing an entire chapter or even an entire book, it would have to be much shorter than that. The longer summary above is one-quarter the length of Alan Blinder's original. Although it shouldn't be very much longer, you have seen (pp. 19–20) that it could be quite a bit shorter.

The length as well as the content of the summary also depends on the *purpose* to which it will be put. Let's suppose you decided to use Blinder's piece in a paper that deals with the loss of manufacturing jobs in the United States and the rise of the service economy. In this case, in an effort to explain the complexities of the service economy to your readers, you might summarize *only* Blinder's core distinction between jobs in personal services and impersonal services, likely mentioning that jobs in the latter category are at risk of offshoring. If, instead, you were writing a paper in which you argued that the forces of globalization will eventually collapse the world's economies into a single, global economy, you would likely give less attention to Blinder's distinction between personal and impersonal services. More to the point might be his observation that highly skilled, highly educated workers in the United States are now finding themselves competing with qualified, lower-wage workers in China and India. Thus, depending on your purpose, you would summarize either selected portions of a source or an entire source. We will see this process more fully demonstrated in the upcoming chapters on syntheses.

Exercise 1.1 ◯

Individual and Collaborative Summary Practice

Turn to Chapter 15 and read Solomon A. Asch's article "Opinions and Social Pressures." Follow the steps for writing summaries outlined above—read, underline, and divide into stages of thought. Write a one-or two-sentence summary of each stage of thought in Asch's article. Then gather in groups of three or four classmates and compare your summary sentences. Discuss the differences in your sentences, and come to some consensus about the divisions in Asch's stages of thought—and the ways in which to best sum them up.

As a group, write a one-or two-sentence thesis statement summing up the entire passage. You could go even further, and, using your individual summary sentences— or the versions of them your group revised—put together a brief summary of Asch's essay. Model your work on the brief summary of Blinder's article, on pp. 19-20.

SUMMARIZING FIGURES AND TABLES

In your reading in the sciences and social sciences, you will often find data and concepts presented in nontext forms—as figures and tables. Such visual devices offer a snapshot, a pictorial overview of material that is more quickly and clearly communicated in graphic form than as a series of (often complicated) sentences. Note that in essence, figures and tables are themselves summaries. The writer uses a graph, which in an article or book is labeled as a numbered "figure," and presents the quantitative results of research as points on a line or a bar or as sections ("slices") of a pie. Pie charts show relative proportions, or percentages. Graphs, especially effective in showing patterns, relate one variable to another: for instance, income to years of education, or sales figures of a product over a period of three years.

Writers regularly draw on graphs, charts, and tables to provide information or to offer evidence for points they are arguing. Consider the following passage from an op-ed article by Michael Klare, arguing that the United States and China should cooperate, rather than compete, in order to supply their future energy needs:

> In 2007, according to Energy Department figures, the United States consumed about 21 million barrels of oil a day, nearly three times as much as China. Even more significant, we imported 13 million barrels every day, a vastly greater amount than China's import tally. So, although it is indeed true that Chinese and American consumers are competing for access to overseas supplies, thereby edging up prices, American consumption still sets the pace in international oil markets.
>
> The reality is that as far as the current run-up in gasoline prices is concerned, other factors are more to blame: shrinking oil output from such key producers as Mexico, Russia and Venezuela; internal violence in Iraq and Nigeria; refinery inadequacies in the U.S. and elsewhere; speculative stockpiling by global oil brokers, and so on. These conditions are likely to persist for the foreseeable future, so prices will remain high.
>
> Peer into the future, however, and the China factor starts looming much larger.
>
> With its roaring economy and millions of newly affluent consumers— many of whom are now buying their first automobiles—China is rapidly catching up with the United States in its net oil intake. According to the most recent projections, Chinese petroleum consumption is expected to jump from 8 million barrels a day in 2008 to an estimated 12 million in 2020 and to 16 million in 2030. American consumption will also climb, but not as much, reaching an estimated 27 million barrels a day in 2030. In terms of oil imports, moreover, the gap will grow even smaller. Chinese imports are projected to hit 10.8 million barrels a day in 2030, compared

with 16.4 million for the United States. Clearly, the Sino-American competition for foreign oil supplies will grow ever more intense with every passing year.*

A good deal of the data Klare provides in this passage likely came from graphs, charts, and tables.

In the following pages, we present four figures and a table from various sources, all related to the world's rising oil consumption and its dwindling supply.

Bar Graphs

Figure 1.1 is a bar graph indicating the world's known oil reserves as of January 2005. The vertical axis of this graph indicates the number of barrels, in billions, estimated to be available. The horizontal axis indicates various regions of the world. The vertical bar above each region indicates the number of billions of barrels. Note that the bar indicating the largest available supplies, representing the Mideast, is subdivided into the nations of that region in control of the largest oil reserves.

Here is a summary of the information presented in Figure 1.1:

As of January 1, 2005, the Middle East had by far the largest quantities of oil reserves in the world, almost 800 billion barrels. North America, the region with the next highest oil reserves, has slightly more than a quarter of this quantity, just over 200 billion barrels. Central and South America and Africa come next, each with about 100 billion

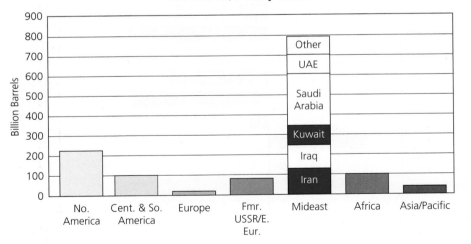

Figure 1.1   World Oil Reserves by Region, January 1, 2005[†]

*Michael T. Klare, "The U.S. and China Are over a Barrel," *Los Angeles Times* 28 Apr. 2008: 17. Klare is professor of peace and world security studies at Hampshire College and the author of *Rising Powers, Shrinking Planet: The New Geopolitics of Energy.*
[†]*Oil and Gas Journal,* 1 Jan. 2005. <http://www.eia.doe.gov/pub/oil_gas/petroleum/analysis_publications/oil_market_basics/sup_image_reserves.htm>.

barrels. Russia and Eastern Europe have slightly less than this quantity. Compared to these oil-rich regions, Asia and the Pacific region and Europe have relatively minimal amounts. Within the Middle East region, Saudi Arabia has the largest oil reserves, about 250 billion barrels. Thus, this one country has more oil than any other entire region in the world. Iran, Iraq, and Kuwait each have at least 100 million barrels of oil. Each of these countries, therefore, has at least as much in oil reserves as all of the African countries or all of the Central and South American countries combined.

Figure 1.2, another bar graph, indicates the number of years (from 2003—the "zero" point on the horizontal axis) until the midpoint of depletion of national oil reserves for fifteen countries. Note that this graph features bars stretching in opposite directions: The bars to the left indicate negative values; the bars to the

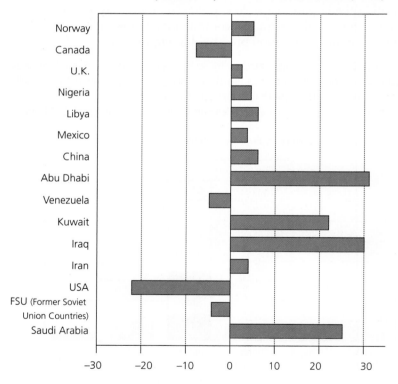

Time to Depletion Midpoint of Oil Reserves, 2003 (Years)

Figure 1.2   This graph illustrates the number of years to the midpoint of the depletion of oil reserves for various major oil-producing nations in 2003. A negative value means that the midpoint was in the past. The only countries a significant distance from their midpoints are the major Middle East producers.*

*The Hubbert Peak for World Oil. Chart updated 2003. <http://www.oilcrisis.com/summary.htm>.

right indicate positive values. Thus, Norway will have used up half of its total oil reserves by 2008, five years after the date the chart was prepared. Canada, by contrast, reached the midpoint of its depletion about eight years *before* 2003.

Exercise 1.2   ◯

Summarizing Graphs

Write a brief summary of the data in Figure 1.2. Use our summary of Figure 1.1 as a model.

Pie Charts

Bar graphs are useful for visually comparing numerical quantities. Pie charts, on the other hand, are useful for visually comparing percentages of a whole. The pie represents the whole; the individual slices represent the relative sizes of the parts. Figure 1.3 is a pie chart indicating the relative oil consumption of various regions of the world in 2007. Each slice represents a percentage of the world's total oil consumption.

In this chart, OECD stands for the Organization for Economic Cooperation and Development.* Note that only two of the five pie slices represent individual

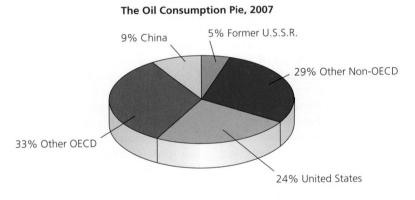

The Oil Consumption Pie, 2007

9% China   5% Former U.S.S.R.

29% Other Non-OECD

33% Other OECD

24% United States

Figure 1.3   The Oil Consumption Pie[†]

---

*The OECD is a Paris-based international group, founded in 1961, that collects and analyzes economic data. According to its Web site <http://www.oecd.org>, "[I]ts mission [is] to help…member countries to achieve sustainable economic growth and employment and to raise the standard of living in member countries while maintaining financial stability…[and contributing] to the development of the world economy." OECD countries, democracies with market economies, include Australia, Austria, Belgium, Canada, the Czech Republic, Denmark, Finland, France, Germany, Greece, Hungary, Iceland, Ireland, Italy, Japan, Korea, Luxembourg, Mexico, the Netherlands, New Zealand, Norway, Poland, the Slovak Republic, Spain, Switzerland, Sweden, Turkey, the United Kingdom, and the United States.
[†]Association for the Study of Peak Oil and Gas—U.S.A. <http://www.aspo-usa.com/index.php?option=com_content&task=view&id=298&Itemid=91>.

countries: the United States (an OECD country) and China. Two additional slices represent "other OECD" countries and "other non-OECD" countries (i.e., countries other than China and the former USSR, which are separately represented in the chart). Finally, note that the "former USSR" slice indicates Russia and Eastern European countries—such as Bulgaria, Romania, and Estonia—that are not presently members of the OECD (as are Hungary and Poland).

Exercise 1.3   ◯

Summarizing Pie Charts

Write a brief summary of the data in Figure 1.3. Use our summary of Figure 1.1 (or your summary of Figure 1.2) as a model.

Line Graphs

Line graphs are useful for showing trends over a period of time. Usually, the horizontal axis indicates years, months, or shorter periods, and the vertical axis indicates a quantity: dollars, barrels, personnel, sales, anything that can be counted. The line running from left to right indicates the changing values, over a given period, of the object of measurement. Frequently, a line graph will feature multiple lines (perhaps in different colors, perhaps some solid, others dotted, etc.), each indicating a separate variable to be measured. Thus, a line graph could show the changing approval ratings of several presidential candidates over the course of a campaign season. Or it could indicate the number of iPhones versus BlackBerrys sold in a given year.

The line graph shown in Figure 1.4 indicates the changes in several U.S. oil consumption variables, over time: (1) total oil demand (in millions of barrels per day), (2) oil consumption demand for transportation alone, and (3) domestic oil production. Note that because the graph was produced in 2001, the fifty-year period before that indicates historical data; the twenty-year period following is a projection based on estimates. Note also that somewhere around 2015, the domestic oil production line splits in two: The upper range indicates the level of oil production if Alaskan oil reserves are included; the lower range indicates domestic production without this particular resource.

Exercise 1.4   ◯

Summarizing Line Graphs

Write a brief summary of the key data in Figure 1.4. Use our summary of Figure 1.1 (or your summary of Figure 1.2) as a model.

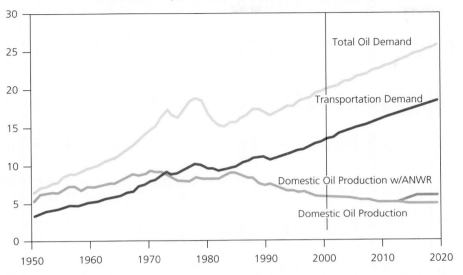

U.S. Oil Consumption, 1950–2020 (million barrels per day)

Figure 1.4   U.S. Oil Consumption, 1950–2020*

Tables

A table presents numerical data in rows and columns for quick reference. If the writer chooses, tabular information can be converted to graphic information. Charts and graphs are preferable when the writer wants to emphasize a pattern or relationship; tables are preferable when the writer wants to emphasize numbers. While the previous charts and graphs represented a relatively small number of factors (regions or countries, quantities of oil produced or consumed in a given year or over a period of time), Table 1.1 breaks down oil production into numerous countries, organized by region.[†] Note that since production is represented in thousands of barrels daily, each number should be multiplied by 1,000. The number at the upper left corner of page 30, 8295, therefore, represents the 8,295,000 barrels a day produced by the United States in 1996. "Total world" production that year (p. 32, lower left) was 69,931,000 barrels per day.

A table may contain so much data that you would not want to summarize *all* of it for a particular paper. In this case, you would summarize the *part* of a

---

*Energy Information Administration (EIA), Annual Energy Outlook, 2001: "Potential Oil Production from the Coastal Plain of ANWR (Arctic National Wildlife Refuge)," EIR Reserves and Production Division. <http://energy.senate.gov/legislation/energybill/charts/chart8.pdf>.
[†]"British Petroleum Statistical Review of World Energy 2006: Oil Production." British Petroleum. 2007.

Table 1.1 Oil Production by Country, 1996–2006*

Producer	Thousands of barrels daily											Change: 2006 over 2005	2006 share of total
	1996	1997	1998	1999	2000	2001	2002	2003	2004	2005	2006		
USA	8295	8269	8011	7731	7733	7669	7626	7400	7228	6895	**6871**	20.5%	8.0%
Canada	2480	2588	2672	2604	2721	2677	2858	3004	3085	3041	**3147**	4.4%	3.9%
Mexico	3277	3410	3499	3343	3450	3560	3585	3789	3824	3760	**3683**	22.1%	4.7%
Total North America	**14,052**	**14,267**	**14,182**	**13,678**	**13,904**	**13,906**	**14,069**	**14,193**	**14,137**	**13,695**	**13,700**	**0.1%**	**16.5%**
Argentina	823	877	890	847	819	830	818	806	754	725	**716**	21.3%	0.9%
Brazil	807	868	1003	1133	1268	1337	1499	1555	1542	1715	**1809**	5.5%	2.3%
Colombia	635	667	775	838	711	627	601	564	551	554	**558**	0.7%	0.7%
Ecuador	393	397	385	383	409	416	401	427	535	541	**545**	0.7%	0.7%
Peru	121	120	116	107	100	98	98	92	94	111	**116**	3.5%	0.1%
Trinidad & Tobago	141	135	134	141	138	135	155	164	152	171	**174**	1.5%	0.2%
Venezuela	3137	3321	3480	3126	3239	3142	2895	2554	2907	2937	**2824**	23.9%	3.7%
Other S. & Cent. America	102	108	125	124	130	137	152	153	144	142	**140**	21.7%	0.2%
Total S. & Cent. America	**6159**	**6493**	**6908**	**6699**	**6813**	**6722**	**6619**	**6314**	**6680**	**6897**	**6881**	**20.4%**	**8.8%**
Azerbaijan	183	182	231	279	282	301	311	313	315	452	**654**	44.9%	0.8%
Denmark	208	230	238	299	363	348	371	368	390	377	**342**	29.3%	0.4%
Italy	104	114	108	96	88	79	106	107	105	117	**111**	25.6%	0.1%
Kazakhstan	474	536	537	631	744	836	1018	1111	1297	1356	**1426**	5.6%	1.7%
Norway	3232	3280	3138	3139	3346	3418	3333	3264	3188	2969	**2778**	26.9%	3.3%
Romania	142	141	137	133	131	130	127	123	119	114	**105**	28.0%	0.1%
Russian Federation	6114	6227	6169	6178	6536	7056	7698	8544	9287	9552	**9769**	2.2%	12.3%
Turkmenistan	90	108	129	143	144	162	182	202	193	192	**163**	215.2%	0.2%
United Kingdom	2735	2702	2807	2909	2667	2476	2463	2257	2028	1809	**1636**	29.6%	2.0%
Uzbekistan	174	182	191	191	177	171	171	166	152	126	**125**	20.7%	0.1%
Other Europe & Eurasia	546	524	506	474	465	465	501	509	496	469	**454**	22.9%	0.5%
Total Europe & Eurasia	**14,003**	**14,226**	**14,190**	**14,473**	**14,943**	**15,444**	**16,281**	**16,965**	**17,570**	**17,533**	**17,563**	**0.2%**	**21.6%**
Iran	3759	3776	3855	3603	3818	3794	3543	4183	4248	4268	**4343**	1.2%	5.4%
Iraq	580	1166	2121	2610	2614	2523	2116	1344	2030	1833	**1999**	9.0%	2.5%
Kuwait	2129	2137	2232	2085	2206	2148	1995	2329	2482	2643	**2704**	2.4%	3.4%
Oman	897	909	905	911	959	961	900	824	756	779	**743**	24.6%	0.9%

Table 1.1 (continued)

Producer	Thousands of barrels daily											Change: 2006 over 2005	2006 share of total
	1996	1997	1998	1999	2000	2001	2002	2003	2004	2005	2006		
Qatar	568	719	747	797	855	854	783	917	990	1045	**1133**	8.1%	1.3%
Saudi Arabia	9299	9482	9502	8853	9491	9209	8928	10,164	10,638	11,114	**10,859**	22.3%	13.1%
Syria	586	577	576	579	548	581	548	527	495	458	**417**	28.9%	0.5%
United Arab Emirates	2438	2567	2643	2511	2626	2534	2324	2611	2656	2751	**2969**	7.3%	3.5%
Yemen	357	375	380	405	450	455	457	448	420	426	**390**	28.7%	0.5%
Other Middle East	50	50	49	48	48	47	48	48	48	34	**32**	27.7%	**
Total Middle East	**20,662**	**21,758**	**23,010**	**22,402**	**23,614**	**23,107**	**21,642**	**23,395**	**24,764**	**25,352**	**25,589**	**0.7%**	**31.2%**
Algeria	1386	1421	1461	1515	1578	1562	1680	1852	1946	2016	**2005**	20.3%	2.2%
Angola	716	741	731	745	746	742	905	862	976	1233	**1409**	14.3%	1.8%
Cameroon	110	124	105	95	88	81	75	68	62	58	**63**	8.6%	0.1%
Chad	–	–	–	–	–	–	–	24	168	173	**153**	211.7%	0.2%
Rep. of Congo (Brazzaville)	200	225	264	266	254	234	231	215	216	246	**262**	6.7%	0.3%
Egypt	894	873	857	827	781	758	751	749	721	696	**678**	22.5%	0.8%
Equatorial Guinea	17	62	85	96	117	173	215	247	343	356	**358**	0.6%	0.5%
Gabon	365	364	337	340	327	301	295	240	235	234	**232**	20.9%	0.3%
Libya	1452	1491	1480	1425	1475	1427	1375	1485	1624	1751	**1835**	4.2%	2.2%
Nigeria	2145	2316	2167	2066	2155	2274	2103	2263	2502	2580	**2460**	24.9%	3.0%
Sudan	5	9	12	63	174	211	233	255	325	355	**397**	11.8%	0.5%
Tunisia	89	81	83	84	78	71	75	68	72	74	**69**	27.1%	0.1%
Other Africa	62	64	63	56	56	53	63	71	75	72	**68**	25.3%	0.1%
Total Africa	**7441**	**7770**	**7644**	**7579**	**7830**	**7887**	**8001**	**8398**	**9263**	**9846**	**9990**	**1.4%**	**12.1%**
Australia	619	669	644	625	809	733	731	624	541	554	**544**	22.1%	0.6%
Brunei	165	163	157	182	193	203	210	214	210	206	**221**	7.1%	0.3%
China	3170	3211	3212	3213	3252	3306	3346	3401	3481	3627	**3684**	1.6%	4.7%
India	778	800	787	788	780	780	801	798	816	784	**807**	3.1%	1.0%

(continued)

Table 1.1 (continued)

Producer	Thousands of barrels daily											Change: 2006 over 2005	2006 share of total
	1996	1997	1998	1999	2000	2001	2002	2003	2004	2005	2006		
Indonesia	1680	1557	1520	1408	1456	1389	1288	1183	1152	1129	1071	25.3%	1.3%
Malaysia	773	777	779	737	735	719	757	776	793	767	747	23.1%	0.9%
Thailand	105	126	130	140	176	191	204	236	223	265	286	8.7%	0.3%
Vietnam	179	205	245	296	328	350	354	364	427	398	367	28.0%	0.5%
Other Asia Pacific	245	229	217	218	200	195	193	195	186	197	215	8.0%	0.3%
Total Asia Pacific	**7615**	**7737**	**7692**	**7608**	**7928**	**7866**	**7884**	**7791**	**7829**	**7926**	**7941**	**0.1%**	**9.7%**
TOTAL WORLD	69,931	72,251	73,626	72,439	75,033	74,932	74,496	77,056	80,244	81,250	**81,663**	0.4%	100.0%
of which:													
European Union 25	3325	3304	3407	3542	3355	3147	3203	2995	2774	2535	**2306**	29.0%	2.8%
OECD	21,355	21,660	21,492	21,095	21,514	21,297	21,422	21,156	20,716	19,825	**19,398**	22.2%	23.3%
OPEC	28,472	29,953	31,207	29,999	31,512	30,857	29,031	30,884	33,175	34,068	**34,202**	0.2%	41.7%
Non-OPEC†	34,288	34,925	35,028	34,887	35,507	35,415	35,933	35,673	35,661	35,343	**35,162**	20.5%	43.0%
Former Soviet Union	7171	7374	7391	7552	8014	8660	9533	10,499	11,407	11,840	**12,299**	3.9%	15.3%

*Includes crude oil, shale oil, oil sands and NGLs (the liquid content of natural gas where this is recovered separately). Excludes liquid fuels from other sources such as biomass and coal derivatives.

**Less than 0.05%

†Excludes former Soviet Union.

Note: Annual changes and shares of total are calculated using million tons per annum figures.

table that you find useful. Here is a summary drawn from the information from Table 1.1 focusing just on the North American and Middle Eastern sections. Notice that the summary requires the writer to read closely and discern which information is significant. The table reports raw data and does not speak for itself. At the end of the summary, the writer, using information not only from this table but also from Figure 1.4,"U.S. Oil Consumption, 1950–2020," draws her own conclusions:

> In 1996, the United States produced 8.3 million barrels of oil daily, or 89% of Saudi Arabia's production of 9.3 million barrels. By 2006, the United States was producing less than 7 million barrels, or 62% of Saudi Arabia's 11 million barrels. If we compare by region, the figures are only marginally more favorable to Americans. In 1996, the countries of North America produced 68% of the oil produced by the countries of the Middle East. Ten years later, that 68% had declined to 54%. Though the years between 1996 and 2006 have seen ups and downs in oil production by both regions, the overall trend is clear: North American production is falling and Middle East production is rising. Further, North American production is falling primarily because of declines in U.S. production; generally, Canadian and Mexican production have seen small but steady rises. Canada, for example, was producing about 2.5 million barrels of oil in 1996 and just over 3 million barrels in 2006. But this half-million-barrel rise was dwarfed by the 1.5-million-barrel rise in production by Saudi Arabia during that same period. The implications are clear: Far from being self-sufficient in oil production, the United States is becoming less self-sufficient every year and is becoming ever more dependent for its petroleum supplies on a region whose political stability and reliability as a petroleum source are in serious question.

Exercise 1.5

Summarizing Tables

Focus on other data in Table 1.1 and write a brief summary of your own. Or locate another table on the general topic of oil production or consumption and summarize part or all of its data. (Suggestion: run an Internet search on the search terms: "cia oil comparison table," and you will find the "Oil Production and Consumption Country Comparison Table" from the World Factbook.)

PARAPHRASE

In certain cases, you may want to *paraphrase* rather than summarize material. Writing a paraphrase is similar to writing a summary: It involves recasting a passage into your own words, so it requires your complete understanding of the material. The difference is that while a summary is a shortened version of the original, the paraphrase is approximately the same length as the original.

Why write a paraphrase when you can quote the original? You may decide to offer a paraphrase of material written in language that is dense, abstract, archaic, or possibly confusing.

Let's consider some examples. If you were writing a paper on bilingual education in the United States, you would likely need to draw on the "Bilingual Education Act" as a source. The language of that law, however, is dense and complex. Had you some actual experience of bilingual education, you might understand this law on a first reading; but those less familiar with the subject or with legal language would have a more difficult time. Suppose that in a section of your paper you decided to discuss with the reader a particularly important section of the law:

TITLE VII—BILINGUAL EDUCATION

SHORT TITLE

SEC. 701. This title may be cited as the "Bilingual Education Act".

POLICY; APPROPRIATIONS

SEC. 702. (a) Recognizing—

(1) that there are large numbers of children of limited English-speaking ability;

(2) that many of such children have a cultural heritage which differs from that of English-speaking persons;

(3) that a primary means by which a child learns is through the use of such child's language and cultural heritage;

(4) that, therefore, large numbers of children of limited English-speaking ability have educational needs which can be met by the use of bilingual educational methods and techniques; and

(5) that, in addition, children of limited English-speaking ability benefit through the fullest utilization of multiple language and cultural resources, the Congress declares it to be the policy of the United States, in order to establish equal educational opportunity for all children (A) to encourage the establishment and operation, where appropriate, of educational programs using bilingual educational practices, techniques, and methods, and (B) for that purpose, to provide financial assistance to local educational agencies, and to State educational agencies for certain purposes, in order to enable such local educational agencies to develop and carry out such programs in elementary and secondary schools, including activities at the preschool level, which are designed to meet the educational needs of such children; and to demonstrate effective ways of providing, for children of limited English-speaking ability, instruction designed to enable them, while using their native language, to achieve competence in the English language.

Like most legal passages, this is somewhat forbidding to lay people: it consists of one sentence more than two hundred words long, with typically impenetrable legal phrasing. To clarify the meaning for the general reader, you proceed to paraphrase the original language. First, of course, you must understand the meaning of the passage, no small task. But having read the material carefully, you might eventually draft a paraphrase such as this one:

The federal guidelines for bilingual education are presented in Public Law 93-380 (Aug. 21, 1974), an amendment to Title VII of the Elementary and Secondary Education Act of 1965. The "Bilingual Education Act"(the short title) is premised on three assumptions: (1) that many children have limited ability to speak English; (2) that many come from ethnical diverse, non-English-speaking backgrounds; and (3) that native language and culture powerfully influence a child's learning. Based on these assumptions, Congress concluded that many children in the United States should be educated through programs in bilingual education. This approach makes full use of a student's native linguistic and cultural resources.

Accordingly, Congress declared that in the interests of establishing equal educational opportunities for all children, the government would encourage the creation of bilingual programs in preschools and in elementary and secondary schools. Congress would fund such programs at the state and local levels with the understanding that these programs would enable students, "while using their native language, to achieve competence in the English language."

In our paraphrase of Congress's one long sentence, we have written six sentences arranged in two paragraphs. Our paragraphs follow the logic and structure of the original, which is presented in two parts. The first part consists of the five "recognizing that" clauses. We've taken these clauses and paraphrased them into two sentences: one dealing with the assumptions underlying the law, the other addressing the conclusions Congress reached based on these assumptions. The second part of the original—and of the paraphrase—presents Congress's two declarations. Notice that to capture some of the tone of the original we ended the paraphrase with a quotation. Although our paraphrase is somewhat briefer than the original, it follows the original's logic and structure. Though it might not stand up in court, this paraphrase accurately conveys the sense of the law to the lay reader.

As you can see, the paraphrase requires a writer to make decisions about the presentation of material. In many, if not most, cases, you will need to do more than simply "translate" from the original, sentence by sentence, to write your paraphrase. When you come across a passage that you don't understand, the temptation is to skip over it. Resist this temptation! Use a paraphrase as a tool for explaining to yourself the main ideas of a difficult passage. By translating another writer's language into your own, you clarify what you understand and pinpoint what you don't. The paraphrase therefore becomes a tool for learning the subject.

The following pointers will help you write paraphrases.

HOW TO WRITE PARAPHRASES

- Make sure that you understand the source passage.
- Substitute your own words for those of the source passage; look for synonyms that carry the same meaning as the original words.
- Rearrange your own sentences so that they read smoothly. Sentence structure, even sentence order, in the paraphrase need not be based on that of the original. A good paraphrase, like a good summary, should stand by itself.

Paraphrases are generally about the same length as (and sometimes shorter than) the passages on which they are based. But sometimes clarity requires that a paraphrase be longer than a tightly compacted source passage. For example, suppose you wanted to paraphrase this statement by Sigmund Freud:

> We have found out that the distortion in dreams which hinders our understanding of them is due to the activities of a censorship, directed against the unacceptable, unconscious wish-impulses.

If you were to paraphrase this statement (the first sentence in the Tenth Lecture of his *General Introduction to Psychoanalysis*), you might come up with something such as this:

> It is difficult to understand dreams because they contain distortions. Freud believed that these distortions arise from our internal censor, which attempts to suppress unconscious and forbidden desires.

Essentially, this paraphrase does little more than break up one sentence into two and somewhat rearrange the sentence structure for clarity.

Like summaries, then, paraphrases are useful devices, both in helping you to understand source material and in enabling you to convey the essence of this source material to your readers. When would you choose to write a summary instead of a paraphrase (or vice versa)? The answer depends on your purpose in presenting the source material. As we've said, summaries are generally based on articles (or sections of articles) or books. Paraphrases are generally based on particularly difficult (or important) paragraphs or sentences. You would seldom paraphrase a long passage, or summarize a short one, unless there were particularly good reasons for doing so. (A lawyer might want to paraphrase several pages of legal language so that his or her client, who is not a lawyer, could understand it.) The purpose of a summary is generally to save your reader time by presenting him or her with a brief version of a lengthy source. The purpose of a paraphrase is generally to clarify a short passage that might otherwise be unclear. Whether you summarize or paraphrase may also depend on the importance of your source. A particularly important source—if it is not too long—may rate a paraphrase. If it is less important, or peripheral to your central argument, you may write a summary instead. And, of course, you may choose to summarize only part of your source—the part that is most relevant to the point you are making.

Exercise 1.6

Paraphrasing

Locate and photocopy three relatively complex, but brief, passages from readings currently assigned in your other courses. Paraphrase these passages, making the language more readable and understandable. Attach the photocopies to the paraphrases.

QUOTATIONS

A *quotation* records the exact language used by someone in speech or writing. A *summary*, in contrast, is a brief restatement in your own words of what someone else has said or written. And a *paraphrase* is also a restatement, although one that is often as long as the original source. Any paper in which you draw upon sources will rely heavily on quotation, summary, and paraphrase. How do you choose among the three?

Remember that the papers you write should be your own—for the most part: your own language and certainly your own thesis, your own inferences, and your own conclusion. It follows that references to your source materials should be written primarily as summaries and paraphrases, both of which are built on restatement, not quotation. You will use summaries when you need a *brief* restatement, and paraphrases—which provide more explicit detail than summaries—when you need to follow the development of a source closely. When you quote too much, you risk losing ownership of your work: More easily than you might think, your voice can be drowned out by the voices of those you've quoted. So *use quotation sparingly*, as you would a pungent spice.

Nevertheless, quoting just the right source at the right time can significantly improve your papers. The trick is to know when and how to use quotations.

Quotations can be direct or indirect. A *direct* quotation is one in which you record precisely the language of another person. An *indirect* quotation is one in which you report what someone has said without repeating the words exactly as spoken (or written):

Direct quotation: Franklin D. Roosevelt said, "The only thing we have to fear is fear itself."

Indirect quotation: Franklin D. Roosevelt said that we have nothing to fear but fear itself.

The language in a direct quotation, which is indicated by a pair of quotation marks (" "), must be faithful to the wording of the original passage. When using an indirect quotation, you have the liberty of changing words (although not changing meaning). For both direct and indirect quotations, *you must credit your sources*, naming them either in (or close to) the sentence that includes the quotation or in a parenthetical citation. (See the "Quick Indexes" at the end of this text for specific rules on citing sources properly.)

Choosing Quotations

You'll find that using quotations can be particularly helpful in several situations.

Quoting Memorable Language

You should quote when the source material is worded so eloquently or powerfully that to summarize or paraphrase it would be to sacrifice much of the impact and significance of the meaning. Here, for example, is the historian John Keegan

WHEN TO QUOTE

- Use quotations when another writer's language is particularly memorable and will add interest and liveliness to your paper.
- Use quotations when another writer's language is so clear and economical that to make the same point in your own words would, by comparison, be ineffective.
- Use quotations when you want the solid reputation of a source to lend authority and credibility to your own writing.

describing how France, Germany, Austria, and Russia slid inexorably into the cataclysm of World War I in 1914:

> In the event, the states of Europe proceeded, as if in a dead march and a dialogue of the deaf, to the destruction of their continent and its civilization.

No paraphrase could do justice to the power of Keegan's words as they appear in his book *The First World War* (1998). You would certainly want to quote them in any paper dealing with the origins of this conflict.

Quoting Clear and Concise Language

You should quote a source when its language is particularly clear and economical—when your language, by contrast, would be wordy. Read this passage from a biology text by Patricia Curtis:

> The honeybee colony, which usually has a population of 30,000 to 40,000 workers, differs from that of the bumblebee and many other social bees or wasps in that it survives the winter. This means that the bees must stay warm despite the cold. Like other bees, the isolated honeybee cannot fly if the temperature falls below 10°C (50°F) and cannot walk if the temperature is below 7°C (45°F). Within the wintering hive, bees maintain their temperature by clustering together in a dense ball; the lower the temperature, the denser the cluster. The clustered bees produce heat by constant muscular movements of their wings, legs, and abdomens. In very cold weather, the bees on the outside of the cluster keep moving toward the center, while those in the core of the cluster move to the colder outside periphery. The entire cluster moves slowly about on the combs, eating the stored honey from the combs as it moves.*

A summary of this paragraph might read:

> Honeybees, unlike many other varieties of bee, are able to live through the winter by "clustering together in a dense ball" for body warmth.

---

*Patricia Curtis, "Winter Organization," *Biology*, 2nd ed. (New York: Worth, 1976): 822–23.

A paraphrase of the same passage would be considerably more detailed:

> Honeybees, unlike many other varieties of bee (such as bumblebees), are able to live through the winter. The 30,000 to 40,000 bees within a honeybee hive could not, individually, move about in cold winter temperatures. But when "clustering together in a dense ball," the bees generate heat by constantly moving their body parts. The cluster also moves slowly about the hive, those on the periphery of the cluster moving into the center, those in the center moving to the periphery, and all eating honey stored in the combs. This nutrition, in addition to the heat generated by the cluster, enables the honeybee to survive the cold winter months.

In both the summary and the paraphrase, we've quoted Curtis's "clustering together in a dense ball," a phrase that lies at the heart of her description of wintering honeybees. For us to describe this clustering in any language other than Curtis's would be pointless, as her description is admirably brief and precise.

Quoting Authoritative Language

You should use quotations that lend authority to your work. When quoting an expert or a prominent political, artistic, or historical figure, you elevate your own work by placing it in esteemed company. Quote respected figures to establish background information in a paper, and your readers will tend to perceive that information as reliable. Quote the opinions of respected figures to endorse a statement that you've made, and your statement becomes more credible to your readers. Here, in a discussion of space flight, the writer David Chandler refers to a physicist and a physicist-astronaut:

> A few scientists—notably James Van Allen, discoverer of the Earth's radiation belts—have decried the expense of the manned space program and called for an almost exclusive concentration on unmanned scientific exploration instead, saying this would be far more cost-effective.
>
> Other space scientists dispute that idea. Joseph Allen, physicist and former shuttle astronaut, says, "It seems to be argued that one takes away from the other. But before there was a manned space program, the funding on space science was zero. Now it's about $500 million a year."

In the first paragraph, Chandler has either summarized or used an indirect quotation to incorporate remarks made by James Van Allen into the discussion on space flight. In the second paragraph, Chandler directly quotes Joseph Allen. Both quotations, indirect and direct, lend authority and legitimacy to the article, for both James Van Allen and Joseph Allen are experts on the subject of space flight. Note that Chandler provides brief but effective biographies of his sources, identifying each one so that their qualifications to speak on the subject are known to all:

James Van Allen, *discoverer of the Earth's radiation belts* . . .

Joseph Allen, *physicist and former shuttle astronaut* . . .

The phrases in italics are *appositives*. Their function is to rename the nouns they follow by providing explicit, identifying detail. Any information about a person that can be expressed in the following sentence pattern can be made into an appositive phrase:

> James Van Allen is the *discoverer of the Earth's radiation belts*.

> He has decried the expense of the manned space program.

Sentence with an appositive:

> James Van Allen, *discoverer of the Earth's radiation belts*, has decried the expense of the manned space program.

Appositives (in the example above, "discoverer of the Earth's radiation belts") efficiently incorporate identifying information about the authors you quote, while adding variety to the structure of your sentences.

Incorporating Quotations into Your Sentences

Quoting Only the Part of a Sentence or Paragraph That You Need

We've said that a writer selects passages for quotation that are especially vivid, memorable, concise, or authoritative. Now put these principles into practice. Suppose that while conducting research on college sports, you've come across the following, written by Robert Hutchins, former president of the University of Chicago:

> If athleticism is bad for students, players, alumni, and the public, it is even worse for the colleges and universities themselves. They want to be educational institutions, but they can't. The story of the famous halfback whose only regret, when he bade his coach farewell, was that he hadn't learned to read and write is probably exaggerated. But we must admit that pressure from trustees, graduates, "friends," presidents, and even professors has tended to relax academic standards. These gentry often overlook the fact that a college should not be interested in a fullback who is a half-wit. Recruiting, subsidizing and the double educational standard cannot exist without the knowledge and the tacit approval, at least, of the colleges and universities themselves. Certain institutions encourage susceptible professors to be nice to athletes now admitted by paying them for serving as "faculty representatives" on the college athletic board.*

Suppose that in this paragraph you find a gem, a sentence with striking language that will enliven your discussion:

> These gentry often overlook the fact that a college should not be interested in a fullback who is a half-wit.

---

*Robert Hutchins, "Gate Receipts and Glory," *Saturday Evening Post* 3 Dec. 1983: 38.

Incorporating the Quotation into the Flow of Your Own Sentence

Once you've selected the passage you want to quote, you need to work the material into your paper in as natural and fluid a manner as possible. Here's how we would quote Hutchins:

> Robert Hutchins, former president of the University of Chicago, asserts that "a college should not be interested in a fullback who is a half-wit."

Note that we've used an appositive to identify Hutchins. And we've used only the part of the paragraph—a single clause—that we thought memorable enough to quote directly.

Avoiding Freestanding Quotations

A quoted sentence should never stand by itself, as in the following example:

> Various people associated with the university admit that the pressures of athleticism have caused a relaxation of standards. "These gentry often overlook the fact that a college should not be interested in a fullback who is a half-wit." But this kind of thinking is bad for the university and even worse for the athletes.

Even if it were followed by a parenthetical citation, a freestanding quotation would be jarring to the reader. You need to introduce the quotation with a *signal phrase* that attributes the source. This should be done not in a parenthetical citation, but in some other part of the sentence—beginning, middle, or end. Thus, you could write:

> As Robert Hutchins notes, "These gentry often overlook the fact that a college should not be interested in a fullback who is a half-wit."

Here's a variation with the signal phrase in the middle:

> "These gentry," asserts Robert Hutchins, "often overlook the fact that a college should not be interested in a fullback who is a half-wit."

Another alternative is to introduce a sentence-long quotation with a colon:

> But Robert Hutchins disagrees: "These gentry often overlook the fact that a college should not be interested in a fullback who is a half-wit."

Use colons also to introduce indented quotations (as when we introduce long quotations in this chapter).

When attributing sources in signal phrases, try to vary the standard *states, writes, says,* and so on. Stronger verbs you might consider are: *asserts, argues, maintains, insists, asks,* and even *wonders.*

Exercise 1.7

Incorporating Quotations

Return to the article (pp. 9–13) by Alan S. Blinder, "Will Your Job Be Exported?" Find sentences that you think make interesting points. Imagine you want to use these points in a paper you're writing on job prospects in the twenty-first century. Write five different sentences that use a variety of the techniques discussed thus far to incorporate whole sentences as well as phrases from Blinder's article.

Using Ellipses

Using quotations becomes somewhat complicated when you want to quote the beginning and end of a passage but not its middle. Here's part of a paragraph from Thoreau's *Walden*:

> To read well, that is to read true books in a true spirit, is a noble exercise, and one that will task the reader more than any exercise which the customs of the day esteem. It requires a training such as the athletes underwent, the steady intention almost of the whole life to this object. Books must be read as deliberately and reservedly as they were written.*

And here is how we can use this material in a quotation:

> Reading well is hard work, writes Henry David Thoreau in *Walden*, "that will task the reader more than any exercise which the customs of the day esteem. . . . Books must be read as deliberately and reservedly as they were written."

Whenever you quote a sentence but delete words from it, as we have done above, indicate this deletion to the reader with three spaced periods—called an "ellipsis"—in the sentence at the point of deletion. The rationale for using an ellipsis mark is that a direct quotation must be reproduced *exactly* as it was written or spoken. When writers delete or change any part of the quoted material, readers must be alerted so they don't think the changes were part of the original. When deleting an entire sentence or sentences from a quoted paragraph, as in the example above, end the sentence you have quoted with a period, place the ellipsis, and continue the quotation.

If you are deleting the middle of a single sentence, use an ellipsis in place of the deleted words:

> "To read well . . . is a noble exercise, and one that will task the reader more than any exercise which the customs of the day esteem."

If you are deleting material from the end of one sentence through to the beginning of another sentence, add a sentence period before the ellipsis:

> "It requires a training such as the athletes underwent. . . . Books must be read as deliberately and reservedly as they were written."

---

*Henry David Thoreau, *Walden* (New York: Signet Classic, 1960): 72.

If you begin your quotation of an author in the middle of his or her sentence, you need not indicate deleted words with an ellipsis. Be sure, however, that the syntax of the quotation fits smoothly with the syntax of your sentence:

> Reading "is a noble exercise," writes Henry David Thoreau.

Using Brackets to Add or Substitute Words

Use brackets whenever you need to add or substitute words in a quoted sentence. The brackets indicate to the reader a word or phrase that does not appear in the original passage but that you have inserted to prevent confusion. For example, when a pronoun's antecedent would be unclear to readers, delete the pronoun from the sentence and substitute an identifying word or phrase in brackets. When you make such a substitution, no ellipsis mark is needed. Assume that you wish to quote either of the underlined sentences in the following passage by Jane Yolen:

> Golden Press's *Walt Disney's Cinderella* set the new pattern for America's Cinderella. This book's text is coy and condescending. (Sample: "And her best friends of all were—guess who—the mice!") The illustrations are poor cartoons. And Cinderella herself is a disaster. She cowers as her sisters rip her homemade ball gown to shreds. (Not even homemade by Cinderella, but by the mice and birds.) <u>She answers her stepmother with whines and pleadings. She is a sorry excuse for a heroine, pitiable and useless.</u> She cannot perform even a simple action to save herself, though she is warned by her friends, the mice. She does not hear them because she is "off in a world of dreams." Cinderella begs, she whimpers, and at last has to be rescued by—guess who—the mice!*

In quoting one of these sentences, you would need to identify to whom the pronoun *she* refers. You can do this inside the quotation by using brackets:

> Jane Yolen believes that "[Cinderella] is a sorry excuse for a heroine, pitiable and useless."

When the pronoun begins the sentence to be quoted, you can identify the pronoun outside the quotation and begin quoting your source one word later:

> Jane Yolen believes that in the Golden Press version, Cinderella "is a sorry excuse for a heroine, pitiable and useless."

Here's another example of a case where the pronoun needing identification occurs in the middle of the sentence to be quoted. Newspaper reporters must use brackets when quoting a source, who in an interview might say this:

> After the fire they did not return to the station house for three hours.

---

*Jane Yolen, "America's 'Cinderella,'" *Children's Literature in Education* 8 (1977): 22.

WHEN TO SUMMARIZE, PARAPHRASE, AND QUOTE

Summarize:
- To present main points of a lengthy passage (article or book)
- To condense peripheral points necessary to discussion

Paraphrase:
- To clarify a short passage
- To emphasize main points

Quote:
- To capture another writer's particularly memorable language
- To capture another writer's clearly and economically stated language
- To lend authority and credibility to your own writing

If the reporter wants to use this sentence in an article, he or she needs to identify the pronoun:

> An official from City Hall, speaking on the condition that he not be identified, said, "After the fire [the officers] did not return to the station house for three hours."

You will also need to add bracketed information to a quoted sentence when a reference essential to the sentence's meaning is implied but not stated directly. Read the following paragraph from Walter Isaacson's biography of Albert Einstein, *Einstein: His Life and Universe*:

> Newton had bequeathed to Einstein a universe in which time had an absolute existence that tick-tocked along independent of objects and observers, and in which space likewise had an absolute existence. Gravity was thought to be a force that masses exerted on one another rather mysteriously across empty space. Within this framework, objects obeyed mechanical laws that had proved remarkably accurate—almost perfect—in explaining everything from the orbits of the planets, to the diffusion of gases, to the jiggling of molecules, to the propagation of sound (though not light) waves.

If you wanted to quote only the underlined sentence above, you would need to provide readers with a bracketed explanation; otherwise, the phrase "this framework" would be unclear. Here is how you would manage the quotation:

> According to Walter Isaacson, Newton's universe was extremely regular and predictable:
>
> > Within this framework [that time and space exist independently of their observation and that gravity results from masses exerting a remote attraction on one another], objects obeyed mechanical laws that had proved remarkably

accurate—almost perfect—in explaining everything from the orbits of the planets, to the diffusion of gases, to the jiggling of molecules, to the propagation of sound (though not light) waves. (223)

Exercise 1.8

Using Brackets

Write your own sentences incorporating the following quotations. Use brackets to clarify information that isn't clear outside its original context—and refer to the original sources to remind yourself of this context.

From the David Chandler paragraph on James Van Allen (pp. 39–40):

a. Other space scientists *dispute that idea.*

b. Now *it's about $500 million a year.*

From the Jane Yolen excerpt on Cinderella (p. 43):

a. *This book's* text is coy and condescending.

b. *She* cannot perform even a simple action to save herself, though she is warned by her friends, the mice.

c. She does not hear *them* because she is "off in a world of dreams."

Remember that when you quote the work of another, you are obligated to credit—or cite—the author's work properly; otherwise, you may be guilty of plagiarism. See the "Quick Indexes" at the end of this text for guidance on citing sources.

INCORPORATING QUOTATIONS INTO YOUR SENTENCES

- **Quote only the part of a sentence or paragraph that you need.** Use no more of the writer's language than necessary to make or reinforce your point.
- **Incorporate the quotation into the flow of your own sentence.** The quotation must fit, both syntactically and stylistically, into your surrounding language.
- **Avoid freestanding quotations.** A quoted sentence should never stand by itself. Use a *signal phrase*—at the beginning, the middle, or the end of the sentence—to attribute the source of the quotation.
- **Use ellipsis marks.** Indicate deleted language in the middle of a quoted sentence with ellipsis marks. Deleted language at the beginning or end of a sentence generally does not require ellipsis marks.
- **Use brackets to add or substitute words.** Put added or substituted words in brackets in a quoted sentence when the meaning of the quotation would otherwise be unclear—for example, when the antecedent of a quoted pronoun is ambiguous.

AVOIDING PLAGIARISM

Plagiarism is generally defined as the attempt to pass off the work of another as one's own. Whether born out of calculation or desperation, plagiarism is the least tolerated offense in the academic world. The fact that most plagiarism is unintentional—arising from an ignorance of the conventions rather than deceitfulness—makes no difference to many professors.

The ease of cutting and pasting whole blocks of text from Web sources into one's own paper makes it tempting for some to take the easy way out and avoid doing their own research and writing. But, apart from the serious ethical issues involved, the same technology that makes such acts possible also makes it possible for instructors to detect them. Software marketed to instructors allows them to conduct Web searches, using suspicious phrases as keywords. The results often provide irrefutable evidence of plagiarism.

Of course, plagiarism is not confined to students. Recent years have seen a number of high-profile cases—some of them reaching the front pages of newspapers—of well-known scholars who were shown to have copied passages from sources into their own book manuscripts, without proper attribution. In some cases, the scholars maintained that these appropriations were simply a matter of carelessness, that in the press and volume of work, they had lost track of which words were theirs and which were the words of their sources. But such excuses sounded hollow: These careless acts inevitably embarrassed the scholars professionally, tarnished their otherwise fine work and reputations, and disappointed their many admirers.

You can avoid plagiarism and charges of plagiarism by following the basic rules provided on page 47.

Following is a passage from an article by Richard Rovere on Senator Joseph P. McCarthy, along with several student versions of the ideas represented.

> McCarthy never seemed to believe in himself or in anything he had said. He knew that Communists were not in charge of American foreign policy. He knew that they weren't running the United States Army. He knew that he had spent five years looking for Communists in the government and that—although some must certainly have been there, since Communists had turned up in practically every other major government in the world—he hadn't come up with even one.*

One student version of this passage reads:

> McCarthy never believed in himself or in anything he had said. He knew that Communists were not in charge of American foreign policy and weren't running the United States Army. He knew that he had spent five years looking for Communists in the government, and although there must certainly have been some there, since Communists were in practically every other major government in the world, he hadn't come up with even one.

---

*Richard Rovere, "The Most Gifted and Successful Demagogue This Country Has Ever Known," *New York Times Magazine*, 30 Apr. 1967.

Clearly, this is intentional plagiarism. The student has copied the original passage almost word for word.

Here is another version of the same passage:

> McCarthy knew that Communists were not running foreign policy or the Army. He also knew that although there must have been some Communists in the government, he hadn't found a single one, even though he had spent five years looking.

This student has attempted to put the ideas into her own words, but both the wording and the sentence structure are so heavily dependent on the original passage that even if it *were* cited, most professors would consider it plagiarism.

In the following version, the student has sufficiently changed the wording and sentence structure, and she uses a *signal phrase* (a phrase used to introduce a quotation or paraphrase, signaling to the reader that the words to follow come from someone else) to properly credit the information to Rovere, so that there is no question of plagiarism:

> According to Richard Rovere, McCarthy was fully aware that Communists were running neither the government nor the Army. He also knew that he hadn't found a single Communist in government, even after a lengthy search (192).

And although this is not a matter of plagiarism, as noted above, it's essential to quote accurately. You are not permitted to change any part of a quotation or to omit any part of it without using brackets or ellipses.

RULES FOR AVOIDING PLAGIARISM

- Cite *all* quoted material and *all* summarized and paraphrased material, unless the information is common knowledge (e.g., the Civil War was fought from 1861 to 1865).
- Make sure that both the *wording* and the *sentence structure* of your summaries and paraphrases are substantially your own.

Chapter 2

Critical Reading and Critique

After completing this chapter, you will be able to:

LO 2.1   Read critically to determine (1) how well an article, editorial, or chapter has succeeded in achieving its purpose and (2) how fully you agree with the author's points.

LO 2.2   Write a critique of an article, editorial, or chapter that expresses (1) how well the passage has succeeded in achieving its purpose and (2) how fully you agree with the author's points.

CRITICAL READING

When writing papers in college, you are often called on to respond critically to source materials. Critical reading requires the abilities to both summarize and evaluate a presentation. As you have seen in Chapter 1, a *summary* is a brief restatement in your own words of the content of a passage; an *evaluation* is a more ambitious undertaking. In your college work, you read to gain and *use* new information. But because sources are not equally valid or equally useful, you must learn to distinguish critically among them by evaluating them.

There is no ready-made formula for determining validity. Critical reading and its written equivalent—the *critique*—require discernment, sensitivity, imagination, knowledge of the subject, and, above all, willingness to become involved in what you read. These skills are developed only through repeated practice. But you must begin somewhere, so we recommend you start by posing two broad questions about passages, articles, and books that you read: (1) To what extent does the author succeed in his or her purpose? (2) To what extent do you agree with the author?

Question 1: To What Extent Does the Author Succeed in His or Her Purpose?

All critical reading *begins with an accurate summary*. Before attempting an evaluation, you must be able to locate an author's thesis and identify the selection's content and structure. You must understand the author's *purpose*. Authors write to inform,

WHERE DO WE FIND WRITTEN CRITIQUES?

Here are just a few of the types of writing that involve critique:

Academic Writing

- **Research papers** critique sources in order to establish their usefulness.
- **Position papers** stake out a position by critiquing other positions.
- **Book reviews** combine summary with critique.
- **Essay exams** demonstrate understanding of course material by critiquing it.

Workplace Writing

- **Legal briefs and legal arguments** critique previous arguments made or anticipated by opposing counsel.
- **Business plans and proposals** critique other less cost-effective, cost-efficient, or reasonable approaches.
- **Policy briefs** communicate strengths and weaknesses of policies and legislation through critique.

to persuade, and to entertain. A given piece may be primarily *informative* (a summary of the research on cloning), primarily *persuasive* (an argument on what the government should do to alleviate homelessness), or primarily *entertaining* (a play about the frustrations of young lovers). Or it may be all three (as in John Steinbeck's novel *The Grapes of Wrath*, about migrant workers during the Great Depression). Sometimes authors are not fully conscious of their purpose. Sometimes their purpose changes as they write. Also, multiple purposes can overlap: A piece of writing may need to inform the reader about an issue in order to make a persuasive point. But if the finished piece is coherent, it will have a primary reason for having been written, and it should be apparent that the author is attempting primarily to inform, persuade, or entertain a particular audience. To identify this primary reason—this purpose—is your first job as a critical reader. Your next job is to determine how successful the author has been in achieving this objective.

As a critical reader, you bring various criteria, or standards of judgment, to bear when you read pieces intended to inform, persuade, or entertain.

Writing to Inform

A piece intended to inform will provide definitions, describe or report on a process, recount a story, give historical background, and/or provide facts and figures. An informational piece responds to questions such as:

What (or who) is _____?

How does _____ work?

What is the controversy or problem about?

What happened?

How and why did it happen?

What were the results?

What are the arguments for and against _____?

To the extent that an author answers these and related questions and that the answers are a matter of verifiable record (you could check for accuracy if you had the time and inclination), the selection is intended to inform. Having identified such an intention, you can organize your response by considering three other criteria: accuracy, significance, and fair interpretation of information.

Evaluating Informative Writing

Accuracy of Information   If you are going to use any of the information presented, you must be satisfied that it is trustworthy. One of your responsibilities as a critical reader, then, is to find out if the information is accurate. This means you should check facts against other sources. Government publications are often good resources for verifying facts about political legislation, population data, crime statistics, and the like. You can also search key terms in library databases and on the Web. Since material on the Web is essentially self-published, however, you must be especially vigilant in assessing its legitimacy. A wealth of useful information is now available on the Internet—as are distorted "facts," unsupported opinion, and hidden agendas.

Significance of Information   One useful question that you can put to a reading is "So what?" In the case of selections that attempt to inform, you may reasonably wonder whether the information makes a difference. What can the reader gain from this information? How is knowledge advanced by the publication of this material? Is the information of importance to you or to others in a particular audience? Why or why not?

Fair Interpretation of Information   At times you will read reports whose sole purpose is to relate raw data or information. In these cases, you will build your response on Question 1, introduced on page 48: To what extent does the author succeed in his or her purpose? More frequently, once an author has presented information, he or she will attempt to evaluate or interpret it—which is only reasonable, since information that has not been evaluated or interpreted is of little use. One of your tasks as a critical reader is to make a distinction between the author's presentation of facts and figures and his or her attempts to evaluate them. Watch for shifts from straightforward descriptions of factual information ("20 percent of the population") to assertions about what this information means ("a *mere* 20 percent of the population"), what its implications are, and so on. Pay attention to whether the logic with which the author connects interpretation with facts is sound. You may find that the information is valuable but the interpretation is not. Perhaps the author's conclusions are not justified. Could you offer a contrary explanation for the same facts? Does more information need to be gathered before firm conclusions can be drawn? Why?

Writing to Persuade

Writing is frequently intended to persuade—that is, to influence the reader's thinking. To make a persuasive case, the writer must begin with an assertion that is arguable, some statement about which reasonable people could disagree. Such an assertion, when it serves as the essential organizing principle of the article or book, is called a *thesis*. Here are two examples:

> Because they do not speak English, many children in this affluent land are being denied their fundamental right to equal educational opportunity.

> Bilingual education, which has been stridently promoted by a small group of activists with their own agenda, is detrimental to the very students it is supposed to serve.

Thesis statements such as these—and the subsequent assertions used to help support them—represent conclusions that authors have drawn as a result of researching and thinking about an issue. You go through the same process yourself when you write persuasive papers or critiques. And just as you are entitled to evaluate critically the assertions of authors you read, so your professors—and other students—are entitled to evaluate *your* assertions, whether they be written arguments or comments made in class discussion.

Keep in mind that writers organize arguments by arranging evidence to support one conclusion and to oppose (or dismiss) another. You can assess the validity of an argument and its conclusion by determining whether the author has (1) clearly defined key terms, (2) used information fairly, and (3) argued logically and not fallaciously (see pp. 55–59).

Exercise 2.1

Informative and Persuasive Thesis Statements

With a partner from your class, identify at least one informative and one persuasive thesis statement from two passages of your own choosing. Photocopy these passages and highlight the statements you have selected.

As an alternative, and also working with a partner, write one informative and one persuasive thesis statement for *three* of the topics listed in the last paragraph of this exercise. For example, for the topic of prayer in schools, your informative thesis statement could read:

> Both advocates and opponents of school prayer frame their position as a matter of freedom.

Your persuasive thesis statement might be worded:

> As long as schools don't dictate what kinds of prayers students should say, then school prayer should be allowed and even encouraged.

Don't worry about taking a position that you agree with or feel you could support; this exercise doesn't require that you write an essay. The topics:

school prayer

gun control

immigration

stem cell research

grammar instruction in English class

violent lyrics in music

teaching computer skills in primary schools

curfews in college dormitories

course registration procedures

Evaluating Persuasive Writing

Read the argument that follows on the cancellation of the National Aeronautics and Space Administration's lunar program. We will illustrate our discussion on defining terms, using information fairly, and arguing logically by referring to Charles Krauthammer's argument, which appeared as an op-ed in the *Washington Post* on July 17, 2009. The model critique that follows these illustrations will be based on this same argument.

THE MOON WE LEFT BEHIND

Charles Krauthammer

Michael Crichton once wrote that if you told a physicist in 1899 that within a hundred years humankind would, among other wonders (nukes, commercial airlines), "travel to the moon, and then lose interest…the physicist would almost certainly pronounce you mad." In 2000, I quoted these lines expressing Crichton's incredulity at America's abandonment of the moon. It is now 2009 and the moon recedes ever further.

Next week marks the 40th anniversary of the first moon landing. We say we will return in 2020. But that promise was made by a previous president, and this president [Obama] has defined himself as the antimatter to George Bush. Moreover, for all of Barack Obama's Kennedyesque qualities, he has expressed none of Kennedy's enthusiasm for human space exploration.

So with the Apollo moon program long gone, and with Constellation,* its supposed successor, still little more than a hope, we remain in retreat from space. Astonishing. After countless millennia of gazing and dreaming, we finally

*Constellation was a NASA human spaceflight program designed to develop post–space shuttle vehicles capable of traveling to the moon and perhaps to Mars. Authorized in 2005, the program was canceled by President Obama in 2010.

got off the ground at Kitty Hawk in 1903. Within 66 years, a nanosecond in human history, we'd landed on the moon. Then five more landings, 10 more moonwalkers and, in the decades since, nothing.

To be more precise: almost 40 years spent in low Earth orbit studying, well, zero-G nausea and sundry cosmic mysteries. We've done it with the most beautiful, intricate, complicated—and ultimately, hopelessly impractical—machine ever built by man: the space shuttle. We turned this magnificent bird into a truck for hauling goods and people to a tinkertoy we call the international space station, itself created in a fit of post-Cold War internationalist absentmindedness as a place where people of differing nationality can sing "Kumbaya" while weightless.

5   The shuttle is now too dangerous, too fragile and too expensive. Seven more flights and then it is retired, going—like the Spruce Goose* and the Concorde[†]— into the Museum of Things Too Beautiful and Complicated to Survive.

America's manned space program is in shambles. Fourteen months from today, for the first time since 1962, the United States will be incapable not just of sending a man to the moon but of sending anyone into Earth orbit. We'll be totally grounded. We'll have to beg a ride from the Russians or perhaps even the Chinese.

So what, you say? Don't we have problems here on Earth? Oh, please. Poverty and disease and social ills will always be with us. If we'd waited for them to be rectified before venturing out, we'd still be living in caves.

Yes, we have a financial crisis. No one's asking for a crash Manhattan Project. All we need is sufficient funding from the hundreds of billions being showered from Washington—"stimulus" monies that, unlike Eisenhower's interstate highway system or Kennedy's Apollo program, will leave behind not a trace on our country or our consciousness—to build Constellation and get us back to Earth orbit and the moon a half-century after the original landing.

Why do it? It's not for practicality. We didn't go to the moon to spin off cooling suits and freeze-dried fruit. Any technological return is a bonus, not a reason. We go for the wonder and glory of it. Or, to put it less grandly, for its immense possibilities. We choose to do such things, said JFK, "not because they are easy, but because they are hard." And when you do such magnificently hard things—send sailing a Ferdinand Magellan or a Neil Armstrong—you open new human possibility in ways utterly unpredictable.

10   The greatest example? Who could have predicted that the moon voyages would create the most potent impetus to—and symbol of—environmental consciousness here on Earth: Earthrise, the now iconic Blue Planet photograph brought back by Apollo 8?

---

*Spruce Goose was the informal name bestowed by critics on the H4 Hercules, a heavy transport aircraft designed and built during World War II by the Hughes Aircraft Company. Built almost entirely of birch (not spruce) because of wartime restrictions on war materials, the aircraft boasted the largest height and wingspan of any aircraft in history. Only one prototype was built, and the aircraft made only one flight, on November 2, 1947. It is currently housed at the Evergreen Aviation Museum in McMinnville, Oregon.
[†]Admired for its elegant design as well as its speed, the Concorde was a supersonic passenger airliner built by a British-French consortium. It was first flown in 1969, entered service in 1976 (with regular flights to and from London, Paris, Washington, and New York), and was retired in 2003, a casualty of economic pressures. Only twenty Concordes were built.

Ironically, that new consciousness about the uniqueness and fragility of Earth focused contemporary imagination away from space and back to Earth. We are now deep into that hyper-terrestrial phase, the age of iPod and Facebook, of social networking and eco-consciousness.

But look up from your BlackBerry one night. That is the moon. On it are exactly 12 sets of human footprints—untouched, unchanged, abandoned. For the first time in history, the moon is not just a mystery and a muse, but a nightly rebuke. A vigorous young president once summoned us to this new frontier, calling the voyage "the most hazardous and dangerous and greatest adventure on which man has ever embarked." And so we did it. We came. We saw. Then we retreated.

How could we?

Exercise 2.2

Critical Reading Practice

Look back at the Critical Reading for Summary box on page 6 of Chapter 1. Use each of the guidelines listed there to examine the essay by Charles Krauthammer. Note in the margins of the selection—or on a separate sheet of paper—the essay's main point, subpoints, and use of examples.

Persuasive Strategies

Clearly Defined Terms   The validity of an argument depends to some degree on how carefully an author has defined key terms. Take the assertion, for example, that American society must be grounded in "family values." Just what do people who use this phrase mean by it? The validity of their argument depends on whether they and their readers agree on a definition of "family values"—as well as what it means to be "grounded in" family values. If an author writes that in the recent past, "America's elites accepted as a matter of course that a free society can sustain itself only through virtue and temperance in the people,"* readers need to know what exactly the author means by "elites" and by "virtue and temperance" before they can assess the validity of the argument. In such cases, the success of the argument—its ability to persuade—hinges on the definition of a term. So, in responding to an argument, be sure you (and the author) are clear on what exactly is being argued. Unless you are, no informed response is possible.

Note that in addition to their *denotative* meaning (their specific or literal meaning), many words carry a *connotative* meaning (their suggestive, associative, or emotional meaning). For example, the denotative meaning of "home" is simply the house or apartment where one lives. But the connotative meaning—with its associations of family, belongingness, refuge, safety, and familiarity—adds a significant emotional component to this literal meaning. (See more on connotation in "Emotionally Loaded Terms," p. 56.)

---

*Charles Murray, "The Coming White Underclass," *Wall Street Journal*, 20 Oct. 1993.

In the course of his argument, Krauthammer writes of "America's abandonment of the moon" and of the fact that we have "retreated" from lunar exploration. Consider the words "abandon" and "retreat." What do these words mean to you? Look them up in a dictionary for precise definitions (note all possible meanings provided). In what contexts are we most likely to see these words used? What emotional meaning and significance do they generally carry? For example, what do we usually think of people who abandon a marriage or military units that retreat? To what extent does it appear to you that Krauthammer is using these words in accordance with one or more of their dictionary definitions, their denotations? To what extent does the force of his argument also depend upon the power of these words' connotative meanings?

When writing a paper, you will need to decide, like Krauthammer, which terms to define and which you can assume the reader will define in the same way you do. As the writer of a critique, you should identify and discuss any undefined or ambiguous term that might give rise to confusion.

Fair Use of Information   Information is used as evidence in support of arguments. When you encounter such evidence, ask yourself two questions: (1) "Is the information accurate and up to date?" At least a portion of an argument becomes invalid when the information used to support it is wrong or stale. (2) "Has the author cited *representative* information?" The evidence used in an argument must be presented in a spirit of fair play. An author is less than ethical when he presents only the evidence favoring his own views even though he is well aware that contrary evidence exists. For instance, it would be dishonest to argue that an economic recession is imminent and to cite only indicators of economic downturn while ignoring and failing to cite contrary (positive) evidence.

"The Moon We Left Behind" is not an information-heavy essay. The success of the piece turns on the author's powers of persuasion, not on his use of facts and figures. Krauthammer does, however, offer some key facts relating to Project Apollo and the fact that President Obama was not inclined to back a NASA-operated lunar-landing program. And, in fact, Krauthammer's fears were confirmed in February 2010, about six months after he wrote "The Moon We Left Behind," when the president canceled NASA's plans for further manned space exploration flights in favor of government support for commercial space operations.

Logical Argumentation: Avoiding Logical Fallacies

At some point, you'll need to respond to the logic of the argument itself. To be convincing, an argument should be governed by principles of *logic*—clear and orderly thinking. This does *not* mean that an argument cannot be biased. A biased argument—that is, an argument weighted toward one point of view and against others, which is in fact the nature of argument—may be valid as long as it is logically sound.

Let's examine several types of faulty thinking and logical fallacies you will need to watch for.

Emotionally Loaded Terms   Writers sometimes attempt to sway readers by using emotionally charged words. Words with positive connotations (e.g., "family values") are intended to sway readers to the author's point of view; words with negative connotations (e.g., "paying the price") try to sway readers away from an opposing point of view. The fact that an author uses emotionally loaded terms does not necessarily invalidate an argument. Emotional appeals are perfectly legitimate and time-honored modes of persuasion. But in academic writing, which is grounded in logical argumentation, they should not be the *only* means of persuasion. You should be sensitive to *how* emotionally loaded terms are being used. In particular, are they being used deceptively or to hide the essential facts?

We've already noted Krauthammer's use of the emotionally loaded terms "abandonment" and "retreat" when referring to the end of the manned space program. Notice also his use of the term "Kumbaya" in the sentence declaring that the international space station was "created in a fit of post-Cold War internationalist absentmindedness as a place where people of differing nationality can sing 'Kumbaya' while weightless." "Kumbaya" is an African-American spiritual dating from the 1930s, often sung by scouts around campfires. Jeffrey Weiss reports on the dual connotations of this word: "The song was originally associated with human and spiritual unity, closeness and compassion, and it still is, but more recently it is also cited or alluded to in satirical, sarcastic or even cynical ways that suggest blind or false moralizing, hypocrisy, or naively optimistic views of the world and human nature."* Is Krauthammer drawing upon the emotional power of the original meaning or upon the more recent significance of this term? How does his particular use of "Kumbaya" strengthen (or weaken) his argument? What appears to be the difference in his mind between the value of the international space station and the value of returning to the moon? As someone evaluating the essay, you should be alert to this appeal to your emotions and then judge whether or not the appeal is fair and convincing. Above all, you should not let an emotional appeal blind you to shortcomings of logic, ambiguously defined terms, or a misuse of facts.

***Ad Hominem* Argument**   In an *ad hominem* argument, the writer rejects opposing views by attacking the person(s) who holds them. By calling opponents names, an author avoids the issue. Consider this excerpt from a political speech:

> I could more easily accept my opponent's plan to increase revenues by collecting on delinquent tax bills if he had paid more than a hundred dollars in state taxes in each of the past three years. But the fact is, he's a millionaire with a millionaire's tax shelters. This man hasn't paid a wooden nickel for the state services he and his family depend on. So I ask you: Is *he* the one to be talking about taxes to *us?*

It could well be that the opponent has paid virtually no state taxes for three years; but this fact has nothing to do with, and is used as a ploy to divert attention

---

*Jeffery Weiss, "'Kumbaya': How did a sweet simple song become a mocking metaphor?" *Dallas Morning News*. 12 Nov. 2006.

from, the merits of a specific proposal for increasing revenues. The proposal is lost in the attack against the man himself, an attack that violates principles of logic. Writers (and speakers) should make their points by citing evidence in support of their views and by challenging contrary evidence.

In "The Moon We Left Behind," Krauthammer's only individual target is President Obama. While he does, at several points, unfavorably compare Obama to Kennedy, he does not do so in an *ad hominem* way. That is, he attacks Obama less for his personal qualities than for his policy decision to close down NASA's manned space program. At most, he laments that Obama "has expressed none of Kennedy's enthusiasm for human space exploration."

Faulty Cause and Effect   The fact that one event precedes another in time does not mean that the first event has caused the second. An example: Fish begin dying by the thousands in a lake near your hometown. An environmental group immediately cites chemical dumping by several manufacturing plants as the cause. But other causes are possible: A disease might have affected the fish; the growth of algae might have contributed to the deaths; or acid rain might be a factor. The origins of an event are usually complex and are not always traceable to a single cause. So you must carefully examine cause-and-effect reasoning when you find a writer using it. In Latin, this fallacy is known as *post hoc, ergo propter hoc* ("after this, therefore because of this").

Toward the end of "The Moon We Left Behind," Krauthammer declares that having turned our "imagination away from space and back to Earth...[w]e are now deep into that hyper-terrestrial phase, the age of iPod and Facebook, of social networking and eco-consciousness." He appears here to be suggesting a pattern of cause and effect: that as a people, we are no longer looking outward but, rather, turning inward; and this shift in our attention and focus has resulted

TONE

Tone refers to the overall emotional effect produced by a writer's choice of language. Writers might use especially emphatic words to create a tone: A film reviewer might refer to a "magnificent performance," or a columnist might criticize "sleazeball politics."

These are extreme examples of tone; tone can also be more subtle, particularly if the writer makes a special effort *not* to inject emotion into the writing. As we indicated in the section on emotionally loaded terms, the fact that a writer's tone is highly emotional does not necessarily mean that the writer's argument is invalid. Conversely, a neutral tone is not proof of an argument's validity.

Many instructors discourage student writing that projects a highly emotional tone, considering it inappropriate for academic or preprofessional work. (One sure sign of emotion: the exclamation mark, which should be used sparingly.)

in—or at least is a significant cause of—the death of the manned space program. Questions for a critique might include the following: (1) To what extent do you agree with Krauthammer's premise that we live in an inward-looking, rather than an outward-looking, age and that it is fair to call our present historical period "the age of iPod and Facebook"? (2) To what extent do you agree that because we may live in such an age, the space program no longer enjoys broad public or political support?

Either/Or Reasoning   Either/or reasoning also results from an unwillingness to recognize complexity. If in analyzing a problem an author artificially restricts the range of possible solutions by offering only two courses of action, and then rejects the one that he opposes, he cannot logically argue that the remaining course of action, which he favors, is therefore the only one that makes sense. Usually, several other options (at least) are possible. For whatever reason, the author has chosen to overlook them. As an example, suppose you are reading a selection on genetic engineering in which the author builds an argument on the basis of the following:

> Research in gene splicing is at a crossroads: Either scientists will be carefully monitored by civil authorities and their efforts limited to acceptable applications, such as disease control; or, lacking regulatory guidelines, scientists will set their own ethical standards and begin programs in embryonic manipulation that, however well intended, exceed the proper limits of human knowledge.

Certainly, other possibilities for genetic engineering exist beyond the two mentioned here. But the author limits debate by establishing an either/or choice. Such a limitation is artificial and does not allow for complexity. As a critical reader, you need to be on the alert for reasoning based on restrictive, either/or alternatives.

Hasty Generalization   Writers are guilty of hasty generalization when they draw their conclusions from too little evidence or from unrepresentative evidence. To argue that scientists should not proceed with the Human Genome Project because a recent editorial urged that the project be abandoned is to make a hasty generalization. That lone editorial may be unrepresentative of the views of most individuals—both scientists and laypeople—who have studied and written about the matter. To argue that one should never obey authority because Stanley Milgram's Yale University experiments in the 1960s showed the dangers of obedience is to ignore the fact that Milgram's experiments were concerned primarily with obedience to *immoral* authority. The experimental situation was unrepresentative of most routine demands for obedience—for example, to obey a parental rule or to comply with a summons for jury duty—and a conclusion about the malevolence of all authority would be a hasty generalization.

False Analogy   Comparing one person, event, or issue to another may be illuminating, but it can also be confusing or misleading. Differences between the two may be more significant than their similarities, and conclusions drawn from one may not necessarily apply to the other. A candidate for governor or president who argues that her experience as CEO of a major business would make her effective in governing a state or the country is assuming an analogy between the business and the political/civic worlds that does not hold up to examination. Most businesses are hierarchical, or top down: When a CEO issues an order, he or she can expect it to be carried out without argument. But governors and presidents command only their own executive branches. They cannot issue orders to independent legislatures or courts (much less private citizens); they can only attempt to persuade. In this case, the implied analogy fails to convince the thoughtful reader or listener.

Begging the Question   To beg the question is to assume as proven fact the very thesis being argued. To assert, for example, that America does not need a new health care delivery system because America currently has the best health care in the world does not prove anything: It merely repeats the claim in different—and equally unproven—words. This fallacy is also known as *circular reasoning*.

Non Sequitur   *Non sequitur* is Latin for "it does not follow"; the term is used to describe a conclusion that does not logically follow from the premise. "Since minorities have made such great strides in the past few decades," a writer may argue, "we no longer need affirmative action programs." Aside from the fact that the premise itself is arguable (*have* minorities made such great strides?), it does not follow that because minorities *may* have made great strides, there is no further need for affirmative action programs.

Oversimplification   Be alert for writers who offer easy solutions to complicated problems. "America's economy will be strong again if we all 'buy American,'" a politician may argue. But the problems of America's economy are complex and cannot be solved by a slogan or a simple change in buying habits. Likewise, a writer who argues that we should ban genetic engineering assumes that simple solutions ("just say no") will be sufficient to deal with the complex moral dilemmas raised by this new technology.

Exercise 2.3

Understanding Logical Fallacies

Make a list of the nine logical fallacies discussed in the preceding section. Briefly define each one in your own words. Then, in a group of three or four classmates, review your definitions and the examples we've provided for each logical fallacy. Collaborate with your group to find or invent additional examples for each of the fallacies. Compare your examples with those generated by the other groups in your class.

Writing to Entertain

Authors write not only to inform and persuade, but also to entertain. One response to entertainment is a hearty laugh, but it is possible to entertain without encouraging laughter: A good book or play or poem may prompt you to reflect, grow wistful, become elated, get angry. Laughter is only one of many possible reactions. Like a response to an informative piece or an argument, your response to an essay, poem, story, play, novel, or film should be precisely stated and carefully developed. Ask yourself some of the following questions (you won't have space to explore all of them, but try to consider the most important ones):

- Did I care for the portrayal of a certain character?
- Did that character (or a group of characters united by occupation, age, ethnicity, etc.) seem overly sentimental, for example, or heroic?
- Did his adversaries seem too villainous or stupid?
- Were the situations believable?
- Was the action interesting or merely formulaic?
- Was the theme developed subtly or powerfully, or did the work come across as preachy or unconvincing?
- Did the action at the end of the work follow plausibly from what had come before? Was the language fresh and incisive or stale and predictable?

Explain as specifically as possible what elements of the work seemed effective or ineffective and why. Offer an overall assessment, elaborating on your views.

Question 2: To What Extent Do You Agree with the Author?

A critical evaluation consists of two parts. The first part, just discussed, assesses the accuracy and effectiveness of an argument in terms of the author's logic and use of evidence. The second part, discussed here, responds to the argument—that is, agrees or disagrees with it.

Identify Points of Agreement and Disagreement

Be precise in identifying where you agree and disagree with an author. State as clearly as possible what *you* believe, in relation to what the author believes, as presented in the piece. Whether you agree enthusiastically, agree with reservations, or disagree, you can organize your reactions in two parts:

- Summarize the author's position.
- State your own position and explain why you believe as you do. The elaboration, in effect, becomes an argument itself, and this is true regardless of the position you take.

Any opinion that you express is effective to the extent you support it by supplying evidence from your reading (which should be properly cited), your observation, or your personal experience. Without such evidence, opinions cannot be authoritative. "I thought the article on inflation was lousy." Or: "It was terrific."

Why? "I just thought so, that's all." Such opinions have no value because the criticism is imprecise: The critic has taken neither the time to read the article carefully nor the time to carefully explore his or her own reactions.

Exploring Your Viewpoints—in Three Paragraphs

Go to a Web site that presents short, persuasive essays on current social issues, such as reason.com, opinion-pages.org, drudgereport.com, or Speakout.com. Or go to an Internet search engine such as Google or Bing and type in a social issue together with the word "articles," "editorials," or "opinion," and see what you find. Locate a selection on a topic of interest that takes a clear, argumentative position. Print out the selection on which you choose to focus.

- Write one paragraph summarizing the author's key argument.
- Write two paragraphs articulating your agreement or disagreement with the author. (Devote each paragraph to a *single* point of agreement or disagreement.)

Be sure to explain why you think or feel the way you do and, wherever possible, cite relevant evidence—from your reading, experience, or observation.

Explore the Reasons for Agreement and Disagreement: Evaluate Assumptions

One way of elaborating your reactions to a reading is to explore the underlying *reasons* for agreement and disagreement. Your reactions are based largely on assumptions that you hold and how those assumptions compare with the author's. An *assumption* is a fundamental statement about the world and its operations that you take to be true. Often, a writer will express an assumption directly, as in this example:

> #1 One of government's most important functions is to raise tax revenues and spend them on projects that improve the housing, medical, and nutritional needs of its citizens.

In this instance, the writer's claim is a direct expression of a fundamental belief about how the world, or some part of it, should work. The argumentative claim *is* the assumption. Just as often, an argument and its underlying assumption are not identical. In these cases, the assumption is some other statement that is implied by the argumentative claim—as in this example:

> #2 Human spaceflight is a waste of public money.

The logic of this second statement rests on an unstated assumption relating to the word *waste*. What, in this writer's view, is a *waste* of money? What is an effective or justified use? In order to agree or not with statement #2, a critical reader must know what assumption(s) it rests on. A good candidate for such an assumption would be statement #1. That is, a person who believes statement #1 about how governments ought to raise and spend money could well make statement #2. This may not be the only assumption underlying statement #2, but it could well be one of them.

Inferring and Implying Assumptions

Infer and *imply* are keywords relating to hidden, or unstated, assumptions; you should be clear on their meanings. A critical reader *infers* what is hidden in a statement and, through that inference, brings what is hidden into the open for examination. Thus, the critical reader infers from statement #2 on human space-flight the writer's assumption (statement #1) on how governments should spend money. At the same time, the writer of statement #2 *implies* (hints at but does not state directly) an assumption about how governments should spend money. There will be times when writers make statements and are unaware of their own assumptions.

Assumptions provide the foundation on which entire presentations are built. You may find an author's assumptions invalid—that is, not supported by factual evidence. You may disagree with value-based assumptions underlying an author's position—for instance, what constitutes "good" or "correct" behavior. In both cases, you may well disagree with the conclusions that follow from these assumptions. Alternatively, when you find that your own assumptions are contradicted by actual experience, you may be forced to conclude that certain of your fundamental beliefs about the world and how it works were mistaken.

An Example of Hidden Assumptions from the World of Finance

An interesting example of an assumption fatally colliding with reality was revealed during a recent congressional investigation into the financial meltdown of late 2008, which was precipitated by the collapse of the home mortgage market—itself precipitated, many believed, by an insufficiently regulated banking and financial system run amuck. During his testimony before the House Oversight Committee in October of that year, former Federal Reserve chairman Alan Greenspan was grilled by committee chairman Henry Waxman (D-CA) about his "ideology"—essentially, an assumption or set of assumptions that become a governing principle. (In the following transcript, you can substitute the word "assumption" for "ideology.")

Greenspan responded, "I do have an ideology. My judgment is that free, competitive markets are by far the unrivaled way to organize economies. We have tried regulation; none meaningfully worked." Greenspan defined an ideology as "a conceptual framework [for] the way people deal with reality. Everyone has one. You have to. To exist, you need an ideology." And he pointed out that the assumptions on which he and the Federal Reserve operated were supported by "the best banking lawyers in the business…and an outside counsel of expert professionals to advise on regulatory matters."

Greenspan then admitted that in light of the economic disaster engulfing the nation, he had found a "flaw" in his ideology—that actual experience had violated some of his fundamental beliefs. The testimony continued:

> Chairman Waxman: You found a flaw?
>
> Mr. Greenspan: I found a flaw in the model that I perceived is the critical functioning structure that defines how the world works, so to speak.
>
> Chairman Waxman: In other words, you found that your view of the world, your ideology, was not right, it was not working.
>
> Mr. Greenspan: Precisely. That's precisely the reason I was shocked, because I had been going for 40 years or more with very considerable evidence that it was working exceptionally well.*

The lesson? All the research, expertise, and logical argumentation in the world will fail if the premise (assumption, ideology) on which it is based turns out to be "flawed."

How do you determine the validity of assumptions once you have identified them? In the absence of more-scientific criteria, you start by considering how well the author's assumptions stack up against your own experience, observations, reading, and values—while remaining honestly aware of the limits of your own personal knowledge.

Readers will want to examine the assumption at the heart of Krauthammer's essay: that continuing NASA's manned space program and, in particular, the program to return human beings to the moon, is a worthwhile enterprise. The writer of the critique that follows questions this assumption. But you may not: You may instead fully support such a program. That's your decision, perhaps made even *before* you read Krauthammer's essay, perhaps as a *result* of having read it. What you must do as a critical reader is to recognize assumptions, whether they are stated or not. You should spell them out and then accept or reject them. Ultimately, your agreement or disagreement with an author will rest on your agreement or disagreement with that author's assumptions.

CRITIQUE

In Chapter 1 we focused on summary—the condensed presentation of ideas from another source. Summary is fundamental to much of academic writing, because such writing relies so heavily on the works of others for the support of its claims. It's not going too far to say that summarizing is the critical thinking skill from which a majority of academic writing builds. However, most academic thinking and writing goes beyond summary. Generally, we use summary to restate our understanding of things we see or read. We then put that summary to use. In academic writing, one typical use of summary is as a prelude to critique.

---

*United States. Cong. House Committee on Oversight and Government Reform. *The Financial Crisis and the Role of Federal Regulators.* 110th Cong., 2nd sess. Washington: GPO, 2008.

A *critique* is a *formalized, critical reading of a passage.* It is also a personal response; but writing a critique is considerably more rigorous than saying that a movie is "great," or a book is "fascinating," or "I didn't like it." These are all responses, and, as such, they're a valid, even essential, part of your understanding of what you see and read. But such responses don't illuminate the subject—even for you—if you haven't explained how you arrived at your conclusions.

Your task in writing a critique is to turn your critical reading of a passage into a systematic evaluation in order to deepen your reader's (and your own) understanding of that passage. When you read a selection to critique, determine the following:

- What an author says
- How well the points are made
- What assumptions underlie the argument
- What issues are overlooked
- What implications can be drawn from such an analysis

When you write a critique, positive or negative, include the following:

- A fair and accurate summary of the passage
- Information and ideas from other sources (your reading or your personal experience and observations), if you think these are pertinent
- A statement of your agreement or disagreement with the author, backed by specific examples and clear logic
- A clear statement of your own assumptions

Remember that you bring to bear on any subject an entire set of assumptions about the world. Stated or not, these assumptions underlie every evaluative comment you make. You therefore have an obligation, both to the reader and to yourself, to clarify your standards by making your assumptions explicit. Not only do your readers stand to gain by your forthrightness, but you do as well. The process of writing a critical assessment forces you to examine your own knowledge, beliefs, and assumptions. Ultimately, the critique is a way of learning about yourself—yet another example of the ways in which writing is useful as a tool for critical thinking.

How to Write Critiques

You may find it useful to organize a critique into five sections: introduction, summary, assessment of the presentation (on its own terms), your response to the presentation, and conclusion.

The next box offers guidelines for writing critiques. These guidelines do not constitute a rigid formula. Most professional authors write critiques that do not follow the structure outlined here. Until you are more confident and practiced in writing critiques, however, we suggest you follow these guidelines. They are meant not to restrict you, but rather to provide a workable sequence for writing critiques until a more fully developed set of experiences and authorial instincts are available to guide you.

GUIDELINES FOR WRITING CRITIQUES

- *Introduce.* Introduce both the passage under analysis and the author. State the author's main argument and the point(s) you intend to make about it.

  Provide background material to help your readers understand the relevance or appeal of the passage. This background material might include one or more of the following: an explanation of why the subject is of current interest; a reference to a possible controversy surrounding the subject of the passage or the passage itself; biographical information about the author; an account of the circumstances under which the passage was written; a reference to the intended audience of the passage.
- *Summarize.* Summarize the author's main points, making sure to state the author's purpose for writing.
- *Assess the presentation.* Evaluate the validity of the author's presentation, distinct from your points of agreement or disagreement. Comment on the author's success in achieving his or her purpose, by reviewing three or four specific points. You might base your review on one or more of the following criteria:

  Is the information accurate?

  Is the information significant?

  Has the author defined terms clearly?

  Has the author used and interpreted information fairly?

  Has the author argued logically?

- *Respond to the presentation.* Now it is your turn to respond to the author's views. With which views do you agree? With which do you disagree? Discuss your reasons for agreement and disagreement, when possible tying these reasons to assumptions—both the author's and your own. Where necessary, draw on outside sources to support your ideas.
- *Conclude.* State your conclusions about the overall validity of the piece—your assessment of the author's success at achieving his or her aims and your reactions to the author's views. Remind the reader of the weaknesses and strengths of the passage.

DEMONSTRATION: CRITIQUE

The critique that follows is based on Charles Krauthammer's op-ed piece "The Moon We Left Behind" (pp. 52–54), which we have already begun to examine. In this formal critique, you will see that it is possible to agree with an author's main point, at least provisionally, yet disagree with other elements of the argument. Critiquing a different selection, you could just as easily accept the author's facts and figures but reject the conclusion he draws from them. As long as you carefully articulate the author's assumptions and your own, explaining in some detail your agreement and disagreement, the critique is yours to take in whatever direction you see fit.

Let's summarize the preceding sections by returning to the core questions that guide critical reading. You will see how, when applied to Charles Krauthammer's argument, they help to set up a critique.

To What Extent Does the Author Succeed in His or Her Purpose?

To answer this question, you will need to know the author's purpose. Krauthammer wrote "The Moon We Left Behind" to persuade his audience that manned space flight must be supported. He makes his case in three ways: (1) He attacks the Obama administration's decision to "retreat" from the moon—i.e., to end NASA's manned space program; (2) he argues for the continuation of this program; and (3) he rebuts criticisms of the program. He aims to achieve this purpose by unfavorably comparing President Obama to President Kennedy, who challenged the nation to put a man on the moon within a decade; by arguing that we should return to the moon for "the wonder and glory of it"; and by challenging the claims that (a) we need first to fix the problems on earth and that (b) we can't afford such a program. One of the main tasks of the writer of a critique of this article is to explain the extent to which Krauthammer has achieved his purpose.

To What Extent Do You Agree with the Author? Evaluate Assumptions

Krauthammer's argument rests upon two assumptions: (1) It is an essential characteristic of humankind to explore—and going to the moon was a great and worthwhile example of exploration; and (2) inspiring deeds are worth our expense and sacrifice—and thus continuing NASA's manned program and returning to the moon is worth our time, effort, and money. One who critiques Krauthammer's op-ed piece must determine the extent to which she or he shares these assumptions. The writer of the model critique does, in fact, share Krauthammer's first assumption, while expressing doubt about the second.

One must also determine the persuasiveness of Krauthammer's arguments for returning to the moon, as well as the persuasiveness of his counterarguments to those who claim this program is too impractical and too expensive. The writer of the model critique believes that Krauthammer's arguments are generally persuasive, even (in the conclusion) judging them "compelling." On the other hand, the critique ends on a neutral note—taking into account the problems with Krauthammer's arguments.

Remember that you don't need to agree with an author to believe that he or she has succeeded in his or her purpose. You may well admire how cogently and forcefully an author has argued, without necessarily accepting her position. Conversely, you may agree with a particular author, while acknowledging that he has not made a very strong case—and perhaps has even made a flawed one—for his point of view. For example, you may heartily approve of the point Krauthammer is making—that the United States should return to the moon. At the same time, you may find problematic the substance of his arguments and/or his strategy for arguing, particularly the dismissive manner in which he refers to the U.S. efforts in space over the last forty years:

> To be more precise: almost 40 years spent in low Earth orbit studying, well, zero-G nausea and sundry cosmic mysteries. We've done it with the most beautiful, intricate, complicated—and ultimately, hopelessly impractical—machine ever built by man: the space shuttle. We turned this magnificent bird into a truck for hauling goods and people to a tinkertoy we call the international space station....

Perhaps you support Krauthammer's position but find his sarcasm distasteful. That said, these two major questions for critical analysis (whether or not the author has been successful in his purpose and the extent to which you agree with the author's assumptions and arguments) are related. You will typically conclude that an author whose arguments have failed to persuade you has not succeeded in her purpose.

The selections you are likely to critique will be those, like Krauthammer's, that argue a specific position. Indeed, every argument you read is an invitation to agree or disagree. It remains only for you to speak up and justify your own position.

MODEL CRITIQUE

Harlan 1

Andrew Harlan

Professor Rose Humphreys

Writing 2

11 January 2011

A Critique of Charles Krauthammer's

"The Moon We Left Behind"

In his 1961 State of the Union address, President John F. Kennedy issued a stirring challenge: "that this nation should commit itself to achieving the goal, before this decade is out, of landing a man on the Moon and returning him safely to the Earth." At the time, Kennedy's proposal seemed like science fiction. Even the scientists and engineers of the National Aeronautics and Space Administration (NASA) who were tasked with the job didn't know how to meet Kennedy's goal. Spurred, however, partly by a unified national purpose and partly by competition with the Soviet Union, which had beaten the United States into space with the first artificial satellite in 1957, the Apollo program to land men on the moon

①

was launched. On July 20, 1969 Kennedy's challenge was met when Apollo 11 astronauts Neil Armstrong and Buzz Aldrin landed their lunar module on the Sea of Tranquility.

(2)　　During the next few years, five more Apollo flights landed on the moon. In all, twelve Americans walked on the lunar surface; some even rode on a 4-wheeled "Rover," a kind of lunar dune buggy. But in December 1972 the Apollo program was cancelled. Since that time, some 40 years ago, humans have frequently returned to space, but none have returned to the moon. In February 2010 President Obama ended NASA's moon program, transferring responsibility for manned space exploration to private industry and re-focusing the government's resources on technological development and innovation. The administration had signaled its intentions earlier, in 2009. In July of that year, in an apparent attempt to rouse public opinion against the President's revised priorities for space exploration, Charles Krauthammer wrote "The Moon We Left Behind." It is these revised priorities that are the focus of his op-ed piece, a lament for the end of lunar exploration and a powerful, if flawed, critique of the administration's decision.

(3)　　Trained as a doctor and a psychiatrist, Charles Krauthammer is a prominent conservative columnist who has won the Pulitzer Prize for his political commentary. Krauthammer begins and ends his op-ed with expressions of dismay and anger at "America's abandonment of the moon." He unfavorably compares the current president, Barack Obama, with the "vigorous young" John F. Kennedy, in terms of their support for manned space exploration. It is inconceivable to Krauthammer that a program that achieved such technical glories and fired the imaginations of millions in so short a span of time has fallen into such decline.

(4)　　Krauthammer anticipates the objections to his plea to keep America competitive in manned space exploration and to return to the moon. We have problems enough on earth, critics will argue. His answer: If we waited to solve these perennial problems before continuing human progress, "we'd still be living in caves." Concerning the expense of continuing the space program, Krauthammer argues that a fraction of the funds being "showered" on the government's stimulus programs (some $1 trillion) would be sufficient to support a viable space program. And as for practicality, he dismisses the idea that we need a practical reason to return to the moon. "We go," he argues, "for the wonder and glory of it. Or, to put it less grandly, for its immense possibilities." Ultimately, Krauthammer urges us to turn away from our mundane preoccupations and look up at the moon where humans once walked. How could Americans have gone so far, he asks, only to retreat?

Harlan 3

⑤ In this opinion piece, Charles Krauthammer offers a powerful, inspiring defense of the American manned space program; and it's hard not to agree with him that our voyages to the moon captured the imagination and admiration of the world and set a new standard for scientific and technical achievement. Ever since that historic day in July 1969, people have been asking, "If we can land a man on the moon, why can't we [fill in your favorite social or political challenge]?" In a way, the fact that going to the moon was not especially practical made the achievement even more admirable: we went not for gain, but rather to explore the unknown, to show what human beings, working cooperatively and exercising their powers of reason and their genius in design and engineering, can accomplish when sufficiently challenged. "We go," Krauthammer reminds us, "for the wonder and glory of it...for its immense possibilities."

⑥ And what's wrong with that? For a relatively brief historical moment, Americans, and indeed the peoples of the world, came together in pride and anticipation as Apollo 11 sped toward the moon and, days later, as the lunar module descended to the surface. People collectively held their breaths after an oxygen tank explosion disabled Apollo 13 on the way to the moon and as the astronauts and Mission Control guided the spacecraft to a safe return. A renewed moon program might similarly help to reduce divisions among people—or at least among Americans—and highlight the reality that we are all residents of the same planet, with more common interests (such as protecting the environment) than is often apparent from our perennial conflicts. Krauthammer's praise of lunar exploration and its benefits is so stirring that many who do not accept his conclusions may share his disappointment and indignation at its demise.

⑦ "The Moon We Left Behind" may actually underestimate the practical aspects of moon travel. "Any technological return," Krauthammer writes, "is a bonus, not a reason." But so many valuable bonuses have emerged from space flight and space exploration that the practical offshoots of lunar exploration may in fact be a valid reason to return to the moon. For instance, the technology developed from the special requirements of space travel has found application in health and medicine (breast cancer detection, laser angioplasty), industrial productivity and manufacturing technology, public safety (radiation hazard detectors, emergency rescue cutters), and transportation (studless winter tires, advanced lubricants, aids to school bus design) ("NASA Spinoffs"). A renewed moon program would also be practical in providing a huge employment stimulus to the economy. According to the NASA Langley Research Center, "At its peak, the Apollo program employed 400,000 people and required the support of over 20,000 industrial firms and universities" ("Apollo Program"). Returning to the moon would create comparable numbers of jobs in aerospace engineering, computer engineering, biology, general engineering, and meteorology, along with hosts of support jobs, from accounting to food service to office automation specialists ("NASA Occupations").

(8)   Krauthammer's emotional call may be stirring, but he dismisses too quickly some of the practical arguments against a renewed moon program. He appears to assume a degree of political will and public support for further lunar exploration that simply does not exist today. First, public support may be lacking—for legitimate reasons. It is not as if with a renewed lunar program we would be pushing boundaries and exploring the unknown: we would not be *going* to the moon; we would be *returning* to the moon. A significant percentage of the public, after considering the matter, may reasonably conclude: "Been there, done that." They may think, correctly or not, that we should set our sights elsewhere rather than collecting more moon rocks or taking additional stunning photographs from the lunar surface. Whatever practical benefits can be derived from going to the moon, many (if not all) have already been achieved. It would not be at all unreasonable for the public, even a public that supports NASA funding, to say, "Let's move on to other goals."

(9)   Second, Krauthammer's argument that poverty and disease and social ills will always be with us is politically flawed. This country faces financial pressures more serious than those at any other time since the Great Depression; and real, painful choices are being made by federal, state, and local officials about how to spend diminished tax dollars. The "vigorous young" JFK, launching the moon program during a time of expansion and prosperity, faced no such restrictions. Krauthammer's dismissal of ongoing poverty and other social ills is not likely to persuade elected representatives who are shuttering libraries, closing fire stations, ending unemployment benefits, and curtailing medical services. Nor will a public that is enduring these cuts be impressed by Krauthammer's call to "wonder and glory." Accurately or not, the public is likely to see the matter in terms of choices between a re-funded lunar program (nice, but optional) and renewed jobless benefits (essential). Not many politicians, in such distressed times, would be willing to go on record by voting for "nice" over "essential"—not if they wanted to keep their jobs.

Finally, it's surprising—and philosophically inconsistent—for a conservative like Krauthammer, who believes in a smaller, less free-spending government, to be complaining about the withdrawal of massive government support for a renewed moon program. After all, the government hasn't banned moon travel; it has simply turned over such projects to private industry. If lunar exploration and other space flights appear commercially viable, there's nothing to prevent private companies and corporations from pursuing their own programs.   ⑩

In "The Moon We Left Behind," Charles Krauthammer stirs the emotions with his call   ⑪ for the United States to return to the moon; and, in terms of practical spinoffs, such a return could benefit this country in many ways. Krauthammer's argument is compelling, even if he too easily discounts the financial and political problems that will pose real obstacles to a renewed lunar program. Ultimately, what one thinks of Krauthammer's call to renew moon exploration depends on how one defines the human enterprise and the purpose of collective agreement and collective effort—what we call "government." To what extent should this purpose be to solve problems in the here and now? To what extent should it be to inquire and to push against the boundaries for the sake of discovery and exploration, to learn more about who we are and about the nature of our universe? There have always been competing demands on national budgets and more than enough problems to justify spending every tax dollar on problems of poverty, social justice, crime, education, national security, and the like. Krauthammer argues that if we are to remain true to our spirit of inquiry, we cannot ignore the investigation of space, because scientific and technological progress is also a human responsibility. He argues that we can—indeed, we must—do both: look to our needs here at home and also dream and explore. But the public may not find his argument convincing.

Works Cited

"Apollo Program." *Apollo Program HSF*. National Aeronautics and Space Administration, 2
    July 2009. Web. 16 Sept. 2010.

Harwood, William. "Obama Kills Moon Program, Endorses Commercial Space." *Spaceflight
    Now*. Spaceflight Now, 1 Feb. 2010. Web. 13 Sept. 2010.

Harlan 7

Kennedy, John F. "Rice University Speech." 12 Sept. 1962. *Public Papers of the Presidents of the United States*. Vol. 1., 1962. 669–70. Print.

---. "Special Message to the Congress on Urgent National Needs." *John F. Kennedy Presidential Library and Museum*. John F. Kennedy Presidential Library and Museum, 25 May 1961. Web. 14 Sept. 2010.

Krauthammer, Charles. "The Moon We Left Behind." *Washington Post* 17 July 2009: A17. Print.

"NASA Occupations." *Nasajobsoccupations*. National Aeronautics and Space Administration, 28 July 2009. Web. 12 Sept. 2010.

"NASA Spinoffs: Bringing Space Down to Earth." *The Ultimate Space Place*. National Aeronautics and Space Administration, 2 Feb. 2004. Web. 18 Sept. 2010.

Exercise 2.5

Informal Critique of the Model Critique

Before reading our analysis of this model critique, write your own informal response to it. What are its strengths and weaknesses? To what extent does the critique follow the general Guidelines for Writing Critiques that we outlined on page 65? To the extent that it varies from the guidelines, speculate on why. Jot down ideas for a critique that takes a different approach to Krauthammer's op-ed.

CRITICAL READING FOR CRITIQUE

- *Use the tips from Critical Reading for Summary on page 6.* Remember to examine the context; note the title and subtitle; identify the main point; identify the subpoints; break the reading into sections; distinguish between points, examples, and counterarguments; watch for transitions within and between paragraphs; and read actively.
- *Establish the writer's primary purpose in writing.* Is the piece meant primarily to inform, persuade, or entertain?
- *Evaluate informative writing. Use these criteria (among others):*
  - Accuracy of information
  - Significance of information
  - Fair interpretation of information

- *Evaluate persuasive writing. Use these criteria (among others):*
  Clear definition of terms
  Fair use and interpretation of information
  Logical reasoning
- *Evaluate writing that entertains. Use these criteria (among others):*
  Interesting characters
  Believable action, plot, and situations
  Communication of theme
  Use of language
- *Decide whether you agree or disagree with the writer's ideas, position, or message.* Once you have determined the extent to which an author has achieved his or her purpose, clarify your position in relation to the writer's.

The Strategy of the Critique

- Paragraphs 1 and 2 of the model critique introduce the topic. They provide a context by way of a historical review of America's lunar-exploration program from 1962 to 1972, leading up to the president's decision to scrub plans for a return to the moon. The two-paragraph introduction also provides a context for Krauthammer's—and the world's—admiration for the stunning achievement of the Apollo program. The second paragraph ends with the thesis of the critique, the writer's overall assessment of Krauthammer's essay.
- Paragraphs 3–4 introduce Krauthammer and summarize his arguments.
  - Paragraph 3 provides biographical information about Krauthammer and describes his disappointment and indignation at "America's abandonment of the moon."
  - Paragraph 4 treats Krauthammer's anticipated objections to the continuation of the manned space program and rebuttals to these objections.
- Paragraphs 5, 6, and 7 support Krauthammer's argument.
  - Paragraphs 5 and 6 begin the writer's evaluation, focusing on the reasons why Krauthammer finds so much to admire in the lunar-exploration program. Most notably: It was a stunning technological achievement that brought the people of the world together (if only briefly). The writer shares this admiration.
  - Paragraph 7 indirectly supports Krauthammer by pointing out that even though he downplays the practical benefits of lunar exploration, the space program has yielded numerous practical technological spinoffs.

- Paragraphs 8–10 focus on the problems with Krauthammer's argument.
  - In paragraph 8, the writer points out that there is little public support for returning to the moon, a goal that many people will see as already accomplished and impractical for the immediate future.
  - Paragraph 9 argues that Krauthammer underestimates the degree to which an electorate worried about skyrocketing deficits and high unemployment would object to taxpayer dollars being used to finance huge government spending on a renewed lunar program.
  - Paragraph 10 points out how surprising it is that a conservative such as Krauthammer would advocate a government-financed manned space program when the same goal could be accomplished by private enterprise.
- Paragraph 11 concludes the critique, summing up the chief strengths and weaknesses of Krauthammer's argument and pointing out that readers' positions will be determined by their views on the "human enterprise" and the purpose of government. How do we balance our "human responsibility" for the expansion of knowledge and technology with the competing claims of education, poverty, crime, and national security?

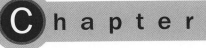

Thesis, Introduction, Conclusion

After completing this chapter, you will be able to:

LO 3.1   Write a thesis that makes an assertion about your topic and provides a structure for your paper.

LO 3.2   Use various strategies to write introductions that provide a context for your readers.

LO 3.3   Use various strategies to write conclusions that move beyond a summary of your paper.

Three features of your paper deserve particular attention: your *thesis*, which presents the paper's underlying rationale; your *introduction*, which draws readers into the world of your subject matter; and your *conclusion*, which leaves readers thinking about your particular take on the subject matter. Here we take a closer look at each of these crucial components.

WRITING A THESIS

A thesis is a one- or two-sentence summary of a paper's content. Whether explanatory, mildly argumentative, or strongly argumentative, the thesis is an assertion about that content—for instance, what the content is, how it works, what it means, if it is valuable, if action should be taken, and so on. A paper's thesis is similar to its conclusion, but it lacks the conclusion's concern for broad implications and significance. The thesis is the product of your thinking; it therefore represents *your* conclusion about the topic on which you're writing. So you have to have spent some time thinking about this conclusion (that is, during the invention stage) in order to arrive at the thesis that will govern your paper.

For a writer in the drafting stages, the thesis establishes a focus, a basis on which to include or exclude information. For the reader of a finished product, the thesis forecasts the author's discussion. A thesis, therefore, is an essential tool for both writers and readers of academic papers.

The Components of a Thesis

Like any other sentence, a thesis includes a subject and a predicate that makes an assertion about the subject. In the sentence "Lee and Grant were different kinds of generals," "Lee and Grant" is the subject and "were different kinds of generals" is the predicate. What distinguishes a thesis from any other sentence with a subject and a predicate is that *the thesis presents the controlling idea of the paper*. The subject of a thesis, and the assertion about it, must present the right balance between the general and the specific, to allow for a thorough discussion within the allotted length of the paper. The discussion might include definitions, details, comparisons, contrasts—whatever is needed to illuminate a subject and support the assertion. (If the sentence about Lee and Grant were a thesis, the reader would assume that the rest of the paper contained comparisons and contrasts between the two generals.)

Bear in mind when writing theses that the more general your subject and the more complex your assertion, the longer your discussion must be to cover the subject adequately. The broadest theses require book-length treatments, as in this case:

> Meaningful energy conservation requires a shrewd application of political, financial, and scientific will.

You couldn't write an effective ten-page paper based on this thesis. The topic alone would require pages just to define what you mean by "energy conservation" and "meaningful." Energy can be conserved in homes, vehicles, industries, appliances, and power plants, and each of these areas would need consideration. Having accomplished this first task of definition, you would then turn your attention to the claim, which entails a discussion of how politics, finance, and science individually and collectively influence energy conservation. Moreover, the thesis requires you to argue that "shrewd application" of politics, finance, and science is required. The thesis may very well be accurate and compelling, yet it promises entirely too much for a ten-page paper.

So to write an effective thesis and therefore a controlled, effective paper, you need to limit your subject and your claims about it. This narrowing process should help you arrive at a manageable topic for your paper. You will convert that topic to a thesis when you make an assertion about it—a *claim* that you will explain and support in the paper.

Making an Assertion

Thesis statements make an assertion or claim *about* your paper's topic. If you have spent enough time reading and gathering information and brainstorming ideas about the assignment, you'll be knowledgeable enough to have something to say based on a combination of your own thinking and the thinking of your sources.

If you have trouble coming up with such an assertion, devote more time to invention strategies: Try writing your subject at the top of a page and then listing everything you now know and feel about it. Often, from such a list you'll venture an assertion you can then use to fashion a working thesis. One good way to gauge the reasonableness of your claim is to see what other authors have asserted about the same topic. Keeping good notes on the views of others will provide you with a useful counterpoint to your own views as you write and think about your claim, and you may want to use those notes in your paper.

Next, make several assertions about your topic, in order of increasing complexity, as in the following:

1. Fuel-cell technology has emerged as a promising approach to developing energy-efficient vehicles.
2. To reduce our dependence on nonrenewable fossil fuel, the federal government should encourage the development of fuel-cell vehicles.
3. The federal government should subsidize the development of fuel-cell vehicles as well as the hydrogen infrastructure needed to support them; otherwise, the United States will be increasingly vulnerable to recession and other economic dislocations resulting from our dependence on the continued flow of foreign oil.

Keep in mind that these are *working theses*. Because you haven't begun a paper based on any of them, they remain *hypotheses* to be tested. You might choose one and use it to focus your initial draft. After completing a first draft, you would revise it by comparing the contents of the paper to the thesis and making adjustments as necessary for unity. The working thesis is an excellent tool for planning broad sections of the paper, but—again—don't let it prevent you from pursuing related discussions as they occur to you.

Starting with a Working Thesis

As a student, you are not yet an expert on the subjects of your papers and therefore don't usually have the luxury of beginning writing tasks with a definite thesis in mind. But let's assume that you *do* have an area of expertise, that you are in your own right a professional (albeit not in academic matters). We'll suppose that you understand some nonacademic subject—say, backpacking—and have been given a clear purpose for writing: to discuss the relative merits of backpack designs. Your job is to write a recommendation for the owner of a sporting-goods chain, suggesting which line of backpacks the chain should carry. Because you already know a good deal about backpacks, you may have some well-developed ideas on the subject before you start doing additional research.

Yet even as an expert in your field, you will find that crafting a thesis is challenging. After all, a thesis is a summary, and it is difficult to summarize a presentation yet to be written—especially if you plan to discover what you want to say during the process of writing. Even if you know your material well, the best you can do at first is to formulate a working thesis—a hypothesis of sorts, a well-informed hunch about your topic and the claim you intend to make about it. After completing a draft, you can evaluate the degree to which your working thesis accurately summarizes the content of your paper. If the match is a good one, the working thesis becomes the final thesis. But if sections of the paper drift from the focus of the working thesis, you'll need to revise the thesis and the paper itself to ensure that the presentation is unified. (You'll know that the match between content and thesis is good when every paragraph directly refers to and develops some element of the thesis.) Later in this chapter, we'll discuss useful revision techniques for establishing unity in your work.

This model works whether dealing with a subject in your area of expertise— backpacking, for example—or one that is more in your instructor's territory, such as government policy or medieval poetry. The difference is that when approaching subjects that are less familiar to you, you'll likely spend more time gathering data and brainstorming in order to make assertions about your subject.

Using the Thesis to Plan a Structure

A working thesis will help you sketch the structure of your paper, because an effective structure flows directly from the thesis. Consider, for example, the third thesis on fuel-cell technology (see p. 79):

> The federal government should subsidize the development of fuel-cell vehicles as well as the hydrogen infrastructure needed to support them; otherwise, the United States will be increasingly vulnerable to recession and other economic dislocations resulting from our dependence on the continued flow of foreign oil.

This thesis is *strongly argumentative*, or *persuasive*. The economic crises mentioned suggest urgency in the need for the solution recommended: the federal subsidy of a national hydrogen infrastructure to support fuel-cell vehicles. A well-developed paper based on this thesis would require you to commit yourself to explaining (1) why fuel-cell vehicles are a preferred alternative to gasoline-powered vehicles; (2) why fuel-cell vehicles require a hydrogen infrastructure (i.e., you must explain that fuel cells produce power by mixing hydrogen and oxygen, generating both electricity and water in the process); (3) why the government needs to subsidize industry in developing fuel-cell vehicles; and (4) how continued reliance on fossil fuel technology could make the country vulnerable to economic dislocations.

This thesis, then, helps you plan the paper, which should include a section on each of the four topics. Assuming that the argument follows the organizational plan we've proposed, the working thesis would become the final thesis. Based on this thesis, a reader could anticipate sections of the paper to come. A focused thesis therefore becomes an essential tool for guiding readers.

At this stage, however, your thesis is still provisional. It may turn out that as you do research or begin drafting, the paper to which this thesis commits you looks to be too long and complex. As a result, you may decide to drop the second clause of the thesis (concerning the country's vulnerability to economic dislocations) and focus instead on the need for the government to subsidize the development of fuel-cell vehicles and a hydrogen infrastructure, relegating the economic

HOW AMBITIOUS SHOULD YOUR THESIS BE?

Writing tasks vary according to the nature of the thesis.

- The *explanatory thesis* is often developed in response to short-answer exam questions that call for information, not analysis (e.g., "How does James Barber categorize the main types of presidential personality?").
- The *mildly argumentative thesis* is appropriate for organizing reports (even lengthy ones), as well as for essay questions that call for some analysis (e.g., "Discuss the qualities of a good speech").
- The *strongly argumentative thesis* is used to organize papers and exam questions that call for information, analysis, *and* the writer's forcefully stated point of view (e.g., "Evaluate the proposed reforms of health maintenance organizations").

The strongly argumentative thesis, of course, is the riskiest of the three, because you must state your position forcefully and make it appear reasonable—which requires that you offer evidence and defend against logical objections. But such intellectual risks pay dividends; and if you become involved enough in your work to make challenging assertions, you will provoke challenging responses that enliven classroom discussions as well as your own learning.

concerns to your conclusion (if at all). With such a change, your final thesis might read: "The federal government should subsidize the development of fuel-cell vehicles as well as the hydrogen infrastructure needed to support them."

This revised thesis makes an assertive commitment to the subject even though the assertion is not as complex as the original. Still, it is more argumentative than the second proposed thesis:

> To reduce our dependence on nonrenewable fossil fuel, the federal government should encourage the development of fuel-cell vehicles.

Here we have a *mildly argumentative* thesis that enables the writer to express an opinion. We infer from the use of the words "should encourage" that the writer endorses the idea of the government's promoting fuel-cell development. But a government that "encourages" development is making a lesser commitment than one that "subsidizes," which means that it allocates funds for a specific policy. So the writer who argues for mere encouragement takes a milder position than the one who argues for subsidies. Note also the contrast between the second thesis and the first one, in which the writer is committed to no involvement in the debate and suggests no government involvement whatsoever:

> Fuel-cell technology has emerged as a promising approach to developing energy-efficient vehicles.

This, the first of the three thesis statements, is *explanatory*, or *informative*. In developing a paper based on this thesis, the writer is committed only to explaining how fuel-cell technology works and why it is a promising approach to energy-efficient vehicles. Given this thesis, a reader would *not* expect to find the writer strongly recommending, for instance, that fuel-cell engines replace internal combustion engines in the near future. Neither does the thesis require the writer to defend a personal opinion; he or she need only justify the use of the relatively mild term "promising."

In sum, for any topic you might explore in a paper, you can make any number of assertions—some relatively simple, some complex. On the basis of these assertions, you set yourself an agenda for your writing—and readers set for themselves expectations for reading. The more ambitious the thesis, the more complex will be the paper and the greater the readers' expectations.

To review: A thesis (a one-sentence summary of your paper) helps you organize your discussion, and helps your reader anticipate it. Theses are distinguished by their carefully worded subjects and predicates, which should be just broad and complex enough to be developed within the length limitations of the assignment. Both novices and experts typically begin the initial draft of a paper with a working thesis—a statement that provides writers with sufficient structure to get started but latitude enough to discover what they want to say, as they write. Once you have completed a first draft, you test the "fit" of your thesis with what you have written. If the fit is good, every element of the thesis will be developed in the paper that follows. Discussions that drift from your thesis should be deleted, or the thesis revised to accommodate the new discussions. These revision concerns will be more fully addressed when we consider the revision stage of the writing process.

Exercise 3.1

Drafting Thesis Statements

Working individually or in small groups, select a topic of current interest on your campus: perhaps the administration's dormitory visitor policy or the role of fraternities and sororities. Draft three theses on this topic: one explanatory, one mildly argumentative, and one strongly argumentative.

INTRODUCTIONS

Writing introductions and conclusions is usually difficult. How to start? What's the best way to approach your topic? With a serious tone, a light touch, an anecdote? And how to end? How to leave the reader feeling satisfied, intrigued, provoked?

Often, writers avoid such decisions by putting them off—and productively so. Bypassing careful planning for the introduction and conclusion, they begin writing the body of the piece. Only after they've finished the body do they go back to write the opening and closing paragraphs. There's a lot to be said for this approach: Because you've presumably spent more time thinking and writing about the topic itself than about how you're going to introduce or conclude it, you're in a better position to set out your ideas. Often it's not until you've actually seen the text on paper or on screen and read it over once or twice that a natural or effective way of introducing or concluding it occurs to you. Also, you're generally in better psychological shape to write both the introduction and the conclusion after the major task of writing is behind you and you've already set down the main body of your discussion or argument.

An effective introduction prepares the reader to enter the world of your paper. It makes the connection between the more familiar world inhabited by the reader and the less familiar world of the writer's topic; it places a discussion in a context that the reader can understand. If you find yourself getting stuck on an introduction at the beginning of a first draft, skip over it for the moment. State your working thesis directly and move on to the body of the paper.

Here are some of the most common strategies for opening a paper:

Quotation

Consider the two introductory paragraphs to an article titled "The Radical Idea of Marrying for Love," from Stephanie Coontz's *Marriage: A History.*

> George Bernard Shaw described marriage as an institution that brings together two people "under the influence of the most violent, most insane, most delusive, and most transient of passions. They are required to swear that they will remain in that excited, abnormal, and exhausting condition continuously until death do them part."
>
> Shaw's comment was amusing when he wrote it at the beginning of the twentieth century, and it still makes us smile today, because it pokes fun at the unrealistic expectations that spring from a dearly held cultural ideal— that marriage should be based on intense, profound love and a couple should maintain their ardor until death do them part. But for thousands of years the joke would have fallen flat.*

Coontz uses the provocative quotation by Shaw to puncture our romantic assumptions about the role of love and passion in marriage. She follows the quotation with an explanation of why Shaw's statement "makes us smile," before setting out on her main undertaking in this article, as indicated in the final sentence of the second paragraph: a historical survey demonstrating that for most of the last few thousand years, love and marriage have had little to do with one another. Quoting the words of others offers many points of departure for your paper: You can agree with the quotation. You can agree and expand. You can sharply disagree. You can use the quotation to set a historical context or establish a tone.

---

*"The Radical Idea of Marrying for Love," from *Marriage: A History*, by Stephanie Coontz, copyright 2005 by the S J Coontz Company. Published by Viking Penguin, a division of Penguin Group (USA), Inc.

Historical Review

Often, the reader will be unprepared to follow the issue you discuss, without some historical background. Consider this introduction to a paper on the film-rating system:

> Sex and violence on the screen are not new issues. In the Roaring Twenties there was increasing pressure from civic and religious groups to ban depictions of "immorality" from the screen. Faced with the threat of federal censorship, the film producers decided to clean their own house. In 1930, the Motion Picture Producers and Distributors of America established the Production Code. At first, adherence to the Code was voluntary; but in 1934 Joseph Breen, newly appointed head of the MPPDA, gave the Code teeth. Henceforth all newly produced films had to be submitted for approval to the Production Code Administration, which had the power to award or withhold the Code seal. Without a Code seal, it was virtually impossible for a film to be shown anywhere in the United States, since exhibitors would not accept it. At about the same time, the Catholic Legion of Decency was formed to advise the faithful which films were and were not objectionable. For several decades the Production Code Administration exercised powerful control over what was portrayed in American theatrical films. By the 1960s, however, changing standards of morality had considerably weakened the Code's grip. In 1968, the Production Code was replaced with a rating system designed to keep younger audiences away from films with high levels of sex or violence. Despite its imperfections, this rating system has proved more beneficial to American films than did the old censorship system.

The paper examines the relative benefits of the rating system. By opening with some historical background on the rating system, the writer helps readers understand his arguments. (Notice the chronological development of details.)

Review of a Controversy

A particular type of historical review provides the background on a controversy or debate. Consider this introduction:

> The *American Heritage Dictionary*'s definition of civil disobedience is rather simple: "the refusal to obey civil laws that are regarded as unjust, usually by employing methods of passive resistance." However, despite such famous (and beloved) examples of civil disobedience as the movements of Mahatma Gandhi in India and the Reverend Martin Luther King, Jr., in the United States, the question of whether or not civil disobedience should be considered an asset to society is hardly clear cut. For instance, Hannah Arendt, in her article "Civil Disobedience," holds that "to think of disobedient minorities as rebels and truants is against the letter and spirit of a constitution whose framers were especially

sensitive to the dangers of unbridled majority rule." On the other hand, a noted lawyer, Lewis Van Dusen, Jr., in his article "Civil Disobedience: Destroyer of Democracy," states that "civil disobedience, whatever the ethical rationalization, is still an assault on our democratic society, an affront to our legal order and an attack on our constitutional government." These two views are clearly incompatible. I believe, though, that Van Dusen's is the more convincing. On balance, civil disobedience is dangerous to society.*

The case against civil disobedience, rather than Van Dusen's article, is the topic of this paper. But to introduce this topic, the writer has provided quotations and references that represent opposing sides of the controversy over civil disobedience. By focusing at the outset on the particular rather than on the abstract qualities of the topic, the writer hopes to secure the attention of her readers and involve them in the controversy that forms the subject of her paper.

From the General to the Specific

Another way of providing a transition from the reader's world to the less familiar world of the paper is to work from a general subject to a specific one. The following introduction begins a paper on improving air quality by urging people to trade the use of their cars for public transportation.

> While generalizations are risky, it seems pretty safe to say that most human beings are selfish. Self-interest may be part of our nature, and probably aids the survival of our species, since self-interested pursuits increase the likelihood of individual survival and genetic reproduction. Ironically, however, our selfishness has caused us to abuse the natural environment upon which we depend. We have polluted, deforested, depleted, deformed, and endangered our earth, water, and air to such an extent that now our species' survival is gravely threatened. In America, air pollution is one of our most pressing environmental problems, and it is our selfish use of the automobile that poses the greatest threat to clean air, as well as the greatest challenge to efforts to stop air pollution. Very few of us seem willing to give up our cars, let alone use them less. We are spoiled by the individual freedom afforded us when we can hop into our gas-guzzling vehicles and go where we want, when we want. Somehow, we as a nation will have to wean ourselves from this addiction to the automobile, and we can do this by designing alternative forms of transportation that serve our selfish interests.[†]

---

*Michele Jacques, "Civil Disobedience: Van Dusen vs. Arendt," unpublished paper, 1993, 1. Used by permission.
[†]Travis Knight, "Reducing Air Pollution with Alternative Transportation," unpublished paper, 1998, 1. Used by permission.

Anecdote and Illustration: From the Specific to the General

The following two paragraphs offer an anecdote in order to move from the specific to a general subject:

> The night of March 24, 1989, was cold and calm, the air crystalline, as the giant *Exxon Valdez* oil tanker pulled out of Valdez, Alaska, into the tranquil waters of Prince William Sound. In these clearest of possible conditions the ship made a planned turn out of the shipping channel and didn't turn back in time. The huge tanker ran aground, spilling millions of gallons of crude oil into the sound. The cost of the cleanup effort was over $2 billion. The ultimate cost of continuing environmental damage is incalculable. Furthermore, when the civil trial was finally over in the summer of 1995, the Exxon Corporation was assessed an additional $5 billion in punitive damages. Everyone I query in my travels vividly recalls the accident, and most have the impression that it had something to do with the master's alcohol consumption. No one is aware of the true cause of the tragedy. In its final report, the National Transportation Safety Board (NTSB) found that sleep deprivation and sleep debt were direct causes of the accident. This stunning result got a brief mention in the back pages of the newspapers.
>
> Out of the vast ocean of knowledge about sleep, there are a few facts that are so important that I will try to burn them into your brain forever. None is more important than the topic of sleep debt. If we can learn to understand sleep indebtedness and manage it, we can improve everyday life as well as avoid many injuries, horribly diminished lives, and premature deaths.*

The previous introduction about pollution went from the general (the statement that human beings are selfish) to the specific (how to decrease air pollution). This one goes from the specific (a calamitous oil spill by a giant oil tanker in Alaskan waters) to the general (the enormous financial and human costs of "sleep debt," or not getting enough sleep). The anecdote is one of the most effective means at your disposal for capturing and holding your reader's attention. It is also one of the most commonly used types of introduction in popular articles. For decades, speakers have begun their remarks with a funny, touching, or otherwise appropriate story. (In fact, plenty of books are nothing but collections of such stories, arranged by subject.)

Question

Frequently, you can provoke the reader's attention by posing a question or a series of questions:

> Which of the following people would you say is the most admirable: Mother Teresa, Bill Gates, or Norman Borlaug? And which do you think is the least admirable? For most people, it's an easy question. Mother Teresa,

---

*From *The Promise of Sleep*, copyright 1999 by William C. Dement. Used by permission of Dell Publishing, a division of Random House, Inc.

famous for ministering to the poor in Calcutta, has been beatified by the Vatican, awarded the Nobel Peace Prize and ranked in an American poll as the most admired person of the 20th century. Bill Gates, infamous for giving us the Microsoft dancing paper clip and the blue screen of death, has been decapitated in effigy in "I Hate Gates" Web sites and hit with a pie in the face. As for Norman Borlaug...who the heck is Norman Borlaug?

Yet a deeper look might lead you to rethink your answers. Borlaug, father of the "Green Revolution" that used agricultural science to reduce world hunger, has been credited with saving a billion lives, more than anyone else in history. Gates, in deciding what to do with his fortune, crunched the numbers and determined that he could alleviate the most misery by fighting everyday scourges in the developing world like malaria, diarrhea and parasites. Mother Teresa, for her part, extolled the virtue of suffering and ran her well-financed missions accordingly: their sick patrons were offered plenty of prayer but harsh conditions, few analgesics and dangerously primitive medical care.

It's not hard to see why the moral reputations of this trio should be so out of line with the good they have done....*

In this introduction to "The Moral Instinct," Steven Pinker asks a question that appears to be easy; but the answer turns out to be more complex than the average reader would have suspected. Pinker uses the rest of the first paragraph to explain why the question appears to be so easy. (After all, no one was more widely admired than Mother Teresa; and for many people—especially Apple partisans!—former Microsoft CEO Bill Gates was an emblem of capitalist greed.) In the second paragraph, Pinker overturns these assumptions as he begins his exploration of the moral sense. Opening your paper with a question is provocative, because it forces the reader to take an active role. Put on the spot by the author, he or she must consider answers—in this case, Who *is* the most admirable? What kind of qualities or activities *should* we admire? An opening question, chosen well, will engage readers and launch them into your paper.

Statement of Thesis

Perhaps the most direct method of introduction is to begin immediately with the thesis:

> The contemporary American shopping mall is the formal garden of late twentieth-century culture, a commodified version of the great garden styles of Western history with which it shares fundamental characteristics. Set apart from the rest of the world as a place of earthly delight like the medieval walled garden; filled with fountains, statuary, and ingeniously devised machinery like the Italian Renaissance garden; designed on grandiose and symmetrical principles like the seventeenth-century French garden; made up of the fragments of cultural and architectural history like the eighteenth-century irregular English garden; and set aside for the public like the nineteenth-century

---

*Steven J. Pinker, "The Moral Instinct," *New York Times Magazine* 12 Jan. 2008.

American park, the mall is the next phase of this garden history, a synthesis of all these styles that have come before. But it is now joined with the shopping street, or at least a sanitized and standardized version of one, something that never before has been allowed within the garden.*

This selection begins with a general assertion—that the American shopping mall is analogous to the great formal gardens of Western history. This idea is Richard Keller Simon's thesis for an article titled "The Formal Garden in the Age of Consumer Culture," which he begins to develop in his second sentence with comparisons between the modern shopping mall and various types of gardens throughout history. In the paragraphs following this introduction, Simon draws correspondences between contemporary shopping malls in Houston, Philadelphia, and Palo Alto and such classic formal gardens as Henry VIII's Hampton Court. The "promenades, walls, vistas, mounts, labyrinths, statues, archways" of classic gardens, he writes, all have their analogs in the modern mall. Beginning with a thesis statement (as opposed to a quotation, question, or anecdote) works well when you want to develop an unexpected, or controversial, argument. The mall as a formal garden? Who would think so? We read on.

Or perhaps you open with the provocative assertion that "Reading is dead" in a paper examining the problem of declining literacy in the digital age. The reader sits up and takes notice, perhaps even protesting, "No, it's not—I read all the time!" This strategy "hooks" a reader, who is likely to want to find out how you will support such an emphatic thesis.

One final note about our model introductions: They may be longer than introductions you have been accustomed to writing. Many writers (and readers) prefer shorter, snappier introductions. The ideal length of an introduction depends on the length of the paper it introduces, and it may also be a matter of personal or corporate style. There is no rule concerning the correct length of an introduction. If you feel that a short introduction is appropriate, use one. Conversely, you may wish to break up what seems like a long introduction into two paragraphs.

Exercise 3.2 ◯

Introductions

Imagine that you are writing a paper using the topic you selected in Exercise 3.1. Conduct some preliminary research on the topic, using an Internet search engine such as Google or Bing, or an article database available at your college. Choose one of the seven types of introductions we've discussed—preferably one you have never used before—and draft an introduction that would work to open a paper on your topic. Use our examples as models to help you draft your introduction.

---

*Excerpted from "The Formal Garden in the Age of Consumer Culture: A Reading of the Twentieth-Century Shopping Mall," copyright 1992 by Richard Keller Simon. Reprinted from *Mapping the American Culture*, ed. Wayne Franklin and Michael Steiner. Published by the University of Iowa Press.

CONCLUSIONS

You might view your conclusion as an introduction in reverse: a bridge from the world of your paper back to the world of your reader. The simplest conclusion is a summary of the paper, but at this point you should go beyond mere summary. You might begin with a summary, for example, and then extend it with a discussion of the paper's significance or its implications for future study, for choices that individuals might make, for policy, and so on. You could urge readers to change an attitude or modify a behavior. Certainly, you're under no obligation to discuss the broader significance of your work (and a summary, alone, will satisfy the formal requirement that your paper have an ending); but the conclusions of effective papers often reveal that their authors are "thinking large" by placing their limited subject into a larger social, cultural, or historical context.

Two words of advice: First, no matter how clever or beautifully executed, a conclusion cannot salvage a poorly written paper. Second, by virtue of its placement, the conclusion carries rhetorical weight: It is the last statement a reader will encounter before turning from your work. Realizing this, writers who expand on the basic summary conclusion often wish to give their final words a dramatic flourish, a heightened level of diction. Soaring rhetoric and drama in a conclusion are fine as long as they do not unbalance the paper and call attention to themselves. Having labored long hours over your paper, you may be inclined at this point to wax eloquent. But keep a sense of proportion and timing. Make your points quickly and end crisply.

Statement of the Subject's Significance

One of the more effective ways to conclude a paper is to discuss the larger significance of your subject. Here, you move from the specific concern of your paper to the broader concerns of the reader's world. A paper on the Wright brothers might end with a discussion of air travel as it affects economies, politics, or families; a paper on contraception might end with a discussion of its effect on sexual mores, population, or the church. But don't overwhelm your reader with the importance of your remarks. Keep your discussion focused.

In this paragraph, June J. Pilcher and Amy S. Walters conclude a paper on how sleep debt hurts college students:

> In sum, our findings suggest that college students are not aware of the extent to which sleep deprivation impairs their ability to complete cognitive tasks successfully because they consistently overrate their concentration and effort, as well as their estimated performance. In addition, the current data suggest that 24 hours of sleep deprivation significantly affects only fatigue and confusion and does not have a more general effect on positive or negative mood states. The practical implication of these findings is that

> many college students are unknowingly sabotaging their own performance by choosing to deprive themselves of sleep [while] they complete complex cognitive tasks.*

The first sentence (as the initial phrase indicates) summarizes the chief finding of the study about which the authors have written. They expand on this conclusion before ending with a statement of the subject's significance ("The practical implication of these findings is that…"). Ending a paper in this way is another way of saying, "The conclusions of this paper matter." If you have taken the trouble to write a good paper, the conclusions *do* matter. Don't be bashful: State the larger significance of the point(s) you have made. Just don't claim too great a significance for your work, lest by overreaching you pop the balloon and your reader thinks, "No, the paper's not *that* important."

Call for Further Research

Scientists and social scientists often end their papers with a review of what has been presented (as, for instance, in an experiment) and the ways in which the subject under consideration needs to be further explored. *A word of caution:* If you raise questions that you call on others to answer, make sure you know that the research you are calling for hasn't already been conducted.

The following conclusion ends a sociological report on the placement of elderly men and women in nursing homes.

> Thus, our study shows a correlation between the placement of elderly citizens in nursing facilities and the significant decline of their motor and intellectual skills over the ten months following placement. What the research has not made clear is the extent to which this marked decline is due to physical as opposed to emotional causes. The elderly are referred to homes at that point in their lives when they grow less able to care for themselves—which suggests that the drop-off in skills may be due to physical causes. But the emotional stress of being placed in a home, away from family and in an environment that confirms the patient's view of himself as decrepit, may exacerbate—if not itself be a primary cause of—the patient's rapid loss of abilities. Further research is needed to clarify the relationship between depression and particular physical ailments as these affect the skills of the elderly in nursing facilities. There is little doubt that information yielded by such studies can enable health care professionals to deliver more effective services.[†]

---

*"How Sleep Deprivation Affects Psychological Variables Related to College Students' Cognitive Performance" by June J. Pilcher and Amy S. Walters, from *Journal of American College Health*, Vol. 46, issue 3, November 1997, pp. 121–126. Published by the Helen Dwight Reid Educational Foundation, Heldref Publications.

[†]Adam Price, "The Crisis in Nursing Home Care," unpublished paper, 2001. Used by permission.

Notice how this call for further study locates the author in a larger community of researchers on whom he depends for assistance in answering the questions that emerge from his own work. The author summarizes his findings (in the first sentence of the paragraph), states what his work has not shown, and then extends his invitation.

Solution/Recommendation

The purpose of your paper might be to review a problem or controversy and to discuss contributing factors. In such a case, after summarizing your discussion, you could offer a solution based on the knowledge you've gained while conducting research, as in the following conclusion. Of course, if your solution is to be taken seriously, your knowledge must be amply demonstrated in the body of the paper.

> The major problem in college sports today is not commercialism—it is the exploitation of athletes and the proliferation of illicit practices which dilute educational standards.
>
> Many universities are currently deriving substantial benefits from sports programs that depend on the labor of athletes drawn from the poorest sections of America's population. It is the responsibility of educators, civil rights leaders, and concerned citizens to see that these young people get a fair return for their labor both in terms of direct remuneration and in terms of career preparation for a life outside sports.
>
> Minimally, scholarships in revenue-producing sports should be designed to extend until graduation, rather than covering only four years of athletic eligibility, and should include guarantees of tutoring, counseling, and proper medical care. At institutions where the profits are particularly large [and the head football coach earns a multi-million-dollar salary], scholarships should also provide salaries that extend beyond room, board, and tuition. The important thing is that the athlete be remunerated fairly and have the opportunity to gain skills from a university environment without undue competition from a physically and psychologically demanding full-time job. This may well require that scholarships be extended over five or six years, including summers.
>
> Such a proposal, I suspect, will not be easy to implement. The current amateur system, despite its moral and educational flaws, enables universities to hire their athletic labor at minimal cost. But solving the fiscal crisis of the universities on the backs of America's poor and minorities is not, in the long run, a tenable solution. With the support of concerned educators, parents, and civil rights leaders, and with the help from organized labor, the college athlete, truly a sleeping giant, will someday speak out and demand what is rightly his—and hers—a fair share of the revenue created by their hard work.*

---

*Mark Naison, "Scenario for Scandal," *Commonweal* 109.16 (1982).

In this conclusion, the author summarizes his article in one sentence: "The major problem in college sports today is not commercialism—it is the exploitation of athletes and the proliferation of illicit practices which dilute educational standards." In paragraph 2, he continues with an analysis of the problem just stated and follows with a general recommendation that "educators, civil rights leaders, and concerned citizens" be responsible for the welfare of college athletes. In paragraph 3, he makes a specific proposal, and in the final paragraph, he anticipates resistance to the proposal. He concludes by discounting this resistance and returning to the general point: that college athletes should receive a fair deal.

Anecdote

As we've seen in our discussion of introductions, an anecdote is a briefly told story or joke, the point of which is to shed light on your subject. The anecdote is more direct than an allusion. With an allusion, you merely refer to a story ("We would all love to go floating down the river like Huck…"); with the anecdote, you retell the story. The anecdote allows readers to discover for themselves the significance of a reference to another source—an effort most readers enjoy because they get to exercise their creativity.

The following anecdote concludes a political–philosophical essay. After the author sums up her argument in a paragraph, she continues—and concludes—with a brief story.

> Ironically, our economy is fueled by the very thing that degrades our value system. But when politicians call for a return to "traditional family values," they seldom criticize the business interests that promote and benefit from our coarsened values. Consumer capitalism values things over people; it thrives on discontent and unhappiness since discontented people make excellent consumers, buying vast numbers of things that may somehow "fix" their inadequacies. We buy more than we need, the economy chugs along, but such materialism is the real culprit behind our warped value systems. Anthony de Mello tells the following story:
>
> > Socrates believed that the wise person would instinctively lead a frugal life, and he even went so far as to refuse to wear shoes. Yet he constantly fell under the spell of the marketplace and would go there often to look at the great variety and magnificence of the wares on display.
> >
> > A friend once asked him why he was so intrigued with the allures of the market. "I love to go there," Socrates replied, "to discover how many things I am perfectly happy without."*

The writer could, at this point, have offered an interpretation instead of an anecdote, but this would have spoiled the dramatic value for the reader. The purpose of an anecdote is to make your point with subtlety, to resist the temptation to

---

*Frances Wageneck, "Family Values in the Marketplace," unpublished paper, 2000. Used by permission.

interpret. When selecting an anecdote, keep in mind four guidelines: The anecdote should fit your content; it should be prepared for (readers should have all the information they need to understand it); it should provoke the readers' interest; and it should not be so obscure as to be unintelligible.

Quotation

A favorite concluding device is the quotation—the words of a famous person or an authority in the field on which you are writing. By quoting another, you link your work to that person's, thereby gaining authority and credibility. The first criterion for selecting a quotation is its suitability to your thesis. But consider carefully what your choice of sources says about you. Suppose you are writing a paper on the American work ethic. If you could use a line either by the comedian Jon Stewart or by the current secretary of labor to make the final point of your conclusion, which would you choose and why? One source may not be inherently more effective than the other, but the choice would affect the tone of your paper. The following paragraph concludes an article on single-sex education:

> But schools, inevitably, present many curriculums, some overt and some subtle; and critics argue that with Sax's* model comes a lesson that our gender differences are primary, and this message is at odds with one of the most foundational principles of America's public schools. Given the myriad ways in which our schools are failing, it may be hard to remember that public schools were intended not only to instruct children in reading and math but also to teach them commonality, tolerance and what it means to be American. "When you segregate, by any means, you lose some of that," says Richard Kahlenberg, a senior fellow at the Century Foundation. "Even if one could prove that sending a kid off to his or her own school based on religion or race or ethnicity or gender did a little bit better job of raising the academic skills for workers in the economy, there's also the issue of trying to create tolerant citizens in a democracy."[†]

In the article leading up to this conclusion, Elizabeth Weil takes a somewhat skeptical view of the virtues of "teaching boys and girls separately." She concludes with an apt quotation by Richard Kahlenberg, who, while conceding some value for single-sex education, supports Weil's own skepticism by suggesting that single-sex education may not create citizens as tolerant as those who have been through classes that include both genders.

Using quotations poses one potential problem, however: If you end with the words of another, you may leave the impression that someone else can make your case more effectively than you. The language of the quotation will put your own prose into relief. If your prose suffers by comparison—if the quotations are the best part of your paper—you need to spend time revising.

---

*Leonard Sax is a psychologist and physician who gave up medicine to devote himself to promoting single-sex public education.

[†]Elizabeth Weil, "Teaching Boys and Girls Separately," *New York Times Magazine* 2 Mar. 2008.

Question

Just as questions are useful for opening papers, they are useful for closing them. Opening and closing questions function in different ways, however. The introductory question promises to be addressed in the paper that follows. But the concluding question leaves issues unresolved, calling on the readers to assume an active role by offering their own answers. Consider the following two paragraphs, written to conclude an article on genetically modified (GM) food:

> Are GM foods any more of a risk than other agricultural innovations that have taken place over the years, like selective breeding? Do the existing and potential future benefits of GM foods outweigh any risks that do exist? And what standard should governments use when assessing the safety of transgenic crops? The "frankenfood" frenzy has given life to a policy-making standard known as the "precautionary principle," which has been long advocated by environmental groups. That principle essentially calls for governments to prohibit any activity that raises concerns about human health or the environment, even if some cause-and-effect relationships are not fully established scientifically. As Liberal Democrat MP [Member of Parliament] Norman Baker told the BBC: "We must always apply the precautionary principle. That says that unless you're sure of adequate control, unless you're sure the risk is minimal, unless you're sure nothing horrible can go wrong, you don't do it."
>
> But can any innovation ever meet such a standard of certainty—especially given the proliferation of "experts" that are motivated as much by politics as they are by science? And what about those millions of malnourished people whose lives could be saved by transgenic foods?*

Rather than end with a question, you may choose to *raise* a question in your conclusion and then answer it, based on the material you've provided in the paper. The answered question challenges a reader to agree or disagree with you and thus places the reader in an active role. The following brief conclusion ends a student paper titled "Is Feminism Dead?"

> So the answer to the question "Is the feminist movement dead?" is no, it's not. Even if most young women today don't consciously identify themselves as "feminists"—due to the ways in which the term has become loaded with negative associations—the principles of gender equality that lie at feminism's core are enthusiastically embraced by the vast number of young women, and even a large percentage of young men.

Speculation

When you speculate, you consider what might happen as well as what has happened. Speculation involves a spinning out of possibilities. It stimulates readers by immersing them in your discussion of the unknown, implicitly challenging

---

*"Frankenfoods Frenzy," *Reason* 13 Jan. 2000.

them to agree or disagree. The following paragraph concludes the brief article "The Incandescent Charisma of the Lonely Light Bulb" by Dan Neil. The author laments the passing of the familiar electric light bulb (in favor of lower-wattage compact fluorescent lights) as one more indication of the end of the analog age and the triumph of the digital: "The demise of the light bulb marks the final transition from electrics to electronics":

> The passing of any technology provokes nostalgia. I'm sure someone bemoaned the rise of the push-button phone and eulogized the rotary dialer. (*What a beautiful sound, the "shickity-shick" of a well-spun number*....) But the Edisonian light bulb is a more fundamental thing—so much the proverbial better idea that it came to symbolize the eureka moment, the flash of insight, when it appeared over a cartoon character's head. The fact is, how we light the world inevitably affects how we see the world. I predict we're going to miss the soft, forgiving light of the incandescent bulb with its celestial geometry. *I predict a more harshly lighted future.**

The author's concluding speculation may not be entirely serious (though a few people do lament the passing of the manual typewriter and the phonograph record), but it does highlight what is often lost, and subsequently missed, in the relentless journey of technological progress. If you have provided the necessary information prior to a concluding speculation, you will send readers back into their lives (and away from your paper) with an implicit challenge: Do they regard the future as you do? Whether they do or not, you have set an agenda. You have got them thinking.

Exercise 3.3 ◯

Drafting Conclusions

Choose one of the seven types of conclusions we've discussed—preferably one you have never used before—and draft a conclusion for the topic you chose for Exercises 3.1 and 3.2. Use our examples as models to help you draft your conclusion.

---

*Dan Neil, "The Incandescent Charisma of the Lonely Light Bulb," *Los Angeles Times Magazine* 3 Feb. 2008: 70.

Chapter 4

Explanatory Synthesis

After completing this chapter, you will be able to:

LO 4.1   View synthesis as a discussion that draws upon an inferred relationship between or among sources.

LO 4.2   Identify the situations in which a synthesis would be useful.

LO 4.3   Use your purpose to guide your use of sources in a synthesis.

LO 4.4   Distinguish between explanatory and argument syntheses.

LO 4.5   Use the guidelines for writing syntheses.

LO 4.6   Write an explanatory synthesis that builds on your purpose, thesis, carefully chosen sources, and a clear plan.

WHAT IS A SYNTHESIS?

A *synthesis* is a written discussion that draws on two or more sources. It follows that your ability to write syntheses depends on your ability to infer relationships among sources such as these:

- Essays
- Fiction
- Interviews
- Articles
- Lectures
- Visual media

This process is nothing new for you because you infer relationships all the time—say, between something you've read in the newspaper and something you've seen for yourself, or between the teaching styles of your favorite and least favorite instructors. In fact, if you've written research papers, you've already written syntheses.

In a *synthesis*, you make explicit the relationships that you have inferred among separate sources.

Summary and Critique as a Basis for Synthesis

The skills you've already learned and practiced in the previous two chapters will be vital in writing syntheses. Before you're in a position to draw relationships between two or more sources, you must understand what those sources say; you must be able to *summarize* those sources. Readers will frequently benefit from at least partial summaries of sources in your synthesis essays. At the same time, you must go beyond summary to make judgments—judgments based on your *critical reading* of your sources: what conclusions you've drawn about the quality and validity of these sources, whether you agree or disagree with the points made in your sources, and why you agree or disagree.

Inference as a Basis for Synthesis: Moving Beyond Summary and Critique

In a synthesis, you go beyond the critique of individual sources to determine the relationships among them. Is the information in source B, for example, an extended illustration of the generalizations in source A? Would it be useful to compare and contrast source C with source B? Having read and considered sources A, B, and C, can you infer something else—in other words, D (not a source, but your own idea)?

Because a synthesis is based on two or more sources, you will need to be selective when choosing information from each. It would be neither possible nor desirable, for instance, to discuss in a ten-page paper on the American Civil War every point that the authors of two books make about their subject. What you as a writer must do is select from each source the ideas and information that best allow you to achieve your purpose.

PURPOSE

Your purpose in reading source materials and then drawing on them to write your own material is often reflected in the wording of an assignment. For instance, consider the following assignments on the Civil War:

American History: Evaluate the author's treatment of the origins of the Civil War.

Economics: Argue the following proposition, in light of your readings: "The Civil War was fought not for reasons of moral principle but for reasons of economic necessity."

Government: Prepare a report on the effects of the Civil War on Southern politics at the state level between 1870 and 1917. Focus on one state.

Mass Communications: Discuss how the use of photography during the Civil War may have affected the perceptions of the war by Northerners living in industrial cities.

Literature: Select two Southern writers of the twentieth century whose work you believe was influenced by the divisive effects of the Civil War. Discuss the ways this influence is apparent in a novel or a group of short stories written by each author. The works should not be *about* the Civil War.

Applied Technology: Compare and contrast the technology of warfare available in the 1860s with the technology available a century earlier.

Each of these assignments creates a particular purpose for writing. Having located sources relevant to your topic, you would select for possible use in a paper only the parts of those sources that helped you in fulfilling this purpose. And how you used those parts—how you related them to other material from other sources—would also depend on your purpose.

Example: Same Sources, Different Uses

If you were working on the government assignment, you might draw on the same source as a student working on the literature assignment by referring to Robert Penn Warren's novel *All the King's Men*, about Louisiana politics in the early part

---

WHERE DO WE FIND WRITTEN SYNTHESES?

Here are just a few of the types of writing that involve synthesis:

Academic Writing

- **Analysis papers** synthesize and apply several related theoretical approaches.
- **Research papers** synthesize multiple sources.
- **Argument papers** synthesize different points into a coherent claim or position.
- **Essay exams** demonstrate understanding of course material through comparing and contrasting theories, viewpoints, or approaches in a particular field.

Workplace Writing

- **Newspaper and magazine articles** synthesize primary and secondary sources.
- **Position papers and policy briefs** compare and contrast solutions for solving problems.
- **Business plans** synthesize ideas and proposals into one coherent plan.
- **Memos and letters** synthesize multiple ideas, events, and proposals into concise form.
- **Web sites** synthesize information from various sources to present in Web pages and related links.

of the twentieth century. But because the purposes of the two assignments are different, you and the other student would make different uses of the source. The parts or aspects of the novel that you find worthy of detailed analysis might be mentioned only in passing—or not at all—by the other student.

USING YOUR SOURCES

Your purpose determines not only what parts of your sources you will use, but also how you will relate those parts to one another. Since the very essence of synthesis is the combining of information and ideas, you must have some basis on which to combine them. *Some relationships among the material in your sources must make them worth synthesizing.* It follows that the better able you are to discover such relationships, the better able you will be to use your sources in writing syntheses. Notice that the mass communications assignment requires you to draw a *cause-and-effect* relationship between photographs of the war and Northerners' perceptions of the war. The applied technology assignment requires you to *compare and contrast* state-of-the-art weapons technology in the eighteenth and nineteenth centuries. The economics assignment requires you to *argue* a proposition. In each case, *your purpose will determine how you relate your source materials to one another.*

Consider some other examples. You may be asked on an exam question or in the instructions for a paper to *describe* two or three approaches to prison reform during the past decade. You may be asked to *compare and contrast* one country's approach to imprisonment with another's. You may be asked to *develop an argument* of your own on this subject, based on your reading. Sometimes (when you are not given a specific assignment) you determine your own purpose: You are interested in exploring a particular subject; you are interested in making a case for one approach or another. In any event, your purpose shapes your essay. Your purpose determines which sources you research, which ones you use, which parts of them you use, at which points in your paper you use them, and in what manner you relate them to one another.

TYPES OF SYNTHESES: EXPLANATORY AND ARGUMENT

In this and the next chapter, we categorize syntheses into two main types: *explanatory* and *argument.* The easiest way to recognize the difference between the two types may be to consider the difference between a news article and an editorial on the same subject. For the most part, we'd say that the main purpose of the news article is to convey *information* and that the main purpose of the editorial is to convey *opinion* or *interpretation.* Of course, this distinction is much too simplified: News articles often convey opinion or bias, sometimes subtly, sometimes openly; and editorials often convey unbiased information along with opinion. But as a practical matter, we can generally agree on the distinction between a news article that primarily conveys information and an editorial that primarily conveys opinion. You should be able to observe this distinction in the selections shown here as "Explanation" and "Argument."

Explanation: News Article from the *New York Times*

WHILE WARNING ABOUT FAT, U.S. PUSHES CHEESE SALES

By Michael Moss
November 6, 2010

Domino's Pizza was hurting early last year. Domestic sales had fallen, and a survey of big pizza chain customers left the company tied for the worst tasting pies.

Then help arrived from an organization called Dairy Management. It teamed up with Domino's to develop a new line of pizzas with 40 percent more cheese, and proceeded to devise and pay for a $12 million marketing campaign.

Consumers devoured the cheesier pizza, and sales soared by double digits. "This partnership is clearly working," Brandon Solano, the Domino's vice president for brand innovation, said in a statement to *The New York Times.*

But as healthy as this pizza has been for Domino's, one slice contains as much as two-thirds of a day's maximum recommended amount of saturated fat, which has been linked to heart disease and is high in calories.

5   And Dairy Management, which has made cheese its cause, is not a private business consultant. It is a marketing creation of the United States Department of Agriculture—the same agency at the center of a federal anti-obesity drive that discourages over-consumption of some of the very foods Dairy Management is vigorously promoting....

Argument: Editorial from the *Boston Globe*

GOT TOO MUCH CHEESE?

By Derrick Z. Jackson
November 9, 2010

...The chief executive of Dairy Management, Thomas Gallagher,...declined to be interviewed by the [*New York*] *Times*, but in a column last year in a trade publication, he wrote, "More cheese on pizza equals more cheese sales. In fact, if every pizza included one more ounce of cheese, we would see an additional 250 million pounds of cheese annually."

Emboldened by its success with cheese, Dairy Management is now reportedly working on bamboozling the public that chocolate milk is a sports recovery drink and persuading children to eat green beans by slathering them with cheese.

A year ago, at a joint press conference held by the USDA, the National Dairy Council and the National Football League to promote exercise, Gallagher said, "Child nutrition, particularly in schools, has been a cornerstone of the National Dairy Council for nearly a century. The program centers on youth taking the lead in changing the school environment."

The truth makes this a galling proclamation. Despite all the nutrition initiatives launched by the Obama administration, the cornerstone of federal policy continues to clog the nation's arteries, making a mockery of programs boasting how youth can take the lead. What is a cornerstone for the USDA is a gravestone for nutrition.

We'll say, for the sake of convenience, that the news article *explains* the contradictory messages on nutrition that the federal government is communicating and that the editorial *argues* that the contradiction is damaging. This important distinction between explanation and argument extends beyond the news to other materials you might consult while doing research. Consider a second set of passages:

What Are Genetically Modified (GM) Foods?

GENETICALLY MODIFIED FOODS AND ORGANISMS

The United States Department of Energy
November 5, 2008

Combining genes from different organisms is known as recombinant DNA technology, and the resulting organism is said to be "genetically modified," "genetically engineered," or "transgenic." GM products (current or those in development) include medicines and vaccines, foods and food ingredients, feeds, and fibers.

Locating genes for important traits—such as those conferring insect resistance or desired nutrients—is one of the most limiting steps in the process. However, genome sequencing and discovery programs for hundreds of organisms are generating detailed maps along with data-analyzing technologies to understand and use them.

In 2006, 252 million acres of transgenic crops were planted in 22 countries by 10.3 million farmers. The majority of these crops were herbicide- and insect-resistant soybeans, corn, cotton, canola, and alfalfa. Other crops grown commercially or field-tested are a sweet potato resistant to a virus that could decimate most of the African harvest, rice with increased iron and vitamins that may alleviate chronic malnutrition in Asian countries, and a variety of plants able to survive weather extremes.

On the horizon are bananas that produce human vaccines against infectious diseases such as hepatitis B; fish that mature more quickly; cows that are resistant to bovine spongiform encephalopathy (mad cow disease); fruit and nut trees that yield years earlier, and plants that produce new plastics with unique properties.

WHY A *GM FREEZE?*

The GM Freeze Campaign
November 11, 2010

Genetic modification in food and farming raises many fundamental environmental, social, health and ethical concerns. There is increasing evidence of contamination of conventional crops and wild plants, and potential damage to wildlife. The effects on human health of eating these foods remain uncertain and some scientists are calling for much more rigorous safety testing. It is clear that further research into all these issues is vital. Furthermore the public has not been properly involved in decision making processes, despite strong public support for the precautionary approach to GM in the [United Kingdom] and the [European Union].

Much more time is needed to assess the need for and implications of using genetic modification in food and farming, in particular the increasing control of corporations who rely on patents to secure their future markets.

Both of these passages deal with the topic of genetically modified (GM) foods. The first is excerpted from a largely informational Web site published by the U.S. Department of Energy, which oversees the Human Genome Project, the government's ongoing effort to map gene sequences and apply that knowledge. We say the DOE account is "largely informational" because readers can find a great deal of information here about genetically modified foods. At the same time, however, the DOE explanation is subtly biased in favor of genetic modification: Note the absence of any language raising questions about the ethics or safety of GM foods; note also the use of terms such as "desired nutrients" and "insect resistance," with their positive connotations. The DOE examples show GM foods in a favorable light, and the passage as a whole assumes the value and importance of genetic manipulation.

As we see in the second passage, however, that assumption is not shared by all. Excerpted from a Web site advocating a freeze on genetically modified crops, the second passage primarily argues against the ethics and safety of such manipulation, calling for more study before modified crops are released widely into the environment. At the same time, the selection provides potentially important explanatory materials: (1) the claim that there is "increasing evidence of contamination of conventional crops and wild plants, and potential damage to wildlife"; (2) the claim that corporations control GM crops, and potentially the food supply, through patents. We can easily and quickly confirm these claims through research; if confirmed, the information—which is nested in a primarily argumentative piece—could prove useful in a paper on GM foods.

So while it is fair to say that most writing can be broadly categorized as explanatory or argumentative, understand that in practice, many of the materials you read will be a mix: *primarily* one or the other but not altogether one or the other. It will be your job as an alert, critical reader to determine when authors are explaining or arguing—sometimes in the same sentence.

For instance, you might read the following in a magazine article: "The use of goats to manufacture anticlotting proteins for humans in their milk sets a dangerous precedent." Perhaps you did not know that scientists have genetically manipulated goats (by inserting human genes) to create medicines. That much of the statement is factual. It is explanatory. Whether or not this fact "sets a dangerous precedent" is an argument. You could agree or not with the argument, but your views would not change the fact about the genetic manipulation of farm animals. Even within a single sentence, then, you must be alert to distinguishing between explanation and argument.

HOW TO WRITE SYNTHESES

Although writing syntheses can't be reduced to a lockstep method, it should help you to follow the guidelines listed in the box below.

In this chapter, we'll focus on explanatory syntheses. In Chapter 5, we'll discuss the argument synthesis.

GUIDELINES FOR WRITING SYNTHESES

- *Consider your purpose in writing*. What are you trying to accomplish in your paper? How will this purpose shape the way you approach your sources?
- *Select and carefully read your sources* according to your purpose. Then reread the passages, mentally summarizing each. Identify those aspects or parts of your sources that will help you fulfill your purpose. When rereading, *label* or *underline* the sources' main ideas, key terms, and any details you want to use in the synthesis.
- *Take notes on your reading.* In addition to labeling or underlining key points in the readings, you might write brief one- or two-sentence summaries of each source. This will help you in formulating your thesis statement and in choosing and organizing your sources later.
- *Formulate a thesis.* Your thesis is the main idea that you want to present in your synthesis. It should be expressed as a complete sentence. You might do some predrafting about the ideas discussed in the readings in order to help you work out a thesis. If you've written one-sentence summaries of the readings, looking over the summaries will help you to brainstorm connections between readings and to devise a thesis.

  When you write your synthesis drafts, you will need to consider where your thesis fits in your paper. Sometimes the thesis is the first sentence, but more often it is *the final sentence of the first paragraph*. If you are writing an *inductively arranged* synthesis (see p. 151), the thesis sentence may not appear until the final paragraphs.

(continued)

- *Decide how you will use your source material.* How will the information and the ideas in the passages help you fulfill your purpose?
- *Develop an organizational plan,* according to your thesis. How will you arrange your material? It is not necessary to prepare a formal outline. But you should have some plan that will indicate the order in which you will present your material and the relationships among your sources.
- *Draft the topic sentences for the main sections.* This is an optional step, but you may find it a helpful transition from organizational plan to first draft.
- *Write the first draft* of your synthesis, following your organizational plan. Be flexible with your plan, however. Frequently, you will use an outline to get started. As you write, you may discover new ideas and make room for them by adjusting the outline. When this happens, reread your work frequently, making sure that your thesis still accounts for what follows and that what follows still logically supports your thesis.
- *Document your sources.* You must do this by crediting sources within the body of the synthesis—citing the author's last name and the page number from which the point was taken—and then providing full citation information in a list of "Works Cited" at the end. Don't open yourself to charges of plagiarism! (See pp. 46–47.)
- *Revise your synthesis,* inserting transitional words and phrases where necessary. Make sure that the synthesis reads smoothly, logically, and clearly from beginning to end. Check for grammatical correctness, punctuation, and spelling.

Note: The writing of syntheses is a recursive process, and you should accept a certain amount of backtracking and reformulating as inevitable. For instance, in developing an organizational plan (Step 6 of the procedure), you may discover a gap in your presentation that will send you scrambling for another source—back to Step 2. You may find that formulating a thesis and making inferences among sources occur simultaneously; indeed, inferences are often made before a thesis is formulated. Our recommendations for writing syntheses will give you a structure that will get you started. But be flexible in your approach; expect discontinuity and, if possible, be assured that through backtracking and reformulating, you will produce a coherent, well-crafted paper.

THE EXPLANATORY SYNTHESIS

Many of the papers you write in college will be more or less explanatory in nature. An explanation helps readers understand a topic. Writers explain when they divide a subject into its component parts and present them to the reader in a clear and orderly fashion. Explanations may entail descriptions that recreate in words some object, place, emotion, event, sequence of events, or state of affairs.

- As a student reporter, you may need to explain an event—to relate when, where, and how it took place.

- In a science lab, you would observe the conditions and results of an experiment and record them for review by others.

- In a political science course, you might review research on a particular subject—say, the complexities underlying the debate over gay marriage—and then present the results of your research to your professor and the members of your class.

Your job in writing an explanatory paper—or in writing the explanatory portion of an argumentative paper—is not to argue a particular point, but rather *to present the facts in a reasonably objective manner.* Of course, explanatory papers, like other academic papers, should be based on a thesis (see pp. 110–112). But the purpose of a thesis in an explanatory paper is less to advance a particular opinion than to focus the various facts contained in the paper.

DEMONSTRATION: EXPLANATORY SYNTHESIS—GOING UP? AN ELEVATOR RIDE TO SPACE

To illustrate how the process of synthesis works, we'll begin with a number of short extracts from several articles on the same subject.

Suppose you were writing a paper on an intriguing idea you came across in a magazine: a space elevator—a machine that would lift objects into earth orbit, and beyond, not by blasting them free of earth's gravity using rockets, but by lifting them in ways similar to (but also different from) the way elevators on earth lift people and material in tall buildings. Once considered a fancy of science fiction, the idea has received serious attention among scientists and even NASA. In fact, an elevator to space could be built relatively soon.

Fascinated by the possibility of an elevator to space being built in your lifetime, you decide to conduct some research with the goal of *explaining* what you discover to interested classmates.

Exercise 4.1

Exploring the Topic

Read the selections that follow on the subject of space elevators. Before continuing with the discussion after the selections, write a page or two of responses. You might imagine the ways an elevator to space might change you and, more broadly, the economy, the military, and international relations. What do you imagine will concern some people about a space elevator? What do you think might be of interest to journalists, the military, politicians, businesspeople, entertainers, artists?

In the following pages, we present excerpts from the kinds of source materials you might locate during the research process.

Note: To save space and for the purpose of demonstration, we offer excerpts from three sources only; a full list of sources appears in the "Works Cited" of the model synthesis on pages 127–128. In preparing your paper, of course, you would draw on the entire articles from which these extracts were taken. (The discussion of how these passages can form the basis of an explanatory synthesis resumes on p. 109.)

The History of the Space Elevator

P. K. Aravind

P. K. Aravind teaches in the Department of Physics at the Worcester Polytechnic Institute, Worcester, Massachusetts. The following is excerpted from "The Physics of the Space Elevator" in the *American Journal of Physics* (May 2007).

I. Introduction

A space elevator is a tall tower rising from a point on the Earth's equator to a height well above a geostationary orbit,* where it terminates in a counterweight (see Figure 1a). Although the idea of such a structure is quite old, it is only within the last decade or so that it has attracted serious scientific attention. NASA commissioned some studies of the elevator in the 1990s that concluded that it would be feasible to build one and use it to transport payload cheaply into space and also to launch spacecraft on voyages to other planets.[1] Partly as a result of this study, a private organization called Liftport[2] was formed in 2003 with the goal of constructing a space elevator and enlisting the support of universities, research labs, and businesses that might have an interest in this venture. Liftport's website features a timer that counts down the seconds to the opening of its elevator on 12 April 2018. Whether that happens or not, the space elevator represents an application of classical mechanics to an engineering project on a gargantuan scale that would have an enormous impact on humanity if it is realized. As such, it is well worth studying and thinking about for all the possibilities it has to offer.

This article explains the basic mechanical principles underlying the construction of the space elevator and discusses some of its principal applications. It should be accessible to anyone who has had a course in undergraduate

*Geostationary orbit, also referred to as geostationary earth orbit (or GEO), marks the altitude above the earth's equator (22,236 miles) at which a satellite will rotate at the same speed as the earth itself and, thus, appear to remain motionless in the sky.

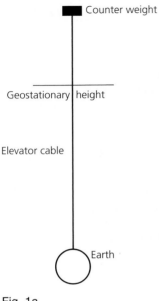

Counter weight

Geostationary height

Elevator cable

Earth

Fig. 1a

mechanics and could help give students in such a course a feeling for some of the contemporary applications of mechanics. Before discussing the physics of the space elevator, we recall some of the more interesting facts of its history. The earliest mention of anything like the elevator seems to have been in the book of Genesis, which talks of an attempt by an ancient civilization to build a tower to heaven—the "Tower of Babel"—that came to naught because of a breakdown of communication between the participants. In more recent times the concept of the space elevator was first proposed by the Russian physicist Konstantin Tsiolkovsky in 1895 and then again by the Leningrad engineer, Yuri Artsutanov, in 1960.[3] The concept was rediscovered by the American engineer, Jerome Pearson,[4] in 1975. In 1978 Arthur Clarke brought the idea to the attention of the general public through his novel *Fountains of Paradise*[5] and at about the same time Charles Sheffield, a physicist, wrote a novel[6] centered on the same concept. Despite this publicity, the idea of the elevator did not really catch on among scientists because an analysis of its structure showed that no known material was strong enough to build it.

This pessimism was largely neutralized by the discovery of carbon nanotubes in 1991.[7] Carbon nanotubes, which are essentially rolled up sheets of graphite, have a tensile strength greatly exceeding that of any other known material. Their high tensile strength, combined with their relatively low density, makes nanotubes an excellent construction material for a space elevator and led to a resurgence of interest in the concept.

Notes

[1] See the story "Audacious and outrageous: Space elevators" at http://science.nasa.gov/headlines/y2000/ast07sep_1.htm.

[2] Liftport, http://www.liftport.com/.

[3] K. Tsiolkovsky, *Dreams of Earth and Sky* 1895, reissue, Athena Books, Barcelona-Singapore, 2004. Y. Artsutanov, "V Kosmos na Elektrovoze" "To the cosmos by electric train" Komsomolskaya Pravda, 31 July 1960.

[4] J. Pearson, "The orbital tower: A spacecraft launcher using the Earth's rotational energy," *Acta Astronaut.* 2, 785–799 1975.

[5] Arthur C. Clarke, *Fountains of Paradise* Harcourt Bruce Jovanovich, New York, 1978.

[6] Charles Sheffield, *The Web Between the Worlds* Baen, Simon and Schuster, Riverdale, NY, 2001.

[7] S. Iijima, "Helical microtubules of graphitic carbon," *Nature London* 354, 56–58 1991.

Applications of the Space Elevator

Bradley C. Edwards

Bradley Edwards, Director of Research for the Institute for Scientific Research (ISR), is the best-known advocate of the space elevator. Rejected as a young man from the astronaut corps due to health concerns, he earned an advanced degree in physics and worked at the Los Alamos National Laboratory on projects related to space technologies. The selection that follows is excerpted from a 2003 report *(The Space Elevator: National Institute for Advanced Concepts Phase II Report)* prepared on the completion of a grant from NASA.

Every development must have some value to be worth doing. In the case of the space elevator there are both short and long-term applications.... The immediate first use of the space elevator is deployment of Earth-orbiting satellites for telecommunications, military, Earth monitoring, etc....

The traditional markets the space elevator will address include:

- Telecommunications
- Remote sensing
- Department of Defense

The U.S. satellite launch market is expected to be at 110 launches per year when we enter the market.[1]

However, we plan to extend this traditional base and target smaller institutions who are interested in space activities—clients who, until now, have been unable to afford it. The new markets we will encourage and target include:

- Solar Energy Satellites (clean, limitless power from space)
- Space-System Test-Bed (universities, aerospace)
- Environmental Assessment (pollution, global change)
- Agricultural Assessment (crop analysis, forestry)
- Private Communications Systems (corporate)
- National Systems (developing countries)
- Medical Therapy (aging, physical handicaps, chronic pain)
- Entertainment/Advertising (sponsorships, remote video adventures)
- Space Manufacturing (biomedical, crystal, electronics)
- Asteroid Detection (global security)
- Basic Research (biomedical, commercial production, university programs)
- Private Tracking Systems (Earth transportation inventory, surveillance)
- Space Debris Removal (international environmental)
- Exploratory Mining Claims (robotic extraction)
- Tourism/Communities (hotels, vacations, medical convalescence)

We expect solar power satellites to be one of the major markets to develop when we become operational and have begun dialogs with [British Petroleum] Solar about launch requirements and interest. Solar power satellites consist of square miles of solar arrays that collect solar power and then beam the power back to Earth for terrestrial consumption. Megawatt systems will have masses of several thousand tons[2] and will provide power at competitive rates to fossil fuels, without pollution, if launch costs get below $500/lb....

Another market we expect to emerge is solar system exploration and development. Initially this would be unmanned but a manned segment, based on the Mars Direct (Zubrin) scenario, could emerge early after elevator operations begin. The exploration market would include:

- Exploratory and mining claims missions to asteroids, Mars, Moon, and Venus
- Science-based, university and private sponsored missions
- In-situ resource production on Mars and Moon
- Large mapping probes for Mars and the asteroids
- Near-Earth object catastrophic impact studies from space

The exploration market would be expected to consist of only a few lifts a year within two years of operations but each mission would be a larger one and produce substantial media attention. In the long-term, such practices will increase our revenue as manned activities in space grow.

Another market to consider in the coming decades is space tourism. We may encourage tourism early on with day-long joyrides to space and later possibly lease a ribbon for long-term, hotels in space. Such activities will produce positive public perception and broaden the long-term market. In a recent survey by Zogby International it was found that "7% of affluent (people) would pay $20 million for 2-week orbital flight; 19% would pay $100,000 for 15-minute sub-orbital flight." These numbers indicate a possible future market that could be tapped as well.

Notes

[1] Zogby International

[2] NASA and ESA studies

GOING UP

Brad Lemley

The following excerpt appeared in the July 2004 issue of *Discover* magazine.

The key to conquering the solar system is inside a black plastic briefcase on Brad Edwards's desk. Without ceremony, he pops open the case to reveal it: a piece of black ribbon about a foot long and a half-inch wide, stretched across a steel frame.

Huh? No glowing infinite-energy orb, no antigravity disk, just a hunk of tape with black fibers. "This came off a five-kilometer-long spool," says Edwards, tapping it with his index finger. "The technology is moving along quickly."

Ocean-based platform for a space elevator

The ribbon is a piece of carbon-nanotube composite. In as little as 15 years, Edwards says, a version that's three feet wide and thinner than the page you are reading could be anchored to a platform 1,200 miles off the coast of Ecuador and stretch upward 62,000 miles into deep space, kept taut by the centripetal force provided by Earth's rotation. The expensive, dangerous business of rocketing people and cargo into space would become obsolete as elevators climb the ribbon and hoist occupants to any height they fancy: low, for space tourism; geosynchronous, for communications satellites; or high, where Earth's rotation would help fling spacecraft to the moon, Mars, or beyond. Edwards contends that a space elevator could drop payload costs to $100 a pound versus the space shuttle's $10,000. And it would cost as little as $6 billion to build—less than half what Boston spent on the Big Dig highway project.

Science fiction writers, beginning with Arthur C. Clarke in his 1979 novel, *The Fountains of Paradise*, and a few engineers have kicked around fantastic notions of a space elevator for years. But Edwards's proposal—laid out in a two-year $500,000 study funded by the NASA Institute for Advanced Concepts—strikes those familiar with it as surprisingly practical. "Brad really put the pieces together," says Patricia Russell, associate director of the institute. "Everyone is intrigued. He brought it into the realm of reality."

"It's the most detailed proposal I have seen so far. I was delighted with the simplicity of it," says David Smitherman, technical manager of the advanced projects office at NASA's Marshall Space Flight Center. "A lot of us feel that it's worth pursuing."

Still, there's many a slip between speculative space proposals and the messy real world. The space shuttle, to name one example, was originally projected to cost $5.5 million per launch; the actual cost is more than 70 times as much. The International Space Station's cost may turn out to be 10 times its original $8 billion estimate. While NASA takes the space elevator seriously, the idea is officially just one of dozens of advanced concepts jostling for tight funding, and it was conspicuously absent from President Bush's January 14 [2004] address, in which he laid out plans for returning to the moon by 2020, followed by a manned mission to Mars.

Space elevator in earth orbit showing tether and laser
power beam

So the United States does not appear to be in a mad rush to build an elevator to heaven anytime soon. On the other hand, for reasons Edwards makes abundantly clear, the United States cannot afford to dither around for decades with his proposal. "The first entity to build a space elevator will own space," he says. And after several hours spent listening to Edwards explain just how and why that is so, one comes away persuaded that he is probably right.

Climber

Ascent vehicles will vary in size, configuration, and power, depending on function. All will climb via tractorlike treads that pinch the ribbon like the wringers of an old-fashioned washing machine. Power for the motors will come from photovoltaic cells on the climbers' undersides that are energized by a laser beamed up from the anchor station. At least two additional lasers will be located elsewhere in case clouds block the anchor station's beam.

Counterweight

A deployment booster, carried aloft in pieces by a vehicle such as the space shuttle and assembled in low Earth orbit, will unfurl two thin strips of ribbon stretching from Earth to deep space. Once the strips are anchored to a site on Earth, 230 unmanned climbers will "zip" together and widen the strips. Those climbers will then remain permanently at the far end of the ribbon, just below the deployment booster, to serve as a counterweight.

Consider Your Purpose

We asked a student, Sheldon Kearney, to read these three selections and to use them (and others) as sources in an explanatory paper on the space elevator. (We also asked him to write additional comments describing the process of developing his ideas into a draft.) His paper (the final version begins on p. 121) drew on seventeen selections on space-elevator technology. How did he—how would you—go about synthesizing the sources?

First, remember that before considering the *how*, you must consider the *why*. In other words, what is your *purpose* in synthesizing these sources? You might use them for a paper dealing with a broader issue—the commercialization of space, for instance. If this were your purpose, any sources on the space elevator would likely be used in only one section devoted to cost-effective options for lifting materials from earth into zero gravity. Because such a broader paper would consider topics other than the space elevator (for instance, a discussion of business opportunities in earth orbit or of possible legal problems among companies operating in space), it would need to draw on sources unrelated to space elevators.

For a business or finance course, you might search for sources that would help you present options for private and government funding of space elevators. The sources gathered by Sheldon Kearney could help explain the technology; but, again, you would need to find other sources to investigate the advantages and disadvantages of public versus private funding or types of private funding. Your overall intention would still be explanatory, yet your focus and your selection of sources would need to broaden from what a space elevator is (the focus of his present paper) to a consideration of the ways in which different classes of investors could pay for actual construction. *Your purpose in writing, then, governs your choice of sources.*

Assume that your goal is to write an explanation of space elevators—a *synthesis* that will explain what the elevator is, how it works, its pros and cons, and why advocates believe it should be built. As part of a larger paper, this explanation would be relatively brief. But if your intention is to explain in greater detail, for an audience of nonspecialists, the basics of space elevator technology and the challenges we can expect with its development, then you will write a paper much like the one Kearney has, the development of which you'll follow in the coming pages. The goal: to present information but not advance a particular opinion or slant on the subject.

Exercise 4.2

Critical Reading for Synthesis

Review the three readings on space elevators and list the ways they explain the technology, address potential advantages and disadvantages, and identify obstacles to construction. Make your list as specific and detailed as you can. Assign a source to each item on the list.

Formulate a Thesis

The difference between a purpose and a thesis is primarily a difference of focus. Your purpose provides direction to your research and gives a focus to your paper. Your thesis sharpens this focus by narrowing it and formulating it in the words of a single declarative statement. (Chapter 3 has more on formulating thesis statements.)

Since Kearney's purpose in this case was to synthesize source material with little or no comment, his thesis would be the most obvious statement he could make about the relationship among the source readings. By "obvious" we mean a statement that is broad enough to encompass the main points of all the readings. Taken as a whole, what do they *mean*? Here Kearney describes the process he followed in coming up with a thesis for his explanatory synthesis:

> I began my writing process by looking over all the readings and noting the main point of each reading in a sentence on a piece of paper.
>
> Then I reviewed all of these points and identified the patterns in the readings. These I recorded underneath my list of main points: All the readings focus on the space elevator: definition, construction, technical obstacles, uses, potential problems. The readings explain a technology that has significant business, military, and environmental implications.
>
> Looking over these points, I drafted what I thought was a preliminary thesis. This thesis summed up for me the information I found in my sources:
>
>> Building a space elevator has garnered the attention of NASA, the U.S. Air Force, foreign nations, private industry, and scientists alike as a feasible and cost effective means of reaching into space.
>
> This was a true statement, the basis of my first draft. What ended up happening, though (I realized this even before my instructor read the draft and commented), was that my supposed thesis wasn't a thesis at all. Instead, I had written a statement that allowed me to write a series of summaries and bullet points and call that a paper. So this first effort was not successful, although one good thing happened: in my conclusion, when I forced myself to sum up, I wrote a sentence that looked more like an organizing thesis statement:
>
>> The development of the space elevator will undoubtedly become a microcosm of the human spirit, for better and for worse.
>
> This statement seemed more promising, and my instructor suggested I use this as my thesis. But the more I thought about "microcosm of the human spirit," the more nervous I got about explaining what the "human spirit" is. That seemed to me too large a project. I figured that might be a trap, so I used a different thesis for my second draft:
>
>> Building the space elevator could lead to innovation and exploration; but there could be problems—caused both by technology and by people—that could derail the project.
>
> This version of the thesis allowed me to write more of a synthesis, to get a conversation going with the sources. After I wrote a second draft, I revised the thesis again. This time, I wanted to hint more directly at the types of problems we could expect. I introduced "earth-bound conflicts" to suggest that the familiar battles we fight down here could easily follow us into space:
>
>> If built, the space elevator would likely promote a new era of innovation and exploration. But one can just as easily imagine progress being compromised by familiar, earth-bound conflicts.

I added "if built" to plant a question that would prepare readers for a discussion of obstacles to constructing the elevator. Originally this thesis was one sentence, but it was long and I split it into two.

Decide How You Will Use Your Source Material

To begin, you will need to summarize your sources—or, at least, be *able* to summarize them. That is, the first step to any synthesis is understanding what your sources say. But because you are synthesizing *ideas* rather than sources, you will have to be more selective than if you were writing a simple summary. In your synthesis, you will not use *all* the ideas and information in every source, only the ones related to your thesis. Some sources might be summarized in their entirety; others, only in part. Look over your earlier notes or sentences discussing the topics covered in the readings, and refer back to the readings themselves. Focusing on the more subtle elements of the issues addressed by the authors, expand your earlier summary sentences. Write brief phrases in the margin of the sources, underline key phrases or sentences, or take notes on a separate sheet of paper or in a word processing file or electronic data-filing program. Decide how your sources can help you achieve your purpose and support your thesis.

For example, how might you use a diagram to explain the basic physics of the space elevator? How would you present a discussion of possible obstacles to the elevator's construction or likely advantages to the country, or business, that builds the first elevators? How much would you discuss political or military challenges?

Develop an Organizational Plan

An organizational plan is your map for presenting material to the reader. What material will you present? To find out, examine your thesis. Do the content and structure of the thesis (that is, the number and order of assertions) suggest an organizational plan for the paper? For example, consider Kearney's revised thesis:

> If built, the space elevator would likely promote a new era of innovation and exploration. But one can just as easily imagine progress being compromised by familiar, earth-bound conflicts.

Without knowing anything about space elevators, a reader of this thesis could reasonably expect the following:

- Definition of the space elevator: What is it? How does it work?
- "If built"—what are the obstacles to building a space elevator?
- What innovations?
- What explorations?
- What problems ("conflicts") on earth would jeopardize construction and use of a space elevator?

Study your thesis, and let it help suggest an organization. Expect to devote at least one paragraph of your paper to developing each section that your thesis promises. Having examined the thesis closely and identified likely sections, think through the possibilities of arrangement. Ask yourself: What information does the reader need to understand first? How do I build on this first section? What block of information will follow? Think of each section in relation to others until you have placed them all and have worked your way through to a plan for the whole paper.

Bear in mind that any one paper can be written—successfully—according to a variety of plans. Your job before beginning your first draft is to explore possibilities. Sketch a series of rough outlines:

- Arrange and rearrange your paper's likely sections until you develop a plan that both enhances the reader's understanding and achieves your objectives as a writer.
- Think carefully about the logical order of your points: Does one idea or point lead to the next?
- If not, can you find a more logical place for the point, or are you just not clearly articulating the connections between the ideas?

Your final paper may well deviate from your final sketch; in the act of writing, you may discover the need to explore new material, to omit planned material, to refocus or to reorder your entire presentation. Just the same, a well-conceived organizational plan will encourage you to begin writing a draft.

Summary Statements

In notes describing the process of organizing his material, Kearney refers to all the sources he used, including the three excerpted in this chapter.

In reviewing my sources and writing summary statements, I detected four main groupings of information:
- The technology for building a space elevator is almost here. Only one major obstacle remains: building a strong enough tether.
- Several sources explained what the space elevator is and how it could change our world.
- Another grouping of articles discussed the advantages of the elevator and why we need it.
- A slightly different combination of articles presented technical challenges and also problems that might arise among nations, such as competition.

I tried to group some of these topics into categories that would have a logical order. What I first wanted to communicate was the sense that the technical obstacles to building a space elevator have been (or soon will be) solved or, in theory, at least, are solvable.

Early in the paper, likely in the paragraph after the introduction, I figured I should explain exactly what a space elevator is.

I would then need to explain the technical challenges—mainly centered on the tether and, possibly, power issues. After covering the technical challenges, I could follow with the challenges that people could pose (based largely on competition and security needs).

I also wanted to give a sense that there's considerable reason for optimism about the space elevator. It's a great idea; but, typically, people could get in the way of their own best interests and defeat the project before it ever got off the ground.

I returned to my thesis and began to think about a structure for the paper.

> Building the space elevator could lead to innovation and exploration; but there could be problems—caused both by technology and by people—that could derail the project.

Based on his thesis, Kearney developed an outline for an eight-paragraph paper, including introduction and conclusion:

1. Introduction: The space elevator <u>can</u> be built a lot sooner than we think.
2. The basic physics of a space elevator is not that difficult to understand.
3. The key to the elevator's success is making a strong tether. Scientists believe they have found a suitable material in carbon nanotubes.
4. Weather and space junk pose threats to the elevator; but these potential problems are solvable with strategic placement of the elevator and sophisticated monitoring systems.
5. Powering the elevator will be a challenge, but one likely source is electricity collected by solar panels and beamed to the climber.
6. Space elevators promise important potential benefits: cost of transporting materials to space will be drastically reduced; industries, including tourism, would take advantage of a zero-gravity environment; and more.
7. Among the potential human-based (as opposed to technology-based) problems to building a space elevator: a new space race; wars to prevent one country from gaining strategic advantage over others, ownership, and access.
8. A space elevator could be inspiring and could usher in a new era of exploration.

Write the Topic Sentences

Writing draft versions of topic sentences (an optional step) will get you started on each main idea of your synthesis and will help give you the sense of direction you need to proceed. Here are Kearney's draft topic sentences for sections, based on the thesis and organizational plan he developed. Note that when read in sequence following the thesis, these sentences give an idea of the logical progression of the essay as a whole.

- A space elevator is exactly what it sounds like.
- A space elevator is not a standard elevator, but a rope—or tether— with a counterweight at the far end kept in place by centrifugal force extending 60,000 miles into space.

- There already exists a single material strong enough to act as a tether for the space elevator, carbon nanotubes.
- Because the space elevator would reach from Earth through our atmosphere and into space, it would face a variety of threats to the integrity of its tether.
- Delivering power to the climbers is also a major point of consideration.
- The ability of a space elevator to lift extremely heavy loads from Earth into space is beneficial for a number of reasons.
- Ownership, as any homeowner can tell you, comes with immense responsibly; and ownership of a technology that could change the world economy would almost certainly create huge challenges.
- The ambition to build a tower so high it would scrape the heavens is an idea stretching back as far as the story of the Tower of Babel.

ORGANIZE A SYTHESIS BY IDEA, NOT BY SOURCE

A synthesis is a blending of sources organized by *ideas*. The following rough sketches suggest how to organize and how *not* to organize a synthesis. The sketches assume you have read seven sources on a topic, sources A–G.

Incorrect: Organizing by Source + Summary

Thesis

Summary of source A in support of the thesis.

Summary of source B in support of the thesis.

Summary of source C in support of the thesis.

(Etc.)

Conclusion

This is *not* a synthesis because it does not blend sources. Each source stands alone as an independent summary. No dialogue among sources is possible.

Correct: Organizing by Idea

Thesis

First idea: Refer to and discuss *parts* of sources (perhaps A, C, F) in support of the thesis.

Second idea: Refer to and discuss *parts* of sources (perhaps B, D) in support of the thesis.

Third idea: Refer to and discuss *parts* of sources (perhaps A, E, G) in support of the thesis.

(continued)

(Etc.)

Conclusion

This *is* a synthesis because the writer blends and creates a dialogue among sources in support of an idea. Each organizing idea, which can be a paragraph or group of related paragraphs, in turn supports the thesis.

Write Your Synthesis

Here is the first draft of Kearney's explanatory synthesis. Thesis and topic sentences are highlighted. Modern Language Association (MLA) documentation style, explained in one of the two "Quick Indexes" at the end of this text, is followed.

Alongside this first draft we have included comments and suggestions for revision from Kearney's instructor. For purposes of demonstration, these comments are likely to be more comprehensive than the selective comments provided by most instructors.

EXPLANATORY SYNTHESIS: FIRST DRAFT

Kearney 1

Sheldon Kearney

Professor Leslie Davis

Technology and Culture

October 1, 2010

The Space Elevator

(1) A space elevator is exactly what it sounds like: an elevator reaching into space. And though some thirty years ago the notion of such an elevator was little more than science fiction, today, building a space elevator has garnered the attention of NASA, the U.S. Air Force, foreign nations, private industry, and scientists alike as a feasible and cost-effective means of reaching into space.

(2) A space elevator is not a standard elevator, but a rope—or tether— with a counterweight at the far end kept in place by centrifugal force extending 60,000 miles into space (citation needed). The rotation of the earth combined with the weight and size of the tether would keep the line taught. As ___notes, imagine a rope hanging down from the earth rather than

Title and Paragraph (1)
Your title could be more interesting and imaginative. Your first paragraph has no organizing statement, no thesis. Devise a statement—or find one in the draft (see your last paragraph, "microcosm of the human spirit")—that can create a map for your readers. Finally, expand the first paragraph and make it an interesting (fascinating?) transition into the world of space elevators.

Paragraph (2)
Consider using an image to help readers understand what a space elevator is and how it works. Also consider using an analogy: What is the space elevator like that readers would understand?

Kearney 2

extending up (citation needed). Rather than having a counterweight moving cargo up and down the tether, as in a conventional elevator, a space elevator would make use of mechanical climbers to move cargo into and down from space. (Image needed for this?)

There already is a material strong enough to act as a tether for the space elevator, carbon nanotubes. Discovered in 1991 by Sumio Iijima, carbon nanotubes have been tested in labs to be X times stronger and X times lighter than steel (get stats). In theory the production of a carbon nanotube ribbon only a meter wide and millimeters thick would be strong enough to act as the space elevator's tether. "Small quantities of some nanotubes have been made that are sufficiently strong enough to be used in a space elevator," though the scale of production would need to be drastically increased to build the tether needed for the space elevator (Olson interview).

Threats. Because the space elevator would reach from Earth through our atmosphere and into space, there are threats it will face to the integrity of its tether. Weather conditions such as hurricanes and lightning pose a threat to the space elevator, as do impacts from Earth-bound objects, i.e. planes, as well as low earth orbit objects such as satellites and meteors and orbital debris. These types of threats have possible solutions. Locating the space elevator off of the Galapagos Islands in open water, if possible, minimizes the likelihood of lightning, wind, and hurricanes damaging the elevator. In this sight, the occurrence of such events are extremely rare (footnote needed, as well as image provided by Edwards). Furthermore, by attaching the space elevator to a large ocean vessel, such as a deep water oil platform, it would be possible to move the tether in the case of severe weather conditions. The ability to move the space elevator is important: NASA estimates that there are some 500,000 objects within the Earth's orbit that could catastrophically damage the space elevator (NASA sight and Edwards).

Delivering power to the climbers is also a major point of consideration. Bringing along the fuel would be prohibitively heavy due to the length of the trip, as would dragging a long power cord. Powering the elevator with laser beams of electricity generated by solar cells on the ground has

③ **Paragraph ③**
The tether is a crucial component of the space elevator. Any obstacles to building? Expand this part of the explanation.

④

⑤ **Paragraphs ④ and ⑤**
Reverse the order of paragraphs 4 and 5. "Power" is a core element of the elevator's success. A discussion of "threats" assumes the space elevator is already functional. Logically, "power" should come first.

Kearney 3

been proposed by advocates of the space elevator. Lasers powerful enough to be used to fuel the climbers are already commercially available (Olsen interview).

⑥ The ability of a space elevator to lift extremely heavy loads from Earth into space is beneficial for a number of reasons. Chemical rockets are only able to carry approximately 6% of their total weight into space as cargo, with the remaining 94% used for fuel to escape the Earth's gravity and launch vehicles (Swan, 2006 2.2). For a space elevator, however, the immense strength of the tether would allow for mechanical climbers to lift extremely heavy loads. There are several obvious advantages to a space elevator:

- As the tether's strength builds over time, there is virtually no limit to the strength and payload capacity of the elevator.
- Inexpensive access to space would quickly permit the development of entirely new space-based industries like tourism and manufacturing.
- The increased ability to place satellites into space would increase the security and amount of digital information needed in the global economy.
- The development of a space elevator could also further act as a launching point for future interplanetary exploration.

⑦ Dr. Edwards notes that "the first entity to build a space elevator will own space" (Edwards 2000 needed). In this he is certainly correct. But ownership, as any homeowner can tell you, comes with immense responsibility; and ownership of a technology that could change the world economy would almost certainly create huge challenges (Eric Westling Interview). Key questions to consider:

- Will the creation of one space elevator create a new space race between nations?
- Will one nation's desire to prevent its construction lead to war?
- Who will own the elevator?
- Who will have access to space via the elevator?

⑧ The ambition to build a tower so high it would scrape the heavens is an idea stretching back as far as the story of the Tower of Babel. For these

Paragraph ⑥
This paragraph, currently in both sentence and bullet format, needs to be split up and expanded. The cost analysis is an important piece of justifying the space elevator. Expand this discussion and explain the expected savings. Also, as part of justifying a new thesis re: "the human spirit," expand your bulleted list of benefits. Possibly develop a full paragraph for each bullet.

Paragraph ⑦
Similar to the comment re: paragraph 6: split the current paragraph and expand bulleted points. If your paper is to account "for better and for worse" elements of the human spirit (see par. 8), then you need a full discussion of problems associated with the elevator. Presently, only these abbreviated bullets suggest possible problems. Expand—possibly a paragraph for each bullet.

Paragraph ⑧
You have found your thesis in this paragraph: "The developments...for better and for worse." Consider moving this sentence to the head of the paper and building out the conclusion to discuss the space elevator and "the human spirit."

Kearney 4

ancient builders their ambition was too great and they were punished. <u>The</u>
<u>development of the space elevator will undoubtedly become a microcosm</u>
<u>of the human spirit, for better and for worse.</u> A space elevator will inspire
untold technological developments and usher in a yet unknown expansion of
the human condition as we begin in earnest to explore beyond the confines
and limitations of the Earth. Yet, the development of a space elevator will
almost certainly act as a lightning rod for international conflict.

Revise Your Synthesis: Global, Local, and Surface Revisions

Many writers find it helpful to plan for three types of revision: global, local, and surface.

Global revisions affect the entire paper: the thesis, the type and pattern of evidence employed, and the overall organization. A global revision may also emerge from a change in purpose—say, when a writer realizes that a paper works better as an argument than as an explanation. In this case, Kearney decided to revise globally based on his instructor's suggestion to use a statement from the conclusion as a thesis in the second draft. The immediate consequence of this decision: Kearney realized he needed to expand substantially the discussion of the benefits of the space elevator and also its potential problems. Such an expansion would make good on the promise of his new thesis for the second draft (a reformulation of his "human spirit" statement at the end of the first draft): "Building the space elevator could lead to innovation and exploration; but there could be problems—caused both by technology and by people—that could derail the project."

Local revisions affect paragraphs: topic and transitional sentences; the type of evidence presented within a paragraph; evidence added, modified, or dropped within a paragraph; logical connections from one sentence or set of sentences within a paragraph to another.

Surface revisions deal with sentence style and construction, word choice, and errors of grammar, mechanics, spelling, and citation form.

Revising the First Draft: Highlights

Global

- At present, the paper has no organizing thesis. Consider moving the sentence underlined in the final paragraph to the first paragraph and letting it serve as your thesis for the revision. "Microcosm of the human spirit" is promising because our reach into space does speak to the human spirit.

- Be careful in your conclusion not to move your explanatory synthesis into the territory of argument. The paragraph as written shifts away from your sources to your personal point of view concerning what might happen post-development of a space elevator.
- Expand the bullet points on the benefits and key challenges facing development of the space elevator (paragraphs 6–7). Expanded, each bullet point could become a paragraph. Considered together, these discussions of benefits and challenges could justify your explanatory claim about "microcosm."
- In paragraph 6, explain in more detail the cost advantages of the space elevator. Relatively inexpensive access to space is one of the key benefits.

Local

- Your introduction needs work. Create more of a context for your topic that moves readers to your (new) thesis. The topic is fascinating. Show your fascination to readers! Work as well on your concluding paragraph; assuming you move the underlined statement in that paragraph to your introduction (where it would serve as a thesis), the remaining conclusion will be weak.
- Expand your discussion of power requirements for the elevator (paragraph 5) and move that before your discussion of threats (currently paragraph 4). Logic: A discussion of threats assumes an operational space elevator, one of the requirements of which is a dependable power supply.
- Expand your discussion of the tether in paragraph 3—a key component of the elevator. We need to know more, including obstacles to making the tether.
- Graphic images could be very helpful to your explanation of the space elevator. You consider using them in paragraphs 2 and 4.
- Assuming you expand the paper and justify your explanatory claim about the development of the elevator providing a "microcosm of the human spirit," you could expand your conclusion. What do you mean, exactly, by "human spirit"—and, also, by "for better and for worse"?

Surface

- Avoid weak verbs (see the first sentence of paragraph 5). Revise passive constructions such as "has been proposed by" in paragraph 5 and "were punished" in paragraph 8.
- Avoid constructions like "there is" and "there are" in paragraphs 3 and 4.
- Watch for errors like "taught" vs. "taut" in paragraph 2 and "sight" vs. "site" in paragraph 4.
- Fix grammatical errors—for instance, subject–verb agreement in paragraph 4: "the occurrence of such events "are" or "is"?

Revising the Explanatory Synthesis

Try your hand at creating a final draft of "The Space Elevator" (on pages 116–119) by following the revision suggestions above and using your own best judgment about how to improve the first draft. Make global, local, and surface changes. After writing your own version of the paper, compare it to the revised version of our student paper below.

MODEL EXPLANATORY SYNTHESIS

Kearney 1

Sheldon Kearney

Professor Leslie Davis

Technology and Culture

October 12, 2010

Going Up? An Elevator Ride to Space

In his 1979 science fiction novel *The Fountains of Paradise*, Arthur C. Clarke introduced his readers to space elevators. While Clarke's idea of a platform that would ride a tether into space (eliminating the need for rockets) was not new, his novel helped focus scientific imaginations on the possibilities. A space elevator is exactly what it sounds like: a platform rising from the ground, not to the top floor of a building but into the weightlessness of earth orbit. It's a real-life Tower of Babel, built to "reach unto heaven" (Gen. 11.4). For thirty years, the elevator has been little more than science fiction hinting at future space tourism, manufacturing in zero gravity, mining of asteroids, abundant solar power beamed to anywhere on earth, and dramatically less expensive inter-planetary travel. Today, however, NASA, the U.S. Air Force, and private industry regard the technology as both feasible and cost-effective. If built, the space elevator would likely promote a new era of innovation and exploration. But one can just as easily imagine progress being compromised by familiar, earth-bound conflicts.

The physics of a space elevator should be familiar to any child who has spun a rope with a rock attached to one end: as the arm spins, the rope remains extended to its full length in the air, apparently defying gravity. The rope and the rock stay up because centrifugal force acts to push the weight outward, while the rope keeps the rock from flying off. In the case of a space elevator, instead of the child spinning the weight, it is the earth that's spinning. And instead of a rope perhaps three feet in length extending taut from the child's

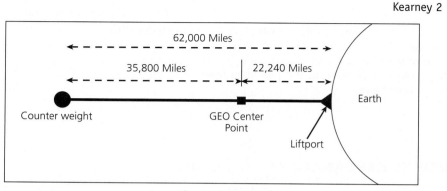

Space Elevator Basic Layout

Fig. 1.   "The space elevator...is a 1-meter wide tether stretching from the surface of the earth out to a point some 62,000 miles in orbit. The base of the ribbon is attached to a platform on the surface (floating at sea) while the space end of the tether extends past geosynchronous orbit to a counter weight. Lifters... would clamp onto the tether and, using a series of rollers powered by lasers, ascend and descend in order to carry people, material, and cargo to and from orbit." (Kent 3)

hand out to the rock, the far end of a space tether would be attached to a weight extending 62,000 miles from earth (Aravind 125–26; Kent 3). Movement up and down the tether would not involve the use of a counterweight and pulley system, as with terrestrial elevators, but rather a mechanical climber to ferry cargo to and from space.

When the space elevator was first envisioned, no known material was strong enough to serve as a tether. Then in 1991, Sumio Iijima, a Japanese physicist and materials scientist at Meijo University in Nagoya, discovered the carbon nanotube: "a material that is theoretically one hundred or more times stronger and ten times lighter than steel" (Kent iii). In principle, the production of a carbon nanotube ribbon only a meter wide and millimeters thick would be strong enough to act as the tether for a space elevator. According to Brad Edwards, a former NASA scientist and leading proponent of space elevators, a nanotube strong enough to serve as a tether will soon be available (Interview, NOVA), though the scale of production would have to increase dramatically to achieve the required 62,000 mile length. Because scaling to that extent could create an "unavoidable presence of defects" (Pugno), materials investigation continues. But Edwards is confident enough to predict an operational space elevator by 2031 (Liftport). Production of nanotubes aside, the major obstacles to construction are not technical but rather financial (funds must be found to build the elevator); legal (the 62,000

Fig. 2. Ocean-based platform for
a space elevator

mile tether cannot interfere with existing satellites); and political (interests representing the chemical rocket industry will object to and likely attempt to thwart the elevator) (Edwards, *Phase II* 40).

NASA has been sufficiently intrigued by the concept to join with the Spaceward Foundation in creating "The Space Elevator Games," which awards cash prizes to promising elevator technologies (Shelef). Key modifications to terrestrial elevators have already been designed. For instance, because carrying the fuel necessary to power the elevator platform would render the project as expensive as chemical rockets (which also carry their own fuel), engineers believe that ground-based lasers, powered by the sun, could aim energy beams that would power the mechanical climber. Such lasers are already produced in the United States (LaserMotive).

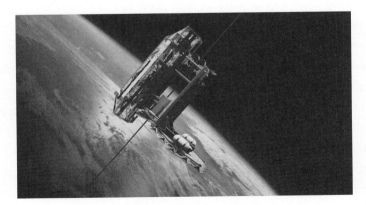

Fig. 3. Space elevator in earth orbit showing tether and laser power beam
Source: Images created by Alan Chan with permission.

(5)   Because the space elevator would reach from Earth through our atmosphere and into space, the tether would be vulnerable to damage or catastrophic failure from airplanes, space debris, meteors, and violent storms. Impact threats like these also have likely solutions, one being to locate the space elevator in a weather-stable climate—for example, off the Galapagos Islands—in open water, which would minimize the likelihood of damage from lightning or wind (SpaceRef). Attaching the earth-end of the elevator to a large ocean vessel, such as a deep water oil platform, would permit moving a tether threatened by impending collisions with space debris or meteors, which would be tracked by an array of telescopes (Edwards, *Phase I* 5.8; *Phase II* 23).

(6)   At present, NASA and other space agencies around the globe are limited to ferrying relatively small quantities of cargo into space, with dozens of launches needed to build (for example) the international space station. Today, at a per-kilogram cost of $11,000, chemical rockets are able to carry only 6% of their total weight into space as cargo, with the remaining 94% used for fuel to escape the Earth's gravity and to launch vehicles (Swan 2.2). For a space elevator, however, the immense strength of the tether would allow mechanical climbers to lift extremely heavy loads for roughly $100 per kilogram. Edwards estimates that within as few as two years of operation, the elevator could be "capable of supporting a 22 ton (20,000 kg) climber with a 14 ton (13,000 kg) payload" (*Phase I* 1.4). He and others estimate the cost of building a space elevator within the next ten to twenty years to be a tiny fraction of the cost of a trip to Mars (*Phase 1* 1.8; Lemley).

(7)   The construction of a space elevator could usher in a new era of exploration and development akin to the reach of the railroad across the continental United States. In this case, however, not only would the economy of a nation be transformed but also, possibly, the global economy. With the low-cost lifting of materials into orbit commonplace, the dreams of science fiction writers could come true, including "mining the asteroid belt, building zero-G hotels, sailing the solar winds to the moon or Mars, [and] disposing of our radioactive waste by shooting it into the sun" (Taylor). Inexpensive access to space would quickly permit the development of entirely new space-based industries. Proposals already exist to use a space elevator to develop orbiting solar arrays capable of providing cheap, abundant, and clean electrical power to almost anywhere in the world (Edwards, *Phase I* 1.7). Such a clean and economically viable energy source made available to much of the world could decrease dependence on fossil fuels and the nations that export them

(Swan 2.3.1.), which in turn could potentially transform the political and economic land-scape here on earth.

The comparatively inexpensive satellite launches made possible by a space elevator would secure global data transfer, including communications. A recent study conducted by the University of California, San Diego, concluded that "the average American consumes about 34 gigabytes of data and information each day" (Bilton). The invention of the iPhone and other Web- and video-capable mobile devices as well as the global prolifera-tion of high-speed Internet in recent years have only increased the need for secure, fast data transfer. Satellites, along with cell towers and fiber-optic cables, form the pillars of this transfer. With regular, relatively inexpensive access to earth orbit provided by a space elevator, military and commercial interests could have replacement satellites ready for deployment in the event of malfunctions (or attack). Sufficient redundancy could be built into these systems to secure the communications and data exchange on which the global economy will increasingly depend.

A space elevator could also prove crucial to the success of future interplanetary explo-ration, since cheap access to space would make manned missions economically feasible. In January 2010 President Obama's proposed federal budget eliminated NASA's Constellation program, which planned for manned missions to the moon within ten years. A working space elevator would significantly reduce the cost of such programs and could make them more at-tractive in the future. Space agencies would be able to build vehicles on earth, where they are more easily and cheaply assembled, and lift large pieces into space for final assembly.

But no one should imagine that the construction of a space elevator will bring only good news or that every predicted benefit will be achieved. The prospect of building a space elevator (like the prospect of building an anti-ballistic missile system) carries with it the potential for fatal misunderstandings and conflicts. For example, a platform in space could provide the builder with enormous military and economic advantages that other nations might find intolerable. We don't need to look much further than the last century to know that nations will launch wars to block rivals from seizing territory that would confer real or perceived advantages. It is not difficult to imagine a scenario in which Russia or China would vigorously protest America's building an elevator capable of creating a military advantage. Even if the United States explained its peaceful intentions, other nations might remain skep-tical and, acting out of self-preservation, rush to build their own elevators.

(11)   And just as nations with nuclear bomb-making capacity strongly discourage other nations from joining that club, one can easily imagine the United States discouraging Iran, for instance, from building a space elevator. Already doubtful of that country's claims for peaceful nuclear development, the United States might also doubt Iran's stated peaceful intentions for a space elevator and move to block its development. The resulting political struggle might look very much like the current effort to keep Iran from becoming a nuclear state. An alternate scenario: other nations, incapable of building the elevator but not willing to see the United States have one, could launch attacks to disable it. Edwards has already considered the implications of a bomb exploding a mechanical climber and severing the nanotube tether (*Phase II* 38).

(12)   Economic gains, real or perceived, of the nation that builds an elevator could also create problems. Not every nation could afford to build its own elevator. Who, then, would control access? Would poor(er) nations be welcomed to share in the expected bounty? Would the elevator become one more resource that separates nations into haves and have-nots? One can imagine the country that builds and operates the elevator saying to others: "You don't cooperate with us here on earth, so we won't grant you cheap access to space." In this scenario, the elevator could become a political and economic weapon.

(13)   Ninety-eight countries, including the United States and Russia, have signed the Outer Space Treaty, which prohibits the placing of nuclear weapons and other weapons of mass destruction into space and establishes the principle that no country can claim sovereignty of space or celestial bodies beyond earth. The spirit of the agreement is hopeful in being "[i]nspired by the great prospects opening up before mankind as a result of man's entry into outer space" (3); but the agreement is somber as well in recognizing implicitly that nations act in their own interests: "The exploration and use of outer space, including the Moon and other celestial bodies, shall be carried out for the benefit and in the interests of all countries, irrespective of their degree of economic or scientific development, and shall be the province of all mankind" (4). Proponents hope that the nations that build space elevators will adhere to these principles and not seek to make earth orbit the ultimate high ground for economic and military advantage.

(14)   The construction of an elevator to space should excite our collective imaginations; but, human nature being what it is, no one should be surprised if conflicts, along with our hopes, follow the platform into orbit. This is no reason not to pursue research and construction: the

elevator and what it makes possible could bring great benefits, including pharmaceuticals and exotic materials manufactured in zero gravity, space tourism, endless supplies of renewable energy, secure communications, and a cost-effective platform from which to explore the solar system and beyond. But the space elevator will likely also act as a lightning rod for international competition. In this way, it could well become just another stage on which to play out our quarrels on earth.

Works Cited

Aravind, P. K. "The Physics of the Space Elevator." *American Journal of Physics* 75.2 (2007): 125–30. PDF file.

The Bible. Introd. and notes by Robert Carroll and Stephen Prickett. Oxford: Oxford UP, 1998. Print. Oxford World's Classics. Authorized King James Vers.

Bilton, Nick. "Part of the Daily American Diet, 34 Gigabytes of Data." *New York Times*. New York Times, 3 Dec. 2009. Web. 14 Sept. 2010.

Clarke, Arthur C. *Fountains of Paradise*. London: V. Gollancz, 1979. Print.

Edwards, Bradley C. Interview. *NOVA: Science Now, Ask the Expert*. PBS, 16 Jan. 2007. Web. 16 Sept. 2010.

---. Interview by Sander Olson. *Nextbigfuture.com*. Lifeboat Foundation, 1 Dec. 2009. Web. 25 Sept. 2010.

---. *The Space Elevator: National Institute for Advanced Concepts Phase I Report*. N.p.: 2000. PDF file.

---. *The Space Elevator: National Institute for Advanced Concepts Phase II Report*. N.p.: 2003. PDF file.

Kent, Jason R. *Getting into Space on a Thread: Space Elevator as Alternative Access to Space*. Maxwell AFB: Air War College, 2007. PDF file.

LaserMotive. Home page. *Lasermotive.com*. LaserMotive, n.d. Web. 14 Sept. 2010.

Lemley, Brad. "Going Up." *Discovermagazine.com*. Discover Magazine, 25 July 2004. Web. 12 Sept. 2010.

Liftport. Home page. *Liftport.com*. Liftport, 2003. Web. 20 Sept. 2010. Kearney 10

Kearney 8

Pugno, Nicola M. "On the Strength of the Carbon Nanotube-based Space Elevator Cable:
From Nanomechanics to Megamechanics." *Journal of Physics: Condensed Matter*
18 (2006): 1971–90. PDF file.

Shelef, Ben. "Did You Just Say 'a Space Elevator'?!" *Spaceward.org*. Spaceward
Foundation, 2008. Web. 18 Sept. 2010.

SpaceRef Interactive. "LiftPort Announces Support of the Space Elevator Concept by the
National Space Society." *SpaceRef.com*. SpaceRef Interactive, 25 June 2003. Web.
12 Sept. 2010.

Swan, Cathy W., and Peter A. Swan. "Why We Need a Space Elevator." *Space Policy* 22.2
(2006): 86–91. *Science Direct*. Web. 12 Sept. 2010.

Taylor, Chris. "Space Elevator Entrepreneurs Shoot for the Starts." *CNN.com*. Cable News
Network, 8 Dec. 2009. Web. 14 Sept. 2010.

United Nations. "Treaty on Principles Governing the Activities of States in the Exploration
and Use of Outer Space, Including the Moon and Other Celestial Bodies." *Treaties
and Principles on Outer Space*. New York: United Nations, 2002: 3–8. PDF file.

CRITICAL READING FOR SYNTHESIS

- *Use the tips from Critical Reading for Summary on page 6.* Remember to examine the context; note the title and subtitle; identify the main point; identify the subpoints; break the reading into sections; distinguish between points, examples, and counterarguments; watch for transitions within and between paragraphs; and read actively and recursively.
- *Establish the writer's primary purpose.* Use some of the guidelines discussed in Chapter 2. Is the piece primarily informative, persuasive, or entertaining? Assess whether the piece achieves its purpose.
- *Read to identify a key idea.* If you begin reading your source materials with a key idea or topic already in mind, read to identify what your sources have to say about the idea.
- *Read to discover a key idea.* If you begin the reading process without a key idea in mind, read to discover a key idea that your sources address.
- *Read for relationships.* Regardless of whether you already have a key idea or you are attempting to discover one, your emphasis in reading should be on noting the ways in which the readings relate to each other, to a key idea, and to your purpose in writing the synthesis.

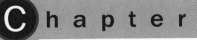

Chapter 5

Argument Synthesis

After completing this chapter, you will be able to:

LO 5.1 Apply the elements of argument (claim, support, and assumption) to the writing of argument synthesis.

LO 5.2 Draw, as needed, upon the appeals to *logos, ethos,* and *pathos.*

LO 5.3 Recognize the limits of argument when writing on controversial subjects.

LO 5.4 As you prepare to write an argument synthesis, consider your purpose, create your thesis, research your sources, and devise a logical plan of development.

LO 5.5 Use various organizational strategies to construct your argument synthesis.

LO 5.6 Avoid common fallacies.

LO 5.7 Use comparison-and-contrast, where appropriate, to develop your argument synthesis.

WHAT IS AN ARGUMENT SYNTHESIS?

An argument is an attempt to persuade a reader or listener that a particular and debatable claim is true. Writers argue in order to establish facts, to make statements of value, and to recommend policies. For instance, answering the question *Why do soldiers sometimes commit atrocities in wartime?* would involve making an argument. To develop this argument, researchers might conduct experiments, interview experts, collect historical evidence, and examine and interpret data. The researchers might then present their findings at professional conferences and in journals and books. The extent to which readers (or listeners) accept these findings will depend on the quality of the supporting evidence and the care with which the researchers have argued their case. What we are calling an *argument synthesis* draws upon evidence from a variety of sources in an attempt to persuade others of the truth or validity of a debatable claim.

By contrast, the explanatory synthesis, as we have seen, is fairly modest in purpose. It emphasizes the sources themselves—not the writer's use of sources—to persuade others. The writer of an explanatory synthesis aims to inform, not persuade. Here, for example, is a thesis devised for an explanatory synthesis on the ubiquity of cell phones in contemporary life:

> Cell phones make it possible for us to be always within reach, though many people would prefer *not* to be always within reach.

This thesis summarizes two viewpoints about the impact of cell phones on contemporary life, arguing neither for nor against either viewpoint.

An argument thesis, however, is *persuasive* in purpose. A writer working with the same source material might conceive and support an opposing thesis:

> Cell phones have ruined our ability to be isolated, to be willfully *out of touch* with the rest of the world.

So the thesis for an argument synthesis is a claim about which reasonable people could disagree. It is a claim with which—given the right arguments—your audience might be persuaded to agree. The strategy of your argument synthesis is therefore to find and use convincing *support* for your *claim*.

The Elements of Argument: Claim, Support, and Assumption

One way of looking at an argument is to see it as an interplay of three essential elements: claim, support, and assumption. A *claim* is a proposition or conclusion that you are trying to prove. You prove this claim by using *support* in the form of fact, statistics, or expert opinion. Linking your supporting evidence to your claim is your *assumption* about the subject. This assumption (as we've discussed in Chapter 2), also called a *warrant*, is an underlying belief or principle about some aspect of the world and how it operates. By their nature, assumptions (which are often unstated) tend to be more general than either claims or supporting evidence.

Here are the essential elements of an argument advocating parental restriction of television viewing for high school students:

Claim

> High school students should be restricted to no more than two hours of TV viewing per day.

Support

> An important new study and the testimony of educational specialists reveal that students who watch more than two hours of TV a night have, on average, lower grades than those who watch less TV.

Assumption

> Excessive TV viewing adversely affects academic performance.

As another example, here's an argumentative claim on the topic of computer-mediated communication (CMC)—a term sociologists use to describe online contacts among friends and family:

> CMC threatens to undermine human intimacy, connection, and ultimately community.

Here are the other elements of this argument:

Support

- People are spending increasing amounts of time in cyberspace: In 1998, the average Internet user spent over four hours per week online, a figure that more than tripled in the last decade.
- College health officials report that excessive Internet use threatens many college students' academic and psychological well-being.
- New kinds of relationships fostered on the Internet often pose challenges to preexisting relationships.

Assumptions

- The communication skills used and the connections formed during Internet contact fundamentally differ from those used and formed during face-to-face contact.
- "Real" connection and a sense of community are sustained by face-to-face contact, not by Internet interactions.

For the most part, arguments should be constructed logically so that assumptions link evidence (supporting facts, statistics, and expert opinions) to claims. As we'll see, however, logic is only one component of effective arguments.

Exercise 5.1

Practicing Claim, Support, and Assumption

Devise two sets of claims, support, and assumptions. First, in response to the example above on computer-mediated communication and relationships, write a one-sentence claim addressing the positive impact (or potentially positive impact) of CMC on relationships—whether you personally agree with the claim or not. Then list the supporting statements on which such a claim might rest, and the assumption that underlies them. Second, write a claim that states your own position on any debatable topic you choose. Again, devise statements of support and relevant assumptions.

The Three Appeals of Argument: *Logos, Ethos, Pathos*

Speakers and writers have never relied on logic alone in advancing and supporting their claims. More than 2,000 years ago, the Athenian philosopher and rhetorician Aristotle explained how speakers attempting to persuade others to their point of view could achieve their purpose by relying on one or more *appeals*, which he called *logos, ethos,* and *pathos.*

Since we frequently find these three appeals employed in political argument, we'll use political examples in the following discussion. All three appeals are also used extensively in advertising, legal cases, business documents, and many other types of argument. Bear in mind that in academic writing, the appeal to logic (*logos*) is by far the most commonly used appeal.

Logos

Logos is the rational appeal, the appeal to reason. Academic presentations, including the papers you will write across the curriculum, build almost exclusively on appeals to logic and evidence. If writers and speakers expect to persuade their audiences, they must argue logically and must supply appropriate evidence to support their case. Logical arguments are commonly of two types (often combined): deductive and inductive.

Deductive Reasoning   The *deductive* argument begins with a generalization, then cites a specific case related to that generalization, from which follows a conclusion. An example of a deductive argument may be seen in President John F. Kennedy's address to the nation in June 1963 on the need for sweeping civil rights legislation. Kennedy begins with the generalizations that it "ought to be possible...for American students of any color to attend any public institution they select without having to be backed up by troops" and that "it ought to be possible for American citizens of any color to register and vote in a free election without interference or fear of reprisal." Kennedy then provides several specific examples (primarily recent events in Birmingham, Alabama) and statistics to show that this was not the case. He concludes:

> We face, therefore, a moral crisis as a country and a people. It cannot be met by repressive police action. It cannot be left to increased demonstrations in the streets. It cannot be quieted by token moves or talk. It is time to act in the Congress, in your state and local legislative body, and, above all, in all of our daily lives.

Underlying Kennedy's argument is this reasoning:

All Americans should enjoy certain rights. (*assumption*)

Some Americans do not enjoy these rights. (*support*)

We must take action to ensure that all Americans enjoy these rights. (*claim*)

Inductive Reasoning   Another form of logical argumentation is *inductive* reasoning. A speaker or writer who argues inductively begins not with a generalization, but with several pieces of specific evidence. The speaker then draws a conclusion from this evidence. For example, in a debate on gun control, Senator Robert C. Byrd cited specific examples of rampant crime involving guns: "I read of young men being viciously murdered for a pair of sneakers, a leather jacket, or $20."

He also offered statistical evidence of the increasing crime rate: "in 1951, there were 3.2 policemen for every felony committed in the United States; this year nearly 3.2 felonies will be committed per every police officer." He concluded, "Something has to change. We have to stop the crimes that are distorting and disrupting the way of life for so many innocent, law-respecting Americans. The bill that we are debating today attempts to do just that."

Senator Edward M. Kennedy also used statistical evidence in arguing for passage of the Racial Justice Act of 1990, which was designed to ensure that minorities are not disproportionately singled out for the death penalty. Kennedy pointed out that between 1973 and 1980, seventeen defendants in Fulton County, Georgia, were charged with killing police officers, but that the only defendant who received the death sentence was a black man. Kennedy also cited statistics to show that "those who killed whites were 4.3 times more likely to receive the death penalty than were killers of blacks," and that "in Georgia, blacks who killed whites received the death penalty 16.7 percent of the time, while whites who killed received the death penalty only 4.2 percent of the time."

Maintaining a Critical Perspective   Of course, the mere piling up of evidence does not in itself make the speaker's case. As Donna Cross explains in "Politics: The Art of Bamboozling,"* politicians are very adept at "card-stacking"—lining up evidence in favor of a conclusion without bothering to mention (or barely mentioning) contrary evidence. And statistics can be selected and manipulated to prove anything, as demonstrated in Darrell Huff's landmark book *How to Lie with Statistics* (1954). Moreover, what appears to be a logical argument may in fact be fundamentally flawed. (See Chapter 2 for a discussion of logical fallacies and faulty reasoning strategies.)

On the other hand, the fact that evidence can be distorted, statistics misused, and logic fractured does not mean that these tools of reason should be dismissed. It means only that audiences have to listen and read critically and to question the use of statistics and other evidence.

Exercise 5.2

Using Deductive and Inductive Logic

Choose an issue currently being debated at your school, or a college-related issue about which you are concerned. Write a claim about this issue. Then write two paragraphs addressing your claim—one in which you organize your points deductively (beginning with your claim and following with support) and one in which you organize them inductively (presenting supporting evidence and following with a claim). Possible issues might include college admissions policies, classroom crowding, or grade inflation. Alternatively, you could base your paragraphs on a claim generated in Exercise 5.1.

---

*Donna Cross, *Word Abuse: How the Words We Use Use Us* (New York: Coward, 1979).

Ethos

Ethos, or the ethical appeal, is based not on the ethics relating to the subject under discussion, but rather on the ethical status of the person making the argument. A person making an argument must have a certain degree of credibility: That person must be of good character, have sound sense, and be qualified to argue based either on expert experience with the subject matter or on carefully conducted research. Students writing in academic settings establish their appeal to *ethos* by developing presentations that are well organized, carefully reasoned, and thoroughly referenced with source citations. These are the hallmarks of writers and speakers who care deeply about their work. If you care, your audience will care and consider your argument seriously.

Appeals to *ethos* are usually most explicit in political contests. For example, Elizabeth Cervantes Barrón, running for senator as the Peace and Freedom candidate, establishes her credibility this way: "I was born and raised in central Los Angeles. I grew up in a multiethnic, multicultural environment where I learned to respect those who were different from me....I am a teacher and am aware of how cutbacks in education have affected our children and our communities." On the other end of the political spectrum, the American Independent gubernatorial candidate Jerry McCready also begins with an ethical appeal: "As a self-employed businessman, I have learned firsthand what it is like to try to make ends meet in an unstable economy being manipulated by out-of-touch politicians." Both candidates are making an appeal to *ethos*, an appeal based on the strength of their personal qualities for the office they seek. Both argue, in effect, "Trust me. My experience makes me a credible, knowledgeable candidate."

L. A. Kauffman is not running for office but writing an article arguing against socialism as an ideology around which to build societies.* To establish his credibility as someone who understands socialism well enough to criticize it meaningfully, Kauffman begins with an appeal to *ethos*: "Until recently, I was executive editor of the journal *Socialist Review*. Before that I worked for the Marxist magazine, *Monthly Review*. My bookshelves are filled with books of Marxist theory, and I even have a picture of Karl Marx up on my wall." Thus, Kauffman establishes his credentials to argue knowledgeably about Marxism.

Exercise 5.3

Using Ethos

Return to the claim you used for Exercise 5.2 and write a paragraph in which you use an appeal to *ethos* to make a case for that claim.

Pathos

Finally, speakers and writers appeal to their audiences by using *pathos*, an appeal to the emotions. Writers in academic settings rely heavily on the force of logic and evidence and rarely make appeals to *pathos*. Beyond academic settings, however,

---

*L. A. Kauffman, "Socialism: No," *Progressive,* 1 Apr. 1993.

appeals to the emotions are commonplace. Nothing is inherently wrong with using an emotional appeal. Indeed, because emotions often move people far more successfully than reason alone, speakers and writers would be foolish not to use emotion. And it would be a drab, humorless world if human beings were not subject to the sway of feeling as well as reason. The emotional appeal becomes problematic only when it is the *sole* or *primary* basis of the argument.

President Ronald Reagan was a master of emotional appeal. He closed his first Inaugural Address with a reference to the view from the Capitol to Arlington National Cemetery, where lie thousands of markers of veterans:

> Under one such marker lies a young man, Martin Treptow, who left his job in a small-town barbershop in 1917 to go to France with the famed Rainbow Division. There, on the western front, he was killed trying to carry a message between battalions under heavy artillery fire. We're told that on his body was found a diary. On the flyleaf under the heading, "My Pledge," he had written these words: "America must win this war. Therefore, I will work, I will save, I will sacrifice, I will endure, I will fight cheerfully and do my utmost, as if the issue of the whole struggle depended on me alone." The crisis we are facing today does not require of us the kind of sacrifice that Martin Treptow and so many thousands of others were called upon to make. It does require, however, our best effort and our willingness to believe in ourselves and to believe in our capacity to perform great deeds, to believe that together with God's help we can and will resolve the problems which now confront us.

Surely, Reagan implies, if Martin Treptow can act so courageously and so self-lessly, we can do the same. His logic is somewhat unclear because the connection between Martin Treptow and ordinary Americans of 1981 is rather tenuous (as Reagan concedes); but the emotional power of the heroism of Martin Treptow, whom reporters were sent scurrying to research, carries the argument.

A more recent president, Bill Clinton, also used *pathos*. Addressing an audience of the nation's governors about his welfare plan, Clinton closed his remarks by referring to a conversation he had had with a welfare mother who had gone through the kind of training program Clinton was advocating. Asked by Clinton whether she thought that such training programs should be mandatory, the mother said, "I sure do." Clinton, in his remarks, explained what she said when he asked her why:

> "Well, because if it wasn't, there would be a lot of people like me home watching the soaps because we don't believe we can make anything of ourselves anymore. So you've got to make it mandatory." And I said, "What's the best thing about having a job?" She said, "When my boy goes to school, and they say, 'What does your mama do for a living?' he can give an answer."

Clinton counts on the emotional power in that anecdote to set up his conclusion: "We must end poverty for Americans who want to work. And we must do it on terms that dignify all of the rest of us, as well as help our country to work better. I need your help, and I think we can do it."

Return to the claim you used for Exercises 5.2 and 5.3, and write a paragraph in which you use an appeal to *pathos* to argue for that claim.

The Limits of Argument

Our discussion of *ethos* and *pathos* indicates a potentially troubling but undeniable reality: Arguments are not won on the basis of logic and evidence alone. In the real world, arguments don't operate like academic debates. If the purpose of argument is to get people to change their minds or to agree that the writer's or speaker's position on a particular topic is the best available, then the person making the argument must be aware that factors other than evidence and good reasoning come into play when readers or listeners are considering the matter.

These factors involve deep-seated cultural, religious, ethnic, racial, and gender identities, moral preferences, and the effects of personal experiences (either pleasant or unpleasant) that are generally resistant to logic and evidence, however well framed. You could try—using the best available arguments—to convince someone who is pro-life to agree with the pro-choice position (or vice versa). Or you could try to persuade someone who opposes capital punishment to believe that state-endorsed executions are necessary for deterrence (or for any other reason). You might even marshal your evidence and logic to try to persuade someone whose family members have had run-ins with the law that police efforts are directed at protecting the law-abiding.

However, on such emotionally loaded topics, it is extremely difficult, if not impossible, to get people to change their minds, because they are so personally invested in their beliefs. As Susan Jacoby, author of *The Age of American Unreason*, notes, "Whether watching television news, consulting political blogs, or (more rarely) reading books, Americans today have become a people in search of validation for opinions that they already hold."*

Fruitful Topics for Argument

The tenacity with which people hold onto longtime beliefs does not mean, however, that they cannot change their minds or that subjects such as abortion, capital punishment, gun control, and gay marriage should be off-limits to reasoned debate. It means only that you should be aware of the limits of argument. The most fruitful topics for argument in a freshman composition setting tend to be those on which most people are persuadable, either because they know relatively little about the topic or because deep-rooted cultural, religious, or moral beliefs are not involved. At least initially in your career as a writer of academic papers,

---

*Susan Jacoby, "Talking to Ourselves: Americans Are Increasingly Close-Minded and Unwilling to Listen to Opposing Views," *Los Angeles Times* 20 Apr. 2008: M10.

it's probably best to avoid hot-button topics that are the focus of broader cultural debates, and to focus instead on topics in which *pathos* plays less of a part.

For example, most people are not heavily invested in the subject of plug-in hybrid or hydrogen-powered vehicles, so an argument on behalf of these promising technologies for the coming decades will not be complicated by deep-seated beliefs. Similarly, most people don't know enough about the mechanics of sleep to have strong opinions on how to deal with sleep deprivation. Your arguments on such topics, therefore, will provide opportunities both to inform your readers or listeners and to persuade them that your arguments, if well reasoned and supported by sound evidence, are at least plausible, if not entirely convincing.

DEMONSTRATION: DEVELOPING AN ARGUMENT SYNTHESIS—BALANCING PRIVACY AND SAFETY IN THE WAKE OF VIRGINIA TECH

To demonstrate how to plan and draft an argument synthesis, let's suppose you are taking a course on Law and Society or Political Science or (from the Philosophy Department) Theories of Justice, and you find yourself considering the competing claims of privacy and public safety. The tension between these two highly prized values burst anew into public consciousness in 2007 after a mentally disturbed student at the Virginia Polytechnic Institute shot to death thirty-two fellow students and faculty members and injured seventeen more. Unfortunately, this incident was only the latest in a long history of mass killings at American schools.* It was later revealed that the shooter had a documented history of mental instability, but because of privacy rules, this information was not made available to university officials. Many people demanded to know why the information had not been shared with campus police or other officials so that Virginia Tech could have taken measures to protect members of the university community. Didn't the safety of those who were injured or killed outweigh the privacy of the shooter? At what point, if any, *does* the right to privacy outweigh the right to safety? What *should* the university have done before the killing started? Should federal and state laws on privacy be changed or even abandoned in the wake of this and other similar incidents?

Suppose, in preparing to write a paper on balancing privacy and safety, you located (among others) the following sources:

- *Mass Shootings at Virginia Tech, April 16, 2007: Report of the Review Panel Presented to Governor Kaine, Commonwealth of Virginia*, August 2007 (a report)
- "Laws Limit Schools Even After Alarms" (a newspaper article)

---

*In 1966, a student at the University of Texas at Austin, shooting from the campus clock tower, killed 14 people and wounded 31. In 2006 a man shot and killed five girls at an Amish school in Lancaster, Pennsylvania.

- "Perilous Privacy at Virginia Tech" (an editorial)
- "Colleges Are Watching Troubled Students" (a newspaper article)
- The Family Educational Rights and Privacy Act (FERPA), Sec. 1232g (a federal statute)

Carefully read these sources (which follow), noting the kinds of evidence—facts, expert opinions, and statistics—you could draw on to develop an *argument synthesis*. Some of these passages are excerpts only; in preparing your paper, you would draw on the entire articles, reports, and book chapters from which these passages were taken. And you would draw on more sources than these in your search for supporting materials (as the writer of the model synthesis has done; see pp. 154–161). But these seven sources provide a good introduction to the subject. Our discussion of how these passages can form the basis of an argument synthesis resumes on page 149.

MASS SHOOTINGS AT VIRGINIA TECH, APRIL 16, 2007

Report of the Review Panel
Presented to Governor Kaine, Commonwealth of Virginia,
August 2007

The following passage leads off the official report of the Virginia Tech shootings by the panel appointed by Virginia Governor Tim Kaine to investigate the incident. The mission of the panel was "to provide an independent, thorough, and objective incident review of this tragic event, including a review of educational laws, policies and institutions, the public safety and health care procedures and responses, and the mental health delivery system." Panel members included the chair, Colonel Gerald Massenghill, former Virginia state police superintendent; Tom Ridge, former director of Homeland Security and former governor of Pennsylvania; Gordon Davies; Dr. Roger L. Depue; Dr. Aradhana A. "Bela" Sood; Judge Diane Strickland; and Carol L. Ellis. The panel's Web site may be found at http://www.vtreviewpanel.org/panel_info/.

Summary of Key Findings

On April 16, 2007, Seung Hui Cho, an angry and disturbed student, shot to death 32 students and faculty of Virginia Tech, wounded 17 more, and then killed himself.

The incident horrified not only Virginians, but people across the United States and throughout the world.

Tim Kaine, Governor of the Commonwealth of Virginia, immediately appointed a panel to review the events leading up to this tragedy; the handling of the incidents by public safety officials, emergency services providers, and the university; and the services subsequently provided to families, survivors, caregivers, and the community.

The Virginia Tech Review Panel reviewed several separate but related issues in assessing events leading to the mass shootings and their aftermath:

- The life and mental health history of Seung Hui Cho, from early childhood until the weeks before April 16.
- Federal and state laws concerning the privacy of health and education records.
- Cho's purchase of guns and related gun control issues.
- The double homicide at West Ambler Johnston (WAJ) residence hall and the mass shootings at Norris Hall, including the responses of Virginia Tech leadership and the actions of law enforcement officers and emergency responders.
- Emergency medical care immediately following the shootings, both onsite at Virginia Tech and in cooperating hospitals.
- The work of the Office of the Chief Medical Examiner of Virginia.
- The services provided for surviving victims of the shootings and others injured, the families and loved ones of those killed and injured, members of the university community, and caregivers.

5   The panel conducted over 200 interviews and reviewed thousands of pages of records, and reports the following major findings:

1. Cho exhibited signs of mental health problems during his childhood. His middle and high schools responded well to these signs and, with his parents' involvement, provided services to address his issues. He also received private psychiatric treatment and counseling for selective mutism and depression.

    In 1999, after the Columbine shootings, Cho's middle school teachers observed suicidal and homicidal ideations in his writings and recommended psychiatric counseling, which he received. It was at this point that he received medication for a short time. Although Cho's parents were aware that he was troubled at this time, they state they did not specifically know that he thought about homicide shortly after the 1999 Columbine school shootings.

2. During Cho's junior year at Virginia Tech, numerous incidents occurred that were clear warnings of mental instability. Although various individuals and departments within the university knew about each of these incidents, the university did not intervene effectively. No one knew all the information and no one connected all the dots.

3. University officials in the office of Judicial Affairs, Cook Counseling Center, campus police, the Dean of Students, and others explained their failures to communicate with one another or with Cho's parents by noting their belief that such communications are prohibited by the federal

laws governing the privacy of health and education records. In reality, federal laws and their state counterparts afford ample leeway to share information in potentially dangerous situations.

4. The Cook Counseling Center and the university's Care Team failed to provide needed support and services to Cho during a period in late 2005 and early 2006. The system failed for lack of resources, incorrect interpretation of privacy laws, and passivity. Records of Cho's minimal treatment at Virginia Tech's Cook Counseling Center are missing.

5. Virginia's mental health laws are flawed and services for mental health users are inadequate. Lack of sufficient resources results in gaps in the mental health system including short term crisis stabilization and comprehensive outpatient services. The involuntary commitment process is challenged by unrealistic time constraints, lack of critical psychiatric data and collateral information, and barriers (perceived or real) to open communications among key professionals.

6. There is widespread confusion about what federal and state privacy laws allow. Also, the federal laws governing records of health care provided in educational settings are not entirely compatible with those governing other health records.

7. Cho purchased two guns in violation of federal law. The fact that in 2005 Cho had been judged to be a danger to himself and ordered to outpatient treatment made him ineligible to purchase a gun under federal law.

8. Virginia is one of only 22 states that report any information about mental health to a federal database used to conduct background checks on would-be gun purchasers. But Virginia law did not clearly require that persons such as Cho—who had been ordered into out-patient treatment but not committed to an institution—be reported to the database. Governor Kaine's executive order to report all persons involuntarily committed for outpatient treatment has temporarily addressed this ambiguity in state law. But a change is needed in the Code of Virginia as well.

9. Some Virginia colleges and universities are uncertain about what they are permitted to do regarding the possession of firearms on campus.

10. On April 16, 2007, the Virginia Tech and Blacksburg police departments responded quickly to the report of shootings at West Ambler Johnston residence hall, as did the Virginia Tech and Blacksburg rescue squads. Their responses were well coordinated.

11. The Virginia Tech police may have erred in prematurely concluding that their initial lead in the double homicide was a good one, or at least in conveying that impression to university officials while continuing their investigation. They did not take sufficient action to deal with what might happen if the initial lead proved erroneous. The police reported to the university emergency Policy Group that the "person of interest" probably was no longer on campus.

12. The VTPD erred in not requesting that the Policy Group issue a campus-wide notification that two persons had been killed and that all students and staff should be cautious and alert.

13. Senior university administrators, acting as the emergency Policy Group, failed to issue an all-campus notification about the WAJ killings until almost 2 hours had elapsed. University practice may have conflicted with written policies.

14. The presence of large numbers of police at WAJ led to a rapid response to the first 9-1-1 call that shooting had begun at Norris Hall.

15. Cho's motives for the WAJ or Norris Hall shootings are unknown to the police or the panel. Cho's writings and videotaped pronouncements do not explain why he struck when and where he did.

16. The police response at Norris Hall was prompt and effective, as was triage and evacuation of the wounded. Evacuation of others in the building could have been implemented with more care.

17. Emergency medical care immediately following the shootings was provided very effectively and timely both onsite and at the hospitals, although providers from different agencies had some difficulty communicating with one another. Communication of accurate information to hospitals standing by to receive the wounded and injured was somewhat deficient early on. An emergency operations center at Virginia Tech could have improved communications.

18. The Office of the Chief Medical Examiner properly discharged the technical aspects of its responsibility (primarily autopsies and identification of the deceased). Communication with families was poorly handled.

19. State systems for rapidly deploying trained professional staff to help families get information, crisis intervention, and referrals to a wide range of resources did not work.

20. The university established a family assistance center at The Inn at Virginia Tech, but it fell short in helping families and others for two reasons: lack of leadership and lack of coordination among service providers. University volunteers stepped in but were not trained or able to answer many questions and guide families to the resources they needed.

21. In order to advance public safety and meet public needs, Virginia's colleges and universities need to work together as a coordinated system of state-supported institutions.

As reflected in the body of the report, the panel has made more than 70 recommendations directed to colleges, universities, mental health providers, law enforcement officials, emergency service providers, lawmakers, and other public officials in Virginia and elsewhere.

LAWS LIMIT SCHOOLS EVEN AFTER ALARMS*

Jeff Gammage and Stacey Burling

This article first appeared in the *Philadelphia Inquirer* on April 19, 2007, just three days after the Virginia Tech shootings. *Inquirer* staff writer Paul Nussbaum contributed to the article.

If Cho Seung-Hui had been a warning light, he would have been blinking bright red.

Two female students complained to campus police that he was stalking them. His poetry was so twisted that his writing professor said she would quit if he weren't removed from her room. Some students found him so menacing that they refused to attend class with him.

Yet Virginia Tech, like other colleges trying to help emotionally troubled students, had little power to force Cho off campus and into treatment.

"We can't even pick up the phone and call their family. They're adults. You have to respect their privacy," said Brenda Ingram-Wallace, director of counseling and chair of the psychology department at Albright College in Reading.

5   In the aftermath of the deadliest shooting in U.S. history, counselors, police authorities, and mental-health professionals say privacy laws prevent colleges from taking strong action regarding students who might be dangerous.

Many at Tech saw Cho as a threat—and shared those fears with authorities. In 2005, after the second stalking complaint, the school obtained a temporary detention order that resulted in Cho undergoing a psychiatric evaluation. But the 23-year-old remained enrolled at the university until the moment he shot himself to death.

Federal laws such as the 1974 Family Educational Rights and Privacy Act (FERPA) and the 1996 Health Insurance Portability and Accountability Act (HIPAA) protect students' right to privacy by banning disclosure of any mental-health problems—even to family members—without a signed waiver.

Patient-therapist confidentiality is crucial, privacy advocates say. Students may shy from treatment for fear of exposure.

FERPA does allow colleges to release information without permission in cases of "health and safety emergencies." But the criteria are so vague, and the potential liability so severe, that administrators say they hesitate to act in any but the most dire circumstances.

10   "The law tends to be protective of individual autonomy rather than getting in there and forcing people to get treatment," said Anthony Rostain, associate professor of psychiatry at the University of Pennsylvania School of Medicine.

Lots of students write violent stories, he noted. How do you distinguish between a future Cho Seung-Hui and a future Quentin Tarantino?[†]

Philadelphia Inquirer 19 Apr. 2007: A01.

[†]Director, screenwriter, and producer of frequently violent films such as *Reservoir Dogs* (1992), *Pulp Fiction* (1994), and *Kill Bill* (vol. 1, 2003; vol. 2, 2004).

"This kind of problem happens all the time across college campuses," Rostain said.

The law puts colleges in a tough position, said Dana Fleming, a lawyer with the college and university practice group at Nelson, Kinder, Mousseau & Saturley in Manchester, N.H. Schools may face legal trouble if they try to keep ill students out, if they try to send them home, or if they let them stay.

"No matter which decision they make," she said, "they can find liability on the other end."

15   Colleges can't screen students for mental illnesses during the admissions process because that violates the Americans With Disabilities Act. As a result, schools know which students will need tutoring or want to play soccer, but have no idea who is likely to need mental-health care, Fleming said.

Virginia Tech and most other universities cannot summarily suspend a student. Formal disciplinary charges must be filed and hearings held. Students who initiate a complaint often end up dropping the matter.

Nor can schools expect courts to hospitalize a student involuntarily without solid evidence that he poses a danger to himself or others.

That has left many colleges trying to find creative ways to identify and help troubled students.

At Albright College, administrators recently updated a program where anyone concerned about a student's behavior—a work supervisor, a professor or another student—can fill out a "student alert form."

20   Perhaps friends notice a student has become withdrawn or has stopped showing up for class. If multiple forms arrive concerning the same person, counseling director Ingram-Wallace said, the counseling center investigates by contacting housing officials or by reaching the student via phone or e-mail.

But the choice to speak with a psychological counselor stays with the student. The center can't send a therapist to knock on the student's door, she said.

"On the surface, it sounds like a caring thing to do," she said, but "if they haven't been dangerous to themselves or others, there's no reason to mandate them into any kind of services."

Among students who have been referred to the counseling center, "the responses are mixed," she said. "Some people felt imposed upon."

At St. Lawrence University in Canton, N.Y., every student who visits the health center—even for a head cold—is screened for depression and signs of other mental illness. The effort follows a national study that showed depression rising among college students.

25   If a screening shows someone needs help from the health center, "we literally walk them over there," said Patricia Ellis, director of counseling services.

More than a year before Monday's massacre of 32 students and staff members, Cho was twice accused of stalking female students and taken to a mental-health facility amid fears he was suicidal, police said yesterday.

After the first incident, in November 2005, police referred him to the university disciplinary system. Ed Spencer, Tech's assistant vice president of student affairs, said he could not comment on any proceedings against the gunman because federal law protects students' medical privacy even after death.

The university obtained the detention order after the second stalking complaint, in December 2005. "His insight and judgment are normal," an examiner at the psychiatric hospital concluded.

Yet poet Nikki Giovanni, one of his professors, told CNN that students were so unnerved by Cho's behavior, which included taking cell-phone photos of them in class, that most stopped attending the course. She insisted that he be removed.

30   Lucinda Roy, a codirector of the creative writing program, tutored Cho after that, and tried to get him into counseling. He always refused. Roy sent samples of Cho's writing, with its images of people attacking each other with chain saws, to the campus police, student-affairs office, and other agencies.

PERILOUS PRIVACY AT VIRGINIA TECH

This editorial appeared in the *Christian Science Monitor* on September 4, 2007.

Colleges didn't need last week's report on the Virginia Tech shootings to address a key finding: a faster alert during the crisis may have saved lives. Many colleges have already set blast-notice plans. But here's what needs careful study: the report's conclusions about privacy.

Privacy is a huge issue on campuses. Colleges and universities are dealing with young people who have just become legal adults, but who may still require supervision and even intervention.

That was the case with Seung-Hui Cho, the student who killed 32 people and then himself on April 16. According to the report, which was commissioned by Virginia Gov. Timothy Kaine, this troubled student's behavior raised serious questions about his mental stability while he was at VT, yet no one contacted his parents, and communication about his case broke down among school, law-enforcement, and mental-health officials.

A big reason? A "widespread perception" that privacy laws make it difficult to respond to troubled students, according to the report. But this is "only partly correct."

5   Lack of understanding about federal and state laws is a major obstacle to helping such students, according to the report. The legal complexity, as well as concerns about liability, can easily push teachers, administrators, police, and mental-health workers into a "default" position of withholding information, the report found.

There's no evidence that VT officials consciously decided not to inform Mr. Cho's parents. But the university's lawyer told the panel investigating Cho's case that privacy laws prevent sharing information such as that relating to Cho.

That's simply not true. The report listed several steps that could quite legally have been taken:

The Virginia Tech police, for instance, could have shared with Cho's parents that he was temporarily detained, pending a hearing to commit him involuntarily to a mental-health institution, because that information was public.

And teachers and administrators could have called Cho's parents to notify them of his difficulties, because only student records—not personal observations or conversations—are shielded by the federal privacy law that covers most secondary schools.

10   Notifying Cho's parents was intuitively the right course. Indeed, his middle school contacted his parents to get him help, and they cooperated. His high school also made special arrangements. He improved.

The report points out that the main federal privacy laws that apply to a college student's health and campus records recognize exceptions for information sharing in emergencies that affect public health and safety.

Privacy is a bedrock of American law and values. In a mental-health case, it gives a patient the security to express innermost thoughts, and protects that person from discrimination. But the federal law, at least, does recognize a balance between privacy and public safety, even when colleges can't, or won't.

The report is to be commended for pointing out this disconnect, and for calling for greater clarification of privacy laws and school policies.

Perhaps now, common sense can match up with legal obligations so both privacy and public safety can be served.

COLLEGES ARE WATCHING TROUBLED STUDENTS

Jeffrey McMurray

During the year following the Virginia Tech shootings, many colleges and universities took a hard look at their policies on student privacy and their procedures for monitoring and sharing information about troubled students. This article, by the Associated Press, was first published on March 28, 2008. AP writer Sue Lindsay contributed to this report.

On the agenda: A student who got into a shouting match with a faculty member. Another who harassed a female classmate. Someone found sleeping in a car. And a student who posted a threat against a professor on Facebook.

In a practice adopted at one college after another since the massacre at Virginia Tech, a University of Kentucky committee of deans, administrators, campus police and mental health officials has begun meeting regularly to discuss a watch list of troubled students and decide whether they need professional help or should be sent packing.

These "threat assessment groups" are aimed at heading off the kind of bloodshed seen at Virginia Tech a year ago and at Northern Illinois University last month.

"You've got to be way ahead of the game, so to speak, expect what may be coming. If you're able to identify behaviors early on and get these people assistance, it avoids disruptions in the classrooms and potential violence," said Maj. Joe Monroe, interim police chief at Kentucky.

5   The Kentucky panel, called Students of Concern, held its first meeting last week and will convene at least twice a month to talk about students whose strange or disturbing behavior has come to their attention.

Such committees represent a change in thinking among U.S. college officials, who for a long time were reluctant to share information about students' mental health for fear of violating privacy laws.

"If a student is a danger to himself or others, all the privacy concerns go out the window," said Patricia Terrell, vice president of student affairs, who created the panel.

Terrell shared details of the four discussed cases with The Associated Press on the condition that all names and other identifying information be left out.

Among other things, the panel can order a student into counseling or bar him or her from entering a particular building or talking to a certain person. It can also order a judicial hearing that can lead to suspension or expulsion if the student's offense was a violation of the law or school policy.

10   Although the four cases discussed last week were the ones administrators deemed as needing the most urgent attention, a database listing 26 other student cases has been created, providing fodder for future meetings.

Students are encouraged during their freshman orientation to report suspicious behavior to the dean of students, and university employees all the way down to janitors and cafeteria workers are instructed to tell their supervisors if they see anything.

Virtually every corner of campus is represented in the group's closed-door meetings, including dorm life, academics, counseling, mental health and police.

"If you look back at the Virginia Tech situation, the aftermath, there were several people who knew that student had problems, but because of privacy and different issues, they didn't talk to others about it," said Lee Todd, UK president.

High schools have been doing this sort of thing for years because of shootings, but only since Virginia Tech, when a disturbed student gunman killed 32 people and committed suicide, have colleges begun to follow suit, said Mike Dorn, executive director of Safe Havens International, a leading campus safety firm.

15   "They didn't think it was a real threat to them," Dorn said.

Virginia Tech has added a threat assessment team since the massacre there. Boston University, the University of Utah, the University of Illinois–Chicago and numerous others also have such groups, said Gwendolyn Dungy, executive director of the National Association of Student Personnel Administrators.

Bryan Cloyd, a Virginia Tech accounting professor whose daughter Austin was killed in the rampage, welcomed the stepped-up efforts to monitor troubled students but stressed he doesn't want to turn every college campus into a "police state."

"We can't afford to overreact," Cloyd said, but "we also can't afford to underreact."

Seung-Hui Cho, the Virginia Tech gunman, was ruled a danger to himself in a court hearing in 2005 that resulted from a roommate's call to police after Cho mentioned suicide in an e-mail. He was held overnight at a mental health center off campus and was ordered into outpatient treatment, but he received no follow-up services, despite his sullen, withdrawn behavior and his twisted, violence-filled writings.

20   Mary Bolin-Reece, director of counseling and testing at Kentucky, attends the threat assessment group's meetings but cannot share what she knows or, in most cases, even whether a student has been undergoing counseling. But participants can share information on other possible red flags.

"We always look at, 'Is there a change in the baseline?'" Bolin-Reece said. "The student had previously gotten very good grades, and then there was a drop-off. Something has happened. Is there some shift in their ability to function? If a student is coming to the attention of various parties around the university, we begin to be able to connect the dots."

The University of Kentucky has not had a murder on campus since 1984. Still, the threat-assessment effort has the strong backing of Carol Graham of Fort Carson, Colo., whose son Kevin was a Kentucky student when he committed suicide before leaving for an ROTC summer camp in 2003.

"UK is such a huge university," Graham said. "It's important to know there's a safety net—that people are looking out for each other. With Kevin, his professors thought he was perfect. He'd be an A student. But the people around him were noticing differences."

As for the four cases taken up by the committee: The student who got into an argument with a faculty member—and had also seen a major dip in grades and exhibited poor hygiene—was ordered to meet with the dean of students.

25   The one accused of harassment was referred to a judicial hearing, during which he was expelled from university housing. The student who made the Facebook threat was given a warning. In the case of the student sleeping in a car, a committee member was dispatched to check on the person. No further details were released.

THE FAMILY EDUCATIONAL RIGHTS AND PRIVACY ACT (FERPA)

United States Code
Title 20. Education
CHAPTER 31. General Provisions Concerning Education
§ 1232g. Family Educational and Privacy Rights

Following are excerpts from the *Family Educational Rights and Privacy Act (FERPA)*, the federal law enacted in 1974 that governs restrictions on the release of student educational records. FERPA provides for the withholding of federal funds to educational institutions that violate its provisions, and it is the federal guarantor of the privacy rights of post-secondary students.

(1) (A) No funds shall be made available under any applicable program to any educational agency or institution which has a policy of denying, or which

effectively prevents, the parents of students who are or have been in attendance at a school of such agency or at such institution, as the case may be, the right to inspect and review the education records of their children. If any material or document in the education record of a student includes information on more than one student, the parents of one of such students shall have the right to inspect and review only such part of such material or document as relates to such student or to be informed of the specific information contained in such part of such material. Each educational agency or institution shall establish appropriate procedures for the granting of a request by parents for access to the education records of their children within a reasonable period of time, but in no case more than forty-five days after the request has been made....

(C) The first sentence of subparagraph (A) shall not operate to make available to students in institutions of postsecondary education the following materials:

(i)   financial records of the parents of the student or any information contained therein;

(ii) confidential letters and statements of recommendation, which were placed in the education records prior to January 1, 1975, if such letters or statements are not used for purposes other than those for which they were specifically intended;

(iii) if the student has signed a waiver of the student's right of access under this subsection in accordance with subparagraph (D), confidential recommendations—

(I)   respecting admission to any educational agency or institution,

(II)   respecting an application for employment, and

(III) respecting the receipt of an honor or honorary recognition.

(B) The term "education records" does not include—

(i)   records of instructional, supervisory, and administrative personnel and educational personnel ancillary thereto which are in the sole possession of the maker thereof and which are not accessible or revealed to any other person except a substitute;

(ii) records maintained by a law enforcement unit of the educational agency or institution that were created by that law enforcement unit for the purpose of law enforcement;

(iii) in the case of persons who are employed by an educational agency or institution but who are not in attendance at such agency or institution, records made and maintained in the normal course of business which relate exclusively to such person in that person's capacity as an employee and are not available for use for any other purpose; or

(iv) records on a student who is eighteen years of age or older, or is attending an institution of postsecondary education, which are made or maintained by a physician, psychiatrist, psychologist, or other recognized professional or paraprofessional acting in his professional or paraprofessional capacity, or assisting in that capacity, and which are made, maintained, or used only in connection with the provision of treatment to the student, and are not available to anyone other than persons providing such treatment, except that such records can be personally reviewed by a physician or other appropriate professional of the student's choice....

(h) Certain disciplinary action information allowable. Nothing in this section shall prohibit an educational agency or institution from—

(1) including appropriate information in the education record of any student concerning disciplinary action taken against such student for conduct that posed a significant risk to the safety or well-being of that student, other students, or other members of the school community; or

(2) disclosing such information to teachers and school officials, including teachers and school officials in other schools, who have legitimate educational interests in the behavior of the student.

Exercise 5.5

Critical Reading for Synthesis

Having read the selections relating to privacy and safety, pages 138–149, write a one-sentence summary of each. On the same page, list two or three topics that you think are common to several of the selections. Beneath each topic, list the authors who have something to say on that topic and briefly note what they have to say. Finally, for each topic, jot down what *you* have to say. Now regard your effort: With each topic you have created a discussion point suitable for inclusion in a paper. (Of course, until you determine the claim of such a paper, you won't know to what end you might put the discussion.) Write a paragraph or two in which you introduce the topic and then conduct a brief conversation among the interested parties (including yourself).

Consider Your Purpose

Your specific purpose in writing an argument synthesis is crucial. What exactly you want to do will affect your claim and how you organize the evidence. Your purpose may be clear to you before you begin research, or it may not emerge until after you have completed your research. Of course, the sooner your purpose is clear to you, the fewer wasted steps you will take. On the other hand, the more you approach research as an exploratory process, the likelier that your conclusions will emerge from the sources themselves rather than from preconceived ideas. Each new writing project will have its own rhythm in this regard. Be flexible in your approach: Through some combination of preconceived structures and invigorating discoveries, you will find your way to the source materials that will yield a promising paper.

Let's say that while reading these seven (and additional) sources on the debate about campus safety and student privacy, you share the outrage of many who blamed the university (and the federal privacy laws on which it relied) for not using the available information in a way that might have spared the lives of those who died. Perhaps you also blame the legislators who wrote the privacy laws, for being more concerned about the confidentiality of the mental health records of the individual person than with the safety of the larger college population. Perhaps, you conclude, society has gone too far in valuing privacy more than it appears to value safety.

On the other hand, in your own role as a student, perhaps you share the high value placed on the privacy of sensitive information about yourself. After all, one of the functions of higher education is to foster students' independence as they make the transition from adolescence to adulthood. You can understand that many students like yourself might not want their parents or others to know details about academic records or disciplinary measures, much less information about therapy sought and undertaken at school. Historically, in the decades since the university officially stood *in loco parentis*—in place of parents—students have struggled hard to win the same civil liberties and rights (including the right to privacy) as their elders.

Further, you may wonder whether federal privacy laws do in fact forbid the sharing of information about potentially dangerous students when the health and safety of others are at stake. A little research may begin to confirm your doubts whether Virginia Tech officials were really as helpless as they claimed they were.

Your purpose in writing, then, emerges from these kinds of responses to the source materials you find.

Making a Claim: Formulate a Thesis

As we indicated in the introduction to this chapter, one useful way of approaching an argument is to see it as making a *claim*. A claim is a proposition, a conclusion you have made, that you are trying to prove or demonstrate. If your purpose is to argue that we should work to ensure campus safety without enacting restrictive laws that overturn the hard-won privacy rights of students, then that claim (generally expressed in one-sentence form as a *thesis*) is at the heart of your argument. You will draw support from your sources as you argue logically for your claim.

Not every piece of information in a source is useful for supporting a claim. You must read with care and select the opinions, facts, and statistics that best advance your position. You may even find yourself drawing support from sources that make claims entirely different from your own. For example, in researching the subject of student privacy and campus safety, you may come across editorials arguing that in the wake of the Virginia Tech shootings, student privacy rights should be greatly restricted. Perhaps you will find information in these sources to help support your own contrary arguments.

You might use one source as part of a *counterargument*—an argument opposing your own—so that you can demonstrate its weaknesses and, in the process, strengthen your own claim. On the other hand, the author of one of your sources may be so convincing in supporting a claim that you adopt it yourself, either partially or entirely. The point is that *the argument is in your hands.* You must devise it yourself and use your sources in ways that will support the claim you present in your thesis.

You may not want to divulge your thesis until the end of the paper, thereby drawing the reader along toward your conclusion, allowing the thesis to flow naturally out of the argument and the evidence on which it is based. If you do this, you are working *inductively.* Or you may wish to be more direct and (after an introduction) *begin* with your thesis, following the thesis statement with evidence and reasoning to support it. If you do this, you are working *deductively.* In academic papers, deductive arguments are far more common than inductive ones.

Based on your reactions to reading sources—and perhaps also on your own inclinations as a student—you may find yourself essentially in sympathy with the approach to privacy taken by one of the schools covered in your sources, M.I.T. At the same time, you may feel that M.I.T.'s position does not demonstrate sufficient concern for campus safety and that Cornell's position, on the other hand, restricts student privacy too much. Perhaps most important, you conclude that we don't need to change the law because, if correctly interpreted, the law already incorporates a good balance between privacy and safety. After a few tries, you develop this thesis:

> In responding to the Virginia Tech killings, we should resist rolling back federal rules protecting student privacy; for as long as college officials effectively respond to signs of trouble, these rules already provide a workable balance between privacy and public safety.

Decide How You Will Use Your Source Material

Your claim commits you to (1) arguing that student privacy should remain protected, and (2) demonstrating that federal law already strikes a balance between privacy and public safety. The sources (some provided here, some located elsewhere) offer information and ideas—evidence—that will allow you to support your claim. The excerpt from the official report on the Virginia Tech shootings reveals a finding that school officials failed to correctly interpret federal privacy rules and failed to "intervene effectively." The article "Virginia Tech Massacre Has Altered Campus Mental Health Systems" outlines some of the ways that campuses around the country have instituted policy changes regarding troubled students and privacy in the wake of Virginia Tech. And the excerpt from the Family Educational Rights and Privacy Act (FERPA), the federal law, reveals that restrictions on revealing students' confidential information have a crucial exception for "the safety or well-being of … students, or other members of the school community." (These and several other sources not included in this chapter will be cited in the model argument paper.)

Develop an Organizational Plan

Having established your overall purpose and your claim, having developed a thesis (which may change as you write and revise the paper), and having decided how to draw upon your source materials, how do you logically organize your paper? In many cases, a well-written thesis will suggest an organization. Thus, the first part of your paper will deal with the debate over rolling back student privacy. The second part will argue that as long as educational institutions behave proactively—that is, as long as they actively seek to help troubled students and foster campus safety—existing federal rules already preserve a balance between privacy and safety. Sorting through your material and categorizing it by topic and subtopic, you might compose the following outline:

I.   Introduction. Recap Va. Tech shooting. College officials, citing privacy rules, did not act on available info about shooter with history of mental problems.

II. Federal rules on privacy. Subsequent debate over balance between privacy and campus safety. Pendulum now moving back toward safety. *Thesis.*

III. Developments in student privacy in recent decades.
   A. Doctrine of *in loco parentis* defines college-student relationship.
   B. Movement away from *in loco parentis* begins in 1960s, in context not only of student rights but also broader civil rights struggles of the period.
   C. FERPA, enacted 1974, establishes new federal rules protecting student privacy.

IV. Arguments *against* student privacy.
   A. In wake of Virginia Tech, many blame FERPA protections and college officials, believing privacy rights have been taken too far, putting campus community at risk.
   B. Cornell rolls back some FERPA privacy rights.

V.   Arguments *for* student privacy.
   A. M.I.T. strongly defends right to privacy.
   B. Problem is not federal law but incorrect interpretation of federal law. FERPA provides health and safety exceptions. Virginia Tech officials erred in citing FERPA for not sharing info about shooter earlier.
   C. Univ. of Kentucky offers good balance between competing claims of privacy and safety.
      1. watch lists of troubled students
      2. threat assessment groups
      3. open communication among university officials

VI. Conclusion.
   A. Virginia Tech incident was an instance of a legal issue students will encounter in the broader world: rights of the individual vs. rights of the larger group.

    B. Virginia Tech incident was tragic but should not cause us to overturn hard-won privacy rights.

    C. We should support a more proactive approach to student mental health problems and improve communication between departments.

Formulate an Argument Strategy

The argument that emerges through this outline will build not only on evidence drawn from sources but also on the writer's assumptions. Consider the bare-bones logic of the argument:

> Laws protecting student privacy serve a good purpose. (*assumption*)
>
> If properly interpreted and implemented, federal law as currently written is sufficient both to protect student privacy and to ensure campus safety. (*support*)
>
> We should not change federal law to overturn or restrict student privacy rights. (*claim*)

The crucial point about which reasonable people will disagree is the *assumption* that laws protecting student privacy serve a good purpose. Those who wish to restrict the information made available to parents are likely to agree with this assumption. Those who favor a policy that allows college officials to inform parents of problems without their children's permission are likely to disagree.

Writers can accept or partially accept an opposing assumption by making a *concession*, in the process establishing themselves as reasonable and willing to compromise (see p. 168). David Harrison does exactly this in the following model synthesis when he summarizes the policies of the University of Kentucky. By raising objections to his own position and conceding some validity to them, he blunts the effectiveness of *counterarguments*. Thus, Harrison concedes the absolute requirement for campus safety, but he argues that this requirement can be satisfied as long as campus officials correctly interpret existing federal law and implement proactive procedures aimed at dealing more effectively with troubled students.

The *claim* of the argument about privacy versus safety is primarily a claim about *policy*, about actions that should (or should not) be taken. An argument can also concern a claim about *facts* (Does X exist? How can we define X? Does X lead to Y?), a claim about *value* (What is X worth?), or a claim about *cause and effect* (Why did X happen?).

The present argument rests to some degree on a dispute about cause and effect. No one disputes that the primary cause of this tragedy was that a disturbed student was not stopped before he killed people. But many have disputed the secondary cause: Did the massacre happen, in part, because federal law prevented officials from sharing crucial information about the disturbed student? Or did it happen, in part, because university officials failed to interpret correctly what they could and could not do under the law? As you read the following paper, observe how these opposing views are woven into the argument.

Draft and Revise Your Synthesis

The final draft of an argument synthesis, based on the outline above, follows. Thesis, transitions, and topic sentences are highlighted; Modern Language Association (MLA) documentation style is used throughout (except in the citing of federal law).

A cautionary note: When writing syntheses, it is all too easy to become careless in properly crediting your sources. Before drafting your paper, always review "Rules for Avoiding Plagiarism" at the end of Chapter 1.

MODEL ARGUMENT SYNTHESIS

David Harrison

Professor Shanker

Law and Society I

21 February 2011

Balancing Privacy and Safety in the Wake of Virginia Tech

(1) On April 16, 2007, Seung Hui Cho, a mentally ill student at Virginia Polytechnic Institute, shot to death 32 fellow students and faculty members, and injured 17 others, before killing himself. It was the worst mass shooting in U.S. history, and the fact that it took place on a college campus lent a special horror to the event. In the days after the tragedy, several facts about Seung Hui Cho came to light. According to the official Virginia State Panel report on the killings, Cho had exhibited signs of mental disturbance, including "suicidal and homicidal ideations" dating back to high school. And during Cho's junior year at Virginia Tech, numerous incidents occurred that provided clear warnings of Cho's mental instability and violent impulses (Virginia Tech Review 1). University administrators, faculty, and officials were aware of these incidents but failed to intervene to prevent the impending tragedy.

(2) In the search for answers, attention quickly focused on federal rules governing student privacy that Virginia Tech officials said prevented them from communicating effectively with each other or with Cho's parents regarding his troubles. These rules, the officials argued, prohibit the sharing of information concerning students' mental health with parents or other students. The publicity about such restrictions revived an ongoing debate over university policies that balance student privacy against campus safety. In the wake of the Virginia

Harrison 2

Tech tragedy, the pendulum seems to have swung in favor of safety. In April 2008, Virginia Governor Tim Kaine signed into law a measure requiring colleges to alert parents when dependent students may be a danger to themselves or to others ("Virginia Tech Massacre" 1). Peter Lake, an educator at Stetson University College of Law, predicted that in the wake of Virginia Tech, "people will go in a direction of safety over privacy" (qtd. in Bernstein, "Mother").

The shootings at Virginia Tech demonstrate, in the most horrifying way, the need for secure college campuses. Nevertheless, privacy remains a crucial right to most Americans— including college students, many of whom for the first time are exercising their prerogatives as adults. Many students who pose no threat to anyone will, and should, object strenuously to university administrators peering into and making judgments about their private lives. Some might be unwilling to seek professional therapy if they know that the records of their counseling sessions might be released to their parents or to other students. In responding to the Virginia Tech killings, we should resist rolling back federal rules protecting student privacy; for as long as college officials effectively respond to signs of trouble, these rules already provide a workable balance between privacy and public safety.

In these days of Facebook and reality TV, the notion of privacy rights, particularly for young people, may seem quaint. In fact, a top lawyer for the search engine Google claimed that in the Internet age, young people just don't care about privacy the way they once did (Cohen A17). Whatever the changing views of privacy in a wired world, the issue of student privacy rights is a serious legal matter that must be seen in the context of the student-college relationship. This relationship has its historical roots in the doctrine of *in loco parentis*, Latin for "in the place of the parents." Generally, this doctrine is understood to mean that the college stands in place of the student's parent or guardian. The college therefore has "a duty to protect the safety, morals, and welfare of their students, just as parents are expected to protect their children" (Pollet).

Writing of life at the University of Michigan before the 1960s, one historian observes that "*in loco parentis* comprised an elaborate structure of written rules and quiet understandings enforced in the trenches by housemothers [who] governed much of the what, where, when, and whom of students' lives, especially women: what to wear to dinner, what time to be home, where, when, and for how long they might receive visitors" (Tobin).

During the 1960s court decisions began to chip away at the doctrine of *in loco parentis*. These rulings illustrate that the students' rights movement during that era was an integral part of a broader contemporary social movement for civil rights and liberties. In *Dixon v. Alabama State Board of Education*, Alabama State College invoked *in loco parentis* to defend its decision to expel six African-American students without due process for participating in a lunchroom counter sit-in. Eventually, a federal appeals court rejected the school's claim to unrestrained power, ruling that students' constitutional rights did not end once they stepped onto campus (Weigel).

7   Students were not just fighting for the right to hold hands in dorm rooms; they were also asserting their rights as the vanguard of a social revolution. As Stetson law professor Robert Bickel notes: "The fall of *in loco parentis* in the 1960s correlated exactly with the rise of student economic power and the rise of student civil rights" (qtd. in Weigel).

8   The students' rights movement received a further boost with the Family Educational Rights and Privacy Act (FERPA), signed into law by President Ford in 1974. FERPA barred schools from releasing educational records—including mental health records—without the student's permission. The Act provides some important exceptions: educational records *can* be released in the case of health and safety emergencies or if the student is declared a dependent on his or her parents' tax returns (*Family*).

9   In the wake of Virginia Tech, however, many observers pointed the finger of blame at federal restrictions on sharing available mental health information. Also held responsible were the school's officials, who admitted knowing of Cho's mental instability but claimed that FERPA prevented them from doing anything about it. The State of Virginia official report on the killings notes as follows:

> University officials . . . explained their failures to communicate with one another or with Cho's parents by noting their belief that such communications are prohibited by the federal laws governing the privacy of health and education records. (Virginia Tech Review 2)

10   Observers were quick to declare the system broken. "Laws Limit Schools Even after Alarms," trumpeted a headline in the *Philadelphia Inquirer* (Gammage and Burling). Commentators attacked federal privacy law, charging that the pendulum had swung too far away from campus safety. Judging from this letter to the editor of the *Wall Street Journal*, many agreed wholeheartedly: "Parents have a right to know if their child has a serious problem, and they need to know the progress of their child's schoolwork, especially if they are paying the cost of the education. Anything less than this is criminal" (Guerriero).

Harrison 4

As part of this public clamor, some schools have enacted policies that effectively curtail   (11)
student privacy in favor of campus safety. For example: after Virginia Tech, Cornell University
began assuming that students were dependents of their parents. Exploiting what the *Wall
Street Journal* termed a "rarely used legal exception" in FERPA allows Cornell to provide parents with confidential information without students' permission (Bernstein, "Bucking" A9).

Conversely, the Massachusetts Institute of Technology lies at the opposite end of the   (12)
spectrum from Cornell in its staunch defense of student privacy. M.I.T. has stuck to its
position even in the wake of Virginia Tech, demanding that the mother of a missing M.I.T.
student obtain a subpoena in order to access his dorm room and e-mail records. That
student was later found dead, an apparent suicide (Bernstein, "Mother"). Even in the face
of lawsuits, M.I.T. remains committed to its stance. Its chancellor explained the school's
position this way:

> Privacy is important.... Different students will do different things they
> absolutely don't want their parents to know about.... Students expect this
> kind of safe place where they can address their difficulties, try out lifestyles,
> and be independent of their parents (qtd. in Bernstein, "Mother").

One can easily understand how parents would be outraged by the M.I.T. position. No parent   (13)
would willingly let his or her child enter an environment where that child's safety cannot be
assured. Just as the first priority for any government is to protect its citizens, the first priority
of an educational institution must be to keep its students safe. But does this responsibility
justify rolling back student privacy rights or returning to a more traditional interpretation of
in loco parentis in the relationship between a university and its students? No, for the simple
reason that the choice is a false one.

As long as federal privacy laws are properly interpreted and implemented, they do   (14)
nothing to endanger campus safety. The problem at Virginia Tech was not the federal government's policy; it was the university's own practices based on a faulty interpretation of
that policy. The breakdown began with the failure of Virginia Tech officials to understand
federal privacy laws. Interpreted correctly, these laws would *not* have prohibited officials
from notifying appropriate authorities of Cho's problems. The Virginia Tech Review Panel report was very clear on this point: "[F]ederal laws and their state counterparts afford ample
leeway to share information in potentially dangerous situations" (2). FERPA does, in fact,
provide for a "health and safety emergencies" exception; educational records *can* be released

without the student's consent "in connection with an emergency, [to] appropriate persons if the knowledge of such information is necessary to protect the health or safety of the student or other person..." (232g (b) (1) (g-h)). But Virginia Tech administrators did not invoke this important exception to FERPA's privacy rules. [Nor did they inform students of Cho's initial murder of two students, according to the Department of Education—an action that might have averted the thirty other murders (Potter).]

(15)   An editorial in the *Christian Science Monitor* suggested several other steps that the university could legally have taken, including informing Cho's parents that he had been briefly committed to a mental health facility, a fact that was public information. The editorial concluded, scornfully, that "federal law, at least, does recognize a balance between privacy and public safety, even when colleges can't, or won't" ("Perilous").

(16)   To be fair, such confusion about FERPA's contingencies appears widespread among college officials. For this reason, the U.S. Department of Education's revised privacy regulations, announced in March 2008 and intended to "clarify" when schools may release student records, are welcome and necessary. But simply reassuring anxious university officials that they won't lose federal funds for revealing confidential student records won't be enough to ensure campus safety. We need far more effective intervention for troubled students than the kind provided by Virginia Tech, which the Virginia Tech Review Panel blasted for its "lack of resources" and "passivity" (2). Yet effective interventions can be difficult to coordinate, and the consequences of inaction are sadly familiar. Three years after the Virginia Tech shootings, a student sued the University of California Regents because administrators at UCLA had allegedly failed to address the troubling behaviors of another student who later slashed and nearly killed her (Gordon).

(17)   Schools like the University of Kentucky offer a positive example of intervention, demonstrating that colleges can adopt a robust approach to student mental health without infringing on privacy rights. At Kentucky, "threat assessment groups" meet regularly to discuss a "watch list" of troubled students and decide what to do about them (McMurray). These committees emphasize proactiveness and communication—elements that were sorely missing at Virginia Tech. The approach represents a prudent middle ground between the extreme positions of M.I.T. and Cornell.

(18)   This middle ground takes full account of student privacy rights. For example, the University of Kentucky's director of counseling attends the threat assessment group's

Harrison 6

meetings but draws a clear line at what information she shares—for instance, whether or not a student has been undergoing counseling. Instead, the group looks for other potential red flags, such as a sharp drop-off in grades or difficulty functioning in the campus environment (McMurray). This open communication between university officials will presumably also help with delicate judgments—whether, for example, a student's violent story written for a creative writing class is an indication of mental instability or simply an early work by the next Stephen King ("Virginia Tech Massacre" 1).

The debate over rights to individual privacy versus public safety is sure to follow students into the wider world because that debate is one instance of a larger issue. The Fourth Amendment protects citizens "against unreasonable searches and seizures." But for more than two centuries, what constitutes *unreasonable* has been vigorously debated in the courts. Such arguments are not likely to end any time soon—on or off college campuses. Consider the recent public controversy over the installation of full body scanners at U.S. airports and intrusive pat-downs of travelers, measures taken by the U.S. Department of Homeland Security to foil terrorist threats. Predictably, many protested what they considered an assault on personal privacy, complaining that the scanners revealed body parts otherwise hidden by clothing and that the pat-downs amounted to sexual groping. On September 1, 2010, a civil liberties group even filed a lawsuit to block deployment of the scanners (Electronic). But many others vigorously defended the Homeland Security measures as essential to ensuring public safety. According to a *Washington Post*-ABC News poll, "Nearly two-thirds of Americans support the new full-body security-screening machines at the country's airports, as most say they put higher priority on combating terrorism than protecting personal privacy" (Cohen and Halsey).

What happened at Virginia Tech was a tragedy. Few of us can appreciate the grief of the parents of the shooting victims at Virginia Tech, parents who trusted that their children would be safe and who were devastated when that faith was betrayed. To these parents, the words of the M.I.T. chancellor quoted earlier—platitudes about students "try[ing] out lifestyles" or "address[ing] their difficulties"—must sound hollow. But we must guard against allowing a few isolated incidents, however tragic, to restrict the rights of millions of students, the vast majority of whom graduate college safely and without incident. Schools must not use Virginia Tech as a pretext to bring back the bad old days of resident assistants snooping on the private lives of students and infringing on their privacy. That step is the first down a slippery slope of dictating morality. Both the federal courts and Congress have rejected that approach and for good reason have established the importance of privacy rights on campus. These rights must be preserved.

(21)   The Virginia Tech shooting does not demonstrate a failure of current policy, but rather a breakdown in the enforcement of policy. In its wake, universities have undertaken important modifications to their procedures. We should support changes that involve a more proactive approach to student mental health and improvements in communication between departments, such as those at the University of Kentucky. Such measures will not only bring confidential help to the troubled students who need it, they will also improve the safety of the larger college community. At the same time, these measures will preserve hard-won privacy rights on campus.

Works Cited

Bernstein, Elizabeth. "Bucking Privacy Concerns, Cornell Acts as Watchdog." *Wall Street Journal* 27 Dec. 2007: A1+. *LexisNexis*. Web. 10 Feb. 2011.

—. "A Mother Takes On MIT." *Wall Street Journal* 20 Sept. 2007: A1. *LexisNexis*. Web. 10 Feb. 2011.

Cohen, Adam. "One Friend Facebook Hasn't Made Yet: Privacy Rights." *New York Times* 18 Feb. 2008: A1+. *Academic Search Complete*. Web. 9 Feb. 2011.

Cohen, Jon, and Ashley Halsey III. "Poll: Nearly Two-Thirds of Americans Support Full-Body Scanners at Airports." *Washington Post*. The Washington Post Co., 23 Nov. 2010. Web. 17 Feb. 2011.

Electronic Privacy Information Center v. Dept. of Homeland Security. No. 10-1157. D.C. Cir. of the US. Sept 1, 2010. *epic.org*. Electronic Privacy Information Center, 1 Sept. 2010. Web. 15 Feb. 2011.

Family Educational Rights and Privacy Act (FERPA). 20 U.S.C. §1232g (b) (1) (g–h) (2006). Print.

Gammage, Jeff, and Stacy Burling. "Laws Limit Schools Even after Alarms." *Philadelphia Inquirer* 19 Apr. 2007: A1. *Academic Search Complete*. Web. 10 Feb. 2011.

Harrison 9

Gordon, Larry. "Campus Stabbing Victim Sues UC Regents." *Los Angeles Times* 8 Dec. 2010. *LexisNexis*. Web. 13 Feb. 2011.

Guerriero, Dom. Letter. *Wall Street Journal* 7 Jan. 2008. *LexisNexis*. Web. 11 Feb. 2011.

McMurray, Jeffrey. "Colleges Are Watching Troubled Students." *AP Online*. Associated Press, 28 Mar. 2008. Web. 11 Feb. 2011.

"Perilous Privacy at Virginia Tech." Editorial. *Christian Science Monitor* 4 Sept. 2007: 8. *Academic Search Complete*. Web. 10 Feb. 2011.

Pollet, Susan J. "Is 'In Loco Parentis' at the College Level a Dead Doctrine?" *New York Law Journal* 288 (2002): 4. Print.

Potter, Dena. "Feds: Va. Tech Broke Law in '07 Shooting Response." *Washington Post*. The Washington Post Co., 10 Dec. 2010. Web. 12 Feb. 2011.

Tobin, James. "The Day 'In Loco Parentis' Died." *Michigan Today*. U of Michigan, Nov. 2007. Web. 10 Feb. 2011.

U.S. Constitution: Fourth Amendment. *Findlaw.com*. Thomson Reuters, n.d. Web. 16 Feb. 2011.

"Virginia Tech Massacre Has Altered Campus Mental Health Systems." *Los Angeles Times* 14 Apr. 2008: A1+. *LexisNexis*. Web. 8 Feb. 2011.

Virginia Tech Review Panel. *Mass Shootings at Virginia Tech, April 16, 2007: Report of the Virginia Tech Review Panel Presented to Timothy M. Kaine, Governor, Commonwealth of Virginia*. Arlington, VA: n.p., 2007. Print.

Weigel, David. "Welcome to the Fun-Free University: The Return of *In Loco Parentis* Is Killing Student Freedom." *Reasononline*. Reason Magazine, Oct. 2004. Web. 7 Feb. 2011.

The Strategy of the Argument Synthesis

In his argument synthesis, Harrison attempts to support a *claim*—one that favors laws protecting student privacy while at the same time helping to ensure campus safety—by offering *support* in the form of facts (what campuses such as the University of Kentucky are doing, what Virginia Tech officials did and failed to do) and opinions (testimony of persons on both sides of the issue). However, because Harrison's claim rests on an *assumption* about the value of student privacy laws, its effectiveness depends partially on the extent to which we, as readers, agree with this assumption. (See our discussion of assumptions in Chapter 2, pp. 61–62.) An assumption (sometimes called a warrant) is a generalization or principle about how the world works or should work—a fundamental statement of belief about facts or values. In this case, the underlying assumption is that college students, as emerging adults and as citizens with civil rights, are entitled to keep their educational records private. Harrison makes this assumption explicit. Though you are under no obligation to do so, stating assumptions explicitly will clarify your arguments to readers.

Assumptions are often deeply rooted in people's psyches, sometimes derived from lifelong experiences and observations and not easily changed, even by the most logical of arguments. People who lose loved ones in incidents such as Virginia Tech, or people who believe that the right to safety of the larger campus community outweighs the right of individual student privacy, are not likely to accept the assumption underlying this paper, nor are they likely to accept the support provided by Harrison. But readers with no firm opinion might well be persuaded and could come to agree with him that existing federal law protecting student privacy is sufficient to protect campus safety, provided that campus officials act responsibly.

A discussion of the model argument's paragraphs, along with the argument strategy for each, follows. Note that the paper devotes one paragraph to developing each section of the outline on pages 152–153. Note also that Harrison avoids plagiarism by the careful attribution and quotation of sources.

- **Paragraph 1:** Harrison summarizes the key events of the Virginia Tech killings and establishes that Cho's mental instability was previously known to university officials.

  Argument strategy: Opening with the bare facts of the massacre, Harrison proceeds to lay the basis for the reaction against privacy rules that will be described in the paragraphs to follow. To some extent, Harrison encourages the reader to share the outrage of many in the general public that university officials failed to act to prevent the killings before they started.

- **Paragraph 2:** Harrison now explains the federal rules governing student privacy and discusses the public backlash against such rules and the new law signed by the governor of Virginia restricting privacy at colleges within the state.

  Argument strategy: This paragraph highlights the debate over student privacy—and in particular the sometimes conflicting demands of student privacy and campus safety that will be central to the rest of the paper. Harrison cites both fact (the new Virginia law) and opinion (the quotation by Peter Lake) to develop this paragraph.

- **Paragraph 3:** Harrison further clarifies the two sides of the apparent conflict between privacy and safety, maintaining that both represent important social values but concluding with a thesis that argues for not restricting privacy.

Argument strategy: For the first time, Harrison reveals his own position on the issue. He starts the paragraph by conceding the need for secure campuses but begins to make the case for privacy (for example, without privacy rules, students might be reluctant to enter therapy). In his thesis, he emphasizes that the demands of both privacy and safety can be satisfied because existing federal rules incorporate the necessary balance.

- **Paragraphs 4–7:** These paragraphs constitute the next section of the paper (see outline, pp. 155–156), covering the developments in student privacy over the past few decades. Paragraphs 4 and 5 cover the doctrine of *in loco parentis*; paragraph 6 discusses how court decisions such as *Dixon v. Alabama State Board of Education* began to erode this doctrine.

  Argument strategy: This section of the paper establishes the situation that existed on college campuses before the 1960s—and that presumably would exist again were privacy laws to be rolled back. By linking the erosion of the *in loco parentis* doctrine to the civil rights struggle, Harrison attempts to bestow upon pre-1960s college students (especially women), who were "parented" by college administrators, something of the *ethos* of African-Americans fighting for full citizenship during the civil rights era. Essentially, Harrison is making an analogy between the two groups—one that readers may or may not accept.

- **Paragraph 8:** This paragraph on FERPA constitutes the final part of the section of the paper dealing with the evolution of student privacy since before the 1960s. Harrison explains what FERPA is and introduces an exception to its privacy rules that will be more fully developed later in the paper.

  Argument strategy: FERPA is the federal law central to the debate over the balance between privacy and safety, so Harrison introduces it here as the culmination of a series of developments that weakened *in loco parentis* and guaranteed a certain level of student privacy. But since Harrison in his thesis argues that federal law on student privacy already establishes a balance between privacy and safety, he ends the paragraph by referring to the "health and safety" exception, an exception that will become important later in his argument.

- **Paragraphs 9–11:** These paragraphs constitute the section of the paper that covers the arguments *against* student privacy. Paragraph 9 discusses public reaction against both FERPA and Virginia Tech officials, who were accused of being more concerned with privacy than with safety. Paragraph 10 cites antiprivacy sentiments expressed in newspapers. Paragraph 11 explains how, in the wake of Virginia Tech, schools such as Cornell have enacted new policies restricting student privacy.

  Argument strategy: Harrison sufficiently respects the sentiments of those whose position he opposes to deal at some length with the counterarguments to his thesis. He quotes the official report on the mass shootings, to establish that Virginia Tech officials believed that they were acting according to the law. He quotes the writer of an angry letter about parents' right to know, without attempting to rebut its arguments. In outlining the newly restrictive Cornell policies on privacy, Harrison also establishes what he considers an extreme reaction to the massacres: essentially gutting student privacy rules. He is therefore setting up one position on the debate that he will later contrast with other positions—those of M.I.T. and the University of Kentucky.

- **Paragraphs 12–16:** These paragraphs constitute the section of the paper devoted to arguments *for* student privacy. Paragraphs 12 and 13 discuss the M.I.T. position on privacy, as expressed by its chancellor. Paragraph 14 refocuses on FERPA and quotes language to demonstrate that existing federal law provides a health and safety exception to the enforcement of privacy rules. Paragraph 15 quotes an editorial supporting this interpretation of FERPA. Paragraph 16 concedes the existence of confusion about federal rules and makes the transition to an argument about the need for more-effective action by campus officials to prevent tragedies such as the one at Virginia Tech.

  Argument strategy: Because these paragraphs express Harrison's position, as embedded in his thesis, this is the longest segment of the discussion. Paragraphs 12 and 13 discuss the M.I.T. position on student privacy, which (given that school's failure to accommodate even prudent demands for safety) Harrison believes is too extreme. Notice the transition at the end of paragraph 13. Conceding that colleges have a responsibility to keep students safe, Harrison poses a question: Does the goal of keeping students safe justify the rolling back of privacy rights? In a pivotal sentence, he responds, "No, for the simple reason that the choice is a false one." Paragraph 14 develops this response and presents the heart of Harrison's argument. Recalling the health and safety exception introduced in paragraph 8, Harrison now explains *why* the choice is false: He quotes the exact language of FERPA to establish that the problem at Virginia Tech was due not to federal law that prevented campus officials from protecting students, but rather to campus officials who *misunderstood* the law.

  Paragraph 15 amplifies Harrison's argument, with a reference to an editorial in the *Christian Science Monitor*. Paragraph 16 marks a transition, within this section, to a position (developed in paragraphs 17 and 18) that Harrison believes represents a sensible stance in the debate over campus safety and student privacy. He bolsters his case by citing here, as elsewhere in the paper, the official report on the Virginia Tech killings. The report, prepared by an expert panel that devoted months to investigating the incident, carries considerable weight as evidence in this argument.

- **Paragraphs 17–18:** These paragraphs continue the arguments in favor of Harrison's position. They focus on new policies in practice at the University of Kentucky that offer a "prudent middle ground" in the debate.

Argument strategy: Having discussed schools such as Cornell and M.I.T., where the reaction to the Virginia Tech killings was inadequate or unsatisfactory, Harrison now outlines a set of policies and procedures in place at the University of Kentucky since April 2007. Following the transition at the end of paragraph 16 on the need for more-effective intervention on the part of campus officials, Harrison explains how Kentucky established a promising form of such intervention: watch lists of troubled students, threat assessment groups, and more-open communication among university officials. Thus, Harrison positions what is happening at the University of Kentucky—as opposed to rollbacks of federal rules—as the most effective way of preventing future killings like those at Virginia Tech. Kentucky therefore becomes a crucial example for Harrison of how to strike a good balance between the demands of student privacy and campus safety.

- **Paragraphs 19–21:** In his conclusion, Harrison both broadens the context of his discussion about Virginia Tech and reiterates points made in the body of the paper. In paragraph 19, he turns from the shooting to the broader world, suggesting that the tension between the individual's right to privacy and the public's right to safety is not unique to college campuses. In paragraph 20, he agrees that what happened at Virginia Tech was a tragedy but maintains that an isolated incident should not become an excuse for rolling back student privacy rights and bringing back "the bad old days" when campus officials took an active, and intrusive, interest in students' private lives. In paragraph 21, Harrison reiterates the position stated in his thesis: that the problem at Virginia Tech was not a restrictive federal policy that handcuffed administrators, but rather a breakdown in enforcement. He concludes on the hopeful note that new policies established since Virginia Tech will both protect student privacy and improve campus safety.

Argument strategy: The last three paragraphs, the conclusion, provide Harrison with an opportunity both to extend his thinking beyond a single case and to reemphasize his main points. In paragraph 19, he moves beyond the world of college and broadens the reach of his argument. The final two paragraphs to some degree parallel the structure of the thesis itself. In paragraph 20, Harrison makes a final appeal against rolling back student privacy rights. This appeal parallels the first clause of the thesis ("In responding to the Virginia Tech killings, we should resist rolling back federal rules protecting student privacy"). In paragraph 21, Harrison focuses not on federal law itself, but rather on the kind of measures adopted by schools such as the University of Kentucky that go beyond mere compliance with federal law—and thereby demonstrate the validity of part two of Harrison's thesis ("...as long as college officials effectively respond to signs of trouble, these rules already provide a workable balance between privacy and public safety"). Harrison thus ends a paper on a grim subject with a note that provides some measure of optimism and that attempts to reconcile proponents on both sides of this emotional debate.

Another approach to an argument synthesis based on the same and additional sources could argue (along with some of the sources quoted in the model paper) that safety as a social value should never be outweighed by the right to privacy. Such a position could draw support from other practices in contemporary society—searches at airports, for example—illustrating that most people are willing to give up a certain measure of privacy, as well as convenience, in the interest of the safety of the community. Whatever your approach to a subject, in first *critically examining* the various sources and then *synthesizing* them to support a position about which you feel strongly, you are engaging in the kind of critical thinking that is essential to success in a good deal of academic and professional work.

DEVELOPING AND ORGANIZING THE SUPPORT FOR YOUR ARGUMENTS

Experienced writers seem to have an intuitive sense of how to develop and present supporting evidence for their claims; this sense is developed through much hard work and practice. Less-experienced writers wonder what to say first, and having decided on that, wonder what to say next. There is no single method of presentation. But the techniques of even the most experienced writers often boil down to a few tried and tested arrangements.

As we've seen in the model synthesis in this chapter, the key to devising effective arguments is to find and use those kinds of support that most persuasively strengthen your claim. Some writers categorize support into two broad types: *evidence* and *motivational appeals.* Evidence—in the form of facts, statistics, and expert testimony—helps make the appeal to reason. Motivational appeals—appeals grounded in emotion and upon the authority of the speaker—are employed to get people to change their minds, to agree with the writer or speaker, or to decide upon a plan of action.

Following are the most common strategies for using and organizing support for your claims.

Summarize, Paraphrase, and Quote Supporting Evidence

In most of the papers and reports you will write in college and in the professional world, evidence and motivational appeals derive from your summarizing, paraphrasing, and quoting of material in sources that either have been provided to you or that you have independently researched. For example, in paragraph 9 of the model argument synthesis, Harrison uses a long quotation from the Virginia Tech Review Panel report to make the point that college officials believed they were prohibited by federal privacy law from communicating with one another about disturbed students like Cho. You will find another long quotation later in the synthesis and a number of brief quotations woven into sentences throughout. In addition, you will find summaries and paraphrases. In each case, Harrison is careful to cite the source.

Provide Various Types of Evidence and Motivational Appeals

Keep in mind that you can use appeals to both reason and emotion. The appeal to reason is based on evidence that consists of a combination of *facts* and *expert testimony*. The sources by Tobin and Weigel, for example, offer facts about the evolution over the past few decades of the *in loco parentis* doctrine. Bernstein and McMurray interview college administrators at Cornell, M.I.T., and the University of Kentucky, who explain the changing policies at those institutions. The model synthesis makes an appeal to emotion by engaging the reader's self-interest: If campuses are to be made more secure from the acts of mentally disturbed persons, then college officials should take a proactive approach to monitoring and intervention.

Use Climactic Order

Climactic order is the arrangement of examples or evidence in order of anticipated impact on the reader, least to greatest. Organize by climactic order when you plan to offer a number of categories or elements of support for your claim. Recognize that some elements will be more important—and likely more persuasive—than others. The basic principle here is that you should *save the most important evidence for the end*, because whatever you say last is what readers are likely to remember best. A secondary principle is that whatever you say first is what they are *next* most likely to remember. Therefore, when you have several reasons to offer in support of your claim, an effective argument strategy is to present the second most important, then one or more additional reasons, and finally the most important reason. Paragraphs 7 to 11 of the model synthesis do exactly this.

Use Logical or Conventional Order

Using a logical or conventional order involves using as a template a preestablished pattern or plan for arguing your case.

- One common pattern is describing or arguing a *problem/solution*. Using this pattern, you begin with an introduction in which you typically define the problem, perhaps explain its origins, then offer one or more solutions, then conclude.
- Another common pattern presents *two sides of a controversy*. Using this pattern, you introduce the controversy and (in an argument synthesis) your own point of view or claim; then you explain the other side's arguments, providing reasons why your point of view should prevail.
- A third common pattern is *comparison-and-contrast*. This pattern is so important that we will discuss it separately in the next section.

The order in which you present elements of an argument is sometimes dictated by the conventions of the discipline in which you are writing. For example, lab reports and experiments in the sciences and social sciences often follow this pattern: *Opening* or *Introduction, Methods and Materials* (of the experiment or study), *Results, Discussion.* Legal arguments often follow the so-called IRAC format: *Issue, Rule, Application, Conclusion.*

Present and Respond to Counterarguments

When developing arguments on a controversial topic, you can effectively use *counterargument* to help support your claims. When you use counterargument, you present an argument *against* your claim and then show that this argument is weak or flawed. The advantage of this technique is that you demonstrate that you are aware of the other side of the argument and that you are prepared to answer it.

Here is how a counterargument is typically developed:

I. Introduction and claim
II. Main opposing argument
III. Refutation of opposing argument
IV. Main positive argument

Use Concession

Concession is a variation of counterargument. As in counterargument, you present an opposing viewpoint, but instead of dismissing that position, you *concede* that it has some validity and even some appeal, although your own position is the more reasonable one. This concession bolsters your standing as a fair-minded person who is not blind to the virtues of the other side. In the model synthesis, Harrison acknowledges the grief and sense of betrayal of the parents of the students who were killed. He concedes that parents have a right to expect that "the first priority of an educational institution must be to keep its students safe." But he insists that this goal of achieving campus safety can be accomplished without rolling back hard-won privacy rights.

Here is an outline for a typical concession argument:

I. Introduction and claim
II. Important opposing argument
III. Concession that this argument has some validity
IV. Positive argument(s) that acknowledge the counterargument and (possibly) incorporate some elements of it

Sometimes when you are developing a counterargument or concession argument, you may become convinced of the validity of the opposing point of view and change your own views. Don't be afraid of this happening. Writing is a tool for learning. To change your mind because of new evidence is a sign of flexibility and maturity, and your writing can only be the better for it.

DEVELOPING AND ORGANIZING SUPPORT FOR YOUR ARGUMENTS

- *Summarize, paraphrase, and quote supporting evidence.* Draw on the facts, ideas, and language in your sources.
- *Provide various types of evidence and motivational appeal.*
- *Use climactic order.* Save the most important evidence in support of your argument for the *end*, where it will have the most impact. Use the next most important evidence *first*.
- *Use logical or conventional order.* Use a form of organization appropriate to the topic, such as problem/solution; sides of a controversy; comparison/contrast; or a form of organization appropriate to the academic or professional discipline, such as a report of an experiment or a business plan.
- *Present and respond to counterarguments.* Anticipate and evaluate arguments against your position.
- *Use concession.* Concede that one or more arguments against your position have some validity; reassert, nonetheless, that your argument is the stronger one.

Avoid Common Fallacies in Developing and Using Support

In Chapter 2, in the section on critical reading, we considered criteria that, as a reader, you may use for evaluating informative and persuasive writing (see pp. 53, 52–59). We discussed how you can assess the accuracy, the significance, and the author's interpretation of the information presented. We also considered the importance in good argument of clearly defined key terms and avoiding the pitfalls of emotionally loaded language. Finally, we saw how to recognize such logical fallacies as either/or reasoning, faulty cause-and-effect reasoning, hasty generalization, and false analogy. As a writer, no less than as a critical reader, you need to be aware of these common problems and how to avoid them.

Be aware, also, of your responsibility to cite source materials appropriately. When you quote a source, double- and triple-check that you have done so accurately. When you summarize or paraphrase, take care to use your own language and sentence structures (though you can, of course, also quote within these forms). When you refer to someone else's idea—even if you are not quoting, summarizing, or paraphrasing it—give the source credit. By being ethical about the use of sources, you uphold the highest standards of the academic community.

THE COMPARISON-AND-CONTRAST SYNTHESIS

A particularly important type of argument synthesis is built on patterns of comparison and contrast. Techniques of comparison and contrast enable you to examine two subjects (or sources) in terms of one another. When you compare, you consider *similarities.* When you contrast, you consider *differences.* By comparing and contrasting, you perform a multifaceted analysis that often suggests subtleties that otherwise might not have come to your (or your reader's) attention.

To organize a comparison-and-contrast argument, you must carefully read sources in order to discover *significant criteria for analysis. A criterion* is a specific point to which both of your authors refer and about which they may agree or disagree. (For example, in a comparative report on compact cars, criteria for *comparison and contrast* might be road handling, fuel economy, and comfort of ride.) The best criteria are those that allow you not only to account for obvious similarities and differences—those concerning the main aspects of your sources or subjects—but also to plumb deeper, exploring subtle yet significant comparisons and contrasts among details or subcomponents, which you can then relate to your overall thesis.

Note that comparison-and-contrast is frequently not an end in itself, but serves some larger purpose. Thus, a comparison-and-contrast synthesis may be a component of a paper that is essentially a critique, an explanatory synthesis, an argument synthesis, or an analysis.

Organizing Comparison-and-Contrast Syntheses

Two basic approaches to organizing a comparison-and-contrast synthesis are organization by *source* and organization by *criteria.*

Organizing by Source or Subject

You can organize a comparative synthesis by first summarizing each of your sources or subjects and then discussing the significant similarities and differences between them. Having read the summaries and become familiar with the distinguishing features of each source, your readers will most likely be able to appreciate the more obvious similarities and differences. In the discussion, your task is to consider both the obvious and the subtle comparisons and contrasts, focusing on the most significant—that is, on those that most clearly support your thesis.

Organization by source or subject works best with passages that can be briefly summarized. If the summary of your source or subject becomes too long, your readers might have forgotten the points you made in the first summary when they are reading the second. A comparison-and-contrast synthesis organized by source or subject might proceed like this:

I. Introduce the paper; lead to thesis.

II. Summarize source/subject A by discussing its significant features.

III. Summarize source/subject B by discussing its significant features.

IV. Discuss in a paragraph (or two) the significant points of comparison and contrast between sources or subjects A and B. Alternatively, begin the comparison-contrast in Section III as you introduce source/subject B.

V. Conclude with a paragraph in which you summarize your points and, perhaps, raise and respond to pertinent questions.

Organizing by Criteria

Instead of summarizing entire sources one at a time with the intention of comparing them later, you could discuss two sources simultaneously, examining the views of each author point by point (criterion by criterion), comparing and contrasting these views in the process. The criterion approach is best used when you have a number of points to discuss or when passages or subjects are long and/or complex. A comparison-and-contrast synthesis organized by criteria might look like this:

I. Introduce the paper; lead to thesis.

II. Criterion 1
   A. Discuss what author 1 says about this point. Or present situation 1 in light of this point.
   B. Discuss what author 2 says about this point, comparing and contrasting 2's treatment of the point with 1's. Or present situation 2 in light of this point and explain its differences from situation 1.

III. Criterion 2
   A. Discuss what author 1 says about this point. Or present situation 1 in light of this point.
   B. Discuss what author 2 says about this point, comparing and contrasting 2's treatment of the point with 1's. Or present situation 2 in light of this point and explain its differences from situation 1.

And proceed so on, criterion by criterion, until you have completed your discussion. Be sure to arrange criteria with a clear method; knowing how the discussion of one criterion leads to the next will ensure smooth transitions throughout your paper. End by summarizing your key points and perhaps raising and responding to pertinent questions.

However you organize your comparison-and-contrast synthesis, keep in mind that comparing and contrasting are not ends in themselves. Your discussion should point to a conclusion, an answer to the question "So what—why bother to compare and contrast in the first place?" If your discussion is part of a larger synthesis, point to and support the larger claim. If you write a stand-alone comparison-and-contrast synthesis, though, you must by the final paragraph answer the "Why bother?" question. The model comparison-and-contrast synthesis that follows does exactly this.

Exercise 5.6

Comparing and Contrasting

Review the model argument synthesis (pp. 154–161) for elements of comparison and contrast—specifically those paragraphs concerning how Cornell University, M.I.T., and the University of Kentucky balance student privacy with the parental right to know about the health and welfare of their children.

1. From these paragraphs in the model paper, extract raw information concerning the positions of the three schools on the issue of student privacy, and then craft your own brief comparison-and-contrast synthesis. Identify criteria for comparison and contrast, and discuss the positions of each school in relation to these criteria. *Note:* For this exercise, do not concern yourself with parenthetical citation (that is, with identifying your source materials).

2. Write a paragraph or two that traces the development of comparison-and-contrast throughout the model paper. Having discussed the *how* and *where* of this development, discuss the *why.* Answer this question: Why has the writer used comparison-and-contrast? (Hint: It is not an end in itself.) To what use is it put?

A Case for Comparison-and-Contrast: World War I and World War II

Let's see how the principles of comparison-and-contrast can be applied to a response to a final examination question in a course on modern history. Imagine that having attended classes involving lecture and discussion, and having read excerpts from John Keegan's *The First World War* and Tony Judt's *Postwar: A History of Europe Since 1945,* you were presented with this examination question:

> Based on your reading to date, compare and contrast the two world wars in light of any four or five criteria you think significant. Once you have called careful attention to both similarities and differences, conclude with an observation. What have you learned? What can your comparative analysis teach us?

Comparison-and-Contrast Organized by Criteria

Here is a plan for a response, essentially a comparison-and-contrast synthesis, organized by *criteria* and beginning with the thesis—and the *claim.*

> *Thesis:* In terms of the impact on cities and civilian populations, the military aspects of the two wars in Europe, and their aftermaths, the differences between World War I and World War II considerably outweigh the similarities.

   I. Introduction. World Wars I and II were the most devastating conflicts in history. *Thesis.*

   II. Summary of main similarities: causes, countries involved, battlegrounds, global scope.

   III. First major difference: Physical impact of war.
      A. WWI was fought mainly in rural battlegrounds.
      B. In WWII cities were destroyed.

   IV. Second major difference: Effect on civilians.
      A. WWI fighting primarily involved soldiers.
      B. WWII involved not only military, but also massive noncombatant casualties: Civilian populations were displaced, forced into slave labor, and exterminated.

V. Third major difference: Combat operations.
   A. World War I, in its long middle phase, was characterized by trench warfare.
   B. During the middle phase of World War II, there was no major military action in Nazi-occupied Western Europe.

VI. Fourth major difference: Aftermath.
   A. Harsh war terms imposed on defeated Germany contributed significantly to the rise of Hitler and World War II.
   B. Victorious allies helped rebuild West Germany after World War II but allowed Soviets to take over Eastern Europe.

VII. Conclusion. Since the end of World War II, wars have been far smaller in scope and destructiveness, and warfare has expanded to involve stateless combatants committed to acts of terror.

The following model exam response, a comparison-and-contrast synthesis organized by criteria, is written according to the preceding plan. (Thesis and topic sentences are highlighted.)

MODEL EXAM RESPONSE

World War I (1914–1918) and World War II (1939–1945) were the most catastrophic and destructive conflicts in human history. For those who believed in the steady but inevitable progress of civilization, it was impossible to imagine that two wars in the first half of the twentieth century could reach levels of barbarity and horror that would outstrip those of any previous era. Historians estimate that more than 22 million people, soldiers and civilians, died in World War I; they estimate that between 40 and 50 million died in World War II. In many ways, these two conflicts were similar: They were fought on many of the same European and Russian battlegrounds, with more or less the same countries on opposing sides. Even many of the same people were involved: Winston Churchill and Adolf Hitler figured in both wars. And the main outcome in each case was the same: total defeat for Germany. However, in terms of the impact on cities and civilian populations, the military aspects of the two wars in Europe, and their aftermaths, the differences between World Wars I and II considerably outweigh the similarities.

The similarities are clear enough. In fact, many historians regard World War II as a continuation--after an intermission of about twenty years--of World War I. One of the main causes of each war was Germany's dissatisfaction and frustration with what it perceived as its diminished place in the world. Hitler launched World War II partly out of revenge for Germany's humiliating defeat in World War I. In each conflict, Germany and its allies (the Central Powers in WWI, the Axis in WWII) went to war against France, Great Britain, Russia (the Soviet Union in WWII), and eventually, the United States. Though neither conflict included literally the entire world, the participation of countries not only in Europe but also in the Middle East, the Far East, and the Western Hemisphere made both conflicts global in scope. And as indicated earlier, the number of casualties in each war was unprecedented in history, partly because modern technology had enabled the creation of deadlier weapons--including tanks, heavy artillery, and aircraft--than had ever before been used in warfare.

3   Despite these similarities, the differences between the two world wars are considerably more significant. One of the most noticeable differences was the physical impact of each war in Europe and in Russia--the western and eastern fronts. The physical destruction of World War I was confined largely to the battlefield. The combat took place almost entirely in the rural areas of Europe and Russia. No major cities were destroyed in the first war; cathedrals, museums, government buildings, urban houses and apartments were left untouched. During the second war, in contrast, almost no city or town of any size emerged unscathed. Rotterdam, Warsaw, London, Minsk, and--when the Allies began their counterattack--almost every major city in Germany and Japan, including Berlin and Tokyo, were flattened. Of course, the physical devastation of the cities created millions of refugees, a phenomenon never experienced in World War I.

4   The fact that World War II was fought in the cities as well as on the battlefields meant that the second war had a much greater impact on civilians than did the first war. With few exceptions, the civilians in Europe during WWI were not driven from their homes, forced into slave labor, starved, tortured, or systematically exterminated. But all of these crimes happened routinely during WWII. The Nazi occupation of Europe meant that the civilian populations of France, Belgium, Norway, the Netherlands, and other conquered lands--along with the industries, railroads, and farms of these countries--were put into the service of the Third Reich. Millions of people from conquered Europe, those who were not sent directly to the death camps, were forcibly transported to Germany and put to work in support of the war effort.

5   During both wars, the Germans were fighting on two fronts: the western front in Europe and the eastern front in Russia. But while both wars were characterized by intense military activity during their initial and final phases, the middle and longest phases--at least in Europe--differed considerably. The middle phase of the First World War was characterized

by trench warfare, a relatively static form of military activity in which fronts seldom moved, or moved only a few hundred yards at a time, even after major battles. By contrast, in the years between the German conquest of most of Europe by early 1941 and the Allied invasion of Normandy in mid-1944, there was no major fighting in Nazi-occupied Western Europe. (The land battles then shifted to North Africa and the Soviet Union.)

And of course, the two world wars differed in their aftermaths. The most significant consequence of World War I was that the humiliating and costly war reparations imposed on the defeated Germany by the terms of the 1919 Treaty of Versailles made possible the rise of Hitler and thus led directly to World War II. In contrast, after the end of the Second World War in 1945, the Allies helped rebuild West Germany (the portion of a divided Germany that it controlled), transformed the new country into a democracy, and helped make it one of the most thriving economies of the world. But perhaps the most significant difference in the aftermath of each war involved Russia. That country, in a considerably weakened state, pulled out of World War I a year before hostilities ended so that it could consolidate its 1917 Revolution. Russia then withdrew into itself and took no significant part in European affairs until the Nazi invasion of the Soviet Union in 1941. In contrast, it was the Red Army in World War II that was most responsible for the crushing defeat of Germany. In recognition of its efforts and of its enormous sacrifices, the Allies allowed the Soviet Union to take control of the countries of Eastern Europe after the war, leading to fifty years of totalitarian rule--and the Cold War.

⑥

While the two world wars that devastated much of Europe were similar in that, at least according to some historians, they were the same war interrupted by two decades, and similar in that combatants killed more efficiently than armies throughout history ever had, the differences between the wars were significant. In terms of the physical impact of the fighting, the impact on civilians, the action on the battlefield at mid-war, and the aftermaths, World Wars I and II differed in ways that matter to us decades later. The wars in Iraq, Afghanistan, and Bosnia have involved an alliance of nations pitted against single nations; but we have not seen, since the two world wars, grand alliances moving vast armies across continents. The destruction implied by such action is almost unthinkable today. Warfare is changing, and "stateless" combatants like Hamas and Al Qaeda wreak destruction of their own. But we may never again see, one hopes, the devastation that follows when multiple nations on opposing sides of a conflict throw millions of soldiers--and civilians--into harm's way.

⑦

The Strategy of the Exam Response

The general strategy of this argument is an organization by *criteria*. The writer argues that although the two world wars exhibited some similarities, the differences between the two conflicts were more significant. Note that the writer's thesis doesn't merely state these significant differences; it also presents them in a way that anticipates both the content and the structure of the response to follow.

In argument terms, the *claim* the writer makes is the conclusion that the two global conflicts were significantly different, if superficially similar. The *assumption* is that key differences and similarities are clarified by employing specific criteria: the impact of the wars upon cities and civilian populations and the consequences of the Allied victories. The *support* comes in the form of historical facts regarding the levels of casualties, the scope of destruction, the theaters of conflict, the events following the conclusions of the wars, and so on.

- **Paragraph 1:** The writer begins by commenting on the unprecedented level of destruction of World Wars I and II and concludes with the thesis summarizing the key similarities and differences.

- **Paragraph 2:** The writer summarizes the key similarities in the two wars: the wars' causes, their combatants, their global scope, and the level of destructiveness made possible by modern weaponry.

- **Paragraph 3:** The writer discusses the first of the key differences: the battlegrounds of World War I were largely rural; the battlegrounds of World War II included cities that were targeted and destroyed.

- **Paragraph 4:** The writer discusses the second of the key differences: the impact on civilians. In World War I, civilians were generally spared from the direct effects of combat; in World War II, civilians were targeted by the Nazis for systematic displacement and destruction.

- **Paragraph 5:** The writer discusses the third key difference: Combat operations during the middle phase of World War I were characterized by static trench warfare. During World War II, in contrast, there were no major combat operations in Nazi-occupied Western Europe during the middle phase of the conflict.

- **Paragraph 6:** The writer focuses on the fourth key difference: the aftermath of the two wars. After World War I, the victors imposed harsh conditions on a defeated Germany, leading to the rise of Hitler and the Second World War. After World War II, the Allies helped Germany rebuild and thrive. However, the Soviet victory in 1945 led to its postwar domination of Eastern Europe.

- **Paragraph 7:** In the conclusion, the writer sums up the key similarities and differences just covered and makes additional comments about the course of more-recent wars since World War II. In this way, the writer responds to the questions posed at the end of the assignment: "What have you learned? What can your comparative analysis teach us?"

SUMMARY OF SYNTHESIS CHAPTERS

In this chapter and in Chapter 4, we've considered three main types of synthesis: the *explanatory synthesis*, the *argument synthesis*, and the *comparison-and-contrast synthesis*. Although for ease of comprehension we've placed these in separate categories, the types are not mutually exclusive. Argument syntheses often include extended sections of explanation and/or comparison-and-contrast. Explanations also commonly include sections of comparison-and-contrast. Which type of synthesis you choose will depend on your *purpose* and the method that you decide is best suited to achieve this purpose.

If your main purpose is to help your audience understand a particular subject, and in particular to help them understand the essential elements or significance of this subject, then you will be composing an explanatory synthesis. If your main purpose, on the other hand, is to persuade your audience to agree with your viewpoint on a subject, or to change their minds, or to decide on a particular course of action, then you will be composing an argument synthesis. If your purpose is to clarify similarities or differences, you will compose a comparison-and-contrast synthesis—which may be a paper in itself (either an argument or an explanation) or part of a larger paper (again, either an argument or an explanation).

In planning and drafting these syntheses, you can draw on a variety of strategies: supporting your claims by summarizing, paraphrasing, and quoting from your sources; using appeals to *logos*, *pathos*, and *ethos*; and choosing from among strategies such as climactic or conventional order, counterargument, and concession the approach that will best help you to achieve your purpose.

The strategies of synthesis you've practiced in these two chapters are common to the research paper. The research paper involves all of the skills in preparing summary, critique, and synthesis that we've discussed thus far, the main difference being that you won't find the sources needed to write the paper in this particular text. We'll discuss approaches to locating and critically evaluating sources, selecting material from among them to provide support for your claims, and, finally, documenting your sources in standard professional formats.

We turn now to analysis, which is another important strategy for academic thinking and writing. Chapter 6, "Analysis," will introduce you to a strategy that, like synthesis, draws upon all the strategies you've been practicing as you move through *Writing and Reading Across the Curriculum.*

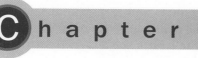

Analysis

6

After completing this chapter, you will be able to:

LO 6.1   Establish the principle, the definition, or the personal perspective on which to base an analysis.

LO 6.2   Write an analysis considering purpose, using an analytical principle, formulating a thesis, and developing a plan.

WHAT IS AN ANALYSIS?

An *analysis* is a type of argument in which you study the parts of something—a physical object, a work of art, a person or group of people, an event, or a scientific, economic, or sociological phenomenon—to understand how it works, what it means, or why it might be significant. The writer of an analysis uses an analytical tool: a *principle* or *definition* on the basis of which the subject of study can be divided into parts and examined.

Here are excerpts from two analyses of the movie version of L. Frank Baum's *The Wizard of Oz*:

> At the dawn of adolescence, the very time she should start to distance herself from Aunt Em and Uncle Henry, the surrogate parents who raised her on their Kansas farm, Dorothy Gale experiences a hurtful reawakening of her fear that these loved ones will be rudely ripped from her, especially her Aunt (Em—M for Mother!).*

> [*The Wizard of Oz*] was originally written as a political allegory about grass-roots protest. It may seem harder to believe than Emerald City, but the Tin Woodsman is the industrial worker, the Scarecrow [is] the struggling farmer, and the Wizard is the president, who is powerful only as long as he succeeds in deceiving the people.†

---

*Harvey Greenberg, *The Movies on Your Mind* (New York: Dutton, 1975).
†Peter Dreier, "Oz Was Almost Reality," *Cleveland Plain Dealer* 3 Sept. 1989.

As these paragraphs suggest, what you discover through analysis depends entirely on the principle or definition you use to make your insights. Is *The Wizard of Oz* the story of a girl's psychological development, or is it a story about politics? The answer is *both*. In the first example, the psychiatrist Harvey Greenberg applies the principles of his profession and, not surprisingly, sees *The Wizard of Oz* in psychological terms. In the second example, a newspaper reporter applies the political theories of Karl Marx and, again not surprisingly, discovers a story about politics.

Different as they are, these analyses share an important quality: Each is the result of a specific principle or definition used as a tool to divide an object into parts in order to see what it means and how it works. The writer's choice of analytical tool simultaneously creates and limits the possibilities for analysis. Thus, working with the principles of Freud, Harvey Greenberg sees *The Wizard of Oz* in

WHERE DO WE FIND WRITTEN ANALYSES?

Here are just a few of the types of writing that involve analysis:

Academic Writing

- **Experimental and lab reports** analyze the meaning or implications of the study results in the Discussion section.
- **Research papers** analyze information in sources or apply theories to material being reported.
- **Process analyses** break down the steps or stages involved in completing a process.
- **Literary analyses** examine characterization, plot, imagery, or other elements in works of literature.
- **Essay exams** demonstrate understanding of course material by analyzing data using course concepts.

Workplace Writing

- **Grant proposals** analyze the issues you seek funding for, in order to address them.
- **Reviews of the arts** employ dramatic or literary analysis to assess artistic works.
- **Business plans** break down and analyze capital outlays, expenditures, profits, materials, and the like.
- **Medical charts** record analytical thinking and writing in relation to patient symptoms and possible options.
- **Legal briefs** break down and analyze facts of cases and elements of legal precedents, and apply legal rulings and precedents to new situations.
- **Case studies** describe and analyze the particulars of a specific medical, social service, advertising, or business case.

psychological, not political, terms; working with the theories of Karl Marx, Peter Dreier understands the movie in terms of the economic relationships among the characters. It's as if the writer of an analysis who adopts one analytical tool puts on a pair of glasses and sees an object in a specific way. Another writer, using a different tool (and a different pair of glasses), sees the object differently.

You might protest: Are there as many analyses of *The Wizard of Oz* as there are people to read the book or to see the movie? Yes, or at least as many analyses as there are analytical tools. This does not mean that all analyses are equally valid or useful. Each writer must convince the reader, using the power of her or his argument. In creating an analytical discussion, the writer must organize a series of related insights using the analytical tool to examine first one part and then another part of the object being studied. To read Harvey Greenberg's essay on *The Wizard of Oz* is to find paragraph after paragraph of related insights—first about Aunt Em, then the Wicked Witch, then Toto, and then the Wizard. All these insights point to Greenberg's single conclusion: that "Dorothy's 'trip' is a marvelous metaphor for the psychological journey every adolescent must make." Without Greenberg's analysis, we would probably not have thought about the movie as a psychological journey. This is precisely the power of an analysis: its ability to reveal objects or events in ways we would not otherwise have considered.

The writer's challenge is to convince readers that (1) the analytical tool being applied is legitimate and well matched to the object being studied; and (2) the analytical tool is being used systematically and insightfully to divide the object into parts and to make a coherent, meaningful statement about these parts and the object as a whole.

HOW TO WRITE ANALYSES

Let's consider a more extended example of analysis, one that approaches excessive TV watching as a type of addiction. This analytical passage illustrates the two defining features of the analysis: a statement of an analytical principle or definition and the use of that principle or definition in closely examining an object, behavior, or event. As you read, try to identify these features. An exercise with questions for discussion follows the passage.

THE PLUG-IN DRUG

Marie Winn

This analysis of television viewing as an addictive behavior appeared originally in Marie Winn's book *The Plug-In Drug: Television, Computers, and Family Life (2002)*. A writer and media critic, Winn has been interested in the effects of television on both individuals and the larger culture. In this passage, she carefully defines the term *addiction* and then applies it systematically to the behavior under study.

The word "addiction" is often used loosely and wryly in conversation. People will refer to themselves as "mystery-book addicts" or "cookie addicts." E. B. White wrote of his annual surge of interest in gardening: "We are hooked and are making an attempt to kick the habit." Yet nobody really believes that reading mysteries or ordering seeds by catalogue is serious enough to be compared with addictions to heroin or alcohol. In these cases the word "addiction" is used jokingly to denote a tendency to overindulge in some pleasurable activity.

People often refer to being "hooked on TV." Does this, too, fall into the light-hearted category of cookie eating and other pleasures that people pursue with unusual intensity? Or is there a kind of television viewing that falls into the more serious category of destructive addiction?

Not unlike drugs or alcohol, the television experience allows the participant to blot out the real world and enter into a pleasurable and passive mental state. To be sure, other experiences, notably reading, also provide a temporary respite from reality. But it's much easier to stop reading and return to reality than to stop watching television. The entry into another world offered by reading includes an easily accessible return ticket. The entry via television does not. In this way television viewing, for those vulnerable to addiction, is more like drinking or taking drugs—once you start it's hard to stop.

Just as alcoholics are only vaguely aware of their addiction, feeling that they control their drinking more than they really do ("I can cut it out any time I want—I just like to have three or four drinks before dinner"), many people overestimate their control over television watching. Even as they put off other activities to spend hour after hour watching television, they feel they could easily resume living in a different, less passive style. But somehow or other while the television set is present in their homes, it just stays on. With television's easy gratifications available, those other activities seem to take too much effort.

5   A heavy viewer (a college English instructor) observes:

> I find television almost irresistible. When the set is on, I cannot ignore it. I can't turn it off. I feel sapped, will-less, enervated. As I reach out to turn off the set, the strength goes out of my arms. So I sit there for hours and hours.

Self-confessed television addicts often feel they "ought" to do other things— but the fact that they don't read and don't plant their garden or sew or crochet or play games or have conversations means that those activities are no longer as desirable as television viewing. In a way, the lives of heavy viewers are as unbalanced by their television "habit" as drug addicts' or alcoholics' lives. They are living in a holding pattern, as it were, passing up the activities that lead to growth or development or a sense of accomplishment. This is one reason people talk about their television viewing so ruefully, so apologetically. They are aware that it is an unproductive experience, that by any human measure almost any other endeavor is more worthwhile.

It is the adverse effect of television viewing on the lives of so many people that makes it feel like a serious addiction. The television habit distorts the sense of time. It renders other experiences vague and curiously unreal while taking on a greater reality for itself. It weakens relationships by reducing and sometimes eliminating normal opportunities for talking, for communicating.

And yet television does not satisfy, else why would the viewer continue to watch hour after hour, day after day? "The measure of health," wrote the psychiatrist Lawrence Kubie, "is flexibility...and especially the freedom to cease when sated." But heavy television viewers can never be sated with their television experiences. These do not provide the true nourishment that satiation requires, and thus they find that they cannot stop watching.

Exercise 6.1

Reading Critically: Winn

In an analysis, an author first presents the analytical principle in full and then systematically applies parts of the principle to the object or phenomenon under study. In her brief analysis of television viewing, Marie Winn pursues an alternative, though equally effective, strategy by *distributing* parts of her analytical principle across the essay. Locate where Winn defines key elements of addiction. Locate where she uses each element as an analytical lens to examine television viewing as a form of addiction.

What function does ¶ 4 play in the analysis?

In the first two paragraphs, how does Winn create a funnel-like effect that draws readers into the heart of her analysis?

Recall a few television programs that genuinely moved you, educated you, humored you, or stirred you to worthwhile reflection or action. To what extent does Winn's analysis describe your positive experiences as a television viewer? (Consider how Winn might argue that from within an addicted state, a person may feel humored, moved, or educated but is in fact—from a sober outsider's point of view—deluded.) If Winn's analysis of television viewing as an addiction does *not* account for your experience, does it follow that her analysis is flawed? Explain.

Locate and Apply an Analytic Tool

The general purpose of all analysis is to enhance one's understanding of the subject under consideration. A good analysis provides a valuable—if sometimes unusual or unexpected—point of view, a way of *seeing*, a way of *interpreting* some phenomenon, person, event, policy, or pattern of behavior that otherwise may appear random or unexplainable. How well the analysis achieves its purpose depends upon the suitability to the subject and the precision of the analytical tools selected and upon the skill with which the writer (or speaker) applies these tools. Each reader must determine for her- or himself whether the analysis enhances understanding or—in the opposite case—is merely confusing or irrelevant. To what extent does it enhance your understanding of *The Wizard of Oz* to view the story in psychological terms? In political terms? To what extent does it enhance your understanding of excessive TV watching to view such behavior as an addiction?

When you are faced with writing an analysis, consider these two general strategies:

- Locate an analytic tool—a principle or definition that makes a general statement about the way something works.
- Systematically apply this principle or definition to the subject under consideration.

Let's more fully consider each of these strategies.

Locate an Analytic Tool

In approaching her subject, Marie Winn finds in the definition of "addiction" a useful principle for making sense of the way some people watch TV. The word "addiction," she notes, "is used jokingly to denote a tendency to overindulge in some pleasurable activity." The question she decides to tackle is whether, in the case of watching TV, such overindulgence is harmless, or whether it is destructive, and thus constitutes an addiction.

Make yourself aware, as both writer and reader, of a tool's strengths and limitations. Pose these questions of the analytical principle and definitions you use:

- Are they accurate?
- Are they well accepted?
- Do you accept them?
- How successfully do they account for or throw light upon the phenomenon under consideration?
- What are the arguments against them?
- What are their limitations?

Since every principle of definition used in an analysis is the end product of an argument, you are entitled—even obligated—to challenge it. If the analytical tool is flawed, the analysis that follows from it will necessarily be flawed.

Some, for example, would question whether addiction is a useful concept to apply to television viewing. First, we usually think of addiction as applying only to substances such as alcohol, nicotine, or drugs (whether legal or illegal). Second, many people think that the word "addiction" carries inappropriate moral connotations: We disapprove of addicts and think that they have only themselves to blame for their condition. For a time, the American Psychiatric Association dropped the word "addiction" from its definitive guide to psychological disorders, the *Diagnostic and Statistical Manual of Mental Disorders* (DSM), in favor of the more neutral term "dependence." (The latest edition of the DSM has returned to the term "addiction.")

On the other hand, "addiction"—also known as "impulse control disorder"—has long been applied to behavior as well as to substances. People are said to be addicted to gambling, to shopping, to eating, to sex, even to hoarding newspapers. The editors of the new DSM are likely to add Internet addiction to the list of impulse control disorders. The term even has national implications: Many argue that this country must break its "addiction" to oil. Thus, there is considerable precedent for Winn to argue that excessive TV watching constitutes an addiction.

Apply the Analytic Tool

Having suggested that TV watching may be an addiction, Winn uses established psychological criteria* to identify the chief components of addictive behavior. She then applies each one of them to the behavior under consideration. In doing so, she presents her case that TV is a "plug-in drug"; and her readers are free to evaluate the success and persuasiveness of her analysis.

In the body of her analysis, Winn systematically applies the component elements of addiction to TV watching. She does this by identifying the major components of addiction and applying them to television watching. Users:

1. Turn away from the real world.
2. Overestimate how much control they have over their addiction.
3. Lead unbalanced lives and turn away from social activities.
4. Develop a distorted sense of time.
5. Are never satisfied with their use.

Analysis Across the Curriculum

The principle that you select can be a theory as encompassing as the statement that *myths are the enemy of truth*. It can be as modest as the definition of a term such as *addiction* or *comfort*. As you move from one subject area to another, the principles and definitions you use for analysis will change, as these assignments illustrate:

Sociology: Write a paper in which you place yourself in American society by locating both your absolute position and relative rank on each single criterion of social stratification used by Lenski and Lenski. For each criterion, state whether you have attained your social position by yourself or have "inherited" that status from your parents.

Literature: Apply principles of Jungian psychology to Hawthorne's "Young Goodman Brown." In your reading of the story, apply Jung's principles of the *shadow*, *persona*, and *anima*.

---

*For example, the Web site AddictionsandRecovery.org, drawing upon the *Diagnostic and Statistical Manual of Mental Disorders* (DSM) criteria, identifies seven components of substance addiction. A person who answers yes to three of the following questions meets the medical definition of addiction: **Tolerance** (increased use of drugs or alcohol increased over time); **Withdrawal** (adverse physical or emotional reactions to not using); **Difficulty controlling your use** (using more than you would like); **Negative consequences** (using even though use negatively affects mood, self-esteem, health, job, or family); **Neglecting or postponing activities** (putting off or reducing social, recreational, work in order to use); **Spending significant time or emotional energy** (spending significant time obtaining, using, concealing, planning, recovering from, or thinking about use); **Desire to cut down**.

Physics: Use Newton's second law ($F = ma$) to analyze the acceleration of a fixed pulley from which two weights hang: m_1 (.45 kg) and m_2 (.90 kg). Explain in a paragraph the principle of Newton's law and your method of applying it to solve the problem. Assume your reader is not comfortable with mathematical explanations: Do not use equations in your paragraph.

Finance: Using Guilford C. Babcock's "Concept of Sustainable Growth" (*Financial Analysis* 26 [May–June 1970]: 108–114), analyze the stock price appreciation of the XYZ Corporation, figures for which are attached.

The analytical tools to be applied in these assignments must be appropriate to the discipline. Writing in response to the sociology assignment, you would use sociological principles developed by Lenski and Lenski. In your literature class,

GUIDELINES FOR WRITING ANALYSES

Unless you are asked to follow a specialized format, especially in the sciences or the social sciences, you can present your analysis as a paper by following the guidelines below. As you move from one class to another, from discipline to discipline, the principles and definitions you use as the basis for your analyses will change, but the following basic components of analysis will remain the same.

- *Create a context for your analysis.* Introduce and summarize for readers the object, event, or behavior to be analyzed. Present a strong case for why an analysis is needed: Give yourself a motivation to write, and give readers a motivation to read. Consider setting out a problem, puzzle, or question to be investigated.
- *Locate an analytic tool—a principle or definition that will form the basis of your analysis.* Plan to devote an early part of your analysis to arguing for the validity of this principle or definition if your audience is not likely to understand it or if they are likely to think that the principle or definition is not valuable.
- *Analyze your topic by applying your selected analytic tool to the topic's component elements.* Systematically apply elements of the analytic tool to parts of the activity or object under study. You can do this by posing specific questions, based on your analytic principle or definition, about the object or phenomenon. Discuss what you find, part by part (organized perhaps by question), in clearly defined subsections of the paper.
- *Conclude by stating clearly what is significant about your analysis.* When considering your analytical paper as a whole, what new or interesting insights have you made concerning the object under study? To what extent has your application of the definition or principle helped you to explain how the object works, what it might mean, or why it is significant?

you would use principles of Jungian psychology; in physics, Newton's second law; and in finance, a particular writer's concept of "sustainable growth." But whatever discipline you are working in, the first part of your analysis will clearly state which (and whose) principles and definitions you are applying. For audiences unfamiliar with these principles, you will need to explain them; if you anticipate objections to their use, you will need to argue that they are legitimate principles capable of helping you conduct the analysis.

Formulate a Thesis

Like any other thesis, the thesis of an analysis compresses into a single sentence the main idea of your presentation. Some authors omit an explicit thesis statement, preferring to leave the thesis implied. Underlying Winn's analysis, for example, is an implied thesis: "By applying my multipart definition, we can understand television viewing as an addiction." Other authors may take two or perhaps even more sentences to articulate their thesis. But stated or implied, one sentence or more, your thesis must be clearly formulated at least in your own mind if your analysis is to hold together.

The analysis itself, as we have indicated, is a two-part argument. The first part states and establishes your use of a certain principle or definition that serves as your analytic tool. The second part applies specific parts or components of the principle or definition to the topic at hand.

Develop an Organizational Plan

You will benefit enormously in the writing of a first draft if you plan out the logic of your analysis. Turn key elements of your analytical principle or definition into questions, and then develop the paragraph-by-paragraph logic of the paper.

Turning Key Elements of a Principle or a Definition into Questions

Prepare for an analysis by phrasing questions based on the definition or principle you are going to apply, and then directing those questions to the activity or object to be studied. The method is straightforward:

- State as clearly as possible the principle or definition to be applied.
- Divide the principle or definition into its parts.
- Using each part, form a question.

For example, Marie Winn develops a multipart definition of addiction, each part of which is readily turned into a question that she directs at a specific behavior: television viewing. Her analysis of television viewing can be understood as *responses* to each of her analytical questions. Note that in her brief analysis, Winn does not first define addiction and then analyze television viewing. Rather, *as* she defines aspects of addiction, she analyzes television viewing.

Developing the Paragraph-by-Paragraph Logic of Your Paper

The following paragraph from Marie Winn's analysis illustrates the typical logic of a paragraph in an analytical paper:

> Self-confessed television addicts often feel they "ought" to do other things—but the fact that they don't read and don't plant their garden or sew or crochet or play games or have conversations means that those activities are no longer as desirable as television viewing. In a way, the lives of heavy viewers are as unbalanced by their television "habit" as drug addicts' or alcoholics' lives. They are living in a holding pattern, as it were, passing up the activities that lead to growth or development or a sense of accomplishment. This is one reason people talk about their television viewing so ruefully, so apologetically. They are aware that it is an unproductive experience, that by any human measure almost any other endeavor is more worthwhile.

We see in this paragraph the typical logic of an analysis:

- *The writer introduces a specific analytical tool.* Winn refers to one of the established components of addiction: The addictive behavior crowds out and takes precedence over other, more fruitful activities.

- *The writer applies this analytical tool to the object being examined.* Winn points out that people who spend their time watching television "don't read and don't plant their garden or sew or crochet or play games or have conversations...."

- *The writer uses the tool to identify and then examine the significance of some aspect of the subject under discussion.* Having applied the analytic tool to the subject of television viewing, Winn generalizes about the significance of what is revealed: "This is one reason people talk about their television viewing so ruefully, so apologetically. They are aware that it is an unproductive experience, that by any human measure almost any other endeavor is worthwhile."

An analytic paper takes shape when a writer creates a series of such paragraphs, links them with an overall logic, and draws a general conclusion concerning what was learned through the analysis. Here is the logical organization of Marie Winn's analysis:

- **Paragraph 1:** Introduces the word "addiction" and indicates how the term is generally used.
- **Paragraph 2:** Suggests that television watching might be viewed as a "destructive addiction."
- **Paragraph 3:** Discusses the first component of the definition of addiction: an experience that "allows the participant to blot out the real world and enter into a pleasurable and passive mental state." Applies this first component to television viewing.

- **Paragraphs 4 and 5:** Discusses the second component of addiction—the participant has an illusion of control—and applies this to the experience of television viewing.

- **Paragraph 6:** Discusses the third component of addiction—because it requires so much time and emotional energy, the addictive behavior crowds out other, more productive or socially desirable activities—and applies this to the experience of television viewing.

- **Paragraph 7:** Discusses the fourth component of addiction—the negative consequences arising from the behavior—and applies this to the experience of television viewing.

- **Paragraph 8:** Discusses the fifth component of addiction—the participant is never satisfied because the experience is essentially empty—and applies this to the experience of television viewing. Note that in this paragraph, Winn brings in for support a relevant quotation by the psychiatrist Lawrence Kubie.

Draft and Revise Your Analysis

You will usually need at least two drafts to produce a paper that presents your idea clearly. The biggest changes in your paper will typically come between your first and second drafts. No paper that you write, analysis or otherwise, will be complete until you revise and refine your single compelling idea—in the case of analysis, your analytical conclusion about what the object, event, or behavior being examined means or how it is significant. You revise and refine by evaluating your first draft, bringing to it many of the same questions you pose when evaluating any piece of writing:

- Are the facts accurate?
- Are my opinions supported by evidence?
- Are the opinions of others authoritative?
- Are my assumptions clearly stated?
- Are key terms clearly defined?
- Is the presentation logical?
- Are all parts of the presentation well developed?
- Are significant opposing points of view presented?

Address these same questions to the first draft of your analysis, and you will have solid information to guide your revision.

Write an Analysis, Not a Summary

The most common error made in writing analyses—an error that is *fatal* to the form—is to present readers with a summary only. For analyses to succeed, you must *apply* a principle or definition and reach a conclusion about the object, event, or behavior you are examining. By definition, a summary (see Chapter 1) includes none of your own conclusions. Summary is naturally a part of analysis; you will need to summarize the object or activity being examined and, depending on the audience's needs, summarize the principle or definition being applied. But in an analysis, you must take the next step and share insights that suggest the meaning or significance of some object, event, or behavior.

Make Your Analysis Systematic

Analyses should give the reader the sense of a systematic, purposeful examination. Marie Winn's analysis illustrates the point: She sets out specific elements of addictive behavior in separate paragraphs and then uses each, within its paragraph, to analyze television viewing. Winn is systematic in her method, and we are never in doubt about her purpose.

Imagine another analysis in which a writer lays out four elements of a definition and then applies only two, without explaining the logic for omitting the others. Or imagine an analysis in which the writer offers a principle for analysis but directs it to only a half or a third of the object being discussed, without providing a rationale for doing so. In both cases the writer fails to deliver on a promise basic to analyses: Once a principle or definition is presented, it should be thoroughly and systematically applied.

Answer the "So What?" Question

An analysis should make readers *want* to read it. It should give readers a sense of getting to the heart of the matter, that what is important in the object or activity under analysis is being laid bare and discussed in revealing ways. If when rereading the first draft of your analysis, you cannot imagine readers saying, "I never thought of _____ this way," then something may be seriously wrong. Reread closely to determine why the paper might leave readers flat and exhausted, as opposed to feeling that they have gained new and important insights. Closely reexamine your own motivations for writing. Have *you* learned anything significant through the analysis? If not, neither will readers, and they will turn away. If you have gained important insights through your analysis, communicate them clearly. At some point, pull together your related insights and say, in effect, "Here's how it all adds up."

Attribute Sources Appropriately

In an analysis, you often work with just a few sources and apply insights from them to some object or phenomenon you want to understand more thoroughly. Because you are not synthesizing large quantities of data, and because the strength of an analysis derives mostly from *your* application of a principle or definition, the opportunities for not appropriately citing sources are diminished. However, take special care to cite and quote, as necessary, those sources that you draw upon throughout the analysis.

CRITICAL READING FOR ANALYSIS

- *Read to get a sense of the whole in relation to its parts.* Whether you are clarifying for yourself a principle or a definition to be used in an analysis, or you are reading a text that you will analyze, understand how parts function to create the whole. If a definition or principle consists of parts, use them to organize sections of your analysis. If your goal is to analyze a text, be aware of its structure: Note the title and subtitle; identify the main point and subordinate points and where they are located; break the material into sections.
- *Read to discover relationships within the object being analyzed.* Watch for patterns. When you find them, be alert, for they create an occasion to analyze, to use a principle or definition as a guide in discussing what the patterns may mean.

> In fiction, a pattern might involve responses of characters to events or to each other, the recurrence of certain words or phrasings, images, themes, or turns of plot (to name a few examples).

> In poetry, a pattern might involve rhyme schemes, rhythm, imagery, figurative or literal language, and more.

The challenge to you as a reader is first to see a pattern (perhaps using a guiding principle or definition to do so) and then to locate other instances of that pattern. Reading carefully in this way prepares you to conduct an analysis.

When *Your* Perspective Guides the Analysis

In some cases, a writer's analysis of a phenomenon or a work of art may not result from anything as structured as a principle or a definition. It may instead follow from the writer's cultural or personal outlook, perspective, or interests. Imagine reading a story or observing the lines of a new building and being asked to analyze it—based not on someone else's definition or principle, but on your own. Your analysis of the story might largely be determined by your preference for fast pacing; intrepid, resourceful heroes; and pitiless, black-hearted villains. Among the principles you might use in analyzing the building are your admiration for curved exterior surfaces and the imaginative use of glass.

Like analyses based on principles or definitions, analyses based on one's personal perspective probe the parts of things to understand how they work and what they mean. They are likewise carefully structured, examining one part of a phenomenon at a time. The essential purpose of the analysis, to *reveal*, remains unchanged. This goal distinguishes the analysis from the critique, whose main purpose is to *evaluate* and *assess validity*.

An intriguing example of how shifts in personal perspective over time may affect one's analysis of a particular phenomenon is offered by Terri Martin Hekker. In 1977, Hekker wrote an op-ed for the *New York Times*, viewing traditional marriage from a perspective very different from that of contemporary feminists, who, she felt, valued self-fulfillment through work more than their roles as traditional housewives:

> I come from a long line of women...who never knew they were unfulfilled. I can't testify that they were happy, but they *were* cheerful.... They took pride in a clean, comfortable home and satisfaction in serving a good meal because no one had explained to them that the only work worth doing is that for which you get paid.

Hekker's view of the importance of what she calls "housewifery"—the role of the traditional American wife and mother—derived from her own personal standards and ideals, which themselves derived from a cultural perspective that she admitted were no longer in fashion in the late 1970s.

Almost thirty years later (2006), Hekker's perspective had dramatically shifted. Her shattering experiences in the wake of her unexpected divorce had changed her view— and as a result, her analysis—of the status, value, and prospects of the traditional wife:

> Like most loyal wives of our generation, we'd contemplated eventual widowhood but never thought we'd end up divorced.... If I had it to do over again, I'd still marry the man I married and have my children.... But I would have used the years after my youngest started school to further my education. I could have amassed two doctorates using the time and energy I gave myself to charitable and community causes and been better able to support myself.*

Hekker's new analysis of the role of the traditional wife derives from her changed perspective, based on her own experience and the similar experiences of a number of her divorced friends.

If you find yourself writing an analysis guided by your own insights, not by someone else's, then you owe your reader a clear explanation of your guiding principles and the definitions by which you will probe the subject under study. Continue using the Guidelines for Writing Analyses (see p. 185), modifying this advice as you think fit to accommodate your own personal outlook, perspective, or interests. Above all, remember to structure your analysis with care. Proceed systematically and emerge with a clear statement about what the subject means, how it works, or why it might be significant.

DEMONSTRATION: ANALYSIS

Linda Shanker wrote the following paper as a first-semester sophomore in response to this assignment from her sociology professor:

> Read Robert H. Knapp's "A Psychology of Rumor" in your course anthology [*see Chapter 11 for excerpt from Knapp*]. Use some of Knapp's observations about rumor to examine a particular rumor that you have read about in your

---

*"Modern Love, Paradise Lost" by Terri Martin Hekker from *The New York Times,* January 1, 2006 © 2006 The New York Times. All rights reserved. Used by permission and protected by the Copyright laws of the United States. The printing, copying, redistribution, or retransmission of this Content without express written permission is prohibited. www.nytimes.com

reading during the first few weeks of this course. Write for readers much like yourself: freshmen or sophomores who have taken one course in sociology. Your object in this paper is to draw upon Knapp to shed light on how the particular rumor you select spread so widely and so rapidly.

MODEL ANALYSIS

Shanker 1

Linda Shanker

Social Psychology 1

UCLA

17 November 2010

The Case of the Missing Kidney: An Analysis of Rumor

> Rumor! What evil can surpass her speed?
>
> In movement she grows mighty, and achieves
>
> strength and dominion as she swifter flies...
>
> [F]oul, whispering lips, and ears, that catch at all...
>
> She can cling
>
> to vile invention and malignant wrong,
>
> or mingle with her word some tidings true.
>
> —Virgil, *The Aeneid* (Book IV, Ch. 8)

1   The phenomenon of rumor has been an object of fascination since ancient times. In his epic poem *The Aeneid*, Virgil noted some insidious truths about rumors: they spread quickly—especially in our own day, by means of phones, TV, e-mail, and Twitter; they can grow in strength and come to dominate conversation with vicious lies; and they are often mixed with a small portion of truth, a toxic combination that provides the rumor with some degree of credibility. In more recent years, sociologists and psychologists have studied various aspects of rumors: why they are such a common feature of any society, how they tie in to our individual and group views of the world, how and why they spread, why people believe them, and finally, how they can be prevented and contained.

2   One of the most important studies is Robert H. Knapp's "A Psychology of Rumor," published in 1944. Knapp's article appeared during World War II (during which he was in charge of rumor control for the Massachusetts Committee of Public Safety), and many of his

examples are drawn from rumors that sprang up during that conflict; but his analysis of why rumors form and how they work remains just as relevant today. First, Knapp defines rumor as an unverified statement offered about some topic in the hope that others will believe it (22). He proceeds to classify rumors into three basic types: the *pipe-dream or wish rumor*, based on what we would like to happen; the *bogie rumor*, based on our fears and anxieties; and the *wedge-driving or aggression rumor*, based on "dividing groups and destroying loyalties" (23–24). He notes that rumors do not spread randomly through the population, but rather through certain "sub-groups and factions" who are most susceptible to believing them. Rumors spread particularly fast, he notes, when these groups do not trust officials to tell them the truth. Most important, he maintains, "rumors express the underlying hopes, fears, and hostilities of the group" (27).

Not all rumors gain traction, of course, and Knapp goes on to outline the qualities ③ that make for successful rumors. For example, a good rumor must be "short, simple, and salient." It must be a good story. Qualities that make for a good story include "a humorous twist...striking and aesthetic detail...simplification of plot and circumstances...[and] exaggeration" (29). Knapp explains how the same rumor can take various forms, each individually suited to the groups among which it is circulating: "[n]ames, numbers, and places are typically the most unstable components of any rumor." Successful rumors adapt themselves to the particular circumstances, anxieties, prejudices of the group, and the details change according to the "tide of current swings in public opinion and interest" (30).

Knapp's insights are valuable in helping us to understand why some contemporary rumors ④ have been so frightening and yet so effective, for instance, the rumor of the missing kidney. One version of this story, current in 1992, is recounted by Robert Dingwall, a sociologist at the University of Nottingham in England:

> A woman friend of another customer had a 17-year-old son who went to a
> night club in Nottingham, called the Black Orchid, one Friday evening. He
> did not come home, so she called the police, who were not very interested
> because they thought that he had probably picked up a girl and gone home
> with her. He did not come back all weekend, but rang his mother from a call
> box on Monday, saying he was unwell. She drove out to pick him up and
> found him slumped on the floor of the call box. He said that he had passed
> out after a drink in the club and remembered nothing of the weekend. There

was a neat, fresh scar on his abdomen. She took him to the Queen's Medical Centre, the main emergency hospital in the city, where the doctors found that he had had a kidney removed. The police were called again and showed much more interest. A senior officer spoke to the mother and said that there was a secret surveillance operation going on in this club and others in the same regional chain in other East Midlands cities because they had had several cases of the same kind and they thought that the organs were being removed for sale by an Asian surgeon. (181)

⑤   It is not clear where this rumor originated, though at around this time the missing kidney story had served as the basis of a *Law and Order* episode in 1992 and a Hollywood movie, *The Harvest*, released in 1992. In any event, within a few months the rumor had spread throughout Britain, with the name of the night club and other details varying according to the city where it was circulating. The following year, the story was transplanted to Mexico; a year later it was set in India. In the Indian version, the operation was performed on an English woman traveling alone who went to a New Delhi hospital to have an appendectomy. Upon returning to England, she still felt ill, and after she was hospitalized, it was discovered that her appendix was still there but that her kidney had been removed. In subsequent years the rumor spread to the United States, with versions of the story set in Philadelphia, New Orleans, Houston, and Las Vegas. In 1997, the following message, addressed "Dear Friends," was posted on an Internet message board:

I wish to warn you about a new crime ring that is targeting business travelers. This ring is well organized, well funded, has very skilled personnel, and is currently in most major cities and recently very active in New Orleans. The crime begins when a business traveler goes to a lounge for a drink at the end of the work day. A person in the bar walks up as they sit alone and offers to buy them a drink. The last thing the traveler remembers until they wake up in a hotel room bath tub, their body submerged to their neck in ice, is sipping that drink. There is a note taped to the wall instructing them not to move and to call 911. A phone is on a small table next to the bathtub for them to call. The business traveler calls 911 who have become quite familiar with this crime. The business traveler is instructed by the 911 operator to very slowly and carefully reach behind

them and feel if there is a tube protruding from their lower back. The
business traveler finds the tube and answers, "Yes." The 911 operator tells
them to remain still, having already sent paramedics to help. The operator
knows that both of the business traveler's kidneys have been harvested.
This is not a scam or out of a science fiction novel, it is real. It is documented and confirmable. If you travel or someone close to you travels,
please be careful. ("You've Got to Be")

Subsequent posts on this message board supposedly confirmed this story ("Sadly, this is very
true"), adding different details.

Is there any truth to this rumor? None, whatsoever—not in any of its forms. Police
and other authorities in various cities have posted strenuous denials of the story in the
newspapers, on official Web sites, and in internal correspondence, as have The National
Business Travel Association, the American Gem Trade Association, and the Sherwin Williams
Co. ("'Stolen' Kidney Myth Circulating"). As reported in the rumor-reporting website Snopes.
com, "the National Kidney Foundation has asked any individual who claims to have had his
or her kidneys illegally removed to step forward and contact them. So far no one's showed
up." The persistence and power of the missing kidney rumor can be more fully understood if
we apply four of Knapp's principles of rumor formation and circulation to this particular
urban legend: his notion of the "bogie"; the "striking" details that help authenticate a
"good story" and that change as the rumor migrates to different populations; the ways
a rumor can ride swings of public opinion; and the mingling of falsehood with truth.

The kidney rumor is first and foremost the perfect example of Knapp's bogie rumor,
the rumor that draws its power from our fears and anxieties. One source of anxiety is being
alone in a strange place. (Recall the scary folk tales about children lost in the forest, soon to
encounter a witch.) These dreaded kidney removals almost always occur when the victim is
away from home, out of town or even out of the country. Most of us enjoy traveling, but we
may also feel somewhat uneasy in unfamiliar cities. We're not comfortably on our own turf,
so we don't quite know our way around; we don't know what to expect of the local population; we don't feel entirely safe, or at least, we feel that some of the locals may resent us
and take advantage of us. We can relate to the 17-year-old in the Nottingham nightclub, to
the young English woman alone in New Delhi, to the business traveler having a drink in a
New Orleans lounge.

Shanker 5

Of course, our worry about being alone in an unfamiliar city is nothing compared to our anxiety about being cut open. Even under the best of circumstances (such as to save our lives), no one looks forward to surgery. The prospect of being drugged, taken to an unknown facility, and having members of a crime ring remove one of our organs without our knowledge or consent—as apparently happened to the various subjects of this rumor—would be our worst nightmare. It's little wonder that this particular "bogie" man has such a powerful grip on our hearts.

Our anxiety about the terrible things that may happen to us in a strange place may be heightened because of the fear that our fate is just punishment for the bad things that we have done. In the Nottingham version of the rumor, the victim "had probably picked up a girl and gone home with her" (Dingwall 181). Another version of the story features "an older man picked up by an attractive woman" (Dingwall 182). Still another version of the story is set in Las Vegas, "Sin City, the place where Bad Things Happen to the Unwary (especially the 'unwary' who were seen as deservedly having brought it upon themselves, married men intent upon getting up to some play-for-pay hanky panky" ("You've Got to Be"). As Dingwall notes of this anxiety about a deserved fate, "[t]he moral is obvious: young people ought to be careful about night clubs, or more generally, about any activity which takes them out of a circle of family and friends" (183).

In addition to being a classic bogie rumor, Knapp would suggest that the missing kidney rumor persists because its "striking and aesthetic detail[s]," while false, have the ring of truth and vary from one version to another, making for a "good story" wherever the rumor spreads. Notice that the story includes the particular names of the bar or nightclub, the medical facility, the hotel; it describes the size and shape of the scar; and it summarizes the instructions of the 911 operator to see if there is a tube protruding from the victim's back. (The detail about the bathtub full of ice and the advice to "call 911" was added to the story around 1995.) As Knapp observes, "[n]ames, numbers, and places are typically the most unstable components of any rumor" (30), and so the particular cities in which the kidney operations are alleged to have been performed, as well as the particular locations within those cities, changed as the rumor spread. Another changing detail concerns the chief villains of this story. Knapp notes that rumors adapt themselves to the particular anxieties and prejudices of the group. Many groups hate or distrust foreigners and so we find different ethnic or racial "villains" named in different cities. In the Nottingham version of the story, the operation is performed by an "Asian surgeon." The English woman's kidney was removed by an Indian doctor. In another version of the story, a Kurdish victim of the kidney operation was lured to Britain "with the promise of a job by a Turkish businessman" ("You've Got to Be").

Third, Knapp observes that successful rumors "ride the tide of current swings in public opinion and interest" (30). From news reports as well as medical and police TV dramas, many people are aware that there is a great demand for organ transplants and that such demand, combined with a short supply, has given rise to a black market for illegally obtained organs. When we combine this awareness with stories that appear to provide convincing detail about the medical procedure involved (the "neat fresh scar," the tube, the name of the hospital), it is not surprising that many people accept this rumor as truth without question. One Internet correspondent, who affirmed that "Yes, this does happen" (her sister-in-law supposedly worked with a woman whose son's neighbor was a victim of the operation), noted that the only "good" thing about this situation was that those who performed the procedure were medically trained, used sterile equipment, made "exact and clean" incisions ("You've Got to Be"), and in general took measures to avoid complications that might lead to the death of the patient.

Finally, this rumor gains credibility because, as Virgil noted, rumor "mingle[s] with her word some tidings true." Although no documented case has turned up of a kidney being removed without the victim's knowledge and consent, there have been cases of people lured into selling their kidneys and later filing charges because they came to regret their decisions or were unhappy with the size of their payment ("You Got to Be").

Rumors can destroy reputations, foster distrust of government and other social institutions, and create fear and anxiety about perceived threats from particular groups of outsiders. Writing in the 1940s about rumors hatched during the war years, Knapp developed a powerful theory that helps us understand the persistence of rumors sixty years later. The rumor of the missing kidney, like any rumor, functions much like a mirror held up to society: it reveals anxiety and susceptibility to made-up but seemingly plausible "facts" related to contemporary social concerns. By helping us to understand the deeper structure of rumors, Knapp's theories can help free us from the "domination" and the "Foul, whispering lips" that Virgil observed so accurately 2,000 years ago.

Shanker 7

Works Cited

Dingwall, Robert. "Contemporary Legends, Rumors, and Collective Behavior: Some Neglected Resources for Medical Technology." *Sociology of Health and Illness* 23.2 (2001): 180–202. Print.

Knapp, Robert H. "A Psychology of Rumor." *Public Opinion Quarterly* 8.1 (1944): 22–37. Print.

"'Stolen' Kidney Myth Circulating: Organ Donation Hurt by Story of Kidney Heist." *UNOS*. United Network for Organ Sharing Newsroom Archive, 20 Aug. 1999. Web. 13 June 2010.

Virgil. *The Aeneid*. Trans. Theodore C. Williams. Perseus 4.0. *Perseus Digital Library*. Web. 17 Oct. 2010.

"You've Got to Be Kidneying." *Snopes.com*. Snopes, 12 Mar. 2008. Web. 12 June 2010.

Exercise 6.2

Informal Analysis of the Model Analysis

Before reading our analysis of this model analysis, write your own informal response. What are its strengths and weaknesses? To what extent does it follow the general Guidelines for Writing Analyses that we outlined on page 185? What function does each paragraph serve in the analysis as a whole?

THE STRATEGY OF THE ANALYSIS

- **Paragraph 1** creates a context for the analysis by introducing the phenomenon of rumor, indicating that it has been an object of fascination and study from ancient times (the poet Virgil is quoted) to the present.

- **Paragraphs 2 and 3** introduce the key principle that will be used to analyze the selected rumor, as explained by Robert H. Knapp in his article "A Psychology of Rumor." The principle includes Knapp's definition of rumor, his classification of rumors into three types, and the qualities that make for a successful rumor.

- **Paragraph 4** begins by indicating how Knapp's principles can be used to help us understand how rumor works, and then presents one particular manifestation of the rumor to be analyzed, the rumor of the missing kidney. Much of the paragraph consists of an extended quotation describing one of the original versions of the rumor, set in Nottingham, England.

- **Paragraph 5** describes how the missing kidney rumor metamorphosed and spread, first throughout England, and then to other countries, including Mexico, India, and the United States. A second extended quotation describes a version of the rumor set in New Orleans.

- **Paragraph 6** explains that the missing kidney rumor has no factual basis, but that its persistence and power can be accounted for by applying Knapp's principles. The final sentence of this paragraph is the thesis of the analysis.

- **Paragraph 7** applies the first of Knapp's principles to the missing kidney rumor: It is a bogie rumor that "draws its power from our fears and anxieties." One such fear is that of being alone in an unfamiliar environment.

- **Paragraph 8** continues to apply Knapp's principle of the bogie rumor, this time focusing on our fears about being unwillingly operated on.

- **Paragraph 9** discusses another aspect of the bogie rumor, the fear that what happens to us is a form of punishment for our own poor choices or immoral actions.

- **Paragraph 10** deals with a second of Knapp's principles, that the "facts" in rumors are constantly changing: names, places, and other details change as the rumor spreads from one city to another, but the reference to specific details lends the rumor a veneer of authenticity.

- **Paragraph 11** deals with a third of Knapp's principles: that successful rumors are often based on topics of current public interest—in this case, organ transplants and that, once again, a surface aura of facts makes the rumor appear credible.

- **Paragraph 12** returns to Virgil (cited in paragraph 1), who notes that successful rumors also appear credible because they often mix truth with fiction.

- **Paragraph 13** concluding the analysis, indicates why it is important to analyze rumor: Shedding light on how and why rumors such as this one spread may help us to counteract rumors' destructive effects.

Part II

Brief Takes

IN THIS SECTION, you'll practice the skills you've learned in summary, critique, synthesis, and analysis. These three "brief take" chapters are—as their name suggests—shorter than the six chapters that make up the main part of the anthology (Part III of this book), and they feature a more limited number of writing assignments. These assignments are sequenced so that the early ones, such as those of summary and critique, can be incorporated into the more complex later ones, for example, analysis and argument synthesis.

The subject matters of these short chapters—artificial intelligence, versions of "Cinderella," and "tiger moms"—span the academic disciplines. Each chapter includes six to nine articles. After reading them, you'll be asked to do some prewriting activities—drawing up lists of topics covered in the articles and establishing connections among topics from one reading to another. Then you'll be prompted to write summaries, critiques, syntheses, and analyses based on the articles, drawing upon the results of your prewriting activities and upon our suggestions for developing and organizing your papers.

This kind of practice will help firm up the skills you've learned in Part I and prepare you both for the lengthier reading and writing assignments of Part III and for the assignments of your other courses. Beyond the value of that preparation, we hope that you'll find yourself pleasantly absorbed by the subject matter of whichever of these brief chapters you decide to pursue.

Chapter 7

Artificial Intelligence

FRANK: Look, Dave, I can't put my finger on it, but I sense something strange about him [the HAL 9000 computer controlling the spaceship]...There isn't a single aspect of ship operations that's not under his control. If he were proven to be malfunctioning, I wouldn't see how we'd have any choice but disconnection.

DAVE: ...Be a bit tricky...We'd have to cut his higher brain functions without disturbing the purely automatic and regulatory systems....as far as I know, no 9000 computer has even been disconnected.

FRANK: Well, no 9000 computer's ever fouled up before.

DAVE: That's not what I mean...I'm not so sure what he'd think about it.

The deep-space explorers of Stanley Kubrick's *2001: A Space Odyssey* (1968) encounter a problem increasingly familiar to us today: They are completely reliant upon properly functioning computers for the success of their objectives; and if these machines don't work the way they're supposed to, people will no longer be able to function in their increasingly complex environments. Of course, we're not yet at the stage where we have to fear intelligent computers planning to disconnect *us*; but could that day arrive sooner than we think?

With the rapid increase in computing power (doubling every two years), we find computers ever more entwined in our lives: translating speech into text and multiple languages, following trends in the financial markets and making lightning-fast—sometimes disastrous—trades, regulating the flow of electricity to our homes, and much, much more. The latest generation of iPhones boasts a feature called Siri, which answers your spoken questions in a way somewhat reminiscent of HAL in a good mood. Ask it if the weather's likely to change, and it may respond, "I don't think the weather is going to get worse." Think of all the ways computers touch your life every day—from the papers you write to the traffic lights that direct your driving to the ubiquitous use of cell phones. Western civilization without computers is unthinkable; "disconnection" isn't an option. What, then, if the computers on which we rely so heavily become able to think for themselves? In which ways would we welcome the development? In what ways might we fear it? How might we grow lazy as computers take over an ever-expanding roster of chores? In a thousand years, or ten thousand, how might our notion of the "human" change?

The science fiction visions of robots and self-aware computers go back almost one hundred years. They include Czech playwright Karel Capek's *Rossum's Universal Robots* (1920), Isaac Asimov's *I Robot* (1950), Ridley Scott's *Blade Runner* (1982), the *Alien* and *Terminator* films, and Steven Spielberg's *A.I.* (2001), about an android who thinks he's really a young boy. In some cases, the intelligent nonhumans are benevolent; in most cases, they are malevolent, or at least have agendas that are at cross-purposes with those of their human creators. But how close are we to creating intelligent robots (machines that take somewhat humanoid form) or self-aware computers? According to futurist Raymond Kurzweil, that time is a little more than thirty years hence. In the year 2045, humankind will see the "Singularity": the point at which "computers will become not just intelligent, but more intelligent than humans. At that point "humanity—our bodies, our minds, our civilization—will be completely and irreversibly transformed."

Could Kurzweil be right? Does the evidence suggest that computer intelligence will soon overtake human intelligence? For that matter, how do we define intelligence? If a human interrogator communicates via computer with both another human being and a computer and cannot tell, from the printed responses, which is which—the famous, so-called Turing test—would we call *that* machine intelligent? Most of the writers represented in this chapter comment on a remarkable recent development: In February 2011, an IBM computer named "Watson" defeated two previous (human) champions in *Jeopardy!* What's the significance of this achievement? What does it portend for the future relationship of humans and computers? Will humans still be necessary—if for no other reason than to serve computers?

Such questions invite real, no longer speculative, answers. This chapter invites you to consider these developments and to contemplate the once unthinkable: the "mind" of a machine.

READ; PREPARE TO WRITE

As you read these selections, prepare for the assignments by marking up the texts: Write notes to yourself in the margins, and comment on what the authors have said.

To prepare for the more ambitious of the assignments that follow—the explanatory and argument syntheses—consider drawing up a topic list of your sources as you read. For each topic about which two or more authors have something to say, jot down notes and page (or paragraph) references. Here's an example entry:

The importance of adaptation in an age of advanced computers

- Levy: Computers with massive databases and powerful algorithms, no longer programmed to mimic human logic but to maximize machine logic, are gaining control of many human tasks. Adaptation is essential. (¶s 11–13)

- Markoff: Physicians are planning to use Watson as "cybernetic assistant." Medical education may need to change and become less memory-based as computers take over. (¶s 29–20)
- Baker: Advanced computers represent a potentially "highly disruptive force," and we must adapt by identifying things they can't do that we can. (¶s 2–8)

Such a topic list, keyed to your sources, will spare you the frustration of reading these three sources and flipping through them later, saying, "Now where did I read that?" At this early point, you don't need to know how you might write a paper based on this or any other topic. But a robust list with multiple topics and accurate notes for each lays the groundwork for your own discussion later and puts you in a good position to write a synthesis.

The example entry above should be useful for explanatory and argument syntheses on the significance of Watson's achievement on the game show *Jeopardy!* You might claim (agreeing with Stephen Baker) that Watson's success has sounded a wake-up call: Humans should leave to computers what computers do well; and humans should identify—and pursue—tasks that only humans can do well. Creating a topic list with multiple entries like the example above will add to your reading time, but it will save time as you prepare to write.

GROUP ASSIGNMENT #1: MAKE A TOPIC LIST

Working in groups of three or four, create a topic list for the selections in this chapter, jotting down notes and page (or paragraph) references. Try several topics to get you started. Find and take notes on other topics common to two or more sources.

- Singularity and its implications
- Science fiction scenarios regarding AI
- Implications of powerful computers for how and what we teach
- Is Watson an AI machine?
- Inevitability (or not) of artificial intelligence
- AI that mimics (or not) the human brain

GROUP ASSIGNMENT #2: CREATE A TOPIC WEB

Working in groups of three or four, create a network, or web, of connections among selected topics. That is, determine which topics relate or "speak" to other topics.

Articulate these connections in a series of different webs, understanding that not all topics will be connected to each web. For example, draw a line from one topic (say, the importance of adaptation in the age of advanced

(continued)

computers) to another (say, implications of powerful computers for how and what we teach). How are these topics related? As a group, generate as many topic webs as possible and, for each, as many connections as possible. At the end of this session, you'll have in hand not only the fruits of Assignment #1, multiple authors discussing common topics, but you'll also have a potential connection *among* topics—basically, the necessary raw material for writing your syntheses.

Note that one synthesis—a single paper—couldn't possibly refer to every topic, or every connection among topics, that you have found. Your skill in preparing and writing a synthesis depends on your ability to *identify* closely related topics and to make and develop a claim that links and is supported by these topics.

Six readings on artificial intelligence follow: a prediction made more than thirty years ago by a noted physicist, followed by selections on the current state of the (digital) art and what we can expect moving forward. Four of these selections debate the achievement of the IBM supercomputer Watson on the television game show *Jeopardy!* After these readings, you'll find a series of linked assignments that prompt you to write some combination of summary, critique, analysis, explanatory synthesis, and argument synthesis.

TOWARD AN INTELLIGENCE BEYOND MAN'S

Robert Jastrow

Physicist Robert Jastrow (1925–2008) was the first director of the National Aeronautic and Space Administration's Goddard Institute for Space Studies, a director of the Mount Wilson Institute and Hale Solar Laboratory, and a writer who made atmospheric and cosmological science accessible to lay audiences in popular books such as *Red Giants and White Dwarfs* (1979) and *Until the Sun Dies* (1977). Born in New York City, Jastrow was educated at Columbia University and did postdoctoral work on astronomy and space exploration at Leiden University, the Princeton Institute of Advanced Study, and the University of California at Berkeley. Jastrow won numerous awards for excellence in his field, including the NASA Exceptional Scientific Achievement Medal.

The following essay, which first appeared in *Time* magazine on February 20, 1978, offers a fascinating prediction of a scientist at the height of his powers, writing early in the digital age, on the prospects for artificial intelligence in the twenty-first century and beyond. As you read his essay thirty-plus years after publication, judge for yourself: How accurate was Jastrow in his predictions? How close have we come to achieving his dreams for artificial intelligence?

As Dr. Johnson said in a different era about ladies preaching, the surprising thing about computers is not that they think less well than a man, but that they think at all. The early electronic computer did not have much going for it except a prodigious memory and some good math skills, but today the best models can be wired up to learn by experience, follow an argument, ask pertinent questions and write pleasing poetry and music. They can also carry on somewhat distracted conversations so convincingly that their human partners do not know they are talking to a machine.

These are amiable qualities for the computer; it imitates life like an electronic monkey. As computers get more complex, the imitation gets better. Finally, the line between the original and the copy becomes blurred. In another 15 years or so[1]—two more generations of computer evolution, in the jargon of the technologists—we will see the computer as an emergent form of life.

The proposition seems ridiculous because, for one thing, computers lack the drives and emotions of living creatures. But when drives are useful, they can be programmed into the computer's brain, just as nature programmed them into our ancestors' brains as a part of the equipment for survival. For example, computers, like people, work better and learn faster when they are motivated. Arthur Samuel made this discovery when he taught two IBM computers how to play checkers. They polished their game by playing each other, but they learned slowly. Finally, Dr. Samuel programmed in the will to win by forcing the computers to try harder—and to think out more moves in advance—when they were losing. Then the computers learned very quickly. One of them beat Samuel and went on to defeat a champion player who had not lost a game to a human opponent in eight years.

Computers match people in some roles, and when fast decisions are needed in a crisis, they often outclass them. The human brain has a wiring defect that prevents it from absorbing several streams of information simultaneously and acting on them quickly. Throw too many things at the brain at one time and it freezes up; it evolved more than 100,000 years ago, when the tempo of life was slower.

5   We are still in control, but the capabilities of computers are increasing at a fantastic rate, while raw human intelligence is changing slowly, if at all. Computer power is growing exponentially; it has increased tenfold every eight years since 1946. Four generations of computer evolution—vacuum tubes, transistors, simple integrated circuits and today's miracle chips—followed one another in rapid succession, and the fifth generation, built out of such esoteric devices as bubble memories and Josephson junctions, will be on the market in the 1980s. In the 1990s, when the sixth generation appears, the compactness and reasoning power of an intelligence built out of silicon will begin to match that of the human brain.

By that time, ultra-intelligent machines will be working in partnership with our best minds on all the serious problems of the day, in an unbeatable combination of brute reasoning power and human intuition. What happens after that? Dartmouth President John Kemeny, a pioneer in computer usage, sees the

---

[1]Writing in 1978, Jastrow is making a prediction for 1993.

ultimate relation between man and computer as a symbiotic union of two living species, each completely dependent on the other for survival. The computer—a new form of life dedicated to pure thought—will be taken care of by its human partners, who will minister to its bodily needs with electricity and spare parts. Man will also provide for computer reproduction, as he does today. In return, the computer will minister to our social and economic needs. Child of man's brain rather than his loins, it will become his salvation in a world of crushing complexity.

The partnership will not last very long. Computer intelligence is growing by leaps and bounds, with no natural limit in sight. But human evolution is a nearly finished chapter in the history of life. The human brain has not changed, at least in gross size, in the past 100,000 years, and while the organization of the brain may have improved in that period, the amount of information and wiring that can be crammed into a cranium of fixed size is limited.

That does not mean the evolution of intelligence has ended on the earth. Judging by the record of the past, we can expect that a new species will arise out of man, surpassing his achievements as he has surpassed those of his predecessor, *Homo erectus*. Only a carbon-chemistry chauvinist would assume that the new species must be man's flesh-and-blood descendants, with brains housed in fragile shells of bone. The new kind of intelligent life is more likely to be made of silicon.

The history of life suggests that the evolution of the new species will take about a million years. Since the majority of the planets in the universe are not merely millions but *billions* of years older than the earth, the life they carry— assuming life to be common in the cosmos—must long since have passed through the stage we are about to enter.

10   A billion years is a long time in evolution; 1 billion years ago, the highest form of life on the earth was a worm. The intelligent life in these other, older solar systems must be as different from us as we are from creatures wriggling in the ooze. Those superintendent beings surely will not be housed in the more or less human shapes portrayed in *Star Wars* and *Close Encounters of the Third Kind*. In a cosmos that has endured for billions of years against man's mere million, the human form is not likely to be the standard form for intelligent life.

In any event, our curiosity may soon be satisfied. At this moment a shell of TV signals carrying old *I Love Lucy* programs and *Tonight* shows is expanding through the cosmos at the speed of light.[2] That bubble of broadcasts has already swept past about 50 stars like the sun. Our neighbors know we are

---

[2]Over-the-air television is broadcast as electric signals, received by earth-based TV sets. These same signals propagate beyond the earth and travel through space at the speed of light. Jastrow refers here to two particularly loved television shows whose broadcasts are being propagated into space: The situation comedy *I Love Lucy* (1951–1957 and in continual reruns thereafter) starred Lucille Ball as Lucy Ricardo, zany and endearing wife to Ricky Ricardo (played by Desi Arnez). The late-night comedy/talk show *Tonight* first aired in 1954, with comedian Steve Allen as host (and with successive hosts Jack Paar, Johnny Carson [for thirty years], Jay Leno, Conan O'Brien, and Jay Leno [again]), and has run continually since.

here, and their replies should be on the way. In another 15 or 20 years we will receive their message and meet our future. Let us be neither surprised nor disappointed if its form is that of Artoo Detoo, the bright, personable canister packed with silicon chips.

THE AI REVOLUTION IS ON

Steven Levy

Steven Levy, a senior writer for *Wired*, has reported on digital technology for a quarter century. His articles have appeared in the *New York Times, Rolling Stone*, and *Macworld*, as well as *Wired*, where this selection appeared on December 27, 2010. Levy is the author of several books, including *In the Plex: How Google Thinks, Works and Shapes Our Lives* (2011), *Hackers* (2010), *Insanely Great: The Life and Times of the Macintosh, the Computer That Changed Everything* (1994), *and Artificial Life: The Quest for a New Creation* (1992). Here, he distinguishes between two visions of artificial intelligence: the kind of AI currently in place (using clever algorithms to access massive databases) and the predictions of futurists who foresee the emergence of thinking machines that will mark our "next step in the evolutionary process."

Diapers.com warehouses are a bit of a jumble. Boxes of pacifiers sit above crates of onesies, which rest next to cartons of baby food. In a seeming abdication of logic, similar items are placed across the room from one another. A person trying to figure out how the products were shelved could well conclude that no form of intelligence—except maybe a random number generator—had a hand in determining what went where.

But the warehouses aren't meant to be understood by humans; they were built for bots. Every day, hundreds of robots course nimbly through the aisles, instantly identifying items and delivering them to flesh-and-blood packers on the periphery. Instead of organizing the warehouse as a human might—by placing like products next to one another, for instance—Diapers.com's robots stick the items in various aisles throughout the facility. Then, to fill an order, the first available robot simply finds the closest requested item. The storeroom is an ever-shifting mass that adjusts to constantly changing data, like the size and popularity of merchandise, the geography of the warehouse, and the location of each robot. Set up by Kiva Systems, which has outfitted similar facilities for Gap, Staples, and Office Depot, the system can deliver items to packers at the rate of one every six seconds.

The Kiva bots may not seem very smart. They don't possess anything like human intelligence and certainly couldn't pass a Turing test.[3] But they represent

---

[3]The "Turing Test" as conceived by mathematician Alan Turing (1912–1954): If a human interrogator communicates via computer with both another human being and a computer and cannot tell, from the printed or on-screen responses, which is which, the machine can be said to exhibit humanlike behavior and therefore passes the Turing Test.

a new forefront in the field of artificial intelligence. Today's AI doesn't try to re-create the brain. Instead, it uses machine learning, massive data sets, sophisticated sensors, and clever algorithms to master discrete tasks. Examples can be found everywhere: The Google global machine uses AI to interpret cryptic human queries. Credit card companies use it to track fraud. Netflix uses it to recommend movies to subscribers. And the financial system uses it to handle billions of trades (with only the occasional meltdown).

This explosion is the ironic payoff of the seemingly fruitless decades-long quest to emulate human intelligence. That goal proved so elusive that some scientists lost heart and many others lost funding. People talked of an AI winter—a barren season in which no vision or project could take root or grow. But even as the traditional dream of AI was freezing over, a new one was being born: machines built to accomplish specific tasks in ways that people never could. At first, there were just a few green shoots pushing up through the frosty ground. But now we're in full bloom. Welcome to AI summer.

5   Today's AI bears little resemblance to its initial conception. The field's trailblazers in the 1950s and '60s believed success lay in mimicking the logic-based reasoning that human brains were thought to use. In 1957, the AI crowd confidently predicted that machines would soon be able to replicate all kinds of human mental achievements. But that turned out to be wildly unachievable, in part because we still don't really understand how the brain works, much less how to re-create it.

So during the '80s, graduate students began to focus on the kinds of skills for which computers were well-suited and found they could build something like intelligence from groups of systems that operated according to their own kind of reasoning. "The big surprise is that intelligence isn't a unitary thing," says Danny Hillis, who cofounded Thinking Machines, a company that made massively parallel supercomputers. "What we've learned is that it's all kinds of different behaviors."

AI researchers began to devise a raft of new techniques that were decidedly not modeled on human intelligence. By using probability-based algorithms to derive meaning from huge amounts of data, researchers discovered that they didn't need to teach a computer how to accomplish a task; they could just show it what people did and let the machine figure out how to emulate that behavior under similar circumstances. They used genetic algorithms, which comb through randomly generated chunks of code, skim the highest-performing ones, and splice them together to spawn new code. As the process is repeated, the evolved programs become amazingly effective, often comparable to the output of the most experienced coders.

MIT's Rodney Brooks also took a biologically inspired approach to robotics. His lab programmed six-legged buglike creatures by breaking down insect behavior into a series of simple commands—for instance, "If you run into an obstacle, lift your legs higher." When the programmers got the rules right, the gizmos could figure out for themselves how to navigate even complicated terrain. (It's no coincidence that iRobot, the company Brooks cofounded with his MIT students, produced the Roomba autonomous vacuum cleaner, which doesn't initially know the location of all the objects in a room or the best way to traverse it but knows how to keep itself moving.)

The fruits of the AI revolution are now all around us. Once researchers were freed from the burden of building a whole mind, they could construct a rich bestiary of digital fauna, which few would dispute possess something approaching intelligence. "If you told somebody in 1978, 'You're going to have this machine, and you'll be able to type a few words and instantly get all of the world's knowledge on that topic,' they would probably consider that to be AI," Google cofounder Larry Page says. "That seems routine now, but it's a really big deal."

10   Even formerly mechanical processes like driving a car have become collaborations with AI systems. "At first it was the automatic braking system," Brooks says. "The person's foot was saying, I want to brake this much, and the intelligent system in the middle figured when to actually apply the brakes to make that work. Now you're starting to get automatic parking and lane-changing." Indeed, Google has been developing and testing cars that drive themselves with only minimal human involvement; by October, they had already covered 140,000 miles of pavement.

In short, we are engaged in a permanent dance with machines, locked in an increasingly dependent embrace. And yet, because the bots' behavior isn't based on human thought processes, we are often powerless to explain their actions. Wolfram Alpha, the website created by scientist Stephen Wolfram, can solve many mathematical problems. It also seems to display how those answers are derived. But the logical steps that humans see are completely different from the website's actual calculations. "It doesn't do any of that reasoning," Wolfram says. "Those steps are pure fake. We thought, how can we explain this to one of those humans out there?"

The lesson is that our computers sometimes have to humor us, or they will freak us out. Eric Horvitz—now a top Microsoft researcher and a former president of the Association for the Advancement of Artificial Intelligence—helped build an AI system in the 1980s to aid pathologists in their studies, analyzing each result and suggesting the next test to perform. There was just one problem—it provided the answers too quickly. "We found that people trusted it more if we added a delay loop with a flashing light, as though it were huffing and puffing to come up with an answer," Horvitz says.

But we must learn to adapt. AI is so crucial to some systems—like the financial infrastructure—that getting rid of it would be a lot harder than simply disconnecting HAL 9000's modules. "In some sense, you can argue that the science fiction scenario is already starting to happen," Thinking Machines' Hillis says. "The computers are in control, and we just live in their world." Wolfram says this conundrum will intensify as AI takes on new tasks, spinning further out of human comprehension. "Do you regulate an underlying algorithm?" he asks. "That's crazy, because you can't foresee in most cases what consequences that algorithm will have."

In its earlier days, artificial intelligence was weighted with controversy and grave doubt, as humanists feared the ramifications of thinking machines. Now the machines are embedded in our lives, and those fears seem irrelevant. "I used to have fights about it," Brooks says. "I've stopped having fights. I'm just trying to win."

COMPUTER WINS ON 'JEOPARDY!': TRIVIAL, IT'S NOT

John Markoff

Journalist John Markoff has covered business and technology news for the *New York Times* for twenty years; before that, he wrote on technology matters for *Byte* magazine. In the following article, Markoff recounts the performance of IBM's supercomputer, Watson, in its much-anticipated faceoff with two human champions of *Jeopardy!* Some took Watson's startling win as a sure sign that artificial intelligence is at our doorstep. Others disagree, as you will see in their observations in the three selections that follow this one. Markoff is the author of several technology-related books, including *The High Cost of High Tech*, (1985), *Cyberpunk: Outlaws and Hackers on the Computer Frontier* (1991), and *What the Dormouse Said: How the 60s Counterculture Shaped the Personal Computer Industry* (2005). The selection first appeared in the *Times* on February 16, 2011.

In the end, the humans on "Jeopardy!" surrendered meekly.

Facing certain defeat at the hands of a room-size I.B.M. computer on Wednesday evening, Ken Jennings, famous for winning 74 games in a row on the TV quiz show, acknowledged the obvious. "I, for one, welcome our new computer overlords," he wrote on his video screen, borrowing a line from a "Simpsons" episode.

From now on, if the answer is "the computer champion on "Jeopardy!," the question will be, "What is Watson?"

For I.B.M., the showdown was not merely a well-publicized stunt and a $1 million prize, but proof that the company has taken a big step toward a world in which intelligent machines will understand and respond to humans, and perhaps inevitably, replace some of them.

5   Watson, specifically, is a "question answering machine" of a type that artificial intelligence researchers have struggled with for decades—a computer akin to the one on "Star Trek" that can understand questions posed in natural language and answer them.

Watson showed itself to be imperfect, but researchers at I.B.M. and other companies are already developing uses for Watson's technologies that could have a significant impact on the way doctors practice and consumers buy products.

"Cast your mind back 20 years and who would have thought this was possible?" said Edward Feigenbaum, a Stanford University computer scientist and a pioneer in the field.

In its "Jeopardy!" project, I.B.M. researchers were tackling a game that requires not only encyclopedic recall, but also the ability to untangle convoluted and often opaque statements, a modicum of luck, and quick, strategic button pressing.

The contest, which was taped in January here at the company's T. J. Watson Research Laboratory before an audience of I.B.M. executives and company clients, played out in three televised episodes concluding Wednesday. At the end of the first day, Watson was in a tie with Brad Rutter, another ace human player, at $5,000 each, with Mr. Jennings trailing with $2,000.

10   But on the second day, Watson went on a tear. By night's end, Watson had a commanding lead with a total of $35,734, compared with Mr. Rutter's $10,400 and Mr. Jennings's $4,800.

Victory was not cemented until late in the third match, when Watson was in Nonfiction. "Same category for $1,200," it said in a manufactured tenor, and lucked into a Daily Double. Mr. Jennings grimaced.

Even later in the match, however, had Mr. Jennings won another key Daily Double it might have come down to Final Jeopardy, I.B.M. researchers acknowledged.

The final tally was $77,147 to Mr. Jennings's $24,000 and Mr. Rutter's $21,600.

More than anything, the contest was a vindication for the academic field of artificial intelligence, which began with great promise in the 1960s with the vision of creating a thinking machine and which became the laughingstock of Silicon Valley in the 1980s, when a series of heavily financed start-up companies went bankrupt.

15   Despite its intellectual prowess, Watson was by no means omniscient. On Tuesday evening during Final Jeopardy, the category was U.S. Cities and the clue was: "Its largest airport is named for a World War II hero; its second largest for a World War II battle."

Watson drew guffaws from many in the television audience when it responded "What is Toronto?????"

The string of question marks indicated that the system had very low confidence in its response, I.B.M. researchers said, but because it was Final Jeopardy, it was forced to give a response. The machine did not suffer much damage. It had wagered just $947 on its result. (The correct answer is, "What is Chicago?")

"We failed to deeply understand what was going on there," said David Ferrucci, an I.B.M. researcher who led the development of Watson. "The reality is that there's lots of data where the title is U.S. cities and the answers are countries, European cities, people, mayors. Even though it says U.S. cities, we had very little confidence that that's the distinguishing feature."

The researchers also acknowledged that the machine had benefited from the "buzzer factor."

20   Both Mr. Jennings and Mr. Rutter are accomplished at anticipating the light that signals it is possible to "buzz in," and can sometimes get in with virtually zero lag time. The danger is to buzz too early, in which case the contestant is penalized and "locked out" for roughly a quarter of a second.

Watson, on the other hand, does not anticipate the light, but has a weighted scheme that allows it, when it is highly confident, to hit the buzzer in as little as 10 milliseconds, making it very hard for humans to beat. When it was less confident, it took longer to buzz in. In the second round, Watson beat the others to the buzzer in 24 out of 30 Double Jeopardy questions.

"It sort of wants to get beaten when it doesn't have high confidence," Dr. Ferrucci said. "It doesn't want to look stupid."

Both human players said that Watson's button pushing skill was not necessarily an unfair advantage. "I beat Watson a couple of times," Mr. Rutter said.

When Watson did buzz in, it made the most of it. Showing the ability to parse language, it responded to, "A recent best seller by Muriel Barbery is called" 'This of the Hedgehog,'" with "What is Elegance?"

25   It showed its facility with medical diagnosis. With the answer: "You just need a nap. You don't have this sleep disorder that can make sufferers nod off while standing up," Watson replied, "What is narcolepsy?"

The coup de grâce came with the answer, "William Wilkenson's 'An Account of the Principalities of Wallachia and Moldavia' inspired this author's most famous novel." Mr. Jennings wrote, correctly, Bram Stoker, but realized that he could not catch up with Watson's winnings and wrote out his surrender.

Both players took the contest and its outcome philosophically.

"I had a great time and I would do it again in a heartbeat," said Mr. Jennings. "It's not about the results; this is about being part of the future."

For I.B.M., the future will happen very quickly, company executives said. On Thursday it plans to announce that it will collaborate with Columbia University and the University of Maryland to create a physician's assistant service that will allow doctors to query a cybernetic assistant. The company also plans to work with Nuance Communications Inc. to add voice recognition to the physician's assistant, possibly making the service available in as little as 18 months.

30   "I have been in medical education for 40 years and we're still a very memory-based curriculum," said Dr. Herbert Chase, a professor of clinical medicine at Columbia University who is working with I.B.M. on the physician's assistant. "The power of Watson-like tools will cause us to reconsider what it is we want students to do."

I.B.M. executives also said they are in discussions with a major consumer electronics retailer to develop a version of Watson, named after I.B.M.'s founder, Thomas J. Watson, that would be able to interact with consumers on a variety of subjects like buying decisions and technical support.

Dr. Ferrucci sees none of the fears that have been expressed by theorists and science fiction writers about the potential of computers to usurp humans.

"People ask me if this is HAL," he said, referring to the computer in "2001: A Space Odyssey." "HAL's not the focus; the focus is on the computer on 'Star Trek,' where you have this intelligent information seek dialogue, where you can ask follow-up questions and the computer can look at all the evidence and tries to ask follow-up questions. That's very cool."

WATSON DOESN'T KNOW IT WON ON 'JEOPARDY!'

John Searle

John R. Searle is the Willis S. and Marion Slusser Professor of the Philosophy of Mind and Language at the University of California, Berkeley. Like Stanley Fish (whose essay follows this one), Searle has developed "a theory of meaning" in an effort to probe how, through various acts of speech, we come to understand the world. In the following op-ed, which appeared originally in the *Wall Street Journal* on February 23, 2011, Searle examines the performance of IBM's Watson on *Jeopardy!* and takes the measure of what, if anything, Watson understood. Searle's numerous books include *Speech Acts* (1969), *The Mystery of*

Consciousness (1997), *Mind, Language and Society: Philosophy in the Real World* (1998), *Rationality in Action* (2001), *Mind* (2004), and *Liberté et Neurobiologie* (2004).

The recent victory of an IBM computer named Watson over human contestants on the TV show "Jeopardy!" has produced a flood of commentaries to the effect that computer understanding now equals—or perhaps even exceeds—human understanding. Thinking computers, at last.

But this interpretation rests on a profound misunderstanding of what a computer is, how it works, and how it differs from a human brain.

A digital computer is a device that manipulates formal symbols. These are usually thought of as zeros and ones, but any symbols will do. An increase in computational power is simply a matter of increasing the speed of symbol manipulation. A computer's effectiveness is a function of the skill of the programmers designing the program.

Watson revealed a huge increase in computational power and an ingenious program. I congratulate IBM on both of these innovations, but they do not show that Watson has superior intelligence, or that it's thinking, or anything of the sort.

5   Computational operations, as standardly defined, could never constitute thinking or understanding for reasons that I showed over 30 years ago with a simple argument.

Imagine that a person—me, for example—knows no Chinese and is locked in a room with boxes full of Chinese symbols and an instruction book written in English for manipulating the symbols. Unknown to me, the boxes are called "the database" and the instruction book is called "the program." I am called "the computer."

People outside the room pass in bunches of Chinese symbols that, unknown to me, are questions. I look up in the instruction book what I am supposed to do and I give back answers in Chinese symbols.

Suppose I get so good at shuffling the symbols and passing out the answers that my answers are indistinguishable from a native Chinese speaker's. I give every indication of understanding the language despite the fact that I actually don't understand a word of Chinese.

And if I do not, neither does any digital computer, because no computer, qua computer, has anything I do not have. It has stocks of symbols, rules for manipulating symbols, a system that allows it to rapidly transition from zeros to ones, and the ability to process inputs and outputs. That is it. There is nothing else.

10   This thought experiment carries over exactly to Watson. But instead of working in Chinese symbols, Watson has proven adept at responding to "Jeopardy!" questions phrased in English.

All the same, as in the original Chinese room, the symbols are meaningless to Watson, which understands nothing. The reason it lacks understanding is that, like me in the Chinese room, it has no way to get from symbols to meanings (or from syntax to semantics, in linguistic jargon). The bottom line can be put in the form of a four-word sentence: Symbols are not meanings.

Of course, Watson is much faster than me. But speed doesn't add understanding. This is a simple refutation of the idea that computer simulations of human cognition are the real thing.

If the computer cannot understand solely by manipulating symbols, then how does the brain do it? What is the difference between the brain and the digital computer? The answer is that the brain is a causal mechanism that causes consciousness, understanding and all the rest of it. It is an organ like any other, and like any other it operates on causal principles.

The problem with the digital computer is not that it is too much of a machine to have human understanding. On the contrary, it is not enough of a machine. Consciousness, the machine process that goes on in the brain, is fundamentally different from what a computer does, which is computation. Computation is an abstract formal process, like addition.

15   Unlike computation, actual human thinking is a concrete biological phenomenon existing in actual human brains. This is as opposed to Watson, which is merely following an algorithm that enables it to manipulate formal symbols.

Watson did not understand the questions, nor its answers, nor that some of its answers were right and some wrong, nor that it was playing a game, nor that it won—because it doesn't understand anything.

IBM's computer was not and could not have been designed to understand. Rather, it was designed to simulate understanding, to act as if it understood. It is an evasion to say, as some commentators have put it, that computer understanding is different from human understanding. Literally speaking, there is no such thing as computer understanding. There is only simulation.

WHAT DID WATSON THE COMPUTER DO?

Stanley Fish

Stanley Fish is a noted literary theorist and a contributor to the "Opinionator" column in the *New York Times*, where the following selection appeared on February 21, 2011. The author of thirteen books, Fish has long been concerned with how we come to understand the world (particularly literary texts). In the following essay, he considers whether or not IBM's Watson understands anything in the sense that humans do. A former professor at Duke University and Dean of Arts and Sciences at the University of Chicago, Fish currently teaches humanities and law at Florida International University. He is particularly well known for his book *Is There a Text in this Class?: The Authority of Interpretive Communities* (1980).

[H]uman beings—have trouble keeping to the rules. Human beings are always thinking, "Yes, I know the rule, but surely those who crafted it would agree that in the situation I now face, it should be relaxed" or "I know the rules of this game but if I obey them slavishly I'm likely to lose, so why don't I bend them creatively and see if I can get away with it." And then there are the familiar conundrums: The rule is no jaywalking, but only by jaywalking will I have a chance of saving the dog that is about to be hit by a car. Or I know the rule is don't lie, but telling the truth now might endanger an innocent person. Or the rule is don't travel at a speed above 25 miles per hour in the city limits, but my wife is about to give birth.

The rule we find unhelpful (or inconvenient) was written with a particular set of circumstances in mind, but circumstances not contemplated by the rule-makers will always turn up. When they do, rule aficionados will say, "Well, we can emend it and make it more supple by adding to the circumstances it covers. But you can never add enough; the proliferation of circumstances always outruns the efforts to take account of them, and after a while you've reached the point when every situation will require a rewriting of the rule, which means that there will no longer be a rule at all.

If you have followed the argument so far, you will have anticipated its next turn, which is to say that the inability or unwillingness of human beings to follow rules or be content with their guidance is not a weakness but a strength; it is the strength of being able to adjust when the rules have nothing helpful to say or produce absurd results in a situation the rule-makers did not anticipate. Only a fool will persist in adhering to a rule or set of directives when its application is clearly counter-intuitive and even disastrous. Those who are not fools will think that this is a new game—a new situation—and it calls for new strategies, different calculations of what will and will not work.

The computer I am writing this column on is a fool. It has a program that directs it to finish words before I do by "consulting" a data base of words I have used that begin with the letters I have already typed. "Consulting" is in quotation marks because the computer isn't doing anything that requires intelligence as opposed to calculation; it is sorting through data and matching the data it has stored with the data of my initially chosen letters. It is almost always wrong because its procedures do not track my practice. I am not self-consciously generating a pattern of statistical frequencies. I am producing words that have been chosen because they contribute to the realization of a governing idea or a compositional plan. In fact, to say that the computer is wrong is to give it more credit than it deserves; for right and wrong are not what it does; what it does is count (faster than I or anyone else could) and match. What it doesn't do is begin with an awareness of a situation and an overall purpose and look around for likely courses of action within that awareness. That is because, as the philosopher Hubert Dreyfus explained almost 40 years ago, a "computer is not in a situation" ("What Computers Can't Do"); it has no holistic sense of context and no ability to survey possibilities from a contextual perspective; it doesn't begin with what Wittgenstein terms a "form of life," but must build up a form of life, a world, from the only thing it has and is, "bits of context-free, completely determinate data." And since the data, no matter how large in quantity, can never add up to a context and will always remain discrete bits, the world can never be built....

5   Watson—the I.B.M.-built computer that won a game of "Jeopardy" last week over two human opponents...[is] just a bigger and fancier version of my

laptop's totally annoying program. It decomposes the question put to it into discrete bits of data and then searches its vast data base for statistically frequent combinations of the bits it is working with. The achievement is impressive but it is a wholly formal achievement that involves no knowledge (the computer doesn't know anything in the relevant sense of "know"); and it does not come within a million miles of replicating the achievements of everyday human thought.

Watson's builders know this; when they are interviewed they are careful to stay away from claims that their creation simulates human mental processes (although they also murmur something about future hopes). But those in charge of the artificial intelligence hype are not so careful and they delight in exciting us and frightening us with the fiction of a machine that can think. It's great theater, or in Watson's case, great television, but that's all it is.

WATSON IS FAR FROM ELEMENTARY

Stephen Baker

Journalist Stephen Baker has reported from Spain, Argentina, Venezuela, and Paris, for *Business Week*, among other publications. His interest in IBM's Watson began in 2009 when, on a visit to the company's headquarters, he heard talk of "the *Jeopardy* computer." He decided to tell the story of its development, as if reporting on a sports team preparing for its upcoming season and big game—in this case, the two-day showdown against former (human) champions of *Jeopardy!* His research took the form of a book, *Final Jeopardy— Man vs. Machine and the Quest to Know Everything* (2011). The following op-ed first appeared in the *Wall Street Journal* on March 14, 2011.

In the weeks since IBM's computer, Watson, thrashed two flesh-and-blood champions in the quiz show "Jeopardy!," human intelligence has been punching back—at least on blogs and opinion pages. Watson doesn't "know" anything, experts say. It doesn't laugh at jokes, cannot carry on a conversation, has no sense of self, and commits bloopers no human would consider. (Toronto, a U.S. city?) What's more, it's horribly inefficient, requiring a roomful of computers to match what we carry between our ears. And it probably would not have won without its inhuman speed on the buzzer.

This is all enough to make you feel reinvigorated to be human. But focusing on Watson's shortcomings misses the point. It risks distracting people from the transformation that Watson all but announced on its "Jeopardy!" debut: These question-answering machines will soon be working alongside us in offices and laboratories, and forcing us to make adjustments in what we learn and how we think. Watson is an early sighting of a highly disruptive force.

The key is to regard these computers not as human wannabes but rather as powerful tools, ones that can handle jobs currently held by people. The "intelligence" of the tools matters little. What counts is the information they deliver.

In our history of making tools, we have long adjusted to the disruptions they cause. Imagine an Italian town in the 17th century. Perhaps there's one man who has a special sense for the weather. Let's call him Luigi. Using his magnificent brain, he picks up on signals—changes in the wind, certain odors, perhaps the flight paths of birds or noises coming from the barn. And he spreads word through the town that rain will be coming in two days, or that a cold front might freeze the crops. Luigi is a valuable member of society.

5   Along comes a traveling vendor who carries a new instrument invented in 1643 by Evangelista Torricelli. It's a barometer, and it predicts the weather about as well as Luigi. It's certainly not as smart as him, if it can be called smart at all. It has no sense of self, is deaf to the animals in the barn, blind to the flight patterns of birds. Yet it comes up with valuable information.

In a world with barometers, Luigi and similar weather savants must find other work for their fabulous minds. Perhaps using the new tool, they can deepen their analysis of weather patterns, keep careful records and then draw conclusions about optimal farming techniques. They might become consultants. Maybe some of them drop out of the weather business altogether. The new tool creates both displacement and economic opportunity. It forces people to reconsider how they use their heads.

The same is true of Watson and the coming generation of question-answering machines. We can carry on interesting discussions about how "smart" they are or aren't, but that's academic. They make sense of complex questions in English and fetch answers, scoring each one for the machines' level of confidence in it. When asked if Watson can "think," David Ferrucci, IBM's chief scientist on the "Jeopardy!" team, responds: "Can a submarine swim?"

As these computers make their way into law offices, pharmaceutical labs and hospitals, people who currently make a living by answering questions must adjust. They'll have to add value in ways that machines cannot. This raises questions not just for individuals but for entire societies. How do we educate students for a labor market in which machines answer a growing percentage of the questions? How do we create curricula for uniquely human skills, such as generating original ideas, cracking jokes, carrying on meaningful dialogue? How can such lessons be scored and standardized?

These are the challenges before us. They're similar, in a sense, to what we've been facing with globalization. Again we will find ourselves grappling with a new colleague and competitor. This time around, it's a machine. We should scrutinize that tool, focusing on the questions it fails to answer. Its struggles represent a road map for our own cognitive migration. We must go where computers like Watson cannot.

SUMMARY

Write three summaries, all of which you will use in subsequent assignments in this chapter.

Summarize Robert Jastrow's "Toward an Intelligence Beyond Man's." Later in this chapter, you will write a critique of—that is, you will formally evaluate—Jastrow's three-decades-old predictions concerning the emergence of artificial intelligence. The summary you write for this exercise will introduce Jastrow's views in that critique and serve as a prelude to evaluating them.

Summarize John Searle's critique of claims that Watson's achievement on *Jeopardy!* represents an advance in artificial intelligence. Searle's essay is brief, appearing originally as an op-ed in the *Wall Street Journal*. Your summary should be briefer still (no longer than, say, five sentences). Be sure to capture the meaning of his key terms "symbols," "meaning," and "computation." You will draw upon Searle's argument in developing your critique of Jastrow.

Summarize Stanley Fish's critique of claims that Watson's achievement on *Jeopardy!* represents an advance in artificial intelligence. Stanley Fish's essay is brief, appearing originally as an "Opinionator" piece on the *New York Times* Web site. Your summary should be briefer still (no longer than, say, than five sentences). Be sure to capture the meaning of his key terms "data" and "context." You will draw upon Fish's argument in developing your critique of Jastrow.

CRITIQUE

Following the guidelines in Chapter 2, particularly the Guidelines for Writing Critiques box (p. 65), write a critique of Robert Jastrow's "Toward an Intelligence Beyond Man's."

Here's a suggested structure for your critique:

1. An introduction, setting the issue in context (see Chapter 3 for advice on creating introductions)

2. A summary of Jastrow's "Toward an Intelligence Beyond Man's." Your summary should note that Jastrow makes two arguments in support of his claim about the emergence of artificial intelligence. His first argument concerns the rate of increase in computing power. His second argument concerns the evolution of life on earth.

3. An evaluation of the first part of Jastrow's argument, especially in ¶ 5. Does Jastrow suggest specifically how artificial intelligence will emerge from exponentially increasing computer power? Does he need to, in your view, to make a valid argument? Consider: How open to critique is Jastrow from arguments such as Searle's and Fish's? Recall that Searle and Fish argue against calling Watson's achievement "intelligence."

4. An evaluation of the second part of Jastrow's argument, especially ¶s 7–11. This is Jastrow's prediction about evolution and what intelligent life might look like, and what form it might take, a million years from now. What is your response to Jastrow's prediction? Does he make a valid point? Whatever your response, develop it as fully as possible. Provide reasons for your conclusions.

5. A conclusion (see Chapter 3 for advice on creating conclusions) in which you assess the overall validity of Jastrow's argument. Take into account the date of this essay (1978) and what you have learned from the other selections in this chapter. What do you make of his prediction more than three decades later? Your overall assessment should respond to the substance of Jastrow's arguments (see 3 and 4, above), not to whether one or another of his predictions has come true in a particular time frame.

In preparing your critique, follow the advice in Chapter 2, particularly the Guidelines for Writing Critiques box (p. 65), along with the hints in Chapter 1 on incorporating summaries, paraphrases, and quoted material into your own writing (p. 44).

EXPLANATORY SYNTHESIS

> What are the differences between the way that humans process information and the way that computers process information? Write an explanatory synthesis that includes a section on the performance of IBM's Watson on the quiz show *Jeopardy!*

Here's a suggested structure for your explanatory synthesis:

1. An introduction, setting the issue in context (see Chapter 3 for advice on creating introductions). End your introduction with a thesis, a single statement that will guide the writing of the paragraphs of explanation that follow.

2. Two or more paragraphs on IBM's achievement with Watson on *Jeopardy!* What did Watson do? Why was the outcome significant? What responses did it generate? (Note: Four sources in the chapter directly address Watson— Markoff, Searle, Fish, and Baker.)

3. Two or more paragraphs on Searle's and Fish's distinctions between human thought and computer processing. Compare and/or contrast the key points of Searle and Fish. Use your comparisons to advance your thesis about differences between human thought and computer processing of information.

4. A paragraph or two on Levy that considers differences between the ways that humans organize and process of information and the ways that computers organize and process information. To what extent, these days, do AI researchers try to mimic human thinking?

5. A conclusion in which you clarify the differences between the ways that humans and computers process information, and the reasons why these differences are important.

Set up the references carefully, using an appropriate citation format, most likely MLA (see the "Quick Index" at the end of this text).

ANALYSIS

Stephen Baker argues that Watson's achievement on *Jeopardy!* represents "an early sighting of a highly disruptive force": computers using natural language to sort through vast quantities of information and deliver precise answers as needed. Watson, says Baker, is a tool that will disrupt our lives just as earlier tools have disrupted the lives of our ancestors (think of the wheel, fire, steam engine, automobile, and airplane).

Extrapolate from Baker's essay—his last paragraph in particular—a principle about the importance of adapting to new tools and the consequences if we do not. (Note that Baker does not use the word *adapt* or *adaptation* in his essay; but for the principle that you infer, *you* can. State what you take to be his principle about adaption in a single, clear sentence.)

Now use Baker's principle to analyze a situation that illustrates how you or people you've observed directly (or read about, perhaps in a history text), did and/or did not adapt successfully to the introduction of a new tool. To what extent did you or others (or did you or others not) "add value," as Baker puts it, in ways beyond what the new tool was designed to do?

Consider using the following structure for your analysis:

1. An introductory paragraph that sets a context for the topic and presents the claim you intend to support in the analysis that follows. Your claim (your thesis) distills the conclusions you've drawn from your analysis. Your claim may appear at the end of the introductory paragraph (or introductory section).

2. A paragraph or two introducing the analytic principle you have borrowed from Baker (concerning our adaptation to new tools). Discuss the key components of this analytic principle.

3. A paragraph or two describing both the situation you will analyze and the tool you will be discussing. Describe the context in which this new tool was used.

4. Several paragraphs (this is the heart of your analysis) in which you systematically apply the key components of Baker's principle to the situation you have described. When you consider the logic implicit in the word *adaptation*, several questions follow. Devote one or more paragraphs to developing answers to these questions. Possibilities:

    • What changes followed from the introduction of this tool?

    • To what extent were these changes disruptive or potentially disruptive?

    • What were the positive consequences of a successful adaptation?

- What were the negative consequences of failing to adapt to the new tool?

- What characteristics of adaptation seemed to matter most in contributing to a successful outcome?

5. A conclusion in which you argue that, based on the insights gained through your analysis, you—and readers—can more fully understand the consequences of introducing a new tool in a specific setting. See Chapter 3 (pp. 87–93) for advice on concluding your papers.

ARGUMENT

One definition of *intelligence* is "the faculty of perceiving and comprehending meaning." Another is "the capacity for reasoning, understanding, and similar forms of mental activity; aptitude in grasping, truths, relationships, facts, meanings, etc." Argue that, based on such definitions, "artificial intelligence" is a contradiction in terms.

ALTERNATE ASSIGNMENT FOR ARGUMENT

Your friend has messaged you from South Korea (or some other remote but high-tech spot not subject to U.S. law). His uncle is a member of a team that's just developed an advanced data-loaded computer chip that can be implanted in one's brain for the purpose of considerably boosting one's intelligence. The chip works seamlessly with existing brain cells to create a super app. Take it as a given that the operation is safe and has no physical side effects; the surgery would be just like cataract surgery, in which doctors implant a new and improved lens in the eye. (Take it as a given also that the operation is not reversible.) Your friend wants to volunteer as a test subject. The operation promises to improve his career prospects and otherwise enhance his life, because afterwards he'll be so much smarter. He asks you what you think, especially since it's not clear to him whether he'll still be thinking like a human being after the operation—or whether he'll care one way or the other. Your e-mailed response is the argument synthesis. Bring in all of the authors in the chapter to debate whether or not your friend will be more "intelligent" as a result of the operation and whether he's likely to be satisfied with the results.

Recall the selections in this chapter. Use them to help make whichever argument you write:

- Jastrow: The emergence of silicon-based intelligence is inevitable, given (1) the exponentially increasing rate of computing power and (2) the likelihood that intelligent life one million years from now will not likely be carbon-based.

- Levy: Experts claim that computers, using organization and processing unique to machines, are already in control.

- Markhoff: IBM's supercomputer, Watson, is capable of astonishing feats of data management and recall.

- Searle and Fish: Watson's achievement does not represent an advance toward artificial intelligence.

- Baker: Debates over whether or not computers are intelligent are meaningless. What matters is how these new tools help us and how successfully we adapt by taking on tasks computers cannot manage.

Also recall the papers you have written thus far. Use all or parts of these as you see fit in developing your argument.

- Three summaries (Jastrow, Searle, and Fish)

- A critique (of Jastrow's predictions regarding artificial intelligence)

- An explanation (of the differences between human and machine processing of information)

- An analysis (of the human adaptation to tools)

A suggested structure for the first argument on whether there can be such a thing as artificial (nonhuman) intelligence, given the meaning of the term "intelligence":

- A paragraph of context that builds on the predictions of Robert Jastrow concerning the emergence of artificial intelligence. State your claim: that "artificial intelligence" is a contradiction in terms.

- A summary of Jastrow's vision of artificial intelligence

- A review of IBM's achievement with Watson and where you see it fitting into Jastrow's predictions

- A critique of Watson's achievement in light of arguments made by Searle and Fish—and your agreement with Searle's and Fish's arguments

- A counterargument built on Jastrow's prediction that, in a million years, intelligent life on Earth is far more likely to be silicon-based than carbon-based. How will you respond to Jastrow in a way that reaffirms your claim?

- A conclusion that restates your claim. In your conclusion, consider referring to Levy and Baker and the point that whether or not we call computer-based information processing "intelligent" matters less than how we use and adapt to these powerful machines.

Where you place the various elements of this argument synthesis will be your decision as writer. Which sources to use and what logic to present in defense of your claim is also yours to decide. See pages 152–153 for help in thinking about structuring and supporting your argument.

A suggested structure for the alternate argument assignment:

The alternate argument will take the form of a personal letter, written with a level of language and a tone appropriate for an e-mail sent to a friend. Consider including these parts in your letter/argument:

- Begin with your first reactions—perhaps shock and awe at the very proposal. Then follow, perhaps, with an expression of concern for your friend's well-being, despite the assurances about the procedure's safety. *Then*, state your claim: Do you advise having the surgery or not?

- Offer some history of the rapid advance of computers—and how your friend's surgery fits into the arc of this history. Consider referring to Jastrow.

- Allow that humans have always developed and adapted to new tools—it's what we do. Consider using part of your analysis for drawing on Baker's notion of adaptation. Consider also a reference to Levy.

- Argue whether or not, in the history of human adaptation to tools, the implanting of a computer into the human brain crosses a barrier that should (or should not) be crossed. Develop your view of "should" or "should not." You might want to argue that "should" has no bearing, that the barrier will be crossed with or without our blessing.

- Counterargue: that is, argue against the position you have just taken and show that you find some merit in this contrary position.

- Notwithstanding these contrary arguments, you counsel to proceed with, or to cancel, the surgery.

Chapter 8

Fairy Tales: A Closer Look at "Cinderella"

In August 2001, when the crown prince of Norway married a single mother and former waitress, hundreds of thousands of Norwegians cheered, along with an estimated 300 million television viewers worldwide. It was said that Mette-Marit Tjessem Hoiby was a "Cinderella figure," and people worldwide understood the reference. But why had the bride's humble beginnings so endeared her to a nation? We can begin to offer answers by examining an ancient and universally known tale in which a humble young woman—heartsick at the death of her mother, deprived of her father's love, and scorned by her new family—is nonetheless recognized for her inner worth and exalted to the highest station.

"Cinderella" appears to be the best-known fairy tale in the world. In 1892, Marian Roalfe Cox published 345 variants of the story, the first systematic study of a single folktale. In her collection, Cox gathered stories from throughout Europe in which recurring elements, or motifs, of "Cinderella" appeared, often mixed with those of other tales. All told, more than seven hundred variants exist throughout the world—in Europe, Africa, Asia, and North and South America. Scholars debate the extent to which such a wide distribution is explained by population migrations, as opposed to some universal quality of imagination that allows people at different times and places to create essentially the same story. Whatever the reason for its wide dissemination, folklorists agree that "Cinderella" has appealed to storytellers and listeners everywhere.

In our own century, fairy tales have come under the scrutiny of anthropologists, linguists, educators, psychologists, and psychiatrists, as well as literary critics, who have come to see them as a kind of social genetic code—a means by which cultural values are transmitted from one generation to the next. Some people may scoff at the idea that charming tales such as "Cinderella" or "Snow White" are anything other than charming tales, at the idea that fairy tales may really be ways of inculcating young and impressionable children with culturally approved values. But even without being aware of it, adults and children respond to fairy tales in complex and subtle ways. Feminists, in particular, have objected to a children's story that promotes the idea—both unrealistic and undesirable—that young women should wait for a handsome prince to carry them off to a happily-ever-after marriage in a magnificent castle.

In this chapter, you will read a general introduction to fairy tales by folklorist Maria Tatar, followed by five versions of "Cinderella" and several writing assignments of the type discussed in the previous chapters. These assignments will culminate in an argument synthesis, a paper that will draw upon what you have already written for the summary, critique, explanatory synthesis, and analysis. A group of activities preceding the reading selections will help prepare you for the writing assignments to come.

READ; PREPARE TO WRITE

As you read these selections, prepare for the assignments by marking up the texts: Write notes to yourself in the margins, and comment on what the authors have said.

To prepare for the more ambitious of the assignments that follow—the explanatory and argument syntheses—consider drawing up a topic list of your sources as you read. For each topic about which two or more authors have something to say, jot down notes and page (or paragraph) references. Here's an example entry:

Cinderella's treatment at the hands of the step-mother / step-sisters

- Perrault version: washes dishes, cleans house, fixes hair, is called "Cinderbottom" (¶s 2–11)
- Grimm version: wears rags, carries water, lights fire, cooks, washes, separates lentils and ashes, is dusty and dirty (¶ 2)
- Native American version: hands and face are burned, is called "little pest"
- Disney version: cooks, bakes, cleans, wears rags (¶s 1–6)
- Sexton version: sleeps in ashes, separates lentils from cinders (lines 30–55)

Such a topic list keyed to your sources will spare you the frustration of reading eight or nine sources and flipping through them later, saying, "Now where did I read that?" In the sample entry, we find all five versions of "Cinderella" establishing the low position of the character in her household. Details of the story change according to the customs of the time and place where the story is set, but Cinderella's abasement is a common element. At this early point, you don't need to know how you might write a paper based on this or any other topic. But a robust list with multiple topics and accurate notes for each lays the groundwork for your own discussion later and puts you in a good position to write a synthesis.

The sample entry above would come in handy if you were preparing to write your own explanatory and argument syntheses on the subject of Cinderella's rising from an abased to an elevated position, taking her seat beside royalty. Creating a topic list with multiple entries will add to your reading time, but it will save time as you prepare to write.

GROUP ASSIGNMENT #1: MAKE A TOPIC LIST

Working in groups of three or four, create a topic list for the selections in this chapter, making sure to jot down notes and page references for each. We suggest several topics to get you started. Find and take notes on other topics common to two or more sources.

- Cinderella's activity or passivity
- The father's role
- The return by midnight
- Levels of violence
- Uses of magic
- The ending

GROUP ASSIGNMENT #2: CREATE A TOPIC WEB

Working in groups of three or four, create a network, or web, of connections among selected topics. That is, determine which topics relate or "speak" to other topics.

Articulate these connections in a series of different webs, understanding that not all topics will be connected to each web. For example, draw a line from one topic (say, levels of violence in versions of "Cinderella") to another (say, the different endings). How are these topics related? As a group, generate as many topic webs as possible and, for each, as many connections as possible. At the end of the session, you'll have in hand not only the fruits of Assignment #1, multiple authors discussing common topics, but you'll also have a potential connection *among* topics—basically, the necessary raw material for writing your syntheses.

Note that one synthesis—a single paper—couldn't possibly refer to every topic, or every connection among topics, that you have found. Your skill in preparing and writing a synthesis depends on your ability to *identify* closely related topics and to make and develop a claim that links and is supported by these topics.

Five versions of "Cinderella" follow, introduced by a selection by folklorist Maria Tatar. After the readings, you will find a series of linked assignments that will lead you to write some combination of summary, critique, analysis, explanatory synthesis, and argument synthesis.

AN INTRODUCTION TO FAIRY TALES

Maria Tatar

Folklorist Maria Tatar is the author of numerous articles on fairy tale literature and ten scholarly books, one of which is *The Annotated Classic Fairy Tales* (2002). The selection that follows is her general introduction to that volume, an overview that will prepare you to read the variants of "Cinderella" to follow. In a recent profile, Tatar said of her life's work: "Fairy tales...face up to the facts of life: nothing is sacred or taboo. Meanwhile they glitter with beauty. I work at the weirdly fascinating intersection of beauty and horror." Tatar teaches folklore at Harvard University.

For many of us childhood books are sacred objects. Often read to pieces, those books took us on voyages of discovery, leading us into secret new worlds that magnify childhood desires and anxieties and address the great existential mysteries. Like David Copperfield, who comforted himself by reading fairy tales, some of us once read "as if for life," using books not merely as consolation but as a way of navigating reality, of figuring out how to survive in a world ruled by adults. In a profound meditation on childhood reading, Arthur Schlesinger, Jr., writes about how the classical tales "tell children what they unconsciously know—that human nature is not innately good, that conflict is real, that life is harsh before it is happy—and thereby reassure them about their own fears and their own sense of self."

"What do we ever get nowadays from reading to equal the excitement and the revelation in those first fourteen years?" Graham Greene once asked. Many of us can recall moments of breathless excitement as we settled into our favorite chairs, our secret corners, or our cozy beds, eager to find out how Dorothy would escape the witch, whether the little mermaid would win an immortal soul, or what would become of Mary and Colin in the secret garden. "I hungered for the sharp, frightening, breath-taking, almost painful excitement that the story had given me," Richard Wright observes in recollecting his childhood encounter with the story "Bluebeard and His Seven Wives." In that world of imagination, we not only escape the drab realities of everyday life but also indulge in the cathartic pleasures of defeating those giants, stepmothers, ogres, monsters, and trolls known as the grown-ups.

Yet much as we treasure the stories of childhood, we also outgrow them, cast them off, and dismiss them as childish things, forgetting their power not only to build the childhood world of imagination but also to construct the adult world of reality. Fairy tales, according to the British illustrator Arthur Rackham, have become "part of our everyday thought and expression, and help to shape our lives." There is no doubt, he adds, "that we should be behaving ourselves very differently if Beauty had never been united to her Beast...or if Sister Anne hadn't seen anybody coming; or if 'Open Sesame!' hadn't cleared the way, or Sindbad sailed." Whether we are aware of it or not, fairy tales have modeled behavioral codes and developmental paths, even as they provide us with terms for thinking about what happens in our world.

Part of the power of these stories derives not just from the words but also from the images that accompany them. In my own childhood copy of the Grimms' fairy tales, held together by rubber bands and tape, there is one picture worth many thousands of words. Each time I open the book to that page, I feel a rush of childhood memories and experience, for a few moments, what it was like to be a child. The images that accompanied "Cinderella," "Little Red Riding Hood," or "Jack and the Beanstalk" in volumes of classic fairy tales from an earlier era have an aesthetic power that produces an emotional hold rarely encountered in the work of contemporary illustrators, and for this reason I have returned to earlier times and places for the images accompanying the stories in this volume.

5   Fairy tales are up close and personal, telling us about the quest for romance and riches, for power and privilege, and, most important, for a way out of the woods back to the safety and security of home. Bringing myths down to earth and inflecting them in human rather than heroic terms, fairy tales put a familiar spin on the stories in the archive of our collective imagination. Think of Tom Thumb, who miniaturizes David's killing of Goliath in the Bible, Odysseus' blinding of the Cyclops in *The Odyssey,* and Siegfried's conquest of the dragon Fafner in Richard Wagner's *Ring of the Nibelung.* Or of Cinderella, who is sister under the skin to Shakespeare's Cordelia and to Charlotte Brontë's Jane Eyre. Fairy tales take us into a reality that is familiar in the double sense of the term— deeply personal and at the same time centered on the family and its conflicts rather than on what is at stake in the world at large.

John Updike reminds us that the fairy tales we read to children today had their origins in a culture of adult storytelling: "They were the television and pornography of their day, the life-lightening trash of preliterate peoples." If we look at the stories in their earliest written forms, we discover preoccupations and ambitions that conform to adult anxieties and desires. Sleeping Beauty may act like a careless, disobedient child when she reaches for the spindle that puts her to sleep, but her real troubles come in the form of a hostile mother-in-law who plans to serve her for dinner with a sauce Robert. "Bluebeard," with its forbidden chamber filled with the corpses of former wives, engages with issues of marital trust, fidelity, and betrayal, showing how marriage is haunted by the threat of murder. "Rumpelstiltskin" charts a woman's narrow escape from a bargain that could cost the life of her first-born. And "Rapunzel" turns on the perilous cravings of a pregnant woman and on the desire to safeguard a girl's virtue by locking her up in a tower.

Fairy tales, once told by peasants around the fireside to distract them from the tedium of domestic chores, were transplanted with great success into the nursery, where they thrive in the form of entertainment and edification for children. These tales, which have come to constitute a powerful cultural legacy passed on from one generation to the next, provide more than gentle pleasures, charming enchantments, and playful delights. They contain much that is "painful and terrifying," as the art historian Kenneth Clark recalled in reminiscing about his childhood encounters with the stories of the Brothers Grimm and Hans Christian Andersen. Arousing dread as well as wonder, fairy tales have, over the centuries, always attracted both enthusiastic advocates, who celebrate their robust charms, and hard-edged critics, who deplore their violence.

Our deepest desires as well as our most profound anxieties enter the folk-loric bloodstream and remain in it through stories that find favor with a community of listeners or readers. As repositories of a collective cultural consciousness and unconscious, fairy tales have attracted the attention of psychologists, most notably the renowned child psychologist Bruno Bettelheim. In his landmark study, *The Uses of Enchantment,* Bettelheim argued that fairy tales have a powerful therapeutic value, teaching children that "a struggle against severe difficulties in life is unavoidable." "If one does not shy away," Bettelheim added with great optimism, "but steadfastly meets unexpected and often unjust hardships, one masters all obstacles and at the end emerges victorious."

Over the past decades child psychologists have mobilized fairy tales as powerful therapeutic vehicles for helping children and adults solve their problems by meditating on the dramas staged in them. Each text becomes an enabling device, allowing readers to work through their fears and to purge themselves of hostile feelings and damaging desires. By entering the world of fantasy and imagination, children and adults secure for themselves a safe space where fears can be confronted, mastered, and banished. Beyond that, the real magic of the fairy tale lies in its ability to extract pleasure from pain. In bringing to life the dark figures of our imagination as ogres, witches, cannibals, and giants, fairy tales may stir up dread, but in the end they always supply the pleasure of seeing it vanquished.

10   Like Bettelheim, the German philosopher Walter Benjamin applauded the feisty determination of fairy-tale heroes and heroines: "The wisest thing—so the fairy tale taught mankind in olden times, and teaches children to this day—is to meet the forces of the mythical world with cunning and with high spirits." If Bettelheim emphasized the value of "struggle" and "mastery" and saw in fairy tales an "experience in moral education," Benjamin reminded us that the morality endorsed in fairy tales is not without complications and complexities. While we may all agree that promoting "high spirits" is a good thing for the child outside the book, we may not necessarily concur that "cunning" is a quality we wish to encourage by displaying its advantages. Early commentators on fairy tales quickly detected that the moral economy of the fairy tale did not necessarily square with the didactic agendas set by parents. The British illustrator George Cruikshank was appalled by the story "Puss in Boots," which seemed to him "a succession of successful falsehoods—a clever lesson in lying!— a system of imposture rewarded by the greatest worldly advantage!" He found Jack's theft of the giant's treasures morally reprehensible and felt obliged to re-write the story, turning the robbery into a reappropriation of the dead father's fortune. Cruikshank would have reacted similarly to Aladdin, that prototypical fairytale hero who is described as "headstrong," as an "incorrigible good-for-nothing," and as a boy who will never amount to anything. Wherever we turn, fairy-tale characters always seem to be lying, cheating, or stealing their way to good fortune.

In stories for children, we have come to desire and expect clear, positive moral direction, along with straightforward messages. The popular success of William Bennett's *Book of Virtues,* a collection of stories chosen for their ability to transmit "timeless and universal" cultural values, reveals just how invested we are in the notion that moral literature can produce good citizens. Bennett is completely at ease with his list of the virtues we all embrace: self-discipline, compassion, responsibility, friendship, work, courage, perseverance, honesty, loyalty, and faith. But he fails to recognize the complexities of reading, the degree to which children often focus on single details, produce idiosyncratic interpretations, or become passionate about vices as well as virtues.

In her memoir *Leaving a Doll's House,* the actress Claire Bloom reminisces about the "sound of Mother's voice as she read to me from Hans Christian Andersen's *The Little Mermaid* and *The Snow Queen.*" Although the experience of reading produced "a pleasurable sense of warmth and comfort and safety," Bloom also emphasizes that "these emotionally wrenching tales…instilled in me a longing to be overwhelmed by romantic passion and led me in my teens and early twenties to attempt to emulate these self-sacrificing heroines." That Bloom played the tragic, self-effacing heroine not only on stage but in real life becomes clear from the painful account of her many failed romances and marriages. The stories, to be sure, may merely have reinforced what was already part of Bloom's character and disposition, but it is troubling to read her real-life history in light of her strong identification with figures like Andersen's Little Mermaid. Bloom's recollection of childhood reading reminds us that reading may yield warmth and pleasure, but that there can be real consequences to reading without reflecting on the effect of what is on the page.

The Book of Virtues, like many anthologies of stories "for children," endorses a kind of mindless reading that fails to interrogate the cultural values embedded in stories written once upon a time, in a different time and place. In its enunciation of a moral beneath each title, it also insists on reducing every story to a flat one-liner about one virtue or another, failing to take into account Eudora Welty's observation that "there is absolutely everything in great fiction but a clear answer." Even fairy tales, with their naïve sense of justice, their tenacious materialism, their reworking of familiar territory, and their sometimes narrow imaginative range, rarely send unambiguous messages.

This lack of ethical clarity did not present a problem for many of the collectors who put fairy tales between the covers of books. When Charles Perrault published his *Tales of Mother Goose* in 1697, he appended at least one moral, sometimes two. Yet those morals often did not square with the events in the story and sometimes offered nothing more than an opportunity for random social commentary and digressions on character. The explicit behavioral directives added by Perrault and others also have a tendency to misfire when they are aimed at children. It did not take Rousseau to discover that when you observe children learning lessons from stories, "you will see that when they are in a position to apply them, they almost always do so in a way opposite to the author's intention." Nearly every former child has learned this lesson through self-observation or through personal experience with children.

15   Do we, then, abandon the notion of finding moral guidance in fairy tales? Is reading reduced to an activity that yields nothing but aesthetic delight or pure pleasure? If fairy tales do not provide us with the tidy morals and messages for which we sometimes long, they still present us with opportunities to think about the anxieties and desires to which the tale gives shape, to reflect on and discuss the values encapsulated in the narrative, and to contemplate the perils and possibilities opened up by the story.

     Today we recognize that fairy tales are as much about conflict and violence as about enchantment and happily-ever-after endings. When we read "Cinderella," we are fascinated more by her trials and tribulations at the hearth than by her social elevation. We spend more time thinking about the life-threatening chant of the giant in "Jack and the Beanstalk" than about Jack's acquisition of wealth. And Hansel and Gretel's encounter with the seemingly magnanimous witch in the woods haunts our imagination long after we have put the story down.

     Through the medium of stories, adults can talk with children about what matters in their lives, about issues ranging from fear of abandonment and death to fantasies of revenge and triumphs that lead to happily-ever-after endings. While looking at pictures, reading episodes, and turning pages, adults and children can engage in what the cultural critic Ellen Handler-Spitz calls "conversational reading," dialogues that meditate on the story's effects and offer guidance for thinking about similar matters in the real world. This kind of reading can take many different turns: earnest, playful, meditative, didactic, empathetic, or intellectual.

     In her recollections of reading "Little Red Riding Hood" with her grandmother, Angela Carter gives us one such scene of reading fairy tales: "My maternal grandmother used to say, 'Lift up the latch and walk in,' when she told it to me when I was a child; and at the conclusion, when the wolf jumps on Little Red Riding Hood and gobbles her up, my grandmother used to pretend to eat me, which made me squeak and gibber with excited pleasure." Carter's account of her experience with "Little Red Riding Hood" reveals the degree to which the meaning of a tale is generated in its performance. This scene of reading—with its cathartic pleasures—tells us more about what the story means than the "timeless truths" that were enunciated by Charles Perrault in his moral to the first literary version of the tale.

     Luciano Pavarotti, by contrast, had a very different experience with "Little Red Riding Hood." "In my house," he recalls, "when I was a little boy, it was my grandfather who told the stories. He was wonderful. He told violent, mysterious tales that enchanted me.... My favorite one was *Little Red Riding Hood*. I identified with Little Red Riding Hood. I had the same fears as she. I didn't want her to die. I dreaded her death—or what we think death is." Charles Dickens had an even more powerful sentiment about the girl in this story. Little Red Riding Hood was his "first love": "I felt that if I could have married Little Red Riding Hood, I should have known perfect bliss."

20   Each of these three readers responded in very different ways to a story that we are accustomed to considering as a cautionary tale warning about the

dangers of straying from the path. Often it is the experience of reading out loud or retelling that produces the most powerful resonances and responses. Since the stories in this collection were once part of an oral tradition and since they are meant to be read aloud and revised, I have sought to recapture the rhythms of oral storytelling in my translations, using phrasing, diction, and pacing that reminds us that these stories were once broadcast, spoken out loud to an audience of young and old.

It is the readers of these fairy tales who will reinvigorate them, making them hiss and crackle with narrative energy with each retelling. Hans Christian Andersen, according to his friend Edvard Collin, had a special way of breathing new life into fairy tales:

> Whether the tale was his own or someone else's, the way of telling it was completely his own, and so lively that the children were thrilled. He, too, enjoyed giving his humor free rein, his speaking was without stop, richly adorned with the figures of speech well known to children, and with gestures to match the situation. Even the driest sentence came to life. He did not say, "The children got into the carriage and then drove away," but "They got into the carriage—'goodbye, Dad! Goodbye, Mum!'—the whip cracked smack! smack! and away they went, come on! gee up!"

Reading these stories in the fashion of Andersen is a way of reclaiming them, turning them into *our* cultural stories by inflecting them in new ways and in some cases rescripting what happened "once upon a time."

The fairy tales in this volume did not require editorial interventions in an earlier age, precisely because they were brought up to date by their tellers and tailored to the cultural context in which they were told. In presenting the "classic" versions of the tales, this volume is offering foundational texts that may not necessarily be completely transparent to readers today. They offer the basis for retelling, but in many cases they will call out for parental intervention. The background material on each fairy tale anchors the story in its historical context, revealing the textual peculiarities and ideological twists and turns taken over time at different cultural sites. Knowing that Cinderella lives happily ever after with her stepsisters in some versions of her story and that doves are summoned to peck out the eyes of the stepsisters in others is something that parents will want to know when they read "Cinderella" to their children. That Little Red Riding Hood outwits the wolf in some versions of her story will be an important point to bear in mind when reading Perrault's version of the story, in which the girl is devoured by the wolf. Understanding something about how Bluebeard's wife is sometimes censured for her curiosity and sometimes praised for her resourcefulness will help adults reflect on how to talk about this story with a child.

The annotations to the stories are intended to enrich the reading experience, providing cues for points in the story where adult and child can contemplate alternative possibilities, improvise new directions, or imagine different endings. These notes draw attention to moments at which adult and child can engage with issues raised, sometimes simply indulging in the pleasures of the narrative, but sometimes also thinking about the values endorsed in the story and questioning whether the plot has to take the particular turn that it does in the printed version.

25 The illustrations for *The Annotated Classic Fairy Tales* have been drawn largely from the image repertoire of nineteenth-century artists, contemporaries of the collectors and editors of the great national anthologies of fairy tales. Arthur Rackham, Gustave Doré, Edmund Dulac, Walter Crane, Edward Burne-Jones, George Cruikshank, and others produced illustrations that provide not only visual pleasure but also powerful commentaries on the tales, interrupting the flow of the story at critical moments and offering opportunities for further reflection and interpretation. For many of us, the most memorable encounters with fairy tales came in the form of illustrated books. Those volumes, as Walter Benjamin points out, always had "one saving grace: their illustration." The pictures in those anthologies escaped the kind of censorship and bowdlerization to which the texts were often subjected. "They eluded the control of philanthropic theories and quickly, behind the backs of the pedagogues, children and artists came together."

The *Annotated Classic Fairy Tales* seeks to reclaim a powerful cultural legacy, creating a storytelling archive for children and adults. While the fairy tales have been drawn from a variety of cultures, they constitute a canon that has gained nearly universal currency in the Western world and that has remained remarkably stable over the centuries. Even those unfamiliar with the details of "The Frog Prince" or "The Little Match Girl" have some sense of what these stories are about and how the salient points in them (attraction and repulsion in the one, compassion in the other) are mobilized in everyday discourse to underscore an argument or to embellish a point. This volume collects the stories that we all think we know—even when we are unable to retell them—providing also the texts and historical contexts that we often do not have firmly in mind.

Disseminated across a wide variety of media, ranging from opera and drama to cinema and advertising, fairy tales have become a vital part of our cultural capital. What keeps them alive and pulsing with vitality and variety is exactly what keeps life pulsing: anxieties, fears, desires, romance, passion, and love. Like our ancestors, who listened to these stories at the fireside, in taverns, and in spinning rooms, we remain transfixed by stories about wicked stepmothers, bloodthirsty ogres, sibling rivals, and fairy godmothers. For us, too, the stories are irresistible, for they offer opportunities to talk, to negotiate, to deliberate, to chatter, and to prattle on endlessly as did the old wives from whom the stories are thought to derive. And from the tangle of that talk and chitchat, we begin to define our own values, desires, appetites, and aspirations, creating identities that will allow us to produce happily-ever-after endings for ourselves and for our children.

FIVE VARIANTS OF "CINDERELLA"

The existence of French, German, and Native American versions of the popular Cinderella tale, along with seven hundred other versions worldwide, comes as a surprise to many. Which is the real "Cinderella"? The question is misleading in that each version is real for a particular audience at a particular place and time. Still, you can choose—you may be hardly able to resist choosing—among versions and selecting your favorite. Indeed, this is your task in the argument assignment that follows: to select a favorite and defend your choice.

CINDERELLA

Charles Perrault

Charles Perrault (1628–1703) was born in Paris of a prosperous family. He practiced law for a short time and then devoted his attention to a job in government, in which capacity he was instrumental in promoting the advancement of the arts and sciences and in securing pensions for writers, both French and foreign. Perrault is best known as a writer for his *Contes de ma mère l'oye (Mother Goose Tales)*, a collection of fairy tales taken from popular folklore. He is widely suspected of having changed these stories in an effort to make them more acceptable to his audience—members of the French court. The version that follows was translated from Perrault's collection of 1696 by Charles Welsh (Boston: D.C. Heath, 1901).

Once upon a time there was a gentleman who married, for his second wife, the proudest and most haughty woman that ever was seen. She had two daughters of her own, who were, indeed, exactly like her in all things. The gentleman had also a young daughter, of rare goodness and sweetness of temper, which she took from her mother, who was the best creature in the world.

The wedding was scarcely over, when the stepmother's bad temper began to show itself. She could not bear the goodness of this young girl, because it made her own daughters appear the more odious. The stepmother gave her the meanest work in the house to do; she had to scour the dishes, tables, etc., and to scrub the floors and clean out the bedrooms. The poor girl had to sleep in the garret, upon a wretched straw bed, while her sisters lay in fine rooms with inlaid floors, upon beds of the very newest fashion, and where they had looking-glasses so large that they might see themselves at their full length. The poor girl bore all patiently, and dared not complain to her father, who would have scolded her if she had done so, for his wife governed him entirely.

When she had done her work, she used to go into the chimney corner, and sit down among the cinders, hence she was called Cinderwench. The younger sister of the two, who was not so rude and uncivil as the elder, called her Cinderella. However, Cinderella, in spite of her mean apparel, was a hundred times more handsome than her sisters, though they were always richly dressed.

It happened that the King's son gave a ball, and invited to it all persons of fashion. Our young misses were also invited, for they cut a very grand figure among the people of the country-side. They were highly delighted with the invitation, and wonderfully busy in choosing the gowns, petticoats, and head-dresses which might best become them. This made Cinderella's lot still harder, for it was she who ironed her sisters' linen and plaited their ruffles. They talked all day long of nothing but how they should be dressed.

5　　"For my part," said the elder, "I will wear my red velvet suit with French trimmings."

"And I," said the younger, "shall wear my usual skirt; but then, to make amends for that I will put on my gold-flowered mantle, and my diamond stomacher, which is far from being the most ordinary one in the world." They sent for the best hairdressers they could get to make up their hair in fashionable style, and bought patches for their cheeks. Cinderella was consulted in all these matters, for she had good taste. She advised them always for the best, and even offered her services to dress their hair, which they were very willing she should do.

As she was doing this, they said to her:—

"Cinderella, would you not be glad to go to the ball?"

"Young ladies," she said, "you only jeer at me; it is not for such as I am to go there."

10　　"You are right," they replied; "people would laugh to see a Cinderwench at a ball."

Any one but Cinderella would have dressed their hair awry, but she was good-natured, and arranged it perfectly well. They were almost two days without eating, so much were they transported with joy. They broke above a dozen laces in trying to lace themselves tight, that they might have a fine, slender shape, and they were continually at their looking-glass.

At last the happy day came; they went to Court, and Cinderella followed them with her eyes as long as she could, and when she had lost sight of them, she fell a-crying. Her godmother, who saw her all in tears, asked her what was the matter.

"I wish I could—I wish I could—" but she could not finish for sobbing.

Her godmother, who was a fairy, said to her, "You wish you could go to the ball; is it not so?"

15　　"Alas, yes," said Cinderella, sighing.

"Well," said her godmother, "be but a good girl, and I will see that you go." Then she took her into her chamber, and said to her, "Run into the garden, and bring me a pumpkin."

Cinderella went at once to gather the finest she could get, and brought it to her godmother, not being able to imagine how this pumpkin could help her to go to the ball. Her godmother scooped out all the inside of it, leaving nothing but the rind. Then she struck it with her wand, and the pumpkin was instantly turned into a fine gilded coach.

She then went to look into the mouse-trap, where she found six mice, all alive. She ordered Cinderella to lift the trap-door, when, giving each mouse, as it went out, a little tap with her wand, it was that moment turned into a fine horse, and the six mice made a fine set of six horses of a beautiful mouse-colored, dapple gray.

Being at a loss for a coachman, Cinderella said, "I will go and see if there is not a rat in the rat-trap—we may make a coachman of him."

20   "You are right," replied her godmother; "go and look."

Cinderella brought the rat-trap to her, and in it there were three huge rats. The fairy chose the one which had the largest beard, and, having touched him with her wand, he was turned into a fat coachman with the finest mustache and whiskers ever seen.

After that, she said to her:—

"Go into the garden, and you will find six lizards behind the watering-pot; bring them to me."

She had no sooner done so than her godmother turned them into six foot-men, who skipped up immediately behind the coach, with their liveries all trimmed with gold and silver, and they held on as if they had done nothing else their whole lives.

25   The fairy then said to Cinderella, "Well, you see here a carriage fit to go to the ball in; are you not pleased with it?"

"Oh, yes!" she cried; "but must I go as I am in these rags?"

Her godmother simply touched her with her wand, and, at the same moment, her clothes were turned into cloth of gold and silver, all decked with jewels. This done, she gave her a pair of the prettiest glass slippers in the whole world. Being thus attired, she got into the carriage, her godmother command-ing her, above all things, not to stay till after midnight, and telling her, at the same time, that if she stayed one moment longer, the coach would be a pumpkin again, her horses mice, her coachman a rat, her footmen lizards, and her clothes would become just as they were before.

She promised her godmother she would not fail to leave the ball before midnight. She drove away, scarce able to contain herself for joy. The King's son, who was told that a great princess, whom nobody knew, was come, ran out to receive her. He gave her his hand as she alighted from the coach, and led her into the hall where the company were assembled. There was at once a profound si-lence; every one left off dancing, and the violins ceased to play, so attracted was every one by the singular beauties of the unknown newcomer. Nothing was then heard but a confused sound of voices saying:—

"Ha! how beautiful she is! Ha! how beautiful she is!"

30   The King himself, old as he was, could not keep his eyes off her, and he told the Queen under his breath that it was a long time since he had seen so beautiful and lovely a creature. All the ladies were busy studying her clothes and head-dress, so that they might have theirs made next day after the same pattern, pro-vided they could meet with such fine materials and able hands to make them.

The King's son conducted her to the seat of honor, and afterwards took her out to dance with him. She danced so very gracefully that they all admired her more and more. A fine collation was served, but the young Prince ate not a morsel, so intently was he occupied with her. She went and sat down beside her sisters, showing them a thousand civilities, and giving them among other things part of the oranges and citrons with which the Prince had regaled her. This very much surprised them, for they had not been presented to her.

Cinderella heard the clock strike a quarter to twelve. She at once made her adieus to the company and hastened away as fast as she could.

As soon as she got home, she ran to find her godmother, and, after having thanked her, she said she much wished she might go to the ball the next day, because the King's son had asked her to do so. As she was eagerly telling her godmother all that happened at the ball, her two sisters knocked at the door; Cinderella opened it. "How long you have stayed!" said she, yawning, rubbing her eyes, and stretching herself as if she had been just awakened. She had not, however, had any desire to sleep since they went from home.

"If you had been at the ball," said one of her sisters, "you would not have been tired with it. There came thither the finest princess, the most beautiful ever was seen with mortal eyes. She showed us a thousand civilities, and gave us oranges and citrons."

35 Cinderella did not show any pleasure at this. Indeed, she asked them the name of the princess; but they told her they did not know it, and that the King's son was very much concerned, and would give all the world to know who she was. At this Cinderella, smiling, replied:—

"Was she then so very beautiful? How fortunate you have been! Could I not see her? Ah! dear Miss Charlotte, do lend me your yellow suit of clothes which you wear every day."

"Ay, to be sure!" cried Miss Charlotte; "lend my clothes to such a dirty Cinderwench as thou art! I should be out of my mind to do so."

Cinderella, indeed, expected such an answer and was very glad of the refusal; for she would have been sadly troubled if her sister had lent her what she jestingly asked for.

The next day the two sisters went to the ball, and so did Cinderella, but dressed more magnificently than before. The King's son was always by her side, and his pretty speeches to her never ceased. These by no means annoyed the young lady. Indeed, she quite forgot her godmother's orders to her, so that she heard the clock begin to strike twelve when she thought it could not be more than eleven. She then rose up and fled, as nimble as a deer. The Prince followed, but could not overtake her. She left behind one of her glass slippers, which the Prince took up most carefully.

40 She got home, but quite out of breath, without her carriage, and in her old clothes, having nothing left her of all her finery but one of the little slippers, fellow to the one she had dropped. The guards at the palace gate were asked if they had not seen a princess go out, and they replied they had seen nobody go out but a young girl, very meanly dressed, and who had more the air of a poor country girl than of a young lady.

When the two sisters returned from the ball, Cinderella asked them if they had had a pleasant time, and if the fine lady had been there. They told her, yes; but that she hurried away the moment it struck twelve, and with so much haste that she dropped one of her little glass slippers, the prettiest in the world, which the King's son had taken up. They said, further, that he had done nothing but look at her all the time, and that most certainly he was very much in love with the beautiful owner of the glass slipper.

What they said was true; for a few days after the King's son caused it to be proclaimed, by sound of trumpet, that he would marry her whose foot this slipper would fit exactly. They began to try it on the princesses, then on the duchesses, and then on all the ladies of the Court; but in vain. It was brought to the two sisters, who did all they possibly could to thrust a foot into the slipper, but they could not succeed. Cinderella, who saw this, and knew her slipper, said to them, laughing:—

"Let me see if it will not fit me."

Her sisters burst out a-laughing, and began to banter her. The gentleman who was sent to try the slipper looked earnestly at Cinderella, and, finding her very handsome, said it was but just that she should try, and that he had orders to let every lady try it on.

45   He obliged Cinderella to sit down, and, putting the slipper to her little foot, he found it went on very easily, and fitted her as if it had been made of wax. The astonishment of her two sisters was great, but it was still greater when Cinderella pulled out of her pocket the other slipper and put it on her foot. Thereupon, in came her godmother, who, having touched Cinderella's clothes with her wand, made them more magnificent than those she had worn before.

And now her two sisters found her to be that beautiful lady they had seen at the ball. They threw themselves at her feet to beg pardon for all their ill treatment of her. Cinderella took them up, and, as she embraced them, said that she forgave them with all her heart, and begged them to love her always.

She was conducted to the young Prince, dressed as she was. He thought her more charming than ever, and, a few days after, married her. Cinderella, who was as good as she was beautiful, gave her two sisters a home in the palace, and that very same day married them to two great lords of the Court.

CINDERELLA

Jakob and Wilhelm Grimm

Jakob Grimm (1785–1863) and Wilhelm Grimm (1786–1859) are best known today for the two hundred folktales they collected from oral sources and reworked in *Kinder- und Hausmärchen* (popularly known as *Grimm's Fairy Tales*), which has been translated into seventy languages. The techniques Jakob and Wilhelm Grimm used to collect and comment on these tales became a model for other collectors, providing a basis for the science of folklore. Although the Grimm brothers argued for preserving the tales exactly as heard from oral sources, scholars have determined that they sought to "improve" the tales by making them more readable. The result, highly pleasing to lay audiences the world over, nonetheless represents a literary reworking of the original oral sources. The following version of the tale was translated from the Grimms' collection by Margaret Hunt (London: George Bell, 1884).

The wife of a rich man fell sick, and as she felt that her end was drawing near, she called her only daughter to her bedside and said, "Dear child, be good and pious, and then the good God will always protect thee, and I will look down on thee from heaven and be near thee." Thereupon she closed her eyes and departed. Every day the maiden went out to her mother's grave and wept, and she remained pious and good. When winter came the snow spread a white sheet over the grave, and when the spring sun had drawn it off again, the man had taken another wife.

The woman had brought two daughters into the house with her, who were beautiful and fair of face, but vile and black of heart. Now began a bad time for the poor step-child. "Is the stupid goose to sit in the parlor with us?" said they. "He who wants to eat bread must earn it; out with the kitchen-wench." They took her pretty clothes away from her, put an old grey bedgown on her, and gave her wooden shoes. "Just look at the proud princess, how decked out she is!" they cried, and laughed, and led her into the kitchen. There she had to do hard work from morning till night, get up before daybreak, carry water, light fires, cook and wash. Besides this, the sisters did her every imaginable injury they mocked her and emptied her peas and lentils into the ashes, so that she was forced to sit and pick them out again. In the evening when she had worked till she was weary she had no bed to go to, but had to sleep by the fireside in the ashes. And as on that account she always looked dusty and dirty, they called her Cinderella.

It happened that the father was once going to the fair, and he asked his two step-daughters what he should bring back for them. "Beautiful dresses," said one, "Pearls and jewels," said the second. "And thou, Cinderella," said he, "what wilt thou have?" "Father, break off for me the first branch which knocks against your hat on your way home." So he bought beautiful dresses, pearls and jewels for his two step-daughters, and on his way home, as he was riding through a green thicket, a hazel twig brushed against him and knocked off his hat. Then he broke off the branch and took it with him. When he reached home he gave his step-daughters the things which they had wished for, and to Cinderella he gave the branch from the hazel-bush. Cinderella thanked him, went to her mother's grave and planted the branch on it, and wept so much that the tears fell down on it and watered it. It grew, however, and became a handsome tree. Thrice a day Cinderella went and sat beneath it, and wept and prayed, and a little white bird always came on the tree, and if Cinderella expressed a wish, the bird threw down to her what she had wished for.

It happened, however, that the King appointed a festival which was to last three days, and to which all the beautiful young girls in the country were invited, in order that his son might choose himself a bride. When the two step-sisters heard that they too were to appear among the number, they were delighted, called Cinderella and said, "Comb our hair for us, brush our shoes and fasten our buckles, for we are going to the festival at the King's palace." Cinderella obeyed, but wept, because she too would have liked to go with them to the dance, and begged her step-mother to allow her to do so. "Thou go, Cinderella!" said she; "Thou art dusty and dirty, and wouldst go to the festival? Thou hast no clothes and shoes, and yet wouldst dance!" As, however,

Cinderella went on asking, the step-mother at last said, "I have emptied a dish of lentils into the ashes for thee, if thou hast picked them out again in two hours, thou shalt go with us." The maiden went through the back-door into the garden, and called, "You tame pigeons, you turtle-doves, and all you birds beneath the sky, come and help me to pick

> *The good into the pot,*
> *The bad into the crop."*

Then two white pigeons came in by the kitchen-window, and afterwards the turtle-doves, and at last all the birds beneath the sky, came whirring and crowding in, and alighted amongst the ashes. And the pigeons nodded with their heads and began pick, pick, pick, pick, and the rest began also pick, pick, pick, pick, and gathered all the good grains into the dish. Hardly had one hour passed before they had finished, and all flew out again. Then the girl took the dish to her step-mother, and was glad, and believed that now she would be allowed to go with them to the festival. But the step-mother said, "No, Cinderella, thou hast no clothes and thou canst not dance; thou wouldst only be laughed at." And as Cinderella wept at this, the step-mother said, "If thou canst pick two dishes of lentils out of the ashes for me in one hour, thou shalt go with us." And she thought to herself, "That she most certainly cannot do." When the step-mother had emptied the two dishes of lentils amongst the ashes, the maiden went through the back-door into the garden and cried, "You tame pigeons, you turtle-doves, and all you birds under heaven, come and help me to pick

> *The good into the pot,*
> *The bad into the crop."*

Then two white pigeons came in by the kitchen-window, and afterwards the turtle-doves, and at length all the birds beneath the sky, came whirring and crowding in, and alighted amongst the ashes. And the doves nodded with their heads and began pick, pick, pick, pick, and the others began also pick, pick, pick, pick, and gathered all the good seeds into the dishes, and before half an hour was over they had already finished, and all flew out again. Then the maiden carried the dishes to the step-mother and was delighted, and believed that she might now go with them to the festival. But the step-mother said, "All this will not help thee; thou goest not with us, for thou hast no clothes and canst not dance; we should be ashamed of thee!" On this she turned her back on Cinderella, and hurried away with her two proud daughters.

5   As no one was now at home, Cinderella went to her mother's grave beneath the hazel-tree, and cried,

> *"Shiver and quiver, little tree,*
> *Silver and gold throw down over me."*

Then the bird threw a gold and silver dress down to her, and slippers embroidered with silk and silver. She put on the dress with all speed, and went to the festival. Her step-sisters and the step-mother however did not know her, and thought she must be a foreign princess, for she looked so beautiful in the golden dress. They never once thought of Cinderella, and believed that she was sitting at home in the dirt, picking lentils out of the ashes. The prince went to meet her, took her by the hand and danced with her. He would dance with no other maiden, and never left loose of her hand, and if any one else came to invite her, he said, "This is my partner."

She danced till it was evening, and then she wanted to go home. But the King's son said, "I will go with thee and bear thee company," for he wished to see to whom the beautiful maiden belonged. She escaped from him, however, and sprang into the pigeon-house. The King's son waited until her father came, and then he told him that the stranger maiden had leapt into the pigeon-house. The old man thought, "Can it be Cinderella?" and they had to bring him an axe and a pickaxe that he might hew the pigeon-house to pieces, but no one was inside it. And when they got home Cinderella lay in her dirty clothes among the ashes, and a dim little oil-lamp was burning on the mantle-piece, for Cinderella had jumped quickly down from the back of the pigeon-house and had run to the little hazel-tree, and there she had taken off her beautiful clothes and laid them on the grave, and the bird had taken them away again, and then she had placed herself in the kitchen amongst the ashes in her grey gown.

Next day when the festival began afresh, and her parents and the step-sisters had gone once more, Cinderella went to the hazel-tree and said

"Shiver and quiver, my little tree,
Silver and gold throw down over me."

Then the bird threw down a much more beautiful dress than on the preceding day. And when Cinderella appeared at the festival in this dress, every one was astonished at her beauty. The King's son had waited until she came, and instantly took her by the hand and danced with no one but her. When others came and invited her, he said, "She is my partner." When evening came she wished to leave, and the King's son followed her and wanted to see into which house she went. But she sprang away from him, and into the garden behind the house. Therein stood a beautiful tall tree on which hung the most magnificent pears. She clambered so nimbly between the branches like a squirrel, that the King's son did not know where she was gone. He waited until her father came, and said to him, "The stranger- maiden has escaped from me, and I believe she has climbed up the pear-tree." The father thought, "Can it be Cinderella?" and had an axe brought and cut the tree down, but no one was on it. And when they got into the kitchen, Cinderella lay there amongst the ashes, as usual, for she had jumped down on the other side of the tree, had taken the beautiful dress to the bird on the little hazel-tree, and put on her grey gown.

On the third day, when the parents and sisters had gone away, Cinderella went once more to her mother's grave and said to the little tree

"Shiver and quiver, my little tree,
Silver and gold throw down over me."

And now the bird threw down to her a dress which was more splendid and magnificent than any she had yet had, and the slippers were golden. And when she went to the festival in the dress, no one knew how to speak for astonishment. The King's son danced with her only, and if any one invited her to dance, he said, "She is my partner."

When evening came, Cinderella wished to leave, and the King's son was anxious to go with her, but she escaped from him so quickly that he could not follow her. The King's son had, however, used a stratagem, and had caused the whole staircase to be smeared with pitch, and there, when she ran down, had the maiden's left slipper remained sticking. The King's son picked it up, and it was small and dainty, and all golden. Next morning, he went with it to the father, and said to him, "No one shall be my wife but she whose foot this golden slipper fits." Then were the two sisters glad, for they had pretty feet. The eldest went with the shoe into her room and wanted to try it on, and her mother stood by. But she could not get her big toe into it, and the shoe was too small for her. Then her mother gave her a knife and said, "Cut the toe off; when thou art Queen thou wilt have no more need to go on foot." The maiden cut the toe off, forced the foot into the shoe, swallowed the pain, and went out to the King's son. Then he took her on his horse as his bride and rode away with her. They were, however, obliged to pass the grave, and there, on the hazel-tree, sat the two pigeons and cried,

"Turn and peep, turn and peep,
There's blood within the shoe,
The shoe it is too small for her,
The true bride waits for you."

Then he looked at her foot and saw how the blood was streaming from it. He turned his horse round and took the false bride home again, and said she was not the true one, and that the other sister was to put the shoe on. Then this one went into her chamber and got her toes safely into the shoe, but her heel was too large. So her mother gave her a knife and said, "Cut a bit off thy heel; when thou art Queen thou wilt have no more need to go on foot." The maiden cut a bit off her heel, forced her foot into the shoe, swallowed the pain, and went out to the King's son. He took her on his horse as his bride, and rode away with her, but when they passed by the hazel-tree, two little pigeons sat on it and cried,

"Turn and peep, turn and peep,
There's blood within the shoe,
The shoe it is too small for her,
The true bride waits for you."

He looked down at her foot and saw how the blood was running out of her shoe, and how it had stained her white stocking. Then he turned his horse and took the false bride home again. "This also is not the right one," said he, "have you no other daughter?" "No," said the man, "There is still a little stunted kitchen-wench which my late wife left behind her, but she cannot possibly be the bride." The King's son said he was to send her up to him; but the mother answered, "Oh no, she is much too dirty, she cannot show herself!" He absolutely insisted on it, and Cinderella had to be called. She first washed her hands and face clean, and then went and bowed down before the King's son, who gave her the golden shoe. Then she seated herself on a stool, drew her foot out of the heavy wooden shoe, and put it into the slipper, which fitted like a glove. And when she rose up and the King's son looked at her face he recognized the beautiful maiden who had danced with him and cried, "That is the true bride!" The step-mother and the two sisters were terrified and became pale with rage; he, however, took Cinderella on his horse and rode away with her. As they passed by the hazel-tree, the two white doves cried,

> "Turn and peep, turn and peep,
> No blood is in the shoe,
> The shoe is not too small for her,
> The true bride rides with you,"

and when they had cried that, the two came flying down and placed themselves on Cinderella's shoulders, one on the right, the other on the left, and remained sitting there.

10   When the wedding with the King's son had to be celebrated, the two false sisters came and wanted to get into favor with Cinderella and share her good fortune. When the betrothed couple went to church, the elder was at the right side and the younger at the left, and the pigeons pecked out one eye of each of them. Afterwards as they came back, the elder was at the left, and the younger at the right, and then the pigeons pecked out the other eye of each. And thus, for their wickedness and falsehood, they were punished with blindness as long as they lived.

OOCHIGEASKW—THE ROUGH-FACED GIRL
(A NATIVE AMERICAN "CINDERELLA")

The following version of the "Cinderella" tale was told, originally, in the Algonquin language. Native Americans who spoke Algonquian lived in the eastern woodlands of what is now the United States and in the northern, semiarctic areas of present-day Canada.

There was once a large village of the MicMac Indians of the Eastern Algonquins, built beside a lake. At the far end of the settlement stood a lodge, and in it lived a being who was always invisible. He had a sister who looked after him, and everyone knew that any girl who could see him might marry him. For that reason there were very few girls who did not try, but it was very long before anyone succeeded.

This is the way in which the test of sight was carried out: at evening-time, when the Invisible One was due to be returning home, his sister would walk with any girl who might come down to the lakeshore. She, of course, could see her brother, since he was always visible to her. As soon as she saw him, she would say to the girls:

"Do you see my brother?"

"Yes," they would generally reply—though some of them did say "No."

5   To those who said that they could indeed see him, the sister would say:

"Of what is his shoulder strap made?" Some people say that she would enquire:

"What is his moose-runner's haul?" or "With what does he draw his sled?"

And they would answer:

"A strip of rawhide" or "a green flexible branch," or something of that kind.

10   Then she, knowing that they had not told the truth, would say:

"Very well, let us return to the wigwam!"

When they had gone in, she would tell them not to sit in a certain place, because it belonged to the Invisible One. Then, after they had helped to cook the supper, they would wait with great curiosity, to see him eat. They could be sure he was a real person, for when he took off his moccasins they became visible, and his sister hung them up. But beyond this they saw nothing of him, not even when they stayed in the place all the night, as many of them did.

Now there lived in the village an old man who was a widower, and his three daughters. The youngest girl was very small, weak, and often ill: and yet her sisters, especially the elder, treated her cruelly. The second daughter was kinder, and sometimes took her side: but the wicked sister would burn her hands and feet with hot cinders, and she was covered with scars from this treatment. She was so marked that people called her *Oochigeaskw*, the Rough-Faced Girl.

When her father came home and asked why she had such burns, the bad sister would at once say that it was her own fault, for she had disobeyed orders and gone near the fire and fallen into it.

15   These two elder sisters decided one day to try their luck at seeing the Invisible One. So they dressed themselves in their finest clothes, and tried to look their prettiest. They found the Invisible One's sister and took the usual walk by the water.

When he came, and when they were asked if they could see him, they answered: "Of course." And when asked about the shoulder strap or sled cord, they answered: "A piece of rawhide."

But of course they were lying like the others, and they got nothing for their pains.

The next afternoon, when the father returned home, he brought with him many of the pretty little shells from which wampum was made, and they set to work to string them.

That day, poor Little Oochigeaskw, who had always gone barefoot, got a pair of her father's moccasins, old ones, and put them into water to soften them so that she could wear them. Then she begged her sisters for a few wampum shells. The elder called her a "little pest," but the younger one gave her some. Now, with no other clothes than her usual rags, the poor little thing went into the woods and got herself some sheets of birch bark, from which she made a dress, and put marks on it for decoration, in the style of long ago. She made a petticoat and a loose gown, a cap, leggings, and a handkerchief. She put on her father's large old moccasins, which were far too big for her, and went forth to try her luck. She would try, she thought, to discover whether she could see the Invisible One.

20   She did not begin very well. As she set off, her sisters shouted and hooted, hissed and yelled, and tried to make her stay. And the loafers around the village, seeing the strange little creature, called out "Shame!"

The poor little girl in her strange clothes, with her face all scarred, was an awful sight, but she was kindly received by the sister of the Invisible One. And this was, of course, because this noble lady understood far more about things than simply the mere outside which all the rest of the world knows. As the brown of the evening sky turned to black, the lady took her down to the lake.

"Do you see him?" the Invisible One's sister asked.

"I do indeed—and he is wonderful!" said Oochigeaskw.

The sister asked:

25   "And what is his sled-string?"

The little girl said:

"It is the Rainbow."

"And, my sister, what is his bow-string?"

"It is The Spirit's Road—the Milky Way."

30   "So you *have* seen him," said his sister. She took the girl home with her and bathed her. As she did so, all the scars disappeared from her body. Her hair grew again, as it was combed, long, like a blackbird's wing. Her eyes were now like stars: in all the world there was no other such beauty. Then, from her treasures, the lady gave her a wedding garment, and adorned her.

Then she told Oochigeaskw to take the *wife's* seat in the wigwam: the one next to where the Invisible One sat, beside the entrance. And when he came in, terrible and beautiful, he smiled and said:

"So we are found out!"

"Yes," said his sister. And so Oochigeaskw became his wife.

WALT DISNEY'S "CINDERELLA"

Adapted by Campbell Grant

Walter Elias Disney (1901–1966), winner of thirty-two Academy Awards, is famous throughout the world for his cartoon animations. After achieving recognition with cartoon shorts populated by such immortals as Mickey Mouse and Donald Duck, he produced the full-length animated film version of *Snow White and the Seven Dwarfs* in 1937. He followed with other animations, including *Cinderella* (1950), which he adapted from Perrault's version of the tale. *A Little Golden Book*, the text of which appears here, was then adapted by Campbell Grant from the film.

Once upon a time in a far-away land lived a sweet and pretty girl named Cinderella. She made her home with her mean old stepmother and her two step-sisters, and they made her do all the work in the house.

Cinderella cooked and baked. She cleaned and scrubbed. She had no time left for parties and fun.

But one day an invitation came from the palace of the king.

A great ball was to be given for the prince of the land. And every young girl in the kingdom was invited.

5   "How nice!" thought Cinderella. "I am invited, too."

But her mean stepsisters never thought of her. They thought only of them-selves, of course. They had all sorts of jobs for Cinderella to do.

"Wash this slip. Press this dress. Curl my hair. Find my fan."

They both kept shouting, as fast as they could speak.

"But I must get ready myself. I'm going, too," said Cinderella.

10   "You!" they hooted. "The Prince's ball for you?"

And they kept her busy all day long. She worked in the morning, while her stepsisters slept. She worked all afternoon, while they bathed and dressed. And in the evening she had to help them put on the finishing touches for the ball. She had not one minute to think of herself.

Soon the coach was ready at the door. The ugly stepsisters were powdered, pressed, and curled. But there stood Cinderella in her workaday rags.

"Why, Cinderella!" said the stepsisters. "You're not dressed for the ball."

"No," said Cinderella. "I guess I cannot go."

15   Poor Cinderella sat weeping in the garden.

Suddenly a little old woman with a sweet, kind face stood before her. It was her fairy godmother.

"Hurry, child!" she said. "You are going to the ball!"

Cinderella could hardly believe her eyes! The fairy godmother turned a fat pumpkin into a splendid coach.

Next her pet mice became horses, and her dog a fine footman. The barn horse was turned into a coachman.

20   "There, my dear," said the fairy godmother. "Now into the coach with you, and off to the ball you go."

"But my dress—" said Cinderella.

"Lovely, my dear," the fairy godmother began. Then she really looked at Cinderella's rags.

"Oh, good heavens," she said. "You can never go in that." She waved her magic wand.

> *"Salaga doola,*
> *Menchicka boola,*
> *Bibbidi bobbidi boo!" she said.*

There stood Cinderella in the loveliest ball dress that ever was. And on her feet were tiny glass slippers!

"Oh," cried Cinderella. "How can I ever thank you?"

25   "Just have a wonderful time at the ball, my dear," said her fairy godmother. "But remember, this magic lasts only until midnight. At the stroke of midnight, the spell will be broken. And everything will be as it was before."

"I will remember," said Cinderella. "It is more than I ever dreamed of."

Then into the magic coach she stepped, and was whirled away to the ball.

And such a ball! The king's palace was ablaze with lights. There was music and laughter. And every lady in the land was dressed in her beautiful best.

But Cinderella was the loveliest of them all. The prince never left her side, all evening long. They danced every dance. They had supper side by side. And they happily smiled into each other's eyes.

30   But all at once the clock began to strike midnight, Bong Bong Bong—

"Oh!" cried Cinderella. "I almost forgot!"

And without a word, away she ran, out of the ballroom and down the palace stairs. She lost one glass slipper. But she could not stop.

Into her magic coach she stepped, and away it rolled. But as the clock stopped striking, the coach disappeared. And no one knew where she had gone.

Next morning all the kingdom was filled with the news. The Grand Duke was going from house to house, with a small glass slipper in his hand. For the prince had said he would marry no one but the girl who could wear that tiny shoe.

35   Every girl in the land tried hard to put it on. The ugly stepsisters tried hardest of all. But not a one could wear the glass shoe.

And where was Cinderella? Locked in her room. For the mean old stepmother was taking no chances of letting her try on the slipper. Poor Cinderella! It looked as if the Grand Duke would surely pass her by.

But her little friends the mice got the stepmother's key. And they pushed it under Cinderella's door. So down the long stairs she came, as the Duke was just about to leave.

"Please!" cried Cinderella. "Please let me try."

And of course the slipper fitted, since it was her very own.

40   That was all the Duke needed. Now his long search was done. And so Cinderella became the prince's bride, and lived happily ever after—and the little pet mice lived in the palace and were happy ever after, too.

CINDERELLA

Anne Sexton

Anne Sexton (1928–1974) has been acclaimed as one of America's outstanding contemporary poets. In 1967, she won the Pulitzer Prize for poetry for *Live or Die*. She published four other collections of her work, including *Transformations*, in which she recast, with a modern twist, popular European fairy tales such as "Cinderella." In her book *All My Pretty Ones*, Sexton quoted Franz Kafka: "The books we need are the kind that act upon us like a misfortune, that make us suffer like the death of someone we love more than ourselves.

A book should serve as the axe for the frozen sea within us." Asked in an interview (by Patricia Marz) about this quotation, Sexton responded: "I think [poetry] should be a shock to the senses. It should almost hurt."

You always read about it;
the plumber with twelve children
who wins the Irish Sweepstakes.
From toilets to riches.
5   That story.

Or the nursemaid,
some luscious sweet from Denmark
who captures the oldest son's heart.
From diapers to Dior.
10   That story.

Or a milkman who serves the wealthy,
eggs, cream, butter, yogurt, milk,
the white truck like an ambulance
who goes into real estate
15   and makes a pile.
From homogenized to martinis at lunch.

Or the charwoman
who is on the bus when it cracks up
and collects enough from the insurance.
20   From mops to Bonwit Teller.
That story.

Once
the wife of a rich man was on her deathbed
and she said to her daughter Cinderella:
25   Be devout. Be good, Then I will smile
down from heaven in the seam of a cloud.
The man took another wife who had
two daughters, pretty enough
but with hearts like blackjacks.
30   Cinderella was their maid.
She slept on the sooty hearth each night
and walked around looking like Al Jolson.
Her father brought presents home from town,
jewels and gowns for the other women
35   but the twig of a tree for Cinderella.
She planted that twig on her mother's grave
and it grew to a tree where a white dove sat.
Whenever she wished for anything the dove
would drop it like an egg upon the ground.
40   The bird is important, my dears, so heed him.
Next came the ball, as you all know.

It was a marriage market.
The prince was looking for a wife.
All but Cinderella were preparing
45   and gussying up for the big event.
Cinderella begged to go too.
Her stepmother threw a dish of lentils
into the cinders and said: Pick them
up in an hour and you shall go.
50   The white dove brought all his friends;
all the warm wings of the fatherland came,
and picked up the lentils in a jiffy.
No, Cinderella, said the stepmother,
you have no clothes and cannot dance.
55   That's the way with stepmothers.

Cinderella went to the tree at the grave
and cried forth like a gospel singer:
Mama! Mama! My turtledove,
send me to the prince's ball!
60   The bird dropped down a golden dress
and delicate little gold slippers.
Rather a large package for a simple bird.
So she went. Which is no surprise.

Her stepmother and sisters didn't
65   recognize her without her cinder face
and the prince took her hand on the spot
and danced with no other the whole day.
As nightfall came she thought she'd better
get home. The prince walked her home
70   and she disappeared into the pigeon house
and although the prince took an axe and broke
it open she was gone. Back to her cinders.
These events repeated themselves for three days.
However on the third day the prince
75   covered the palace steps with cobbler's wax
and Cinderella's gold shoe stuck upon it.
Now he would find whom the shoe fit
and find his strange dancing girl for keeps.
He went to their house and the two sisters
80   were delighted because they had lovely feet.
The eldest went into a room to try the slipper on
but her big toe got in the way so she simply
sliced it off and put on the slipper.
The prince rode away with her until the white dove
85   told him to look at the blood pouring forth.
That is the way with amputations.
They don't just heal up like a wish.
The other sister cut off her heel

but the blood told as blood will.
90   The prince was getting tired.
He began to feel like a shoe salesman.
But he gave it one last try.
This time Cinderella fit into the shoe
like a love letter into its envelope.

95   At the wedding ceremony
the two sisters came to curry favor
and the white dove pecked their eyes out.
Two hollow spots were left
like soup spoons.

100   Cinderella and the prince
lived, they say, happily ever after,
like two dolls in a museum case
never bothered by diapers or dust,
never arguing over the timing of an egg,
105   never telling the same story twice,
never getting a middle-aged spread,
their darling smiles pasted on for eternity.

Regular Bobbsey Twins.
That story.

SUMMARY

Write two summaries. You will use both in the argument synthesis that follows.

(a) Following the guidelines in Chapter 1, particularly the Guidelines for Writing Summaries box (pp. 7–8), summarize Maria Tatar's "Introduction to Fairy Tales." In preparation for writing the summary, review the model summary (pp. 19–20) and consult the advice on note-taking (pp. 13–15).

Read Tatar's "Introduction" carefully enough to identify four sections, or groupings, of related paragraphs: ¶s 1–5, 6–9, 10–14, and 15–20. Write a sentence summarizing each section. Then write a one-sentence summary of Tatar's main point and place it at the head of your section summaries. Note that her "Introduction" is an argument. The lead sentence of your summary should restate this argument.

(b) Summarize the version of "Cinderella" that most appeals to you—that you would read to a favorite child if you could choose only *one* version. Your summary should be a single, brief paragraph that restates main plot points. Write in the present tense, and begin (for example) as follows: "In the Native American version of 'Cinderella,' the Cinderella character is a young maiden who lives…"

CRITIQUE

Following the guidelines in Chapter 2, particularly the Guidelines for Writing Critiques box (p. 65), write a critique of Maria Tatar's "Introduction to Fairy Tales." The early part of the critique should draw on the summary of Tatar that you prepared for the previous assignment. In preparation for writing the critique, review the model critique (pp. 67–72).

Your summary of Tatar's "Introduction" has (or should have) restated her argument *against* the position of William Bennett (see ¶s 10–14) regarding the moral ambiguity of fairy tales. Your task in writing a critique of Tatar is to evaluate this argument. Do you agree or disagree with her criticism of Bennett? In answering the question, draw on both your experience of having fairy tales read to you as a child and your experience of reading fairy tales to children. Shape the insights from your experiences with fairy tales into an argument that will either support or challenge Tatar's argument regarding the moral ambiguity of these tales.

In reflecting on your experiences, you may want to consider several questions that may help you to clarify your response to Tatar's (and Bennett's) positions.

- Did you, as a child, have trouble with the violence of fairy tales—or the pain, fear, envy, or other "dark" emotions common to these tales?

- Especially if you haven't read (or heard) one of these tales in awhile, do you now have trouble with the darker emotions associated with them?

- Contact an adult who read fairy tales to you as a child. Ask how s/he approached the tales. Were there expectations, for instance, of a moral to be learned? Were there concerns about violence, etc.?

- Is a story for children just a story? Should it have moral content? If not, why not? If so, why? And who gets to decide this content?

Here's a suggested organizational plan for your critique:

1. An introduction, setting the issue in context (see Chapter 3 for advice on creating introductions)

2. A summary of Tatar's "Introduction to Fairy Tales" (a version of your response to the summary assignment above)

3. An evaluation of Tatar's piece for clarity, logic, and/or fairness

4. An account of your own agreement or disagreement with Tatar's argument against Bennett

5. A conclusion (see Chapter 3 for advice on creating conclusions)

In preparing your critique, follow the advice in Chapter 2, particularly the Guidelines for Writing Critiques box (p. 65), along with the hints in Chapter 1 on incorporating summaries, paraphrases, and quoted material into your own writing (p. 44).

EXPLANATORY SYNTHESIS

The five versions of the tale presented in this chapter differ. Still, we have no trouble agreeing that each is a form of "Cinderella." Why? Write a synthesis that explains the main plot elements that make each of at least three of the stories a recognizable version of "Cinderella." Another way of getting at the same question: Were you to read a story that a friend wrote about a character named Kate, what plot elements would need to be present for you to conclude that "Kate's Tale" is an updated version of "Cinderella"?

Key requirements for the explanatory synthesis:

- Craft a thesis for your paper, a single statement that will guide the writing of the paragraphs of explanation that follow.

- Devote a section, or grouping of related paragraphs, to a specific plot point. Discuss at least three versions of "Cinderella" in relation to this plot point. Introduce the section with a clear statement that defines the plot point. Begin each subsequent paragraph within the section with a clear topic sentence.

- Develop groupings of paragraphs as above, introducing as many plot points as you think necessary to explain the essential elements of "Cinderella."

- Set up the references carefully, using an appropriate citation format, most likely MLA (see the "Quick Index" at the end of this text).

ANALYSIS

Maria Tatar's "Introduction to Fairy Tales" is rich with statements that could serve as principles for analysis. Some examples:

> ¶ 1 Arthur Schlesinger, Jr., writes about how the classical tales "tell children what they unconsciously know—that human nature is not innately good, that conflict is real, that life is harsh before it is happy—and thereby reassure them about their own fears and their own sense of self."

> ¶ 5 "Fairy tales are up close and personal, telling us about the quest for romance and riches, for power and privilege, and, most important, for a way out of the woods back to the safety and security of home."

You will find at least four other such statements that could serve as principles for analysis. Use one such statement as a tool to understand more deeply the version of "Cinderella" you summarized in the earlier (summary) assignment. Your analysis will prepare you to write an argument in which you defend this version of "Cinderella" as your preferred version.

Consider using the following structure for your analysis:

1. An introductory paragraph that sets a context for the topic and presents the claim you intend to support in the analysis that follows. Your claim (your thesis) distills the conclusions you've drawn from your analysis. Your claim may appear at the end of the introductory paragraph (or introductory section).

2. A paragraph or two introducing the analytic tool or principle you intend to use and discussing its key components. Suppose you decided to use Tatar's statement that fairy tales tell us "about the quest for romance and riches, for power and privilege, and, most important, for a way out of the woods back to the safety and security of home." You would need to define "quest for romance and riches," then use your definitions to help you select and afterwards discuss specific parts of "Cinderella." You would do the same for "power and privilege" and the same again for "out of the woods...home."

   It may be that using every term of Tatar's quotation would commit you to too lengthy an analysis. In this case, choose one term (perhaps "a way out of the woods back to the safety and security of home").

3. A paragraph or two describing the situation that you will analyze—drawn from the variant of "Cinderella" you have chosen.

4. Several paragraphs (this is the heart of your analysis) in which you systematically apply the key components of the principle you have selected to the situation you have described. Staying with "for a way out of the woods back to the safety and security of home," you would need to stretch your thinking. Some fairy tales place characters literally in a forest, or woods. You would need to think metaphorically about this language when considering "Cinderella." What might *woods* represent in the tale, if not a literal forest? In what woods does Cinderella find herself? What in the variant of the tale you've selected would count as "the safety and security of home"? (Doesn't she already have a home?) Your paragraphs of analysis would respond to these and related questions.

5. A conclusion in which you argue that, based on the insights gained through your analysis, the story can now be understood more deeply. See Chapter 3 (pp. 87–93) for advice on concluding your papers.

ARGUMENT

Which of the five versions of "Cinderella" that you've read in this chapter would you choose, above others, to read to a favorite child—if you could read only *one* version? Write an argument in which you defend your choice.

You will find it useful to draw upon the products of your earlier assignments on summary, critique, explanatory synthesis, and analysis. Follow the guidelines in Chapter 5 and also the Guidelines for Writing Synthesis box in Chapter 4 (pp. 101–102); review also the model argument synthesis (pp. 154–161).

In planning your synthesis, review the master list of topics and notes that you and your classmates generated for Group Assignment #1 on page 228. Which topics now seem most important to you in deciding on one variant of "Cinderella?" Compare how different variants treat these topics—for instance, levels and kinds of violence. What emerges from your consideration? What leads you to prefer one variant over others? Examine your reasoning and then write.

Note that one synthesis—a single paper—could not possibly refer to every topic, or every connection among topics, that you have found. The craft of preparing and writing a synthesis depends on your ability to *select* closely related topics and then to make and develop a claim that links and can be supported by them—in this case, the claim that one version of the story is preferable to others. You don't have to refer to *all* of the selections in this chapter while developing your paper, but you should refer to at least four. You may even want to research additional sources.

Here's one way of structuring such an argument synthesis:

- An introductory paragraph that sets a context for the topic: You've read five variants of "Cinderella," and you are going to choose one, above others, to read to a favorite child. At the end of this introduction, state your choice. Make your claim: State (in one sentence) why you've chosen as you have. You will devote the remainder of the paper to developing and defending this statement.

- A paragraph or two summarizing the variant you have selected. Use your summary of the variant you selected for the summary assignment, above.

- Key reasons for preferring one variant over others. Base the first reason for your selection on the analysis you have written in the preceding assignment. Likely, this section of the paper will consist of several paragraphs.

- Base additional reasons for supporting your choice on topics you developed in Group Assignment #1 (p. 228). Consider one example: levels of violence in the tale. Perhaps you find good cause for the violence; perhaps not. In either case, argue that violence is a significant reason for selecting or rejecting a variant. In a second paragraph, discuss your preferred version of "Cinderella" with respect to this reason. In a third paragraph, discuss how the other versions fall short, in your view, with respect to this reason.

- A section, two or more paragraphs, of counterargument in which you concede that others might disagree with the version of "Cinderella" that you've chosen. Acknowledge some validity to their reasoning, if possible.

- A "nevertheless" section, in which you respond to the counterarguments and reaffirm your own position.

- A paragraph or two of conclusion. See Chapter 3 (pp. 87–93) for advice on concluding your papers.

Where you place the various elements of this argument synthesis will be your decision as writer. Which sources to use and what logic to present in defense of your claim is also yours to decide. See pages 152–153 for help in thinking about structuring and supporting your argument.

A Note on Incorporating Quotations and Paraphrases   Identify the sources you intend to use for your synthesis. Working with a phrase, sentence, or brief passage from each, use a variety of the techniques discussed in the section Incorporating Quotations into Your Sentences, Chapter 1 (pp. 40–45), to write sentences that you can use to advance your argument. Some of these sentences should demonstrate the use of ellipsis marks and brackets. See pages 42–45. Paraphrase passages, as needed, and incorporate these as well into your papers.

Chapter 9

The Roar of the Tiger Mom

"Chinese Mothers Are Superior" announced an op-ed in the *Wall Street Journal* in January 2011. That piece by Yale Law School professor Amy Chua and the book from which it was drawn, *The Battle Hymn of the Tiger Mother*, ignited a furious national debate over parenting methods. The online edition of the *Journal* records over 8,800 responses to the initial op-ed in which Chua lists the activities she does not allow her children to do (including attend a sleepover, watch TV or play computer games, or get any grade less than A). In the piece, Chua also describes her efforts to motivate her children to excellence (by calling one child "garbage," rejecting an amateurish birthday card as unworthy, and driving her 7-year-old to tears after she is unable, after hours of practice, to perfectly execute a complex piano piece). A cover story in *Time* magazine reports that when Chua appeared on the *Today* show, "the usually sunny host Meredith Viera could hardly contain her contempt as she read aloud a sample of viewer comments: 'She's a monster'; 'The way she raised her kids is outrageous'; 'Where is the love, the acceptance?'"

But Chua's ideas and methods resonated with many readers. At a time when American students are ranked seventeenth in the world in reading, twenty-third in science, and thirty-first in math, can the country settle for anything less than excellence? Can American citizens hope to compete with China and other rising economies in the global marketplace if they find academic mediocrity acceptable? And on the personal level, are parents helping their children if they accept anything less than the best, if they strive, in "Western" manner, not to damage their children's unearned self-esteem and to protect them from the consequences of failure?

And yet—what are the psychological consequences of the "Chinese" parenting methods advocated by Chua? To what extent should we allow children a childhood that is filled with play and exploration, not rigid goals? What is Chua's goal beyond strictly defined academic excellence? Does academic excellence correspond with success in one's profession? With one's broader happiness in life? Does a relentless focus on academic excellence in any way limit developing social skills?

These issues are the subject of the readings that follow. You'll be asked to consider such questions as you prepare several writing assignments of the type discussed in the previous chapters. These assignments will culminate in an argument synthesis, a paper that will draw upon what you have already written for the summary, the critique, the explanatory synthesis, and the analysis.

Preceding the reading selections is a group of activities that will help prepare you for the writing assignments to come. The writing assignments themselves follow the readings.

READ; PREPARE TO WRITE

As you read these selections, prepare for the assignments by marking up the texts: Write notes to yourself in the margins and comment on what the authors have said.

And to prepare for the more ambitious of the assignments that follow—the explanatory and argument syntheses—consider drawing up a topic list of your sources as you read. For each topic about which two or more authors have something to say, jot down notes and page references. Here's an example entry:

> *Shaming/threatening children who underperform*
>
> Amy Chua: Sophia incident ("garbage") (p. 262); Lulu incidents ("Little White Donkey") (p. 264)
>
> Hanna Rosin: birthday card; rejection of Chua's approach (p. 266)
>
> Elizabeth Kolbert: Kolbert's sons' reaction to the Sophia episode (p. 275)

Such a topic list, keyed to your sources, will spare you the frustration of reading eight or nine sources and flipping through them later, saying, "Now where did I read that?" In the sample entry, we see four authors speaking to the wisdom of shaming or threatening underperforming children. At this early point, you don't need to know how you might write a paper based on this or any other topic. But a robust list with multiple topics and accurate notes for each lays the groundwork for your own discussion later and puts you in a good position to write a synthesis.

As it happens, the sample entry above should come in handy when you're preparing to write your own explanatory and argument syntheses on the subject of tiger moms. Creating a topic list with multiple entries will take you a bit more time as you read, but it will save you time as you write.

GROUP ASSIGNMENT #1: MAKE A TOPIC LIST

Working in groups of three or four, create a topic list for the selections in this chapter, making sure to jot down notes and page references for each. Here are some entries to get you started; find other topics common to two or more sources.

- overriding importance of children excelling academically—and musically
- importance for children in not wasting time (according to Chua) on non-academic activities
- importance of practice and hard work for a child's sense of achievement and self-esteem
- effects of relentless academic focus on a child's creativity and/or social skills
- factors contributing to American competitiveness (or decline) in a global economy

GROUP ASSIGNMENT #2: CREATE A TOPIC WEB

Working in groups of three or four, create a network, or web, of connections among selected topics. That is, determine which topics relate or "speak" to other topics.

Articulate these connections in a series of different webs, understanding that not all topics will be connected to each web. For example, draw a line from one topic (say, the overriding importance of children excelling academically) to another (say, factors contributing to American competitiveness in a global economy). How are these topics related? As a group, generate as many topic webs as possible and, for each, as many connections as possible. At the conclusion of the session, you'll have in hand not only the fruits of Assignment #1, multiple authors discussing common topics, but you'll also have a potential connection *among* topics—basically, the necessary raw material for writing your syntheses.

Note that one synthesis—a single paper—couldn't possibly refer to every topic, or every connection among topics, that you have found. Your skill in preparing and writing a synthesis depends on your ability to *identify* closely related topics and to make and develop a claim that links and is supported by these topics.

The readings on "tiger moms" follow. After the readings, you will find a series of linked assignments that will lead you to write some combination of summary, critique, analysis, explanatory synthesis, and argument synthesis.

WHY CHINESE MOTHERS ARE SUPERIOR

Amy Chua

Amy Chua, a professor at Yale Law School, is the author of *The World on Fire: How Exporting Free Market Democracy Breeds Ethnic Hatred and Global Instability* (2002), *Day of Empire: How Hyperpowers Rise to Global Dominance—and Why They Fall* (2007), and *Battle Hymn of the Tiger Mother* (2011), from which the following selection was excerpted as an op-ed in the *Wall Street Journal* on January 8, 2011. The title "Why Chinese Mothers are Superior" was written by the editors of the *Journal*, not by Chua, most likely in an attempt (a successful one) to attract attention and encourage controversy.

A lot of people wonder how Chinese parents raise such stereotypically successful kids. They wonder what these parents do to produce so many math whizzes and music prodigies, what it's like inside the family, and whether they could do it too. Well, I can tell them, because I've done it. Here are some things my daughters, Sophia and Louisa, were never allowed to do:

- attend a sleepover
- have a playdate
- be in a school play
- complain about not being in a school play
- watch TV or play computer games
- choose their own extracurricular activities
- get any grade less than an A
- not be the No. 1 student in every subject except gym and drama
- play any instrument other than the piano or violin
- not play the piano or violin.

I'm using the term "Chinese mother" loosely. I know some Korean, Indian, Jamaican, Irish and Ghanaian parents who qualify too. Conversely, I know some mothers of Chinese heritage, almost always born in the West, who are not Chinese mothers, by choice or otherwise. I'm also using the term "Western parents" loosely. Western parents come in all varieties.

All the same, even when Western parents think they're being strict, they usually don't come close to being Chinese mothers. For example, my Western friends who consider themselves strict make their children practice their instruments 30 minutes every day. An hour at most. For a Chinese mother, the first hour is the easy part. It's hours two and three that get tough.

Despite our squeamishness about cultural stereotypes, there are tons of studies out there showing marked and quantifiable differences between Chinese and Westerners when it comes to parenting. In one study of 50 Western American mothers and 48 Chinese immigrant mothers, almost 70% of the Western mothers said either that "stressing academic success is not good for children" or that "parents need to foster the idea that learning is fun." By contrast, roughly 0% of the Chinese mothers felt the same way. Instead, the vast majority of the Chinese mothers said that they believe their children can be "the best" students, that "academic achievement reflects successful parenting," and that if children did not excel at school then there was "a problem" and parents "were not doing their job." Other studies indicate that compared to Western parents, Chinese parents spend approximately 10 times as long every day drilling academic activities with their children. By contrast, Western kids are more likely to participate in sports teams.

5   What Chinese parents understand is that nothing is fun until you're good at it. To get good at anything you have to work, and children on their own never want to work, which is why it is crucial to override their preferences. This often requires fortitude on the part of the parents because the child will resist; things are always hardest at the beginning, which is where Western parents tend to give up. But if done properly, the Chinese strategy produces a virtuous circle. Tenacious practice, practice, practice is crucial for excellence; rote repetition is underrated in America. Once a child starts to excel at something—whether it's math, piano, pitching or ballet—he or she gets praise, admiration and satisfaction. This builds confidence and makes the once not-fun activity fun. This in turn makes it easier for the parent to get the child to work even more.

Chinese parents can get away with things that Western parents can't. Once when I was young—maybe more than once—when I was extremely disrespectful to my mother, my father angrily called me "garbage" in our native Hokkien dialect. It worked really well. I felt terrible and deeply ashamed of what I had done. But it didn't damage my self-esteem or anything like that. I knew exactly how highly he thought of me. I didn't actually think I was worthless or feel like a piece of garbage.

As an adult, I once did the same thing to Sophia, calling her garbage in English when she acted extremely disrespectfully toward me. When I mentioned that I had done this at a dinner party, I was immediately ostracized. One guest named Marcy got so upset she broke down in tears and had to leave early. My friend Susan, the host, tried to rehabilitate me with the remaining guests.

The fact is that Chinese parents can do things that would seem unimaginable—even legally actionable—to Westerners. Chinese mothers can say to their daughters, "Hey fatty—lose some weight." By contrast, Western parents have to tiptoe around the issue, talking in terms of "health" and never ever mentioning the f-word, and their kids still end up in therapy for eating disorders and negative self-image. (I also once heard a Western father toast his adult daughter by calling her "beautiful and incredibly competent." She later told me that made her feel like garbage.)

Chinese parents can order their kids to get straight As. Western parents can only ask their kids to try their best. Chinese parents can say, "You're lazy. All your classmates are getting ahead of you." By contrast, Western parents have to struggle with their own conflicted feelings about achievement, and try to persuade themselves that they're not disappointed about how their kids turned out.

10   I've thought long and hard about how Chinese parents can get away with what they do. I think there are three big differences between the Chinese and Western parental mind-sets.

First, I've noticed that Western parents are extremely anxious about their children's self-esteem. They worry about how their children will feel if they fail at something, and they constantly try to reassure their children about how good they are notwithstanding a mediocre performance on a test or at a recital. In other words, Western parents are concerned about their children's psyches. Chinese parents aren't. They assume strength, not fragility, and as a result they behave very differently.

For example, if a child comes home with an A-minus on a test, a Western parent will most likely praise the child. The Chinese mother will gasp in horror and ask what went wrong. If the child comes home with a B on the test, some Western parents will still praise the child. Other Western parents will sit their child down and express disapproval, but they will be careful not to make their child feel inadequate or insecure, and they will not call their child "stupid," "worthless" or "a disgrace." Privately, the Western parents may worry that their child does not test well or have aptitude in the subject or that there is something wrong with the curriculum and possibly the whole school. If the child's grades do not improve, they may eventually schedule a meeting with the school principal to challenge the way the subject is being taught or to call into question the teacher's credentials.

If a Chinese child gets a B—which would never happen—there would first be a screaming, hair-tearing explosion. The devastated Chinese mother would then get dozens, maybe hundreds of practice tests and work through them with her child for as long as it takes to get the grade up to an A.

Chinese parents demand perfect grades because they believe that their child can get them. If their child doesn't get them, the Chinese parent assumes it's because the child didn't work hard enough. That's why the solution to substandard performance is always to excoriate, punish and shame the child. The Chinese parent believes that their child will be strong enough to take the shaming and to improve from it. (And when Chinese kids do excel, there is plenty of ego-inflating parental praise lavished in the privacy of the home.)

15   Second, Chinese parents believe that their kids owe them everything. The reason for this is a little unclear, but it's probably a combination of Confucian filial piety and the fact that the parents have sacrificed and done so much for their children. (And it's true that Chinese mothers get in the trenches, putting in long grueling hours personally tutoring, training, interrogating and spying on their kids.) Anyway, the understanding is that Chinese children must spend their lives repaying their parents by obeying them and making them proud.

By contrast, I don't think most Westerners have the same view of children being permanently indebted to their parents. My husband, Jed, actually has the opposite view. "Children don't choose their parents," he once said to me. "They don't even choose to be born. It's parents who foist life on their kids, so it's the parents' responsibility to provide for them. Kids don't owe their parents anything. Their duty will be to their own kids." This strikes me as a terrible deal for the Western parent.

Third, Chinese parents believe that they know what is best for their children and therefore override all of their children's own desires and preferences. That's why Chinese daughters can't have boyfriends in high school and why Chinese kids can't go to sleepaway camp. It's also why no Chinese kid would ever dare say to their mother, "I got a part in the school play! I'm Villager Number Six. I'll have to stay after school for rehearsal every day from 3:00 to 7:00, and I'll also need a ride on weekends." God help any Chinese kid who tried that one.

Don't get me wrong: It's not that Chinese parents don't care about their children. Just the opposite. They would give up anything for their children. It's just an entirely different parenting model.

Here's a story in favor of coercion, Chinese-style. Lulu was about 7, still playing two instruments, and working on a piano piece called "The Little White Donkey" by the French composer Jacques Ibert. The piece is really cute—you can just imagine a little donkey ambling along a country road with its master—but it's also incredibly difficult for young players because the two hands have to keep schizophrenically different rhythms.

20   Lulu couldn't do it. We worked on it nonstop for a week, drilling each of her hands separately, over and over. But whenever we tried putting the hands together, one always morphed into the other, and everything fell apart. Finally, the day before her lesson, Lulu announced in exasperation that she was giving up and stomped off.

"Get back to the piano now," I ordered.
"You can't make me."
"Oh yes, I can."

Back at the piano, Lulu made me pay. She punched, thrashed and kicked. She grabbed the music score and tore it to shreds. I taped the score back together and encased it in a plastic shield so that it could never be destroyed again. Then I hauled Lulu's dollhouse to the car and told her I'd donate it to the Salvation Army piece by piece if she didn't have "The Little White Donkey" perfect by the next day. When Lulu said, "I thought you were going to the Salvation Army, why are you still here?" I threatened her with no lunch, no dinner, no Christmas or Hanukkah presents, no birthday parties for two, three, four years. When she still kept playing it wrong, I told her she was purposely working herself into a frenzy because she was secretly afraid she couldn't do it. I told her to stop being lazy, cowardly, self-indulgent and pathetic.

25   Jed took me aside. He told me to stop insulting Lulu—which I wasn't even doing, I was just motivating her—and that he didn't think threatening Lulu was helpful. Also, he said, maybe Lulu really just couldn't do the technique—perhaps she didn't have the coordination yet—had I considered that possibility?

"You just don't believe in her," I accused.
"That's ridiculous," Jed said scornfully. "Of course I do."
"Sophia could play the piece when she was this age."
"But Lulu and Sophia are different people," Jed pointed out.

30   "Oh no, not this," I said, rolling my eyes. "Everyone is special in their special own way," I mimicked sarcastically. "Even losers are special in their own special way. Well don't worry, you don't have to lift a finger. I'm willing to put in as long as it takes, and I'm happy to be the one hated. And you can be the one they adore because you make them pancakes and take them to Yankees games."

I rolled up my sleeves and went back to Lulu. I used every weapon and tactic I could think of. We worked right through dinner into the night, and I wouldn't let Lulu get up, not for water, not even to go to the bathroom. The house became a war zone, and I lost my voice yelling, but still there seemed to be only negative progress, and even I began to have doubts.

Then, out of the blue, Lulu did it. Her hands suddenly came together—her right and left hands each doing their own imperturbable thing—just like that.

Lulu realized it the same time I did. I held my breath. She tried it tentatively again. Then she played it more confidently and faster, and still the rhythm held. A moment later, she was beaming.

"Mommy, look—it's easy!" After that, she wanted to play the piece over and over and wouldn't leave the piano. That night, she came to sleep in my bed, and we snuggled and hugged, cracking each other up. When she performed "The Little White Donkey" at a recital a few weeks later, parents came up to me and said, "What a perfect piece for Lulu—it's so spunky and so *her*."

35   Even Jed gave me credit for that one. Western parents worry a lot about their children's self-esteem. But as a parent, one of the worst things you can do for your child's self-esteem is to let them give up. On the flip side, there's nothing better for building confidence than learning you can do something you thought you couldn't.

There are all these new books out there portraying Asian mothers as scheming, callous, overdriven people indifferent to their kids' true interests. For their part, many Chinese secretly believe that they care more about their children and are willing to sacrifice much more for them than Westerners, who seem perfectly content to let their children turn out badly. I think it's a misunderstanding on both sides. All decent parents want to do what's best for their children. The Chinese just have a totally different idea of how to do that.

Western parents try to respect their children's individuality, encouraging them to pursue their true passions, supporting their choices, and providing positive reinforcement and a nurturing environment. By contrast, the Chinese believe that the best way to protect their children is by preparing them for the future, letting them see what they're capable of, and arming them with skills, work habits and inner confidence that no one can ever take away.

MOTHER INFERIOR?

Hanna Rosin

Hanna Rosin is a contributing editor at the *Atlantic* and is working on a book based on her recent *Atlantic* cover story, "The End of Men." "Mother Inferior?" first appeared in the *Wall Street Journal* on January 15, 2011.

The other day I was playing a game called "Kids on Stage" with my 2-year-old. I had to act out "tiger," so I got down on all fours and roared. He laughed, so I roared even louder, which only made him laugh more. Eventually he came up to me, patted my head and said "kitty kat" with benevolent condescension. This perfectly sums up my status in the animal pack of mothers defined by Amy Chua's *Battle Hymn of the Tiger Mother*. There are the fierce tigers who churn out child prodigies, and then there are the pussycats who waste their afternoons playing useless board games and get bested by their own toddlers.

In pretty much every way, I am the weak-willed, pathetic Western parent that Ms. Chua describes. My children go on playdates and sleepovers; in fact I wish they would go on more of them. When they give me lopsided, hastily drawn birthday cards, I praise them as if they were Matisse, sometimes with tears in my eyes. (Ms. Chua threw back one quickly scribbled birthday card, saying "I reject this," and told her daughters they could do better.) My middle son is skilled at precisely the two extracurricular activities Ms. Chua most mocks: He just got a minor part in the school play as a fisherman, and he is a master of the drums, the instrument that she claims leads directly to using drugs (I'm not sure if she is joking or not).

I would be thrilled, of course, if my eldest child made it to Carnegie Hall at 14, which is the great crescendo of the Chua family story (although I would make sure to tell my other two children that they were fabulous in other ways!). But the chances that I would threaten to burn all her stuffed animals unless she played a piano piece perfectly, or to donate her favorite doll house to the Salvation Army piece by piece, as Ms. Chua did with her daughter, are exactly zero. It's not merely that such vigilant attention to how my daughter spends every minute of her afternoon is time-consuming and exhausting; after all, it takes time to play "Kids on Stage" and to drive to drum lessons, too. It's more that I don't have it in me. I just don't have the demented drive to pull it off.

Many American parents will read *Battle Hymn of the Tiger Mother* and feel somewhat defensive and regretful. *Well, I do make my Johnny practice his guitar twice a week! Or, Look, I have this nice discipline chart on my refrigerator with frowny faces for when he's rude at dinner!* But I don't feel all that defensive. In fact, I think Ms. Chua has the diagnosis of American childhood exactly backward. What privileged American children need is not more skills and rules and math drills. They need to lighten up and roam free, to express themselves in ways not dictated by their upright, over-invested parents. Like Ms. Chua, many American parents suffer from the delusion that, with careful enough control, a child can be made perfect. Ms. Chua does it with Suzuki piano books and insults, while many of my friends do it with organic baby food and playrooms filled with fully curated wooden toys. In both cases, the result is the same: an excess of children who are dutiful proto-adults, always responsible and good, incapable of proper childhood rebellion.

5   In the days since Ms. Chua's book has come out, the media have brought up horror stories of child prodigies gone bad, including this 16-year-old who stabbed her mother to death after complaining that her Chinese immigrant parents held her to impossibly high standards. Most prodigy stories, I imagine, involve more complicated emotions. (The Amy Chua of the book, by the way, is more seductive than the distilled media version. She is remarkably self-aware. "The truth is, I'm not good at enjoying life," she writes, and she never hesitates

to tell stories that she knows make her look beastly. It's worth noting that, in TV and radio interviews about the book, she's been trending more pussycat).

I have a good friend who was raised by a Chinese-style mother, although her parents were actually German. Her mother pushed her to practice the violin for eight hours a day, and she rarely saw other people her age. Now she is my age, and she does not hate her mother or even resent her. She is grateful to her mother for instilling in her a drive and focus that she otherwise would have lacked. What she does hate is music, because it carries for her associations of loneliness and torture. She hasn't picked up the violin in a decade, and these days, she says, classical music leaves her cold. It's not an uncommon sentiment among prodigies: "I hate tennis," Andre Agassi says on the first page of his autobiography, "Open," "hate it with a dark and secret passion, and always have."

The oddest part of Ms. Chua's parenting prescription is that it exists wholly apart from any passion or innate talent. The Chua women rarely express pure love of music; instead they express joy at having mastered it. Ms. Chua writes that she listened to CDs of Itzhak Perlman to figure out "why he sounded so good." This conception of child prodigies is not just Chinese. It is the extreme expression of the modern egalitarian notion of genius, as described by Malcolm Gladwell in *Outliers*. Anyone can be a genius, if they just put in 10,000 hours of practice! It doesn't matter if they can carry a tune or have especially limber fingers. They don't even have to like music.

But why not wait for your children to show some small spark of talent or interest in an activity before you force them to work at it for hours a day? What would be so bad if they followed their own interests and became an expert flutist, or a soccer star or even a master tightrope walker? What's so special about the violin and the piano?

Ms. Chua's most compelling argument is that happiness comes from mastery. "What Chinese parents understand is that nothing is fun until you're good at it." There is some truth to this, of course. But there is no reason to believe that calling your child "lazy" or "stupid" or "worthless" is a better way to motivate her to be good than some other more gentle but persistent mode. There is a vast world between perfection and loserdom. With her own children, Ms. Chua does not just want them to be good at what they do; she wants them to be better than everyone else.

10   "Children on their own never want to work," Ms. Chua writes, but in my experience this is not at all true. Left to their own devices, many children of this generation still have giant superegos and a mad drive to succeed. They want to run faster than their siblings, be smarter than their classmates and save the world from environmental disaster. In my household, it's a struggle to get my children to steal a cookie from the cookie jar without immediately confessing.

Before I had children, I worried about all the wrong things. I was raised by (immigrant) parents who did not have a lot of money, and so I spent my childhood roaming the streets of Queens looking for an open handball court. My children, by contrast, have been raised by relatively well-off parents who can afford to send them to good schools and drum lessons. I wanted them to be coddled and never to experience hardship. But childhood, like life, doesn't work that way. Privilege does not shield a child from being painfully shy or awkward around peers or generally ostracized. There are a thousand ways a child's life can be difficult, and it's a parent's job to help them navigate through them.

Because Ms. Chua really likes bullet points, I will offer some of my own:

- Success will not make you happy.
- Happiness is the great human quest.
- Children have to find happiness themselves.
- It is better to have a happy, moderately successful child than a miserable high-achiever.

"Western parents," Ms. Chua writes, "have to struggle with their own conflicted feelings about achievement and try and persuade themselves that they're not disappointed in how their kids turned out." With that, she really has our number. At the present moment in Western parenting, we believe that our children are special and entitled, but we do not have the guts or the tools to make that reality true for them. This explains, I think, a large part of the fascination with Ms. Chua's book.

But *Battle Hymn of the Tiger Mother* will lead us down the wrong path. The answer is not to aim for more effective child-perfecting techniques; it is to give up altogether on trying to perfect our children. Now I look upon those aimless days wandering the streets of Queens with fondness, because my life since then, starting the moment I entered a competitive high school, has been one ladder rung after another.

15   In her book, Ms. Chua refers, with some disdain, to her mother-in-law's belief that childhood should be full of "spontaneity, freedom, discovery and experience." My mother-in-law believes that, too, and she is especially gifted at facilitating it with whatever tools are at hand: a cardboard box, some pots and pans, torn envelopes. One afternoon I watched her play with my then-2-year old daughter for hours with some elephant toothpick holders and Play-Doh. I suppose that I could quantify what my daughter learned in those few hours: the letter E, the meaning of "pachyderm," who Hannibal was and how to love her grandmother 2% more. But the real point is that they earned themselves knee scabs marching across those imaginary Alps, and pretty soon it was time for a nap.

AMY CHUA IS A WIMP

David Brooks

David Brooks is a columnist for the *New York Times* and a commentator on the PBS *News Hour* and National Public Radio. He has written for the *Wall Street Journal* and the *Washington Times* and has been an editor for *The Weekly Standard, The Atlantic*, and *Newsweek. His books include the anthology* Backward and Upward: The New Conservative Writing (1996), *a book of cultural commentary,* Bobos in Paradise: The New Upper Class and How They Got There (2000), *and* On Paradise Drive: How We Live Now (And Always Have) in the Future Tense (2004). *This article appeared in the* New York Times *on January 17, 2011.*

Sometime early last week, a large slice of educated America decided that Amy Chua is a menace to society. Chua, as you probably know, is the Yale professor who has written a bracing critique of what she considers the weak, cuddling American parenting style.

Chua didn't let her own girls go out on play dates or sleepovers. She didn't let them watch TV or play video games or take part in garbage activities like crafts. Once, one of her daughters came in second to a Korean kid in a math competition, so Chua made the girl do 2,000 math problems a night until she regained her supremacy. Once, her daughters gave her birthday cards of insufficient quality. Chua rejected them and demanded new cards. Once, she threatened to burn all of one of her daughter's stuffed animals unless she played a piece of music perfectly.

As a result, Chua's daughters get straight As and have won a series of musical competitions.

In her book, *Battle Hymn of the Tiger Mother*, Chua delivers a broadside against American parenting even as she mocks herself for her own extreme "Chinese" style. She says American parents lack authority and produce entitled children who aren't forced to live up to their abilities.

5   The furious denunciations began flooding my in-box a week ago. Chua plays into America's fear of national decline. Here's a Chinese parent working really hard (and, by the way, there are a billion more of her) and her kids are going to crush ours. Furthermore (and this Chua doesn't appreciate), she is not really rebelling against American-style parenting; she is the logical extension of the prevailing elite practices. She does everything over-pressuring upper-middle-class parents are doing. She's just hard core.

Her critics echoed the familiar themes. Her kids can't possibly be happy or truly creative. They'll grow up skilled and compliant but without the audacity to be great. She's destroying their love for music. There's a reason Asian-American women between the ages of 15 and 24 have such high suicide rates.

I have the opposite problem with Chua. I believe she's coddling her children. She's protecting them from the most intellectually demanding activities because she doesn't understand what's cognitively difficult and what isn't.

Practicing a piece of music for four hours requires focused attention, but it is nowhere near as cognitively demanding as a sleepover with 14-year-old girls. Managing status rivalries, negotiating group dynamics, understanding social norms, navigating the distinction between self and group—these and other social tests impose cognitive demands that blow away any intense tutoring session or a class at Yale.

Yet mastering these arduous skills is at the very essence of achievement. Most people work in groups. We do this because groups are much more efficient at solving problems than individuals (swimmers are often motivated to have their best times as part of relay teams, not in individual events). Moreover, the performance of a group does not correlate well with the average I.Q. of the group or even with the I.Q.'s of the smartest members.

10   Researchers at the Massachusetts Institute of Technology and Carnegie Mellon have found that groups have a high collective intelligence when members of a group are good at reading each others' emotions—when they take turns

speaking, when the inputs from each member are managed fluidly, when they detect each others' inclinations and strengths.

Participating in a well-functioning group is really hard. It requires the ability to trust people outside your kinship circle, read intonations and moods, understand how the psychological pieces each person brings to the room can and cannot fit together.

This skill set is not taught formally, but it is imparted through arduous experiences. These are exactly the kinds of difficult experiences Chua shelters her children from by making them rush home to hit the homework table.

Chua would do better to see the classroom as a cognitive break from the truly arduous tests of childhood. Where do they learn how to manage people? Where do they learn to construct and manipulate metaphors? Where do they learn to perceive details of a scene the way a hunter reads a landscape? Where do they learn how to detect their own shortcomings? Where do they learn how to put themselves in others' minds and anticipate others' reactions?

These and a million other skills are imparted by the informal maturity process and are not developed if formal learning monopolizes a child's time.

15   So I'm not against the way Chua pushes her daughters. And I loved her book as a courageous and thought-provoking read. It's also more supple than her critics let on. I just wish she wasn't so soft and indulgent. I wish she recognized that in some important ways the school cafeteria is more intellectually demanding than the library. And I hope her daughters grow up to write their own books, and maybe learn the skills to better anticipate how theirs will be received.

IN THE EYE OF THE TIGER

Meghan Daum

Meghan Daum is a columnist for the *Los Angeles Times*, where this piece first appeared on January 20, 2011. Her work has also appeared in the *New Yorker*, *Harper's*, *GQ*, and the *Village Voice*. Daum has also published a novel, *The Quality of Life Report* (2004), a collection of essays, *My Misspent Youth* (2001), and a memoir, *Life Would Be Perfect if I Lived in That House* (2010).

Amy Chua, a Yale law professor and mother of two, was unknown to most of the world until two weeks ago. On Jan. 8, the *Wall Street Journal* published an excerpt from her then-forthcoming, now-bestselling book, *Battle Hymn of the Tiger Mother*. Part memoir and part manifesto, the excerpt was titled "Why Chinese Mothers Are Superior" and led with a list of activities and behaviors that Chua's two daughters, now teenagers, have never been allowed to engage in. These include "attend a sleepover," "have a play date," "be in a school play," "complain about not being in a school play" and "get anything less than an A."

That wasn't all. Chua's stratospherically demanding parenting technique, a carryover from her own Chinese immigrant parents, required playing violin or piano and practicing several hours a day, even if that meant rising before dawn. In a particularly harrowing passage, Chua forces her 7-year-old into learning a difficult piano piece. When the child screamed and kicked and tore up the music score, Chua hauled the girl's dollhouse to the car and threatened to donate it to the Salvation Army.

"I told her she was purposely working herself into a frenzy because she was secretly afraid she couldn't do it," Chua writes. "I told her to stop being lazy, cowardly, self-indulgent and pathetic." She also denied the girl a bathroom break as they worked on the piece well into the evening.

Needless to say, the excerpt went viral. Though many readers were appalled by her methods, others praised her for bucking the trend of parents wanting to be their kids' best friend.

5   But Chua, who's reportedly received death threats, now appears to be trying to soften her message. At Vroman's Bookstore in Pasadena on Tuesday night, she was in defense mode and even a bit flustered, saying repeatedly that the excerpt had been misleading and that the book, which "poured" out of her over eight weeks, was meant to be funny in places. But even as she backed away from the deadpan, inflammatory tone of the book—and chose to read from the ending so we could see she'd changed her ways—Chua stood her ground about the effectiveness (if not necessarily the superiority) of her parenting philosophy.

"We talk about giving our kids freedom," she said, "but the way to be free is to be able to get a good job and have the opportunities that come from hard work."

I can't argue with that. And, yes, I feel her pain that the *Wall Street Journal* went for the most incendiary stuff in "Tiger Mother" and topped it with a headline she didn't write. But once I read the book—this can be done, cover to cover, in a few hours—it became painfully clear that Chua's image problem isn't really due to her mothering style. It's due to her inability as a writer to handle the provocative tone of her book, particularly the ostensibly self-parodying aspects. (I think the dollhouse bit was an attempt to make fun of herself.) Where in real life she might be endearingly wacky, she comes across in the book as possibly crazy. For all her controlling impulses, as a writer she lacks the wit, pacing and emotional honesty to effectively control her own material.

Which is a shame really, because Chua has important things to say. Her book raises necessary questions about how permissive parenting affects not just children but society. She talks unflinchingly about the anxieties of the immigrant experience and the way the attendant work ethic feeds the myth that Asians are simply genetically smarter than Westerners.

In the end, though, I have to wonder if her lack of sensitivity to the tone and impact of her words doesn't in fact deliver a judgment about the very upbringing she espouses.

10   Chua's parenting method might garner perfect grades and test scores and multiple Harvard degrees (which she has, thank you very much). But maybe what gets sacrificed along the way is the ability to genuinely laugh at yourself, to recognize the absurd and to weave it into your existence—in other words, to

hone the tools necessary for effectively seeing yourself in full, so that you can make others understand where you're coming from.

That's less a skill that can be learned than a gift that can come from only one source: the experience of failure. Surely no kid should be denied that.

TIGER MOM VS. TIGER MAILROOM

Patrick Goldstein

Patrick Goldstein writes "The Big Picture," a *Los Angeles Times* column dealing with the film industry. This article first appeared in the *Times* on February 6, 2011.

It's hard to go anywhere these days, especially if you're a parent with young kids, where the conversation doesn't eventually turn to Amy Chua's red-hot child-rearing memoir, *Battle Hymn of the Tiger Mother*. It offers a provocative depiction of Chinese-style extreme parenting—her daughters are not allowed to watch TV, have playdates or get any grade below an A, all as preparation for success in life, beginning with getting into an Ivy League school, like their Tiger Mom, who went to Harvard and now teaches at Yale Law School.

But of all the heated reaction to Chua's parenting strategy, none was as compelling as what former Harvard President Larry Summers had to say when he discussed parenting with Chua at the recent World Economic Forum in Davos, Switzerland. Summers made a striking point, arguing that the two Harvard students who'd had the most transformative impact on the world in the past 25 years were Bill Gates and Mark Zuckerberg, yet neither had, ahem, graduated from college. If they had been brought up by a Tiger Mom, Summers imagined, she would've been bitterly disappointed.

I have no beef with Chua's parenting code, which hardly seems any more extreme than the neurotic ambitions of mothers and fathers I'm exposed to living on the Westside of Los Angeles. But if Chua wants a radically different perspective on the relationship between higher education and career achievement, she should spend some time in Hollywood, a place that's been run for nearly a century by men who never made it through or even to college. The original moguls were famously uneducated, often having started as peddlers and furriers before finding their perches atop the studio dream factories. But even today, the industry is still dominated by titanic figures, both on the creative and on the business side, who never got anywhere near Harvard Yard.

A short list of the industry leaders who never finished or even attended college would include Steve Jobs, David Geffen, Steven Spielberg, Jeffrey Katzenberg, James Cameron, Clint Eastwood, Barry Diller, Ron Meyer, Peter Jackson, Harvey Weinstein, Scott Rudin and Quentin Tarantino. Some of this is clearly a generational thing, since everyone on that list is over 40. On the other hand, the younger new-media icons seem as likely to be degree-free as their Hollywood brethren, whether it's Zuckerberg or the founders of Twitter, who didn't graduate from college either. (Though it's true that Zuckerberg might not have even thought of Facebook if he hadn't been in the sexually charged freshman swirl at Harvard.)

Common Thread

5 But in showbiz, you learn by doing. If there is a common denominator to all of those success stories, it's that they were all men in a hurry, impatient with book learning, which could only take them so far in the rough-and-tumble world of Hollywood. Ron Meyer, a founder of Creative Artists Agency and now president of Universal Studios, dropped out of high school, served in the Marines and proudly notes on his résumé that his first job was as a messenger boy for the Paul Kohner Agency.

"The truth is that if you have a particular talent and the will to succeed, you don't really need a great education," Meyer told me last week. "In showbiz, your real college experience is working in a talent agency mail-room. That's the one place where you can get the most complete understanding of the arena you're playing in and how to deal with the complicated situations you'll come across in your career."

There are plenty of successful lawyers and MBAs in Hollywood, but the raw spirit of can-do invention and inspiration will take people further than the ability to read a complex profit and loss statement. Years ago, Geffen, who dropped out of night school at Brooklyn College before eventually landing a job in the William Morris mail-room, once told me that his early success was rooted in the ability to develop relationships. "It's not about where you went to college or how good-looking you are or whether you could play football—it's about whether you can create a relationship."

To produce a film or create a TV show or found a company requires the same kind of raw entrepreneurial zeal that it must have taken the '49ers who came west in search of gold. "You often feel like you're surrounded by a do-it-yourself ethic, almost a pioneer spirit," says Michael De Luca, producer of *The Social Network*, who dropped out of NYU four credits short of graduation to take a job at New Line Cinema, where he rose to become head of production. "All those successful guys you're talking about—they had an intense desire to create something big, new and different. They didn't need to wait around for the instruction manual."

In David Rensin's wonderful oral history *The Mailroom: Hollywood History From the Bottom Up*, survivors of the Mike Ovitz-era CAA experience tell war stories about how, as mail-room flunkies, they had to replenish Ovitz's candy dishes, stock his jars with raw cashews and fill his water jar with Evian. It seemed like hellish drudgery but, as the agents recalled, it prepared you for all the craziness of later Hollywood life, where multimillion-dollar movie star deals could fall a part if someone's exercise trainer or makeup specialist wasn't provided.

Do the Hustle

10 Even today, people in Hollywood are far more impressed by, say, your knack for finding new talent than by what your grades were like. "Show business is all about instinct and intuition," says Sam Gores, head of the Paradigm Agency,

who went to acting school but never to college, having joined a meat-cutters' union by the time he was 18. "To succeed, you need to have a strong point of view and a lot of confidence. Sometimes being the most well-informed person in your circle can almost get in your way."

In show business, charm, hustle and guile are the aces in the deck. When New York Times columnist David Brooks was dissecting Chua's book recently, he argued that "managing status rivalries, negotiating group dynamics, understanding social norms, navigating the distinction between self and group" imposed the kind of cognitive demands that far exceed what's required of students in a class at Yale. He probably picked that up reading a fancy sociology text, but it was a letter-perfect description of the skill set for a gifted filmmaker, agent or producer.

In Hollywood, whether you were a C student or *summa cum laude*, it's a level playing field. "When you're working on a movie set, you've got 50 film professors to learn from, from the sound man to the cinematographer," says producer David Permut, who dropped out of UCLA to work for Roger Corman. "I've never needed a résumé in my whole career. All you need a 110-page script that some one is dying to make and you're in business."

AMERICA'S TOP PARENT

Elizabeth Kolbert

Elizabeth Kolbert is a staff writer for the *New Yorker*, where this article first appeared on January 20, 2011. Kolbert has also written for the *New York Times* and is the author of *Field Notes from a Catastrophe: Man and Nature and Climate Change* (2006).

"Call me garbage."

The other day, I was having dinner with my family when the subject of Amy Chua's new book, *Battle Hymn of the Tiger Mother* (Penguin Press; $25.95), came up. My twelve-year-old twins had been read an excerpt from the book by their teacher, a well-known provocateur. He had been sent a link to the excerpt by another teacher, who had received it from her sister, who had been e-mailed it by a friend, and, well, you get the point. The excerpt, which had appeared in the *Wall Street Journal* under the headline "WHY CHINESE MOTHERS ARE SUPERIOR," was, and still is, an Internet sensation—as one blogger put it, the "Andromeda Strain of viral memes." Within days, more than five thousand comments had been posted, and "Tiger Mother" vaulted to No. 4 on Amazon's list of best-sellers. Chua appeared on NPR's "All Things Considered" and on NBC's "Nightly News" and "Today" show. Her book was the topic of two columns in last week's Sunday *Times*, and, under the racially neutral headline "IS EXTREME PARENTING EFFECTIVE?," the subject of a formal debate on the paper's Web site.

Thanks to this media blitz, the basic outlines of *Tiger Mother*'s story are by now familiar. Chua, the daughter of Chinese immigrants, is a Yale Law School professor. She is married to another Yale law professor and has two daughters, whom she drives relentlessly. Chua's rules for the girls include: no sleepovers, no playdates, no grade lower than an A on report cards, no choosing your own extracurricular activities, and no ranking lower than No. 1 in any subject. (An exception to this last directive is made for gym and drama.)

In Chua's binary world, there are just two kinds of mother. There are "Chinese mothers," who, she allows, do not necessarily have to be Chinese. "I'm using the term 'Chinese mothers' loosely," she writes. Then, there are "Western" mothers. Western mothers think they are being strict when they insist that their children practice their instruments for half an hour a day. For Chinese mothers, "the first hour is the easy part." Chua chooses the instruments that her daughters will play—piano for the older one, Sophia; violin for the younger, Lulu—and stands over them as they practice for three, four, sometimes five hours at a stretch. The least the girls are expected to do is make it to Carnegie Hall. Amazingly enough, Sophia does. Chua's daughters are so successful—once, it's true, Sophia came in second on a multiplication test (to a Korean boy), but Chua made sure this never happened again—that they confirm her thesis: Western mothers are losers. I'm using the term "losers" loosely.

5   Chua has said that one of the points of the book is "making fun of myself," but plainly what she was hoping for was to outrage. Whole chapters of "Tiger Mother"—admittedly, many chapters are only four or five pages long—are given over to incidents like that of the rejected smiley face.

"I don't want this," she tells Lulu, throwing back at her a handmade birthday card. "I want a better one."

In another chapter, Chua threatens to take Lulu's doll house to the Salvation Army and, when that doesn't work, to deny her lunch, dinner, and birthday parties for "two, three, four years" because she cannot master a piece called "The Little White Donkey." The kid is seven years old. In a third chapter, Chua tells Sophia she is "garbage." Chua's own father has called her "garbage," and she finds it a highly effective parenting technique. Chua relates this at a dinner party, and one of the guests supposedly gets so upset that she breaks down in tears. The hostess tries to patch things up by suggesting that Chua is speaking figuratively.

"You didn't actually call Sophia garbage," the hostess offers.

"Yes, I did," Chua says.

10   When the dinner-party episode was read in class, my sons found it hilarious, which is why they were taunting me. "Call me garbage," one of the twins said again. "I dare you."

"O.K.," I said, trying, for once, to be a good mother. "You're garbage."

If Chua's tale has any significance—and it may not—it is as an allegory. Chua refers to herself as a Tiger because according to the Chinese zodiac she was born in the Year of the Tiger. Tiger people are "powerful, authoritative, and magnetic," she informs us, just as tigers that walk on four legs inspire "fear and respect." The "tiger economies" of Asia aren't mentioned in the book, but they growl menacingly in the background.

It's just about impossible to pick up a newspaper these days—though who actually *picks up* a newspaper anymore?—without finding a story about the rise of the East. The headlines are variations on a theme: "SOLAR PANEL MAKER MOVES WORK TO CHINA"; "CHINA DRAWING HIGH-TECH RESEARCH FROM

U.S."; "IBM CUTTING 5,000 SERVICE JOBS; MOVING WORK TO INDIA." What began as an outflow of manufacturing jobs has spread way beyond car parts and electronics to include information technology, legal advice, even journalism. (This piece could have been written much more cost-effectively by a team in Bangalore and, who knows, maybe next month it will be.)

On our good days, we tell ourselves that our kids will be all right. The new, global economy, we observe, puts a premium on flexibility and creativity. And who is better prepared for such a future than little Abby (or Zachary), downloading her wacky videos onto YouTube while she texts her friends, messes with Photoshop, and listens to her iPod?

15   "Yes, you can brute-force any kid to learn to play the piano—just precisely like his or her billion neighbors" is how one of the comments on the *Wall Street Journal's* Web site put it. "But you'll never get a Jimi Hendrix that way."

On our bad days, we wonder whether this way of thinking is, as Chua might say, garbage. Last month, the results of the most recent Programme for International Student Assessment, or PISA, tests were announced. It was the first time that Chinese students had participated, and children from Shanghai ranked first in every single area. Students from the United States, meanwhile, came in seventeenth in reading, twenty-third in science, and an especially demoralizing thirty-first in math. This last ranking put American kids not just behind the Chinese, the Koreans, and the Singaporeans but also after the French, the Austrians, the Hungarians, the Slovenians, the Estonians, and the Poles.

"I know skeptics will want to argue with the results, but we consider them to be accurate and reliable," Arne Duncan, the U.S. Secretary of Education, told the *Times*. "The United States came in twenty-third or twenty-fourth in most subjects. We can quibble, or we can face the brutal truth that we're being out-educated."

Why is this? How is it that the richest country in the world can't teach kids to read or to multiply fractions? Taken as a parable, Chua's cartoonish narrative about browbeating her daughters acquires a certain disquieting force. Americans have been told always to encourage their kids. This, the theory goes, will improve their self-esteem, and this, in turn, will help them learn.

After a generation or so of applying this theory, we have the results. Just about the only category in which American students outperform the competition is self-regard. Researchers at the Brookings Institution, in one of their frequent studies of education policy, compared students' assessments of their abilities in math with their scores on a standardized test. Nearly forty per cent of American eighth graders agreed "a lot" with the statement "I usually do well in mathematics," even though only seven per cent of American students actually got enough correct answers on the test to qualify as advanced. Among Singaporean students, eighteen per cent said they usually did well in math; forty-four per cent qualified as advanced. As the Brookings researchers pointed out, even the least self-confident Singaporean students, on average, outscored the most self-confident Americans. You can say it's sad that kids in Singapore are so beaten down that they can't appreciate their own accomplishments. But you've got to give them this: at least they get the math right.

20   Our problems as a country cannot, of course, be reduced to our problems as educators or as parents. Nonetheless, there is an uncomfortable analogy. For some time now, the U.S. has, in effect, been drawing crappy, smiley-face birthday cards and calling them wonderful. It's made us feel a bit better about ourselves without improving the basic situation. As the cover story on China's ascent in this month's *Foreign Policy* sums things up: "American Decline: This Time It's Real."

It's hard to believe that Chua's book would be causing quite as much stir without the geopolitical subtext. (Picture the reaction to a similar tale told by a Hungarian or an Austrian über-mom.) At the same time, lots of people have clearly taken "Tiger Mother" personally.

Of the zillions of comments that have been posted on the Web, many of the most passionate are from scandalized "Western" mothers and fathers, or, as one blogger dubbed them, "Manatee dads." Some have gone as far as to suggest that Chua be arrested for child abuse. At least as emotional are the posts from Asians and Asian-Americans.

"Parents like Amy Chua are the reason why Asian-Americans like me are in therapy," Betty Ming Liu, who teaches journalism at N.Y.U., wrote on her blog.

"What's even more damning is her perpetuation of the media stereotypes of Asian-Americans," Frank Chi, a political consultant, wrote in the Boston *Globe's* opinion blog.

25   "Having lived through a version of the Chinese Parenting Experience, and having been surrounded since birth with hundreds of CPE graduates, I couldn't not say something," a contributor to the Web site Shanghaiist wrote after the *Wall Street Journal* excerpt appeared. "The article actually made me feel physically ill."

Chua's response to some of the unkind things said about her—she has reported getting death threats—has been to backpedal. "RETREAT OF THE 'TIGER MOTHER'" was the headline of one *Times* article. (It, too, quickly jumped to the top of the paper's "most e-mailed" list.) Chua has said that it was not her plan to write a parenting manual: "My actual book is not a how-to guide." Somehow or other, her publisher seems to be among those who missed this. The back cover spells out, in black and red type, "How to Be a Tiger Mother."

According to Chua, her "actual book" is a memoir. Memoir is, or at least is supposed to be, a demanding genre. It requires that the author not just narrate his or her life but reflect on it. By her own description, Chua is not a probing person. Of her years studying at Harvard Law School, she writes:

> I didn't care about the rights of criminals the way others did, and I froze whenever a professor called on me. I also wasn't naturally skeptical and questioning; I just wanted to write down everything the professor said and memorize it.

Battle Hymn of the Tiger Mother exhibits much the same lack of interest in critical thinking. It's breezily written, at times entertaining, and devoid of anything approaching introspection. Imagine your most self-congratulatory friend holding forth for two hours about her kids' triumphs, and you've more or less got the narrative. The only thing that keeps it together is Chua's cheerful faith that whatever happened to her or her daughters is interesting just because it happened to happen to them. In addition to all the schlepping back and forth to auditions, there are two chapters on Chua's dogs (Samoyeds named Coco and Pushkin), three pages of practice notes that she left behind for Lulu when she could not be there to berate her in person, and a complete list of the places that she had visited with her kids by the time they were twelve and nine:

> London, Paris, Nice, Rome, Venice, Milan, Amsterdam, The Hague, Barcelona, Madrid, Málaga, Liechtenstein, Monaco, Munich, Dublin, Brussels, Bruges, Strasbourg, Beijing, Shanghai, Tokyo, Hong Kong, Manila, Istanbul, Mexico City, Cancún, Buenos Aires, Santiago, Rio de Janeiro, São Paulo, La Paz, Sucre, Cochabamba, Jamaica, Tangier, Fez, Johannesburg, Cape Town, and the Rock of Gibraltar.

Chua's husband is not Chinese, in either sense of the word. He makes occasional appearances in the book to try—ineffectually, it seems—to shield the girls. Chua has said that she wrote more about their arguments, but her husband didn't like those passages, so they've been cut. Perhaps had more of his voice been included it would have provided some grit and at least the semblance of engagement. As it is, though, it's just her. "I'm happy to be the one hated," she tells her husband at one point, and apparently she means it.

30   Parenting is hard. As anyone who has gone through the process and had enough leisure (and still functioning brain cells) to reflect on it knows, a lot of it is a crapshoot. Things go wrong that you have no control over, and, on occasion, things also go right, and you have no control over those, either. The experience is scary and exhilarating and often humiliating, not because you're disappointed in your kids, necessarily, but because you're disappointed in yourself.

Some things do go wrong in Chua's memoir. Her mother-in-law dies; her younger sister develops leukemia. These events get roughly the same amount of space as Coco and Pushkin, and yet they are, on their own terms, moving. More central to the story line is a screaming fit in a Moscow restaurant during which a glass is thrown. The upshot of the crisis is that Lulu is allowed to take up tennis, which Chua then proceeds to micromanage.

Chua clearly wants to end her book by claiming that she has changed. She knows enough about the conventions of memoir-writing to understand that some kind of transformation is generally required. But she can't bring herself to do it. And so in the final pages she invokes the Founding Fathers. They, too, she tells her daughters, would not have approved of sleepovers.

In Defense of Being a Kid

James Bernard Murphy

James Bernard Murphy is a professor of government at Dartmouth College, where he teaches the philosophy of law, ethics, and education, subjects on which he has written extensively. The following piece first appeared as an op-ed in the *Wall Street Journal* on February 9, 2011.

Amy Chua, the "tiger mother," is clearly hitting a nerve—especially among the anxious class (it used to be called the upper class), which understands how much skill and discipline are necessary for success in the new economy.

What Ms. Chua and her critics agree on is that childhood is all about preparation for adulthood. Ms. Chua claims that her parenting methods will produce ambitious, successful and happy adults—while her critics argue that her methods will produce neurotic, self-absorbed and unhappy ones.

It took economist Larry Summers, in a debate with Ms. Chua at the World Economic Forum in Davos, to point out that part of the point of childhood is childhood itself. Childhood takes up a quarter of one's life, Mr. Summers observed, and it would be nice if children enjoyed it.

Bravo, Larry.

5   Children are not merely adults in training. They are also people with distinctive powers and joys. A happy childhood is measured not only by the standards of adult success, but also by the enjoyment of the gifts given to children alone.

What are the unique blessings of childhood?

First is the gift of moral innocence: Young children are liberated from the burdens of the knowledge of the full extent of human evil—a knowledge that casts a pall over adult life. Childhood innocence permits children to trust others fully. How wonderful to live (even briefly) with such confidence in human goodness. Childhood innocence teaches us what the world ought to be.

Second is the gift of openness to the future. We adults are hamstrung by our own plans and expectations. Children alone are free to welcome the most improbable new adventures.

Third, children are liberated from the grim economy of time. Children become so absorbed in fantasy play and projects that they lose all sense of time. For them, time is not scarce and thus cannot be wasted.

10   Finally, we parents are so focused on adult superiority that we forget that most of us produced our best art, asked our deepest philosophical questions, and most readily mastered new gadgets when we were mere children.

Tragically, there is a real conflict within childhood between preparation for adulthood and the enjoyment of the gifts of youth. Preparation for adulthood requires the adoption of adult prudence, discipline and planning that undermine the spontaneous adventure of childhood.

Parents are deeply conflicted about how to balance these two basic demands: raising good little ladies and gentlemen, while also permitting children to escape into the irresponsible joys of Neverland.

Our wisest sages also disagree fundamentally about the nature of childhood. The ancient Greek philosopher Aristotle famously declared that "no child is happy" on the grounds that children are incapable of the complex moral and intellectual activities that constitute a flourishing life. Aristotle said that when we describe a child as happy, what we mean is that he or she is anticipating the achievements of adult life. For him, the only good thing about childhood is that we leave it behind.

By contrast, Jesus frequently praised children, welcomed their company, and even commanded adults to emulate them: "Unless you become like a little child, you shall not enter the kingdom of God."

15   Tom Sawyer enjoyed a childhood of nearly pure adventure with minimal preparation for adult life. The 19th-century philosopher John Stuart Mill, by contrast, barely survived a "tiger father" who enforced a regime of ruthless discipline and learning that would make Ms. Chua blanche.

    Most of us would like Tom's childhood followed by Mill's adulthood. But as parents we are stuck with trying to balance the paradoxical demands of both preparing our children for adulthood and protecting them from it.

    As the current dustup shows, many parents today would benefit hugely by taking a reflective time-out from teaching our children to discover how much we might learn from them.

SUMMARY

Following the guidelines in Chapter 1, particularly the Guidelines for Writing Summaries box (pp. 7–8), summarize "Chinese Mothers are Superior" by Amy Chua. In preparation for writing the summary, review the model summary (pp. 19–20) and consult the advice on note-taking (pp. 13–15).

As an alternative, summarize one of the other selections in this chapter. The article by Kolbert would also be a good subject for summary.

CRITIQUE

Following the guidelines in Chapter 2, particularly the Guidelines for Writing Critiques box (p. 65), write a critique of "Chinese Mothers are Superior." The early part of the critique should draw upon the summary of Chua that you prepared for the previous assignment. In preparation for writing the critique, review the model critique (p. 67–72).

You've probably already noticed that most of the articles following Chua are to some extent critiques of either "Why Chinese Mothers Are Superior" or the book from which this selection was drawn, *Battle Hymn of the Tiger Mother*. Some authors argue with her basic premise, some support it, though perhaps with reservations, and others discuss related issues such as the preparedness of America's youth to compete with their counterparts in China. In developing your own critique, you're free to draw upon these other authors; but you should also stake out your own position based upon your own observations and experience and your own understanding of the issues Chua discusses. Doing so will help ensure that your critique isn't merely a compendium of other authors' observations and arguments.

    Begin preparing for the critique by reflecting on your own observations and experiences in relation to Chua's main assumption (expressed in the two sentences that open ¶ 5): "What Chinese parents understand is that nothing is fun until you're good at it. To get good at anything you have to work, and children on their own never want to work, which is why it is crucial to override their preferences." Ask yourself:

- To what extent do you agree that "nothing is fun until you're good at it"? Do your own experiences and the experiences of your friends and relatives bear out this assumption? What have you read that supports or refutes it?

- Do you agree that "children on their own never want to work"? Cite examples in support or to the contrary.

- Consider the proposition that it is crucial for parents to override children's natural disinclination to work, in light of your own experiences, observations, and reading.

Throughout Chua's op-ed, you'll encounter controversial statements such as this one, along with anecdotes about the ways she has driven her children, sometimes mercilessly, in pursuit of her standards of excellence and success. And you'll find numerous comparisons between "Chinese" and "Western" approaches to child rearing. Your assessment of these statements should provide a rich source of material for your own critique.

Here's a suggested organizational plan for your critique:

1. An introduction, setting the issue in context (see Chapter 3 for advice on creating introductions)

2. A summary of Chua's op-ed (a brief version of your response to the summary assignment above)

3. An evaluation of Chua's piece for clarity, logic, and/or fairness (the Question #1 topics in Chapter 2, pp. 48–49)

4. An account of your own agreement or disagreement with Chua's argument (the Question #2 topics in Chapter 2, pp. 60–63)

5. A conclusion (see Chapter 3 for advice on creating conclusions)

In preparing your critique, follow the advice in Chapter 2, see particularly the Guidelines for Writing Critiques box (p. 65), along with the hints in Chapter 1 on incorporating summaries, paraphrases, and quoted material into your own writing (p. 44).

 ## EXPLANATORY SYNTHESIS

Based on the readings in this chapter, write an explanatory synthesis that you might use in a broader argument on the subject of varying approaches to child rearing and preparing children to be competitive in the workplace of the future. The synthesis should each consist of three to five well-developed paragraphs on the following topics: (1) an account of the controversy over Chua's op-ed and the book from which it was drawn; (2) an account of the two different approaches to parenting represented by the "Chinese" and "Western" models; and (3) an account of the different approaches to preparing children to be competitive in the current and future marketplace. Follow the guidelines in Chapter 4, particularly the Guidelines for Writing Syntheses box (pp. 101–102); review also the model explanatory synthesis (pp. 121–128), though your assignment here calls for a considerably briefer paper.

Key requirements for the explanatory synthesis:

- Craft a thesis for your paper, a single statement that will guide the writing of the paragraphs of explanation that follow.

- Begin each paragraph of explanation that follows the explanatory thesis with a clear topic sentence.

- Refer in each paragraph of explanation to *at least two* different sources. Set up the references carefully, using an appropriate citation format, most likely MLA (see the "Quick Index" at the end of this text).

- In developing your explanatory synthesis, draw on facts, examples, statistics, and expert opinions from your sources.

ANALYSIS

Select a principle or definition discussed in one of the readings in "The Roar of the Tiger Mom" and apply this principle or definition to either (1) a particular situation of which you have personal knowledge or (2) a situation that you have learned about in the course of your reading. Follow the guidelines in Chapter 6, particularly the Guidelines for Writing Analyses box (p. 185); review also the model analysis (pp. 192–198).

First, review the topic list you created in Group Assignment #1 after reading the selections in this chapter. At least one of the items on the list may point the way to an analytic principle that resonates with you. If so, follow through by locating a particular quotation that articulates this principle. Here are some examples of such quotations from the readings:

- "But as a parent, one of the worst things you can do for your child's self-esteem is to let them give up. On the flip side, there's nothing better for building confidence than learning you can do something you thought you couldn't." (Chua, p. 265)

- "What privileged American children need is not more skills and rules and math drills. They need to lighten up and roam free, to express themselves in ways not dictated by their uptight, over-invested parents." (Rosin, p. 266)

- "Managing status rivalries, negotiating group dynamics, understanding social norms, navigating the distinction between self and group—these and other social tests impose cognitive demands that blow away any intense tutoring session or a class at Yale." (Brooks, p. 269).

- "For some time now, the U.S. has, in effect, been drawing crappy, smiley-faced birthday cards and calling them wonderful." (Kolbert, p. 277)

- "A happy childhood is measured not only by standards of adult success, but also by the enjoyment of the gifts given to children alone." (Murphy, p. 279)

Consider using the following structure for your analysis:

1. An introductory paragraph that sets a context for the topic and presents the claim you intend to support in the analysis that follows. Your claim (your thesis) distills the conclusions you've drawn from your analysis. Your claim may appear at the end of the introductory paragraph (or introductory section).

2. A paragraph or two introducing the analytic tool or principle you intend to use and discussing its key components. Suppose you decided to use Brooks' quotation as an analytic principle. You would need to explain what he means by one or more of these skills: "[m]anaging status rivalries," "negotiating group dynamics," "understanding social norms," and "navigating the distinction between self and group." You would also need to explain how successfully managing such social tests imposes "cognitive demands that blow away any intense tutoring session or a class at Yale." Note, however, that you're not required to establish that one set of tasks is *more* difficult or important than the other. It may be sufficient for your purpose to establish simply that the social skills are at least *as* important as the academic skills. Once you establish this analytic principle, you can proceed with the analysis.

3. A paragraph or two describing the situation that you will analyze—drawn from your own personal experience or observation or from your reading.

4. Several paragraphs (this is the heart of your analysis) in which you systematically apply the key components of the principle you have selected to the situation you have described. Staying with Brooks, you would apply such key components as managing status rivalries, negotiating group dynamics, and so on to the situation you have described. As you apply these key components each in turn, in separate paragraphs or groupings of paragraphs, you would discuss why such skills are, if not *more* difficult than undergoing a demanding class or tutoring session, then at least *as valuable* for success in later life as academic skills.

5. A conclusion in which you argue that, based on the insights gained through your analysis, the experience or situation in question can now be understood more deeply. See Chapter 3 (pp. 87–93) for advice on concluding your papers.

ARGUMENT

Write an argument synthesis based upon the selections in "The Roar of the Tiger Mom." You may find it useful to draw upon the products of your earlier assignments in this section on summary, critique, explanatory synthesis, and analysis. Follow the guidelines in Chapter 5, particularly the Guidelines for Writing Synthesis box in Chapter 4 (pp. 101–102); review also the model argument synthesis (pp. 121–128).

In planning your synthesis, review the master list of topics and notes that you and your classmates generated for Group Assignment #1 above (p. 260), and draw upon what the authors of the passages have written about these topics in developing your outline. Devise a claim, a thesis that distills your argument to a sentence or two. Plan to support your claim with facts, opinions, and statistics from the passages.

Note that one synthesis—a single paper—could not possibly refer to every topic, or every connection among authors, that you have found. The craft of preparing and writing a synthesis depends on your ability to *select* closely related topics and then to make and develop a claim that links and can be supported by them. You don't have to refer to *all* of the selections in this chapter while developing your paper; but you will likely want to refer to most. You may even want to research additional sources.

In formulating arguments on a controversial issue—for example, immigration, abortion, the size of government, or capital punishment—the immediate temptation is to adopt one strong (and uncompromising) position or to adopt its counterpart on the opposite side. Many commentators on Chua's book or op-ed tend to divide themselves into pro-Chua or anti-Chua camps: she's either dead right about her approach to parenting or she's dead wrong. Arguments supporting such polarized positions may be forceful, even eloquent, but seldom persuade those predisposed to the opposite point of view. (See "The Limits of Argument" in Chapter 5, pp. 136–137.)

After considering all the facts and the assertions, strive yourself for a more nuanced approach. This doesn't necessarily mean adopting a straight-down-the-middle/split-the-difference position, which is likely to persuade no one. It does mean acknowledging opposing arguments and dealing with them in good faith. (See "Present and Respond to Counterarguments" in Chapter 5, pp. 168–169.) It does mean considering the issue afresh, thinking about the implications of the problems and the possible solutions, and coming up with your own insights, your own distinctive take on the subject. Such thought, such nuance, should be reflected in your thesis. (See "Writing a Thesis" in Chapter 3, pp. 75–76.)

Without writing your thesis for you, we'll suppose for the sake of example that the subject of your argument synthesis concerns how the debate over Chua's ideas clarifies how parents can best help their children to succeed as they prepare for adulthood. An arguable claim on the subject would likely state which approach to child rearing, in your opinion, would best prepare children. Here's one way of structuring such an argument synthesis:

- An introductory paragraph that sets a context for the topic—in the example above, the debate over Chua's op-ed and the best pathway to success—and presents the claim you intend to support in the argument that follows. Your claim (that is, your argumentative thesis) may appear at the end of this paragraph (or introductory section).

- A paragraph or two summarizing Chua's ideas. This section may be an abbreviated version of the summary you wrote earlier.

- One to three paragraphs discussing some of the commentary on Chua's ideas, organized by topic, rather than author. That is, identify two or three main categories of response to Chua—favorable, unfavorable, and neutral—and take up each category in turn. You may have created topic webs for these categories when preparing to write. See Group Assignments #1 and #2.

- A paragraph or two discussing your own assessment of the best pathway (or pathways) to success, supported in part by the comments of some of the authors in this chapter. Relate this assessment to ideas contained within the articles by Chua and her critics. For this section you may want to draw upon your responses to the earlier analysis or critique assignments. You may even elect to consult additional sources on the subject (for example, Chua's op-ed in the online edition of the *Wall Street Journal* is followed by almost nine thousand reader comments).

- A counterargument section, in which you concede the validity of positions on the subject different from your own and acknowledge the ideas of authors in this section with whom you disagree.

- A "nevertheless" section, in which you respond to the counterarguments and reaffirm your own position.

- A paragraph or two of conclusion. See Chapter 3 (pp. 87–93) for advice on concluding your papers.

Where you place the various elements of this argument synthesis will be your decision as writer. Which sources to use and what logic to present in defense of your claim is also yours to decide. See pages 152–153 for help in thinking about structuring and supporting your argument.

A Note on Incorporating Quotations and Paraphrases   Identify the sources you intend to use for your synthesis. Working with a phrase, sentence, or brief passage from each, use a variety of the techniques discussed in the section Incorporating Quotations into Your Sentences, Chapter 1 (pp. 40–45), to write sentences that you can use to advance your argument. Some of these sentences should demonstrate the use of ellipsis marks and brackets. See pages 42–45 in Chapter 1. Paraphrase passages, as needed, and incorporate these as well into your papers.

Part III

An Anthology of Readings

10

The Changing Landscape of Work in the Twenty-First Century

You attend college for many reasons, but perhaps none is so compelling as the hope and expectation that higher education offers a passport to a better future, a future based on meaningful employment and financial independence—especially in an uncertain economy.

As fate would have it, you will enter the American workforce at a particularly dynamic and (most would acknowledge) stressful time. The recent "Great Recession" (January 2007–June 2009) continues to roil the economy. But long before the recession took hold, the twin forces of globalization and computer-driven technology began to alter the workplace of your future. If the wisdom of the analysts and economists collected in this chapter could be reduced to a single statement of advice, it would be this: Think strategically about your future working life.

As you begin, some recent history can provide perspective. In the second half of the twentieth century, since the end of World War II, the labor market rewarded the educated, conferring on those who attended college an "education premium." Even as the forces of globalization reshaped the American economy and workers began losing manufacturing jobs to competitors offshore in China and India, college-educated workers were generally spared major career disruptions. Today, higher education no longer promises such protection. The relentless search for cheap labor and plentiful raw materials, together with advances in technology, have opened the information-based service economy to foreign competition. Increasingly, the American college-educated workforce will face the same relentless pressures that decades ago unsettled the automotive and manufacturing sectors. Employers are already offshoring computer coding, certain types of accounting, and medical consultation (the reading of X-rays, MRIs, CT scans, and such)—services that require extensive training. Experts predict that more

American jobs will be lost to foreign competition and fewer will entail a lifelong commitment between employer and employee. What are the implications of these developments for you and your intended career? Will they affect the courses you take, the major (and minors) you choose, the summer jobs and internships you pursue? Could you investigate *now* how to anticipate and avoid major disruptions to your working life tomorrow?

This chapter provides an opportunity to learn what economists, policy analysts, sociologists, educators, statisticians, and journalists are forecasting about the world of work in the twenty-first century. You'll find ten selections presented in four components, beginning with *Prospects for Graduates*. Jenna Brager's "A Post-College Flow Chart of Misery and Pain" might cut a little close to the bone for those pursuing a humanities degree. Next, reporter Catherine Rampell takes a snapshot of job prospects for graduates in May 2011, concluding that "Many with New College Degree Find Job Market Humbling." But writing just six months later, Lacey Johnson reports that the "Job Outlook for College Graduates Is Slowly Improving."

The second component of readings, *Data on the Job Market*, opens with a recent report showing that when it comes time for graduating seniors to find a job, "Not All College Degrees Are Created Equal." Next you'll find the U.S. Bureau of Labor Statistics summary of its employment projections for 2010–2020. This summary and the accompanying tables point you to vast online resources for determining which sectors of the economy are adding jobs and which are eliminating jobs.

What you do with this information as you chart a course of study is up to you; and what you decide will affect your sense of yourself—if, that is, you accept the premise of sociologist Richard Sennett, writing on *Work and Identity*. In this third component of the chapter, Sennett relates the story of a man whose talents for business allowed him to succeed in modern corporate life but at the cost of "corroding" his character. The selection will provoke you to consider how your job choices may affect your sense of self.

The final component of selections addresses *Trends Affecting Work*. Here, you will read what an economist, a former hedge-fund manager, and reporters predict about coming changes in the workforce. Adam Davidson investigates tectonic changes in American manufacturing, which (though surprising to many) is booming at present—in ways that benefit workers with specific skill sets. Next, former presidential advisor Alan Blinder traces the migration of service jobs (even those requiring a college degree) away from American shores. The chapter concludes with two writers who predict winners and losers in the evolving workplace. Former hedge-fund manager Andy Kessler asks "Is Your Job an Endangered Species?" Finally, economist and Nobel laureate Paul Krugman questions the widely assumed link between a college degree and job security.

The workplace you'll be entering is doubly uncertain as it struggles to emerge from a long recession and morphs due to global and technological forces that will continue to play out in the years to come. As you search for employment now and in the near future, the selections in this chapter may help inform your choices.

PROSPECTS FOR GRADUATES

That perfect job: It's out there, you hope—even in these distressed times. And now, you're taking the first steps to get it. In part, isn't this why you've come to college—to acquire skills that will lead to satisfying, well-paid work? You know the economy is uncertain, and you're more than curious: Just what are the job prospects these days for new college graduates?

This first component of readings will help to provide some answers. We begin with a provocative teaser—"A Post-College Flow Chart of Misery and Pain" by Jenna Brager, who writes a weekly webcomic for curmudgeoncomic.com. In this satiric look at job possibilities for humanities majors, Brager raises an important question: If the job market is so tough for humanities majors, why would anyone study the humanities? People do, of course—for many reasons, not always related to employability. This graphic first appeared on the shareable.com Web site and in its online book *Share or Die: Youth in Recession*.

Rounding out the "Prospects" component are two selections on job prospects for recent graduates. Writing for the *New York Times* on May 18, 2011, economics reporter Catherine Rampell concludes that "Many with New College Degree Find Job Market Humbling." Just six months later, Lacey Johnson reports in the *Chronicle of Higher Education* (November 17, 2011) that the "Job Outlook for College Graduates [is] Slowly Improving." Notwithstanding this brightening picture, the job market remains in flux. After reading these selections, you may want to update what you've learned by running a quick Internet search on "job prospects for college students."

A POST-COLLEGE FLOW CHART OF MISERY AND PAIN

Jenna Brager

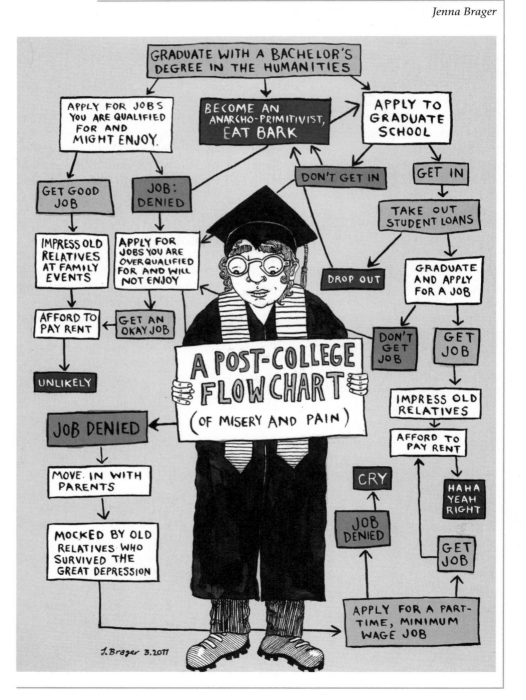

Many with New College Degree Find the Job Market Humbling

Catherine Rampell

The individual stories are familiar. The chemistry major tending bar. The classics major answering phones. The Italian studies major sweeping aisles at Wal-Mart.

Now evidence is emerging that the damage wrought by the sour economy is more widespread than just a few careers led astray or postponed. Even for college graduates—the people who were most protected from the slings and arrows of recession—the outlook is rather bleak.

Employment rates for new college graduates have fallen sharply in the last two years, as have starting salaries for those who can find work. What's more, only half of the jobs landed by these new graduates even require a college degree, reviving debates about whether higher education is "worth it" after all.

"I have friends with the same degree as me, from a worse school, but because of who they knew or when they happened to graduate, they're in much better jobs," said Kyle Bishop, 23, a 2009 graduate of the University of Pittsburgh who has spent the last two years waiting tables, delivering beer, working at a bookstore and entering data. "It's more about luck than anything else."

5   The median starting salary for students graduating from four-year colleges in 2009 and 2010 was $27,000, down from $30,000 for those who entered the work force in 2006 to 2008, according to a study released on Wednesday by the John J. Heldrich Center for Workforce Development at Rutgers University. That is a decline of 10 percent, even before taking inflation into account.

Of course, these are the lucky ones—the graduates who found a job. Among the members of the class of 2010, just 56 percent had held at least one job by this spring, when the survey was conducted. That compares with 90 percent of graduates from the classes of 2006 and 2007. (Some have gone for further education or opted out of the labor force, while many are still pounding the pavement.)

Even these figures understate the damage done to these workers' careers. Many have taken jobs that do not make use of their skills; about only half of recent college graduates said that their first job required a college degree.

The choice of major is quite important. Certain majors had better luck finding a job that required a college degree, according to an analysis by Andrew M. Sum, an economist at Northeastern University, of 2009 Labor Department data for college graduates under 25.

Young graduates who majored in education and teaching or engineering were most likely to find a job requiring a college degree, while area studies majors—those who majored in Latin American studies, for example—and humanities majors were least likely to do so. Among all recent education graduates, 71.1 percent were in jobs that required a college degree; of all area studies majors, the share was 44.7 percent.

10   An analysis by the *New York Times* of Labor Department data about college graduates aged 25 to 34 found that the number of these workers employed in food service, restaurants and bars had risen 17 percent in 2009 from 2008, though the sample size was small. There were similar or bigger employment increases at gas stations and fuel dealers, food and alcohol stores, and taxi and limousine services.

This may be a waste of a college degree, but it also displaces the less-educated workers who would normally take these jobs.

"The less schooling you had, the more likely you were to get thrown out of the labor market altogether," said Mr. Sum, noting that unemployment rates for high school graduates and dropouts are always much higher than those for college graduates. "There is complete displacement all the way down."

Meanwhile, college graduates are having trouble paying off student loan debt, which is at a median of $20,000 for graduates of classes 2006 to 2010.

Mr. Bishop, the Pittsburgh graduate, said he is "terrified" of the effects his starter jobs might have on his ultimate career, which he hopes to be in publishing or writing. "It looks bad to have all these short-term jobs on your résumé, but you do have to pay the bills," he said, adding that right now his student loan debt was over $70,000.

15   Many graduates will probably take on more student debt. More than 60 percent of those who graduated in the last five years say they will need more formal education to be successful.

"I knew there weren't going to be many job prospects for me until I got my Ph.D.," said Travis Patterson, 23, a 2010 graduate of California State University, Fullerton. He is working as an administrative assistant for a property management company and studying psychology in graduate school. While it may not have anything to do with his degree, "it helps pay my rent and tuition, and that's what matters."

Going back to school does offer the possibility of joining the labor force when the economy is better. Unemployment rates are also generally lower for people with advanced schooling.

Those who do not go back to school may be on a lower-paying trajectory for years. They start at a lower salary, and they may begin their careers with employers that pay less on average or have less room for growth.

"Their salary history follows them wherever they go," said Carl Van Horn, a labor economist at Rutgers. "It's like a parrot on your shoulder, traveling with you everywhere, constantly telling you 'No, you can't make that much money.' "

20   And while young people who have weathered a tough job market may shy from risks during their careers, the best way to nullify an unlucky graduation date is to change jobs when you can, says Till von Wachter, an economist at Columbia.

"If you don't move within five years of graduating, for some reason you get stuck where you are. That's just an empirical finding," Mr. von Wachter said. "By your late 20s, you're often married, and have a family and have a house. You stop the active pattern of moving jobs."

JOB OUTLOOK FOR COLLEGE GRADUATES IS SLOWLY IMPROVING

Lacey Johnson

The job outlook for college students is expected to improve by a modest 4 percent this academic year [2011–2012], according to a major annual survey of employers released on Thursday. This is the second year in a row that the hiring of new graduates is predicted to increase, following drops of 35 percent to 40 percent in 2008. Bachelor's degree graduates should see the most hiring, with a 7-percent increase in available jobs.

Many employers overestimated their hiring growth last year, anticipating a 10-percent increase in new bachelor's degree hires; but this year's data appear to be "a little deeper" and show "a more consistent pattern of growth," says the survey, which is administered by the Collegiate Employment Research Institute at Michigan State University.

Between baby boomers retiring, the exhaustion of today's work force, and employers' need to revitalize their skill base, "this trend will only accelerate over the next decade," wrote Phil Gardner, director of the institute, in the latest report. "All these factors are nudging the college labor market out of the doldrums, ahead of other segments of the labor market."

Of the more than 3,300 employers surveyed, nearly 40 percent said they planned to hire graduates from all fields of study, regardless of their major. And, despite overall growth, one-third had decided to cut back on hiring.

5   Some industries look more promising than others, according to the report. Accounting, engineering, finance, and supply chain are all expected to do well, while state and local agencies are less likely to hire, because of budget cuts. The strongest job sector was agriculture/food processing, predicted to grow by 14 percent this year. Marketing, advertising, and public relations were also expecting to see strong hiring growth.

One of the most employable degrees continues to be in computer science—a field that will have more available positions than qualified graduates. The opposite is true in most other occupations, and competition will stay fierce, says the study.

While more graduates may be employed, it is unlikely that they will be earning more money than their predecessors; 70 percent of employers said they had no intention of raising salaries for new workers.

The results of this year's survey showed consistency across economic sector, organizational size, academic major, location, and are "basically boring," wrote Mr. Gardner. "But you know what? Boring is good." This kind of stability means the upcoming job market may "have legs," he said.

● Review Questions

1. Summarize Jenna Brager's "A Post-College Flow Chart of Misery and Pain."

2. According to Rampell's article in the *New York Times*, how have graduates in 2010 fared in comparison with those graduating in the preceding four years?

3. According to Rampell, what are the dangers of having a low-paying "starter job"?

4. As discussed in Rampell, how can those landing a job in a challenging market improve their (initially low) salaries?

5. What data does Johnson point to in justifying the title of her article in the *Chronicle of Higher Education*: "Job Outlook for College Graduates Is Slowly Improving"?

● Discussion and Writing Suggestions

1. The topic of marginal job prospects for college graduates is no laughing matter. Yet Brager's "A Post-College Flow Chart of Misery and Pain" brings a smile. Why? What is the role of humor in Brager's "flow chart"? Reread your summary of Brager. Which format—prose or graphic—do you find more compelling? Why? How does the graphic convey Brager's observations on job prospects in way that (1) your summary and (2) Catherine Rampell's article in the *New York Times* (especially ¶s 9–10) do not?

2. Johnson reports in mid-November 2011 that the hiring of college graduates will accelerate regardless of their field of study. Writing six months earlier, Rampell reports that the employment outlook for graduates "is rather bleak." Both writers cite authoritative sources, and both write for reputable papers. As a prospective job seeker, what do you make of the conflicting reports: Are you left hopeful, dejected, confused? As someone who may draw on these sources for a paper, how would you plan to use such conflicting evidence?

3. Brager premises her "Flow Chart" on a trend obvious to many who major in the humanities: Finding a job can be difficult when you haven't learned an immediately applicable skill such as accounting or engineering. Rampell draws on sources reporting the same phenomenon. Why, then, do you think that students continue to major in the humanities?

4. Rampell and Johnson cite conflicting data regarding job opportunities for students graduating college. Will you take either of their reports into account in choosing a major? Do you expect to conduct research on postcollege employment prospects relating to your major? Explain.

DATA ON THE JOB MARKET

What do we know about thousands of possible occupations—how much they pay, the ten-year prospects, the kind of education and training needed to land you that interview, what's involved in the job, the working conditions you'll experience? You don't have to guess at the answers, because clear, reliable information is out there. In the second component of this chapter, we take a close look at some of that information.

First, you'll examine unemployment and wage statistics associated with different academic majors, in tables from a report by the Georgetown University Center for Education and the Workforce. The report's coauthors, Anthony Carnevale, Ban Cheah, and Jeff Strohl, sum up their findings in the title "Not all College Degrees Are Created Equal." If such is the case, what effect (if any) will this data have on your choice of major?

Information about almost every possible type of occupation is readily available online, courtesy of the Bureau of Labor Statistics, a division of the U.S. Department of Labor. Every two years, the BLS releases ten-year employment projections as part of a "60-year tradition of providing information to individuals who are making education and training choices, entering the job market, or changing careers." What follows is a summary of the BLS data published as a news release on February 1, 2012. At the end of this summary, look for ten online tables sure to interest anyone contemplating a job search. For instance, one table reveals which industries over the next ten years have the potential for the largest growth, both in total job numbers and in wages.

COLLEGE MAJORS, UNEMPLOYMENT AND EARNINGS: NOT ALL COLLEGE DEGREES ARE CREATED EQUAL

Anthony P. Carnevale, Ban Cheah, and Jeff Strohl

The question, as we slowly dig out from under the wreckage left by the Great Recession, is unavoidable: "Is college worth it?" Our answer: "Yes, extensive research, ours included, finds that a college degree is still worth it." A Bachelor's degree is one of the best weapons a job seeker can wield in the fight for employment and earnings. And staying on campus to earn a graduate degree provides safe shelter from the immediate economic storm, and will pay off with greater employability and earnings once the graduate enters the labor market. Unemployment for students with new Bachelor's degrees is an unacceptable 8.9 percent, but it's a catastrophic 22.9 percent for job seekers with a recent high school diploma—and an almost unthinkable 31.5 percent for recent high school dropouts.

Here is a look at several factors that current and future college students should consider as they choose their courses:

The risk of unemployment among recent college graduates depends on their major. The unemployment rate for recent graduates is highest in Architecture (13.9 percent) because of the collapse of the construction and home building industry in the recession. Unemployment rates are generally higher in non-technical majors, such as the Arts (11.1 percent), Humanities and Liberal Arts (9.4 percent), Social Science (8.9 percent) and Law and Public Policy (8.1 percent).

Unemployment in majors related to computers and mathematics vary widely depending on the technical and scientific content of the major. Employers are still hiring technical computer specialists who can write software and invent new applications. But for information specialists who use software to manipulate, mine, and disseminate information, hiring slows down in recessions. We can see the difference in unemployment between people who invent computer technology as opposed to people who use computer technology. The unemployment rate for recent college graduates in Information Systems has spiked to 11.7 percent, while the rates for majors in Computer Science and Mathematics are 7.8 percent and 6.0 percent, respectively.

Computer majors are likely to bounce back strongly as the recovery proceeds. For example, the unemployment rate for recent college graduates who major in information systems is a hefty 11.7 percent, but only 5.4 percent for experienced workers who major in Information Systems.

5   **The Education, Healthcare, Business and Professional Services industries have been the most stable employers for recent college graduates.** Unemployment rates are relatively low (5.4 percent) for recent college students who majored in Healthcare and Education because these majors are attached to stable or growing industry sectors. Recent graduates in Psychology and Social Work have relatively low unemployment rates (7.3 percent) nearly half work in Healthcare and Education. The same is true for unemployment among recent college graduates who majored in the Life and Physical Sciences (7.7 percent). More than 60 percent of these recent college graduates who are working have landed in the Healthcare, Professional Contracting Businesses or Education sectors.

Business majors have low unemployment rates (7.4 percent) with the exception of those who specialize in Hospitality Management (9.1 percent), which is hampered by the ongoing slump in Travel and Tourism. Similarly, recent graduates in Engineering do relatively well (7.5 percent unemployment), except for Civil and Mechanical Engineers who are still suffering from the deep dive in manufacturing and construction activity.

Majors that are more closely aligned with particular occupations and industries tend to experience lower unemployment rates. Majors such as Healthcare, Education and those related to technical occupations tend to have lower unemployment rates than more general majors, like Humanities and Liberal Arts, where graduates are broadly dispersed across occupations and industries. Unemployment rates for recent graduates in Healthcare and Education are 5.4 percent compared to 9.4 percent for people who majored in Humanities and the Liberal Arts. More than three out of four people who major in Education work in the Education industry while no more than 20 percent of Liberal Arts graduates are concentrated in any single industry.

At the same time, majors that are closely aligned with occupations and industries can misfire. For example, tying oneself to a particular major can be a problem if the associated occupations or industries collapse. Unemployment rates for recent college graduates who majored in Architecture start high at 13.9 percent and, due to its strong alignment with the collapse in construction and housing, unemployment remains high even for experienced college graduates at 9.2 percent.

As the recovery proceeds and recent college graduates gain access to work, especially in their major fields, their unemployment rates will drop substantially. Employment patterns among experienced workers who have been out of college for a while suggest that recent graduates will fare better as the recovery continues. With the exception of majors in Architecture, International Business and Theater Arts, more experienced workers have substantially lower unemployment rates and higher earnings than recent college graduates.

10   **Graduate degrees make a quantum difference in employment prospects across all majors.** Sometimes, when unemployment is high, the best strategy to increase future employability is to go to graduate school. The unemployment rate for people with graduate degrees is 3 percent compared with a 5 percent unemployment rate for those with a BA (recent college graduates and experienced workers holding a Bachelor's degree). With the exception of majors in the arts and Architecture, unemployment rates for people with graduate degrees range between 1.9 percent and 4.0 percent. Graduate degrees tend to outperform BA's on employment in part because advanced degrees represent higher levels of human capital development and because those degrees are more closely aligned with career pathways in particular occupations and industries.

For example, experienced workers with BA's in healthcare have lower unemployment rates than people with graduate degrees in every other field, except the Life and Physical Sciences. Similarly, a BA in Education can make a job seeker more employable than majors in Architecture, Humanities, Journalism, Computers, Social Science, Arts and Business who go on to graduate school.

What college graduates earn also depends on what they take. Median earnings among recent college graduates vary from $55,000 among Engineering majors to $30,000 in the Arts, as well as Psychology and Social Work. In our more detailed data—which drills into the broad categories to look at results for more individual, specialized majors—the variation is even more pronounced, ranging from $60,000 for Computer Engineering graduates to $24,000 for Physiology majors.

Majors with high technical, business and healthcare content tend to earn the most among both recent and experienced college graduates. Engineering majors lead both in earnings for recent and experienced college graduates followed by Computer and Mathematics majors, and Business majors. Recent graduates in Healthcare majors start out with high earnings, but begin to lose ground to Science, Business and Engineering as college graduates gain experience and graduate degrees. Graduate school further differentiates earnings among majors.

Majors that are most closely aligned with particular industries and occupations tend to have low unemployment rates but not necessarily the highest earnings. Some majors offer both high security and high earnings, while other majors trade off earnings for job security. Healthcare, Science and Business majors have both low unemployment and the highest earnings

Unemployment Rates Decline as Recent College Graduates Gain Experience and Graduate Education*

Unemployment Rates

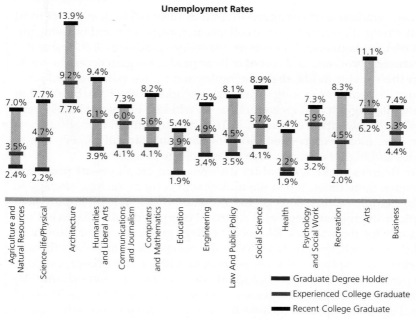

Graduate Degree Holder
Experienced College Graduate
Recent College Graduate

Earnings Increase As Recent College Graduates Gain Experience and Graduate Education*

Earnings

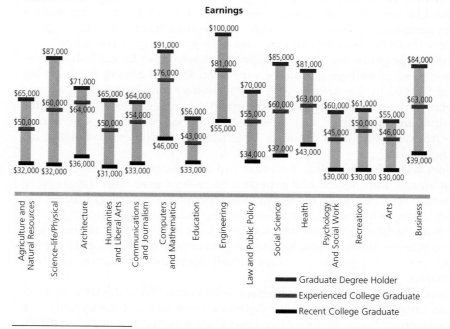

Graduate Degree Holder
Experienced College Graduate
Recent College Graduate

*ACS 2009–2010, pooled sample. Recent college graduates are 22–26 years of age, experienced workers are 30–54 years of age. Percent unemployed are computed based on total employed and unemployed. Earnings based on full-time, full-year workers.

boost from experience and graduate education. At the same time, Education, Psychology and Social Work majors have relatively low unemployment, but earnings are also low and only improve marginally with experience and graduate education.

15 **Although differences remain high among majors, graduate education raises earnings across the board.** The average earnings for BA's now stands at $48,000 compared with $62,000 for graduate degrees. With the exception of the Arts and Education, earnings for graduate workers range between $60,000 and $100,000.

It is easy to look at unemployment rates for new college graduates or hear stories about degree-holders forced to tend bar and question the wisdom of investing in higher education when times are bad. But those questions should last only until you compare how job seekers with college degrees are doing compared to those without college degrees.

Today's best advice, then, is that high school students who can go on to college should do so—with one caveat. They should do their homework before picking a major because, when it comes to employment prospects and compensation, not all college degrees are created equal.

EMPLOYMENT PROJECTIONS: 2010–2020 SUMMARY

U.S. Bureau of Labor Statistics

Industries and occupations related to health care, personal care and social assistance, and construction are projected to have the fastest job growth between 2010 and 2020, the U.S. Bureau of Labor Statistics reported [on February 1, 2012]. Total employment is projected to grow by 14.3 percent over the decade, resulting in 20.5 million new jobs. Despite rapid projected growth, construction is not expected to regain all of the jobs lost during the 2007–09 recession. The 2010–20 projections...depict education, training, and related work experience typically needed for occupations. In occupations in which a master's degree is typically needed for entry, employment is expected to grow by 21.7 percent, faster than the growth rate for any other education category. In occupations in which apprenticeship is the typical on-the-job training, employment is expected to grow by 22.5 percent, faster than for any other on-the-job training category. This news release focuses on five areas: labor force and the macroeconomy, industry employment, occupational employment, education and training, and replacement needs.

Labor force and the macroeconomy*

— Slower population growth and a decreasing overall labor force participation rate are expected to lead to slower civilian labor force growth from 2010 to 2020: 0.7 percent annually, compared with 0.8 percent for 2000–10, and 1.3

---

*Macroeconomics: the study of the economy as a whole, considering such factors as unemployment, inflation, interest rates, national income, and debt.

percent for 1990–2000. The projected 0.7 percent growth rate will lead to a civilian labor force increase of 10.5 million by 2020. (See table 1).[†]

— The baby-boom generation moves entirely into the 55-years-and-older age group by 2020, increasing that age group's share of the labor force from 19.5 percent in 2010 to 25.2 percent in 2020. The "prime-age" working group (ages 25 to 54) is projected to drop to 63.7 percent of the 2020 labor force. The 16- to 24-year-old age group is projected to account for 11.2 percent of the labor force in 2020. (See table 1.)

— By 2020, the number of Hispanics in the labor force is projected to grow by 7.7 million, or 34.0 percent, and their share of the labor force is expected to increase from 14.8 percent in 2010 to 18.6 percent in 2020. The labor force shares for Asians and blacks are projected to be 5.7 and 12.0 percent, respectively, up slightly from 4.7 and 11.6 percent in 2010. (See table 1.)

— Gross domestic product (GDP) is projected to grow by 3.0 percent annually, consistent with slow labor force growth, the assumption of a full-employment economy in 2020, and labor productivity growth of 2.0 percent annually.

Industry employment

— Nonagriculture wage and salary employment, which accounts for more than 9 in 10 jobs in the economy, is projected to expand to 150.2 million by 2020, up from 130.4 million in 2010. (See table 2.)

— The health care and social assistance sector is projected to gain the most jobs (5.6 million), followed by professional and business services (3.8 million), and construction (1.8 million). Despite rapid growth in the construction sector, employment in 2020 is not expected to reach its pre-recessionary annual average peak of 7.7 million in 2006. (See table 2.)

— About 5.0 million new jobs—25 percent of all new jobs—are expected in the three detailed industries projected to add the most jobs: construction, retail trade, and offices of health practitioners. Seven of the 20 industries gaining the most jobs are in the health care and social assistance sector, and five are in the professional and business services sector. (See table 3.)

— The 20 detailed industries projected to lose the largest numbers of jobs are primarily in the manufacturing sector (11 industries) and the federal government (3 industries). The largest job losses are projected for the Postal Service (–182,000), federal non-defense government (–122,000), and apparel knitting mills (–92,000). (See table 4.)

Occupational employment

— Of the 22 major occupational groups, employment in healthcare support occupations is expected to grow most rapidly (34.5 percent), followed by personal care and services occupations (26.8 percent), and healthcare practitioners and technical occupations (25.9 percent). However, the office and administrative support occupations group, with projected slower than average

---

[†]Directions for locating Tables 1–10 online can be found on page 305.

growth of 10.3 percent, is expected to add the largest number of new jobs (2.3 million). (See table 5.)
— The four detailed occupations expected to add the most employment are registered nurses (712,000), retail salespersons (707,000), home health aides (706,000), and personal care aides (607,000). All have large employment in 2010 and are expected to grow faster than the average of 14.3 percent. (See table 6.)
— One-third of the projected fastest growing occupations are related to health care, reflecting expected increases in demand as the population ages and the health care and social assistance industry grows. (See table 7.)
— More than one-fourth of the projected fastest growing occupations are related to construction. Employment in most of these occupations, still at low levels in 2010 because of the 2007–09 recession, will recover along with the construction industry. But employment in most construction occupations is not expected to reach pre-recession levels. (See table 7.)
— Production occupations and office and administrative support occupations dominate the list of detailed occupations with the largest projected employment declines. However, farmers, ranchers, and other agricultural managers top the list, with a projected loss of 96,100 jobs. (See table 8.)

Education and training
— Occupations that typically need some type of postsecondary education for entry are projected to grow the fastest during the 2010–20 decade. Occupations classified as needing a master's degree are projected to grow by 21.7 percent, followed by doctoral or professional degree occupations at 19.9 percent, and associate's degree occupations at 18.0 percent. (See table 9.)
— In terms of typical on-the-job training, occupations that typically require apprenticeships are projected to grow the fastest (22.5 percent). (See table 9.)
— Of the 30 detailed occupations projected to have the fastest employment growth, 17 typically need some type of postsecondary education for entry into the occupation. (See table 7.)
— Two-thirds of the 30 occupations projected to have the largest number of new jobs typically require less than a postsecondary education, no related work experience, and short- or moderate-term on-the-job training. (See table 6.)
— Only 3 of the 30 detailed occupations projected to have the largest employment declines are classified as needing postsecondary education for entry. (See table 8.)

Replacement needs
— Over the 2010–20 decade, 54.8 million total job openings are expected. (See table 9.) While growth will lead to many openings, more than half—61.6 percent—will come from the need to replace workers who retire or otherwise permanently leave an occupation.
— In 4 out of 5 occupations, openings due to replacement needs exceed the number due to growth. Replacement needs are expected in every occupation, even in those that are declining.

— More than two-thirds of all job openings are expected to be in occupations that typically do not need postsecondary education for entry. (See table 9.)
— Eighteen of the 30 occupations with the largest number of projected total job openings are classified as typically needing less than a postsecondary education and needing short-term on-the-job training. (See table 10.)

Interpreting the projections in light of the 2007–09 recession and recovery

The BLS projections are built on the assumption of a full employment economy in 2020. The 2007–09 recession represented a sharp downturn in the economy—and the economy, especially the labor market, has been slow to recover. As a result, the 2010–20 projections reach a robust 2020 target year largely because the 2010 base year began from a relatively low point. Rapid growth rates for some measures reflect recovery from the recession and, with some important exceptions, growth beyond recovery.

A note about labor shortages and surpluses in the context of long-term economic projections

Users of these data should not assume that the difference between the projected increase in the labor force and the projected increase in employment implies a labor shortage or surplus. The BLS projections assume labor market equilibrium, that is, one in which labor supply meets labor demand except for some degree of frictional unemployment. In addition, the employment and labor force measures use different concepts. Employment is a count of jobs, and one person may hold more than one job. Labor force is a count of people, and a person is counted only once regardless of how many jobs he or she holds. For a discussion of the basic projections methodology, see "Overview of projections to 2020," Dixie Sommers and James C. Franklin, January 2012 issue of the *Monthly Labor Review*.

More information

The BLS projections are used by high school students and their teachers and parents, college students, career changers, and career development and guidance specialists. The projections are the foundation of the *BLS Occupational Outlook Handbook*, the nation's most widely used career information resource. The projections also are used by state workforce agencies to prepare state and area projections that, together with the national projections, are widely used by policymakers and education and training officials to make decisions about education and training policy, funding, and program offerings. In addition, other federal agencies, researchers, and academics use the projections to understand trends in the economy and labor market. The projections are updated every two years. More detailed information on the 2010–20 projections appears in five articles in the January 2012 issue of the Monthly Labor Review, published by the Bureau of Labor Statistics, U.S. Department of Labor. The *Monthly Labor Review* is available online at www.bls.gov/opub/mlr/mlrhome.htm.

The 2012–13 edition of the *Occupational Outlook Handbook* will feature the 2010–20 projections in assessing job outlook, work activities, wages, education and training requirements, and more for detailed occupations in 341 profiles. The updated *Handbook* will be available online in late March 2012, at www.bls .gov/ooh. A graphic representation of the highlights of the projections appears in the Winter 2011–12 issue of the *Occupational Outlook Quarterly*, available online at www.bls.gov/ooq.

For ready access to Tables 1–10, listed below, go to the BLS Web site.

> **Go to: www.bls.gov**
> ***Search terms: "news release February 1, 2012"***

You will find the following tables at the end of this online version of "Employment Projections: 2010–2020 Summary."

- Table 1. Civilian labor force, by age, sex, race, and ethnicity, 1990, 2000, 2010, and projected 2020
- Table 2. Employment by major industry sector, 2000, 2010, and projected 2020
- Table 3. The 20 industries with the largest projected wage and salary employment growth, 2010–20
- Table 4. The 20 industries with the largest projected wage and salary employment declines, 2010–20
- Table 5. Employment by major occupational group, 2010 and projected 2020, and median annual wage, May 2010
- Table 6. The 30 occupations with the largest projected employment growth, 2010–20
- Table 7. The 30 occupations with the fastest projected employment growth, 2010–20
- Table 8. The 30 occupations with the largest projected employment declines, 2010–20
- Table 9. Employment and total job openings by education, work experience, and on-the-job training category, 2010 and projected 2020
- Table 10. The 30 occupations with the largest projected number of total job openings due to growth and replacements, 2010–20

● Review Questions

1. When asked if college is worth the expense and time commitment, why do Carnevale et al. strongly recommend a student's getting a college degree, even in times of recession?

2. The research of Carnevale et al. shows what key relationships between the selection of an undergraduate major and employability?

3. Carnevale et al. include two summary charts presenting multiple comparative data. Review these charts. What data is being compared? What broad conclusions can you draw from these comparisons?

4. According to the Bureau of Labor Statistics *Summary*, what are the employment prospects for those with postsecondary education?

5. According to the Bureau of Labor Statistics, how much of the projected gain in employment will result from growth of the new economy, as opposed to retirement among baby-boom workers?

6. Which employment areas are projected to grow the most, according to the Bureau of Labor Statistics? Which are expected to suffer greatest declines?

7. Examine BLS Tables 6 and 7. What is the difference between the "largest employment projected growth" and the "fastest employment projected growth"?

● Discussion and Writing Suggestions

1. Carnevale et al. report some sobering facts about the job prospects for recent college graduates with degrees in the arts and liberal arts. Do you consider these findings an argument against pursuing degrees in these majors? Explain.

2. Carnevale et al. present two charts summarizing their research. You've likely come to college with some idea about which major(s) you expect to pursue. To what extent might you reassess your employment prospects in your intended career field, in light of the data in these charts? Do you see anything here that argues for—or against—pursuing your intended major?

3. Describe the ways in which you might use the Bureau of Labor Statistics *Summary* and Web site to investigate either broad career areas or specific jobs within a broad area.

4. The Bureau of Labor Statistics *Summary 2010–2020* is a vast resource that can provide you with credible statistical information as you complete writing assignments associated with this chapter. Take a moment to skim the synthesis assignments on pages 336–338. For any *one* assignment, locate on these Web pages a statistic that might prove useful in your writing.

5. Use information from this Bureau of Labor Statistics *Summary* to assess the accuracy of employment projections by Krugman or Kessler in this chapter or Blinder in Chapter 1. To what extent do the predictions of the writer you've selected match the projections of the BLS *Summary*?

6. Group work: Join with four classmates and study the ten tables referred to in the Bureau of Labor Statistics *Summary*. Each group member should study the content of two tables and then make an oral presentation of that content to group members.

WORK AND IDENTITY

A significant portion of your life will be spent at work. Your job will make demands of you—complex and often unanticipated demands—and you'll need to adapt in order to succeed. You may need to develop new skills and new ways of interacting with colleagues. This will change you, sometimes in subtle ways. Any activity in which you invest so much of your energy, your creativity, your intellect, and your resourcefulness will, for better or for worse, affect your life far beyond the scope of that activity. It will potentially recreate your sense of self, your sense of the kind of person you've become. If, twenty years from now, a stranger asks you who you are (beyond your name), you may well reply that you're an engineer, or a graphic designer, or a history professor—as opposed, say, to a husband or a mother. In other words, you'll define yourself in terms of your occupation; you'll think of yourself as someone who does a particular job or has a particular career.

In the third component of this chapter, sociologist Richard Sennett investigates the links between work and our sense of identity by relating the story of a man who adapted successfully to the modern workplace but paid dearly in terms of his self-worth. Sennett is best known for his writing about cities, labor, and culture. He is Centennial Professor of Sociology at the London School of Economics and Professor of the Humanities at New York University. During the 1980s, he served as president of the American Council on Work. Sennett is the author of three novels and numerous scholarly studies, including the much-cited *The Corrosion of Character: The Personal Consequences of Work in the New Capitalism* (1998), in which the following passage initially appeared.

No Long Term: New Work and the Corrosion of Character

Richard Sennett

Recently I met someone in an airport whom I hadn't seen for fifteen years. I had interviewed the father of Rico (as I shall call him) a quarter century ago when I wrote a book about blue-collar workers in America, *The Hidden Injuries of Class*. Enrico, his father, then worked as a janitor, and had high hopes for this boy, who was just entering adolescence, a bright kid good at sports. When I lost touch with his father a decade later, Rico had just finished college. In the airline lounge, Rico looked as if he had fulfilled his father's dreams. He carried a computer in a smart leather case, dressed in a suit I couldn't afford, and sported a signet ring with a crest.

Enrico had spent twenty years by the time we first met cleaning toilets and mopping floors in a downtown office building. He did so without complaining, but also without any hype about living out the American Dream. His work had one single and durable purpose, the service of his family. It had taken him fifteen years to save the money for a house, which he purchased in a suburb near Boston, cutting ties with his old Italian neighborhood because a house in the suburbs was better for the kids. Then his wife, Flavia, had gone to work, as a presser in a dry-cleaning plant; by the time I met Enrico in 1970, both parents were saving for the college education of their two sons.

What had most struck me about Enrico and his generation was how linear time was in their lives: year after year of working in jobs which seldom varied from day to day. And along that line of time, achievement was cumulative: Enrico and Flavia checked the increase in their savings every week, measured their domesticity by the various improvements and additions they had made to their ranch house. Finally, the time they lived was predictable. The upheavals of the Great Depression and World War II had faded, unions protected their jobs; though he was only forty when I first met him, Enrico knew precisely when he would retire and how much money he would have.

Time is the only resource freely available to those at the bottom of society. To make time accumulate, Enrico needed what the sociologist Max Weber called an "iron cage," a bureaucratic structure which rationalized the use of time; in Enrico's case, the seniority rules of his union about pay and the regulations organizing his government pension provided this scaffolding. When he added to these resources his own self-discipline, the result was more than economic.

5   He carved out a clear story for himself in which his experience accumulated materially and psychically; his life thus made sense to him as a linear narrative. Though a snob might dismiss Enrico as boring, he experienced the years as a dramatic story moving forward repair by repair, interest payment by interest payment. The janitor felt he became the author of his life, and though he was a man low on the social scale, this narrative provided him a sense of self-respect.

Though clear, Enrico's life story was not simple. I was particularly struck by how Enrico straddled the worlds of his old immigrant community and his new suburban-neutral life. Among his suburban neighbors he lived as a quiet, self-effacing citizen; when he returned to the old neighborhood, however, he received much more attention as a man who had made good on the outside, a worthy elder who returned each Sunday for Mass followed by lunch followed by gossipy coffees. He got recognition as a distinctive human being from those who knew him long enough to understand his story; he got a more anonymous kind of respect from his new neighbors by doing what everyone else did, keeping his home and garden neat, living without incident. The thick texture of Enrico's particular experience lay in the fact that he was acknowledged in both ways, depending in which community he moved: two identities from the same disciplined use of his time.

If the world were a happy and just place, those who enjoy respect would give back in equal measure the regard which has been accorded them. This was Fichte's idea in "The Foundations of National Law"; he spoke of the "reciprocal effect" of recognition. But real life does not proceed so generously.*

Enrico disliked blacks, although he had labored peaceably for many years with other janitors who were black; he disliked non-Italian foreigners like the

---

*Johann Gottlieb Fichte (1762–1814): a German philosopher.

Irish, although his own father could barely speak English. He could not acknowledge kindred struggles; he had no class allies. Most of all, however, Enrico disliked middle-class people. We treated him as though he were invisible, "as a zero," he said; the janitor's resentment was complicated by his fear that because of his lack of education and his menial status, we had a sneaking right to do so. To his powers of endurance in time he contrasted the whining self-pity of blacks, the unfair intrusion of foreigners, and the unearned privileges of the bourgeoisie.

Though Enrico felt he had achieved a measure of social honor, he hardly wanted his son Rico to repeat his own life. The American dream of upward mobility for the children powerfully drove my friend. "I don't understand a word he says," Enrico boasted to me several times when Rico had come home from school and was at work on math. I heard many other parents of sons and daughters like Rico say something like "I don't understand him" in harder tones, as though the kids had abandoned them. We all violate in some way the place assigned us in the family myth, but upward mobility gives that passage a peculiar twist. Rico and other youngsters headed up the social ladder sometimes betrayed shame about their parents' working-class accents and rough manners, but more often felt suffocated by the endless strategizing over pennies and the reckoning of time in tiny steps. These favored children wanted to embark on a less constrained journey.

10   Now, many years later, thanks to the encounter at the airport, I had the chance to see how it had turned out for Enrico's son. In the airport lounge, I must confess, I didn't much like what I saw. Rico's expensive suit could have been just business plumage, but the crested signet ring—a mark of elite family background—seemed both a lie and a betrayal of the father. However, circumstances threw Rico and me together on a long flight. He and I did not have one of those American journeys in which a stranger spills out his or her emotional guts to you, gathers more tangible baggage when the plane lands, and disappears forever. I took the seat next to Rico without being asked, and for the first hour of a long flight from New York to Vienna had to pry information out of him.

Rico, I learned, has fulfilled his father's desire for upward mobility, but has indeed rejected the way of his father. Rico scorns "time-servers" and others wrapped in the armor of bureaucracy; instead he believes in being open to change and in taking risks. And he has prospered; whereas Enrico had an income in the bottom quarter of the wage scale, Rico's has shot up to the top 5 percent. Yet this is not an entirely happy story for Rico.

After graduating from a local university in electrical engineering, Rico went to a business school in New York. There he married a fellow student, a young Protestant woman from a better family. School prepared the young couple to move and change jobs frequently, and they've done so. Since graduation, in fourteen years at work Rico has moved four times.

Rico began as a technology adviser to a venture capital firm on the West Coast, in the early, heady days of the developing computer industry in Silicon

Valley; he then moved to Chicago, where he also did well. But the next move was for the sake of his wife's career. If Rico were an ambition-driven character out of the pages of Balzac, he would never have done it, for he gained no larger salary, and he left hotbeds of high-tech activity for a more retired, if leafy, office park in Missouri. Enrico felt somewhat ashamed when Flavia went to work; Rico sees Jeannette, his wife, as an equal working partner, and has adapted to her. It was at this point, when Jeannette's career took off, that their children began arriving.

In the Missouri office park, the uncertainties of the new economy caught up with the young man. While Jeannette was promoted, Rico was downsized—his firm was absorbed by another, larger firm that had its own analysts. So the couple made a fourth move, back East to a suburb outside New York. Jeannette now manages a big team of accountants, and he has started a small consulting firm.

15   Prosperous as they are, the very acme of an adaptable, mutually supportive couple, both husband and wife often fear they are on the edge of losing control over their lives. This fear is built into their work histories.

In Rico's case, the fear of lacking control is straightforward: it concerns managing time. When Rico told his peers he was going to start his own consulting firm, most approved; consulting seems the road to independence. But in getting started he found himself plunged into many menial tasks, like doing his own photocopying, which before he'd taken for granted. He found himself plunged into the sheer flux of networking; every call had to be answered, the slightest acquaintance pursued. To find work, he has fallen subservient to the schedules of people who are in no way obliged to respond to him. Like other consultants, he wants to work in accordance with contracts setting out just what the consultant will do. But these contracts, he says, are largely fictions. A consultant usually has to tack one way and another in response to the changing whims or thoughts of those who pay; Rico has no fixed role that allows him to say to others, "This is what I do, this is what I am responsible for."

Jeannette's lack of control is more subtle. The small group of accountants she now manages is divided among people who work at home, people usually in the office, and a phalanx of low-level back-office clerks a thousand miles away connected to her by computer cable. In her present corporation, strict rules and surveillance of phones and e-mail disciplines the conduct of the accountants who work from home; to organize the work of the back-office clerks a thousand miles away, she can't make hands-on, face-to-face judgments, but instead must work by formal written guidelines. She hasn't experienced less bureaucracy in this seemingly flexible work arrangement; indeed, her own decisions count for less than in the days when she supervised workers who were grouped together, all the time, in the same office.

As I say, at first I was not prepared to shed many tears for this American Dream couple. Yet as dinner was served to Rico and me on our flight, and he began to talk more personally, my sympathies increased. His fear of losing control, it developed, went much deeper than worry about losing power in his job. He feared that the actions he needs to take and the way he has to live in order to survive in the modern economy have set his emotional, inner life adrift.

Rico told me that he and Jeannette have made friends mostly with the people they see at work, and have lost many of these friendships during the moves of the last twelve years, "though we stay 'netted.'" Rico looks to electronic communications for the sense of community which Enrico most enjoyed when he attended meetings of the janitors' union, but the son finds communications on-line short and hurried. "It's like with your kids—when you're not there, all you get is news later."

20   In each of his four moves, Rico's new neighbors have treated his advent as an arrival which closes past chapters of his life; they ask him about Silicon Valley or the Missouri office park, but, Rico says, "they don't *see* other places"; their imaginations are not engaged. This is a very American fear. The classic American suburb was a bedroom community; in the last generation a different kind of suburb has arisen, more economically independent of the urban core, but not really town or village either; a place springs into life with the wave of a developer's wand, flourishes, and begins to decay all within a generation. Such communities are not empty of sociability or neighborliness, but no one in them becomes a long-term witness to another person's life.

The fugitive quality of friendship and local community form the background to the most important of Rico's inner worries, his family. Like Enrico, Rico views work as his service to the family; unlike Enrico, Rico finds that the demands of the job interfere with achieving the end. At first I thought he was talking about the all too familiar conflict between work time and time for family. "We get home at seven, do dinner, try to find an hour for the kids' homework, and then deal with our own paperwork." When things get tough for months at a time in his consulting firm, "it's like I don't know who my kids are." He worries about the frequent anarchy into which his family plunges, and about neglecting his children, whose needs can't be programmed to fit into the demands of his job.

Hearing this, I tried to reassure him; my wife, stepson, and I had endured and survived well a similarly high-pressure life. "You aren't being fair to yourself," I said. "The fact you care so much means you are doing the best for your family you can." Though he warmed to this, I had misunderstood.

As a boy, I already knew, Rico had chafed under Enrico's authority; he had told me then he felt smothered by the small-minded rules which governed the janitor's life. Now that he is a father himself, the fear of a lack of ethical discipline haunts him, particularly the fear that his children will become "mall rats," hanging out aimlessly in the parking lots of shopping centers in the afternoons while the parents remain out of touch at their offices.

He therefore wants to set for his son and daughters an example of resolution and purpose, "but you can't just tell kids to be like that"; he has to set an example. The objective example he could set, his upward mobility, is something they take for granted, a history that belongs to a past not their own, a story which is over. But his deepest worry is that he cannot offer the substance of his work life as an example to his children of how they should conduct themselves ethically. The qualities of good work are not the qualities of good character.

25   As I came later to understand, the gravity of this fear comes from a gap separating Enrico and Rico's generations. Business leaders and journalists emphasize the global marketplace and the use of new technologies as the hallmarks of the capitalism of our time. This is true enough, but misses another dimension of change: new ways of organizing time, particularly working time.

The most tangible sign of that change might be the motto "No long term." In work, the traditional career progressing step by step through the corridors of one or two institutions is withering; so is the deployment of a single set of skills through the course of a working life. Today, a young American with at least two years of college can expect to change jobs at least eleven times in the course of working, and change his or her skill base at least three times during those forty years of labor.

An executive for ATT points out that the motto "No long term" is altering the very meaning of work:

> In ATT we have to promote the whole concept of the work force being contingent, though most of the contingent workers are inside our walls. "Jobs" are being replaced by "projects" and "fields of work."[1]

Corporations have also farmed out many of the tasks they once did permanently in-house to small firms and to individuals employed on short-term contracts. The fastest-growing sector of the American labor force, for instance, is people who work for temporary job agencies.[2]

"People are hungry for [change]," the management guru James Champy argues, because "the market may be 'consumer-driven' as never before in history."[3] The market, in this view, is too dynamic to permit doing things the same way year after year, or doing the same thing. The economist Bennett Harrison believes the source of this hunger for change is "impatient capital," the desire for rapid return; for instance, the average length of time stocks have been held on British and American exchanges has dropped 60 percent in the last fifteen years. The market believes rapid market return is best generated by rapid institutional change.

The "long-term" order at which the new regime takes aim, it should be said, was itself short-lived—the decades spanning the mid-twentieth century. Nineteenth-century capitalism lurched from disaster to disaster in the stock markets and in irrational corporate investment; the wild swings of the business cycle provided people little security. In Enrico's generation after World War II, this disorder was brought somewhat under control in most advanced economies; strong unions, guarantees of the welfare state, and large-scale corporations combined to produce an era of relative stability. This span of thirty or so years defines the "stable past" now challenged by a new regime.

30   A change in modern institutional structure has accompanied short-term, contract, or episodic labor. Corporations have sought to remove layers of bureaucracy, to become flatter and more flexible organizations. In place of organizations as pyramids, management wants now to think of organizations as networks. "Networklike arrangements are lighter on their feet" than pyramidal hierarchies, the sociologist Walter Powell declares; "they are more readily

decomposable or redefinable than the fixed assets of hierarchies."[4] This means that promotions and dismissals tend not to be based on clear, fixed rules, nor are work tasks crisply defined; the network is constantly redefining its structure.

An IBM executive once told Powell that the flexible corporation "must become an archipelago of related activities."[5] The archipelago is an apt image for communications in a network, communication occurring like travel between islands—but at the speed of light, thanks to modern technologies. The computer has been the key to replacing the slow and clogged communications which occur in traditional chains of command. The fastest-growing sector of the labor force deals in computer and data-processing services, the area in which Jeanette and Rico work; the computer is now used in virtually all jobs, in many ways, by people of all ranks. . . .

For all these reasons, Enrico's experience of long-term, narrative time in fixed channels has become dysfunctional. What Rico sought to explain to me—and perhaps to himself—is that the material changes embodied in the motto "No long term" have become dysfunctional for him too, but as guides to personal character, particularly in relation to his family life.

Take the matter of commitment and loyalty. "No long term" is a principle which corrodes trust, loyalty, and mutual commitment. Trust can, of course, be a purely formal matter, as when people agree to a business deal or rely on another to observe the rules in a game. But usually deeper experiences of trust are more informal, as when people learn on whom they can rely when given a difficult or impossible task. Such social bonds take time to develop, slowly rooting into the cracks and crevices of institutions.

The short time frame of modern institutions limits the ripening of informal trust. A particularly egregious violation of mutual commitment often occurs when new enterprises are first sold. In firms starting up, long hours and intense effort are demanded of everyone; when the firms go public—that is, initially offer publicly traded shares—the founders are apt to sell out and cash in, leaving lower-level employees behind. If an organization whether new or old operates as a flexible, loose network structure rather than by rigid command from the top, the network can also weaken social bonds. The sociologist Mark Granovetter says that modern institutional networks are marked by "the strength of weak ties," by which he partly means that fleeting forms of association are more useful to people than long-term connections, and partly that strong social ties like loyalty have ceased to be compelling.[6] These weak ties are embodied in teamwork, in which the team moves from task to task and the personnel of the team changes in the process.

35 Strong ties depend, by contrast, on long association. And more personally they depend on a willingness to make commitments to others. Given the typically short, weak ties in institutions today, John Kotter, a Harvard Business School professor, counsels the young to work "on the outside rather than on the inside" of organizations. He advocates consulting rather than becoming "entangled" in long-term employment; institutional loyalty is a trap in an economy where "business concepts, product designs, competitor intelligence, capital equipment, and all kinds of knowledge have shorter credible life spans."[7]

A consultant who managed a recent IBM job shrinkage declares that once employees "understand [they can't depend on the corporation] they're marketable."[8] Detachment and superficial cooperativeness are better armor for dealing with current realities than behavior based on values of loyalty and service.

It is the time dimension of the new capitalism, rather than high-tech data transmission, global stock markets, or free trade, which most directly affects people's emotional lives outside the workplace. Transposed to the family realm, "No long term" means keep moving, don't commit yourself, and don't sacrifice. Rico suddenly erupted on the plane, "You can't imagine how stupid I feel when I talk to my kids about commitment. It's an abstract virtue to them; they don't see it anywhere." Over dinner I simply didn't understand the outburst, which seemed apropos of nothing. But his meaning is now clearer to me as a reflection upon himself. He means the children don't see commitment practiced in the lives of their parents or their parents' generation.

Similarly, Rico hates the emphasis on teamwork and open discussion which marks an enlightened, flexible workplace once those values are transposed to the intimate realm. Practiced at home, teamwork is destructive, marking an absence of authority and of firm guidance in raising children. He and Jeannette, he says, have seen too many parents who have talked every family issue to death for fear of saying "No!," parents who listen too well, who understand beautifully rather than lay down the law; they have seen as a result too many disoriented kids.

"Things have to hold together," Rico declared to me. Again, I didn't at first quite get this, and he explained what he meant in terms of watching television. Perhaps unusually, Rico and Jeannette make it a practice to discuss with their two sons the relation between movies or sitcoms the boys watch on the tube and events in the newspapers. "Otherwise it's just a jumble of images." But mostly the connections concern the violence and sexuality the children see on television. Enrico constantly spoke in little parables to drive home questions of character; these parables he derived from his work as a janitor—such as "You can ignore dirt but it won't go away." When I first knew Rico as an adolescent, he reacted with a certain shame to these homely snippets of wisdom. So now I asked Rico if he too made parables or even just drew ethical rules from his experience at work. He first ducked answering directly—"There's not much on TV about that sort of thing"—then replied, "And well, no, I don't talk that way."

Behavior which earns success or even just survival at work thus gives Rico little to offer in the way of a parental role model. In fact, for this modern couple, the problem is just the reverse: how can they protect family relations from succumbing to the short-term behavior, the meeting mind-set, and above all the weakness of loyalty and commitment which mark the modern workplace? In place of the chameleon values of the new economy, the family—as Rico sees it—should emphasize instead formal obligation, trustworthiness, commitment, and purpose. These are all long-term virtues.

40   This conflict between family and work poses some questions about adult experience itself. How can long-term purposes be pursued in a short-term society? How can durable social relations be sustained? How can a human being develop a narrative of identity and life history in a society composed of episodes

and fragments? The conditions of the new economy feed instead on experience which drifts in time, from place to place, from job to job. If I could state Rico's dilemma more largely, short-term capitalism threatens to corrode his character, particularly those qualities of character which bind human beings to one another and furnishes each with a sense of sustainable self.

•   •   •

Rico's experiences with time, place, and work are not unique; neither is his emotional response. The conditions of time in the new capitalism have created a conflict between character and experience, the experience of disjointed time threatening the ability of people to form their characters into sustained narratives.

At the end of the fifteenth century, the poet Thomas Hoccleve declared in *The Regiment of Princes*, "Allas, wher ys this worldes stabylnesse?"—a lament that appears equally in Homer or in Jeremiah in the Old Testament.[9] Through most of human history, people have accepted the fact that their lives will shift suddenly due to wars, famines, or other disasters, and that they will have to improvise in order to survive. Our parents and grandparents were filled with anxiety in 1940, having endured the wreckage of the Great Depression and facing the looming prospect of a world war.

What's peculiar about uncertainty today is that it exists without any looming historical disaster; instead it is woven into the everyday practices of a vigorous capitalism. Instability is meant to be normal, Schumpeter's entrepreneur served up as an ideal Everyman. Perhaps the corroding of character is an inevitable consequence. "No long term" disorients action over the long term, loosens bonds of trust and commitment, and divorces will from behavior.

I think Rico knows he is both a successful and a confused man. The flexible behavior which has brought him success is weakening his own character in ways for which there exists no practical remedy. If he is an Everyman for our times, his universality may lie in that dilemma.

Notes

[1] Quoted in *New York Times*, Feb. 13, 1996, pp. D1, D6.

[2] Corporations like Manpower grew 240 percent from 1985 to 1995. As I write, the Manpower firm, with 600,000 people on its payroll, compared with the 400,000 at General Motors and 350,000 at IBM, is now the country's largest employer.

[3] James Champy, *Re-engineering Management* (New York: HarperBusiness, 1995) p. 119, pp. 39–40.

[4] Walter Powell and Laurel Smith-Doerr, "Networks and Economic Life," in Neil Smelser and Richard Swedberg, eds., *The Handbook of Economic Sociology* (Princeton: Princeton University Press, 1994), p. 381.

[5] Ibid.

[6] Mark Granovetter, "The Strength of Weak Ties, " *American Journal of Sociology* 78 (1973), 1360–80.

[7] John Kotter, *The New Rules* (New York: Dutton, 1995) pp. 81, 159.

[8] Anthony Sampson, *Company Man* (New York: Random House, 1995), pp. 226–27.

[9] Quoted in Ray Pahl, *After Success: Fin de Siècle Anxiety and Identity* (Cambridge, U.K.: Polity Press, 1995), pp. 163–64.

Review Questions

1. What does "No long term" mean—as compared to "Long term"? How does Sennett use "No long term" as a "motto" to describe changes in the new economy?

2. Sennett describes Rico and his father, Enrico, as having different life narratives. What are these narratives? How do they differ? How do they lead to Rico's distress?

3. In the new economy, according to Sennett, what changes have occurred in the structure of businesses and the ways in which workers are assigned and do work?

4. Why does Rico feel that he needs to protect his family from behavior patterns and values now commonplace in the new economy?

5. Reread ¶s 39 and 43, in which Sennett summarizes Rico's "dilemma." What is that dilemma?

Discussion and Writing Suggestions

1. Sennett compares the old world of work and its values to modern work and its values. He suggests that workers in the new "knowledge" economy pay a psychic price for their labor. What is that price? Does the loss of those values associated with "old" work seem like a loss to you? Explain.

2. Sennett argues that a person's identity is intimately tied to the work s/he does. How so? In what ways have you (or have you not) found this connection to be true?

3. Rico's "deepest worry," according to Sennett, "is that he cannot offer the substance of his work life as an example to his children of how they should conduct themselves ethically. The qualities of good work are not the qualities of good character" (¶ 24). In your experience, is this so? If you don't feel you have the life experience to respond, pose this question to someone who you think does—someone who has worked a decade or more.

4. Is there any sense in which you find Sennett to be nostalgic—that is, longing for a world of work that is largely gone? Have you experienced in your own work any of the "old work" values discussed here? Are these values disappearing? Are they worth fighting for? Do you, as a worker, have any say in the matter? If you don't feel you have the life experience to respond, pose these questions to someone who you think does—someone who has worked a decade or more.

5. According to Sennett, "a young American with at least two years of college can expect to change jobs at least eleven times in the course of working, and change his or her skill base at least three times during those forty years of labor" (¶ 25). What is your "gut level" response to these projections concerning changes in jobs and skill base?

6. In these times, most college graduates would be happy to find a job—period. Is it too much to ask that your first job be "meaningful" in the sense Sennett describes?

7. Sennett describes Rico as a man in crisis. Do you sense a "crisis" in the modern workplace? To what extent does the work demanded of people in this economy place a burden on or confuse our identities? If you don't feel you have the life experience to respond, pose these questions to someone who you think does—someone who has worked a decade or more.

TRENDS AFFECTING WORK

The authors in this fourth and final component of readings don't use crystal balls to predict the future of working life in America. Instead, these analysts—an investigative reporter, an economist, and a former hedge-fund manager—rely on research and their own professional experience to anticipate coming changes in a dynamic job market. They are making informed guesses; and though they approach their common topic from various points of view, many of their guesses overlap. If they are right, the implications for your own working life will be substantial.

MAKING IT IN AMERICA

Adam Davidson

Despite the conventional wisdom, American manufacturing is booming. But this boom is, for the most part, limited to the fabrication of precision parts such as fuel injectors (for cars), which require the use of computer-aided machines. Gone are the days when an American worker could step off the farm or arrive at the shop door with (or without) a high school diploma and learn skills on the job that would secure an income for life. Now, the machines are too complicated for that, and the unskilled or low-skilled jobs have moved offshore to low-cost-labor countries such as China and India. Those jobs that survive in America's manufacturing sector require technical know-how—which means education beyond high school. As the following article illustrates, this industrial shift has created opportunities for some workers and eliminated opportunities for others.

Adam Davidson is a broadcast and print journalist who specializes in reporting on the impact of major economic trends. He cofounded and cohosts NPR's *Planet Money*, has won numerous awards in broadcast journalism, and contributes to print publications including the *New York Times Magazine*, *Harper's*, and *GQ*. This article first appeared in the January/February 2012 issue of *The Atlantic*.

I first met Madelyn "Maddie" Parlier in the "clean room" of Standard Motor Products' fuel-injector assembly line in Greenville, South Carolina. Like everyone else, she was wearing a blue lab coat and a hairnet. She's so small that she seemed swallowed up by all the protective gear.

Tony Scalzitti, the plant manager, was giving me the grand tour, explaining how bits of metal move through a series of machines to become precision fuel injectors. Maddie, hunched forward and moving quickly from one machine to another, almost bumped into us, then shifted left and darted away. Tony, in passing, said, "She's new. She's one of our most promising Level 1s."

Later, I sat down with Maddie in a quiet factory office where nobody needs to wear protective gear. Without the hairnet and lab coat, she is a pretty, intense woman, 22 years old, with bright blue eyes that seemed to bore into me as she talked, as fast as she could, about her life. She told me how much she likes her job, because she hates to sit still and there's always something going on in the factory. She enjoys learning, she said, and she's learned how to run a lot of the different machines. At one point, she looked around the office and said she'd really like to work there one day, helping to design parts rather than stamping them out. She said she's noticed that robotic arms and other machines seem to keep replacing people on the factory floor, and she's worried that this could happen to her. She told me she wants to go back to school—as her parents and grandparents keep telling her to do—but she is a single mother, and she can't leave her two kids alone at night while she takes classes.

I had come to Greenville to better understand what, exactly, is happening to manufacturing in the United States, and what the future holds for people like Maddie—people who still make physical things for a living and, more broadly, people (as many as 40 million adults in the U.S.) who lack higher education, but are striving for a middle-class life. We do still make things here, even though many people don't believe me when I tell them that. Depending on which stats you believe, the United States is either the No. 1 or No. 2 manufacturer in the world (China may have surpassed us in the past year or two). Whatever the country's current rank, its manufacturing output continues to grow strongly; in the past decade alone, output from American factories, adjusted for inflation, has risen by a third.

5   Yet the success of American manufacturers has come at a cost. Factories have replaced millions of workers with machines. Even if you know the rough outline of this story, looking at the Bureau of Labor Statistics data is still shocking. A historical chart of U.S. manufacturing employment shows steady growth from the end of the Depression until the early 1980s, when the number of jobs drops a little. Then things stay largely flat until about 1999. After that, the numbers simply collapse. In the 10 years ending in 2009, factories shed workers so fast that they erased almost all the gains of the previous 70 years; roughly one out of every three manufacturing jobs—about 6 million in total—disappeared. About as many people work in manufacturing now as did at the end of the Depression, even though the American population is more than twice as large today.

I came here to find answers to questions that arise from the data. How, exactly, have some American manufacturers continued to survive, and even thrive, as global competition has intensified? What, if anything, should be done to halt the collapse of manufacturing employment? And what does the disappearance of factory work mean for the rest of us?

Across America, many factory floors look radically different than they did 20 years ago: far fewer people, far more high-tech machines, and entirely different demands on the workers who remain. The still-unfolding story of manufacturing's transformation is, in many respects, that of our economic age. It's a story with much good news for the nation as a whole. But it's also one that is decidedly less inclusive than the story of the 20th century, with a less certain role for people like Maddie Parlier, who struggle or are unlucky early in life.

The Life and Times of Maddie Parlier

The Greenville Standard Motor Products plant sits just off I-85, about 100 miles southwest of Charlotte, North Carolina. It's a sprawling beige one-story building, surrounded by a huge tended lawn. Nearby are dozens of other similarly boxy factory buildings. Neighbors include a big Michelin tire plant, a nutrition-products factory, and, down the road, BMW's only car plant on American soil. Greenville is at the center of the 20-year-old manufacturing boom that's still taking place throughout the "New South." Nearby, I visited a Japanese-owned fiber-optic-material manufacturer, and a company that makes specialized metal parts for intercontinental ballistic missiles.

Standard makes and distributes replacement auto parts, known in the industry as "aftermarket" parts. Companies like Standard directly compete with Chinese firms for shelf space in auto-parts retail stores. This competition has intensified the pressure on all parts makers—American, Chinese, European. And of course it means that Maddie is, effectively, competing directly with workers in China who are willing to do similar work for much less money.

10   When Maddie says something important, something she wants you to really hear, she repeats it. She'll say it one time in a flat, matter-of-fact voice, and then again with a lot of upstate South Carolina twang.

"I'm a redneck," she'll say. "I'm a *reeeeeedneck.*"

"I'm smart," she told me the first time we met. "There's no other way to say it. I am *smaaaart.* I am."

Maddie flips back and forth between being a stereotypical redneck and being awfully smart. She will say, openly, that she doesn't know all that much about the world outside of Easley, South Carolina, where she's spent her whole life. Since her childhood, she's seen Easley transform from a quiet country town to a busy suburb of Greenville. (It's now a largely charmless place, thick with chain restaurants and shopping centers.) Maddie was the third child born to her young mother, Heather. Her father left when Maddie was young, never visited again, and died after he drove drunk into a car carrying a family of four, killing all of them as well.

Until her senior year of high school, Maddie seemed to be headed for the American dream—a college degree and a job with a middle-class wage. She got good grades, and never drank or did drugs or hung out with the bad kids. For the most part, she didn't hang out with anybody outside her family; she went to school, went home, went to church on Sundays. When she was 17, she met a boy who told her she should make friends with other kids at school. He had an easy way with people and he would take Maddie to Applebee's and cookouts and other places where the cool kids hung out. He taught her how to fit in, and he told her she was pretty.

15   Maddie's senior year started hopefully. She had finished most of her high-school requirements and was taking a few classes at nearby Tri-County Technical College. She planned to go to a four-year college after graduation, major in criminal justice, and become an animal-control officer. Around Christmas, she found out she was pregnant. She did finish school and, she's proud to say, graduated with honors. "On my graduation, I was six months pregnant," she says. "*Six months.*" The father and Maddie didn't stay together after the birth, and Maddie couldn't afford to pay for day care while she went to college, so she gave up on school and eventually got the best sort of job available to high-school graduates in the Greenville area: factory work.

If Maddie had been born in upstate South Carolina earlier in the 20th century, her working life would have been far more secure. Her 22 years overlap the final collapse of most of the area's once-dominant cotton mills and the birth of an advanced manufacturing economy. Hundreds of mills here once spun raw cotton into thread and then wove and knit the thread into clothes and textiles. For about 100 years, right through the 1980s and into the 1990s, mills in the Greenville area had plenty of work for people willing to put in a full day, no matter how little education they had. But around the time Maddie was born, two simultaneous transformations hit these workers. After NAFTA* and, later, the opening of China to global trade, mills in Mexico and China were able to produce and ship clothing and textiles at much lower cost, and mill after mill in South Carolina shut down. At the same time, the mills that continued to operate were able to replace their workers with a new generation of nearly autonomous, computer-run machines. (There's a joke in cotton country that a modern textile mill employs only a man and a dog. The man is there to feed the dog, and the dog is there to keep the man away from the machines.)

Other parts of the textile South have never recovered from these two blows, but upstate South Carolina—thanks to its proximity to I-85, and to foresighted actions by community leaders—attracted manufacturers of products far more complicated than shirts and textiles. These new plants have been a godsend for the local economy, but they have not provided the sort of wide-open job opportunities that the textile mills once did. Some workers, especially those with advanced manufacturing skills, now earn higher wages and have more opportunity, but there are not enough jobs for many others who, like Maddie, don't have training past high school.

Maddie got her job at Standard through both luck and hard work. She was temping for a local agency and was sent to Standard for a three-day job washing

---

*NAFTA: The North American Free Trade Agreement was implemented in January 1994. It eliminated most trade and investment barriers among the United States, Canada, and Mexico.

walls in early 2011. "People came up to me and said, 'You have to hire that girl—she is working so hard,'" Tony Scalzitti, the plant manager, told me. Maddie was hired back and assigned to the fuel-injector clean room, where she continued to impress people by working hard, learning quickly, and displaying a good attitude. But, as we'll see, this may be about as far as hustle and personality can take her. In fact, they may not be enough even to keep her where she is.

The Transformation of the Factory Floor

20 To better understand Maddie's future, it's helpful, first, to ask: Why is anything made in the United States? Why would any manufacturing company pay American wages when it could hire someone in China or Mexico much more cheaply?

I came to understand this much better when I learned how Standard makes fuel injectors, the part that Maddie works on. Like so many parts of the modern car engine, the fuel injector seems mundane until you sit down with an engineer who can explain how amazing it truly is.

A fuel injector is a bit like a small metal syringe, spraying a tiny, precise mist of gasoline into the engine in time for the spark plug to ignite the gas. The small explosion that results pushes the piston down, turning the crankshaft and propelling the car. Fuel injectors have replaced the carburetor, which, by comparison, sloppily sloshed gasoline around the engine. They became common in the 1980s, helping to solve a difficult engineering problem: how to make cars more efficient (and meet ever-tightening emission standards) without sacrificing power or performance.

To achieve maximum efficiency and power, a car's computer receives thousands of signals every second from sensors all over the engine and body. Based on the car's speed, ambient temperature, and a dozen other variables, the computer tells a fuel injector to squirt a precise amount of gasoline (anywhere from one to 100 10,000ths of an ounce) at the instant that the piston is in the right position (and anywhere from 10 to 200 times a second). For this to work, the injector must be perfectly constructed. When squirting gas, the syringe moves forward and back a total distance of 70 microns—about the width of a human hair—and a microscopic imperfection in the metal, or even a speck of dust, will block the movement and disable the injector. The tip of the plunger—a ball that meets a conical housing to create a seal—has to be machined to a tolerance of a quarter micron, or 10 millionths of an inch, about the size of a virus. That precision explains why fuel injectors are likely to be made in the United States for years to come. They require up-to-date technology, strong quality assurance, and highly skilled workers, all of which are easier to find in the United States than in most factories in low-wage countries.

The main factory floor of Standard's Greenville plant is, at first, overwhelming. It has the feel of a very crowded high-school gym: a big space with high ceilings but not a lot of light, a gray cement floor that's been around for a long time, and row after row of machines, going back farther than the eye can see, some the size of a washing machine, others as big as a small house. The first two machines, in the first row as you enter, are the newest: the Gildemeister seven-axis turning machines, two large off-white boxes each about the size of a small car turned on its side. Costing just under half a million dollars apiece, they gleam next to all the older machines. Inside each box is a larger, more precise version of the lathe you'd find in any high-school metal shop: a metal rod is spun rapidly while a cutting tool approaches it to cut at an exact angle. A special computer language tells the Gildemeisters how fast to spin and how close to bring the cutting tool to the metal rod.

25   A few decades ago, "turning machines" like these were operated by hand; a machinist would spin one dial to move the cutting tool large distances and another dial for smaller, more precise positioning. A good machinist didn't need a lot of book smarts, just a steady, confident hand and lots of experience. Today, the computer moves the cutting tool and the operator needs to know how to talk to the computer.

Luke Hutchins is one of Standard's newest skilled machinists. He is somewhat shy and talks quietly, but when you listen closely, you realize he's constantly making wry, self-deprecating observations. He's 27, skinny in his dark-blue jacket and jeans. When he was in his teens, his parents told him, for reasons he doesn't remember, that he should become a dentist. He spent a semester and a half studying biology and chemistry in a four-year college and decided it wasn't for him; he didn't particularly care for teeth, and he wanted to do something that would earn him money right away. He transferred to Spartanburg Community College hoping to study radiography, like his mother, but that class was full. A friend of a friend told him that you could make more than $30 an hour if you knew how to run factory machines, so he enrolled in the Machine Tool Technology program.

At Spartanburg, he studied math—a lot of math. "I'm very good at math," he says. "I'm not going to lie to you. I got formulas written down in my head." He studied algebra, trigonometry, and calculus. "If you know calculus, you definitely can be a machine operator or programmer." He was quite good at the programming language commonly used in manufacturing machines all over the country, and had a facility for three-dimensional visualization—seeing, in your mind, what's happening inside the machine—a skill, probably innate, that is required for any great operator. It was a two-year program, but Luke was the only student with no factory experience or vocational school, so he spent two summers taking extra classes to catch up.

After six semesters studying machine tooling, including endless hours cutting metal in the school workshop, Luke, like almost everyone who graduates, got a job at a nearby factory, where he ran machines similar to the Gildemeisters. When Luke got hired at Standard, he had two years of technical schoolwork and five years of on-the-job experience, and it took one more month of training before he could be trusted alone with the Gildemeisters. All of which is to say that running an advanced, computer-controlled machine is extremely hard. Luke now works the weekend night shift, 6 p.m. to 6 a.m., Friday, Saturday, and Sunday.

When things are going well, the Gildemeisters largely run themselves, but things don't always go well. Every five minutes or so, Luke takes a finished part to the testing station—a small table with a dozen sets of calipers and other precision testing tools—to make sure the machine is cutting "on spec," or matching the requirements of the run. Standard's rules call for a random part check at least once an hour. "I don't wait the whole hour before I check another part," Luke says. "That's stupid. You could be running scrap for the whole hour."

30   Luke says that on a typical shift, he has to adjust the machine about 20 times to keep it on spec. A lot can happen to throw the tolerances off. The most common issue is that the cutting tool gradually wears down. As a result, Luke needs to tell the computer to move the tool a few microns closer, or make some other adjustment. If the operator programs the wrong number, the tool can cut right into the machine itself and destroy equipment worth tens of thousands of dollars.

Luke wants to better understand the properties of cutting tools, he told me, so he can be even more effective. "I'm not one of the geniuses on that. I know a little bit. A lot of people go to school just to learn the properties of tooling." He also wants to learn more about metallurgy, and he's especially eager to study industrial electronics. He says he will keep learning for his entire career.

In many ways, Luke personifies the dramatic shift in the U.S. industrial labor market. Before the rise of computer-run machines, factories needed people at every step of production, from the most routine to the most complex. The Gildemeister, for example, automatically performs a series of operations that previously would have required several machines—each with its own operator. It's relatively easy to train a newcomer to run a simple, single-step machine. Newcomers with no training could start out working the simplest and then gradually learn others. Eventually, with that on-the-job training, some workers could become higher-paid supervisors, overseeing the entire operation. This kind of knowledge could be acquired only on the job; few people went to school to learn how to work in a factory.

Today, the Gildemeisters and their ilk eliminate the need for many of those machines and, therefore, the workers who ran them. Skilled workers now are required only to do what computers can't do (at least not yet): use their human judgment. This change is evident in the layout of a factory. In the pre-computer age, machines were laid out in long rows, each machine tended constantly by one worker who was considered skilled if he knew the temperament of his one, ornery ward. There was a quality-assurance department, typically in a lab off the factory floor, whose workers occasionally checked to make sure the machinists were doing things right. At Standard, today, as at most U.S. factories, machines are laid out in cells. One skilled operator, like Luke, oversees several machines, performing on-the-spot quality checks and making appropriate adjustments as needed.

The combination of skilled labor and complex machines gives American factories a big advantage in manufacturing not only precision products, but also those that are made in small batches, as is the case with many fuel injectors. Luke can quickly alter the program in a Gildemeister's computer to switch from making one kind of injector to another. Standard makes injectors and other parts for thousands of different makes and models of car, fabricating and shipping in small batches; Luke sometimes needs to switch the type of product he's making several times in a shift. Factories in China, by contrast, tend to focus on long runs of single products, with far less frequent changeovers.

35   It's no surprise, then, that Standard makes injectors in the U.S. and employs high-skilled workers, like Luke. It seems fairly likely that Luke will have a job for a long time, and will continue to make a decent wage. People with advanced skills like Luke are more important than ever to American manufacturing.

But why does Maddie have a job? In fact, more than half of the workers on the factory floor in Greenville are, like Maddie, classified as unskilled. On average, they make about 10 times as much as their Chinese counterparts. What accounts for that?

The Remnant Workforce

Tony Scalzitti, the factory manager, guides me through the logic of Maddie's employment. He's bookish and thoughtful—nothing like my mental image of a big, hulking factory manager. Trained as an engineer, he is constantly drawing charts and making lists as he talks, in order to explain modern American manufacturing. Sitting at a table in his office in the administrative area off the factory floor, Tony takes out a pen and writes down the definitions.

"Unskilled worker," he narrates, "can train in a short amount of time. The machine controls the quality of the part."

"High-skill worker," on the other hand, "can set up machines and make a variety of small adjustments; they use their judgment to assure product quality."

40   To show me the difference between the two, Tony takes me from Luke's station through an air lock and into Standard's bright-white clean room—about a quarter the size of the dirtier, louder factory floor—where dozens of people in booties, hairnets, and smocks, most of them women, stand at a series of workstations.

Tony points out that most of the factory's parts go through roughly the same process. Metal is cut into a precise shape in the "unclean" part of the factory and is then washed in a huge industrial washing machine to remove any bits of dirt, flakes of skin, or other contaminants, and, pristine, enters the clean room. Here, machines build the outer housing of the fuel injector, the part that is open to the engine and doesn't require anything like the precision of the inner workings.

The injectors progress through a series of stations, at each of which an unskilled worker and a simple machine perform one task. The machines here are much smaller, and are in one key respect the opposite of the Gildemeisters; these machines can work in only one way and require little judgment from the operator. This is not a throwback to the old system, in which workers manually ran single-purpose machines. This new technology is the other side of the computer revolution in manufacturing. Computers eliminate the need for human discretion; the person is there only to place the parts and push a button.

•   •   •

For Maddie [a Level 1 employee earning about $13 an hour] to achieve her dreams—to own her own home, to take her family on vacation to the coast, to have enough saved up so her children can go to college—she'd need to become one of the advanced Level 2s [like Luke, who earns about $20 an hour]. A decade ago, a smart, hard-working Level 1 might have persuaded management to provide on-the-job training in Level-2 skills. But these days, the gap between a Level 1 and a 2 is so wide that it doesn't make financial sense for Standard to spend years training someone who might not be able to pick up the skills or might take that training to a competing factory.

45   It feels cruel to point out all the Level-2 concepts Maddie doesn't know, although Maddie is quite open about these shortcomings. She doesn't know the computer-programming language that runs the machines she operates; in fact, she was surprised to learn they are run by a specialized computer language. She doesn't know trigonometry or calculus, and she's never studied the properties of cutting tools or metals. She doesn't know how to maintain a tolerance of 0.25 microns, or what *tolerance* means in this context, or what a micron is.

Tony explains that Maddie has a job for two reasons. First, when it comes to making fuel injectors, the company saves money and minimizes product damage by having both the precision and non-precision work done in the same place. Even if Mexican or Chinese workers could do Maddie's job more cheaply, shipping fragile, half-finished parts to another country for processing would make no sense. Second, Maddie is cheaper than a machine. It would be easy to buy a robotic arm that could take injector bodies and caps from a tray and place them precisely in a laser welder. Yet Standard would have to invest about $100,000 on the arm and a conveyance machine to bring parts to the welder and send them on to the next station. As is common in factories, Standard invests only in machinery that will earn back its cost within two years. For Tony, it's simple: Maddie makes less in two years than the machine would cost, so her job is safe—for now. If the robotic machines become a little cheaper, or if demand for fuel injectors goes up and Standard starts running three shifts, then investing in those robots might make sense.

"What worries people in factories is electronics, robots," she tells me. "If you don't know jack about computers and electronics, then you don't have anything in this life anymore. One day, they're not going to need people; the machines will take over. People like me, we're not going to be around forever."

•   •   •

Is there a crisis in manufacturing in America? Looking just at the dollar value of manufacturing output, the answer seems to be an emphatic no. Domestic manufacturers make and sell more goods than ever before. Their success has been grounded in incredible increases in productivity, which is a positive way of saying that factories produce more with fewer workers.

Productivity, in and of itself, is a remarkably good thing. Only through productivity growth can the average quality of human life improve. Because of higher agricultural productivity, we don't all have to work in the fields to make enough food to eat. Because of higher industrial productivity, few of us need to work in factories to make the products we use. In theory, productivity growth should help nearly everyone in a society. When one person can grow as much food or make as many car parts as 100 used to, prices should fall, which gives everyone in that society more purchasing power; we all become a little richer. In the economic models, the benefits of productivity growth should not go just to the rich owners of capital. As workers become more productive, they should be able to demand higher salaries.

50 Throughout much of the 20th century, simultaneous technological improvements in both agriculture and industry happened to create conditions that were favorable for people with less skill. The development of mass production allowed low-skilled farmers to move to the city, get a job in a factory, and produce remarkably high output. Typically, these workers made more money than they ever had on the farm, and eventually, some of their children were able to get enough education to find less-dreary work. In that period of dramatic change, it was the highly skilled craftsperson who was more likely to suffer a permanent loss of wealth. Economists speak of the middle part of the 20th century as the "Great Compression," the time when the income of the unskilled came closest to the income of the skilled.

The double shock we're experiencing now—globalization and computer-aided industrial productivity—happens to have the opposite impact: income inequality is growing, as the rewards for being skilled grow and the opportunities for unskilled Americans diminish.

I went to South Carolina, and spent so much time with Maddie, precisely because these issues are so large and so overwhelming. I wanted to see how this shift affected regular people's lives. I didn't come away with a handy list of policies that would solve all the problems of unskilled workers, but I did note some principles that seem important to improving their situation.

It's hard to imagine what set of circumstances would reverse recent trends and bring large numbers of jobs for unskilled laborers back to the U.S. Our efforts might be more fruitfully focused on getting Maddie the education she needs for a better shot at a decent living in the years to come. Subsidized job-training programs tend to be fairly popular among Democrats and Republicans, and certainly benefit some people. But these programs suffer from all the ills in our education system; opportunities go, disproportionately, to those who already have initiative, intelligence, and—not least—family support.

I never heard Maddie blame others for her situation; she talked, often, about the bad choices she made as a teenager and how those have limited her future. I came to realize, though, that Maddie represents a large population: people who, for whatever reason, are not going to be able to leave the workforce long enough to get the skills they need. Luke doesn't have children, and his parents could afford to support him while he was in school. Those with the right ability and circumstances will, most likely, make the right adjustments, get the right skills, and eventually thrive. But I fear that those who are challenged now will only fall further behind. To solve all the problems that keep people from acquiring skills would require tackling the toughest issues our country faces: a broken educational system, teen pregnancy, drug use, racial discrimination, a fractured political culture.

55 This may be the worst impact of the disappearance of manufacturing work. In older factories and, before them, on the farm, there were opportunities for almost everybody: the bright and the slow, the sociable and the awkward, the people with children and those without. All came to work unskilled, at first, and then slowly learned things, on the job, that made them more valuable. Especially

in the mid-20th century, as manufacturing employment was rocketing toward its zenith, mistakes and disadvantages in childhood and adolescence did not foreclose adult opportunity.

For most of U.S. history, most people had a slow and steady wind at their back, a combination of economic forces that didn't make life easy but gave many of us little pushes forward that allowed us to earn a bit more every year. Over a lifetime, it all added up to a better sort of life than the one we were born into. That wind seems to be dying for a lot of Americans. What the country will be like without it is not quite clear.

Review Questions

1. Summarize Davidson's assessment of the current state of manufacturing in the United States, taking into account his responses to these questions: (1) What is the global ranking of the United States in terms of manufacturing output? (2) In what types of manufacturing does the United States excel? (3) What type of manufacturing jobs has the country lost—and when did these losses begin? (4) Despite job losses in manufacturing, to what extent is U.S. manufacturing output rising—and at what cost, according to Davidson?

2. Maddie Parlier, one of the workers featured in Davidson's article, faces an uncertain future in manufacturing. Why?

3. What two developments in the early 1990s fundamentally changed manufacturing in the United States? Which types of manufacturing jobs were lost? Which survived? Which workers survived the change? Which lost?

4. Davidson writes that Luke "personifies" changes in the world of U.S. manufacturing. How so? What's the key distinction between Luke, a "high-skill worker," and Parlier, an "unskilled worker"?

5. How did jobs through much of the twentieth century favor the low-skilled worker and help to create a land of opportunity for all? What is likely to follow, according to Davidson, from the loss of these types of jobs?

Discussion and Writing Suggestions

1. If you have worked in manufacturing, how true to your experience is what you've read in Davidson's article? Did you find the same divide between low- and high-skilled jobs? Did computers play a role on the factory floor? (If you haven't worked in manufacturing, perhaps you know someone who has. Interview this person and record your responses.)

2. "Especially in the mid-20th century," writes Davidson (¶ 50), "as manufacturing employment was rocketing toward its zenith, mistakes and disadvantages in childhood and adolescence did not foreclose adult

opportunity." Something has been lost in America, writes Davidson; and he does not name any new developments in the manufacturing sector that could recreate the opportunities that less-educated and less-skilled Americans lost with the death of precomputerized manufacturing. Davidson is both troubled by this development and (as we find in his last sentence) confused. Are you? What's at stake here?

3. Economists maintain that the technological changes that destroy jobs in one sector of the economy create jobs in other sectors. (Economist Joseph Schumpeter coined the term "creative destruction" for this process.) Davidson is doubtless aware of this principle, and still he's concerned about prospects for American workers. Why? Does he doubt that this fundamental principle will apply in the case of computer-driven manufacturing?

4. Use the information you've learned in this article as the basis of a letter that you write to a younger sibling, cousin, or friend, in which you urge him or her not only to stay in school, but also to seek post high school training. Be as specific as you care to be about the nature of this training.

5. What surprised you most about Davidson's account of manufacturing capabilities in the United States? Would you consider pursuing a job in manufacturing? Which ones? Why? How confident are you that you could not only retain your manufacturing job, but also stay ahead of inevitable changes and flourish?

WILL YOUR JOB BE EXPORTED? [SUMMARY]

Alan S. Blinder

Alan S. Blinder is the Gordon S. Rentschler Memorial Professor of Economics at Princeton University. He has served as vice chairman of the Federal Reserve Board and was a member of President Clinton's original Council of Economic Advisers. This article first appeared in *The American Prospect* in November 2006. The following summary of "Will Your Job Be Exported?" appears in Chapter 1, in the context of a discussion on how to write summaries. See pp. 8–13 for the complete text of this important article.

In "Will Your Job Be Exported?" economist Alan S. Blinder argues that the quality and security of future jobs in America's services sector will be determined by how "offshorable" those jobs are. For the past 25 years, the greater a worker's skill or level of education, the better and more stable the job. No longer. Advances in technology have brought to the service sector the same pressures that forced so many manufacturing jobs offshore to China and India. The rate of offshoring in the service sector will accelerate, and jobs requiring both relatively little education (like call-center staffing) and extensive education (like software development) will increasingly be lost to workers overseas.

These losses will "eventually exceed" losses in manufacturing, but not all service jobs are equally at risk. While "personal services" workers (like barbers and surgeons) will be relatively safe from offshoring because their work requires close physical proximity to customers, "impersonal services" workers (like call-center operators and radiologists), regardless of their skill or education, will be at risk because their work can be completed remotely without loss of quality and then delivered via phone or computer. "[T]he relative demand for labor in the United States will [probably] shift away from impersonal services and toward personal services."

Blinder recommends three courses of action: He advises young people to plan for "a high-end personal services occupation that is not offshorable." He urges educators to prepare the future workforce by anticipating the needs of a personal services economy and redesigning classroom instruction and vocational training accordingly. Finally, he urges the government to adopt policies that will improve existing personal services jobs by increasing wages for low-wage workers; retraining workers to take on better jobs; and increasing opportunities in high-demand, well-paid areas like nursing and carpentry. Ultimately, Blinder wants America to prepare a new generation to "lead and innovate" in an economy that will continue exporting jobs that require "following and copying."

● Review Questions

1. What is "offshoring"? Why have service jobs been thought "immune to foreign competition"?

2. Explain Blinder's distinction between "personal services" and "impersonal services." Why is this distinction important?

3. In the past 25 years, what role has education played in preparing people for work? How does Blinder see that role changing in the coming decades?

4. What advice does Blinder offer to young people preparing for future work in the coming decades?

5. Why will the United States eventually lose more service-sector than manufacturing-sector jobs?

● Discussion and Writing Suggestions

1. Identify a worker (real or imagined) in a job that may be at risk for offshoring, according to Blinder. Write a letter to that person, apprising him or her of the potential danger and offering advice you think appropriate.

2. What is your reaction to Blinder's claim that educational achievement, in and of itself, will be less of a predictor of job quality and security than it once was?

3. Describe a well-paying job that would not require a college education but that should, according to Blinder, be immune to offshoring. Compare your responses to those of your classmates.

4. What work can you imagine doing in ten years? Describe that work in a concise paragraph. Now analyze your description as Blinder might. How secure is your future job likely to be?

5. Approach friends who have not read the Blinder article with his advice on preparing for future work (see Review Question 4). Report on their reactions.

6. What were your *emotional* reactions to Blinder's article? Did the piece leave you feeling hopeful, anxious, apprehensive, excited? Explain.

Is Your Job an Endangered Species?

Andy Kessler

Which types of jobs are most likely to go away in the new economy? This former chip designer, programmer, and hedge-fund manager presents likely candidates—in fact, a whole category of candidates. Kessler contributes frequently to the op-ed pages of the *New York Times* and the *Wall Street Journal,* in which this piece first appeared on February 17, 2011. His most recent book is *Eat People and Other Unapologetic Rules for Game-Changing Entrepreneurs* (2011). In nominating Kessler's *Eat People* for its annual award of best business books, the publisher of 800ceoread.com writes that "Kessler has made a career out of seeing the future of business, as an analyst, investment banker, venture capitalist, and hedge fund manager. Now he explains how the world's greatest entrepreneurs don't just start successful companies—they overturn entire industries."

So where the heck are all the jobs? Eight-hundred billion in stimulus and $2 trillion in dollar-printing and all we got were a lousy 36,000 jobs last month. That's not even enough to absorb population growth.

You can't blame the fact that 26 million Americans are unemployed or underemployed on lost housing jobs or globalization—those excuses are played out. To understand what's going on, you have to look behind the headlines. That 36,000 is a net number. The Bureau of Labor Statistics shows that in December some 4,184,000 workers (seasonally adjusted) were hired, and 4,162,000 were "separated" (i.e., laid off or quit). This turnover tells the story of our economy—especially if you focus on jobs lost as a clue to future job growth.

With a heavy regulatory burden, payroll taxes and health-care costs, employing people is very expensive. In January, the Golden Gate Bridge announced that it will have zero toll takers next year: They've been replaced by wireless FastTrak payments and license-plate snapshots.

Technology is eating jobs—and not just toll takers.

5   Tellers, phone operators, stock brokers, stock traders: These jobs are nearly extinct. Since 2007, the New York Stock Exchange has eliminated 1,000 jobs. And when was the last time you spoke to a travel agent? Nearly all of them have been displaced by technology and the Web. Librarians can't find 36,000 results in 0.14 seconds, as Google can. And a snappily dressed postal worker can't instantly deliver a 140-character tweet from a plane at 36,000 feet.

So which jobs will be destroyed next? Figure that out and you'll solve the puzzle of where new jobs will appear.

Forget blue-collar and white-collar. There are two types of workers in our economy: creators and servers. Creators are the ones driving productivity—writing code, designing chips, creating drugs, running search engines. Servers, on the other hand, service these creators (and other servers) by building homes, providing food, offering legal advice, and working at the Department of Motor Vehicles. Many servers will be replaced by machines, by computers and by changes in how business operates. It's no coincidence that Google announced it plans to hire 6,000 workers in 2011.

But even the label "servers" is too vague. So I've broken down the service economy further, as a guide to figure out the next set of unproductive jobs that will disappear. (Don't blame me if your job is listed here; technology spares no one, not even writers.)

- *Sloppers* are those that move things—from one side of a store or factory to another. Amazon is displacing thousands of retail workers. DMV employees and so many other government workers move information from one side of a counter to another without adding any value. Such sloppers are easy to purge with clever code.

- *Sponges* are those who earned their jobs by passing a test meant to limit supply. According to this newspaper, 23% of U.S. workers now need a state license. The Series 7 exam is required for stock brokers. Cosmetologists, real estate brokers, doctors and lawyers all need government certification. All this does is legally bar others from doing the same job, so existing workers can charge more and sponge off the rest of us.

   But eDiscovery is the hottest thing right now in corporate legal departments. The software scans documents and looks for important keywords and phrases, displacing lawyers and paralegals who charge hundreds of dollars per hour to read the often millions of litigation documents. Lawyers, understandably, hate eDiscovery.

   Doctors are under fire as well, from computer imaging that looks inside of us and from Computer Aided Diagnosis, which looks for patterns in X-rays to identify breast cancer and other diseases more cheaply and effectively than radiologists do. Other than barbers, no sponges are safe.

- *Supersloppers* mark up prices based on some marketing or branding gimmick, not true economic value. That Rolex Oyster Perpetual

Submariner Two-Tone Date for $9,200 doesn't tell time as well as the free clock on my iPhone, but supersloppers will convince you to buy it. Markups don't generate wealth, except for those marking up. These products and services provide a huge price umbrella for something better to sell under.

- *Slimers* are those that work in finance and on Wall Street. They provide the grease that lubricates the gears of the economy. Financial firms provide access to capital, shielding companies from the volatility of the stock and bond and derivative markets. For that, they charge hefty fees. But electronic trading has cut into their profits, and corporations are negotiating lower fees for mergers and financings. Wall Street will always exist, but with many fewer workers.

- *Thieves* have a government mandate to make good money and a franchise that could disappear with the stroke of a pen. You know many of them: phone companies, cable operators and cellular companies are the obvious ones. But there are more annoying ones—asbestos testing and removal, plus all the regulatory inspectors who don't add value beyond making sure everyone pays them. Technologies like Skype have picked off phone companies by lowering international rates. And consumers are cutting expensive cable TV services in favor of Web-streamed video.

Like it or not, we are at the beginning of a decades-long trend. Beyond the demise of toll takers and stock traders, watch enrollment dwindle in law schools and medical schools. Watch the divergence in stock performance between companies that actually create and those that are in transition—just look at Apple, Netflix and Google over the last five years as compared to retailers and media.

10   But be warned that this economy is incredibly dynamic, and there is no quick fix for job creation when so much technology-driven job destruction is taking place. Fortunately, history shows that labor-saving machines haven't decreased overall employment even when they have made certain jobs obsolete. Ultimately the economic growth created by new jobs always overwhelms the drag from jobs destroyed—if policy makers let it happen.

● Review Questions

1. What is the main development that drives job destruction, according to Kessler? What impact does this development have on the overall economy, over time?

2. What are the two main types of workers in our economy, according to Kessler? What type of worker is in greater danger of losing his/her job today? What further subdivisions does Kessler make?

3. How is eDiscovery representative, for Kessler, of important changes underway in our economy?

● Discussion and Writing Suggestions

1. What associations do you make with the category names Kessler invents for his article? Why might Kessler have chosen these particular names in his analysis of the economy? What effect do these names have on your understanding of (and your emotional response to) the subject under discussion?

2. Conservatives generally favor a smaller, less-intrusive government with lower taxes, fewer regulations, and fewer social welfare benefits. What language does Kessler use that suggests his conservative leanings?

3. Kessler claims that an entire class of jobs is at risk. Based on what you have read in this chapter and have seen for yourself, how convincing do you find Kessler's analysis of our economy? What evidence do you see that he may be wrong or has overstated his case?

4. Describe Kessler's overall tone (see p. 57), or stance, in this article. For instance, does he lament the jobs he reports being lost in the way Davidson laments the loss of opportunity for certain Americans? How well matched do you find Kessler's tone for the analysis he is presenting to readers of the *Wall Street Journal*?

5. Consider the jobs you see yourself pursuing upon graduation. Where do these jobs fit into Kessler's two broadest categories; and where, if at all, into his sub-categories? Does Kessler's analysis of the economy give you confidence that the jobs that interest you will exist in ten, twenty, or thirty years?

DEGREES AND DOLLARS

Paul Krugman

Paul Krugman, Professor of Economics and International Affairs at Princeton University, won the Nobel Prize for economics in 2008 for his work on free trade and globalization. As a columnist for the *New York Times*, Krugman writes regularly on economic trends. In this piece, published in the *Times* on March 6, 2011, he sticks a pin in the conventional wisdom that to secure a good job these days, job seekers need "ever higher levels" of education. In fact, writes Krugman, jobs that require many years of schooling are vulnerable to elimination by new technologies and competition from overseas. Winner of numerous awards in addition to the Nobel, Krugman has written twenty books for both scholarly and lay audiences.

It is a truth universally acknowledged that education is the key to economic success.* Everyone knows that the jobs of the future will require ever higher levels of skill. That's why, in an appearance Friday with former Florida Gov. Jeb

*Krugman makes a sly allusion to the opening line of Jane Austen's *Pride and Prejudice* ("It is a truth universally acknowledged, that a single man in possession of a good fortune must be in want of a wife").

Bush, President Obama declared that "If we want more good news on the jobs front then we've got to make more investments in education."

But what everyone knows is wrong.

The day after the Obama-Bush event, *The Times* published an article about the growing use of software to perform legal research. Computers, it turns out, can quickly analyze millions of documents, cheaply performing a task that used to require armies of lawyers and paralegals. In this case, then, technological progress is actually reducing the demand for highly educated workers.

And legal research isn't an isolated example. As the article points out, software has also been replacing engineers in such tasks as chip design. More broadly, the idea that modern technology eliminates only menial jobs, that well-educated workers are clear winners, may dominate popular discussion, but it's actually decades out of date.

5   The fact is that since 1990 or so the U.S. job market has been characterized not by a general rise in the demand for skill, but by "hollowing out": both high-wage and low-wage employment have grown rapidly, but medium-wage jobs—the kinds of jobs we count on to support a strong middle class—have lagged behind. And the hole in the middle has been getting wider: many of the high-wage occupations that grew rapidly in the 1990s have seen much slower growth recently, even as growth in low-wage employment has accelerated.

Why is this happening? The belief that education is becoming ever more important rests on the plausible-sounding notion that advances in technology increase job opportunities for those who work with information—loosely speaking, that computers help those who work with their minds, while hurting those who work with their hands.

Some years ago, however, the economists David Autor, Frank Levy and Richard Murnane argued that this was the wrong way to think about it. Computers, they pointed out, excel at routine tasks, "cognitive and manual tasks that can be accomplished by following explicit rules." Therefore, any routine task—a category that includes many white-collar, nonmanual jobs—is in the firing line. Conversely, jobs that can't be carried out by following explicit rules—a category that includes many kinds of manual labor, from truck drivers to janitors—will tend to grow even in the face of technological progress.

And here's the thing: Most of the manual labor still being done in our economy seems to be of the kind that's hard to automate. Notably, with production workers in manufacturing down to about 6 percent of U.S. employment, there aren't many assembly-line jobs left to lose. Meanwhile, quite a lot of white-collar work currently carried out by well-educated, relatively well-paid workers may soon be computerized. Roombas are cute, but robot janitors are a long way off; computerized legal research and computer-aided medical diagnosis are already here.

And then there's globalization. Once, only manufacturing workers needed to worry about competition from overseas, but the combination of computers and telecommunications has made it possible to provide many services at long range. And research by my Princeton colleagues Alan Blinder and Alan Krueger suggests that high-wage jobs performed by highly educated workers are, if anything, more "offshorable" than jobs done by low-paid, less-educated workers. If they're right, growing international trade in services will further hollow out the U.S. job market.

10   So what does all this say about policy?

Yes, we need to fix American education. In particular, the inequalities Americans face at the starting line—bright children from poor families are less likely to finish college than much less able children of the affluent—aren't just an outrage; they represent a huge waste of the nation's human potential.

But there are things education can't do. In particular, the notion that putting more kids through college can restore the middle-class society we used to have is wishful thinking. It's no longer true that having a college degree guarantees that you'll get a good job, and it's becoming less true with each passing decade.

So if we want a society of broadly shared prosperity, education isn't the answer—we'll have to go about building that society directly. We need to restore the bargaining power that labor has lost over the last 30 years, so that ordinary workers as well as superstars have the power to bargain for good wages. We need to guarantee the essentials, above all health care, to every citizen.

What we can't do is get where we need to go just by giving workers college degrees, which may be no more than tickets to jobs that don't exist or don't pay middle-class wages.

● Review Questions

1. According to Krugman, what key attribute of a job will determine whether or not that job is likely to be replaced by technology?

2. Why does Krugman believe that those who argue that education is becoming ever more important in securing a good job are mistaken?

3. What has happened to the middle class in America in the past twenty years, according to Krugman?

● Discussion and Writing Suggestions

1. "It's no longer true that having a college degree guarantees that you'll get a good job, and it's becoming less true with each passing decade." Does this statement (in ¶ 12) alarm you? After all, you are (likely) attending college with an eye to finding a good job. Political liberals generally favor government programs that protect poor and working-class Americans, creating the conditions that they (liberals) think will lead to economic opportunities. Liberals are willing to raise taxes in order to provide these benefits. What evidence do you find in this op-ed of Krugman's liberal leanings?

2. Reread the first four paragraphs of this op-ed. What strategy does Krugman use to get the reader's attention? Do you find this strategy effective? Why?

SYNTHESIS ACTIVITIES

1. Write an explanatory synthesis that reviews the impacts of globalization and technology on the twenty-first-century workplace. What jobs are most—and least—at risk from these two forces? In developing your paper, draw on the selections by Davidson, Blinder, Kessler, and Krugman.

2. Writing on trends in the twenty-first-century workplace, three authors in this chapter make distinctions that, they argue, provide the keys to future employ-ability: Krugman writes of routine and non-routine work; Blinder, of personal services and impersonal services; and Kessler, of creators and servers. Write a comparison-contrast synthesis that explains this terminology. To what extent are these writers identifying the same trends, while using different terms? To what extent are they describing different trends?

3. Assuming that you are fortunate enough to get a job upon graduation, is it reasonable to expect this job to be personally meaningful? Draw on the selection by Sennett in developing your paper. *Note:* Relatively early in your paper, you should define (both for you and your reader) the word *meaningful*.

4. What are the attributes of workers who are likeliest to succeed in the new economy? Develop your answer into an explanation that synthesizes the attributes for success discussed by Kessler, Krugman, Rampell, Carnevale et al., and Blinder. In the second part of your paper, analyze your own prospects for workplace success based on these same attributes. Respond to two questions: To what extent do you possess these attributes now? To what extent will your intended course of study prepare you to develop these attributes?

5. Sennett concludes that the skills needed to succeed in the new economy may "corrode" one's character. He writes that the "qualities of good work [in the new economy] are not the qualities of good character." He argues that our work affects our character and, ultimately, our prospects for personal fulfill-ment. Do you accept this connection between work and psychic health? Use the article by Sennett along with examples from your own work experience (or the experience of someone you know well) to develop an argument.

6. In reading the articles by Sennett and Davidson, you may detect a tone of lament—a sense that something of value from the old world of work has been lost in the new economy. Other writers such as Kessler and Blinder look at the economy and see a dynamic transformation (or "creative destruction") taking place. Compare and contrast the degrees of optimism and pessimism among authors in this chapter, considering their reasons (stated or not) for taking the positions they do. This paper could be an explanatory or an argument synthe-sis. If an argument, agree or disagree that the authors' optimism or pessimism is warranted. Include arguments supporting your own optimism or pessimism. Remember to organize your synthesis by idea, not by source.

7. Sennett writes that "a young American with at least two years of college can expect to change jobs at least eleven times in the course of working, and change his or her skill base at least three times during those forty years of labor" (¶ 26). Assuming the accuracy of this claim, how can a college student like you prepare for a life of work in which change is constant? As you develop your paper, address the following tension: On the one hand, you can major in a subject that leads you to master a specific skill (like engineering) in current demand in the workplace. (On this point, see Carnevale et al., Rampell, and Johnson.) On the other hand, assuming that the economy will require you to change skill sets, you'll need a broader training. What mix of specific and general skills will you seek in order to prepare yourself for the labor force of the twenty-first century? Develop your response into an argument synthesis that draws on the work of Davidson, Sennett, and Blinder.

8. Carnevale et al. and Rampell establish that students who major in the liberal arts have more trouble finding jobs postgraduation than do those who major in more skills-specific subjects, like engineering. Moreover, when liberal arts majors do find work, they earn less than their counterparts. Why, then, do students continue to major in the liberal arts? What is the value of such an education in a work environment such as the one you now face? Develop your answer in an argument synthesis. Draw on the authors in this chapter to help you make your case. (As part of your argument, you might respond to Sennett's observation about changing "skill sets," as detailed in the Synthesis Activity 7.)

9. What is the importance of your ability to adapt in the twenty-first-century workplace? First consider adaptations you can make as a student still in school—that is, *prior* to entering the workforce. Would you, for instance, consider changing what you study based on the information learned in this chapter and in related labor analyses and reports? Second, as you contemplate future employment, consider adaptations you may be called on to make *during* your working life. What adaptations are possible *as* you are working? Finally, consider both the positive and negative consequences of adaptation. Sennett, for instance, relates the story of a man whose adaptability allowed him to succeed in a corporate culture of downsizing but at the same time "corroded" his character. Develop your responses into an argument that draws on the selections in this chapter.

10. Training beyond high school can lead to a variety of degrees and certifications: the bachelor's degree from four-year institutions; a two-year associate's degree that demonstrates competence in a particular field; a license that gains one access to a trade; apprenticeships that gain one access to a union; and more. Given the discussions of Blinder, Kessler, and Krugman concerning changes in the new economy and good jobs that are likely to remain for American workers, what are the relative values of these degrees? What can one expect, in terms of employability when pursuing one type of post–high school education over another? In addition to referencing the authors just noted,

consider drawing on Davidson, who writes about good jobs to be found in American manufacturing, given the right training.

11. Blinder, Davidson, and Krugman find public educators failing in their mission to train students for the types of jobs demanded by the twenty-first-century workplace. How do these authors think we should reform our public schools to better prepare students? Based on what you've read in this chapter, what do *you* think must be done to train students for the jobs of tomorrow? How do we fix education? Develop your answer into an argument.

12. Blinder, Kessler, and Krugman make predictions about employability in the American workplace. Choose any one of these authors. Then, using the Bureau of Labor Statistics *Summary* (with its accompanying tables), assess that author's predictions. Do you see evidence in the BLS *Summary*, for instance, of what Blinder thinks will be an accelerating loss of jobs in the impersonal services economy? Of Krugman's assessment that more education is not necessarily the ticket to stable employment? Of Kessler's categorization of the economy into creators and servers? Each of these authors makes projections that rest on assumptions about the economy. Your task is to consider these arguments in light of the BLS data. Your paper will be a critique to the extent that you are evaluating the arguments of an author; your paper will also be an argument synthesis to the extent that you are using data from one source in your evaluation of another.

13. How do the selections in this chapter illustrate the serious reality underlying "A Post-College Flow Chart of Misery and Pain" by Jenna Brager? The graphic prompts both a smile and a groan. Why? At the risk of destroying a good joke by analyzing it to death, how can the selections by Blinder, Carnevale et al., Kessler, and others help you to appreciate Brager's humor? How would you describe that humor?

RESEARCH ACTIVITIES

1. Interview several workers you know who are in their forties or, preferably, in their fifties. Ask them to describe changes they've seen in the workplace and ask how they're adapting to these changes. Frame the results of your interview in the context of several of the readings in this chapter. That is, use the readings to help make sense of the information you record in the interviews. Your research paper could take the form of an argument or an analysis.

2. Take a thorough accounting of the "Occupational Outlook Handbook" at the Bureau of Labor Statistics Web site. Prepare a report that presents (1) the range of information available at the OOH site—and closely linked sites; (2) a strategy for mining useful information. Essentially, you will be preparing a "user's guide" to the OOH.

3. Find a copy of Studs Terkel's *Working*, select one of the interviewees reporting on his or her experiences at a particular job, and research the current status of this job or career field at the Bureau of Research Statistics Web site. Compare and contrast the experiences of the Terkel subject (mid-1970s) with those of a present-day worker.

4. Visit the career counseling office at your school; interview one or more of the staff people there, and survey the publications available at the office to determine facts about the interests and employment prospects of the student body at your school. Write a report on the success your fellow students have had in securing internships at local businesses or job placements with local employers.

5. Research the term "creative destruction" as developed by Joseph Schumpeter and report on its acceptance by present-day economists.

6. Trace the changing attitudes toward work in Western culture. Authors of interest will likely include Herbert Applebaum, Melvin Kranzberg and Joseph Gies, Richard Donkin, and Joanne Ciulla.

7. Research the origins of the Puritan work ethic and its persistence in American culture. Puritans, writes Melvin Kranzberg, "regard[ed] the accumulation of material wealth through labor as a sign of God's favor as well as of the individual's religious fervor." Be sure, in your research, to look at *The Protestant Ethic and the Spirit of Capitalism* by economist and sociologist Max Weber.

8. Research and report on one jobs-related aspect of the "Great Recession" of December 2007–June 2009, the most significant downturn in the American economy since the Great Depression of the 1930s. Here are five jobs-related topics on which you might report: "underemployment"; the fate of older, laid-off workers; the impact of the recession on American youth employment; job losses in the industries and businesses hardest hit by the recession; the emergence of "Top 10" (or 8 or 20, etc.) lists of "recession-proof" jobs.

11

Have You Heard This?
The Latest on Rumor

Beneath the streets of New York City, countless alligators live in the sewers. Entire packs of these menacing reptiles roam the subterranean waterways, waiting to swallow unsuspecting citizens above. These are no ordinary alligators. Flushed down toilets after growing too large for their owners, fed on an endless supply of New York City rats and trash shoved from the streets into grates, they are huge, fearsome creatures. No one has actually seen these nightmarish beasts, but they are certainly lurking below, their sharp teeth just hidden from view.

The alligator rumor might be the high concept for a horror movie if it were true. But of course it isn't. This classic story is a quintessential rumor, having developed over the decades into urban legend. As it circulated and gradually took hold of public consciousness, it became, for many, as good as fact. Then, both New Yorkers and tourists began nervously watching their toes as they approached sewer grates.

How fast do rumors spread? Consider a math problem: On January 1, you tell a story to a couple of your friends. On January 2, each of your friends tells two others. On January 3, each of these tells two more. And so on, for twenty days. The spread of the rumor during the first two days can be diagrammed as follows (P = person):

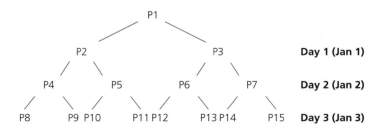

P1		
P2 P3		**Day 1 (Jan 1)**
P4 P5 P6 P7		**Day 2 (Jan 2)**
P8 P9 P10 P11 P12 P13 P14 P15		**Day 3 (Jan 3)**

By the 20th of January, how many people will know the rumor? Answer: 2,097,151.

At some moment, a spreading rumor eventually crosses what rumor expert Cass Sunstein calls a "tipping point," the point at which so many people believe the story that it's hard to separate rumor from reality. The alligator rumor began in the 1920s but didn't reach that key moment until it hit fever pitch in the early 1980s. Of course, during the first few decades of this intervening period, there was no TV, much less cable news, and the Internet didn't become an efficient agent of rumor spreading until the '90s. Otherwise, the tipping point for the Big Apple's subterranean alligators would likely have been reached much earlier.

Reconsider the math problem above, which assumes one-day-at-a-time distribution via word of mouth. How would the same problem work in the digital age? In 2012, we can e-mail an entire address book with a simple touch of the "Send" button or "share" with all of our Facebook friends with a quick tap of "Enter." Within seconds, minutes, or hours, a rumor can "go viral," moving from a whispered piece of gossip to an e-mail chain, a Twitter feed, or a recurring story on cable news. As the transition from rumor to perceived reality becomes near-instantaneous, rumors become virtually uncontrollable, both by those who originate them and those who are targeted.

What do rumors tell us about those who start and spread them? Or, as psychologist Nicholas DiFonzo asks, "What is it about being human that sets the stage for rumor activity?" As you will discover in this chapter, rumors can be understood as expressions of our collective fears, hopes, and attitudes about the community and the world we live in. They are outward signs of the way we view one another, individually and in groups. They help us make sense of a sometimes confusing or threatening world by confirming the truth of our world views or our beliefs about how particular groups of people behave. Some rumors encapsulate what Robert H. Knapp calls our "pipe dreams"—our fervent, if unrealistic, hopes. Others offer thinly veiled covers for our anxieties, our concerns about the bad things that might happen. They often confirm what we already believe to be true (even if it isn't). They also drive further apart individuals and groups who are already suspicious of one another. In examining rumors, we discern the psychological, emotional, and intellectual life of our personal and business relationships, our popular culture, our politics, and our society.

Consider political rumors, which often arise out of fears about what a president or political party might do unless stopped. During the health care debate of 2009, so many rumors were competing for public attention (among them, the government's "death panels") that the White House eventually created a Web site to attempt to set the record straight. Two years later, President Obama felt compelled to release his long-form birth certificate to put to rest the stubbornly persistent rumor that he was not born in the United States. But as *Los Angeles Times* columnist Gregory Rodriguez explains, once we accept as true a rumor that is supported by our own belief system, even hard evidence is unlikely to sway us. The release of the president's birth certificate counted for nothing to some of his opponents, who went to great lengths to explain why the released document was not real or was of suspect origin.

The falsehoods about Barack Obama's citizenship are the most prominent recent manifestations of rumor in American presidential politics. As former John

McCain presidential campaign manager Richard H. Davis explains, political rumors have long been a feature of American history. During the 1828 presidential campaign, supporters of Andrew Jackson spread a rumor that his opponent, incumbent President John Quincy Adams, had procured an American woman to provide sexual services for the czar of Russia. Later that century, rumors circulated that Abraham Lincoln was actually the illegitimate son of a Smoky Mountain man named Abram Elroe. Other presidential rumors are rooted in religious bigotry: that Lincoln was a Catholic, that Franklin Roosevelt was a Jew, that Barack Obama is a Muslim. Among the more bizarre recent political rumors was the Clinton "body count," a list of more than fifty suspicious deaths of colleagues, friends, advisors, and other citizens who were allegedly preparing to testify against the Clintons in the wake of the Monica Lewinsky scandal.

Rumors driven by anxiety, fear, and prejudice also proliferate in the immediate wake of national disasters. After the Japanese attack on Pearl Harbor in December 1941, rumors spread that Roosevelt and Churchill had actually plotted the raids as a pretext for U.S. entry into World War II, and even that some of the attacking airplanes were piloted by British and American flyers. After 9/11, rumors spread that the American and Israeli governments were involved in planning the attacks on the World Trade Center and the Pentagon, and that 4,000 Jews stayed home from work that day because they had been told in advance of the targeting of the twin towers. (In fact, such beliefs are almost conventional wisdom among many in the Middle East.)

Many other rumors are focused on the personal—on what is happening, or what could happen, to ordinary people: Dave and his next door neighbor are having a fling; the company where we work is closing down next month (or, if actually scheduled to close down, will stay in business, after all); school jobs in the community are being given to illegal aliens from Jamaica; vaccinations cause autism (or cancer); or—to look back at our model analysis in Chapter 6—travelers abroad who are rash enough pick up sexual companions in lounges risk having their kidneys surgically removed.

In the following pages, then, we explore this problematic but ubiquitous phenomenon of rumor. Among our chief concerns:

- How and why do rumors start?
- How do rumors spread? What are their mechanisms, and what can we do to stop them—or at least, to neutralize them?
- Why do rumors spread? Why are people apt to believe them, even when the evidence suggests they are false? How may rumors confirm what people already believe or suspect to be true?
- In what ways do people use rumors for political, professional, or personal gain?
- What do our rumors suggest about *us*?

The chapter consists of three types of selections: works of art or literature, case studies of particular rumors, and theoretical or reflective pieces that attempt to explain how rumors work. The works of art serve as bookends to the chapter.

We begin with the famous *Saturday Evening Post* cover "The Gossips" by the beloved American painter Norman Rockwell, which vividly—and humorously—illustrates the communal spread of rumor. We end by directing readers online to a short story by John Updike, famed chronicler of twentieth-century middle-class suburban angst. In "The Rumor," Updike creates a tale of a long-married couple dealing in unexpected ways with an amusing but potentially damaging rumor.

The case studies offer extended examples of particular rumors. "Frankenchicken" discusses one of the first Internet-fueled rumors, the supposedly genetically modified chicken offered by a popular fast food chain. In "What Really Cost Chris Dussold His Job?" Thomas Bartlett tells the story of a college teacher who saw his career devastated by rumors that spread through the hallways of academia. In "That Old Devil Moon," Sandra Salmans explores the supposed satanic company logo of a major American company. Alan Glenn's "Paul is Dead (said Fred)" traces the life of a Beatles rumor. And focusing on presidential politics, the selections by Richard H. Davis, Samuel G. Freedman, and Jeremy W. Peters dissect the long-standing nature of political rumor mongering, that rare aspect of political discourse that's truly bipartisan.

The theoretical selections attempt to explain how and why rumors work and how they can be fought. In "Truth Is in the Ear of the Beholder," Gregory Rodriguez examines how we accept rumors that confirm our worldview (and reject facts that don't). The classic "A Psychology of Rumor" by Robert H. Knapp explores three particular types of rumor and their causes and responds to the question "What are the qualities that make for a good rumor?" In "It's Clear That It's Unclear," Nicholas DiFonzo explores the ways in which rumors help us to make sense of a complex and sometimes threatening world. Next, in a chapter from his recent book *On Rumors*, Cass Sunstein discusses the manner in which rumors expand through "cascades" and how they are reinforced by "group polarization." Finally, in "Managing Rumors," public relations experts John Doorley and Helio Fred Garcia offer businesspeople a systematic approach to counteracting false stories and reports.

Together, these selections should help you understand rumors in many of their forms and venues: why they're created, how they work, and how we all contribute to their enduring power.

THE GOSSIPS

Norman Rockwell

As children, most of us have played the "telephone game." One person shares a piece of information with a friend, who tells it to another, who tells it to another, and so on. By the time the last person hears the news, the original story has changed into something else entirely. "The sky is blue" can turn somewhere along the line into "the sky is going to fall on you." In the painting below, which originally appeared as the cover of the March 6, 1948, edition of the *Saturday Evening Post*, Norman Rockwell (1894–1978) humorously traces this kind of error-compounding pattern.

One of America's most beloved artists, Rockwell created quintessential, wholesome, and often whimsical images of American life, many of them originally appearing in the *Saturday Evening Post* (322 of his paintings were published as *Post* covers over a period of 47 years). As his career progressed, Rockwell began to explore the complex issues of his time: civil rights, poverty, and even space travel. His critics sometimes accused him of idealizing and sentimentalizing American life; but Rockwell's reputation has grown in recent years, culminating with exhibitions in art museums in New York, Washington, Raleigh, Chicago, Phoenix, Tacoma, and San Diego, as well as in the White House. Whether depicting an archetypal Thanksgiving meal, a father seeing his son off to military service, or a young African-American girl accompanied by federal marshals as she enrolls in a previously all-white school, Rockwell's work indelibly memorialized mainstream American life. In "The Gossips," he shows the sometimes amusing, sometimes insidious play of that most mainstream of American, indeed human, activities—rumor.

Printed by permission of the Norman Rockwell Family Agency, Copyright © 1948
The Norman Rockwell Family Entities

Discussion and Writing Suggestions

1. Rockwell's painting is called "The Gossips." In your own mind and experience, what are the main similarities and differences between gossip and rumor?

2. Most of us have found ourselves in a situation similar to the one Rockwell portrays here, at least once in our lives. Where was your placement in the line? How did the initial message change during the course of the communication?

3. When a piece of information is transmitted on a wave of gossip, the content of that information—its meaning and implications—often changes drastically. Think about an event from your own life affected by a rumor. In what ways did changes in the informational content of the rumor affect your life? Can you think of a current (or historical) event that has been affected by the mutating nature of gossip?

4. Several figures in this painting are clearly pleased by the gossip. Why do you think some people enjoy getting and passing along salacious information (of sometimes dubious reliability) about their friends and neighbors?

5. Aside from pleasure, what other responses are represented by the figures in the painting?

6. The last two figures in the painting suggest that the end result of gossip is negative. Can you think of any *positive* aspects of sharing information in this manner?

7. Rockwell was known for painting "American" scenes and images. What does this particular piece suggest about American culture—at least in the era (the late 1940s) when this painting was created?

FRANKENCHICKEN

One of life's guilty pleasures is occasionally digging into a plate of crispy fried chicken. But suppose someone told you that what you were eagerly ingesting wasn't really chicken, but a "frankenfood" bird, genetically engineered to have shrunken bones, no beak, and no feet and to be technologically optimized for preparing and cooking? According to the rumor described in the following selection, frankenbirds are exactly what the popular fast food chain KFC uses for its chicken. This rumor has the distinction of being one of the first to spread worldwide via e-mail. In the following selection, the popular site Snopes.com tackles this rampant early Internet rumor and explains why it was just that—a rumor, not the truth. A vast cornucopia of fascinating rumor lore, Snopes.com was formed in 1995 to help Web surfers get to the bottom of online rumors.

Go to: Snopes.com

Search terms: "tastes like chicken"

● Review Questions

1. As it worked its way across the Internet, many people accepted this apparently absurd rumor without question. Why did they find it so plausible? What "facts" were offered in support?

2. What elements of the story (e.g., about corporate practices and corporate deception) seemed reasonable to readers and to those spreading the rumor?

3. While this rumor implies a distrust of corporate practices, how does it also reflect a lack of faith in government?

4. In what ways did contemporary scientific developments contribute this particular rumor?

● Discussion and Writing Suggestions

1. Reading about this rumor in hindsight can make it seem absurd. But plenty of people believed it when it worked its way across the Internet. Why do you think that people found it so plausible?

2. The piece alludes to other popular fast food restaurant rumors, including worms at McDonald's and roaches at Taco Bell. What other restaurant-focused rumors have you heard about? Did you believe them? Why or why not?

3. Snopes.com offers some reasons for the spread of this rumor. Which reason seems most persuasive—and why? What might motivate someone to help spread a rumor like this?

4. Considering how quickly Internet stories can spread, a company can find itself on the wrong side of a rumor in the blink of an eye. If you were running a business, how would you respond to this sort of rumor? (For instance, would you respond at all?)

5. Clearly, the KFC rumor may have affected the public's eating patterns—or at least those of a segment of the population. Have you ever altered your behavior based on a rumor? Tell the story—in a paragraph.

6. What does the wide reach of this particular rumor suggest about rumor transmission in general?

TRUTH IS IN THE EAR OF THE BEHOLDER

Gregory Rodriguez

In this op-ed, published on September 28, 2009, in the *Los Angeles Times*, columnist Gregory Rodriguez argues that rumors thrive because those who hear them are "predisposed to believe them." Drawing upon rumor theorists such as Robert H. Knapp and Cass Sunstein, represented later in this chapter, he explores the ways in which rumors emerge from our anxieties and belief systems. Rumors that support and validate our prior convictions are hard to disprove, even when countered with cold hard facts and solid reasoning. A founding director of Arizona State University's Center for Social Cohesion, Rodriguez writes about civic engagement and political and cultural trends.

Rumors and conspiracy theories can only thrive in the minds of people who are predisposed to believe them. Successful propagators of fringe theories don't just send random balloons into the atmosphere. Rather, they tap into the preexisting beliefs and biases of their target audiences.

Plenty of studies have shown that people don't process information in a neutral way—"biased assimilation" they call it. In other words, rather than our opinions being forged by whatever information we have available, they tend to be constructed by our wants and needs. With all their might, our minds try to reduce cognitive dissonance—that queasy feeling you get when you are confronted by contradictory ideas simultaneously. Therefore, we tend to reject theories and rumors—and facts and truths—that challenge our worldview and embrace those that affirm it.

It's easy to assume that lack of education is the culprit when it comes to people believing rumors against logic and evidence—for instance, that Barack Obama, whose mother was an American citizen and whose state of birth has repeatedly said his birth records are in good order, isn't a legitimate American citizen. But one 1994 survey on conspiracy theories found that educational level or occupational category were not factors in whether you believed in them or not.

What was significant? Insecurity about employment. That finding ties into psychologist Robert H. Knapp's 1944 thesis that rumors "express and gratify the emotional needs" of communities during periods of social duress. They arise, in his view, to "express in simple and rationalized terms the uncertainties and hostilities which so many feel."

5   If, on the one hand, you think you should blame rumormongers and rumor believers for not doing their homework, you can, on the other hand, give them credit for striving pretty hard to explain phenomena they find threatening. Rumors and conspiracy theories often supply simplified, easily digestible explanations (and enemies) to sum up complex situations. However crass, they're both fueled by a desire to make sense of the world.

Can false rumors and off-the-wall theories be corrected by broadcasting the truth? Sometimes, but not always. Access to information, evidently, is not a silver bullet. In his just-published book, *On Rumors,* legal scholar (and new head of the White House Office of Information and Regulatory Affairs) Cass R. Sunstein argues that efforts at correcting rumors can sometimes even hurt the cause of truth.

He cites a 2004 experiment in which liberals and conservatives were asked to examine their views on the existence of weapons of mass destruction in Iraq After reading a statement that declared that Iraq had WMD, the subjects were asked to reveal their views on a five-point scale, from "strongly agree" to "strongly disagree."

Then they were handed a mock news article in which President George W. Bush defended the war, in part by suggesting that Saddam Hussein had weapons of mass destruction. After reading that article, participants were also asked to read about the CIA's Duelfer report, which showed that the Bush administration was wrong to think Iraq had such weapons. Finally, they were again asked their opinion of the original statement on the same five-point scale.

What the researchers found is that the outcome depended on the participants' political point of view. The liberals shifted in the direction of greater disagreement, while the conservatives showed a significant shift in agreeing with the original statement. As the researchers put it, "The correction backfired—conservatives who received the correction telling them that Iraq did not have WMD were more likely to believe that Iraq had WMD."

10   Are you scared yet? I am.

Sunstein's book goes on to explore ways that society can hold rumor-mongers accountable without eliciting a chilling effect on the freedom of speech. He's concerned that crazy rumors in the Internet Age can gum up the machinery of democracy itself.

I applaud the effort, but I'd prefer to do away with the insecurity and uncertainty that feed wacko theories and rumors in the first place. A modicum of stability, a fair and functioning economy and polity—those have to be what we strive for.

But in the meantime, don't forget psychologist Knapp. "To decry the ravages of rumor-mongering is one thing," he wrote, "to control it is yet an other." Pass it on.

● Review Questions

1. Define "biased assimilation."

2. Which factors concerning rumors were found *not* to be of importance, according to a 1994 study? Which *were* found significant?

3. In what ways are the views of psychologist Robert H. Knapp supported by the 1994 findings discussed here?

4. How did researchers draw a connection between the political stance of participants and their beliefs about the justification for the Iraq War?

● Discussion and Writing Suggestions

1. Rodriguez suggests that when confronted with information that flies in the face of our personal ideologies, we often ignore the new information and stick with what we already believe. Discuss an occasion when you changed your mind on a subject based on new information or—conversely—a time when you ignored or rationalized away new data in order to justify sticking with your existing belief or set of values.

2. Rodriguez describes a 2004 study concerning participants' changing views about the justification of the U.S. war in Iraq—both before and after participants were presented with the "facts" about Iraq's weapons of mass destruction. What other recent events or controversies have sparked broad, vocal opinions about "facts" that have since been discredited? Consider stories such as the controversies over the president's birth certificate and religious beliefs. In these or other like cases, to what extent do you find that facts, when eventually revealed, make a difference to people's convictions?

3. Rodriguez summarizes Cass Sunstein's view that trying to correct false rumors is often counterproductive. Cite examples of situations in which attempts to clarify a rumor only reinforces it.

4. How does the Internet affect both the spread and the attempted refutation of rumors? What seem to you the differences between reading a correction online, reading a correction in a traditional print source, and being given the correction face-to-face by another person?

5. Discussing those who don't change their opinions after being confronted with the facts, Rodriguez says that we can at least "give them credit for striving pretty hard to explain phenomena they find threatening." What does he mean? To what extent do you agree?

WHAT COST CHRIS DUSSOLD HIS DREAM JOB?

Thomas Bartlett

Some rumors are simply odd stories that thread their way through public consciousness before disappearing without a trace. Whether or not KFC is "real chicken" may intrigue us, but unless we regularly eat at the franchise, it does not have a direct and significant impact on our lives. Other rumors are like tornados: Starting small but gradually picking up momentum, over time they grow more powerful and destructive. We see the latter pattern in Thomas Bartlett's article, below. A senior writer for the *Chronicle of Education*, Bartlett has been a finalist for the National Magazine Award for reporting on some of the darker elements of college life, including plagiarism and diploma mills. In this article, originally published in the *Chronicle* on February 10, 2006, Bartlett explores the case of Professor Chris Dussold, who saw his career derailed as a rumor spread across his department. What started as a whisper culminated in a lawsuit and upended lives.

He has told the story before. How he was fired from his dream job. How he cleaned out his office under police escort. How he felt hopeless, crushed, as if his career—and maybe his life—was over.

But even after two years and numerous retellings, the emotion still sneaks up on him. He pauses in midsentence, puts his face in his hands, and begins to weep.

Chris Dussold has been through a lot. In 2004 the assistant professor of finance was fired by Southern Illinois University at Edwardsville for copying another professor's teaching statement. It was two pages of boilerplate about the need to "practice life-long learning" and such. The word plagiarism had never crossed his mind.

Besides, he says, that was not the real reason he was fired.

5   What brought him down, he believes, was a persistent rumor that he was sleeping with an undergraduate. A rumor that was false, according to both Mr. Dussold and a university investigation. A rumor, he believes, that cost him not only his job, but his good name and his peace of mind.

Now Mr. Dussold is on a crusade to restore his reputation and to expose what he sees as widespread hypocrisy among academics. No matter what you think of Mr. Dussold or his motives, you can't deny his zeal: He is a man on a mission.

And he is starting to make his former colleagues very nervous.

Landing a Dream Job

Chris Dussold loves math, wears a big digital watch, and quotes Star Trek characters. In other words, he is a geek. Even he thinks so.

He majored in finance at Edwardsville and stuck around to get his master's in economics. He earned his Ph.D. just up the road at the University of Missouri at Columbia. After completing his doctorate, he fielded several offers, including one from North Carolina State University.

10   He turned them all down to return to Edwardsville in 2001, even though it offered less money and less prestige (though his salary at Southern Illinois—just over $100,000—wasn't bad). "I used to tell them I would take this job for nothing," he says. "It felt like coming home."

His first couple of years at the university were among the happiest of his life. He found that he really liked teaching and research. He tried to steer clear of any controversy. He did not take sides in departmental conflicts. He did not discuss politics or religion with his colleagues. He did his best to remain above the fray.

Then, in the fall of 2003, he heard a rumor. The story going around was that he was sleeping with an undergraduate in his financial-management club. At first he thought the rumor might have something to do with the fact that his fiancée, Sara Bennett, was a former student. But they had not started dating—or even become friends—until after she graduated. Their relationship was no secret anyway: Ms. Bennett accompanied him to university functions and dinners with other professors. Everyone knew they were together.

The woman mentioned in the rumor, Jennifer Peyla, was in the club, but Mr. Dussold says he barely knew her. His only social contact with her, he says, was once giving her a ride to her car. That was it. There were students he considered friends, those who stopped by his office or lingered after class to chat, but she wasn't one of them.

So at first he shrugged it off.

15   Then he heard the rumor again from someone else. And again, the same name: Jennifer Peyla.

He began to be concerned. Mr. Dussold, who is now 35, asked an older colleague for advice. "This happens to every young male professor," he says the colleague told him. "Rumors come, rumors go. Ignore it."

This was news to him. But maybe it did happen to others, he thought. Maybe he was naïve.

A Meeting With the Accuser

Later in the fall, another colleague approached him privately. "This needs to stop in case she's ever in one of your classes," he says the colleague told him. Those words hit him like a punch. People assumed the story was true. "I realized this was beyond rumors," he says. "This was career-jeopardizing."

He set up a meeting with Ms. Peyla in late October. He also invited Radcliffe G. Edmonds Jr., an associate professor of economics. to attend. In the meeting, according to Mr. Dussold, Ms. Peyla denied that there was any inappropriate relationship and denied starting the rumors. This was reassuring.

20   (Mr. Edmonds declined to comment for this article. So did Ms. Peyla—who has since married and changed her last name to Schuette—saying that she didn't want to put herself "in the position where something could be used against" her. She is now a graduate student at Southern Illinois.)

Mr. Dussold then asked for a meeting with the university's human-resources director, Angelo G. Monaco. He wanted an official record in case the matter ever came up again. Ms. Bennett, his fiancée, accompanied him to the meeting. Mr. Monaco told them that rumors had a "life cycle" and that they should wait it out, according to both of them.

Maybe everyone was right: There was nothing to worry about. This was a self-correcting problem. It would go away on its own.

But he was starting to feel the strain. Every interaction now carried a question mark: Who believes the rumor? What have they heard? One rumor had it that he was having sex with Ms. Peyla in his office. Another that they were having sex in his truck. Were there more? What exactly were people saying?

Mr. Monaco had advised him to require every visitor to his office to sign a log. He also suggested meeting with female students in a conference room, rather than his office. Such actions were supposed to quell the whispers. But Mr. Dussold worried they only made it seem like something was wrong. Other professors did not have a log. Other professors met with students in their offices. Why was he different?

25   "Everyone started noticing that I was the only one doing this stuff," he says.

The once-outgoing professor started keeping to himself. Maybe he was paranoid, he admits. Then again, people talking behind his back. As the semester drew to a close, Mr. Dussold hoped that the Christmas break would end the rumors. A new year, a new semester. Everything would be OK.

Exonerated?

For a while it seemed like that might be true. Then, in mid-January, Ms. Peyla showed up unannounced at his office door. He describes the conversation that followed as "surreal."

She told him, he says, that other professors were encouraging her to file a complaint. She told him she thought it might be in her best interest to follow their advice, even though she again acknowledged that nothing had happened, according to Mr. Dussold. He remembers her saying that the complaint would not harm him and might somehow help her get into graduate school.

"I told her that filing a false complaint would be unethical," he remembers saying. She was standing in the doorway to his office so he kept his voice low, fearing that the conversation would be overheard. "I said, 'Of course it's going to harm me. It would ruin my career.' I said, 'You need to stand up to them and tell them it's false. And you need to leave me alone,'" he says he told her.

30 Then came January 28, a day Mr. Dussold says he will never forget. He and his fiancée live on a small farm about a half-hour outside of Edwardsville. They awoke that morning to find that eight of their 22 cows had fallen into a partially frozen pond overnight and drowned.

It was, he thought, a bad sign.

That morning he was told to report to the provost's office.

It turned out to be good news. Mr. Dussold was informed that the university had investigated the rumors and found no evidence to support them. The letter he was later sent said that "Ms. Peyla denied they ever had a sexual relationship." A friend of Ms. Peyla's was interviewed and told officials that the relationship between the two seemed "friendly and professional."

Other professors were also interviewed, none of whom had knowledge of any inappropriate relationship, according to the letter.

35 In short, he was exonerated. What was strange, though, was that he had never been told of any investigation before that day. Still, he could not help feeling relieved.

His relief would not last long. A couple of hours later, according to Mr. Dussold, he was summoned to the office of Gary A. Giamartino, dean of the business school. Mr. Giamartino had heard about the provost's investigation, and he was not pleased. According to Mr. Dussold, the dean told him he was beginning his own investigation. Then, Mr. Dussold says, the dean began asking detailed questions about his sex life.

"You can't ask me this!" he remembers telling him. "I thought this nightmare was over."

"I don't know why you would think this was over," was the dean's reply, according to Mr. Dussold. (Mr. Giamartino declined to comment for this article.)

The professor says he made it clear that he thought the dean had no right to conduct an investigation. He reiterated his innocence. And then he went home to deal with the dead cows.

Scared

40 A couple of weeks later, Ms. Peyla returned to his office. She was very upset. She accused him of starting the rumors to draw attention to himself, according to Mr. Dussold. "First you're saying you want to file a false complaint, and then you're accusing me of starting the rumors. I mean, holy crap!" he says now.

There was no discussion. "You need to leave my office," he remembers telling her.

She refused, insisting that he apologize. She said her life was miserable and that it was his fault. Mr. Dussold called a fellow professor and asked him to come immediately to his office. When he arrived, Ms. Peyla left. (The colleague, who asked not to be named, confirms Mr. Dussold's account.)

"At this point, I'm thinking she's unstable," he says.

A few days later, he received a call on his cellphone. It was Ms. Peyla. He asked her how she got his number.

45 "Are you mad at me?" Ms. Peyla said, according to Mr. Dussold.

He hung up the phone.

"Sara and I were both freaked out," he says. (Ms. Bennett, who was with him at the time, confirms his account).

The call was followed by a "long, convoluted" message left by Ms. Peyla on his university voice mail. In it, he says, she apologized for the trouble she caused him.

Mr. Dussold remembers this as a dark time. The rumors were not going away, and he wasn't sure what Ms. Peyla would do or say next. Plus, what would the dean's investigation conclude? When would this end?

50 A former student of Mr. Dussold's, Amanda Bemis, recalls seeing him during this period and thinking he looked "gaunt" and that "the stress was taking its toll."

While Ms. Bemis only met Ms. Peyla a few times, she felt uneasy around her. "You know how you meet people and you think something isn't quite right? That's how it was," she says. When asked if Mr. Dussold was often flirtatious with students or seemed like a womanizer, Ms. Bemis laughs. "No," she says. "That's not Chris."

Another former student, Tyson Giger, who was in the same financial-management club as Ms. Peyla, says he never saw any hint of a relationship between them.

Mr. Dussold was sure that no matter what he did, the rumors wouldn't stop. The dean seemed convinced of his guilt, he thought. University officials had asked Mr. Dussold to let them know if the rumors continued. So, in February, he called the provost's office and explained that they were not going away; if anything, they were getting worse.

"I'm scared at this point," he says. "I don't know what the next thing will be."

Ready to Jump

55 Over spring break, Mr. Dussold arrived at a big decision: He was going to quit. He had already submitted his three-year tenure-review package, but when he returned to the campus he would ask to withdraw it. He would stay for his lame-duck year while he looked for a job. He called his friend Jim Wilkerson, an assistant professor of management and marketing. "He let me know he had made the decision to leave the university," says Mr. Wilkerson, who has since left Southern Illinois to become a consultant. "He said, 'I'm not going to request renewal. I'm going on the market.'"

Mr. Dussold told several other colleagues of his decision, all of whom tried to talk him out of it, he says. But he was firm. He could not go on living like this. Anyway, he was sure that the rumors and the investigations were never going to end, no matter what he did.

On the Monday after spring break, he informed the dean, Mr. Giamartino, and his department chairman of his decision to resign. He told them that it was because the rumor, and the dean's investigation, had become too much.

A couple of hours later, he says, he was called into the dean's office. Mr. Dussold assumed that the dean would try to talk him into staying. Instead, the dean fired him [using as a pretext Dussold's use of another instructor's teaching statement, found on the Internet; see paragraph 3. Dussold argued that the real reason he was fired was because of the effects of the rumor]....

"I don't know what they're talking about," he recalls thinking.

60 He asked what would happen to his classes. The dean told him the classes would be taken care of. Mr. Dussold says he was also offered the opportunity to resign with two months of pay, but only if he signed a letter promising not to sue the university.

"Is there anything I can do to express my point of view on this?" he said he asked.

No. This was final, he says they told him.

• • •

He was told that he could clean out his office in the presence of campus police officers.

There would be no lame-duck year, no. graceful exit. Instead, Mr. Dussold left the campus in shame.

65 When his students discovered that the popular professor was not coming back, they held a demonstration. A petition was passed around. Students made T-shirts that asked "Where's Dussold?"

But he was already gone.

Glass Houses

The next week, he says, he received a call from Ms. Peyla. She told him she was sorry about what had happened.

He hung up.

A month later he received a letter signed by Ms. Peyla and several other students thanking him for leading the financial-management club. "Your assistance aided us in what became one of the most rewarding experiences in our professional, academic, and personal lives," it said.

70 By then, Mr. Dussold says, his life was a mess. "I'm trying to make a life with a wonderful girl," he says. "We have our own little hobby farm, and then one day—no income, no benefits, and in my mind no hope for a comparable job. How often are professors fired midsemester?"

He was, he admits, extremely depressed.

• • •

A New Start

Mr. Dussold has sued university officials, fellow professors, and Ms. Peyla, all of whom he believes were responsible for his dismissal. In the lawsuit, he accuses them of making false statements about him and failing to follow university policy. (Six of the people named in the lawsuit declined to comment when contacted by the *Chronicle.*) He remains convinced that it was the rumor—and the fear that he would sue—that led to his firing. And he believes he can prove that in court.

"This isn't about getting back at SIUE," Mr. Dussold says. "I just want my name cleared. That's all I want."

He was recently hired by nearby McKendree College. He says the college has been kind and welcoming, even after everything that happened at Southern Illinois. "I can't say enough good things about McKendree," he says. He does note that his salary is less than half what it was at Southern Illinois and that his tenure clock has been reset. He is, in effect, starting over.

75   And he is much more cautious now about even the slightest appearance of impropriety. The chairs in his office are closer to the door than to his desk, He tries to work at home whenever he can. And he says he would never allow a student in his car because that might be enough to start a rumor. "Do I take it to the extreme? Yes," he says. "I take no chances."

● Review Questions

1. Some of Dussold's colleagues advised him to just let the rumor run the course of its "life cycle." What did he eventually learn about that life cycle?

2. What rumor management problem did Dussold confront after taking a colleague's advice to have students sign in for office hours?

3. Peyla filed a complaint with the college administration against Dussold while claiming to others that nothing untoward had happened. What explains the contradiction?

4. How did the particular nature of Dussold's dismissal affect his choices for clearing his name?

● Discussion and Writing Suggestions

1. How do you suppose that this particular rumor started? How and why do you think it began to spread until none of the main participants could control it?

2. When Dussold first heard rumblings of the rumor in the fall of 2003, he "shrugged it off." In what ways do you think that the rumor's life span and reach might have been different had he addressed it more quickly and directly?

3. It could be argued that all three principal participants in this episode—Dussold, the student, and the university administration—made one or more serious mistakes and miscalculations in dealing with this rumor. How might each participant—or all of them, collectively—have handled things better? What actions by any or all concerned might have resulted in a different outcome or in a fairer, more reasonable resolution?

4. Suggestions of sexual harassment spark particularly sensitive and salacious gossip and accusations. In what ways might some of the major participants in this case have exploited that fact? Explain.

5. Cases such as Dussold's always pique public interest: Sexual harassment is reported and discussed in the news, dramatized on TV shows (ranging from *Law and Order* to *The Simpsons*) and in the theater (David Mamet's acclaimed play *Oleanna*, for example), and fought over in actual courtrooms. Why is this subject of such great public interest? How does the degree of public fascination affect the spread of this type of rumor?

FIGHTING THAT OLD DEVIL RUMOR

Sandra Salmans

Might buying a can of coffee be a way of supporting "black magic?" Could baking a cake be a form of devil worship? If we are to believe a long-standing rumor about Procter & Gamble, the company behind products such as Folger's coffee and Duncan Hines baking mixes, the answer is yes. Rumors suggesting that the company's distinctive moon and stars logo was a sign of some satanic affiliation became so widespread that the company had to go to court to clear its name. Over the years, P&G sued a number of individuals and other companies it claimed were spreading this devil-worship rumor, including the Amway Corporation. After a court process that dragged on for seventeen years, P&G was awarded over $19 million in damages. By that time, the company had already modified its logo in an attempt to put the rumors to rest. That attempt—a major concession to the rumormongers—helped to quiet the story; it also illustrated that once a rumor takes hold, its grip remains tenacious. In this October 1982 *Saturday Evening Post* article, Sandra Salmans traces the ongoing reverberations of a rumor that grew out of reactions to a simple line drawing. *Note:* To view the logo in question, Google or Bing "procter and gamble logo controversy."

Cathy Gebing's telephone rings every few minutes, and the question is always the same: Is the moon-and-stars design on Procter & Gamble's 70-odd products the mark of the devil?

"No, sir, that's a false rumor," Mrs. Gebing answers patiently. "That's our trademark, we've had it about 100 years."

Normally the consumer services department, this is now the rumor control center for Procter, the consumer goods giant that has lately become the focus of a nationwide rumor campaign.

The rumors, first appearing about two years ago, essentially contend that Procter's 132 year-old trademark, which shows the man in the moon and 13 stars representing the original colonies, is a symbol of Satanism and devil worship. The rumor-mongering also urges a Christian boycott of Procter's products, which include Pampers, Duncan Hines and Folgers, plus dozens of other well-known names.

5   After a great deal of indecision about how to combat the rumors, Procter took formal action in July, filing libel suits against seven individuals for spreading "false and malicious" rumors. The company has said that it may file more suits. "What we have to do is make people realize that we mean business," said Robert Norrish, Procter's public relations director.

It is, in fact, a public relations problem and a difficult one.

"Legal recourse isn't a happy way to go," said Robert Schwartz, president of Manning, Selvage & Lee, a leading New York public relations firm, "but they probably had very few alternatives. The company was diverting resources to deal with this, and at some point, you have to call a halt." However, Mr. Schwartz added, if Procter loses the suits, its image will certainly suffer.

Procter has firmly rejected suggestions that it simply remove the offending symbol from its packages. That, however, increases the suspicions of some consumers.

"If it causes controversy, I don't see why they have to have it." said Faye Dease, a clinic supervisor at Womack Army Hospital in Fort Bragg, North Carolina. Mrs. Dease said that, when a mirror is held up to the logo, the curlicues in the man's beard become 666—the sign of the Antichrist.

10   Procter is not the only company to have fallen siege to rumors. McDonald's has found itself subject to whisper campaigns contending alternately that the restaurant chain was giving to Satan or that it was putting worms in its hamburgers. Entenmann's, the bakery owned by the Warner-Lambert Company, was rumored to be owned by the Rev. Sun Myung Moon's Unification Church.

But the rumors have been more enduring at Procter, and the company's course—to go not only to news organizations and clergy for help, but also the courts—has been more aggressive.

Procter is going after the rumor with all the diligence that it devotes to a new product introduction. A three-inch-thick file documents the company's strategy: a map of the United States, showing the geographical sweep of the rumors; tallies, state by state, of the queries to the consumer services department; tallies, day by day, of the nature of the complaint ("Satanic"; "Mentions lawsuits"; "Has heard/seen media reports"; "Check more than one if appropriate").

At the consumer services department, whose toll-free telephone number is printed on every Procter package, the calls first began trickling in two years ago, the company said.

Individuals in a handful of Middle Western states said they had heard that Procter was owned by the Rev. Sun Myung Moon's followers. In November 1980 Procter felt compelled to answer the charges by writing to news organizations in those states.

15   But in December 1981, there were suddenly 1,152 queries, by the company's tally, mainly from the West Coast, and the focus shifted from the Moon church to the devil. "In the beginning, God made the tree," a 75-year-old woman wrote the company. "Where did Satan get Charmin?"

Many callers reported hearing that Procter's "owner" had appeared on a television talk show where he admitted selling his soul to the devil in order to gain the company's success.

Anonymous fliers, usually misspelling the company's name, began to appear at supermarkets. "Proctor & Gamble," one said, "announced on *The Phil Donahue Show* Friday that they contribute 10 percent of their earnings to the Satanic religion (which is devil worship)."

"Do you realize," another anonymous flier said, "that if all the Christians in the world would stop buying Proctor and Gamble Products this Company would soon be out of business?"

Procter did a second mailing, to news organizations on the West Coast. But this time there was no letup. By last spring, Procter was getting 12,000 queries monthly about its relationship with the devil. There were reports of ministers, mainly in small Fundamentalist churches, attacking Procter from the pulpit and urging their congregations to boycott its products.

20   Given the dubious results of the news media campaign, John Smale, Procter's president, decided on a less public line of attack. The company wrote to local clergy and enclosed testaments of faith from very prominent clerics, including preachers who led an earlier attack on Procter for sponsoring television shows of what they regarded as questionable morality. The Rev. Jerry Falwell, leader of Moral Majority, a church-based conservative political-action group, wrote that he had talked with Procter's chairman, "and I am certain neither he nor his company is associated in any way with Satanism or devil worship."

By June, however, the center was receiving more than 15,000 queries monthly, including a few from Alaska and Hawaii.

Mr. Smale told Procter's public relations department to forget his earlier cautions. On June 10, "We presented our recommendations to Mr. Smale." William Dobson, of the public relations department, recalled. "It was essentially to go on the offensive."

On July 1, Procter announced its first lawsuits. The litigation was "a very hard-nosed way to generate publicity." Mr. Dobson said. "We were working on the traditional Procter concepts: reach and frequency."

The subjects of those lawsuits and a second wave later in the month—Mike Campbell of Atlanta, William and Linda Moore of Pensacola, Florida, Guy Sharpe of Atlanta, Elma and Ed Pruitt of Clovis, New Mexico, and Sherman and Margaret McCord of Tullahoma, Tennessee—were chosen simply because "they just happened to be the first people where we felt we had enough evidence to go to court," Mr. Dobson said.

25   Most of the leads to ministers had evaporated, and in any case, a suit against a member of the clergy, "frankly, wasn't our optimum choice," Mr. Dobson said.

All but one of the defendants sell products of competing consumer-goods companies, according to Procter. The Moores and Mr. Pruitt are distributors for the Amway Corporation, which sells soap and other consumer products door-to-door. The McCords are distributors for Shaklee, which sells vitamins, household cleaners and personal care products. Mr. Campbell works for a grocery brokerage firm that represents manufacturers of household cleaning products.

However, "there is no evidence that companies are pushing this rumor," Mr. Norrish said. Nor is it clear that they were economically inspired. "We didn't try to figure out motives," he added. "We just want to stop them."

Most of the defendants denied the charges or said that they were convinced the rumors were false.

Mrs. McCord said that she had printed the rumor in her newsletter to other Shaklee distributors, but had realized her mistake and apologized in both the newsletter and a letter to Procter. Mrs. Pruitt said she and her husband stopped distributing anti-Procter leaflets after learning that the rumor was false.

30   William Hurst, the lawyer for Mr. Campbell, said that his client did hand an anti-Procter circular to a supermarket clerk when he was stocking the shelves with Clorox, but it was his only copy, and "he did not believe it."

Mr. Sharpe, a well-known weatherman for WXIA-TV in Atlanta and a Methodist lay preacher, issued a denial that he had made defamatory remarks against Procter & Gamble.

The lawsuits provoked the hoped for flurry of publicity, including network television coverage, and the number of queries to the consumer services department has fallen by half, Procter says. But few of the remaining 250 or so callers each day have heard of the lawsuits. "How do you reach them?" Mr. Norrish wonders.

 Review Questions

1. What do the images in the Procter & Gamble logo actually represent?

2. Which component of the logo occasioned the "devil worship" rumor?

3. Aside from exercising its legal recourse, what did P&G hope to accomplish with its first lawsuits?

4. Why did Procter president John Smale reach beyond the usual media outlets in an effort to deflate the rumor?

 Discussion and Writing Suggestions

1. The logo rumor led many people to boycott Procter & Gamble. Have you ever been asked to boycott a company? Why? In hindsight, to what extent was the boycott based on rumor?

2. Why do you think that the Procter & Gamble rumor was so persuasive and so resistant over the years to the company's attempts at refuting it? In formulating your response, speculate on some of the possible motivations of those who began the rumor and those who spread it; speculate also on the worldviews of those who were so receptive to its content.

3. P&G took a variety of approaches over the years to handling the charges of Satanism, ultimately filing lawsuits that took years to resolve. In the meantime, the company changed its logo. Assume you worked at Procter & Gamble during the years that the devil-worship rumor took hold. How might you have advised the company to adopt a different rumor-fighting strategy? In developing your answer, draw upon both your business sense and what you understand about human nature. In the final analysis, how well (or badly) do you think the company dealt with this persistent rumor?

4. The Procter & Gamble rumor is intertwined with religious beliefs and fears. History is filled with rumors of this nature—for example, the Salem witch trials of 1692. What other rumors have you personally encountered, or do you know

of, that you can attribute to religious belief, fear, or just simple misunderstanding? How did these rumors spread, and what were their outcomes?

5. This particular rumor spread in the early 1980s, before the widespread availability of the Internet. At that time, rumors were not spread with the same instantaneous pace as they are now; similarly, companies could not simply respond within seconds by "tweeting" a response in an effort to deflate the rumor. How might the slower exchange of information during the 1980s have affected both the life of this rumor and the company's attempts at refutation? Had the rumor started today, do you think its life span would have been as long as it turned out to be?

A PSYCHOLOGY OF RUMOR

Robert H. Knapp

During World War II, psychologist Robert H. Knapp attempted to classify and identify the numerous rumors circulating at the time (rumors being everywhere in time of war). In his classic article "A Psychology of Rumor," Knapp examined some of the rumors currently or recently in circulation and attempted to create a framework for further study. In this selection, he classifies three main types of rumor, each based on the human emotion that drives it: wish, fear, or hostility. At the time he wrote this paper, Knapp headed rumor control for the Massachusetts Committee on Public Safety. Though the paper (excerpted here) was published nearly seventy years ago, Knapp's classification system continues to be influential in the academic study of rumor and remains useful in accounting for the features of the countless rumors we encounter daily.

[W]e shall define rumor as a *proposition for belief of topical reference disseminated without official verification.* So formidably defined, rumor is but a special case of informal social communications, including myth, legend, and current humor. From myth and legend it is distinguished by its emphasis on the topical. Where humor is designed to provoke laughter, rumor begs for belief.

So defined, rumors have three basic characteristics. They have, first, a distinct and characteristic mode of transmission—mostly by word of mouth. Being spread by means of this primitive medium, rumors are more subject than the formal modes of transmission to inaccuracy and capricious distortion.

A second characteristic of rumors is that they provide "information." A rumor is always about some particular person, happening, or condition.

Finally, rumor satisfies. Mythology, folklore, and humor gather impetus from the emotional gratifications which they afford. The same may be said of rumor. Rumors *express* and *gratify* the emotional needs of the community in much the same way as day dreams and fantasy fulfill the needs of the individual. For convenience of notation, this importance aspect of rumors will be called the "expressive" characteristic.

•   •   •

Knapp, Robert H., "A Psychology of Rumor" from *The Public Opinion Quarterly* 8:1 (Spring 1944): pages 22–31, by permission of Oxford University Press.

The Classification of Rumors

5 We present here a three-fold classification, based upon the already observed fact that rumors almost invariably gratify some emotional need. In practice it has been found that the emotional needs most frequently served by rumors are wish, fear, and hostility. Accordingly, three basic types of rumors can be delineated.

The *Pipe-dream or Wish Rumor*. Such rumors express the wishes and hopes of those among they circulate. They can be popularly identified with "wishful thinking." The following, found in circulation in Boston during the winter of 1942, are typical examples:

> The Japanese do not have enough oil to last six months.
> There will be a revolution in Germany before summer.
> Lloyd's of London Wall Street are betting 10 to 1 that the war will be over by autumn.

The *Bogie Rumor*. The precise opposite of the pipe-dream rumor is the bogie rumor. Just as the former mirrors the wishes and hopes of the group, so the bogie is essentially derived from fears and anxieties. Bogies range all the way from rumors with a dour and pessimistic quality to the panic rumors so familiar to social psychologists. Typical examples of this type are these:

> The entire Pacific Fleet was destroyed at Pearl Harbor.
> Several thousand bodies of soldiers have washed up off the town of X.
> Crab meat packed by the Japanese contains ground glass.

The *Wedge-driving Aggression Rumor*. The wedge-driving rumor is so termed because of its effect in dividing groups and destroying loyalties; its essential motivation is aggression or hatred. In practice almost all aggression rumors turn out to be directed against elements of our own population or our allies. The following are typical examples:

> Churchill blackmailed Roosevelt into provoking war with Japan.
> The British are sabotaging their own ships in American ports so that they will not have to put out to sea.
> The Catholics in America are trying to evade the draft.

● ● ●

What Makes a Good Rumor

10 1. No successful rumor may exceed a length or complexity greater than the memory span of the group through which it passes Rumor by its very nature must depend upon the memory of its successive tellers. Typically the successful rumor is short, simple and salient. . . .

2. As perception and memory simplify the things we see, so do they simplify the rumors we hear and read. In time, a successful rumor becomes a "good story." This process of heightening some elements, of leveling or deleting others, is accomplished by the following typical distortions:

    addition of a humorous twist
    addition of striking and aesthetic detail

deletion of qualifications and syntactic complexities
simplification of plot and circumstances
assumption of a more familiar form
exaggeration

Through the operation of these several processes, the successful rumor emerges with the same vigor that characterizes the folk ballad, the popular witticism, and other products of extensive oral transmission.

3. There are conditions which make it easier for rumors to become distorted. The farther a rumor is removed from known or confirmed fact, the more easily does it seem to get twisted when passed on. Distortion appears to take its greatest toll when a rumor is kept entirely on the person-to-person level and does not appear in the press or on the air. Finally, when there is either great unrest (as in panic) or an acute need for information, rumor tends to undergo its most drastic changes.

4. Names, numbers, and places are typically the most unstable components of any rumor. There are abundant examples of rumors circulating in different totalitarian nations, all of identical plot, yet each employing the names and places familiar to the local populations. Similarly with respect to numbers, rumors are notoriously capricious.

5. From whatever humble beginning a rumor may spring, it is soon attributed to a high authoritative source. This gives the rumor both prestige and the appearance of veracity.

6. Rumors become harmonized with the cultural traditions of the group in which they circulate. The rumors of the secret weapon, rife in France during the early days of the present war, were cast in terms of the Big Bertha* of the last war....

7. The successful rumor, to thrive, must always adapt *itself* to the *immediate* as well as to the traditional circumstances of the group; it must ride the tide of current swings in public opinion and interest. Typically, rumors come in clusters dealing with a single subject. Thus in Boston, rumors of anti-semitic character would dominate the grapevine for one month, only to subside and be replaced with anti-British rumors. The primitive grapevine mentality seems almost incapable of sustaining more than three or four basic ideas at a time. Similarly, in respect to expressive character, rumors at a given time tend to follow a single expressive pattern. This was very clearly demonstrated in England during the last war when waves of "bogie" rumors of defeat or of military disaster were dispelled almost over night by waves of "pipe-dream" rumors telling of the arrival of Russian troops in England.

---

*Big Bertha was a howitzer—a heavy artillery piece with a 16.5-inch diameter barrel—developed by the German armament manufacturer Krupp just before World War I.

Review Questions

1. Identify the three basic characteristics of rumor as established by Knapp.

2. Describe Knapp's classification system for rumor.

3. How do successful rumors become heightened into "good stories" as time goes on?

4. Which aspects of a rumor tend to be the most unstable?

Discussion and Writing Suggestions

1. Use each of Knapp's categories to classify a rumor you've read about in this chapter.

2. Based on your own experience, and using Knapp's categories, classify at least one rumor that you have heard or helped spread. How does this rumor meet the criteria of the particular category?

3. Knapp's examples of rumor are a product of the public anxieties associated with wartime. What recent rumors can you think of that spring from uneasiness about contemporary events?

4. The World War II examples used here are specific to Knapp's time. Since then, the United States has been involved in a number of wars and other conflicts. What role do you think rumor plays in this country's current military engagements? Consider both rumors that develop on the home front and rumors that develop among soldiers, sailors, and airmen.

5. Knapp states that rumor is transmitted "mostly by word of mouth." To what extent have you found this still to be the case? How is information that is spread by various methods of transmission interpreted in different ways?

6. Knapp suggests that all rumors grow out of basic human emotions such as hope or anxiety. In what ways have you found his observation to be true (or false) in your own experience or the experiences of people you know?

"PAUL IS DEAD!" (SAID FRED)

Alan Glenn

In the late 1960s, The Beatles were the most commercially successful rock band in the world, and Paul McCartney perhaps its most well-known and beloved singer. So when a rumor started in 1969 that Paul might have died three years earlier, music fans were jolted. According to the rumor, Paul's death had been hushed up, but (in the spirit of imaginative fun) the band had left "clues" about the truth throughout its albums for their fans to decipher. Of course, this morbid scheme would have been outrageous if true.

But was it? Originating at a college radio station, the rumor, initially intended as a lark for local audiences, spread across the country. In the pre-Internet age, the rumor moved at record speed, inviting audiences to research the "clues" and find their own. Here, in an article from the November 11, 2009, edition of the University of Michigan's *Michigan Today*, Alan Glenn, a columnist for the *Ann Arbor Chronicle*, explores the relatively innocent beginnings of the rock world's most enduring rumor: "Paul is dead." What happened subsequently is a textbook case of how rumor can spread across the pop-culture landscape. Note: additional illustrations to accompany this selection can be found online. Google or Bing "paul is dead said fred."

In the fall of 1969 a strange and mysterious rumor was circulating on the fringes of college campuses in the Midwest: Paul McCartney of the Beatles was dead.

According to the rumor, McCartney had died three years previously in a horrific car crash. His death—so the story went—was covered up, the surviving Beatles found a double to replace him, and ever since had been hiding clues in their songs and album covers that revealed the truth about their ex-bandmate's grisly fate.

No one knows for certain how the rumor started, or where. But in mid-October it exploded on to the national scene, sweeping the ranks of youth from coast to coast in a matter of days. Suddenly it seemed as if everyone under the age of 30 was either debating the possibility of McCartney's demise or poring over their Beatles records, searching for clues.

The power of the rumor was such that, four decades later, plenty of Baby Boomers still vividly recall the tingling sensation they felt when they first heard an eerie backwards voice emanating from their turntables, and began to consider that Paul might actually be dead.

5   What many do not know is that the rumor might not have come to their attention at all except for a mischievous young U-M natural resources student named Fred LaBour. Indeed, if the McCartney death rumor can be called a modern myth, then Beatles expert Devin McKinney may be correct to identify LaBour as its Homer.

Today, Fred LaBour is best known as "Too Slim," bassist-cum-jokester for the country and western act Riders in the Sky. Forty years ago he was an equally jocular staff writer for the *Michigan Daily* who had been assigned to review *Abbey Road*, the Beatles' latest album.

On October 12, 1969, LaBour was tuned in to radio station WKNR from Detroit when disc jockey Russ Gibb took a call from a listener who wanted to talk about a rumor going around that Paul McCartney was dead. Gibb was skeptical at first, but became intrigued when the caller explained that there were clues pointing to McCartney's death hidden in the Beatles' music.

For the next hour thousands of listeners, including LaBour, stayed glued to their radios as Gibb and his callers discussed the supposed evidence and what could be behind it. The following day LaBour got out his Beatles records, lined them up on his desk, and sat down to write one of the oddest and most influential record reviews ever printed.

On the morning of October 14, the university community awoke to the shocking and incredible report that one of the world's most popular and beloved

According to rumors, the Beatles left clues to Paul's death. Abbey Road's album cover (above) was supposedly flush with such clues, such as Paul's bare feet, and a cigarette in his right hand.

entertainers was no more. The headline blazoned across the second page of the Michigan Daily proclaimed the awful news:

"McCartney dead; new evidence brought to light."

"Paul McCartney was killed in an automobile accident in early November, 1966," began Fred LaBour's accompanying full-page article, "after leaving EMI recording studios tired, sad, and dejected." McCartney was found four hours later, "pinned under his car in a culvert with the top of his head sheared off. He was deader than a doornail."

10 What LaBour had written was less record review than conspiracy-age fable. He related in detail how the accident had been covered up and a look-alike found to replace the dead musician—not as a rumor, but as if it were fact The mysterious clues were held to be part of a strange and disturbing plot orchestrated by John Lennon, who had it in mind to found a new religion with himself as god and the "reborn" McCartney a Christ-like figure at his side.

LaBour's story electrified the campus. The *Daily* sold out its entire run by mid-morning, and a second printing was ordered to meet demand. "I remember walking down Ann Arbor streets hearing Beatles music from every single apartment and house," LaBour says. He also recalls occasionally hearing someone trying to play a record backwards—listening for clues.

Indeed, the enigmatic clues seemed to draw most people into the rumor's web—and LaBour's article contained an abundance of evidence for clue-hungry readers to digest.

For instance, the inside cover of *Sgt. Pepper's Lonely Hearts Club Band* features a photo in which McCartney is wearing an arm patch that seems to read O.P.D.—according to LaBour, an abbreviation for "Officially Pronounced Dead," the British equivalent of DOA. On the album's back cover is a photo in which McCartney is the only one of the Beatles facing away from the camera.

15   LaBour also pointed out that on the front cover of *Abbey Road* McCartney is barefoot, signifying death because that is how corpses are buried. Furthermore, in the photo Paul holds a cigarette in his right hand, whereas the "real" McCartney is left-handed.

Then there were the now-famous clues to be found by playing certain songs backwards. When reversed, "Revolution 9" reveals something that sounds eerily like "Turn me on, dead man," while from the outro of "I Am the Walrus" seems to emerge a creepy chorus of "Ha ha! Paul is dead."

"I cannot tell you how many times I listened to those records backwards," says actress Christine Lahti (*Chicago Hope*), who in the fall of 1969 was a nineteen-year-old U-M theater student. Dubious at first, after many repetitions—and the encouragement of friends—she found herself more willing to believe. "After a point you started to hear it," she explains, "just by the power of suggestion."

Lahti suspects that this Rorschach-like nature of the clues accounts for much of the rumor's appeal. "It might also have had something to do with the mind-altering drugs that many people were involved with," she adds with a laugh.

Filmmaker Ric Burns (*New York: A Documentary Film*), then a teenaged Beatlemaniac attending Ann Arbor's Pioneer High School, remembers spending hours hunting for clues and debating the rumor with friends. Like Lahti, he believes that a major part of the attraction was the ambiguity of the purported evidence.

20   "It was not some 'x-marks-the-spot' clue," Burns explains. "You could sort of hear it, but you couldn't. It was like you were seeing the tip of the iceberg of a larger reality."

But most people did not realize that many of the clues were nothing more than a college prank.

Fred LaBour's article in the *Daily* presented more than two-dozen clues, most of which he originated himself. Of those, many went on to become an integral part of the rumor.

But LaBour admits—and has always admitted—that he made up his clues on the spot, as a joke. A prime example is his assertion that "walrus"—as in the lyric "the walrus was Paul"—is Greek for "corpse." (It isn't.) LaBour also brazenly fabricated many other "facts": identifying, for instance, McCartney's replacement as a Scottish orphan named William Campbell. (He had considered calling the impostor "Glen" Campbell, after the country singer, but decided it would be too obvious.)

LaBour never expected his article to be taken at face value, and was astonished when the national press picked it up as a serious piece of news. "The story was quoted extensively everywhere," he recalls. "First the Detroit papers, then Chicago, then, by the weekend, both coasts."

25   After this the rumor truly seemed to catch fire. Suddenly LaBour's playful inventions were being soberly, discussed on the evening news of all three major television networks, and in prestigious national magazines such as *Time* and *Life*.

Exactly why LaBour's story was so influential is unclear. It was not the only article on the rumor, nor was it the first. The rumor was also being heavily promoted on alternative radio. But many agree with Beatleologist Andru J. Reeve, who opines that LaBour's story was "the single most significant factor in the breadth of the rumor's spread."

LaBour recalls being worried about his unintentional role in sending the rumor spiraling out of control. "But after a few days," he says, "the theatrical aspect became clearer to me, and, shy as I was in the face of all the attention, I began to enjoy the ride."

The culmination of that ride was being invited to Hollywood in early November to participate in an RKO television special that featured celebrity attorney F. Lee Bailey conducting a mock trial in which he examined various expert "witnesses" on the subject of McCartney's alleged death.

30   "I was a nervous college kid, way out of my league," LaBour recalls. "I told Bailey during our pre-show meeting that I'd made the whole thing up. He sighed, and said, 'Well, we have an hour of television to do. You're going to have to go along with this.' I said okay."

By the time the program was scheduled for broadcast, however, public interest in the rumor had cooled. It received only a single airing, on a local television station in New York City on November 30, 1969.

The popular mania surrounding the "Paul is dead" rumor was short-lived—but even today, despite the thorough debunking of nearly all the so-called evidence, it continues to circulate, mainly among conspiracy buffs and inquisitive Beatles fans.

Fred LaBour doesn't think his adoptive brainchild will ever completely disappear. "Like it or not," he says, "the rumor will be with us as long as the Beatles are with us."

Which will be a very long time indeed.

● Review Questions

1. After LaBour published his article, the campus was "electrified" by the story. Given that the McCartney rumor was already in verbal circulation before his piece was published, why did it have such a galvanizing force?

2. What quality of LaBour's "clues" appeared to draw in the most readers, and ultimately spread the rumor further?

3. The speed and popularity of this particular rumor taught LaBour a lesson about being the "source" of a rumor. What did he learn?

4. What did LaBour discover, through his experience on television, about the popular media's attitude toward rumor?

● Discussion and Writing Suggestions

1. This rumor highlights two aspects of human nature: a fascination with celebrity and a morbid curiosity with death. What does this intersection of rumor, fame, and mortality suggest about human nature?

2. How do you account for the remarkable success of the "Paul is dead" rumor in spreading so quickly and persuading so many people of its truth? To what distinctive elements do you attribute its appeal and its power? Compare this rumor—and the evidence offered for its support—to one or more other rumors you have heard or read about concerning particular celebrities today.

3. To what extent is a rumor more or less believable when its details are ambiguous, as compared, say, to the very particular details associated with the missing-kidney rumor discussed in Chapter 6 (pp. 192–198)? Based on your own experience, compare and contrast examples of ambiguous rumors and rumors in which details are precise.

4. On its surface, the "Paul is dead" rumor seems worlds away from the political and military nature of Knapp's examples and his theoretical framework for classifying rumors. Still, can you detect ways in which this case falls within Knapp's framework of rumor? Consider his three types of rumor, along with his analyses of what happens to a rumor as it spreads. Consider, too, Knapp's discussion of the factors that create successful rumors.

POLITICAL SMEAR RUMORS: THREE CASE STUDIES

During a particularly tense town hall meeting in 2008, a prospective voter declared to Republican presidential candidate John McCain that his Democratic opponent, Barack Obama, was "an Arab." This kind of charge had been floating for months across segments of the political landscape: Obama was a Muslim, a socialist, even a terrorist conspirator. While some Obama opponents tried to capitalize on such sentiments shared by certain segments of the electorate, the Republican candidate himself demurred, and to the disapproval of many of his listeners, gently corrected the audience member. Through personal experience, McCain knew both how unfair and how damaging to a presidential campaign such a rumor could be. In 2000 he himself had been the victim of malicious rumor when anonymous political opponents falsely charged that McCain had fathered a child outside of marriage.

We may think that this kind of strategic rumor mongering is a relatively recent development of a hyper-partisan era; unfortunately, such smears have a long history in American politics. During their presidential campaigns, both Thomas Jefferson and Grover Cleveland were accused of fathering out of wedlock offspring. (Both men were elected, despite the rumors, which in Jefferson's case were probably true.)

The three selections in this cluster focus on the specific cases of Obama, McCain, and South Carolina governor Nikki R. Haley, but two of them also look back to rumors of a previous era. *New York Times* columnist Samuel Freedman, author of six acclaimed books about journalism and American history, explores the 2008 rumors about Obama. His piece, "In Untruths About Obama," sets those untruths in the context of a campaign run 80 years earlier. In "Anatomy of a Smear Campaign" (available online), Richard H. Davis, who served twice as John McCain's national campaign manager, shares his inside knowledge of the smears that derailed McCain's 2000 presidential bid. Finally, in "A Lie Races Across Twitter Before the Truth Can Boot Up," *New York Times* reporter Jeremy W. Peters demonstrates how quickly, in this age of Twitter, an unsubstantiated rumor can be transformed "from hearsay to mainstream journalism."

In Untruths About Obama, Echoes of a Distant Time

Samuel G. Freedman

During the presidential campaign of 1928, a photograph began circulating in rural areas of the Southwest showing Alfred E. Smith shaking hands with a fellow politician on the roadway of a tunnel. The image depicted Smith as he was officially opening the Holland Tunnel, which had been built during his tenure as governor of New York.

The people thousands of miles away who received copies of the picture were given a decidedly different explanation: Smith planned to extend the tunnel under the Atlantic Ocean all the way to the Vatican, so he could take secret orders from the pope. As just about any informed voter that year already knew, Smith was the first Roman Catholic ever to win a major party's presidential nomination.

At the remove of 80 years, it is tempting to laugh off such a crude attempt at fearmongering and character assassination. With Catholics unquestionably part of the American mainstream—one of the most coveted swing groups of voters in the current race [2008] for the White House—the misrepresentation of the photo might seem the artifact of a benighted past.

Except for two things.

5   The first is that the climate of anti-Catholic bigotry, which ran from the refined arena of the *Atlantic* magazine to the cross burnings of the Ku Klux Klan, not only contributed to Smith's crushing defeat by Herbert Hoover but also helped keep any other Catholic from mounting a serious run for the presidency until John F. Kennedy in 1960. The hate campaign, in other words, worked.

As for the second point, scholars of Smith's career and of American Catholicism say nothing in presidential history since 1928 more closely resembles the smearing of Al Smith than the aura of anti-Muslim agitation that has swirled around Barack Obama these past two years.

The insinuations of disloyalty to America, the caricature of the candidate as less than genuinely American—these tactics could have come from the playbook of Smith's basest opponents, the scholars say.

The biggest single difference may be the postmodern aspect of the attacks against Mr. Obama. He is vilified not for the religion he follows but for the one he doesn't, and much of his campaign's energy has gone into reiterating that he is a Christian. Either way, the underlying premise of the rumors remains that a Muslim is unfit to be president.

"What is similar in Smith's time is that there was a widespread belief there was something dangerous about electing a Catholic as president," said Allan J. Lichtman, an American University historian who is the author of *Prejudice and the Old Politics: The Presidential Election of 1928.* "You couldn't be a good American and serve American interests if you were a Catholic, because you were beholden to a foreign potentate called the pope and Catholicism held autocratic tenets.

10   "Likewise today, there is a widespread belief that somehow you cannot be a good American and be a Muslim at the same time, that being a Muslim means you have loyalties outside the United States—and, like Catholics in the 1920s, they are dangerous loyalties to militant groups seeking to do harm. There's no truth to the allegations, then or now, but they are tenaciously held."

In Smith's case, foes from the highbrow end of society, as well as K.K.K. bottom feeders, disparaged Catholic faith as incompatible with democracy. Admittedly, the smears against Mr. Obama have not achieved the comparable legitimacy in elite circles.

In the blogosphere and through mass e-mail, however, and even on Fox News and in *Insight* magazine, the disinformation has proliferated that Mr. Obama was raised as a Muslim, educated in a madrassa, influenced by an Islamist stepfather and sworn into the Senate holding a Koran.

These calumnies, no matter how often contradicted, have nourished virulent behavior at Republican campaign rallies. At an event for John McCain and Sarah Palin in Bethlehem, Pa., National Public Radio captured the voice of one participant shouting: "Obama's a Muslim! He's a terrorist himself!"

Robert A. Slayton, author of the Smith biography *Empire Statesman,* suggested in a recent interview that the religious bias against Smith and Mr. Obama served in part as a proxy for nativist resistance to an increasingly diverse nation. The United States in both the 1920s and the 2000s has been bitterly divided over mass immigration—by Jews and Catholics then, Hispanics and Muslims now.

15   Smith's opponents conflated his Catholic faith with his Irish heritage, urban roots and even New York accent to cast him outside the Anglo-Saxon, Protestant, small-town norms of America. Mr. Obama, of course, is of mixed race and has a Muslim middle name, Hussein, which has been flourished by some Republicans as proof of his foreignness.

"The most remarkable parallel to 1928 has to do with the idea that Smith was one of 'those people,' that the people he represented weren't real Americans," said Mr. Slayton, a professor of American history at Chapman University in Orange, Calif. "And when Sarah Palin talks about the 'real America' now, I hear an echo of that."

If there is a lesson from Al Smith about all this, then it came during a speech he delivered on Sept. 20, 1928, in Oklahoma City.

"This country, to my way of thinking, cannot be successful if it ever divides on sectarian lines," he declared. "If there are any considerable number of our people that are going to listen to appeals to their passion and to their prejudice, if bigotry and intolerance and their sister vices are going to succeed, it is dangerous for the future life of the Republic. And the best way to kill anything un-American is to drag it out into the open, because anything un-American cannot live in the sunlight."

THE ANATOMY OF A SMEAR CAMPAIGN: THE CASE OF JOHN MCCAIN

Richard H. Davis

Go to: Google or Bing

Search terms: "mccain campaign smear spurstalk"

A LIE RACES ACROSS TWITTER BEFORE THE TRUTH CAN BOOT UP

Jeremy W. Peters

It took only two minutes. An unfounded report on a little-known blog claiming that Gov. Nikki R. Haley was about to be indicted rocketed from South Carolina political circles into national circulation, along the way becoming the latest lesson in the perils of an instantaneous news culture.

The item's rapid journey from hearsay to mainstream journalism, largely via Twitter, forced Ms. Haley to rush to defend herself against a false rumor. And it left news organizations facing a new round of questions about accountability and standards in the fast and loose "retweets do not imply endorsement" ethos of today's political journalism.

There were elements of old-fashioned South Carolina sabotage: an embattled Republican governor and possible vice-presidential contender dogged by unproven accusations of impropriety. And there were modern twists: a liberal-leaning 25-year-old blogger eager to make a name for his new Web site, and a buzz-seeking political press corps that looks to the real-time, unedited world of Twitter as the first place to break news.

In retrospect, there were clear reasons to doubt the March 29 report, from a blog called the *Palmetto Public Record*, that Ms. Haley was facing indictment on tax fraud charges. The blog's editor, Logan Smith, never asked the governor's office for comment before he posted his report. Later, in an e-mail, Mr. Smith said he could not be sure whether his sources were correct.

5   "I reported that credible sources said they believed the governor would be indicted—not that I knew she would be indicted, or even whether or not I personally believed she would be indicted," he said. (He did not respond to questions asking for further clarification.)

But journalists from news outlets that reposted Mr. Smith's report on Twitter—including establishments old and venerable (the *Washington Post*, CBS News) as well as new and widely read (the *Huffington Post* and *BuzzFeed*)—had no way of knowing that in the minutes after it went online, and did not stop to check first.

March 29, 12:52 p.m.: The *Palmetto Public Record* publishes an article online with the headline "Haley indictment imminent? Stay tuned...." It cites two unidentified "well-placed legal experts" who said they expected the federal Department of Justice to indict Ms. Haley "as early as this week" on charges stemming from her involvement with a local Sikh temple.

12:54 p.m.: A blogger for *The Hill*, a Washington newspaper that focuses on government and politics, sends a Twitter post about the article to his 1,500 followers, who include several prominent political journalists with large Twitter followings that reach into the tens of thousands. Some then repost the item—BuzzFeed just two minutes later; the *Washington Post* 18 minutes after that.

1:03 p.m.: The *Daily Beast* posts a short article, which it later removes, about the *Palmetto Public Record* report, becoming one of many online outlets to write lengthier items, including *Daily Kos* and the *Daily Caller*. Headlines like one on the *Atlantic Wire's* post, "Nikki Haley Probably Won't Win Republican Veepstakes," are common.

10   1:12 p.m.: A *USA Today* reporter contacts Ms. Haley's office with a request for comment, the first of dozens of such inquiries that will deluge the governor and her staff for the rest of the day.

1:22 p.m.: The Romney campaign, which is reported to be considering Ms. Haley as one of many possible vice-presidential choices, receives a request for comment from ABC News.

1:25 p.m.: Mr. Smith seems bemused by all the attention his report is getting, posting on Twitter: "Well, now I know what it's like to watch a story go viral in real time."

3:29 p.m.: Matt Drudge, whose heavily visited *Drudge Report* can help drive decisions in newsrooms around the country, links to a *Daily Caller* article under the headline "REPORT: DOJ targets S.C. Gov. Nikki Haley."

By the next morning, South Carolina's largest newspaper, the *State* in Columbia, had an article on its front page.

15   Ms. Haley had tried in vain to persuade the reporter at the *State* not to write anything. "I remember getting on the phone, and I usually don't do this, but I just yelled at her," the governor said in an interview. "I said, 'Why are you doing this? There are no facts here.' "

Her office, which chalked the report up to a plant by a political opponent, later released a letter from the Internal Revenue Service declaring that there was no tax investigation.

This episode is not the first time that a questionable Twitter report has roiled the 2012 elections—the first presidential campaign in which the microblogging service has been used broadly by news outlets as a way to report and break news.

And although many news organizations have set standards for the use of Twitter by their journalists, reporters remain largely free to exercise their own, unedited news judgment. (At least one staff member from the *New York Times* sent out a Twitter post about the initial report.)

For many, that is Twitter's beauty: it is a conversational device where words are impermanent and always revisable. And as the *Palmetto Public Record* episode shows, anyone can inject himself into that conversation.

20   Ben Smith, editor in chief of *BuzzFeed*, which mixes the silly ("Amazing Dog Lifeguard Rescues Pup From Drowning") with serious original political reporting, said he believed Twitter users expected the news they read there was in a state of constant evolution and should not be taken as gospel.

"I think what you get is a running conversation and a chance to keep talking about it," he said. "The beauty of all this is the speed of the self-correction. If it had been a newspaper report, it could have hung out there for a day."

Reporters for *BuzzFeed* and most of the other news outlets that sent Twitter posts about the initial *Palmetto Public Record* report did later post about the governor's denials and the letter she produced from the Internal Revenue Service. Tucker Carlson, editor in chief of the *Daily Caller*, apologized personally to Ms. Haley.

But even those who embrace Twitter's value as a conversational reporting tool questioned what is ultimately gained by introducing illegitimate news into the conversation.

"I saw the original Tweets, and my first thought was that I'd never heard of the Web site that reported it," said Byron York, the chief political correspondent for the *Washington Examiner*. Mr. York, a prolific Twitter poster, decided not to send the item out to his 30,000 followers. "It was a pretty easy decision to stay away from it," he said.

25   Ms. Haley, who has lived with an unfounded blog report of marital infidelity since before she took office, fears that the episode may have done lasting damage to her reputation. She said she was not certain that it could be easily repaired. But she is certain of one thing.

"There will be another one," she said, predicting another attempt to smear her online. "I'm not one that thinks this is going to stop."

● Review Questions

1. What method did political operatives use to spread the rumor about McCain in 2000?

2. Why did the McCain campaign choose not to directly refute the rumor?

3. Aside from the fact that the Obama rumor was untrue, what thinly veiled underlying fear does it represent for some members of the public?

4. Despite the similarities between the rumors concerning Al Smith and Barack Obama, in what key way did they differ, according to Freedman?

5. In what ways did experienced editors and reporters, who should have known better, contribute to the rapid spread of the Nikki Haley rumor?

6. How is the rumor about Haley different in kind from the ones that swirled around McCain, Al Smith, and Obama?

● Discussion and Writing Suggestions

1. Davis asserts that "if you're responding, you're losing." What do you think of this approach—that is, doing nothing to handle "tawdry attacks"? In what ways is doing nothing effective from a political and/or personal perspective? In what ways is doing nothing ineffective? Compare this no-response policy to Dussold's strategy in "What Cost Chris Dussold His Dream Job?" How are the situations similar? Different?

2. Contorting facts into a rumor for political use clearly worked against McCain in 2000. Is "all fair" in politics? To what extent should candidates be prepared to handle such situations? What do these methods, and responses, indicate about the participants?

3. Freedman asserts that a deeper anxiety lay beneath the Smith and Obama rumors. Can you think of other cases, whether in politics or in your personal life, where rumors about an individual are rooted in a deeper anxiety? How did these rumors operate?

4. Considering the cases of both McCain and Obama, do you think the responses of their campaigns were appropriate? Is it possible for a response to be appropriate, but not effective? Explain.

5. Put yourself in the shoes of a campaign manager, whether for McCain or Obama. Create a plan of action for responding to the rumors faced by their respective campaigns.

6. Assess the degree of blame that should attach to some of the parties involved in the Nikki Haley rumor—blogger Logan Smith, other bloggers who transmitted the rumor without verification, and mainstream media outlets like the *Washington Post* and CBS News. In retrospect, what lessons should bloggers and print and Web reporters draw from this incident?

7. Compare and contrast the motivations and methods of Logan Smith, the blog editor who first transmitted the rumor about South Carolina governor Nikki R. Haley, and Fred LaBour, who originated the "Paul is dead" rumor.

8. How do the rumors discussed in these two selections fit within Knapp's framework? How would you classify them, according to his scheme? To what extent do they exhibit the qualities that make for "good" or successful rumors?

How Rumors Help Us Make Sense of an Uncertain World

Nicholas DiFonzo

On general principle we may disapprove of rumors, but their pervasiveness throughout history and across cultures suggests that they serve important personal and social purposes. In the following selection, Nicholas DiFonzo, Professor of Psychology at Rochester Institute of Technology and the author of numerous books and articles on rumor, discusses why both individuals and groups find it necessary and even desirable to create and spread rumors. "How Rumors Help Us Make Sense of an Uncertain World" forms Chapter 3 of DiFonzo's best-known book *The Watercooler Effect* (2008). Offering examples from his own experience, together with other cultural and historical examples, DiFonzo shows how rumors develop on both personal and social levels.

I was proofreading a manuscript about the history of rumor research on the morning of September 11, 2001, when my wife called and told me to turn on the television. As I sat in spellbound silence, I saw jetliners crash into the World Trade Center, erupt into fireballs, and each of the Twin Towers collapse. The TV announcers were silent at that moment—too stunned to even comment. That morning in Sarasota, Florida, the president called for a moment of silence to honor those killed in the attacks. And in the week that followed, the sky was also eerily silent—no planes were permitted to fly.

These spaces of silence punctuated the long expanses of conversation—and conjecture—in the aftermath of that memorable day. America had been attacked; she felt physically and psychologically threatened and a heightened sense of unity and patriotism. We spontaneously gathered in houses of worship to pray. We monitored the Internet, radio, and television news for information. We talked to one another and wondered aloud: Why? What's next? During these very unusual days rumors flourished: "The Justice Department has advised all employees to avoid using the [Washington, D.C.] Metro to get home because of a subway attack." "Arabs employed at Dunkin' Donuts and International House of Pancakes celebrated in reaction to news of the attacks." "A hijacked plane is headed for the Sears Tower in Chicago." None of these rumors were true, but they were part of how we tried to make sense of the new (to us) threat of terrorism.

These 9/11 rumors dramatically illustrate some of the key elements of rumors that I will explore in this chapter. Up to this point I've tried to show that rumors are prevalent, that various types of rumors exist, and that rumors cause or contribute to a variety of outcomes. But exactly what do we mean by the term "rumor"? In the introduction, I described rumor as shared human sensemaking par excellence, but *how* do rumor help people make sense of their worlds? . . .

Let's begin by defining our term. Rumors are unverified information statements that circulate about topics that people perceive as important; arise in situations of ambiguity, threat, or potential threat; and are used by people attempting to make sense or to manage risk. There are three questions that this definition addresses: What do rumor statements consist of? What types of situations do they tend to arise from? And what are people trying to do with them?

5   First, rumors consist of information statements—noun and verb statements that purport to inform us. "Harry Potter is dead" proposes that J. K. Rowling, the author of the famed children's book series, "killed off" the hero in its last installment. (This rumor—uncertain at the time—lured Potter fans into clicking Web links that contained a computer worm.) "Tropical Fantasy Fruit Punch is owned by the KKK" alleges that the Brooklyn Bottling Company is controlled by the Ku Klux Klan. (False—it is owned by Eric Miller.) "As part of a grisly initiation rite, gang members in Illinois—driving with their headlights off—have killed unsuspecting motorists who blink their headlights at them." (False— the Illinois State Police call this the "headlights hoax.") These rumors are all declarative—they tell us something.

Second, rumors consist of statements that circulate among people; they are never merely a private thought held by an individual. Rumor is a group phenomenon, something that happens between at least two people (usually more). I may know that my boss is unhappy in his job, that he was recently scolded unfairly by his superiors, and that he has taken a few days off. I may speculate to myself that he has flown to another city for a job interview, but this thought is not yet a rumor until I share it with another person. Rumors are therefore not synonymous with another person. Rumors are therefore not synonymous with prejudices, stereotypes, beliefs, or attitudes, although each of these may be conveyed in a rumor. Rather, rumors are fundamentally acts of communication.

Third, rumors consist of statements in circulation that people generally consider significant or of interest to tellers and hearers. They tend to be about topics that we regard as relatively more urgent, vital, consequential, or imperative. The classic rumor is often embedded in the anxiety-filled utterance "I heard that our department is being downsized; did you hear anything?" Obviously, a department layoff would be of great importance to employees because unemployment is a threat to well-being. Or, rumors about stocks that I own are important to me because they're relevant to my financial bottom line. This sense of importance can stem from our interest in anything we hold dear or cherish. For example, sports rumors reflect the intense interest of fans. Soccer player Michael Owen was beset by many rumors of his supposed intention to leave his Newcastle team, perhaps originating from his absence from play due to many injuries over two seasons. In the realm of political games, if I'm a solid Democrat or Republican, rumors about politicians from either group greatly interest me. Ralph Rosnow called these sorts of concerns "outcome relevant"— the outcome of a particular situation or issue is relevant to me, my welfare, my well-being, or my sense of self.

Fourth, and most important, these information statements in circulation are not verified—they are not supported, buttressed, checked, or authenticated. A verified statement has a stamp of approval on it: an imprimatur if you will; a person or source that will vouch for the validity of the information. A verified statement is not necessarily the same as a true statement: True means that the information corresponds with objective reality, while verified means that someone vouches for its correspondence with objective reality. News is typically—though not always—verified; rumor is not.

Some examples will help clarify what "unverified" means. Let's consider the two possibilities: statements that a person thinks are unverified, and those he or she classifies as verified. Perhaps most readily identified as unverified are statements that the sender himself classifies as unverified—that is, those he is openly unsure of: "I'm not sure that this is true, but I heard that management is now requiring that nurses in our department be 'on call' nights and weekends." The cautionary prefix "I'm not sure that this is true..." is a dead giveaway that the statement is unverified. It doesn't matter whether the information following the prefix is true or false; at the moment of transmission it's imparted as a rumor. Of course, this unverified rumor could be true or false.

10   Next, consider statements that a person classifies as verified. These could also be true or false. Verified statements that are true are certainly not rumors. What about "verified" statements that are false? That is, statements that are false, but which people—the transmitter, the receivers, or both—vouch for as true. False statements might be vouched for as true by con men and propagandists, or by the misinformed and mistaken. Verification in all such cases is necessarily weak—because the statement is false—even if it has been vouched for by the most impeccable source. The impeccable source is either lying or mistaken. Misinformation spread by propagandists is rumor. Saddam Hussein regularly spread rumors about his ability to spy on and punish ordinary Iraqi citizens to discourage potential rebels. A less intentional example are the exaggerated reports of raping, killing, and pillaging by the citizens of New Orleans following Hurricane Katrina that were reported by credible news agencies—it seemed a reasonable course of action to believe them at the time—yet they turned out to be objectively false. They were therefore rumors—the evidence that buttressed these statements crumbled. Statements that are *apparently* verified also fall into this category. Flyers and e-mails circulating in the 1980s and 1990s proclaimed that the head of Procter & Gamble (P&G) announced on the *Phil Donahue Show* that the corporation donates to the Church of Satan. The flyers urged recipients to contact the show for a transcript as proof. Anyone who took the time to do so found out, of course, that P&G's CEO has never been on this show (indeed—on any talk show). The "evidence" upon which the statement rested failed on closer examination. False statements that people believe to be verified are ultimately unverifiable—and are therefore always properly considered rumors.

So, rumors consist of unverified information statements in circulation that are perceived to be important or of interest. What types of situations give rise to these kinds of statements?

Recall the GM automotive factory workers in Ypsilanti, Michigan. These workers were told that by the end of the summer of 1993, the plant would close. Not much else was revealed, leaving employees with a lot of questions: When will it happen? How will the shutdown proceed? Who will be laid off? How will these decisions be made? Information was also missing in a large consumer loan corporation where I interviewed managers several years ago. This corporation faced an extensive restructuring involving the relocation of one large division to another city. Motivated to give only solid information to employees, managers were quite secretive about the reorganization plans. They actually gave the reorganization effort a secret code name and were instructed not to discuss it with workers. Rumors abounded.

Rumors tend to arise in situations that are ambiguous and/or pose a threat or potential threat—situations in which meanings are uncertain, questions are unsettled, information is missing, and/or lines of communication are absent.

Similarly, during natural disasters lines of communication are sometimes knocked out, often resulting in an information blackout. One wintry day in the early 1990s, I had difficulty returning home on my daily commute because a severe ice storm had disrupted transportation—including my train—throughout all of southeastern Pennsylvania and New Jersey. My fellow passengers and I were unable to gather information that would have helped us answer some key questions: How long will the storm last? Are there any other trains running in my direction? Are the roads safe enough to drive on?

15 Even the prevalence of cell phones doesn't necessarily disambiguate such weather-related snafus. Traveling through O'Hare airport on a recent summer day, I—along with thousands of other passengers—looked at the departing flights roster and read "FLIGHT CANCELED." No other information was given. Clearly, it was an unclear situation. I started talking with perfect strangers and, through rumor, I learned that the reason for cancellations was high winds, that the proper response was to "get in line" at the United Airlines desk, and that in these situations it was best to make hotel reservations immediately for that night. (I made it home after a couple of days in Chicago.)

Ambiguous situations also occur when one bit of information contradicts another—a common occurrence in life. Not long ago, I happened to be in Memphis, Tennessee, and I took the opportunity to visit the National Civil Rights Museum. The museum is housed in the Lorraine Motel, where Dr. Martin Luther King Jr. was assassinated on April 4, 1968. Across the street is another part of the museum: the Main Street rooming house where James Earl Ray allegedly fired the fatal shot resulting in King's death. In March 1969, Ray confessed to shooting Dr. King and was sentenced to ninety-nine years in prison. However, he recanted three days after he confessed and hinted that he had been an unwilling patsy as part of a conspiracy. He spent the rest of his life seeking a retrial and denying his alleged part in Dr. King's murder.

Lloyd Jowers, a restaurant owner in Memphis, claimed in 1993 that King's death was the result of a conspiracy involving the Mafia and the U.S. government. In 1999, a civil suit against Jowers found that a conspiracy to kill Dr. King did exist. Dr. King's family also became convinced of Ray's innocence and issued a statement to that effect that same year. Despite this, a U.S. Justice Department investigation completed in 2000 disagreed. It didn't find any of these allegations to be credible. Confused? So are many people, and as a result, rumors about what happened to Dr. King on that April day in 1968 are alive and well.

Rumors also tend to arise in situations that pose a threat or potential threat—possibly to one's welfare or even survival. This explains why rumor statements are generally considered important by rumor discussants.

At the beginning of this chapter I recounted some of the rumors that arose out of the widespread feelings of vulnerability in the weeks following September 11, 2001. Continued terrorist activity and ubiquitous security checking have refreshed this unease and fueled more rumors. In July 2007, police arrested a suspected terrorist in the port city of Santander, northern Spain, who had been found with a gun and a timer. Unsubstantiated reports then circulated that plans had been found on him to bomb a ferry line to the United Kingdom. Rumors then flourished that the *Pont-Aven*, a vessel connecting Santander and Plymouth, was the target of a terrorist bombing plot. The potential threat posed in this situation was obviously to human life

20   But anything that challenges one's welfare or well-being is a potential threat. A computer consultant company owner I once interviewed, recounted how his organization was the target of a negative rumor campaign. The campaign was orchestrated by employees who preyed upon fears that the new computer system would make job duties more difficult and even lead to layoffs. Rumors were spread purposely that the consultant was "incompetent."

Similar, rumors circulated among staff in an organization I helped change toward a measurement culture. Some employees feared that the proposed changes would make it much more difficult to do their jobs, and even that they might not be able to perform the new tasks at all. Negative rumors about the change surfaced: "Management will not adequately support the change." The rumors were an attempt to identify and cope with potential threats. Change of any stripe can be scary—it may lead us into situations that we can't handle.

The threat posed can be psychological in nature. A situation may challenge a belief, attitude, mind-set, or sense of identity. Strong feelings of defensiveness can be called forth when we—or groups that we identify with—are criticized or derogated; we can *feel* very threatened indeed. Rumors can neutralize such threats, for example, by denigrating the source of the challenge or by bolstering our own position, cause, or group.

In 2007, WorldPublicOpinion.org conducted an in-depth survey of citizens from four predominately Muslim countries—Egypt, Morocco, Pakistan, and Indonesia; the sample was representative of the population of each of these countries. The survey explored sentiments toward the United States and Al Qaeda, and attitudes about the use of violence on civilian populations. Very large majorities of participants opposed violence against civilians, as exemplified in the acts of September 11, 2001, perpetrated by Al Qaeda. However, because American intentions are widely believed to be hostile to Islam, respondents were motivated not to criticize any group—including Al Qaeda—antagonistic to the United States.

Among a number of interesting findings were the perceptions of who was responsible for the attacks of September 11. A very small minority—2 percent of Pakistanis, for example—thought that Al Qaeda orchestrated the attacks. When pressed in focus groups that Osama bin Laden had taken responsibility for the attacks on videotape, many participants became visibly uncomfortable and defensive, expressed disbelief, and suggested that the video was fake. A common response was that "Hollywood can create anything."

25   Instead, many thought that unknown persons, Israel, or even the United States was behind the events. To wit, rumors persist that four thousand Jews were told by the Israeli Secret Service on September 10, 2001, not to report to work at the World Trade Center the next day—the implication being that Israel bombed the buildings to incite anti-Arab sentiment. Rumors portraying Israel or the United States as masterminding September 11 are likely to spring up in situations where participants feel defensive about Al Qaeda's role in the attacks. Arab nations, of course, do not have a monopoly on such rumors—they circulate among all people whenever defensive sentiments arise.

So, rumors arise in situations that are ambiguous, or pose some threat or potential threat. But how do they help people deal with ambiguity and threat?

In the early summer of 2007, five happy and carefree young women died in a horrible head-on collision with a tractor-trailer on a two-lane highway near Rochester, New York. One week earlier, they had graduated from high school. They were in an SUV headed to a summer house at 10:00 p.m. along a two-lane rural road, when they passed a sedan, then inexplicably swerved into the path of the oncoming eighteen-wheeler. Fuel lines were broken and their vehicle erupted in a terrible conflagration. The force of the impact was so great that the young women were killed instantly. Why had their SUV swerved into the path of the oncoming truck?

The answer to that question will probably never be definitively known, but a grieving community tried to answer it as part of an effort to make sense of the tragedy. Out of this sensemaking, two false rumors were fashioned. One was that the driver of the sedan had sped up as he was being passed, forcing the SUV into the truck's path. This was in fact the opposite of what happened: The sedan slowed down to allow the SUV to safely pass. Another was that the oncoming eighteen-wheeler didn't reduce its speed before the collision. False again: The truck driver jammed on the brakes as soon as he saw the SUV enter his lane—he left more than 120 feet of skid marks before the impact. These rumors were put to rest weeks later at a news conference during which it was revealed that the SUV driver's cell phone had sent and received text messages just seconds before the crash. It appears likely that distraction due to cell phone usage was at the heart of this sad event. The rumors that arose served as hypotheses to people trying to make sense of what happened.

It's clear that rumors help people make some sort of sense out of unclear situations. The GM workers in Ypsilanti circulated rumors in an attempt to achieve clarity about the impending plant closing. Employees in the lending institution I interviewed passed rumors as a way of ferreting out the facts of the restructuring situation. My fellow stranded train and plane travelers and I used rumors to sift a picture of the weather, transportation routes, and appropriate courses of action. People set forth rumors about the death of Dr. King in order to resolve the contradictory statements associated with this national tragedy.

Human nature abhors an explanation vacuum. People in groups use rumors to construct, evaluate, and refine explanations for the ambiguous situation.

30   In situations that pose a threat or potential threat, rumors also help people manage that threat by encouraging them to deal with it through positive action, or by simply making them feel better about it. Rumors about the bombing of the *Pont-Aven* alerted patrons not to travel via that ferry; passengers could avoid the possibility of a sudden death by delaying their trip or choosing another route. Rumors that a computer consultant is incompetent warned clients not to use that consultant; company officials could avoid years of computer-related troubles by simply choosing a different consultant or by not installing a computer system at all. A rumor that "the Port Jervis dam is breaking!" instructs Port Jervis residents to flee the scene immediately if they know what's good for them; they could preserve their lives by acting quickly.

A rumor in 2001 warned: "Avoid Boston on September 22 because drunken Arabs at a bar let it slip that there would be a second wave of attacks that day." By staying out of town on the twenty-second, Bostonians and others could evade the dangers encountered by people living and working in New York City on September 11. Rumors among college students about professors—"Milgram is a hard but fair grader"; "Rogers is an easy A"; "Allport is a phenomenal lecturer"—help students avoid unfavorable experiences such as unfair grades, low marks, and boring lectures. In all of these examples, the rumor implies a course of action that—if available—will supposedly aid the hearer in avoiding a negative or achieving a positive out come.

Many negative outcomes in life are, of course, unavoidable. For these, rumors assist people by helping them emotionally cope with the dreaded event or state of affairs. Rumors can help do this by, again, simply helping people make sense of an unclear situation. Merely understanding why a bad thing is happening is a good emotional coping strategy.

Understanding that the GM plant will be closing down this summer because foreign labor is cheaper won't alter the negative outcome for employees—losing employment—but is will remove a sense of arbitrariness from the situation. The plant closing can be understood as the result of larger economic forces, globalization, or corporate greed. Understanding how the SUV with five young women crossed into the opposing lane will not bring them back to life or lessen the feelings of loss felt by family and community—but it will set the event into a larger context. The crash could have come about, for example, as part of larger patterns of cell phone distraction, aggressive driving, or time pressures faced by truck drivers. We search for explanations in part because the very presence of an explanation is comforting. Rumors often often help people by providing a ready-made explanation.

Rumors can also help people cope emotionally by neutralizing a psychological threat—especially a challenge to our positive view of ourselves. In conflict situations, this is particularly so. In the study investigating sentiments toward Al Qaeda, focus group respondents presumably latched on to rumors that the United States or Israel organized the events of September 11 because they deflect the threatening idea that Al Qaeda was responsible for killing nearly three thousand civilians. Similarly, negative racial attitudes are distasteful—we don't like to think of ourselves as judgmental toward a person based solely on the color of his skin, her gender, or country of origin. We consider ourselves fair-minded people. How is it that we sometimes exhibit racial prejudice, then?

35   Wedge-driving rumors—negative stories about members of the rival or targeted group—can justify distasteful attitudes. In the aftermath of Hurricane Katrina, false rumors about black individuals in New Orleans engaged in looting, raping, and shooting at rescuers were widespread. False rumors that groups of unruly black persons vandalized rest stop facilities while being bussed from New Orleans at taxpayer expense were also common. Such rumors can make prejudiced individuals feel better about their negative racial attitudes toward African-Americans. Conversely, false rumors that New Jersey State troopers and their dogs chased a black child, causing the boy to fall into the Raritan Canal near Princeton and drown, spread quickly in the African-American community one hot summer in the late 1980s. Such rumors can make prejudiced persons feel better about having negative racial attitudes toward European Americans.

In a similar vein, we don't like to think of ourselves as prejudiced against even a rival group. But prejudice against any rival group can be legitimated by negative rumors about that group. Politics has always been a hot topic, but what can explain the current acrimony between Democrats and Republicans? Negative rumors about politicians from the opposing party help people justify their intense biases. I receive negative political e-rumors from both sides of the aisle. These rumors are always of "the other side is bad" variety. They are never checked for veracity, but simply forwarded to friends believed to be like-minded. These rumors serve a purpose—to justify negative prejudice toward the rival group—in this case, the opposing political party. We would normally consider such bias for what it is—unfair and distasteful; rumors, however, can make it palatable.

Central to our discussion of rumors is their role in human sense-making. So, to better understand what rumor is, we need to understand how we make sense generally and the role of rumors in that process. More specifically, how do individuals make sense and how do rumors affect this individual sense-making? And how do groups make sense together and how do rumors affect this group sense-making?

Not long ago, my wife and I were exiting a movie theater just past midnight. The theater was located near a large Barnes and Noble bookstore, around which stood a huge crowd alternately cheering and clapping as they awaited their turn to purchase *Harry Potter and the Deathly Hallows*, the seventh and last installment of J. K. Rowling's amazingly popular children's book series. I slowly drove by the fringe of the crowd; it was New Year's Eve in the middle of July. People of all ages had waited in line the entire day in order to be among the first to receive the coveted volume. Three news stations were also present, adding to the circus-like fanfare. It was a happy event. My wife and I couldn't recall such excitement over the release of a book. Many would stay up all night to read the 784-page tome and then attend a brunch to discuss it with other bleary-eyed enthusiasts. Some would go straight from the bookstore to parties where the main social activity was sitting and reading. What could *explain* the Harry Potter phenomenon?

40   What was it about this children's book, our culture, or media that led to this unprecedented interest and fanfare at this moment in time? Any satisfactory explanation would convey the desires, beliefs, and aims of the many people involved in Pottermania, and clarify the underlying psychological, sociological, and literary underpinnings of this muggle (ordinary human) event. Good candidate explanations might appeal to the literary quality of Rowling's epic, an increasing desire for a sense of wonder in our modern age, contagion phenomena, global interconnectedness resulting from the growth of the Internet, or the increasing media savvy of marketers.

To ask how individuals make sense of things is really to ask how they go about the task of explanation. Explanation is aimed at increasing comprehension and understanding. It can involve offering details of a situation that enable us to understand it, or the reasons—i.e., the desires, beliefs, or aims—of the actors involved. Good explanations clarify meanings, ideas, or thoughts.

Psychologists have outlined the process an individual undergoes when seeking to explain an event, situation, or feature of their experience that is unclear. The process has a common-sense flavor to it; explanation is a universal human activity. A person first becomes aware of an event—it is noticed. It is then interpreted—an initial explanation is set forth. If so motivated and able, the person can then iteratively test and revise this interpretation, or generate alternatives for testing and revision. This iterative testing may involve searching for additional information. At some point, the individual settles on a final explanation. Noticing and interpreting happen automatically; that is, they occur in an almost reflex fashion, without effort or thought. Testing, revising, generating alternatives, and selecting a final explanation, however, take effort.

Whether automatic or effortful, each of the tasks in the explanation process is guided by cognitive structures. I introduced this term in Chapter 2; it refers to associations of ideas, such as stereotypes or frameworks. Cognitive structures are activated by bringing ideas to mind. For example, if I say the word "Italian," several ideas are brought to mind or become more accessible in our awareness: pasta, large close-knit families, Roman noses, expressive gestures, espresso coffee, medieval art, Mediterranean climate, and Mafia. These elements are associated with one another around the concept "Italian"; they form a stereotype.

Cognitive structures guide the explanation process at each step. For example, they help us notice events. Upon learning that our new neighbor's name is DiFonzo, their facial features, expressive gestures, and many children become more salient to us—we notice them. When we encounter an event that puzzles us, cognitive structures help us interpret the event automatically—without thinking. We learn that Mr. Difonzo's uncle in Sicily was found dead from a gunshot wound; we privately wonder if it was a Mafia-related killing. Cognitive structures guide us in the effortful generation of alternate explanations as well. We know that the Sicilian uncle collected guns for a hobby and—guided by the cognitive structure "gun collecting"—we inquire as to whether he accidentally shot himself while cleaning his guns.

45   Rumors affect this process of explanation at several points along the way, often by simply delivering the relevant cognitive structure. First of all, they help us to notice events. Many times this is a simple matter of the rumor calling attention to a particular incident, theme, characteristic, or situation. False rumors that Snapple is owned by the Ku Klux Klan brought attention to the kosher symbol—signified on the Snapple label by the letter *K* with a circle around it. In addition, rumors often also convey an initial interpretation of an event. To continue our Snapple example, the presence of the *K* symbol on the Snapple label, according to the rumor, indicated that the company was owned by the KKK.

The false rumors of Paul McCartney's death both called attention to and interpreted why he was barefoot on the cover of the *Abbey Road* album: according to the rumor, the deceased are customarily interred without shoes in Britain. (Actually, this isn't true.) Rumors activated the cognitive structures that guided the noticing and interpreting in each of these examples. This "rumor guidance" often happens automatically—without effort, intention, or thought.

Rumors may also activate the cognitive structures that motivate and guide the effortful search for new information to help us evaluate an explanation. A rumor that American Home Mortgage Investment Corporation had shut down part of its lending operation inspired information-seeking about the company's lending practices. The company had indeed engaged in risky practices; it had issued many loans to borrowers without requiring extensive documentation. The rumor resulted in a 23 percent reduction in the company's stock value in one day, despite protests by company officials that the rumor was untrue.

One particular type of cognitive structure that rumors frequently deliver to individuals is the stable cause—a cause that lasts over time. In the previous chapter, I discussed how a rumor that "Goodyear profits are up because of good management practices" activated the stable cause idea that good management will continue, thereby leading to the prediction that Goodyear stock would continue to rise. In experiments, these rumors did indeed lead to predictions that Goodyear stock would continue to rise and in this way systematically affected buying behavior—but, as it turns out, unprofitably.

In another study I discussed in Chapter 2, rumors that Sophie (a fictional character) has some form of mental illness conveyed the idea that Sophie was mentally ill, activated the stable cause idea that mental illness lasts over time, and thereby led to the conclusion that her mental illness was likely to continue. Mental illness would presumably impair her judgments and adversely affect her desirability as a friend. Students (not educated about mental illness) were then less likely to vote for Sophie as class president and to desire to be socially close with her.

50   The point is that rumors often affect individual sensemaking by activating a stable, lasting cause to explain events; this frequently leads to predicting that the recent events, behaviors, or conditions will continue. Put another way, rumors often lead to this kind of sensemaking simply because they often supply a lasting cause for the current state of affairs or trend of events: The way things are going now will continue into the future.

For individuals, then, rumors make us think about some events, affect how we frame these events, and affect what we continue to learn about these events.

But what about collections of connected individuals? That is, what about groups? How do groups make sense together and how do rumors affect group sensemaking?

In the mid-1990s, Internet discussion groups were a new phenomenon. A small percentage of people at that time participated in email Listservs. My colleague, Prashant Bordia, was one of them. He noticed that discussions of rumors on these groups were sensemaking activities and he carefully recorded and analyzed these electronic posts.

One discussion in particular intrigued him and became the subject of his master's thesis: people on one particular Usenet site were concerned that Prodigy—a large Internet service provider at the time—was spying on customers' personal files. The false rumor asserted that this profit-driven corporation was uploading private information from subscribers' hard drives without their knowledge or consent. Prodigy then allegedly sifted through this information for marketing purposes—that is, to develop a clearer demographic and psychological picture of their customers so that they might be more successful at selling them additional products and services. Demographic and psychological profiling was not new at this time, but the idea that a large company would, without permission, upload private customer files was a key part of the rumor that sparked concern and discussion.

Broadly speaking, group sensemaking resembles individual sensemaking in that particular tasks are performed by many different people rather than just one. There is a division of labor. That noticing, interpreting, revising, and settling on a final explanation are performed by members of the group rather than by a Single person. One task, for example, is to first bring a rumor to the group. The sociologist Tamotsu Shibutani called this the messenger role. After analysis of the types of statements that people actually include in their posts, Prashant and I categorized such roles as "communicative postures." For example, the messenger role is best represented in an explanation delivering posture. In the Prodigy rumor discussion, a discussant might post "I don't know if this is true, but I heard that Prodigy is uploading our private files for use by their marketing departments"—the person delivers an explanation to the group along with a cautionary statement that it might be false.

55   We dubbed such tasks "postures" because they represent the temporary role that a person may play while "taking their turn" at any given point in the discussion. That is, "posture" conveys that the role that one plays in a discussion may change over time. A person might cautiously deliver an explanation at one stage of a discussion, but then later perform a different role in that same discussion. She might, for example, later express disbelief in that explanation and present an argument supporting her contention that Prodigy was not surreptitiously uploading customer data (we dubbed this an explanation falsifying posture): "I don't believe that Prodigy is uploading information because to do so would take up too much bandwidth."

Prashant's analysis detected other communicative postures displayed in these discussions. A post that was explanation evaluating would analyze and interpret the rumor explanation. For example: "Perhaps the Prodigy cache file grows over time because they are first compressing the user's personal files, then adding it into the cache file before uploading!" Explanation accepting posts would express belief in the rumor: "I believe they are doing this." Explanation verifying postures would go further and express belief in the rumor along with a supporting argument: "I believe Prodigy is doing this because they are solely interested in making a profit and would not hesitate to violate our privacy rights." Of course, when people are collectively analyzing a rumor explanation, they need to search for, find, deliver, and analyze additional information.

A directing posture would provide information and suggest a strategy for further information gathering: "Whenever I dial in to Prodigy, my modem light turns on intermittently, even if I'm not sending or receiving information; someone should find out if this is the way modems ordinarily operate." Information-seeking postures would simply state the gaps in knowledge needed in order to generate or evaluate a rumor and would often be in the form of a question: "What do we know about the Prodigy cache file?" Information reporting postures would share information and personal experience: "Ever since I subscribed to Prodigy, my computer has been operating more slowly." Other postures performed the functions of motivating participants to continue sense-making by either considering negative outcomes ("I'm scared about what this could mean about my privacy") or positive ones ("I wish our private files would remain private")....

The point in pondering these postures is that people, when they "take their turn" in an electronic discussion by posting a message, perform a particular function in service of the group's goal of making sense of the situation. Clearly, rumor discussions are not simply telephone game transmissions, otherwise known as "whispers down the lane"—A tells B a rumor, who then tells C, who then tells D...and so on down the line. This common conception of rumor is simplistic and individualistic—it frames rumor as something that primarily happens with an individual rather than a group. Instead, a group sensemaking discussion around a rumor consists of a sometimes confusing interchange of news, information statements, opinions, explanations, commands, questions, motivators, and digressions.

But even though the discussion seems unwieldy, there are clear trends as it moves forward. At first, people display explanation delivering and directing postures: they cautiously bring the rumor to the group, and strategies are proposed to find out more information. Supported by information seeking and reporting, and motivated to continue by considering negative or positive outcomes, they engage in explanation evaluating postures—they are actively sifting, sorting, and making sense of the rumor. Finally, people participate more casually as a consensus in reached or interest dies down. They move on to other topics or simply stop participating. Despite the apparent chaos and confusion, these discussions are colorful and purposeful interchanges that—collectively— proceed in a fairly predictable fashion around the central task of sensemaking.

Review Questions

1. Summarize the four major characteristics of rumor, according to DiFonzo.

2. Explain the difference between unverified and verified rumor.

3. DiFonzo explains that rumors sometimes help us cope with the fact that "negative outcomes in life are . . . unavoidable." How does he support this assertion?

4. Define wedge-driving rumors. Cite two examples of such rumors, according to DiFonzo.

5. What is the "messenger role?" Define what DiFonzo calls "postures."

 Discussion and Writing Suggestions

1. How does DiFonzo's analysis of rumor square with your own understanding of rumor? Recall a particular rumor that concerned you, someone you know, or some group of which you are (or were) a member. In your response, address some of the following questions: (1) What event(s) or concern(s) sparked this rumor? (2) To what extent did this rumor fulfill the terms of DiFonzo's definition of rumor? (3) Who took on the "messenger role"? (4) How did the rumor affect "group sensemaking"? (5) What "postures" were involved? (6) How did these postures operate to spread and transform the rumor? Drawing on DiFonzo's insights, explain how this rumor helped you or others "make sense of an uncertain world."

2. DiFonzo explains that "in situations that pose a threat . . . rumors also help people manage that threat by encouraging them to deal with it through positive action, or by simply making them feel better about it." In what ways can rumors make us "feel better?" Alternately, how might threat-managing rumors have a negative impact? Provide examples from your own experience.

3. DiFonzo's account of the accident in which five young women in an SUV died . demonstrates how people use rumor to help make sense of tragedy. The initial stories concerning the accident misrepresented key facts but may have helped the grief-stricken community of the victims better come to terms with the accident. The actual cause of the accident was more difficult for the community to accept. Can you think of other examples from your own experience, or the experiences of people you know, demonstrating the ways in which rumors sometimes provide comfort in the face of realities we prefer to avoid?

4. Through his example of the airport mishap, DiFonzo demonstrates how rumor can lead to useful "positive action." What other occasions come to mind, whether from your own life or from social situations in your experience, suggesting that rumors sometimes serve a useful purpose?

5. DiFonzo explains that group rumor making is more complex than a game of "telephone." Based on your own experiences and observations, recount an example of how a rumor develops through group discussion.

6. This selection begins by referencing the events of 9/11 and continues throughout discussing the rumors involving the events of that day. To what extent, positively and/or negatively, did these rumors help "people deal with ambiguity and threat"?

7. Recall once again a rumor from your own experience. Reconstruct a stretch of dialogue between you and a group of friends that illustrates how the rumor was created, transformed, and spread. Incorporate into the dialogue some of the phenomena DiFonzo discusses: threat neutralization, communicative postures, group sensemaking, and so on.

RUMOR CASCADES AND GROUP POLARIZATION

Cass R. Sunstein

Picture a snowball rolling down a steep hill. As it gathers momentum, collecting more snow, its diameter rapidly swells. By the time it hits bottom, its mass is considerably larger than it was at the top. According to legal scholar Cass Sunstein, rumors operate in a like manner. Sunstein asserts that rumors move and grow in various types of "cascades," pulling in new believers in the process. Before long, rumors have reached the point at which a majority of listeners or readers believes them. This dynamic can have positive effects: As Sunstein points out, informational cascades helped spur the worldwide movement for sexual equality into near-universal acceptance. But the dynamic can just as easily spread misinformation as rumors cascade into believability and take on an aura of "fact" to large groups of people. These cascaded "truths" might be relatively innocuous urban myths (such as alligators living in city sewers); they might just as easily be political smears that damage or destroy campaigns. Cass Sunstein is the author of numerous books, including *Risk and Reason* (2002), *Why Societies Need Dissent* (2003), and *Infotopia: How Many Minds Produce Knowledge* (2006). Much of his recent work has focused on the impact of rumor cascades involving government conspiracy theories and how to best counteract them. The following selection first appeared as a chapter in Sunstein's book *On Rumors* (2009), published shortly after he was chosen to head the Obama White House Office of Information and Regulatory Affairs.

Learning from Others 1: Informational Cascades

Rumors frequently spread through informational cascades. The basic dynamic behind such cascades in simple: once a certain number of people appear to believe a rumor, others will believe it too, unless they have good reason to believe that it is false. Most rumors involve topics on which people lack direct or personal knowledge, and so most of us defer to the crowd. As more people defer, thus making the crowd grow, there is a real risk that large groups of people will believe rumors even though they are entirely false.

Imagine a group of people who are deciding whether Senator Jones has done something scandalous.[1] Each member of the group is announcing his view in sequence. Andrew is the first to speak; perhaps he is the propagator of the rumor. Andrew states that Senator Jones has indeed done something scandalous. Barbara now knows Andrew's judgment. Exercising her own independent judgment on the basis of what she knows of the senator, she might agree with Andrew. If she has no knowledge at all about Senator Jones, she might also agree with Andrew; perhaps she accepts Andrew's claim that he knows what he is talking about. Or suppose that her independent judgment is that Senator Jones probably did not engage in the scandalous conduct. Even if so, she still might end up believing the rumor, just because of what Andrew has said. If she trusts Andrew no more and no less than she trusts herself, she might not know what to think or do; she might simply flip a coin.

Now consider a third person, Carl. Suppose that both Andrew and Barbara suggest that they believe the rumor, but that Carl's own information, though far from conclusive, indicates that their belief is wrong. Even in that event, Carl might well ignore what he knows and follow Andrew and Barbara. It is likely, after all, that both Andrew and Barbara had reasons for reaching their conclusion, and unless Carl thinks that his own information is better than theirs, he may follow their lead. If he does, Carl is in a cascade.

Now suppose that Carl is agreeing with Andrew and Barbara; lacking any personal information about Senator Jones, he thinks they are probably right. Suppose too that other group members—Dennis, Ellen, and Frances—know what Andrew, Barbara, and Carl think and said, and believe that their judgments are probably reasonable. In that event, they will do exactly what Carl did: accept the rumor about Senator Jones even if they have no relevant knowledge. Our little group might accept the rumor even if Andrew initially said something that he knew to be false or spoke honestly but erroneously. Andrew's initial statement, in short, can start a cascade in which a number of people accept and spread serious misinformation.

5   All this might seem unrealistic, but cascades often do occur in the real world. In fact, this little account helps to explain the transmission of many rumors. Even among specialists, cascades are common. Thus an article in *The New England Journal of Medicine* explores "bandwagon diseases," in which doctors act like "lemmings, episodically and with a blind infectious enthusiasm pushing certain diseases and treatments primarily because everyone else is doing the same."[2] There can be serious consequences in the real world. "Most doctors are not at the cutting edge of research; their inevitable reliance upon what colleagues have done and are doing leads to numerous surgical fads and treatment-caused illnesses."[3] Some medical practices, including tonsillectomy, "seem to have been adopted initially based on weak information," and extreme differences in tonsillectomy frequencies (and other procedures, including vaccinations) provide good evidence that cascades are at work.[4]

On the Internet, informational cascades happen every day, and even when they involve baseless rumors, they greatly affect our beliefs and our behavior. Consider the fact that YouTube videos are far more likely to attract many more viewers if they have already attracted many viewers—a clear example of a cascade.

It is also true that many cascades spread truth, and they can do a lot of good. Cascades help account for the beliefs that the earth is round, that racial segregation is wrong, that people should be allowed to engage in free speech, and that democracy is the best form of government. A bank might really be failing, and a politician might really be corrupt, and if a cascade spreads these facts, so much the better. The belief that the earth is round, the attack on apartheid in South Africa, and the global movement for sexual equality were all fueled by informational cascades. But false rumors often also set off cascades, and when they do, two major social problems occur. First and most important, people can come to believe a falsehood, possibly a damaging one. Such cascades can ruin relationships, businesses, and even careers. Second, those who are in the cascade generally do not disclose their private doubts. People may know that Senator Jones is unlikely to have done what he is accused of doing, but they follow the lead of those who came before them. Recall the self-interested or malicious motivations of many propagators; we can now have a better sense of why it is important to chill the falsehoods they circulate.

With respect to rumors, of course, people start with different levels of information. Many of us lack any relevant information at all. Once we hear something that seems plausible but alarming, those of us who lack information may believe what we hear if we do not know anything to the contrary. Other people are not ignorant; they do know something that is relevant, but not enough to overcome the shared beliefs of many others, at least when those others are trusted. Still other people have a significant amount of relevant information, but are nonetheless motivated to accept the false rumor. Recall the importance of tipping points: rumors often spread through a process in which they are accepted by people with low thresholds first, and, as the number of believers swells, eventually by others with higher thresholds who conclude, not unreasonably, that so many people cannot be wrong.[5] The ultimate result is that large numbers of people end up accepting a false rumor even though it is quite baseless. Return to the Internet. A propagator makes a statement on a blog; other blogs pick up the statement; and eventually the accumulation of statements makes a real impression, certainly among people within specific social networks, and perhaps far more generally. Both truths and falsehoods spread in this fashion.

A study not of rumors but of music downloads is revealing about this process. The Princeton sociologist Matthew Salganik and his coauthors[6] created an artificial music market among 14,341 participants who were visitors to a website that was popular among young people. The participants were given a list of previously unknown songs from unknown bands. They were asked to listen to selections of any of the songs that interested them, to decide which songs (if any) to download, and to assign a rating to the songs they chose. About half the participants made their decisions based on their own independent judgments about the quality of the music. This was the control group. The participants outside that group were randomly assigned to one of eight possible "worlds." Within these worlds, participants could see how many times each song had been downloaded. Each of these worlds evolved on its own; participants in any particular world could see only the downloads in their own world.

The key question was whether people would be affected by the visible choices of others—and whether different music would become popular in different worlds. What do you expect would happen? Would people be affected by the judgments of others?

10   It turned out that people were dramatically influenced by the choices of their predecessors. In every one of the eight worlds, people were far more likely to download songs that had been previously downloaded in significant numbers—and far less likely to download songs that had not been so popular. Most strikingly, the success of songs was highly unpredictable. The songs that did well or poorly in the control group, where people did not see other people's judgments, could perform very differently in the "social influence" worlds. In those worlds, a song could become very popular or very unpopular, with everything depending on the choices of the first participants to decide whether to download it. The identical song could be a hit or a failure, simply because other people, at the start, chose to download it or not. As Salganik and his coauthors put it: "In general, the 'best' songs never do very badly, and the 'worst' songs never do extremely well," but—and this is the remarkable point—"almost any other result is possible."[7]

In a related study, Salganik and his coauthors, acting not unlike propagators, attempted to influence the process. They told people, falsely, that certain songs had been downloaded in large numbers, even though they had actually proved unpopular.[8] More particularly, the researchers actually inverted true popularity, so that people would see the least popular songs as having the most downloads and the most popular songs as having the fewest. Their key finding was that they were able to produce self-fulfilling prophecies, in which false perceptions of popularity produced actual popularity over time. When people think songs are popular, songs actually become popular, at least in the short run. True, the most popular songs did in fact recover their popularity, but it took a while, and songs that had previously been among the least popular—before the inversion—continued to be at or toward the top of the list. This is a striking demonstration of how people's behavior can be affected by an understanding, even a false one, what other people think and do.

The music download experiments help to explain how rumors spread. Alleged facts about a politician or a country or a company do move far more in some "worlds" than in others—and in different worlds, people will believe different "facts." The variable success of rumors provides a real-world analogue to the concept, so popular in science fiction novels, of "parallel worlds. "Even without self-conscious efforts at manipulation, certain rumors will become entrenched in some places and have no success at all in others. If propagators are clever, they will attempt to convince people that others have come to believe the rumor that they are creating or spreading. One propagator will have terrific success in some worlds but none at all in others; another propagator will show a radically different pattern of success and failure. Quality, assessed in terms of correspondence to the truth, might not matter a great deal or even at all. Recall that on YouTube, cascades are common, as popular videos attract increasing attention not necessarily because they are good but because they are popular.

In light of this, we can see why some social groups hold quite tenaciously to false rumors while other groups treat them as implausible or even ridiculous. An example is the existence of widely divergent judgments among differing groups about the origins and causes of AIDS—with some groups believing, falsely, that the first cases were observed in Africa as a result of sexual relations between human beings and monkeys, and other groups believing, also falsely, that the virus was produced in government laboratories.[9] Another example is the existence of widely divergent views about the causes of the 9/11 attacks—views that attribute the attacks to many sources, including Israel and the United States.

The multiple views about AIDS and the attacks of 9/11 are products of social interactions and in particular of informational cascades. The same process occurs when groups come to believe some alleged fact about the secret beliefs, foolishness, or terrible misdeeds of a public or private figure. In each instance, an informational cascade is often at work. And when cascade-propelled rumors turn into firm beliefs, the combination can be devastating. Recall that people holding similar beliefs are especially likely to accept some rumors and to discount others. Suppose that one group (in, say, Utah or Iran) has been subject to a rumor-driven cascade, while another group (in, say, New York or Canada) has not. If so, those in the different "worlds" will develop strong prior beliefs with which they will approach whatever they hear later—beliefs that may make corrections hard to accept....

Learning from Others 2: Conformity Cascades

15 Sometimes people believe rumors because other people believe them. But sometimes people just act as if they do.

They censor themselves so that they can appear to agree with the crowd. Conformity pressures offer another account of how rumors spread.

To see how conformity works, let us consider some classic experiments by Solomon Asch, who explored whether people would be willing to overlook the unambiguous evidence of their own senses.[10] In these experiments, the subject was placed into a group of seven to nine people who seemed to be other subjects in the experiment but who were actually Asch's confederates. Their ridiculously simple task was to match a particular line, shown on a large white card, to the one of three "comparison lines" that was identical to it in length. The two nonmatching lines were substantially different, with the differential varying from an inch and three quarters to three quarters of an inch.

In the first two rounds of the Asch experiments, everyone agreed about the right answer. "The discriminations are simple; each individual monotonously calls out the same judgment."[11] But "suddenly this harmony is disturbed at the third round."[12] All other group members made what is obviously, to the subject and to any reasonable person, a glaring error, matching the line at issue to one that is conspicuously longer or shorter. In these circumstances, the subject had a choice: she could maintain her independent judgment or instead accept the view of the unanimous majority.

What happened? Remarkably, most people ended up yielding to the group at least once in a series of trials. When asked to decide on their own, without seeing judgments from others, people erred less than 1 percent of the time. But in rounds in which group pressure supported the incorrect answer, people erred 36.8 percent of the time.[13] Indeed, in a series of twelve questions, no less than 70 percent of people went along with the group, and defied the evidence of their own senses, at least once.[14]

20   Why did this happen? Several conformists stated, in private interviews, that their own opinions must have been wrong—an answer suggesting that they were moved not by peer pressure but instead by a belief that the shared belief of others is probably correct. On the other hand, experimenters using the same basic circumstances of Asch's experiments have generally found significantly reduced error when the subject is asked to give a private answer.[15] In short, when people know that conformity or deviation will be easily identified, they are more likely to conform.[16] These findings suggest that peer pressure matter—and that it induces what the economist Timur Kuran has called *knowledge falsification*, that is, public statements in which people misrepresent their actual knowledge.[17] Here, then, is a clue to the relationship between successful rumors and conformity pressures. People will falsify their own knowledge, or at least squelch their own doubts, in the face of the apparent views of a crowd.

Rumors often spread as a result of conformity cascades, which are especially important in social networks made up of tightly knit groups or in which there is a strong stake in a certain set of beliefs. In a conformity cascade, people go along with the group in order to maintain the good opinion of others—no matter their private views or doubts. Suppose that Albert suggests that a certain political figure is corrupt and that Blanche concurs with Albert, not because she actually thinks that Albert is right, but because she does not wish to seem, to Albert, to be ignorant or indifferent to official corruption. If Albert and Blanche say that the official is corrupt, Cynthia might not contradict them publicly and might even appear to share their judgment. She does so not because she believes that judgment to be correct, but because she does not want to face their hostility or lose their good opinion.

It should be easy to see how this process might generate a special kind of cascade. Once Albert, Blanche, and Cynthia offer a united front on the issue, their friend David might be reluctant to contradict them even if he thinks that they are wrong. The apparently shared view of Albert, Blanche, and Cynthia imparts its own information: their view might be right. But even if David is skeptical or has reason to believe that they are wrong, he might not want to break with them publicly.

Conformity cascades can certainly produce convergence on truth. Maybe unduly skeptical people are silencing themselves—not the worst thing if their skepticism is baseless. But conformity cascades often help to account for the spread of false rumors. Especially when people operate within a tightly knit group or live in some kind of enclave, they may silence themselves in the face of an emerging judgment or opinion even if they are not sure whether it is right. Often people will be suspicious of a rumor, or believe that it is not true, but they will not contradict the judgment of the relevant group, largely in order to avoid social sanctions. Consider far-left and far-right groups, in which well-organized social networks often spread damaging falsehoods, frequently about their political opponents, with the indispensable aid of conformity pressures.

In the actual world of group decisions, people are of course uncertain whether publicly expressed statements are a product of independent knowledge, participation in an informational cascade, or the pressure of conformity. Much of the time, we overestimate the extent to which the actions of others are based on independent information rather than on social pressures. False rumors become entrenched as a result. And here too, of course, diverse thresholds matter a great deal. Blanche may silence herself and agree with the group only when the pressure to conform is intense; David might be more easily led to go along with the crowd. But if most of the world consists of people like David, then the Blanches are more likely eventually to yield. There are tipping points for conformity no less than for information.

Learning from Others 3: Group Polarization

25   Deliberation among like-minded people often entrenches false rumors.[18] The explanations here overlap with those that account for social cascades, but the dynamics are distinctive. Here again, we can understand why some groups will end up firmly believing rumors that seem ludicrously implausible to others.

The Basic Finding

In the summer of 2005, a small experiment in democracy was held in Colorado.[19] Sixty American citizens were brought together and assembled into ten groups, each consisting of six people. Members of each group were asked to deliberate on several issues, including one of the most controversial of the day: Should the United States sign an international treaty to combat global warming? To answer that question, people had to come to terms with what were, in a loose sense, rumors. They had to ask whether climate change was real or a hoax, whether the American economy would be badly harmed by participation in an international agreement, and whether such an agreement was necessary to prevent an imminent or long-term disaster for the United States.

As the experiment was designed, the groups consisted of "liberal" and "conservative" members—the former from Boulder, the latter from Colorado Springs. In the parlance of election years, there were five "blue state" groups and five "red state" groups—five groups whose members initially tended toward liberal positions on climate change and five whose members tended toward conservative positions on that issue. People were asked to state their opinions anonymously both before and after fifteen minutes of group discussion. What was the effect of discussion?

The results were simple. In almost every group, members ended up holding more extreme positions after they spoke with one another. Most of the liberals in Boulder favored an international treaty to control global warming before discussion; they favored it more strongly after discussion. Many of the conservatives in Colorado Springs were somewhat skeptical about that treaty before discussion; they strongly opposed it after discussion. Aside from increasing extremism, the experiment had an independent effect: it made both liberal groups and conservative groups significantly more homogeneous—and thus squelched diversity. Before their members started to talk, both the red and the blue groups displayed a fair bit of internal disagreement. The disagreements were reduced as a result of a mere fifteen-minute discussion. Even in their anonymous statements, group members showed far more consensus after discussion than before.

30   Moreover, the rift between liberals and conservatives widened as a result of discussing. And after discussion, opinions among like-minded group members narrowed to the point where everyone mostly agreed with everyone else.

The Colorado experiment is a case study in group polarization: when like-minded people deliberate, they typically end up adopting a more extreme position in line with their pre-deliberation inclinations.[20] Group polarization is pervasive in human life. If a group of people tends to believe that the nation's leader is a criminal, or that some corporate executive is a scoundrel, or that one of their own members has betrayed them, their belief to this effect will be strengthened after they speak among themselves. In the context of rumor transmission, the implication is simple: when group members begin with an antecedent commitment to a rumor, internal deliberations will strengthen their belief in its truth. The antecedent commitment might involve a specific claim, including a bit of gossip about an apparently powerful person. Or it might involve a more general belief with which the rumor easily fits. The key point is that internal deliberations further entrench the rumor.

Notes

[1]I draw here on David Hirshleifer, "The Blind Leading the Blind: Social Influence, Fads, and Information Cascades," in *The New Economics of Human Behavior*, edited by Mariano Tommasi and Kathryn Ierulli (Cambridge, Mass.: Cambridge University Press, 1995), 188, 193–95, and on the discussion in Cass R. Sunstein, *Why Societies Need Dissent* (Cambridge, Mass.: Harvard University Press, 2003), 55–73.

[2]John F. Burnham, "Medical Practice á la Mode: How Medical Fashions Determine Medical Care," *The New England Journal of Medicine* 317 (1987): 1220, 1201.

[3]Hirshleifer, "Blind Leading the Blind," 204.

[4]Sushil Bikhchandani et al., "Learning from the Behavior of Other: Conformity, Fads, and Informational Caseades." *The Journal of Economic Perspectives* 12 (1998): 151, 167. On YouTube cascades, see Clarice Sim and W. Wayne Fu, "Riding the 'Hits' Wave: Informational Cascades in Viewership of Online Videos" (unpublished manuscript, 2008), available at www.isu.uzh.ch/enterpreneurship/workshop/fu.pdf.

[5]For many illustrations, see Terry Ann Knof, *Rumors, Race, and Riots* (New York: Transaction, 2006).

[6]Matthew J. Salganik et al., "Experimental Study of Inequality and Unpredictability in an Artificial Cultural Market," *Science* 311 (2006): 854–56.

[7]Ibid.

[8]Matthew J. Salganik et al., "Leading the Herd Astray: An Experimental Study of Self-Fulfilling Prophecies in an Artificial Cultural Market," *Social Psychology Quarterly* (forthcoming).

[9]Fabio Lorenzi-Cioldi and Alain Clèmence, "Group Processes and the Construction of Social Representations," in *Blackwell Handbook of Group Psychology: Group Processes*, edited by Michael A. Hogg and R. Scott Tindale (Oxford: Blackwell Publishing, 2011), 311, 315–17.

[10]See the overview in Solomon Asch, "Opinions and Social Pressure," in *Readings About the Social Animal*, edited by Elliott Aronson (New York: W. H. Freeman, 1995), 13.

[11]Solomon Asch, *Social Psychology* (Oxford: Oxford University Press, 1952), 453.

[12]Asch, "Opinions and Social Pressure," 13.

[13]Ibid., 16.

[14]Ibid.

[15]Aronson, *Readings About the Social Animal*, 23–24.

[16]Robert Baron and Norbert Kerr, *Group Process, Group Decision, Group Action* (Pacific Grove, Calif.: Brooks/Cole, 1992), 66.

[17]Kuran, *Private Truths, Public Lies*.

[18]Allport and Postman, *Psychology of Rumor*, 35.

[19]Reid Hastie, David Schkade, and Cass R. Sunstein, "What Really Happened in Deliberation Day", *California Law Review* 95 (2007): 915–40.

[20]Roger Brown, *Social Psychology*, 2nd ed. (New York: Free Press, 1986).

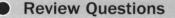

Review Questions

1. What are the various types of cascades?

2. What is "the basic dynamic behind" rumor cascades, according to Sunstein?

3. How does Sunstein draw from an article in the *New England Journal of Medicine* to reinforce the concept of rumor cascades?

4. In what way does YouTube act as an ideal example of cascade movement?

5. Cite some examples offered by Sunstein to explain how cascades can also spread and reinforce truth, thereby having a positive impact on the world.

6. What kind of problems can occur, according to Sunstein, when false rumors spark cascades?

7. What paradox arises during the group polarization process?

Discussion and Writing Suggestions

1. Patients may suffer harm when physicians allow medical cascades to influence their diagnoses and prescriptions. Drawing on your own experiences and observations, as well as on your reading, discuss other ways in which cascades can cause personal damage.

2. Cascades don't spread false rumors only; they may also spread beliefs about important social and scientific developments. In recent years, we have seen social media help spread news of democracy and help mobilize social movements. In what ways have you witnessed or read about positive information spread through a cascade?

3. Sunstein identifies three specific cascades in this selection. Consider each type—the root cause, the methods of delivery, the audience, and the impact. Which type of cascade do you believe has the greatest impact on the public at large? Explain, using specific examples and drawing upon Sunstein's text.

4. Sunstein describes an experiment conducted by Princeton sociologist Matthew Salganik, who used music sharing as a way of illustrating cascade thinking. The experiment showed the workings of a self-fulfilling prophecy through which "false perceptions of popularity produced actual popularity over time." Were you surprised by the results of this experiment? To what extent do you think that cascade thinking might have affected your own musical tastes or your assessment of particular songs—or the artists who created these songs?

5. Referencing Solomon Asch's famous experiments (see "Opinions and Social Pressure," pp. 655–659), Sunstein suggests that people conform to the views of a crowd even when they doubt the crowd's collective judgment. Why do you think the pressure to conform is so strong? On a personal level, discuss an occasion when you have been faced with a conformity cascade. What were the circumstances? Write a narrative describing how you gave into the group thinking, or stood up to it. Did you express your reservations?

6. In "Truth Is in the Ear of the Beholder," Rodriguez refers to and expands upon Sunstein's discussion of group polarization, particularly the latter's point that during the process of speaking with each other, individuals in political groups become ever more entrenched in their beliefs. Using one or more examples from your own experience, discuss how this phenomenon works, both in terms of the impact upon individuals in the group and upon the progress of the rumor itself.

MANAGING RUMORS

John Doorley and Helio Fred Garcia

We see the pattern repeatedly in the media: A rumor breaks into the news, and the embarrassed or outraged subject hires a public relations firm, releases a statement (or appears at a press conference, his pained but supportive spouse by his side), appears on a talk show, and attempts in various—and often fruitless—ways to stop the rumor in its tracks. The subject may be a business (such as a Procter & Gamble representative appearing on *Donahue*), a personality (Paul McCartney performing a concert to prove that he is, in fact, alive), a public official, or a candidate for office. Battling rumor has reached all the way to the White House. As a candidate, Barack Obama featured a "Fighting Rumors" link on his Web site, tasked with tackling rumors about his religion or his birthplace as they appeared. More recently, as the President worked toward his health care reform, White House staff launched a Web site specifically designed to address rumors about the plan.

These developments are emblematic of the concepts John Doorley and Helio Fred Garcia, authors of *Reputation Management* (2006), explore in "Understanding and Managing Rumors." Using a formula devised by rumor experts Gordon Allport and Leo Postman in the 1940s, these experts create a schedule for responding to rumor, for minimizing negative impact. The next time you see a company spokesperson clarifying a rumor on CNN, chances are he or she is following the kind of guidelines suggested by Doorley and Garcia.

The Morphing of Rumors

One of the defining elements of rumors is that they are not static. As a rumor passes from person to person, it tends to change through processes that social psychologists call leveling, sharpening and assimilation.

In the 1940s, two Harvard University psychologists, Gordon W. Allport and Leo Postman, conducted experiments on how the content of rumors changes as the rumor passes from person to person. They concluded that as a rumor travels, it tends to grow shorter, more concise and more easily told: In subsequent versions [of the rumor] more and more original details are leveled out, fewer words are used and fewer items are mentioned...As the leveling of details proceeds, the remaining details are necessarily sharpened. Sharpening refers to the selective perception, retention and reporting of a few details from the originally larger context. Although sharpening, like leveling, occurs in every series of reproductions, the same items are not always emphasized. Much depends on the constitution of the group in which the tale is transmitted. Those items will be selected for sharpening which are of particular interest to the reporter. Assimilation has to do with the powerful attractive force exerted upon the rumor by habits, interests and sentiments existing in the reader's mind. Items become sharpened or leveled to fit the leading motif of the story, and they become consistent with this motif in such a way as to make the resultant story more coherent.

Allport and Postman emphasize that while leveling, sharpening and assimilation are independent mechanisms, they function simultaneously. The result is that a story becomes more coherent and interesting, and therefore, more believable with each retelling.

•   •   •

Controlling Rumors Mathematically

Fortunately, rumors tend to follow predictable patterns, and intervention in specific ways can help an organization overcome, or even kill, a rumor.

5   Breakthrough research on rumors was conducted during World War II by Allport and Postman. Much of their work was classified, but after the war it was published, first in *Public Opinion Quarterly* in 1946 and then in their 1947 book, *The Psychology of Rumor*. One of their most significant contributions to the study of rumors was a mathematical formula that described the way a rumor works. The formula further suggests ways to control or eliminate a rumor.

The two factors that influence a rumor are its importance to the listener and its ambiguity. To control a rumor, one must either diminish the importance assigned to the rumor if true, or eliminate the ambiguity around the factual basis of the rumor, or both. Eliminating ambiguity is particularly important if the rumor is completely false. But even when the rumor has a mixture of truth and fiction, eliminating ambiguity about the fiction can control the rumor and ground it in reality. Once an unambiguous reality is established, it may be possible to reduce the importance of the information in the rumor, thereby decelerating its transmission.

The Basic Law of Rumor

Allport and Postman elaborate below on how the two factors of importance and ambiguity work together and note that there is a mathematical relationship:

> The two essential conditions of importance and ambiguity seem to be related to rumor transmission in a roughly quantitative manner. A formula for the intensity of rumor might be written as follows: $R \sim i \times a$
>
> In words, this formula means that the amount of rumor in circulation will vary with the importance of the subject to the individuals concerned (i) times the ambiguity of the evidence pertaining to the topic at issue (a). The relation between importance and ambiguity is not additive but multiplicative, for if either importance or ambiguity is zero, there is no rumor. Ambiguity alone does not sustain rumor. Nor does importance.

Because the relationship between importance and ambiguity is multiplicative, an incremental decline in either can result in a greater-than-incremental decline in the scope of the rumor.

Here's how the math works: Assume a scale of zero to 10, zero being nonexistent and 10 being certain. If both importance and ambiguity are high, say 10, the scope of the rumor will be quite strong:

$R \sim i \times a$ $R \sim 10 \times 10$ $R \sim 100$

10   In other words, when both importance and ambiguity are at their highest, the scope of the rumor will be at its highest. But reduce just one of the factors, and the scope of the rumor declines considerably. Assume that importance remains at 10 but that ambiguity can be reduced to 3.

The scope of the rumor has declined from 100 to 30, or by more than two-thirds. And because anything multiplied by zero equals zero, if either ambiguity or importance is reduced to zero, the rumor disappears.

In practical terms, this formula lets a professional communicator and a management team do several powerful things. Knowing that importance and ambiguity drive a rumor, a company can more efficiently identify what it needs to do and say. Second, knowing the formula gives clients and bosses confidence that they can influence the interpretation of events. The formula empowers management to focus communications in ways that can impact how the company is perceived. Best of all, the formula can disarm negative information, killing a rumor and preventing further damage.

Dynamics of Controlling a Rumor in the News Cycle

When applying the $R \sim i \times a$ formula, one critical element of success is how early one can influence importance and ambiguity. Corporate management often has little appreciation for the need to pre-empt rumors or for the seemingly arbitrary and somewhat confusing deadlines under which journalists work. The Allport and Postman model empowers crisis communicators and companies to disclose more information sooner, controlling the rumor and decreasing the likelihood of a negative story.

The Rule of 45 Minutes, Six Hours, Three Days and Two Weeks

At specific points in a news cycle it is possible to kill a negative story or control a partially accurate story. Miss one of these points and you will suffer reputational damage. Worse, the distance between the points, the intensity of the crisis and the potential for reputational harm grow in an almost exponential fashion as bad news spreads.

15   And while these points result from careful observation of how the news cycles and the rumor formula interact, the same orders of magnitude apply beyond the media, when progressively larger groups of people, overtime, become invested in a rumor.

The first 45 minutes: You have maximum influence on the outcome of a story in the first moments after the rumor arises. During this time, only a small number of people, and possibly only one reporter, know about a rumor or are working on a story. If you follow the $R \sim i \times a$ formula to persuade a reporter not to pursue a story in those first 45 minutes, chances are high that the story will disappear. On the other hand, if you are unable to respond within that 45-minute time frame, a number of negative things happen. First, the original reporter is likely to be on the phone trying to confirm the rumor, retelling it to sources who can pass it along to other reporters. Second, given the proliferation of all-news media, chances are good that the story will break quickly. Third, in the retelling of the rumor from the first reporter to other sources, the substance of the rumor will change. As the rumor becomes known in slightly different forms by many different people, it will become harder to find a definitive demonstration to put the rumor to rest.

Controlling the rumor now becomes less a function of persuasion—a private intervention with a single reporter—than of a public statement to influence your constituencies.

Six hours: Once a story crosses a wire service, is broadcast on television or radio, or appears on the Internet, it may still be possible to eventually control the rumor, but now it will be much more difficult. As a general rule, once a story is broadcast you can expect to have at least six hours of negative coverage.

During these six hours, more reporters come to the story and more people become aware of the rumor. Your customers, employees, suppliers, competitors, regulators and local community hear about it and begin to react.

20   If, during this part of the cycle, you consider the $R \sim i \times a$ formula as you plan your public statements, chances are high that the rumor can be controlled and the story will fade, though reputational damage may have been done.

If you are unable to control the story during this phase of the cycle, expect several days of negative news—all the while, the processes of leveling, sharpening, assimilating and snowballing are morphing the rumor into something far less manageable.

Three days: Once a story hits the daily newspapers, you can expect it to be alive for several days. The day the story appears, there is likely to be television and radio commentary about the story, as well as gossip among your customers, employees and competitors, with all the attendant distortion.

During this period it is still possible to use the $R \sim i \times a$ formula to your advantage. You will have suffered several days of reputational damage and will have seen a wide range of people exposed to the negative rumor. If you cannot control the story during these three days, expect at least two weeks of negative coverage.

Two weeks: After the daily newspapers have had their run, there is still a further news cycle that includes weekly and bimonthly magazines, industry trade publications, and the Sunday-morning talk shows. During this period you can still use the $R \sim i \times a$ formula to kill the rumor. You will have suffered several weeks of negative coverage and reputational harm. If you are unable to control the story in this time frame, expect continuous coverage. A company is unlikely to recover quickly from this kind of scrutiny.

25   All of this suggests that it is a fundamental mistake for corporations to make decisions about crisis communications on their own timelines. They need to recognize that however arbitrary and at times irrational media deadlines may seem, companies can control their destinies better if they can kill rumors as early as possible in a news cycle.

Failure to recognize the power of both the $R \sim i \times a$ formula and the rule of 45 minutes, six hours, three days and two weeks puts the company at the mercy of the rumor mill, gossipmongers and the irrational-seeming dynamics of the news media. Successfully employing them can help prevent reputational damage and keep the company focused on its own agenda.

 Review Questions

1. According to Allport and Postman, what three processes occur as a rumor develops? Describe what is involved in these processes.

2. What two factors most influence a rumor? Express the relationship between these factors as a formula.

3. Indicate the time frames Doorley and Garcia establish as the benchmarks in rumor management.

● **Discussion and Writing Suggestions**

1. Doorley and Garcia establish clear time-frame benchmarks for dealing with rumor. Consider some of the previous readings in this chapter about particular rumors. To what extent did the subjects attempt to meet these time frames? How did their success—or failure—in meeting these deadlines affect the spread and effectiveness of the rumors?

2. The writers indicate that the longer we wait to address a rumor, the more difficult it becomes to control. Can you think of any public cases (either recent or historical) where swift response failed to help? What about cases where delayed responses did, in fact, settle the matter? How were those situations handled?

3. Consider a recent rumor from any realm of public interest (politics, entertainment, business, etc.). How did the target address the rumor? To what extent was the chosen strategy effective? How closely did the subject use Doorley and Garcia's rumor-control framework?

4. Put yourself in the shoes of a public figure (business executive, celebrity, public official, etc.) at the heart of a rumor. Identify yourself and describe the rumor. Using the four time frames established in this selection, create a plan of action for each level.

5. Doorley and Garcia discuss Allport and Postman's concepts of leveling, sharpening, and assimilation. Select any of the rumors discussed in this chapter—or another rumor with which you are familiar—and explain how any or all of these processes may apply.

THE RUMOR

John Updike

We've become familiar with the public face of rumor: the instantaneous surge of an allegation across the Internet and onto YouTube, the press releases on company letterhead, the politician's talk show appearances. But what happens behind closed doors—when, for example, a rumor ricochets inside the home, affecting both a couple and their circle of friends and colleagues? In the following story, John Updike traces the effects of gossip on a marriage. Updike (1932–2009) was a "Renaissance man" among American writers of the second half of the twentieth century: novelist, short-story writer, poet, essayist, literary critic, art critic. A two-time Pulitzer Prize winner, he is best known for his "Rabbit" novels—*Rabbit, Run* (1960), *Rabbit Redux* (1971), *Rabbit is Rich* (1981), and *Rabbit at Rest* (1990)—which trace the life of Harry C. ("Rabbit") Angstrom, former high school basketball star, car salesman, and indifferent husband and father, as he struggles to make sense of—and break free from—his middle class, suburban life. Like Norman Rockwell earlier in this chapter, Updike is best known for his portrayal of "average" Americans and mainstream life. In this story, originally published by *Esquire* in June 1991, he presents a vivid portrait of a marriage. While initially dismissing as falsehood a rumor that comes to engulf their life, the couple is nonetheless quietly enthralled by it.

Go to: Google or Bing
Search terms: "updike rumor"

● **Discussion and Writing Suggestions**

1. Even as she dismisses the rumors, Sharon is surprised by her friends' certainty about its truth. Do you think she has doubts? Why? Is she bothered—or excited—by the rumor?

2. The rumor in this story is "factually untrue." During the course of the story, however, Frank begins to wonder whether it might be at least partially true. He even wonders whether it would be a good thing for the rumor to be *perceived* as true by his wife and his colleagues. Can you think of other rumors, whether from your own life or from the public stage, that may have been false but have been accepted or even embraced by the subjects?

3. How do Frank's feelings toward his mother and father, as well as his feelings about the kind of men he admires, lend support to his feelings about the rumor?

4. Most of the previous selections in this chapter have focused on rumor functioning on a societal scale. This story, however, deals with the personal life of the Whittiers. How do some of the theories explored in the chapter (by Knapp, Sunstein, and DiFonzo) apply here? Consider specific moments in the story: How do the phone calls link up with Sunstein's "cascades"? Which of Knapp's categories does the rumor fit (from the perspective of the friends, as well as Frank himself)?

5. Frank entertains the notion that there may be value, or at least allure, in the rumor's spread. Create a rumor about yourself that you would like to see circulate among your friends and community. What is it? Why would you want people to believe this rumor?

6. Do you like Frank and Sharon Whittier? Why or why not? Do their thoughts and actions seem plausible? Explain.

7. This story is centered on married life, not on a larger societal context like most of the other readings in this chapter. That said, the implications of "The Rumor" might also be applied to larger arenas. What other situations come to mind, whether from other chapter selections or from your own experience, where a company, a politician, or a celebrity indulges in or even encourages a rumor instead of correcting it?

◯ **SYNTHESIS ACTIVITIES**

1. Write a synthesis that explains *why* and *how* rumors spread. In your discussion, refer to the theories of Knapp, Sunstein, and DiFonzo. Use any of the example rumors treated in this chapter (as well as the stolen-kidney case in Chapter 6, "Analysis," pp. 192–198) to support your discussion.

2. Select one of the rumors treated at length in this chapter. Briefly analyze this rumor from the perspective of the theoretical approaches of Knapp (three categories of rumor; qualities of good rumors), Rodriguez ("biased assimilation"), Sunstein (cascades and group polarization), and DiFonzo (dealing with ambiguity and threat). Then, in an argument synthesis, explain which theoretical approach most compellingly reveals the whys and wherefores of the rumor you have selected.

3. Some rumors are created in the spirit of fun and are relatively harmless in their effects—for example, those New York alligators that led off our introduction or the "Paul is dead" rumor described by Alan Glenn. Other rumors arise from malicious intent and often devastate their targets. In an argument synthesis, rank several types of rumors on a scale of benevolence/malevolence, according to the motives of those who create and spread them. Draw upon some of the case studies treated in this chapter, as well as the "missing kidney" rumor. Don't hesitate to bring into the discussion rumors based on your own personal knowledge and experience. Also use some of the theoretical pieces such as those of Rodriguez, Knapp, Sunstein, and DiFonzo to help account for and justify your rankings.

4. Select any three of the cases of rumor from this chapter or from Chapter 6, "Analysis" (the missing kidney). Compare and contrast these rumors, taking account of their origins (and the rationales behind their creation), their spread, and their impact. Try to select cases that appear similar on the surface but may have subtle or even major differences below the surface. Alternately, choose cases that appear quite different but that, according to your analysis, are essentially similar in nature. A key part of your comparison-contrast synthesis will be answering the *So what?* question. Having worked the comparison, what observations can you make about the three rumors you have discussed—and, provisionally (based on your small sample size), about rumor itself?

5. In his article on McCain's presidential bid of 2000, Davis writes of the campaign manager's feeling that to respond to a rumor would only give it weight. Considering everything you have read in this chapter—not just that particular piece—to what extent do you agree with this cautious approach? Should a rumor be addressed at its first sign, or should it be allowed to run its course, however long that takes? What factors should bear most on how best to counteract damaging rumors? Use examples from the readings, as well as the ideas of theorists such as Sunstein and DiFonzo to support your argument.

6. In 2011, President Obama and his aides attempted to quell the long-standing rumor that he was not born in the United States. Attempting to put the claim to rest, he eventually released the full-length version of his birth certificate. Even in the face of this hard evidence, the rumor persisted, and public figures such as Donald Trump and Rick Perry suggested that the evidence presented by the new document was insufficient or questionable. What does the refusal to accept concrete evidence suggest about human nature and political affiliation? In drafting your response, an argument synthesis, consider the points made by at least two of the following: Rodriguez, Knapp, Sunstein.

7. Conventional wisdom suggests that our digital lifestyle (think e-mail, Facebook, Twitter, computers, smartphones, and so on) has accelerated the spread of rumor. To what extent do you find this belief true? In the digital age, can attempts to quell rumors move at the same speed as the rumors themselves? Use examples from the selections in this chapter, along with cases of rumor known to you personally, to develop an argument in response to this question. It might be helpful to consider a rumor from the pre-Internet era, as well as one from the present day.

8. Knapp and DiFonzo explain that rumors are often symptoms of our hopes and fears. What hopes and fears are reflected by one of the following rumors: (1) the genetically modified chicken, (2) the "satanic logo," or (3) "Paul is dead"? Model your response on the analysis paper in Chapter 6, which applied Knapp's categories to the "missing kidney" rumor.

9. Imagine that you work for a public relations firm, hired by someone targeted by a rumor. This might be a rumor similar to one covered in this chapter or another you have come across outside of class. Create an argument synthesis that takes the form of an action plan for your client. (A model for such an action plan might be the one offered by Doorley and Garcia.)

10. You work for a book publisher that is preparing a new edition of Sunstein's *On Rumors*. For this latest edition, the author wants to update the examples offered, to demonstrate various types of "cascades." Considering the readings from this chapter (and elsewhere), write a memo to Sunstein offering current examples for his discussions of "informational cascades," "conformity cascades," and "group polarization." In your memo, be sure to explain how each example fulfills Sunstein's criteria.

11. After the "Paul is dead" rumor spread, as documented by Glenn, the Beatles seemed to have fun playing along with the story. In John Updike's "The Rumor," we see an untrue rumor spark a sense of excitement in its subject and a surprising determination to keep the rumor alive. What is it about a rumor that, occasionally, might be alluring to its subject? Drawing upon some of the particular cases covered in this chapter, or cases known to you personally, develop your response into an argument synthesis.

RESEARCH ACTIVITIES

1. Throughout his discussion, DiFonzo refers to the numerous rumors that grew out of the terrorist attacks of September 11, 2001. As he explains, some of these rumors were developed as a coping mechanism, and some grew out of newly discovered anxieties and fears about the identity and the nature of our enemies. Research another catastrophic event in American history, and identify some of the rumors that were created in its wake. Knapp offers a glimpse into the rumors circulating around World War II. What about the Vietnam War? The Kennedy assassination? The Martin Luther King assassination? Explore

some of the rumors associated with these events (or another such national calamity) and the ways in which theories by Knapp, DiFonzo, or Sunstein help account for them.

2. While some rumors eventually go national and even global, others affect a more limited group of people: employees of a particular company, customers of local establishments, soldiers in a particular military unit, students at a particular school. In the fall of 2011, Smith College was overrun with an explosive culinary news item: All campus dining services were going vegan. This announcement sparked Twitter feeds, campus protests, and even coverage from the leading vegan lifestyle magazine. But the news was a hoax, fueled by the power of rumor. Research two or three other hoaxes of limited impact, and discuss their spread and their impact (try searching for "local rumors" on Snopes.com or the archives of local newspapers). How and why did these rumors spread so fast and alarm so many? Draw upon Sunstein's concept of "cascades" to support your discussion, as well as DiFonzo's ideas about how rumors help us make sense of an uncertain world. What does public willingness to accept these hoaxes as true say about human nature?

3. Some rumors, such as "the missing kidney" (see Chapter 6), have entered popular culture as "urban legends." Urban legends (which often have nothing to do with cities) are defined by DiFonzo as "narratives about strange, funny, or horrible events that could have happened, the details of which change to fit particular locales or time periods, and which frequently contain a moral lesson." There's even a horror film named *Urban Legend*. Picture yourself as a film executive or screenwriter looking for an idea to develop into a movie. Research other urban legends (start with Snopes.com), and write a pitch for a movie based on one that appeals to you. Why do you think audiences will connect to this story? What features about it will engage viewers? What does it have in common with other rumors?

4. In an op-ed for the *Washington Post* (November 17, 2011), Paul Farhi asserts that "the e-mail rumor mill is run by conservatives." While he discusses political rumors associated with both Republicans and Democrats, Farhi claims that "when it comes to generating and sustaining specious and shocking stories, there's no contest. The majority of the junk comes from the right, aimed at the left." Research some of the more notorious rumors that have been a feature of recent politics. Describe and characterize them. To what extent are their agendas and political purposes clear? Based on your research, do you agree with Farhi? Develop your argument using Knapp's scheme. What do your findings suggest about political discourse in both parties?

5. Samuel Freedman draws parallels between the anti-Muslim sentiment in the 2008 election and anti-Catholicism in the 1930s, showing us that political rumormongering has a long, dishonorable history. The targets may change, but for centuries the rumor mill has operated the same way. Research two or three politically connected rumors from earlier historical periods. (Again, a good starting point is Snopes.com, along with works by the authors in this

chapter, such as DiFonzo and Sunstein, and the bibliographies or endnotes in their articles and books.) Discuss the rumors themselves and explain how they affected the political landscape at the time. Consider the causes, agendas, and hopes and fears expressed by the rumors.

6. If you were to receive an e-mail sharing a story about a "missing kidney," you might assume that the alleged events in the story represented a new phenomenon. As Robert Dingwall explains, however (see the model analysis in Chapter 6), the kidney rumor stretches back many years, undergoing transformations in different countries and at different periods of its development. During this transformative process, particularly potent rumors go through what rumor scholars Gordon Allport and Leo Postman describe as "leveling, sharpening, and assimilation" (as discussed by Doorley and Garcia in "Managing Rumor").

   Research and discuss another fear-driven rumor. (Once again, a good starting point is Snopes.com. Then learn more about your selected rumor from additional sources). How far back does the rumor go in the public consciousness? How has it changed over the years? How has it—to use Allport and Postman's terms—leveled, sharpened, and assimilated?

7. The Chris Dussold case involved charges of sexual harassment. Research the sexual harassment guidelines in place at various colleges and universities. Based on these guidelines, what do you conclude is the appropriate way to handle allegations based on rumors of sexual harassment? Locate other cases similar to Dussold's, taking account of both their similarities and differences.

8. Robert H. Knapp's theory of rumor, included in this chapter, was written over half a century ago, a fact that accounts for his choice of examples relating to World War II. Imagine that you work for a publisher looking to release an updated version of his article, with content footnotes providing examples more likely to be familiar to contemporary readers. Locate new examples of rumor (not treated in this chapter) that illustrate each of Knapp's three categories. In your memo to the publisher, identify each rumor, categorize it, and explain how it fulfills the criteria for that type of rumor.

9. Research the new crop of "reputation defender" services available to those who find their online identities under siege. (Start by googling terms like "managing rumor.") Based on your findings, discuss these services and explain how they work and why they may or may not be effective. To what extent do these services follow an approach similar to the one recommended by Doorley and Garcia?

Chapter 12

The Pursuit of Happiness

Enshrined in the Declaration of Independence are the unalienable rights to "Life, Liberty, and the pursuit of Happiness." The founders believed that a nation should guarantee its citizens' physical safety and freedom—preconditions for the right to life and liberty. As for happiness, they understood that while a government can create the necessary conditions—including the right to vote and to worship freely—ultimately it falls to individuals to *be* happy.

Which, of course, begs one of humankind's oldest, most vexing questions: *What is happiness?* Any attempt to define the word draws on the teachings of our major religious and ethical systems. In the Western tradition, the attempt raises familiar questions and points us toward well-known thinkers, including these:

- Is happiness found in living a virtuous life (Aristotle)?
- Is happiness found in wrestling with life (Marcus Aurelius)?
- Is happiness found not in this world but the next (St. Augustine)?
- Is happiness whatever provides the greatest good for the greatest number (Bentham/Mill)
- Is happiness possible, given the tradeoffs we make to enjoy the benefits of civilization (Freud)?
- Can happiness be found by searching for it (Camus)?

Humankind has debated definitions of happiness for thousands of years, and still a single, acceptable definition eludes us. Perhaps, as some philosophers suggest, the question *What is happiness?* is flawed. Perhaps the answer is ultimately trivial, as Samuel Beckett implies in his absurdist masterpiece *Waiting for Godot*:

> VLADIMIR: Say you are [happy], even if it's not true.
>
> ESTRAGON: What am I to say?
>
> VLADIMIR: Say, I am happy.
>
> ESTRAGON: I am happy.
>
> VLADIMIR: So am I.

ESTRAGON: So am I.

VLADIMIR: We are happy.

ESTRAGON: We are happy. (*Silence.*) What do we do now, now that we are happy?*

Beckett wrote in the mid-twentieth century. Sixty years later, we still seek answers—no surprise. But what *is* surprising is that today answers are increasingly couched in the language of science. One recent study shows that people who reported being happy throughout the day, over a five-year span, were 35% less likely to die over that span than those who reported being unhappy. Multiple studies have reached a similar conclusion: Happiness, which researchers term *subjective well-being*, is a positive, contributing factor to long, healthy lives.

Claims such as this one differ in kind from ones that have occupied history's philosophers, theologians, and artists—for the social scientists study happiness by conducting experiments. Calling themselves *positive psychologists* (and building on the pioneering work of Abraham Maslow [1908–1970] in self-actualization and peak experiences), they hope to complement psychology's traditional focus on mental *dis*order by investigating conditions that "lead to well-being…[and] positive individuals." Their efforts to understand happiness—and some rather heated challenges to their efforts—provide the focus of this chapter.

As data concerning the correlation between happiness and longevity emerged, two lines of criticism followed: the first, a criticism not of positive psychology, per se, but of the get-happy-quick industry that has skimmed off legitimate research findings and promised gullible consumers easy formulas for the Happy Life. These programs inevitably fail, claim the critics; worse, they mislead the vulnerable into thinking that *if* they read self-help books and attend expensive seminars and *if* they still are feeling sad, then they must somehow be defective. Not true—and the psychologists actually conducting the studies make no claims about quickly transforming gloomy faces to smiley ones.

A second line of criticism directed at happiness studies challenges both its methods and assumptions. Among the questions you will find debated in this chapter:

- Can happiness be measured? Are such measurements reliable and replicable—and, if not, how can we call positive psychology a science?

- To what extent does positive psychology assume that states such as sadness and anger are harmful? Might these states, unpleasant though they are, play a beneficial role in human development?

- Given ongoing human suffering, is the desire to be extremely happy defensible?

- In what ways does an emphasis on positive psychology risk turning ordinary sadness into a psychiatric disorder for which pills are the proffered cure?

The literature on happiness is vast, and we have limited the focus of this chapter to three elements: the emerging science of happiness, critiques of this science, and selections on happiness from the humanist (that is, *non*scientific)

---

*From *Waiting for Godot,* London: Faber and Faber, 1956.

tradition. The chapter opens with two readings that set a context for what follows. Philosopher Lynne McFall's "Pig Happiness?" presents a playful yet serious run of questions on happiness, a teaser to get your mind primed for engagement. In the "Pursuit of Happiness," cultural critic Mark Kingwell (also a philosopher) claims that while the question "What is Happiness?" never leads to definitive answers, the question remains an important one that is worth pursuing.

Four readings on positive psychology follow. "A Balanced Psychology and a Full Life" by Martin Seligman, one of the founders of the field, sets out an agenda for the new discipline. Next, journalist Jennifer Senior, writing for *New York* magazine, reviews some of the important findings of positive psychology while at the same time exposing potential contradictions. "Flow"—as in "being in the flow" or "zone" while engaged in an activity—describes the key contribution of Mihaly Csikszentmihalyi, another founder of the discipline. Elizabeth Dunn, Daniel Gilbert, and Tim Wilson follow with "If Money Doesn't Make You Happy, Then You Probably Aren't Spending It Right." Though the nominal topic of their paper is spending money, the article serves as a fascinating, entertaining overview of key findings in positive psychology.

Critics then challenge the methods and assumptions of positive psychology. In "Happy Like God," philosopher Simon Critchley takes a swipe at the effort to measure happiness scientifically (while meditating on the philosophy of Rousseau). Richard Schoch follows with a stinging "Critique of Positive Psychology." Sharon Begley then reports on a growing backlash to happiness studies in "Happiness: Enough Already."

As a reminder that social scientists are not the only ones investigating happiness these days, we conclude with three readings from the humanistic tradition. Former New Hampshire poet laureate Jane Kenyon compares happiness to an unknown uncle who suddenly appears in one's life. Human geographer Yi-Fu Tuan illustrates varieties of happy experience with rich anecdotes. And, in an excerpt from *Zen and the Art of Motorcycle Maintenance*, a humanistic view of "flow," Robert Pirsig writes about motorcycle repair in unexpected ways that transcend engine parts and point to profound contentment.

The authors in this chapter are both approachable and provocative. They offer new terms and fresh ideas through which you can reflect on your own happiness—past, present, and future.

PIG HAPPINESS?

Lynne McFall

Aristotle wrote that happiness follows from living a virtuous life. Two thousand years later, dramatist and storyteller William Saroyan claimed that the "greatest happiness you can have is knowing that you do not necessarily require happiness." What happiness might be, no one can say for certain; but the question has occupied thinkers and writers for millennia. Philosopher Lynne McFall, emerita associate professor of philosophy at Syracuse University, takes a playful yet serious run at understanding happiness in this introduction to our chapter. Her questions will amuse and confound you. The passage appeared first in *Happiness* (1989), the first volume in *Studies in Moral Philosophy*.

It is better to be a human being dissatisfied than a pig satisfied; better
to be Socrates dissatisfied than a fool satisfied.

John Stuart Mill
Utilitarianism

Is it? And if it is, which is happier?

Let's call a person, P, *pig-happy*, just in case *P* is satisfied as a consequence of
the belief that *P*'s life is going the way *P* wants it to go. [But suppose] *P*'s life is
one many would judge unfit for persons: *P*'s desires, values, beliefs, capacities,
or circumstances are radically defective in some way. The question I want to
raise is: Is someone who is pig-happy really happy[? Is] pig-happiness enough
for human happiness? More positively, by what standard should we judge that a
person is leading or has led a happy life?

Pig-happiness takes different forms. There are many ways in which a person's life might be seen as defective, but the following five examples illustrate
different categories of defect which, in conjunction with satisfaction, present us
with conflicting intuitions on the question of happiness.

The *"happy" idiot*. Consider the severely retarded person, one who lacks many
of the capacities we regard as characteristically human (e.g., the capacity for self-
reflection), and assume she is content for the most part. Is this a happy life?

5   *The incompetent bottlecap collector*. Say someone's only end in life is to amass
the largest collection of bottlecaps in the world. He's considered the matter thoroughly, looked into other options, and this is the one goal that inspires him. He
thinks he has an impressive collection of bottlecaps (actually it's pretty paltry),
and so is satisfied with his life. Is he happy?

The *deluded fool*. Suppose a woman's ideal is the love of a good man. If the
man she loves despises her and is despicable, is she happy so long as she is de-
ceived? If she dies believing in his undying affection and moral perfection, was
hers a happy life? Is the fool's paradise paradise, or at least happiness?

The *successful immoralist*. Take any conventionally evil person, e.g., Hitler,
Mata Hari, or Idi Amin, and suppose he or she found this life rewarding. Is this
"true" happiness?

The *impossible idealist*. Imagine a woman with a noble ideal: she desires universal peace, perfect justice, and happiness for all. Given that this ideal is unreal-
izable, could her life be a happy one?

Our intuitions in these cases conflict. On the one hand, we may be inclined
to say of such persons that they are not (or could not be) *truly* happy. On the
other hand, there is a fairly clear sense in which they are ("At least the poor
thing is happy"; "He's happy collecting bottlecaps"; "Ignorance is bliss";
"Hitler doesn't deserve to be happy"; "She's happy with her dreams, let her
keep them").

10   But this is not the only problem in sorting out the confusions in our talk
about happiness: the explanations of our conflicting intuitions may themselves
conflict. If we are inclined to call the retarded, the crazy, the deluded, the immoral, and the too-idealistic happy, to say that they may lead happy lives, is this
because no "objective" standard for appraising persons' lives is defensible (Who

are we to say?), because happiness is only one good among others, or simply because this is *one* of the ways we use the word—as a report on someone's state of mind? If we refuse to say that such people can lead happy lives, is this because we do not think they will *remain* happy in such circumstances, because happiness is the greatest good and these are clearly defective lives, because they do not meet *our* standards [for happiness], fail [at happiness], even by their own [standards], or have [no standards]?

● Review Questions

1. Briefly summarize the five categories of ways in which a person's life may be viewed as "defective."

2. In ¶ 2, McFall asks if "pig-happiness" is "enough" for human happiness. What does "enough" mean, in the context of the epigraph by John Stuart Mill?

3. In ¶ 10, the most challenging of the selection, McFall lays out key criteria by which we might judge—or refuse to judge—a person's life as happy. Outline the logic of this paragraph. How is it structured?

● Discussion and Writing Suggestions

1. Philosophers pose difficult, sometimes uncomfortable questions. Of the questions that McFall poses about human defects that bear on a discussion of happiness, which unsettles you most—and why?

2. After discussing each of the ways a person's life may be defective, McFall asks: Is this person, P, happy? Choose one of these defects and answer McFall's question. Explain your answer.

3. John Stuart Mill, quoted by McFall, has no qualms in judging the relative value of types of happiness. Do you? Are you comfortable stating unequivocally that one person's happiness is superior to another's? Why? In your answer, discuss the standards you would use to make the judgment—or the reasons why you might distrust such standards.

4. Using McFall's questions on happiness as an example, discuss what it means to be "seriously playful" in the philosophical sense.

5. Philosophical discussion about the world differs from we might call "ordinary" discussion—the kind of talk that might transpire between friends discussing, say, happiness. Assume that you know *nothing* about the discipline of philosophy. Reread this selection and attempt to define the topics philosophers study and the methods they use to investigate these topics.

IN PURSUIT OF HAPPINESS

Mark Kingwell

Mark Kingwell is an award-winning social critic, essayist, and professor of philosophy at the University of Toronto. In the following excerpt from his book *In Pursuit of Happiness: Better Living From Plato to Prozac* (1998), Kingwell calls the quest for a universal definition of happiness "a mug's game"—that is, a game no one can win. Still, he argues, the question of what happiness is remains important; and so the mug's game continues, as vital to us in the twenty-first century as it was to philosophers in the first. Kingwell's essays have appeared in the *New York Times* and *Harper's*. His numerous books in include *Rites of Way: The Politics and Poetics of Public Space* (2009), *Nearest Thing to Heaven* (2006), and *The World We Want* (2000).

The desire to understand happiness, to get hold of it, is one that is common in our culture, central to our many daily judgments about life, love, work, politics, and play. We do not always confront happiness head on, as it were, but it is nonetheless implicit in our decisions and undertakings, the ordering principle or end of our human projects. But if the desire to understand happiness is common, there is every kind of disagreement about what constitutes a good answer. Everyone thinks they know something about what happiness is; very few people manage to convince anyone else that they are right. Indeed, happiness seems to be one of those "essentially contestable concepts" that philosophers love to unleash upon an unsuspecting world. You know the sort of thing: justice, goodness, virtue, beauty, love. Thinkers since Plato have thought they could say what those things were, sometimes in great detail, but the fact that we are still asking questions about them demonstrates that no single answer is good enough.

Just so with happiness. Often we are inclined . . . to *demand a definition* of it. But, paradoxically, all offered definitions are waved aside like so many feeble tennis lobs, reducing the question itself to a mere ploy, a rhetorical device to confound the speaker. . . . Nor is that sort of thing much improvement on the kinds of uselessly precise definitions you are likely to find in the dictionary. The *New English Dictionary*, for example, offers the famously unhelpful "state of pleasurable content of mind, which results from success of the attainment of what is considered good." Samuel Johnson neatly evaded the notorious problem in his own *Dictionary* by defining "happiness" as felicity and "felicity" as happiness.

The first thing to realize about happiness, I think, is that trying to provide a one-sentence definition of it is always a mug's game. (One critic of such vacuous definitions noted they mostly worked by "in effect defining happiness as wanting what you want and getting what you get and hoping that the two will coincide."[1]) There are many more questions than answers in this particular quarter of the philosophical field, and we must learn to accept that. No sentence beginning "Happiness is . . ." is likely to do us much good.

There is also a related and larger problem, as many a philosopher of happiness has discovered over the centuries. It is difficult to say anything intelligent about a subject that is at once so apparently clear and yet so resistant to explication. There is something about the implicit profundity of the issue of happiness, in other words, combined with the nearly inevitable banality of most sentiments given to it, that makes of happiness-talk a din of misfiring attempts at eloquence. Getting a grip on happiness is therefore far from easy. Indeed, for many, the concept is the paragon of ineffability, something about which nothing meaningful can be said or written. "Happiness writes white," said Henri de Montherlant of the banality of contentment when it came to literature.

5   John Stuart Mill fingered an even more troubling problem. "Ask yourself whether you are happy," he wrote in his 1873 *Autobiography,* "and you cease to be so." The search for happiness is one of the chief sources of unhappiness," agreed twentieth-century essayist Eric Hoffer, while novelist Nathaniel Hawthorne famously compared happiness to a butterfly which, if pursued, always eludes your grasp, but which, if you sit quietly, may just land upon you.[2] The contemporary critic John Ralston Saul argues that notions of happiness have suffered such a decline from their ancient philosophical robustness that they now speak of mere material comfort or simply "pursuit of personal pleasure or an obscure sense of inner contentment"; accordingly, he suggests dropping the world from our lexicon altogether. "As economic and social conditions have gradually sunk, happiness, with its twisted meaning at the ethical and legal centre of our society, has seemed increasingly lugubrious and out of place," he writes. "In a more practical world, there would be a formal process for retiring a world from active use until it finds itself again."[3]

On this view, asking about happiness can only result in unhapiness or confusion, and therefore the project must succumb to its own self-contradiction. The question "What is happiness?" is judged by these thinkers to be a bad one, logically ill formed, misleading, or maybe just pointless. Pursuing it can only bring vexation and misery, the opposite of what we desire. (I don't know about Hoffer or Hawthorne, but Mill wasn't a very happy type: a celebrated child prodigy who learned Greek at three and had read all of Plato at seven, he suffered a nervous breakdown at nineteen.)

Those who would turn their backs on the pursuit of a definition for happiness would even seem to have scientific authority on their side. In 1996, several genetic and behavioral studies appeared in scientific journals that offered evidence to support the conclusion that one's achievable degree of happiness is genetically determined. You are either happy or you're not, and there is nothing that talking or writing about it is going to do to change that; indeed, nothing in your own life plans or aspirations and accomplishments will alter a built-in, hard-wired capacity for contentment. Try as you might, you cannot overcome the fact that, when it comes to happiness, biology is destiny.

Edward and Carol Diener, psychologists at the University of Illinois, reported in *Psychological Science* magazine that their study of surveys from more than forty countries demonstrated that money, education, and family background were less important in determining one's level of happiness than was basic genetic predisposition. David Lykken, a behavior geneticist at the University of Minnesota, concurred in his report on a survey of more than 1,300 sets of twins. "People who have to go to work in overalls on the bus can feel as happy as people who wear suits and ties and drive a Mercedes," Lykken said (as if that should be surprising).[4]

The geneticists were far from confident in predicting a solution to the problem of happiness, but they nevertheless demonstrated a high degree of scientific confidence—a confidence shared by those who had reviewed the studies, including Dr. Jerome Kagan, a well-known developmental psychologist at Harvard University. "It's clear that T. S. Eliot was by nature dour, and Jay Leno is congenitally upbeat," Kagan told the *New York Times*. "But we're far from filling in the biological blanks. [Lykken's study] is a brilliant idea—it's well worth pursuing." The studies, and others that demonstrated a correlation between dopamine levels in the brain and expressions of subjective satisfaction, were widely reported in articles in publications as diverse as scientific journals and glossy in-flight magazines, often with jaunty titles like "How Your Genes Put a Smile on Your Face" or (rather illogically, considering the evidence) the old imperative "Get Happy!"[5]

10   Hawthorne's brand of common sense and these new genetic-predisposition theories, both of which seek to ground the happiness inquiry before it is launched, sound good—but only until you recognize their essential conservatism. If followed honestly and to their logical conclusion, such views would mark the end of rational human life, suspending us in intellectual nullity. So, while there is some measure of truth in the observation that questioning happiness will result in a certain kind of unhappiness, Mill, Hawthorne, Hoffer, and the rest of the nay-sayers are unnecessarily and preemptively pessimistic. So are the geneticists, who condemn us to a prison of biological limitation without ever raising the deeper question of what they, or we, mean by happiness—a failure that says more about the current popularity of this kind of reductive genetic "explanation" of human behavior than it does about the real limits of human life and experience. The happiness question is a good one, indeed a very good one. It is both answerable and important. . . . We can speak meaningfully about happiness, in short, and we can do so with intelligence and with reasonable prospect of results—not perhaps the kind of results that some happy-merchants promise you, but results nonetheless.

Notes

[1] Howard Mumford Jones, *The Pursuit of Happiness* (Cambridge: Harvard University Press, 1953), p. 6, in a chapter on what he calls "The Glittering Generality," borrowing the phrase from Rufus Choate's wry 1856 comment on the natural law provisions of the U.S. Constitution. Copyright © 1957 by the President and Fellows of Harvard College. Reprinted by permission of Harvard University Press. This and all further quotations used by permission.

[2] Eric Hoffer, *The Passionate State of Mind and Other Aphorisms* (New York: Harper & Row, 1955). See also Paul Nowell Elbin, *The Paradox of Happiness* (New York: Hawthorn Books, 1975).

[3] John Ralston Saul, *The Doubter's Companion: A Dictionary of Aggressive Common Sense* (Toronto: Viking, 1994), pp. 153–54.

[4] Quoted in Sanjida O'Connell, "How Your Genes Put a Smile on Your Face," *Toronto Star* (1 September 1996), pp. Al and A4.

[5] Rae Corelli, "Get Happy!" *Maclean's* (16 September 1996). Also Daniel Goleman, "Forget Money: Nothing Can Buy Happiness," *USAir* (November 1996), pp. 70–90 (inter.); and Goleman, "Happiness Is... Genetic, Researchers Say," *New York Times* (15 July 1996), reprinted in *Globe and Mail* (16 July 1996).

● Review Questions

1. In what way is happiness an "essentially contestable concept"?

2. "Happiness writes white," suggests one commentator. What does this mean?

3. Compare and contrast Mill's, Hawthorne's, and Saul's comments on happiness in ¶ 5.

4. What do studies of genetics add to the discussion of happiness?

5. Kingwell disagrees with the findings of geneticists and the opinions of Mill, Hawthorne, and Hoffer. Why?

● Discussion and Writing Suggestions

1. If, as Kingwell writes, "no single answer [to the question of happiness] is good enough" and "[n]o sentence beginning 'Happiness is . . .' is likely to do us much good," what accounts for humankind's endless attempts to define the term?

2. Reread ¶ 5 and the lines quoted from Hawthorne and Saul. How might the search for happiness be self-defeating? Why would those who search for happiness fail to grasp it or, worse, turn unhappy *because* of the search?

3. Reread ¶ 5. Use Kingwell's references to John Stuart Mill, Nathaniel Hawthorne, or Eric Hoffer as a principle with which to analyze an experience of your own. What do you discover?

4. Consider Kingwell's quotation of John Stuart Mill: "Ask yourself whether you are happy, and you cease to be so." In your experience, is Mill correct?

5. Kingwell rescues the possibility of an inquiry into happiness from the "conservatism" of the geneticists and Hawthorne, concluding that "[w]e can speak meaningfully about happiness." Based on your experience, do you think it useful to discuss happiness? Is it better not to inquire and simply embrace the experience of happiness when it comes? Explain.

A BALANCED PSYCHOLOGY AND A FULL LIFE

Martin E. P. Seligman, Acacia C. Parks, and Tracy Steen

Philosophers, theologians, and artists have long pondered happiness, unable to agree on what the word might mean. For thousands of years, they have based their observations and arguments on appeals to logic, personal reflection, and speculation. Recently, however, social scientists have entered the discussion with a new investigative tool—experiments designed to clarify behaviors that "help people become lastingly happier." Martin Seligman is one of the founders of this new inquiry, called positive psychology.

Zellerbach Family Professor of Psychology and director of the Positive Psychology Center at the University of Pennsylvania and past president of the American Psychological Association, Seligman has won dozens of awards and is widely credited for his work on positive psychology. Seligman's research on happiness has been supported by numerous foundations and institutions, among them the National Institute of Mental Health, the National Science Foundation, the Department of Education, and the MacArthur Foundation. He has authored and coauthored hundreds of articles, including this introduction to positive psychology in the *Philosophical Transactions of the Royal Society* (London, 2004). His many books, translated into multiple languages, include *Authentic Happiness: Using the New Positive Psychology to Realize Your Potential for Lasting Fulfillment* (2002) and *Flourish: A Visionary New Understanding of Happiness and Well-Being* (2011). Coauthor Acacia C. Parks teaches psychology and conducts research on happiness at Hiram College in Ohio. Tracy Steen grounds her work as a personal coach on the principles of positive psychology.

1. A Balanced Psychology

American psychology before World War II had three objectives: the first was to cure mental illness, the second was to make relatively untroubled people happier, and the third was to study genius and high talent. All but the first fell by the wayside after the war. Researchers turned to the study of mental disorders because that was where the funding was. The biggest grants were coming from the newly founded National Institute of Mental Health, whose purpose was to support research on mental illness, not mental health. At the same time, practitioners suddenly became able to earn a good living treating mental illness as a result of the Veterans Administration Act of 1946. Psychopathology became a primary focus of psychology in America because it made sense at that time. Many very distressed people were left in the wake of World War II, and the high incidence of mental disorders had become a pressing and immediate problem.

A wealth of excellent research resulted from this chain of events. In 1946, there were no effective treatments for any of the psychological disorders, whereas now we can cure two and treat another 12 via psychotherapy and/ or pharmacology (Seligman 1993). Furthermore, the intensive study of psychopathology has given rise to methods of classifying the mental disorders (*International classification of diseases,* 9th edition, and *Diagnostic and statistical manual of mental disorders*, 4th edition), and these methods have allowed clinical psychologists to produce diagnoses with acceptable accuracy, and to reliably measure symptoms that were once quite difficult to pinpoint. After 50 years and 30 billion dollars of research, psychologists and psychiatrists can boast that we are now able to make troubled people less miserable, and that is surely a significant scientific accomplishment.

The downside of this accomplishment is that a 50-year focus on disease and pathology has taken its toll on society and on science. In our efforts to fix the worst problems that people face, we have forgotten about the rest of our mission as psychologists. Approximately 30% of people in the USA suffer from a severe mental disorder at one time or another (Kessler *et al.* 1994) and we have done an excellent job of helping that 30%. It is time now to turn to the other 70%. Although these people may not be experiencing severe pathology, there is good evidence to indicate that the absence of maladies does not constitute happiness (Diener & Lucas 2000). Even if we were asymptotically successful at removing depression, anxiety and anger, that would not result in happiness. For we believe 'happiness' is a condition over and above the absence of unhappiness.

That said, we know very little about how to improve the lives of the people whose days are largely free of overt mental dysfunction but are bereft of pleasure, engagement and meaning. We do not know much about what makes a person optimistic, kind, giving, content, engaged, purposive or brilliant. To address this, the first author proposed, during his term as President of the American Psychological Association in 1998, that psychology be just as concerned with what is right with people as it is with what is wrong. As a supplement to the vast research on the disorders and their treatment, we suggest that there should be an equally thorough study of strengths and virtues, and that we should work towards developing interventions that can help people become lastingly happier.

2. What Is Happiness?

5 Towards this goal, our first order of business is to determine what it is we were trying to increase. What is happiness? More words have been written about this great philosophical question than perhaps any other. Science can no more presume to answer this question than other classic philosophical questions, such as 'what is the meaning of life'? But science can illuminate components of happiness and investigate empirically what builds those components. With that said, a review of the literature led us to identify three constituents of happiness: (i) pleasure (or positive emotion); (ii) engagement; and (iii) meaning. We define these three routes to happiness in the paragraphs that follow.

The first route to greater happiness is hedonic, increasing positive emotion. When people refer in casual conversation to being happy, they are often referring to this route. Within limits, we can increase our positive emotion about the past (e.g. by cultivating gratitude and forgiveness), our positive emotion about the present (e.g. by savouring and mindfulness) and our positive emotion about the future (e.g. by building hope and optimism). However, unlike the other two routes to happiness, the route relying on positive emotions has clear limits. Positive affectivity is heritable, and we speculate that, for important evolutionary reasons, our emotions fluctuate within a genetically determined range. It is possible (and worthwhile) to increase the amount of positive emotion in our lives, but we can boost our hedonics only so high. Further, when people fluctuate within a relatively 'down' range of positive emotion, but live in a society like the USA that promotes an upbeat disposition, they can feel discouraged and even defective. Fortunately, positive emotion is not the sole determinant of happiness, and our most liberating goal is to offer a broader conception of happiness than mere hedonics (Seligman 2002).

A second route to happiness involves the pursuit of 'gratification'. The key characteristic of a gratification is that it engages us fully. It absorbs us. Individuals may find gratification in participating in a great conversation, fixing a bike, reading a good book, teaching a child, playing the guitar or accomplishing a difficult task at work. We can take shortcuts to pleasures (e.g. eating ice cream, masturbating, having a massage or using drugs), but no shortcuts exist to gratification. We must involve ourselves fully, and the pursuit of gratifications requires us to draw on character strengths such as creativity, social intelligence, sense of humour, perseverance, and an appreciation of beauty and excellence.

Although gratifications are activities that may be enjoyable, they are not necessarily accompanied by positive emotions. We may say afterwards that the concert was 'fun', but what we mean is that during it, we were one with music, undistracted by thought or emotion. Indeed, the pursuit of a gratification may be, at times, unpleasant. Consider, for example, the gratification that comes from training for an endurance event such as a marathon. At any given point during the gruelling event, a runner may be discouraged or exhausted or even in physical pain; however, they may describe the overall experience as intensely gratifying.

Finding flow in gratifications need not involve anything larger than the self. Although the pursuit of gratifications involves deploying our strengths, a third route to happiness comes from using these strengths to belong to and in the service of something larger than ourselves; something such as knowledge, goodness, family, community, politics, justice or a higher spiritual power. The third route gives life meaning. It satisfies a longing for purpose in life and is the antidote to a 'fidgeting until we die' syndrome.

10   Peterson *et al.* (2005) develop reliable measures for all three routes to happiness and demonstrate that people differ in their tendency to rely on one rather than another. We call a tendency to pursue happiness by boosting positive emotion, 'the pleasant life'; the tendency to pursue happiness via the gratifications, 'the good life'; and the tendency to pursue happiness via using our strengths towards something larger than ourselves, 'the meaningful life'. A person who uses all three routes to happiness leads the 'full life', and recent empirical evidence suggests that those who lead the full life have much the greater life satisfaction (Peterson *et al.* 2005).

3. Interventions to Nurture Happiness?

We have designed and tested interventions to nurture each of the three routes to happiness (pleasure, gratification and meaning). Positive emotions are increased and the pleasant life is promoted by exercises that increase gratitude, that increase savouring, that build optimism and that challenge discouraging beliefs about the past. Interventions that increase the good life identify participants' signature strengths and use them more often and in creative new ways. Meaningful life interventions aim toward participants' identifying and connecting with something larger than themselves by using their signature strengths. Some of these interventions can be found at *www.authentichappiness.org.*

We are in the process of testing the efficacy of these interventions by randomly assigning individuals to interventions or to a placebo control, and measuring their level of happiness and depression before the intervention, immediately after it, one week later, one month later, and three months later. Early results demonstrate that (i) it is possible to boost individuals' levels of happiness, and (ii) these effects do not fade immediately after the intervention (as is the case with the placebo). The 'good things in life' exercise provides an example of an efficacious intervention. Designed to increase positive emotion about the past, this exercise requires individuals to record, every day for a week, three good things that happened to them each day and why those good things occurred. After completing this exercise, individuals were happier and less depressed at the three-month follow-up (Seligman & Steen 2005). Note that these research designs are exactly parallel to the random-assignment, placebo-controlled experiments that are the bulwark of the medication and psychotherapy outcome literature, except that the intervention is targeted to increase happiness rather than just to decrease suffering.

Our research places us among a growing number of positive psychologists who are committed to understanding and cultivating those factors that nurture human flourishing, and we are encouraged that the field of positive psychology seems to be thriving as well. Researchers who were studying positive strengths, emotions and institutions long before the term 'positive psychology' was coined are receiving increased recognition and support for their work, while young researchers worldwide can apply for research and intellectual support via positive psychology research awards and conferences.

One reason for optimism that the field of positive psychology may make substantial gains in the next several years is that it does not start from square one. Rather, it draws on the proven methodologies that advanced the understanding and treatment of the mental illnesses. When it is no longer necessary to make distinctions between 'positive psychology' and 'psychology as usual', the field as a whole will be more representative of the human experience. Our goal is an integrated, balanced field that integrates research on positive states and traits with research on suffering and pathology. We are committed to a psychology that concerns itself with repairing weakness as well as nurturing strengths, a psychology that concerns itself with remedying deficits as well as promoting excellence, and a psychology that concerns itself with reducing that which diminishes life as well as building that which makes life worth living. We are committed to a balanced psychology.

References

Diener, E. & Lucas, R. E. 2000 Subjective emotional wellbeing. In *Handbook of emotions* (ed. M. Lewis & J. M. Haviland-Jones), pp. 325–337. New York: Guilford.

Kessler, R. C., McGonagle, K. A., Zhao, S., Nelson, C. B., Hughes, M., Eshelman, S., Wittchen, H. & Kendler, K. S. 1994 Lifetime and 12-month prevalence of DSM-III-R psychiatric disorders in the United States. *Arch. Gen. Psychiatry* 51, 8–19.

Peterson, C., Park, N. & Seligman, M.E.P. 2005 Approaches to happiness: the full life versus the empty life. Unpublished manuscript, University of Michigan. *Am. Psychol.* (Submitted.)

Seligman, M. 1993 *What you can change and what you can't.* New York: Knopf.

Seligman, M. 2002 *Authentic happiness.* New York: Free Press.

Seligman, M. E. P. & Steen, T. 2005 Making people happier: a randomized controlled study of exercises that build positive emotion, engagement, and meaning. *Am. Psychol.* (Submitted.)

 ## Review Questions

1. What is the broadest goal of positive psychology?

2. Instead of defining the word "happiness," which Seligman, Parks, and Steen recognize as a notoriously difficult, if not impossible, task, the authors explore what three "components of happiness"?

3. How do the results of positive psychology differ from the results of meditations on happiness by philosophers, theologians, and artists? (Reread ¶ 5 in developing your response; when writing, be sure you understand and discuss the word *empirical.*)

4. What are the limits of positive emotion, and why are these limits not necessarily an obstacle to a person's overall happiness?

5. How do the authors define the pleasant life? The good life? The meaningful life? The full life?

Discussion and Writing Suggestions

1. Illustrate the authors' three components of happiness with accounts of brief experiences from your life (or the life of someone you know personally). Write one-paragraph narratives focused on each component of happiness.

2. In ¶ 7, the authors write that "no shortcuts exist to gratification." What do the authors mean? Given their definition of gratification, do you find their statement true to your experience?

3. In ¶ 12, the authors report that routes to happiness are teachable; that is, you can learn to be happy by practicing specific activities such as "'the good things in life' exercise." What do you think of this suggestion? Could you learn to be happier? Before answering, consider this: Seligman, Parks, and Steen are not reporting stories when they make their claim about the teachability of happiness. They say they are reporting scientific *evidence*: measurable, objective evidence that could be reproduced in other studies. In their view, this evidence is no less valid or authoritative than evidence from experiments in medicine or physics.

4. "There is good evidence," write the authors, "to indicate that the absence of maladies does not constitute happiness." Reflect on your own experiences or those of others you know well. Use this insight to analyze that experience.

SOME DARK THOUGHTS ON HAPPINESS

Jennifer Senior

In the following selection, Jennifer Senior recounts the founding of positive psychology, probes the extent to which happiness can be taught, and highlights basic findings—including one that surprised her: The "young are not happier than the elderly." With a journalist's sure instinct, Senior also investigates the more unsettling implications of happiness studies, the so-called "dark thoughts" of her title. Senior has written dozens of articles for *New York* magazine from 2004 through 2011. This selection first appeared on July 9, 2006.

They say you can't really assign a number to happiness, but mine, it turns out, is 2.88. That's not as bad as it sounds. I was being graded on a scale of 1 to 5. My score was below average for my age, education level, gender, and occupation, sure, but at exactly the 50 percent mark for my Zip Code. Liking my job probably helped, being an atheist did not, and neither did my own brain chemistry, which, in spite of my best efforts to improve it, remains more acidic than I'd like. Unhappy thoughts can find surprisingly little resistance up there, as if they've found some wild river to run along, while everything else piles up along the banks.

The test I took was something called the Authentic Happiness Inventory, and the man who designed it, Chris Peterson, is one of the first people I meet at the Positive Psychology Center at the University of Pennsylvania. Unlike many who study happiness for a living, he seems to embody it, though he tells me that's a recent development. He offers me an impromptu tour of the place (walls of salmon and plum and turquoise; tables piled high with complimentary granola bars), then wanders toward his office, absently hugging an orange-juice bottle to his stomach as he drifts, having graciously offered to check, at my request, which Zip Codes are the happiest and the most miserable in his 350,000-person database. At the end of the day, I check in with him.

The happiest, he reports, is Branson, Missouri's.

"But please appreciate—and this is a formal disclaimer—that these are not representative respondents," he says. "These are just people who logged on to our Website and took our happiness measure." In other words, hundreds of mental patients from Chicago could have decided to take the test, while only fifteen Buddhists in Baja did the same, which would result in a very skewed perception of the well-being of Chicagoans and Bajans. I ask how many people from Branson took the test. "A small number," he warns. "I think it was two or three. And the other happiest Zip Codes are also represented by a very small number of respondents. Nonetheless, I think the results are kind of interesting. Missoula, Montana. Rural Minnesota. Rural Indiana. Rural Alabama. Savannah, Georgia.

The Outer Banks. Is there a theme here? There's a theme here. It seems to run through the Bible Belt and go straight up north. And if you want to know the absolutely most miserable Zip Code—and this is based on a very large number of people—it seems to start with 101."

5   That's the prefix assigned to many of the office buildings in midtown Manhattan. "Staten Island is also miserable," he adds.

So what does this say about New York? I ask.

"I don't know," he says. "Maybe that if you make it there, you can make it anywhere, but you won't be happy doing it."

This past spring, the *Boston Globe* reported that the single most popular course at Harvard was about positive psychology, or the study of well-being. Its immense appeal took everyone by surprise. Just one year before, the instructor, Tal Ben-Shahar, offered the course for the first time, and although it was certainly a hit, with 380 students enrolled, no one could have imagined that the following year the number would have jumped to 855.

There's a theme here, too. Back in the mid-1840s, a Scot by the irresistible name of Samuel Smiles was invited to lecture before a class in "mutual improvement" in the north of England—a class, he later noted in a book, that also began with two or three young men but grew so large it took over a former cholera hospital. That book is called *Self-Help*, published in 1859. It is considered by many to be the first of its genre. Today, it's still in print, and has even come up in Ben-Shahar's Harvard class. He has tremendous respect for it.

10   "For many years," says Ben-Shahar, "the people who were writing about happiness were the self-help gurus. It had a bad rap. It was all 'five easy steps,' rather than dignity and hard work. What I'm trying to do in my class is to regain respectability for the concept of self-help. It's a great thing, if you think about it literally. It's what this country was built on."

The pursuit of happiness was indeed at the heart of America's conception. But the study of happiness—as a science, with random-assignment, placebo-controlled testing—is a far more recent phenomenon. And right now, it's booming. At least two basic positive-psychology textbooks are being published this fall, one written by Peterson, the other by a University of Kansas professor named Shane Lopez, whose publisher estimates that roughly 150 colleges will be offering some kind of positive-psychology course next year. Since 2000, the University of Erasmus at Rotterdam has been publishing the *Journal of Happiness Studies* (whose editorial board is represented in curious disproportion by Californians and Germans). At Barnes & Noble, there are three excellent books about happiness now sitting on the shelves: the divinely readable *Stumbling on Happiness*, by Harvard professor Daniel Gilbert, about how hopeless we are at predicting our moods; *The Happiness Hypothesis*, by University of Virginia professor Jonathan Haidt, about the ways that ancient wisdom about flourishing intersects with the modern; and *Happiness: A History*, an intellectually elegant work by historian Darrin McMahon, which is exactly as it sounds, but darker.

Ellen Langer, a professor at Harvard, ventures that the explosive interest in positive psychology is, like so many cultural curiosities involving self-obsession, a boomer phenomenon. "There's a feeling of, 'I'm not going off to some nursing home,'" she says. (And she should know: During the seventies, she found that the more control nursing-home patients had—over watering their plants, for example—the longer they were apt to live.) And there are undoubtedly other factors at work. Universities, for example, have become more sensitive today to the intense pressures on their students (at Harvard, the chief of mental-health services recently came out with a book called *The College of the Overwhelmed*). Economics has also started to take the discipline of psychology seriously again— Malcolm Gladwell's books are a sure testimony to this—and the psychology of positivity and productivity were a perfect fit for the ethos of the bubble years. (Recently, I've come to wonder whether positive psychology isn't also the perfect discipline for the era of George Bush, the decider, the man who remains shinily optimistic no matter how many red lights are glowing on his dashboard.)

But the happiness-studies boom may have an even simpler explanation: In 1998, an enterprising, highly established, and press-savvy psychologist from the University of Pennsylvania, Martin Seligman, convened a group of his peers in Mexico, hoping to help shift the emphasis of psychology away from pathology and toward functionality, resilience, and well-being. He coined the term *positive psychology* to describe the scientific study of these things—the study of happiness, in short—and because he was president of the American Psychological Association, he was able to shore up prestige and grant money for its pursuit.

"What's unique about Seligman is that he's not only a great psychologist but a great organizer, a leader," says Ben-Shahar, who's also got a book about happiness in the [works.] After five minutes on the phone with Ben-Shahar, I can already sense that he's a warm, intelligent man and that the plants in his house grow faster than those in my own. But convincing people that positive psychology is not merely the cryptoscience of sunniness—or its featherbrained pursuit—is one of the most persistent challenges he and some of his colleagues, particularly those closely associated with Seligman, face. No longer should we think of ourselves as tin cans of sexual chaos, as echoing caverns of repressed wishes and violent desires; rather, we should think of ourselves as the shining sum of our strengths and virtues, forceful, masters of our fates. All that nattering we've been doing in therapists' armchairs, trying to know and exorcise our darker selves—it's been misguided. It's our better selves we want to know.

15   Peterson, the inventor of the Authentic Happiness Inventory, is clearly aware of how easily these ideas can be trivialized. The afternoon I visit him in Philadelphia, he lingers in his doorway before saying good-bye, telling me he has one final request.

"Harvey Ball," he says, "was a Massachusetts graphic designer who was commissioned to do an ad for an insurance company. He was paid a whopping $45 for it. Neither he nor the company thought to trademark it. It belongs to the world."

Interesting, I tell him, though I'm uncertain where this is going.

"He created the yellow smiley face," he says. "Please don't use it to illustrate your story."

To wade into the literature on happiness is to wade into a world of control groups and volunteers, questionnaires and ratings scales, cases of the fortunate and cases of the medically extreme. From Seligman's *Authentic Happiness*, I learn about a perverse form of facial paralysis called Moebius syndrome, which makes it impossible for its sufferers to smile; from *Stumbling on Happiness*, I learn about something called alexithymia, whose literal meaning is "absence of words to describe emotional states." From many sources, too many to count, I read about a survey of nuns, which showed that those who expressed faith and optimism in their journals were apt to live far longer than those who didn't. And from Barry Schwartz's *The Paradox of Choice: Why More Is Less*, I come across the most compelling, persuasive, and revolting study of them all: Two separate groups of men, when given colonoscopies, reported less discomfort if the instrument sat in place for a few seconds after the procedure, even though it prolonged the exam. The reason is that the final moment involved less pain. Apparently, we define and remember our experiences by their highs, lows, and how they end.

20   Other findings from the emerging field of happiness studies: Married people are happier than those who are not, while people who believe in God are happier than those who don't. On the former point, Seligman's book cites a 35,000-person poll from the National Opinion Research Center, in which 40 percent of married Americans described themselves as "very happy," compared with just 24 percent of unmarried Americans who said the same. (Of course, he allows, happy people may be the ones who get married to begin with.) On the latter point, he cites a study showing that the faithful are less likely to abuse drugs, commit crimes, or to kill themselves. The act of worshipping builds community—itself another source of happiness—and belief systems provide structure, meaning, and the promise of relief from pain in this life.

Smarter people aren't any happier, but those who drink in moderation are. Attractive people are slightly happier than unattractive people. Men aren't happier than women, though women have more highs and more lows. Surprisingly, the young are not happier than the elderly; in fact, it's the other way round, with older people reporting slightly higher levels of life satisfaction and fewer dark days.

Money doesn't buy happiness—or even upgrade despair, as the playwright Richard Greenberg once wrote—once our basic needs are met. In one well-known survey, Ed Diener of the University of Illinois determined that those on the Forbes 100 list in 1995 were only slightly happier than the American public as a whole; in an even more famous study, in 1978, a group of researchers determined that 22 lottery winners were no happier than a control group (leading one of the authors, Philip Brickman, to coin the scarily precise phrase "hedonic treadmill," the unending hunger for the next acquisition).

As a general rule, human beings adapt quickly to their circumstances because all of us have natural hedonic "set points," to which our bodies are likely to return, like our weight. This is true whether our experiences are marvelous—like winning the lottery—or shattering. Not only did Brickman and his colleagues look at lottery winners but also at 29 people who'd recently become paraplegic or quadriplegic. It turned out the victims of these accidents reported no more unhappy moments than a control group. (This exceptionally counterintuitive finding, however, has not been replicated in a published paper—and subsequent studies have certainly shown that the loss of a spouse or a child can dramatically depress our happiness thermostats, as can sustained unemployment.)

There's surprisingly little in the happiness literature about raising children, which in and of itself is odd. Odder still is that most of it suggests children don't make parents any happier. Gilbert wrote only three scant pages about this in *Stumbling on Happiness*. But he says he's been asked about it on his book tour more than almost anything else. "It really violates our intuition," he says. "Yet every bit of data says children are an extreme source of negative affect, a mild source of negative affect, or none at all. It's hard to find a study where there's one net positive." (One possible explanation, he says, is that children are sources of transcendent moments, and those highs are what people remember.)

25   Paradoxes abound. Nebraskans think that Californians are happier, but a study done by the Princeton Nobel Prize winner Daniel Kahneman suggests they aren't. One might expect the homeless of Fresno to be happier than the slum-dwellers of Calcutta, but another study suggests they aren't (probably because Indians don't live in social isolation, as our homeless do). In a 2003 poll by the Roper organization, the Danes, the Americans, and the Australians rated themselves the happiest (Australian buoyancy, such an enduring mystery—they're like an entire nation of people who can't relate to Chekhov). Other polls have found the Swiss happiest, and the Canadians always do well (hardly a surprise to anyone who knows Canadians). Compared with their purchasing power, Latin and South Americans are much happier than one would imagine, and the Japanese are less so, though being happy in Japan might not be a value per se. And every survey agrees on one point: That the people of Eastern European nations—Lithuania, Estonia, Romania, Latvia, Belarus, and Bulgaria—consistently rank themselves the least happy, with Russia coming in especially low. (This might explain my own desolate moods. *You can take the girl out of Vladivostok, but you can't take Vladivostok out of the girl.*) Yet people in the happiest countries are more likely to kill themselves.

And no matter where they live, human beings are terrible predictors of what will make them happy. If *Stumbling on Happiness* tells us anything, it's this. "Imagination," says Gilbert, "is the poor man's wormhole." Our imagination has an odd knack for Photoshopping things in and airbrushing things out, which is why we think that getting back together with our exes is a good idea; it also tends to mistake our present feelings for future ones, which is why, when we decide to marry the right person, we find it unthinkable we'll ever be tempted to sleep with anyone else. At the same time, we forget that our imagination has a miraculous ability to rationalize its way out of grim situations—which is why we're more likely to take a positive view of things we did than things we didn't (so go ahead and ask that woman to marry you), more comfortable with decisions we can't reverse than ones we can, and more apt to make the best of a terrible situation than a merely annoying one.

Because our imaginations are limited, we can be disappointed by the things we covet most. But it also means—and this is the gorgeous part—that we're much more likely to cope well with situations we never thought we'd be able to survive. Perhaps the most profound study Gilbert cites is about the disabled, showing that those who are permanently injured say they'd be willing to pay far less to undo their injuries than able-bodied people say they'd pay to prevent them. It's possible, as Gilbert notes, that they may even find some silver lining in their experiences, as when the late Christopher Reeve memorably said, "I didn't appreciate others nearly as much as I do now."

Like every religion, movement, and interesting idea, positive psychology has its own creation myth. One day, says Seligman, his daughter Nikki took him to task for scolding her while he was working in his garden, when it was clear she'd done little to annoy him. She reminded him that she'd given up whining on her 5th birthday, and it was the hardest thing she'd ever done; he, on the other hand, remained a grouch. That was the day, Seligman says, that he realized two things: First, he had to change, and second, raising children didn't just mean correcting their failings but isolating and nurturing their strengths.

It makes sense that a man like Seligman would come to this conclusion. He has tremendous faith in the power of human agency. During our interview, he describes himself as a "launcher of ships" and an "intellectual entrepreneur." He knows lots of people, moves around in high places; in the course of our conversation, he refers to Jeffrey Epstein, a money manager and close friend of Bill Clinton's, as "Jeffrey," and talks about going swimming with Michael Crichton. His desk at work has two computer screens to maximize his efficiency, and at home, he has four. When we get to the subject of Methodism, he waxes rhapsodic: "I think what Methodism did is take this terrifically important premise, which is that we can participate in our own grace. That we can do things to be better people."

30   But is change something that can come about by a simple act of will? Agency requires start-up energy, something depressives aren't necessarily going to have if they've spent their time rattling around a bell jar. I mention this to him.

"I have to fight to get up in the morning, too."

I ask when he wakes up.

"Between six and nine. If I could, I'd stay in bed until nine, but usually I'm up at six or six-thirty."

Seligman's an interesting standard-bearer for his cause. He's thoroughly engaged with the world, a huge success, and an extremely generous and creative conversationalist. But managing anger seems like a key part of managing depression, and so does maintaining a healthy sense of proportion about one's own needs. At some point, I ask whether his kids from his first marriage feel robbed, because he had his epiphany about changing his own behavior during his second marriage. Did he ever write them notes of apology or explanation?...

35   There are about eight seconds of silence. "No, we've never really talked about it. Huh. That's a good idea. There's no reason not to..."

Well, there's no reason to do it, either, I say, if it's not something you feel particularly guilty about...

"Well, my first wife and I made this agreement that we would not bad-mouth each other, which she violated from day one, but I never did. And a real conversation with my kids about it would involve some bad-mouthing of her."

Why would a conversation about your regrets as a father involve bad-mouthing your ex-wife?

"I don't have regrets," he says. "I would choose to do the same thing. That was the time of my life in which I needed to do my work, the foundation, and I would do it again. And it just happened they were victims of that. No, it'd be a conversation much more about what the marriage and the child-rearing was like and how we felt about each other."

40   Even if you don't have regrets, you can feel bad, I say.

"Yes. I feel bad. But I would do it the same way. I was married to my work, and I should have been married to my work."

A launcher of ships.

•   •   •

Philip Brickman, the man who did the famous lottery study, was also a launcher of ships—or at least a launcher of careers, a mentor to many. In his work, he focused a lot on happiness and what it took to achieve it. He was creative, collegial, a nurturer; his obituary mentions that one of his favorite topics of discussion was what constituted "the perfect day." On May 13, 1982, when he was 38 years old, he climbed to the roof of the tallest building in Ann Arbor and jumped. His colleagues were stunned. There's an untold distance between knowing happiness and knowing about it. And sometimes, to our blinking incomprehension, that distance can only be measured in the space between this life and the next.

•   •   •

[C]an happiness be taught? Literature based on twin studies seems to suggest that roughly 50 percent of our affect is determined by genetics. If you're like me, a pessimist, that seems like a depressing lot. Optimists, of course, would argue that 50 percent is a lot of room to play with, and that through a combination of acts of will and shifts in fortune, our happiness levels can change substantially. (In fact, happiness researchers frequently use the equation $H = S + C + V$, or happiness equals our genetic set point plus our circumstances plus what we voluntarily change—a tad too reminiscent, for my taste, of a certain "Far Side" cartoon: *Einstein discovers time actually is money.*)

45   Seligman is most interested in V. And because he's a self-identified depressive, or perhaps because he's a philosopher, his idea of happiness is much more comprehensive than positive emotion. By engaging and cultivating our strengths, he says, and by deploying our virtues, we can lead a fulfilling, meaningful life—a notion not unlike Aristotle's, who defined happiness as "an activity of the soul that expresses virtue." He makes the critical distinction between pleasures, which make us feel good, and gratifications, which, oddly, may not involve positive emotions at all, but rather the blunting of them. Eating a Mars Bar is a pleasure; doing something that engages or enhances our strengths is a gratification, whether it's swimming, welding, or listening to a friend in need. Optimally, when we're in a state of high gratification, we're experiencing what Seligman's colleague, Mihaly Csikszentmihalyi (pronounced "cheeks sent me

high"), calls flow—a state of total absorption, when time seems to stop and the self deserts us completely.

• • •

"There's no credible evidence that dispositional optimism is changeable," says Julie Norem, a Wellesley professor and author of *The Positive Power of Negative Thinking*. Norem is one of the more outspoken critics of the positive-psychology movement. "And the research shows that it's dispositional optimism that makes your life better," she continues. "So if it's not clear you can change this kind of disposition, it's not especially useful to tell people about it."

Norem is a researcher. One of her most interesting studies involved giving anagrams to solve to both optimists and pessimists, first listening to Mozart, then listening to a dirge. The pessimists did better when they were listening to the dirge. "I've come to think of them as the French," she says. She has also given them a name: "defensive pessimists."

Another very vivid critic of the positive-psychology movement is Barbara Held, author of *Stop Smiling, Start Kvetching*. She's more of a culture critic. She detects a certain high-handed moralism in Seligman's work—a presumption that happiness is itself virtuous. "Can Seligman's claim that virtuous action produces well-being be tested scientifically?" she asked during a 2003 positive-psychology conference, at which both she and Norem were asked to speak. Unlike Harvey Ball, who forgot to trademark the yellow smiley face, Held trademarked the yellow smiley face with a slash running through it. She made Seligman wear a T-shirt with it throughout her talk.

Until extremely recently, happiness wasn't even a value, much less an inalienable right. Instead, it was something one got to experience only in death, after leading a virtuous, and often self-denying, life. As McMahon points out in *Happiness: A History*, the words for happiness in both ancient Greek—eudaimonia—and every Indo-European language include, at the root, a cognate for "luck." In English, it's *happ*, or *chance*—as in *happenstance, haphazard, perhaps*. The implication is that being happy means being lucky. And luck is not something we can entirely will.

50 "Happiness is fine as a side effect," says Adam Phillips, the British psychoanalyst and lay philosopher whose latest work, *Going Sane*, examines functionality and well-being, but from a much more literary and ruminative perspective. "It's something you may or may not acquire, in terms of luck. But I think it's a cruel demand. It may even be a covert form of sadism. Everyone feels themselves prone to feelings and desires and thoughts that disturb them. And we're being persuaded that by acts of choice, we can dispense with these thoughts. It's a version of fundamentalism."

Unlike Seligman, Phillips declares happiness "the most conformist of moral aims." "For me," he continues, "there's a simple test here. Read a really good book on positive psychology, and read a great European novel. And the difference is evident in one thing—the complexity and subtlety of the moral and emotional life of the characters in the European novel are incomparable. Read a positive-psychology book, and what would a happy person look like? He'd look like a Moonie. He'd be empty of idiosyncrasy and the difficult passions.

"It seems to me that if you were to take a rather stringent line here," concludes Phillips, "then anyone who could maintain a state of happiness, given the state of the world, is living in a delusion."

Funny he should mention this: One of the most interesting bits of American research to surface—repeatedly—in books about happiness is a study that shows depressives are far more likely to be realists, while happy people are more likely to walk around in a mild state of delusion. The study itself was fairly simple: A group of undergraduates was given varying degrees of control over turning on a green light. Some members of the group had perfect control; others had none—the light went on and off of its own accord. The depressives accurately predicted, in each instance, whether they were in control of the situation or not. The non-depressives, on the other hand, thought they had control about 35 percent of the time over the situation in which they were, in fact, 100 percent helpless.

To me, this study more or less explains our current president [George W. Bush]—sunny and optimistic and full of faith, certainly, but not quite able to see the world as it is. After I read it, I couldn't help but think that a different man, a slightly more pessimistic man, may have been less inclined to believe that Iraq could be conquered, subdued, and rebuilt as a flourishing democracy with just 150,000 troops.

55   I mention this to Seligman. He declines to discuss Bush specifically, but says that he and his colleagues have analyzed political speeches before and discovered that although more optimistic candidates are likely to win presidential elections, it was the presidents who gave the most pessimistic inaugural speeches who went down in history as being great. "You have to be optimistic enough to get voters to vote for you," he says, "but you have to be pessimistic enough to do serious, great stuff."

At this moment, it doesn't occur to me to stop Seligman and ask him to further explain this observation. But later, as I listen to our discussion on tape, the implication seems clear: Even the director of the Positive Psychology Center associates pessimism with seriousness and greatness. He sounds as divided about the question as his critics. It's a conundrum, certainly. A psychoanalyst might even call him conflicted.

● Review Questions

1. What is the "hedonic set point"? the "hedonic treadmill"?

2. Cite four findings from happiness studies that you find particularly intriguing.

3. Senior reports that "human beings are terrible predictors of what will make them happy." How so? And why is this significant?

4. What distinction does Martin Seligman make between pleasure and gratification?

5. In ¶s 28–56, Senior explores what in her title she refers to as "Dark Thoughts on Happiness." Summarize these dark thoughts.

● Discussion and Writing Suggestions

1. Studies show that lottery winners are not as happy as nonwinners imagine, nor are those who lose the use of their limbs as unhappy as fully abled people imagine. Are you surprised? Explain your answer.

2. Consider applying the happiness equation $H = S + C + V$ to your own life. What do imagine your genetic set point (S) to be? Are you fundamentally an optimist? A pessimist? Do you find any need to change your life's circumstances (C) in order to increase happiness? Could you make voluntary changes (V) in how you spend time or money to improve your happiness? Having worked through this exercise, do you find it a useful tool to boost your happiness?

3. In her interview with Martin Seligman (see ¶s 28–42), Senior asks about his feelings concerning his first wife and the children of that marriage. She concludes this section with a one-phrase paragraph: "A launcher of ships." What comment is she making with this phrase? What is your response?

4. Reread ¶ 43, on the life—and death—of Philip Brickman. Senior writes: "There's an untold distance between knowing happiness and knowing about it." Comment on this distance and your response to learning of Brickman's suicide.

5. Adam Phillips writes: "anyone who could maintain a state of happiness, given the state of the world, is living in a delusion." Your response? To what degree is individual happiness tied to "the state of the world"?

6. Senior concludes her interview of Seligman by drawing out of him a fascinating observation: "you have to be pessimistic enough to do serious, great stuff." That is, Seligman, a founder of happiness studies, "associates pessimism with seriousness and greatness." What does he mean? Do you agree?

FINDING FLOW

Mihaly Csikszentmihalyi

As a child growing up in an Italian prison camp during the late 1930s and early 1940s, Mihaly Csikszentmihalyi (pronounced, as Jennifer Senior helpfully suggests, as "cheeks sent me high") watched many adults become "empty shells" when the world war upended the comfortable routines of their lives. Yet some people, he observed, maintained their dignity and values in the face of extreme hardship. When the war ended, Csikszentmihalyi immigrated to the United States to learn why. Winner of numerous awards and honorary degrees, he is best known for his theory of "flow," which he explains in the following excerpt from *Flow: The Psychology of Engagement with Everyday Life* (1997). Csikszentmihalyi is C. S. and D. J. Davidson Professor of Psychology and management director of Quality of Life Research Center at the Claremont Graduate University. Along with Martin Seligman, Csikszentmihalyi is credited with founding positive psychology. He has written hundreds of articles and nineteen books, one of which was translated into twenty-five languages.

If we really want to live, we'd better start at once to try;
If we don't, it doesn't matter, but we'd better start to die.

—W. H. Auden

The lines by Auden reproduced above compress precisely what this book is about. The choice is simple: between now and the inevitable end of our days, we can choose either to live or to die. Biological life is an automatic process, as long as we take care of the needs of the body. But to live in the sense the poet means it is by no means something that will happen by itself. In fact everything conspires against it: if we don't take charge of its direction, our life will be controlled by the outside to serve the purpose of some other agency. Biologically programmed instincts will use it to replicate the genetic material we carry; the culture will make sure that we use it to propagate its values and institutions; and other people will try to take as much of our energy as possible to further their own agenda—all of this without regard to how any of this will affect us. We cannot expect anyone to help us live; we must discover how to do it by ourselves.

So what does "to live" mean in this context? Obviously, it doesn't refer simply to biological survival. It must mean to live in fullness, without waste of time and potential, expressing one's uniqueness, yet participating intimately in the complexity of the cosmos. This book will explore ways of living in this manner, relying as much as possible on findings in contemporary psychology and my own research, as well as on the wisdom of the past, in whatever form it was recorded.

I will reopen the question of "What is a good life?" in a very modest fashion. Instead of dealing in prophecies and mysteries I will try to stay as close to reasonable evidence as possible, focusing on the mundane, the everyday events that we typically encounter throughout a normal day.

A concrete example may illustrate best what I mean by leading a good life. Years ago my students and I studied a factory where railroad cars were assembled. The main workplace was a huge, dirty hangar where one could hardly hear a word because of the constant noise. Most of the welders who worked there hated their jobs, and were constantly watching the clock in anticipation of quitting time. As soon as they were out of the factory they hurried to the neighborhood saloons, or took a drive across the state line for more lively action.

5   Except for one of them. The exception was Joe, a barely literate man in his early sixties, who had trained himself to understand and to fix every piece of equipment in the factory, from cranes to computer monitors. He loved to take on machinery that didn't work, figure out what was wrong with it, and set it right again. At home, he and his wife built a large rock garden on two empty lots next to their house, and in it he built misty fountains that made rainbows—even at night. The hundred or so welders who worked at the same plant respected Joe, even though they couldn't quite make him out. They asked his help whenever there was any problem. Many claimed that without Joe the factory might just as well close.

Throughout the years I have met many CEOs of major companies, powerful politicians, and several dozen Nobel Prize-winners—eminent people who in many ways led excellent lives, but none that was better than Joe's. What makes a life like his serene, useful, and worth living?

•   •   •

In everyday life, it is rare for the different contents of experience to be in synchrony with each other. At work my attention might be focused, because the boss gave me a job to do that requires intense thinking. But this particular job is not one I ordinarily would want to do, so I am not very motivated intrinsically. At the same time, I am distracted by feelings of anxiety about my teenage son's erratic behavior. So while part of my mind is concentrated on the task,. I am not completely involved in it. It is not that my mind is in total chaos, but there is quite a bit of entropy in my consciousness—thoughts, emotions, and intentions come into focus and then disappear, producing contrary impulses, and pulling my attention in different directions. Or, to consider another example, I may enjoy a drink with friends after work, but I feel guilty about not going home to the family and mad at myself for wasting time and money.

Neither of these scenarios is particularly unusual. Everyday life is full of them: rarely do we feel the serenity that comes when heart, will, and mind are on the same page. Conflicting desires, intentions, and thoughts jostle each other in consciousness, and we are helpless to keep them in line.

But now let us consider some alternatives. Imagine, for instance, that you are skiing down a slope and your full attention is focused on the movements of the body, the position of the skis, the air whistling past your face, and the snow-shrouded trees running by. There is no room in your awareness for conflicts or contradictions; you know that a distracting thought or emotion might get you buried facedown in the snow. And who wants to get distracted? The run is so perfect that all you want is for it to last forever, to immerse yourself completely in the experience.

10   If skiing does not mean much to you, substitute your favorite activity for this vignette. It could be singing in a choir, programming a computer, dancing, playing bridge, reading a good book. Or if you love your job, as many people do, it could be when you are getting immersed in a complicated surgical operation or a close business deal. Or this complete immersion in the activity may occur in a social interaction, as when good friends talk with each other, or when a mother plays with her baby. What is common to such moments is that consciousness is full of experiences, and these experiences are in harmony with each other. Contrary to what happens all too often in everyday life, in moments such as these what we feel, what we wish, and what we think are in harmony.

These exceptional moments are what I have called *flow experiences*. The metaphor of "flow" is one that many people have used to describe the sense of effortless action they feel in moments that stand out as the best in their lives. Athletes refer to it as "being in the zone," religious mystics as being in "ecstasy," artists and musicians as aesthetic rapture. Athletes, mystics, and artists do very different things when they reach flow, yet their descriptions of the experience are remarkably similar.

Flow tends to occur when a person faces a clear set of goals that require appropriate responses. It is easy to enter flow in games such as chess, tennis, or poker, because they have goals and rules for action that make it possible for the player to act without questioning what should be done, and how. For the duration of the game the player lives in a self-contained universe where everything is black and white. The same clarity of goals is present if you perform a religious ritual, play a musical piece, weave a rug, write a computer program, climb a mountain, or perform surgery. Activities that induce flow could be called "flow activities" because they make it more likely for the experience to occur. In contrast to normal life, flow activities allow a person to focus on goals that are clear and compatible.

Another characteristic of flow activities is that they provide immediate feedback. They make it clear how well you are doing. After each move of a game you can tell whether you have improved your position or not. With each step, the climber knows that he has inched higher. After each bar of a song you can hear whether the notes you sang matched the score. The weaver can see whether the last row of stitches fits the pattern of the tapestry as it should. The surgeon can see as she cuts whether the knife has avoided cutting any arteries, or whether there is sudden bleeding. On the job or at home we might go for long periods without a clue as to how we stand, while in flow we can usually tell.

Flow tends to occur when a person's skills are fully involved in overcoming a challenge that is just about manageable. Optimal experiences usually involve a fine balance between one's ability to act, and the available opportunities for action (see Figure 1). If challenges are too high one gets frustrated, then worried, and eventually anxious. If challenges are too low relative to one's skills one gets relaxed, then bored. If both challenges and skills are perceived to be low, one gets to feel apathetic. But when high challenges are matched with high skills, then the deep involvement that sets flow apart from ordinary life

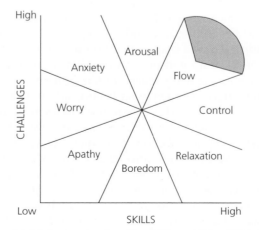

Figure 1 The quality of experience as a function of the relationship between challenges and skills. Optimal experience, or flow, occurs when both variables are high.

Sources: Adapted from Massimini & Carli 1988; Csikszentmihalyi 1990.

is likely to occur. The climber will feel it when the mountain demands all his strength, the singer when the song demands the full range of her vocal ability, the weaver when the design of the tapestry is more complex than anything attempted before, and the surgeon when the operation involves new procedures or requires an unexpected variation. A typical day is full of anxiety and boredom. Flow experiences provide the flashes of intense living against this dull background.

15   When goals are clear, feedback relevant, and challenges and skills are in balance, attention becomes ordered and fully invested. Because of the total demand on psychic energy, a person in flow is completely focused. There is no space in consciousness for distracting thoughts, irrelevant feelings. Self-consciousness disappears, yet one feels stronger than usual. The sense of time is distorted: hours seem to pass by in minutes. When a person' entire being is stretched in the full functioning of body and mind, whatever one does becomes worth doing for its own sake; living becomes its own justification. In the harmonious focusing of physical and psychic energy, life finally comes into its own.

It is the full involvement of flow, rather than happiness, that makes for excellence in life. When we are in flow, we are not happy, because to experience happiness we must focus on our inner states, and that would take away attention from the task at hand. If a rock climber takes time out to feel happy while negotiating a difficult move, he might fall to the bottom of the mountain. The surgeon can't afford to feel happy during a demanding operation, or a musician while playing a challenging score. Only after the task is completed do we have the leisure to look back on what has happened, and then we are flooded with gratitude for the excellence of that experience—then, in retrospect, we are happy. But one can be happy without experiencing flow. We can be happy experiencing the passive pleasure of a rested body, a warm sunshine, the contentment of a serene relationship. These are also moments to treasure, but this kind of happiness is very vulnerable and dependent on favorable external circumstances. The happiness that follows flow is of our own making, and it leads to increasing complexity and growth in consciousness.

The graph in Figure 1 can also be read to indicate why flow leads to personal growth. Suppose a person is in the area marked "Arousal" on the graph. This is not a bad condition to be in; in arousal a person feels mentally focused, active, and involved—but not very strong, cheerful, or in control. How can one return to the more enjoyable flow state? The answer is obvious: by learning new skills. Or let us look at the area labeled "Control." This is also a positive state of experience, where one feels happy, strong, satisfied. But one tends to lack concentration, involvement, and a feeling that what one does is important. So how does one get back to flow? By increasing challenges. Thus arousal and control are very important states for learning. The other conditions are less favorable. When a person is anxious or worried, for example, the step to flow often seems too far, and one retreats to a less challenging situation instead of trying to cope.

Thus the flow experience acts as a magnet for learning—that is, for developing new levels of challenges and skills. In an ideal situation, a person would be constantly growing while enjoying whatever he or she did. Alas, we know this is not the case. Usually we feel too bored and apathetic to move into the flow zone, so we prefer to fill our mind with ready-made, prepackaged stimulation off the video shelf or some other kind of professional entertainment. Or we feel too overwhelmed to imagine we could develop the appropriate skills, so we prefer to descend into the apathy engendered by artificial relaxants like drugs or alcohol. It takes energy to achieve optimal experiences, and all too often we are unable, or unwilling, to put out the initial effort.

How often do people experience flow? That depends on whether we are willing to count even mild approximations of the ideal condition as instances of flow. For example, if one asks a sample of typical Americans: "Do you ever get involved in something so deeply that nothing else seems to matter, and you lose track of time?" roughly one in five will say that yes, this happens to them often, as much as several times a day; whereas about 15 percent will say that no, this never happens to them. These frequencies seem to be quite stable and universal. For instance, in a recent survey of a representative sample of 6,469 Germans the same question was answered in the following way: Often, 23 percent; Sometimes, 40 percent; Rarely, 25 percent; Never or Don't Know, 12 percent. Of course if one were to count only the most intense and exalted flow experiences, then their frequency would be much more rare.

20   Flow is generally reported when a person is doing his or her favorite activity—gardening, listening to music, bowling, cooking a good meal. It also occurs when driving, when talking to friends, and surprisingly often at work. Very rarely do people report flow in passive leisure activities, such as watching television or relaxing. But because almost any activity can produce flow provided the relevant elements are present, it is possible to improve the quality of life by making sure that clear goals, immediate feedback, skills balanced to action opportunities, and the remaining conditions of flow are as much as possible a constant part of everyday life.

● Review Questions

1. What is flow? Summarize its main characteristics.

2. Summarize Figure 1, using your own language. Explain in your summary how the figure can be used as a tool for "personal growth."

3. What are the reasons that a person in flow is not happy—though he or she might recall the experience of being in flow as a happy one?

4. Csikszentmihalyi writes that "one can be happy without experiencing flow." What are some other sources of happiness? How do these compare with the happiness that follows from flow experiences?

5. How can the experience of flow be increased, and why might people not seize opportunities to increase flow?

Discussion and Writing Suggestions

1. Use Csikszentmihalyi's concept of flow to analyze an experience in your own life. To what extent does this principle help you to understand your experience?

2. Csikszentmihalyi remarks that of all the CEOs and Nobel laureates he has met, none led a life "that was better than Joe's"—that is, Joe the welder. What does the author mean, "better than"? Do you know any people like Joe? Describe them.

3. Csikszentmihalyi opens with a meditation on living fully, with intention. He claims that if we do not "choose" to live, our biology, our culture, and other people will use us to their own ends. What does Csikszentmihalyi mean by "live"—and what does his definition have to do with the epigraph by W. H. Auden, which opens the selection?

4. Csikszentmihalyi writes that "Flow experiences provide the flashes of intense living against a dull background." To what extent would you find it desirable for most if not all of your experiences to be flow experiences—such that there would be no "dull background"? Explain.

IF MONEY DOESN'T MAKE YOU HAPPY, THEN YOU PROBABLY AREN'T SPENDING IT RIGHT

Elizabeth W. Dunn, Daniel T. Gilbert, and Timothy D. Wilson

Research shows that happiness rises along with income, due largely to improved living conditions and access to quality education, healthcare, and increased leisure time. The correlation, however, holds only to about $75,000. Beyond this amount, increasing wealth does not improve people's self-reports of day-to-day happiness. Though income above $75,000 boosts people's overall satisfaction with their lives (reflected in statements like "I'm pleased with my general circumstances"), their daily happiness depends on other factors. The selection that follows reviews these factors, distilled by the authors into eight principles. Elizabeth Dunn is an associate professor of psychology at the University of British Columbia. Daniel Gilbert is a professor of psychology at Harvard University. Timothy Wilson is professor of psychology at the University of Virginia. All three are major contributors to the research on happiness. This paper first appeared in the *Journal of Consumer Psychology* in March 2011.*

Scientists have studied the relationship between money and happiness for decades and their conclusion is clear: Money buys happiness, but it buys less than most people think. The correlation between income and happiness is positive but modest, and this fact should puzzle us more than it does. After

---

*To save space, this reprinted selection appears without the authors' original parenthetical citations or references.

all, money allows people to do what they please, so shouldn't they be pleased when they spend it? Why doesn't a whole lot more money make us a whole lot more happy? One answer to this question is that the things that bring happiness simply aren't for sale. This sentiment is lovely, popular, and almost certainly wrong. Money allows people to live longer and healthier lives, to buffer themselves against worry and harm, to have leisure time to spend with friends and family, and to control the nature of their daily activities—all of which are sources of happiness. Wealthy people don't just have better toys; they have better nutrition and better medical care, more free time and more meaningful labor—more of just about every ingredient in the recipe for a happy life. And yet, they aren't that much happier than those who have less. If money can buy happiness, then why doesn't it?

Because people don't spend it right. Most people don't know the basic scientific facts about happiness—about what brings it and what sustains it—and so they don't know how to use their money to acquire it. It is not surprising when wealthy people who know nothing about wine end up with cellars that aren't that much better stocked than their neighbors', and it should not be surprising when wealthy people who know nothing about happiness end up with lives that aren't that much happier than anyone else's. Money is an opportunity for happiness, but it is an opportunity that people routinely squander because the things they think will make them happy often don't.

•   •   •

In this article, we will use insights gleaned from the affective forecasting literature to explain why people often spend money in ways that fail to maximize their happiness, and we will offer eight principles that are meant to remedy that.

Principle 1: Buy Experiences Instead of Things

"Go out and buy yourself something nice." That's the consoling advice we often give to friends who have just gotten bad news from their employer, their doctor, or their soon-to-be-ex spouse. Although the advice is well-meant, research suggests that people are often happier when they spend their money on experiences rather than things.

5   Van Boven and Gilovich defined experiential purchases as those "made with the primary intention of acquiring a life experience: an event or series of events that one lives through," while defining *material purchases* as those "made with the primary intention of acquiring a material good: a tangible object that is kept in one's possession." Although there is a "fuzzy boundary" between these two types of purchases, with many purchases (e.g., a new car) falling somewhere in the hazy middle, consumers are consistently able to describe past purchases that clearly fit these definitions, both in their own minds and the minds of coders trained in this distinction. In one study, these definitions were presented to a nationwide sample of over a thousand Americans, who were asked to think of a material and an experiential purchase they had made with the intention of increasing their own happiness. Asked which of the two purchases made them happier,

fully 57% of respondents reported that they had derived greater happiness from their experiential purchase, while only 34% reported greater happiness from their material purchase. Similar results emerged using a between-subjects design in which participants were randomly assigned to reflect on either a material or experiential purchase they had made; individuals experienced elevated mood when contemplating a past experiential purchase (relative to those contemplating a past material purchase), suggesting that experiential purchases produce more lasting hedonic benefits.

•   •   •

Experiences are good; but why are they better than things? One reason is that we adapt to things so quickly. After devoting days to selecting the perfect hardwood floor to install in a new condo, homebuyers find their once beloved Brazilian cherry floors quickly become nothing more than the unnoticed ground beneath their feet. In contrast, their memory of seeing a baby cheetah at dawn on an African safari continues to provide delight. Testing this idea in an experimental context, Nicolao, Irwin, and Goodman randomly assigned participants to spend several dollars on either a material or experiential purchase, tracking participants' happiness with their purchase over a 2 week period. Over time, participants exhibited slower adaptation to experiential purchases than to material purchases.[1] One reason why this happens is that people adapt most quickly to that which doesn't change. Whereas cherry floorboards generally have the same size, shape, and color on the last day of the year as they did on the first, each session of a year-long cooking class is different from the one before.

Another reason why people seem to get more happiness from experiences than things is that they anticipate and remember the former more often than the latter. Surveying a sample of Cornell students, Van Boven and Gilovich found that 83% reported "mentally revisiting" their experiential purchases more frequently than their material purchases. Things bring us happiness when we use them, but not so much when we merely think about them. Experiences bring happiness in both cases—and some (e.g., climbing a mountain or making love to a new partner) may even be better contemplated than consummated. We are more likely to mentally revisit our experiences than our things in part because our experiences are more centrally connected to our identities. In a survey of 76 adults, Van Boven and Gilovich found that the vast majority of adults viewed their experiential purchases as more self-defining than their material purchases. What's more, because experiences often seem as unique as the people who are having them, it can be difficult to compare the butt-numbing bicycle ride we decided to take through the Canadian Arctic to the sunny Sonoma wine tour we could have taken instead—thereby saving us from troubling ruminations about the road less travelled. As

---

[1]Of course, if people adapt more slowly to experiential than material purchases, then they may also experience more lasting distress from a terrible experiential (versus material purchase). Indeed, Nicolao et al. found suggestive evidence that experience purchases that turn out badly may produce somewhat more lasting unhappiness than material purchases that turn out badly.

such, it is possible to reduce our proclivity for making these kinds of distressing comparisons simply by thinking of our purchases in experiential terms; if we view a new car not as something we *have*, but as something that expands what we can *do*, then discovering that a shinier, faster, less expensive model has just come out may be a little less frustrating. A final reason why experiences make us happier than things is that experiences are more likely to be shared with other people, and other people—as we are now about to see—are our greatest source of happiness.

Principle 2: Help Others Instead of Yourself

Human beings are the most social animal on our planet. Only three other animals (termites, eusocial insects, and naked mole rats) construct social networks as complex as ours, and we are the only one whose complex social networks include unrelated individuals. Many scientists believe that this "hypersociality" is what caused our brains to triple in size in just 2 million years. Given how deeply and profoundly social we are, it isn't any wonder that the quality of our social relationships is a strong determinant of our happiness.

Because of this, almost anything we do to improve our connections with others tends to improve our happiness as well—and that includes spending money. Dunn, Aknin, and Norton asked a nationally representative sample of Americans to rate their happiness and to report how much money they spent in a typical month on (1) bills and expenses, (2) gifts for themselves, (3) gifts for others, and (4) donations to charity. The first two categories were summed to create a personal spending composite, and the latter two categories were summed to create a prosocial spending composite. Although personal spending was unrelated to happiness, people who devoted more money to prosocial spending were happier, even after controlling for their income. An experiment revealed a similar pattern of results. Researchers approached individuals on the University of British Columbia (UBC) campus, handed them a $5 or $20 bill, and then randomly assigned them to spend the money on themselves or on others by the end of the day. When participants were contacted that evening, individuals who had been assigned to spend their windfall on others were happier than those who had been assigned to spend the money on themselves. The benefits of prosocial spending appear to be cross-cultural. Over 600 students attending universities in Canada and in the East African nation of Uganda were randomly assigned to reflect on a time they had spent money on themselves or on others. Participants felt significantly happier when they reflected on a time they had spent money on others, and this effect emerged consistently across these vastly different cultural contexts—even though the specific ways in which participants spent their money varied dramatically between cultures.[2] The emotional rewards of prosocial spending are also detectable at the neural level. Participants in an MRI were given the opportunity to donate money to a local food bank. Choosing to give money away—or even being forced to do so—led to activation in brain areas typically associated with receiving rewards.

---

[2]Providing evidence that the benefits of prosocial spending emerge regardless of whether purchases are material or experiential, the effect of prosocial spending remained significant even when controlling for the extent to which the purchase was material versus experiential.

10   Why does prosocial spending produce such strong and consistent benefits for well-being? Diener and Seligman argue that strong social relationships are universally critical for happiness, and prosocial spending has a surprisingly powerful impact on social relationships. Research shows that receiving a gift from a romantic partner has a significant impact on college students' feelings about the likelihood that the relationship will continue over the long-term and lead to marriage. Spending money on a friend or romantic partner also provides an opportunity for positive self presentation, which has been shown to produce benefits for mood. Giving to charity may facilitate such positive self-presentation as well, and may even facilitate the development of social relationships, considering that most charitable donations are made by individuals who are directly connected to the beneficiaries (e.g., churches, arts organizations).

Although the benefits of prosocial spending are robust across cultures and methodologies, they are invisible to many people. Surveying UBC students, Dunn et al. found that a significant majority made an affective forecasting error: they thought that spending money on themselves would make them happier than spending on others. Indeed, simply thinking about money has been shown to undermine prosocial impulses, making people less likely to donate to charity or help acquaintances. Although money can and should promote happiness, the mere thought of money may undermine its ability to do so.

Principle 3: Buy Many Small Pleasures Instead of Few Big Ones

Adaptation is a little bit like death: we fear it, fight it, and sometimes forestall it, but in the end, we always lose. And like death, there may be benefits to accepting its inevitability. If we inevitably adapt to the greatest delights that money can buy, than it may be better to indulge in a variety of frequent, small pleasures—double lattes, uptown pedicures, and high thread-count socks—rather than pouring money into large purchases, such as sports cars, dream vacations, and front-row concert tickets. This is not to say that there's anything *wrong* with large purchases. But as long as money is limited by its failure to grow on trees, we may be better off devoting our finite financial resources to purchasing frequent doses of lovely things rather than infrequent doses of lovelier things. Indeed, across many different domains, happiness is more strongly associated with the frequency than the intensity of people's positive affective experiences. For example, no one finds it surprising that people who have sex are happier than people who don't, but some do find it surprising that the optimal number of sexual partners to have in a 12-month period is one. Why would people who have one partner be happier than people who have many? One reason is that multiple partners are occasionally thrilling, but regular partners are regularly enjoyable. A bi-weekly ride on a merry-go-round may be better than an annual ride on a roller coaster.

One reason why small frequent pleasures beat infrequent large ones is that we are less likely to adapt to the former. The more easily people can understand and explain an event, the quicker they adapt to it, and thus anything that makes a pleasurable event more difficult to understand and explain will delay adaptation.

These variables include novelty (we've never experienced the event before), surprise (we didn't expect it to happen), uncertainty (we're not entirely sure what the event is), and variability (the event keeps changing). Each of these variables makes an event harder to understand and as a result we pay more attention to it and adapt more slowly. And, small pleasures are more likely to satisfy these conditions than are large ones. Having a beer after work with friends, for example, is never exactly the same as it was before; this week the bar had a new India Pale Ale from Oregon on tap, and Sam brought along his new friend Kate who told a funny story about dachshunds. If we buy an expensive dining room table, on the other hand, it's pretty much the same table today as it was last week. Because frequent small pleasures are different each time they occur, they forestall adaptation.

*   *   *

The happiness provided by frequent small pleasures helps make sense of the modest correlation between money and happiness. In a study of Belgian adults, individuals who had a strong capacity to savor the mundane joys of daily life were happier than those who did not. This capacity to savor, however, was reduced among wealthy individuals. Indeed, the positive impact of wealth on happiness was significantly undercut by the negative impact of wealth on savoring. Quoidbach et al. argue that wealth promises access to peak experiences, which in turn undermine the ability to savor small pleasures. Indeed, when participants are exposed to photographs of money (thereby priming the construct of wealth) they spend significantly less time eating a piece of chocolate and exhibit less pleasure while doing it. In short, not only are the small pleasures of daily life an important source of happiness, but unfettered access to peak experiences may actually be counterproductive.

Principle 4: Buy Less Insurance

15 If the bad news is that we adapt to good things, the good news is that we adapt to bad things as well. Research on how well people cope with a wide variety of traumas and tragedies—from heart attacks to terrorist attacks—suggests that people are not the emotionally fragile creatures they often imagine themselves to be. Just as the physical immune system wards off maladies, the "psychological immune system" wards off malaise by marshalling the remarkable human capacities of reconstrual and rationalization. But research suggests that people don't know much about their own psychological immune systems, and as a result they overestimate their vulnerability to negative affect.

Businesses often trade on that ignorance by offering various forms of insurance against unhappiness, from extended warranties to generous return policies. With price tags reaching as high as 50% of a product's original cost, extended warranties sold by retailers and manufacturers provide huge benefits to the seller and are widely acknowledged to be "bad bets" for the buyer. Why are consumers willing to pay so much for these overpriced warranties? Owning something instantly makes it more delightful, and as such, a plasma TV that has just become *my* plasma TV may seem worthy of protection. The prospect of loss is highly aversive to people, who expect the pain of losing $5 to exceed the pleasure of gaining $5. But research shows that this expectation is wrong. Kermer et al. gave participants $5, and then flipped a coin. Participants were told that if the coin came up one way they would get an additional $5, and if it came up the other way they would lose $3 of their initial endowment. Although participants expected to be more emotionally affected by the loss of $3 than by the gain of $5, they were not. Participants who lost $3 out of their initial $5 endowment were significantly less upset than they expected because they instantly framed the event as a $2 gain. Research like this suggests that buying expensive extended warranties to guard against the loss of consumer goods may be unnecessary emotional protection.

The psychological immune system also provides the key to understanding a phrase uttered by embattled politicians, reality show rejects, and Olympic athletes who just missed the podium: "I have no regrets." When former British Prime Minister Tony Blair invoked this familiar refrain in reference to getting his country involved in the divisive Iraq War, a heckler yelled, "What, no regrets? Come on!" (The Independent, 2010). Like the heckler, Blair himself might have found it hard to believe years ago that he would not regret his actions, had he been able to preview how the future would unfold. The ability to "spin" events in a positive direction after they have occurred—thereby dodging regret—is not limited to politicians. Recent research demonstrates that ordinary people are remarkably adept at reconstruing events in order to avoid self-blame and the regret that accompanies it, a capacity that these same individuals may fail to appreciate in prospect. When passengers on a train were asked to estimate how much regret they would feel have felt if they had missed the train by 5 minutes or 1 minute, they estimated that they would have felt more regret in the latter case than the former. And yet, passengers who had actually missed their trains by 1 and 5 min reported remarkably little regret, and equally little regret regardless of whether they had missed the train by 5 min or by 1. What explains this discrepancy? When passengers who had made their trains were asked to imagine having missed them by a minute, they imagined blaming themselves for the near miss (e.g., "I would not have missed the train if only I'd woken up earlier and gotten out of the house faster"). Passengers who had actually missed their trains, however, tended to blame anyone or anything but themselves (e.g., "I would not have missed the train if only all the gates were open instead of just one"). Because people are highly skilled at dodging self-blame, they experience less regret than they predict.

• • •

Principle 5: Pay Now and Consume Later

In 1949, a businessman named Frank McNamara found himself without any cash after dining at a New York City restaurant. The mortification he experienced as his wife paid the bill provided the impetus for him to create one of the earliest credit cards, establishing the foundation for today's multibillion dollar credit card industry. Just as credit card companies allow customers to "consume now and pay later," so do merchants whose offers include phrases such as "No money down!" and "Don't pay for six months!" Meanwhile, consumers are provided with the chance to satisfy their desires faster than ever, instantly downloading music and movies through iTunes or obtaining same-day delivery of everything from books to jewelry through Amazon.

This shift toward immediate enjoyment and delayed payment represents a fundamental change in our economic system that undermines well-being in two important ways. The first and most obvious is that the "consume now and pay later" heuristic leads people to engage in shortsighted behavior—to rack up debts, to save little for retirement, etc. In the end, the piper must be paid, and when that happens, lives are often ruined. Vast literatures on delay of gratification, intertemporal choice, and delay discounting show that when people are impatient, they end up less well off.

20 But there is a second reason why "consume now, pay later" is a bad idea: it eliminates anticipation, and anticipation is a source of "free" happiness. The person who buys a cookie and eats it right away may get X units of pleasure from it, but the person who saves the cookie until later gets X units of pleasure when it is eventually eaten plus all the additional pleasure of looking forward to the event. Research shows that people can reap substantial enjoyment from anticipating an upcoming event even if the event itself is not entirely enjoyable. Examining three different vacations ranging from a trip to Europe to a bicycle trip through California, Mitchell et al. found that people viewed the vacation in a more positive light before the experience than during the experience, suggesting that anticipation may sometimes provide more pleasure than consumption simply because it is unsullied by reality. Not surprisingly, then, people who devote time to anticipating enjoyable experiences report being happier in general.

• • •

Delaying consumption provides the benefit of anticipation, but it may also promote happiness in two other ways. First, it may alter what consumers choose. When people select goods for immediate consumption, they are tempted by "vices," such as fattening food and lowbrow entertainment, which produce pleasure right away but lack long-term benefits—or even carry long-term costs—for well-being. By comparison, delayed consumption is more likely to promote the selection of "virtues," which produce more lasting (if less immediate) well-being. For example, when asked to choose a snack from an array that included apples, bananas, paprika-flavored crisps, and Snickers bars, people overwhelmingly selected an unhealthy snack if it was to be consumed immediately, but drifted toward the healthier options when selecting a snack to be consumed the following week. Because the present seems to be viewed under an emotional magnifying glass, people gave in to the temptation of salty, sweet satiation when it was immediately available, but when such satiation receded into the future, this temptation no longer loomed large, freeing people to select more virtuous options—and perhaps to appreciate the abstract health benefits of a banana at least as much as the more concrete deliciousness of nutty, chocolaty nougat.

A second way in which delayed consumption may promote happiness is that it may create uncertainty. Before purchasing a product, consumers generally face some degree of uncertainty about which product they will select, what it will be like, and how they will use it. This uncertainty may help to counteract the process of adaptation by keeping attention focused on the product. Consider, for example, a little boy in Toys R Us eagerly clutching both a stunt kite and a water gun. While the boy would probably experience immediate delight if his mother offered to buy both toys for him, new research suggests that more lasting pleasure would ensue if his mother told him that she would return to the store the next day and buy him one of the two toys. Demonstrating this idea, Kurtz et al. told undergraduates that they had the opportunity to receive small gifts, such as Godiva chocolates, coffee mugs, and disposable cameras. At the beginning of the experiment, participants in the certainty condition were told which gift or gifts they would receive, whereas those in the uncertainty condition were told only that they would receive a gift, but were not told which one until the end of the session. Compared to those in the certainty condition, participants who were uncertain about which gift they would receive spent more time looking at pictures of the gifts and experienced a more lasting boost in mood during the experimental session. Indeed, at the end of the experimental session, participants in the uncertain condition who received just one gift were happier than those participants in the certain condition who received two gifts. When provided with a detailed description of the experimental conditions, however, most people predicted that they would be happier in the certain condition. Thus, our Toys R Us kid would likely entreat his mother to reveal which of the toys she was planning to buy him the following day, sincerely believing that this knowledge would make him happy, but his mother would be wise to keep mum, thereby treating her son to a pleasurable day of fantasizing about water fights and flying kites.

Principle 6: Think About What You're Not Thinking About

According to a recent poll, a majority of adult Canadians dream of owning a vacation home, preferably by a lake. The features they highlight as important for their dream cottage include peace and quiet, access to fishing and boating, and sunset vistas. These are features that are central to the very essence of a lakeside cottage, and they naturally come to mind when people envision owning a vacation home. But, taking a broader view, there are many other, less essential aspects of cottage ownership that are likely to influence owners' happiness, from the mosquitoes buzzing just outside, to the late-night calls about a plumbing disaster in the lakeside area, to the long drives back home after a vacation weekend with sleepy children scratching their mosquito bites. Cast in the soft light of imagination, these unpleasant, inessential details naturally recede from view, potentially biasing consumers' predictions about the degree of happiness that their purchases will provide.

This phenomenon stems from a peculiar property of imagination. The farther away an experience lies in time, the more abstractly we tend to think of it. Like airplane passengers viewing a city just as they begin their descent, we see the distant future in simple, high-level ways rather than in fine detail.

Fully 89% of Canadians think of a cottage as "a great place for family to gather," and although this high-level construal is not inaccurate, it is certainly incomplete inasmuch as it lacks important details about family gatherings—from whether to invite Aunt Mandy whose snoring will keep everyone awake, to what to make for dinner that will satisfy both the meat-lovers and the glutenallergic vegaquarians in the clan.

25   This oversight matters because happiness is often in the details. On any given day, affective experience is shaped largely by local features of one's current situation—such as experiencing time pressure at work or having a leisurely dinner with friends—rather than by more stable life circumstances (e.g., having high job security, being married). Over time, psychological distress is predicted better by the hassles and "uplifts" of daily life than by more major life events. Thus, in thinking about how to spend our money, it is worthwhile to consider how purchases will affect the ways in which we spend our time. For example, consider the choice between a small, well-kept cottage and a larger "fixer upper" that have similar prices. The bigger home may seem like a better deal, but if the fixer upper requires trading Saturday afternoons with friends for Saturday afternoons with plumbers, it may not be such a good deal after all.

•   •   •

Principle 7: Beware of Comparison Shopping

Each month, as many as 20 million people visit bizrate.com, a top comparison-shopping website that entices consumers with the slogan, "Search. Compare. Conquer." Sites like this one offer consumers the opportunity to search for everything from mattresses and remote control cars to educational degrees, comparing a vast range of available options within a given category. The comparison shopping facilitated by these sites offers obvious benefits to consumers, who can find the best deal on the product most ideally suited to their needs. But recent research suggests that comparison shopping may sometimes come at a cost. By altering the psychological context in which decisions are made, comparison shopping may distract consumers from attributes of a product that will be important for their happiness, focusing their attention instead on attributes that distinguish the available options.

•   •   •

In a particularly vivid demonstration of this idea, Hsee presented participants with a choice between receiving a larger (2.0 oz.) chocolate valued at $2 that was shaped like a real cockroach and a smaller (0.5 oz.) chocolate valued at 50 cents that was shaped like a heart. Although only 46% participants of participants predicted that they would enjoy the larger roach-shaped chocolate more than the smaller heart-shaped one, fully 68% of participants reported that they would choose the roach-shaped chocolate. This suggests that comparison shopping may lead people to seek out products that provide the "best deal" (i.e., why accept a chocolate valued at 50 cents when I could have one valued at $2?).

•   •   •

Principle 8: Follow the Herd Instead of Your Head

By visiting the Internet Movie Database at imdb.com, consumers can access a huge array of information to help them choose a movie, including trailers, plot summaries, and detailed information about the cast and crew. This information allows consumers to simulate the experience of watching a movie, potentially enabling them to make more accurate affective forecasts and better movie choices. Alternatively, however, consumers could choose to ignore all of this detailed information about a movie's content, and instead click on "user ratings" to find out how thousands of other visitors to the site rated the movie. It is possible to break down these ratings by demographics so, for example, a 32 year old woman could find out how women ages 30–44 liked the movie. So which method is better?

Research suggests that the best way to predict how much we will enjoy an experience is to see how much someone else enjoyed it. In one study, Gilbert, Killingsworth, Eyre, and Wilson asked women to predict how much they would enjoy a speed date with a particular man. Some of the women were shown the man's photograph and autobiography, while others were shown only a rating of how much a previous woman had enjoyed a speed date with the same man a few minutes earlier. Although the vast majority of the participants expected that those who were shown the photograph and autobiography would make more accurate predictions than those who were shown the rating, precisely the opposite was the case. Indeed, relative to seeing the photograph and autobiography, seeing the rating reduced inaccuracy by about 50%. It appears that the 17th century writer François de La Rochefoucauld was correct when he wrote: "Before we set our hearts too much upon anything, let us first examine how happy those are who already possess it."

• • •

Conclusion

30 When asked to take stock of their lives, people with more money report being a good deal more satisfied. But when asked how happy they are at the moment, people with more money are barely different than those with less. This suggests that our money provides us with satisfaction when we think about it, but not when we use it. That shouldn't happen. Money can buy many, if not most, if not all of the things that make people happy, and if it doesn't, then the fault is ours. We believe that psychologists can teach people to spend their money in ways that will indeed increase their happiness, and we hope we've done a bit of that here.

⬤ Review Questions

1. Cite the observation from prior research that launched the present study. What do Dunn, Gilbert, and Wilson set out to do in this article?

2. Summarize the authors' eight principles for spending money in ways likely to produce happiness.

● Discussion and Writing Suggestions

1. The authors emphasize the importance of "savoring" (see ¶ 14). Reread their account of the relationship between money and savoring and describe an experience from your own life that illustrates—or contradicts—their point.

2. Consider the case of the hypothetical child (in ¶ 22) who would like a kite and a water gun from a toy store. Working with the principle of "pay now and consume later," the authors analyze the mother's purchasing decision and suggest a course of action to maximize the child's happiness. What do you think of this application of social science? Do you believe that the child's pleasure would, indeed, be maximized? Do you imagine yours would, were you the child?

3. Which of the authors' eight principles surprised you most? Why?

4. Select any of the eight principles for spending money in Dunn et al. in ways that promote happiness. Then use that principle to analyze an event in your life. Why were you (or were you not) happy at that time?

Happy Like God

Simon Critchley

Those committed to the humanist tradition—including the study of philosophy, literature, and religion—have little patience for a science of happiness that attempts to measure well-being. Simon Critchley's essay and the two that follow offer a critique (in one case a savage critique) of happiness studies. Critchley is a British philosopher who teaches at The New School for Social Research. He has written numerous books on philosophy, including *On Humor* (2002), *Things Merely Are: Philosophy in the Poetry of Wallace Stevens* (2005), and *The Book of Dead Philosophers* (2008). The essay below first appeared in the *New York Times* on May 25, 2009. You will find in Critchley's humanist reflections on happiness an approach far different from that of positive psychologists. Consider the differences as you read, and consider which perspective on the question of happiness appeals to you more.

What is happiness? How does one get a grip on this most elusive, intractable and perhaps unanswerable of questions?

I teach philosophy for a living, so let me begin with a philosophical answer. For the philosophers of Antiquity, notably Aristotle, it was assumed that the goal of the philosophical life—the good life, moreover—was happiness and that the latter could be defined as the *bios theoretikos*, the solitary life of contemplation. Today, few people would seem to subscribe to this view. Our lives are filled with the endless distractions of cell phones, car alarms, commuter woes and the traffic in Bangalore. The rhythm of modern life is punctuated by beeps, bleeps and a generalized attention deficit disorder.

But is the idea of happiness as an experience of contemplation really so ridiculous? Might there not be something in it? I am reminded of the following extraordinary passage from Rousseau's final book and his third (count them—he still beats Obama 3-to-2) autobiography, "Reveries of a Solitary Walker":

> If there is a state where the soul can find a resting-place secure enough to establish itself and concentrate its entire being there, with no need to remember the past or reach into the future, where *time is nothing to it*, where the present runs on indefinitely but this duration goes unnoticed, with no sign of the passing of time, and no other feeling of deprivation or enjoyment, pleasure or pain, desire or fear than the simple *feeling of existence*, a feeling that fills our soul entirely, as long as this state lasts, we can call ourselves happy, not with a poor, incomplete and relative happiness such as we find in the pleasures of life, but with a sufficient, complete and perfect happiness which leaves no emptiness to be filled in the soul. (emphases mine)

This is as close to a description of happiness as I can imagine. Rousseau is describing the experience of floating in a little rowing boat on the Lake of Bienne close to Neuchâtel in his native Switzerland. He particularly loved visiting the Île Saint Pierre, where he used to enjoy going for exploratory walks when the weather was fine and he could indulge in the great passion of his last years: botany. He would walk with a copy of Linneaus under his arm, happily identifying plants in areas of the deserted island that he had divided for this purpose into small squares.

5   On the way to the island, he would pull in the oars and just let the boat drift where it wished, for hours at a time. Rousseau would lie down in the boat and plunge into a deep reverie. How does one describe the experience of reverie: one is awake, but half asleep, thinking, but not in [a]...calculative or ordered way, simply letting the thoughts happen, as they will.

Happiness is not quantitative or measurable and it is not the object of any science, old or new. It cannot be gleaned from empirical surveys or programmed into individuals through a combination of behavioral therapy and anti-depressants. If it consists in anything, then I think that happiness is this *feeling of existence*, this sentiment of momentary self-sufficiency that is bound up with the experience of time.

Look at what Rousseau writes above: floating in a boat in fine weather, lying down with one's eyes open to the clouds and birds or closed in reverie, one feels neither the pull of the past nor does one reach into the future. Time is nothing, or rather time is nothing but the experience of the present through which one passes without hurry, but without regret. As Wittgenstein writes in what must be the most intriguing remark in the "Tractatus," "the eternal life is given to those who live in the present." Or, as Whitman writes in "Leaves of Grass": "Happiness is not in another place, but in this place...not for another hour...but this hour."

Rousseau asks, "What is the source of our happiness in such a state?" He answers that it is nothing external to us and nothing apart from our own existence. However frenetic our environment, such a feeling of existence can be achieved. He then goes on, amazingly, to conclude, "as long as this state lasts we are self-sufficient like God."

God-like, then. To which one might reply: Who? Me? Us? Like God? Dare we? But think about it: If anyone is happy, then one imagines that God is pretty happy, and to be happy is to be like God. But consider what this means, for it might not be as ludicrous, hubristic or heretical as one might imagine. To be like

God is to be without time, or rather in time with no concern for time, free of the passions and troubles of the soul, experiencing something like calm in the face of things and of oneself.

10   Why should happiness be bound up with the presence and movement of water? This is the case for Rousseau and I must confess that if I think back over those experiences of blissful reverie that are close to what Rousseau is describing then it is often in proximity to water, although usually saltwater rather than fresh. For me, it is not so much the stillness of a lake (I tend to see lakes as decaffeinated seas), but rather the never-ending drone of the surf, sitting by the sea in fair weather or foul and feeling time disappear into tide, into the endless pendulum of the tidal range. At moments like this, one can sink into deep reverie, a motionlessness that is not sleep, but where one is somehow held by the sound of the surf, lulled by the tidal movement.

Is all happiness solitary? Of course not. But one can be happy alone and this might even be the key to being happy with others. Wordsworth wandered lonely as a cloud when walking with his sister. However, I think that one can also experience this feeling of existence in the experience of love, in being intimate with one's lover, feeling the world close around one and time slips away in its passing. Rousseau's rowing boat becomes the lovers' bed and one bids the world farewell as one slides into the shared selfishness of intimacy.

...And then it is over. Time passes, the reverie ends and the feeling for existence fades. The cell phone rings, the e-mail beeps and one is sucked back into the world's relentless hum and our accompanying anxiety.

● Discussion and Writing Suggestions

1. Describe an experience of reverie in your own life, an experience that calls to mind the state of happiness described by Rousseau. Where were you? (In the presence of water, like Rousseau and Critchley?) How common is this experience of reverie for you? Can you go "there" any time, at will? If not, under what conditions can you achieve this state?

2. In ¶ 8, Critchley writes: "However frenetic our environment, such a feeling of existence can be achieved." How is this possible—to be in a "frenetic" environment, yet to be happy in the sense Rousseau is describing?

3. In ¶ 6, Critchley directly challenges a key premise of positive psychology: that happiness can be quantified and measured. How persuasive do you find Critchley on this point? As you consider this question, make notes and anticipate (if you're interested) a paper-long response. See Synthesis Activity #1.

4. In ¶ 7, Critchley quotes the philosopher Ludwig Wittgenstein and the poet Walt Whitman. Considered together, these quotations suggest that one can live an "eternal life." *Eternal* in what sense?

5. Critchley acknowledges that the claim that we could be "self-sufficient like God" is provocative. Do you find this assertion to be "ludicrous, hubristic or heretical"? Explain.

6. Reflecting on the work of Rousseau, Critchley writes: "[H]appiness is this *feeling of existence*, this sentiment of momentary self-sufficiency that is bound up with the experience of time." Use Critchley's statement as a principle with which to analyze an experience of your own. What do you discover?

A CRITIQUE OF POSITIVE PSYCHOLOGY

Richard Schoch

Cultural critic Richard Schoch has no patience for experiment-based attempts by positive psychologists to penetrate the secrets of happiness—secrets that have resisted the probing of philosophers and religious thinkers for thousands of years. Skeptical that psychologists even understand what they seek to measure, Schoch offers a stinging critique. Schoch is professor of the history of culture and director of the Graduate School in Humanities and Social Sciences at Queen Mary, University of London. He is a prolific writer and researcher whose interests include cultural history and performances of the plays of Shakespeare. The following passage first appeared in his introduction to *The Secrets of Happiness: Three Thousand Years of Searching for the Good Life* (2006).

Over the past decade, behavioural scientists, neuroscientists and psychologists (including a Nobel laureate from Princeton) have been working to measure reported levels of happiness and to identify its causes. Their methods are droll. In one 'experience sampling', participants carry internet-ready palmtop computers twenty-four hours a day. When an alarm sounds on their palmtops, the participants—who have been trained to respond with Pavlovian mechanicity to aural stimulation—stop what they're doing and complete an on-line survey about how they feel about what they've just stopped doing. Back in the laboratory of happiness, technicians download this data and then plot a graph showing each participant's happiness peaks and troughs over time. In case the guinea pigs have tried to outfox their masters—pretending to be happier or unhappier than they actually are—brain scans are used to confirm their testimony. (The participants, it can be revealed, are honest.)

What do the surveys say? Sex, no surprise, makes everyone feel better. The second best thing is having a drink after work with your friends. Work itself—challenging, rewarding and secure employment—also contributes greatly to happiness. Commuting, however, makes us miserable. Well, almost all of us. Four percent of respondents claimed to *enjoy* traffic jams. (Who could these people be?) If you believe the statistics, it's pretty easy to make yourself happy: live within walking distance of an enjoyable and secure job, prop up the bar with your friends, and then go home and have sex. Happiness, the secret revealed!

Enter the economists. Suddenly, they care about how you feel. Which is odd because generally they care about what you buy. Actually, the real oddity is that economists *do* regard happiness as something you can buy. As some of them now propose, we should stop looking for happiness in material prosperity and start looking for it in whatever gives us satisfaction, whether rewarding work, a supportive family or a vibrant community. At a time when financial prosperity is assured for many, though by no means all, in the industrialised world, happiness has become the ultimate luxury item.

Happiness is also a growth industry. Self-help books generate $1 billion in annual sales, while the global market for anti-depressants (O true apothecary!) stands valued at an astounding $17 billion. The 'desire industry'—whose titans are Botox jabbers, personal trainers and lifestyle gurus—rakes in even more. (So reports the earnestly named Work Foundation.) As the snake-oil salesman with a Harvard MBA would say, it's one vast marketing opportunity. Yet it hardly matters which product you choose, the economists tell us, because what you value is not the product but what it can do for you. You drink the elixir of happiness not because you like elixirs but because you like happiness.

5 The happiness economists are part of the new breed of neo-Benthamites. Now some explanation for those of us who are not experts in microeconomics. Jeremy Bentham, the eighteenth-century English legal philosopher, believed that every person strives to become happy by maximising pleasure and minimising pain. (He, in turn, had relied upon a distorted view of Epicureanism, the ancient Greek philosophy of living for pleasure....) Bentham wanted the government to enact laws that would give people the freedom to pursue happiness in whatever way they judged best.

Today's *neo*-Benthamites believe that governments should implement an interventionist 'happiness-based approach to public policy'. Supportively, they want politicians to stop worrying about our income and start worrying about our emotions. They lobby for legislation to foster not wealth and prosperity but feelings of satisfaction and contentment. Surprisingly, the political secrets of happiness include higher marginal tax rates (to stop us from working so hard), restrictions on labour mobility (to keep families together) and redistribution of wealth (to makes us less anxious about income disparity). But what next? A Department of Happiness?

Quitting the laboratory and the library, I found myself both amused and dejected. On the one hand, I had fun learning about the latest trends in 'hedonic psychology' and a 'happiness-based approach to public policy'. On the other hand, I found that none of this helped me to find the secret of happiness. Not that the results of the research were unclear. What could be more lucid than the expression of happiness brainwaves along the graphed co-ordinates of 'x' (intensity) and 'y' (time)? No, the flaw was introduced much earlier in the process: not in the answers generated but the questions posed. For, as surely as tock follows tick, if you ask the wrong question you will get the wrong answer. The hedonic psychologists asked 'How happy are you?' when they should have asked 'What is happiness?' As a result, they could do no more than measure and calibrate happiness, and this they did with a precision to rival the anonymous stonemasons who built the Great Pyramid at Giza.

'Happiness,' as Richard Layard, the United Kingdom's leading happiness economist recently explained,

> can be measured. We can ask people how they feel. We can ask their friends or observers for an independent assessment. Also, remarkably, we can now take measurements of the electrical activity in the relevant part of a person's brain. All of these different measurements give consistent answers about a person's happiness.*

But what *is* this thing called happiness? The scientists and the social scientists do not stop to ask the question because they presume to know its answer. As a team of eminent psychologists from the American Midwest has spelled out, '[a]ll attempts to comprehend, explain, and predict happiness presuppose that researchers can define [it]'. Presuppose away. Nearly every scientific study allots a single, begrudged paragraph to explaining what happiness actually is. So unencumbered by complexity are these definitions that their articulation requires no profusion of words. Happiness is...well, it's just 'feeling good—enjoying life and wanting the feeling to be maintained'. So say the economists. In the genial patois of researchers this is called 'subjective well-feeling'. Those now in kindergarten, or who once were, will doubtless be familiar with its romping musical expression, 'If you're happy, and you know it, clap your hands'. Maybe the mystery of happiness has *not* been solved by the palmtop experience sampling. They had the experience but missed the meaning.

● Review Questions

1. Who was Jeremy Bentham—and what is a *neo*-Benthamite? In what ways did Bentham's thinking influence happiness studies and its applications?

2. Summarize Schoch's major criticism of happiness studies.

● Discussion and Writing Suggestions

1. In the last line of the selection, Schoch writes that happiness researchers and subjects reporting on happiness have "the experience but [miss] the meaning." What does he mean?

2. Schoch (and also Critchley) emphatically rejects the claim that happiness can be measured. Gilbert, Seligman, and other positive psychologists have based their careers on the premise that it can. While you may lack the experience to support one side of the argument or the other, you can consider the argument itself. Why is it important? What's at stake?

3. Schoch strikes an ironic tone throughout this selection. Point to some examples of his irony. How effective do you find his use of this rhetorical device?

---

*Richard Layard, *Happiness: Lessons from a New Science* (London: Allen Lane, 2005), p. 12.

HAPPINESS: ENOUGH ALREADY

Sharon Begley

Humanists such as Critchley and Schoch criticize happiness studies on the grounds that positive psychology assumes a simplistic definition of happiness and attempts to quantify the unknowable. Yet even some psychologists have their doubts—though on different grounds. Perhaps, they suggest, humans have put sadness, fear, and anxiety to good use over the millennia. In the selection that follows, Sharon Begley, an award-winning staff writer at *Newsweek*, surveys critiques of happiness studies from within the profession of psychology. Begley has written scores of articles that decode the complexities of science for lay readers. In a five-year break from *Newsweek*, she wrote the "Science Journal" column for the *Wall Street Journal*. The selection here first appeared on the *Newsweek*-affiliated Web site the *Daily Beast* on February 2, 2008.

[C]onsider these snapshots of the emerging happiness debate.... Lately, Jerome Wakefield's students have been coming up to him after they break up with a boyfriend or girlfriend, and not because they want him to recommend a therapist. Wakefield, a professor at New York University, coauthored the 2007 book "The Loss of Sadness: How Psychiatry Transformed Normal Sorrow Into Depressive Disorder," which argues that feeling down after your heart is broken—even so down that you meet the criteria for clinical depression—is normal and even salutary. But students tell him that their parents are pressuring them to seek counseling and other medical intervention—"some Zoloft, dear?"—for their sadness, and the kids want no part of it. "Can you talk to them for me?" they ask Wakefield. Rather than "listening to Prozac," they want to listen to their hearts, not have them chemically silenced.

University of Illinois psychologist Ed Diener, who has studied happiness for a quarter century, was in Scotland recently, explaining to members of Parliament and business leaders the value of augmenting traditional measures of a country's wealth with a national index of happiness. Such an index would measure policies known to increase people's sense of well-being, such as democratic freedoms, access to health care and the rule of law. The Scots were all in favor of such things, but not because they make people happier. "They said too much happiness might not be such a good thing," says Diener. "They like being dour, and didn't appreciate being told they should be happier."

Eric Wilson tried to get with the program. Urged on by friends, he bought books on how to become happier. He made every effort to smooth out his habitual scowl and wear a sunny smile, since a happy expression can lead to genuinely happy feelings. Wilson, a professor of English at Wake Forest University, took up jogging, reputed to boost the brain's supply of joyful neurochemicals, watched uplifting Frank Capra and Doris Day flicks and began sprinkling his conversations with "great!" and "wonderful!", the better to exercise his capacity for enthusiasm. When none of these made him happy, Wilson not only jumped off the happiness bandwagon—he also embraced his melancholy side and decided to blast a happiness movement that "leads to half-lives, to bland existences," as he argues in *Against Happiness*, a book now reaching stores. Americans' fixation on happiness, he writes, fosters "a craven disregard for the value of sadness" and "its integral place in the great rhythm of the cosmos."

It's always tricky to identify a turning point, at least in real time. Only in retrospect can you accurately pinpoint when a financial market peaked or hit bottom, for instance, or the moment when the craze for pricey coffee drinks crested. But look carefully, and what you are seeing now may be the end of the drive for ever-greater heights of happiness. Fed by hundreds of self-help books, including the current *The How of Happiness: A Scientific Approach to Getting the Life You Want*, magazine articles and an industry of life coaches and motivational speakers, the happiness movement took off in the 1990s with two legitimate developments: discoveries about the brain activity underlying well-being, and the emergence of "positive psychology," whose proponents urged fellow researchers to study happiness as seriously as they did pathological states such as depression. But when the science of happiness collided with pop culture and the marketplace, it morphed into something even its creators hardly recognized. There emerged "a crowd of people out there who want you to be happier," write Ed Diener and his son, Robert Biswas-Diener, in their book, *Rethinking Happiness*, due for publication later this year. Somewhere out there a pharmaceutical company "is working on a new drug to make you happier," they warn. "There are even people who would like to give you special ozone enemas to make you happier." Although some 85 percent of Americans say they're pretty happy, the happiness industry sends the insistent message that moderate levels of well-being aren't enough: not only can we all be happier, but we practically have a duty to be so. What was once considered normal sadness is something to be smothered, even shunned.

5   The backlash against the happiness rat race comes just when scientists are releasing the most-extensive-ever study comparing moderate and extreme levels of happiness, and finding that being happier is not always better. In surveys of 118,519 people from 96 countries, scientists examined how various levels of subjective well-being matched up with income, education, political participation, volunteer activities and close relationships. They also analyzed how different levels of happiness, as reported by college students, correlated with various outcomes. Even allowing for imprecision in people's self-reported sense of well-being, the results were unambiguous. The highest levels of happiness go along with the most stable, longest and most contented relationships. That is, even a little discontent with your partner can nudge you to look around for someone better, until you are at best a serial monogamist and at worst never in a loving, stable relationship. "But if you have positive illusions about your partner, which goes along with the highest levels of happiness, you're more likely to commit to an intimate relationship," says Diener.

In contrast, "once a moderate level of happiness is achieved, further increases can sometimes be detrimental" to income, career success, education and political participation, Diener and colleagues write in the journal *Perspectives on Psychological Science*. On a scale from 1 to 10, where 10 is extremely happy,

8s were more successful than 9s and 10s, getting more education and earning more. That probably reflects the fact that people who are somewhat discontent, but not so depressed as to be paralyzed, are more motivated to improve both their own lot (thus driving themselves to acquire more education and seek ever-more-challenging jobs) and the lot of their community (causing them to participate more in civic and political life). In contrast, people at the top of the jolliness charts feel no such urgency. "If you're totally satisfied with your life and with how things are going in the world," says Diener, "you don't feel very motivated to work for change. Be wary when people tell you you should be happier."

The drawbacks of constant, extreme happiness should not be surprising, since negative emotions evolved for a reason. Fear tips us off to the presence of danger, for instance. Sadness, too, seems to be part of our biological inheritance: apes, dogs and elephants all display something that looks like sadness, perhaps because it signals to others a need for help. One hint that too much euphoria can be detrimental comes from studies finding that among people with late-stage illnesses, those with the greatest sense of well-being were more likely to die in any given period of time than the mildly content were. Being "up" all the time can cause you to play down very real threats.

Eric Wilson needs no convincing that sadness has a purpose. In his *Against Happiness,* he trots out criticisms of the mindless pursuit of contentment that philosophers and artists have raised throughout history—including that, as Flaubert said, to be chronically happy one must also be stupid. Less snarkily, Wilson argues that only by experiencing sadness can we experience the fullness of the human condition. While careful not to extol depression—which is marked not only by chronic sadness but also by apathy, lethargy and an increased risk of suicide—he praises melancholia for generating "a turbulence of heart that results in an active questioning of the status quo, a perpetual longing to create new ways of being and seeing." This is not romantic claptrap. Studies show that when you are in a negative mood, says Diener, "you become more analytical, more critical and more innovative. You need negative emotions, including sadness, to direct your thinking." Abraham Lincoln was not hobbled by his dark moods bordering on depression, and Beethoven composed his later works in a melancholic funk. Vincent van Gogh, Emily Dickinson and other artistic geniuses saw the world through a glass darkly. The creator of "Peanuts," Charles M. Schulz, was known for his gloom, while Woody Allen plumbs existential melancholia for his films, and Patti Smith and Fiona Apple do so for their music.

Wilson, who asserts that "the happy man is a hollow man," is hardly the first scholar to see melancholia as muse. A classical Greek text, possibly written by Aristotle, asks, "Why is it that all those who have become eminent in philosophy or politics or poetry or the arts are clearly melancholic?" Wilson's answer is that "the blues can be a catalyst for a special kind of genius, a genius for exploring dark boundaries between opposites." The ever-restless, the chronically discontent, are dissatisfied with the status quo, be it in art or literature or politics.

10   For all their familiarity, these arguments are nevertheless being crushed by the happiness movement. Last August, the novelist Mary Gordon lamented to the *New York Times* that "among writers...what is absolutely not allowable is sadness.

People will do anything rather than to acknowledge that they are sad." And in a "My Turn" column in *Newsweek* last May, Jess Decourcy Hinds, an English teacher, recounted how, after her father died, friends pressed her to distract herself from her profound sadness and sense of loss. "Why don't people accept that after a parent's death, there will be years of grief?" she wrote. "Everyone wants mourners to 'snap out of it' because observing another's anguish isn't easy."

It's hard to say exactly when ordinary Americans, no less than psychiatrists, began insisting that sadness is pathological. But by the end of the millennium that attitude was well entrenched. In 1999, Arthur Miller's *Death of a Salesman* was revived on Broadway 50 years after its premiere. A reporter asked two psychiatrists to read the script. Their diagnosis: Willy Loman was suffering from clinical depression, a pathological condition that could and should be treated with drugs. Miller was appalled. "Loman is not a depressive," he told the *New York Times*. "He is weighed down by life. There are social reasons for why he is where he is." What society once viewed as an appropriate reaction to failed hopes and dashed dreams, it now regards as a psychiatric illness.

That may be the most damaging legacy of the happiness industry: the message that all sadness is a disease. As NYU's Wakefield and Allan Horwitz of Rutgers University point out in *The Loss of Sadness*, this message has its roots in the bible of mental illness, the *Diagnostic and Statistical Manual of Mental Disorders*. Its definition of a "major depressive episode" is remarkably broad. You must experience five not-uncommon symptoms, such as insomnia, difficulty concentrating and feeling sad or empty, for two weeks; the symptoms must cause distress or impairment, and they cannot be due to the death of a loved one. Anyone meeting these criteria is supposed to be treated.

Yet by these criteria, any number of reactions to devastating events qualify as pathological. Such as? For three weeks a woman feels sad and empty, unable to generate any interest in her job or usual activities, after her lover of five years breaks off their relationship; she has little appetite, lies awake at night and cannot concentrate during the day. Or a man's only daughter is suffering from a potentially fatal blood disorder; for weeks he is consumed by despair, cannot sleep or concentrate, feels tired and uninterested in his usual activities.

Horwitz and Wakefield do not contend that the spurned lover or the tormented father should be left to suffer. Both deserve, and would likely benefit from, empathic counseling. But their symptoms "are neither abnormal nor inappropriate in light of their" situations, the authors write. The DSM definition of depression "mistakenly encompasses some normal emotional reactions," due to its failure to take into account the context or trigger for sadness.

15   That has consequences. When someone is appropriately sad, friends and colleagues offer support and sympathy. But by labeling appropriate sadness pathological, "we have attached a stigma to being sad," says Wakefield, "with the result that depression tends to elicit hostility and rejection" with an undercurrent of " 'Get over it; take a pill.' The normal range of human emotion is not being tolerated." And insisting that sadness requires treatment may interfere with the natural healing process. "We don't know how drugs react with normal sadness and its functions, such as reconstituting your life out of the pain," says Wakefield.

Even the psychiatrist who oversaw the current DSM expresses doubts about the medicalizing of sadness. "To be human means to naturally react with feelings of sadness to negative events in one's life," writes Robert Spitzer of the New York State Psychiatric Institute in a foreword to *The Loss of Sadness.* That would be unremarkable if it didn't run completely counter to the message of the happiness brigades. It would be foolish to underestimate the power and tenacity of the happiness cheerleaders. But maybe, just maybe, the single-minded pursuit of happiness as an end in itself, rather than as a consequence of a meaningful life, has finally run its course.

 Review Questions

1. In what way has happiness become a "rat race," according to Begley?

2. According to research, how might happiness beyond a moderate level have a detrimental effect?

3. In what ways has the definition of normal or appropriate sadness changed over time?

 Discussion and Writing Suggestions

1. Most, if not all, of us have suffered a broken heart at some point with the loss of another's affections. How reasonable and appropriate would you find it to take medication to lessen feelings of sadness in such an unhappy state?

2. Begley quotes Eric Wilson: America's "fixation on happiness fosters 'a craven disregard for the value of sadness and its integral place in the great rhythm of the cosmos.' " What is the value of sadness, in your view? If you care to speculate, what might "the great rhythm of the cosmos" be—and what integral role might sadness play?

3. If you've read or seen a production of *Death of a Salesman,* comment on Arthur Miller's response to the verdict of two psychiatrists who find Willy Loman clinically depressed. *Note:* Two of the most celebrated productions of this play, available on DVD, are those featuring Lee J. Cobb (1966), who appeared as Willy Loman in the original Broadway production (1949), and—and in a considerably different interpretation of the same role—Dustin Hoffman (1986).

4. Begley makes a distinction between "the single-minded pursuit of happiness as an end in itself" and happiness that comes "as a consequence of a meaningful life." Why is this distinction important?

5. Begley writes that we respond differently to those who are sad and those who receive a medical diagnosis of clinical depression. Is this distinction meaningful to you? Explain.

6. Begley quotes Ed Diener, one of the founders of happiness studies: "If you're totally satisfied with your life and with how things are going in the world, . . . you don't feel very motivated to work for change. Be wary when people tell you you should be happier." Use Diener's observation as a principle to analyze an experience in your life.

HAPPINESS

Jane Kenyon

We now transition from the psychological to the literary perspective. So far, you have read attempts to quantify happiness and name its key elements. You have read critiques of these efforts. Notice how both positive psychologists and their critics directly approach their topic: They define happiness, argue the definition, and also argue the very methods of investigation—experiment versus reflection. Literature, by contrast, suggests and evokes. Literature is indirect, achieving its effects not by appeals to logic but by engaging the reader's desire to discover what happens next and by tapping into the reader's emotions and memories. Literature takes on the topic of happiness because happiness is fundamental to human experience, and literature is about nothing if not that. To the extent literature argues, it diffuses argument among characters and explores it through literary devices such as metaphor.

Writing in a different context elsewhere in this text, folklorist Maria Tatar quotes the short story writer Eudora Welty, who says that "there is absolutely everything in great fiction but a clear answer." Answers are what psychologists such as Seligman and Gilbert and humanists such as Critchley and Schoch attempt to provide in their research and writing on happiness. Not so writers of literature.

For you to better appreciate the radical challenge that positive psychology presents in the discussion of happiness (a discussion that has been ongoing for thousands of years), we offer three selections from the literary tradition. The contrast, the ways of investigating the nature of happiness, could not be clearer. The first selection is a poem by the (nearly) contemporary poet, Jane Kenyon (1947–1995). Poetry distills emotions and impressions; unlike fiction, it frequently lacks a narrative. But poetry, like fiction (and the mediations by Tuan and Pirsig that follow), operates indirectly. You will not find answers; but you will consider what happiness is.

Kenyon wrote four books of poetry: *From Room to Room* (1978), *The Boat of Quiet Hours* (1986), *Let Evening Come* (1990), and *Constance* (1993). The poem "Happiness" first appeared in *Poetry* magazine (February 1995) and is collected in the posthumously published *Otherwise: New and Selected Poems* (1996). When she died of cancer at the age of forty-seven, Kenyon was poet laureate of New Hampshire.

> There's just no accounting for happiness,
> or the way it turns up like a prodigal*
> who comes back to the dust at your feet
> having squandered a fortune far away.

---

*Kenyon refers to the biblical parable of the "Prodigal (or Lost) Son." A man has two sons. One takes his inheritance, goes off, squanders the money, and returns ashamed and defeated while the other son remains at home, diligently working. When the father celebrates the return of the one son, the other protests that his long-absent brother should be a cause for joy. See Luke 15:11–32.

5   And how can you not forgive?
    You make a feast in honor of what
    was lost, and take from its place the finest
    garment, which you saved for an occasion
    you could not imagine, and you weep night and day
10 to know that you were not abandoned,
    that happiness saved its most extreme form
    for you alone.

    No, happiness is the uncle you never
    knew about, who flies a single-engine plane
15 onto the grassy landing strip, hitchhikes
    into town, and inquires at every door
    until he finds you asleep midafternoon
    as you so often are during the unmerciful
    hours of your despair.

20 It comes to the monk in his cell.
    It comes to the woman sweeping the street
    with a birch broom, to the child
    whose mother has passed out from drink.
    It comes to the lover, to the dog chewing
25 a sock, to the pusher, to the basketmaker,
    and to the clerk stacking cans of carrots
    in the night.
    It even comes to the boulder
    in the perpetual shade of pine barrens,
30 to rain falling on the open sea,
    to the wineglass, weary of holding wine.

● Discussion and Writing Suggestions

1. Read the biblical story of the "prodigal son" (Luke 15:11–32). What do you learn from the story that can help you understand the poem?

2. In her comparison of happiness and the prodigal child, Kenyon adopts the point of view of the father to whom the son returns. That is, she equates happiness with the prodigal son and the recipient of happiness with the father. Why?

3. In lines 13–19, Kenyon shifts the comparison: Happiness is now like a previously unknown uncle come to visit. Consider the details of the uncle's landing and search—for example, the "single-engine plane" and the hitchhiking into town. In what ways does this mini-narrative suggest the approach and arrival of happiness?

4. Review your answers to Discussion and Writing Suggestions #2 and #3, above. Kenyon offers two comparisons. How is happiness like *both* an unknown uncle *and* a prodigal son? Another way of thinking about this: What qualities do the prodigal son and uncle share that suggest an essential feature of happiness?

5. Reread lines 20–31, images of people and places visited by happiness. Does happiness visiting a boulder tell you more about the boulder or about the nature of happiness? Does happiness visiting a person tell you more about the person or about the nature of happiness? What qualities of happiness is Kenyon exploring here?

6. "[H]ow can you not forgive?" In what sense is forgiveness called for when happiness arrives?

7. Reread the last line. What could it mean, in relation to the rest of the poem?

8. Do you find any connections between the view of happiness embodied in Kenyon's poem and some of the approaches to happiness by the psychologists and journalists who wrote the earlier selections of the chapter? Explain.

THE GOOD LIFE

Yi-Fu Tuan

Yi-Fu Tuan was born in Tianjin, China in 1930. The son of a diplomat, he traveled extensively as a child and was educated in London and, later, in Berkeley, California. He is best known for his contributions to humanist geography, a discipline that synthesizes traditional geography with insights from religion and the social sciences. He has written twenty-three books, including *Human Goodness* (2008), *Place, Art, and Self* (2004), and *The Good Life* (1986), in which this selection first appeared. A vocabulary note: Tuan uses the expressions "good life" and "happiness" interchangeably.

When we try to recall memorable experiences from our past they emerge as separate pictures rather than as linked stories. The dense connective tissues of life are largely forgotten. As we show our family album to a friend, we say, "Look at this one. I was only three years old then." And then, "look at that," and "that." The pictures are of good times—winning a race at school, wedding, the proud smile of parenthood, chatting with neighbors one sunny afternoon. A friend who has not had the same experiences can nevertheless look at pictures and smile in recognition. What does this suggest? It suggests that individual experiences of import can be shared to a degree that whole life stories, with their unique yet dull routines and accidental twists and turns, cannot: the disappearance of connective tissues between climactic moments may help rather than hinder the feeling of participation in a common world.

We are able to appropriate other people's experiences for our own. An event in the life of a stranger can hit us with such force and vividness that it is as though it has happened to ourself. Needless to say, a good life must contain stirring moments that are directly experienced. But a reason for this is that such direct brushes with benign reality enable us to possess the happiness of others. We do so through the empathetic imagination, by which I mean the ability not only to see but to "live and feel" from another person's standpoint.

In a human life, what experiences may be considered good? Which of them stay in the memory? Which do we recall fondly from time to time? Which of them, if we have not known them ourselves, would we deeply regret?

• • •

I now present a sample of experiences, beginning with those of childhood and moving on to those of maturity—experiences of time, space, and place, of the body, human relations, and nature. They can all have come out of the lifetime of one individual. Happy that individual! But they do not. They are taken from separate lives in various parts of the Western world. A man or woman raised in that world is therefore more likely to identify with them than will someone from elsewhere. But, if these experiences are deeply human notwithstanding their cultural coloring—as I believe them to be—then they are potentially accessible to all. Significantly, although only one of them is my own it no more stands out in my mind than do the others. So all of them are now mine. Without such supplementary wealth, my life (perhaps any individual human life) would be too constrained and monotone to be wholly satisfactory.

5   Childhood. Is not timelessness—the sense that time moves slowly if at all—an important component of the child's ease in the world, his contentment? When the playwright Eugène Ionesco was eight years old, everything to him was joy, everything was *presentness*. The seasons seemed to spread out in space. They are a decorative background that expanded and contracted around a circular arena at the center of which stood the child. Now the flowers and grass moved toward him, now they moved away. Time passed but young Ionesco was outside of time. "At fifteen or sixteen it was all over," says Ionesco. "I was in time, in flight, in finiteness. The present had disappeared, there was nothing left for me but a past and a tomorrow which I was already conscious of as past."[1]

Children's experiences are often intense. It is not surprising that adults can recall them while forgetting those of maturer years. One reason for the intensity is that it comes to the child undiluted by context. When adults go fishing they have to prepare for it, making sure a day ahead that the car is in good shape. On the way there they worry about the effect of the corded country roads on the mayonnaise jars in the trunk. Throughout the day they may wonder whether they can really afford to take the day off from work. None of these worries nag the young child. Fishing for him is a pure experience cut off from what had taken place before and may happen after. The physician Percival Bailey recalls the happiest moment of his life as catching fish. "I cannot have been more than four years old," he writes. "The whole setting is still a vivid picture in my mind—the creek which ran across my grandfather's farm, the big willow tree, my mother and my grandfather, who had prepared the hook and line and given the pole to me to hold. When the cork bobbed, I pulled as I had been told, and out came a little sliver of silver which danced in the sunshine at the end of the line. I ran around like one possessed, shrieking in a delirium of joy." Bailey did not become henceforth an avid fisherman. His favorite treatise on the art is not *The Compleat Angler* but a more modern one titled *To Hell With Fishing!* "Can it be," Bailey asks, "that there is a subconscious wish to protect this ancient memory? At any rate, on that day I was completely happy, for I was too young to realize the tragic destiny of mankind, and no one to whom that realization has come can ever be completely happy again."[2]

The total absorption of children at play, in blissful ignorance of the problematical world around them, is noted by Reginald Turner in a letter dated May 1937. "I have decided that the ideal age to be is ten, since two days ago I saw three urchins of (seemingly) that age splashing about in the Arno* and then rolling down a bank of dirty sand while the people on the bridge watched them—some disapprovingly, for they were stark naked and Florence had become puritan, though they had no sex showing as amounted to more than a pin point.... But there they were, quite ravenously happy with no thought of the Gold Standard,[†] or disarmament** or even the status of Mrs. Warfield Simpson[††]—only caring for being covered with dirty sand and then plunging into the still cool water like tadpoles."[3]

For children and athletes life is joyous in its vitality, and vitality is motion during which time is forgotten, space becomes freedom, self and world unite. In his autobiography, *The Four Minute Mile* (1955), Roger Bannister recalls a moment in childhood when he stood "barefoot on firm dry sand by the sea." He had just taken a few tentative, running steps. "I was startled," he wrote, "and frightened, by the tremendous excitement that so few steps could create. I glanced around uneasily to see if anyone was watching. A few more steps—selfconsciously now and firmly gripping the original excitement. The earth seemed almost to move with me. I was running now, and a fresh rhythm entered my body. No longer conscious of my movement I discovered a new unity with nature. I had found a new source of power and beauty, a source I never dreamed existed."[4]

We are not always vigorous and on top of the world. For all of us a time comes when we feel the need to withdraw, sink self-indulgently into a passive state that attracts to it sympathy and care. But in modern society adults, even when sick, cannot really count on the solicitous care of others. They are expected to stand on their feet—the posture of action. Children in modern society, by contrast, have no such demands placed upon them. They fulfill their end by simply living and growing. The protection they receive is never more evident than when sick. Here is a sketch by John Updike of a boy suffering from flu. It captures a tender moment in middle-class childhood. In the story, a man lived with a boy who had awoken with a sore throat and stayed home from school. Turning the newspaper pages, the man heard the boy's mother mounting to him with breakfast on a tray and remembered those mornings when he too stayed home from school, remembered "the fresh orange juice seedy from its squeezing, the toast warm from its toasting and cut into strips, the Rice Krispies, the blue cream

---

*The Arno River flows through Florence, Italy.

[†]The value of world currency was historically backed by gold. Whether or not the Gold Standard contributed to the Great Depression, or its end, was hotly debated in the run-up to World War II.

**In the years prior to World War II, nations debated whether or not to increase military spending in response to Hitler's massive arms buildup.

[††]The King of England caused an international uproar in 1936 when he abdicated his throne to marry the twice-divorced American socialite, Wallace Simpson.

pitcher, the sugar, the japanned tray where his mother had arranged these good things like the blocks in an intelligence test, the fever-swollen mountains and valleys of the blankets where books and crayons and snub-nosed scissors kept losing themselves, the day outside the windows making its irresistible arc from morning to evening, the people of the town traveling to their duties and back, running to the trolley and walking wearily back, his father out suffering among them, yet with no duty laid on the child but to live, to stay safe and get well, to do that huge something called nothing."[5]

10   Heaven is other people. The gallery of the good life is necessarily filled with pictures of human contact—erotic, affectional, courtly, and intellectual. Erotic contact is accessible to the very young, as the following story told by Nikos Kazantzakis indicates. Kazantzakis was three years old, his girl friend a year older. One day the little girl took his hand and brought him into her mother's house. "Without losing a moment, we took off our socks, lay down on our backs, and glued our bare soles together. We did not breathe a word. Closing my eyes, I felt Emine's warmth pass from her soles to mine, then ascend little by little to my knees, belly, breast, and fill me entirely. The delight I experienced was so profound that I thought I would faint.... Even now, seventy years later, I close my eyes and feel Emine's warmth rise from my soles and branch out through my entire body, my entire soul."[6]

So many eloquent and passionate words have been spent on erotic love that we do well to present here an abstract statement rather than a detailed picture. The hero in an Iris Murdoch novel wonders what after all does love consist in, and answers: "Suddenly the reorientation of the world round one illumined point, all else in shadow. The total alteration of corporeal being, the minute electric sensibility of the nerves, the tender expectancy of the skin. The omnipresence of a ghostly sense of touch. The awareness of organs. The absolute demand for the presence of the beloved, the categorical imperative, the beauty of all things. The certainty; and with it the great sad knowledge of change and decay."[7]

Experiences that make for the good life can be quite ordinary. They can, of course, also be exceptional. When affection between two brothers is joined to deep intellectual sympathy, the combination is rare enough to seem an extraordinary gift of fortune. "What a happiness it was for me to have such a brother!—a brother who, moreover, loved me passionately," wrote Peter Kropotkin (1842–1921) in his memoirs. When Kropotkin was sixteen years old and a cadet in the Imperial School for Pages and his brother, one year older, was a cadet in another military school, they could seldom meet. One night Alexander escaped from his school, walked five miles through rough country haunted by wild dogs, in order to see Peter. (If the older boy had been caught the punishment could be whipping and then exile to Siberia.) The servants of their Moscow home hid the two brothers in the coachman's house.

> They looked at us, and took seats at a distance, along the walls, exchanging words in a subdued tone, so as not to disturb us; while we two, in each other's arms, sat there till midnight, talking about nebulae and Laplace's hypothesis, the structure of matter, the struggles of the papacy under Boniface VIII with the imperial power, and so on.[8]

In the small world of a traditional community, one sees few strangers. What it offers is human warmth and entanglements along settled paths rather than the poignancy of the chance encounter, at an unfamiliar place, with a stranger. In the large world of our time, such encounters are possible—even likely—and they are among the human blessings of contemporary life. Encounters of even the briefest sort may leave an indelible impression. Because they are unlikely ever to be repeated, they can have the luminous import of an epiphany. "I arrive," says W. N. P. Barbellion, "toward evening at a village thirty miles in the country and enter a baker's shop for a loaf of bread for my supper. There is the baker, fat, bald, and sleepy—waiting for me. He has been waiting there all day—for weeks past—perhaps all his life! He hands me the loaf, our courses touch and then we sweep away again out into the infinite. What would he say if I told him his life was a beautiful parabolic curve?"[9]

Barbellion called on a professor of zoology. He was inadvertently shown by the maid into the drawing room in which a little boy lay on a rug sound asleep, with his head framed in one arm and his curls hanging loosely down over his face. "I looked down upon his little form and upon his face and marvelled. He never stirred and I stepped softly from the room and never saw him again."[10]

15   Pablo Neruda recalls an incident from his childhood—an exchange of gifts with a young stranger—that is to become for him a lifelong inspiration—the "light of his poetry." Playing in the lot behind the house one day, young Neruda discovered a hole in the fence board.

> I looked through the hole and saw a landscape like that behind our house, uncared for, and wild. I moved back a few steps, because I sensed vaguely that something was about to happen. All of a sudden a hand appeared—a tiny hand of a boy about my own age. By the time I came close again, the hand was gone, and in its place there was a marvelous white toy sheep.
>
> The sheep's wool was faded. Its wheels had escaped. All of this only made it more authentic. I have never seen such a wonderful sheep. I looked back through the hole but the boy had disappeared. I went into the house and brought out a treasure of my own: a pine cone, opened, full of odor and resin, which I adored. I set it down in the same spot and went off with the sheep. I never saw either the hand or the boy again.[11]

Courtesy is an aristocratic gesture extended to people we do not know, or do not know well. Louis XIV was a courteous man. When he encountered a charwoman in a corridor of Versailles, he doffed his hat. In time, it became a mark of common civility to extend these gestures of respect and of concern to strangers and acquaintances that one met on the public stages of life. "Every customer is a lady" was not only the slogan but the normal practice of the great department store in the latter half of the nineteenth century. "Have a nice day!" is the compulsive benediction of the marketplace in contemporary America. Of course, such gestures easily turn routine and insincere. Yet there is something wonderful in the notion that courtesy can become as unexamined and automatic as breathing. When a mark of concern from an acquaintance or stranger is touched by genuine warmth, it seems a miracle.

Courtesy is not restricted to the courtly life or to urban culture. Rousseau speaks of the "noble savage." There is also the expression "nature's aristocrat" or the "natural aristocrat." Despite the somewhat condescending tone of these well-intentioned labels, they do address an important fact—that an exquisite gentilesse is not the exclusive possession of any people. A journalist explores the Ituri rain forest of central Africa. Of his guide—a native villager—the journalist notes: "Once, as he walked beside me, with his hands clasped shyly in front of him, I tripped and he said, with a look of real distress, as if it were *his* fault, '*Oh, pardon, monsieur.*'" The villager identifies with the forest. The journalist is his guest, and if he trips in the villager's home, an expression of regret is appropriate.[12]

Polite exchange and erotic love are at two extremes of intensity in human relationship. Somewhere in between is friendship. Yet a meeting of minds can be as intimate and intoxicating as a meeting of bodies: indeed minds interpenetrate far more fully than do bodies. Bertrand Russell records his remarkable relationship with Joseph Conrad thus: "At our very first meeting, we talked with continually increasing intimacy. We seemed to sink through layer after layer of what was superficial, till gradually both reached the central fire. It was an experience unlike any other that I have known. We looked into each other's eyes half appalled and half intoxicated to find ourselves together in such a region. The emotion was as intense as passionate love, and at the same time all-embracing. I came away bewildered, and hardly able to find my way among ordinary affairs."[13]

The good life and nature are intertwined in the mythos of civilizations. When we ask what aspects or images of nature are identified with the good life, the answer at the cultural level is fairly standard: they are variants of the garden and the farm, which we shall explore in the next chapter. At the individual level, predictably, the beloved face of nature is extraordinarily varied. Turgenev worships nature. What aspects? Not its "greedy, egoistic power," says he in a letter, but "the hurried movements of a duck at the edge of a lake as it scratches the back of its head with its moist foot, or the long gleaming drops of water, slowly falling from the mouth of a cow after it has drawn its fill from the pond."[14] For John Cowper Powys, "the curious metallic whiteness of water just before nightfall" arouses a strong emotion. He is also strangely stirred by the sight of any fragment of rooftop or wall-coping bathed in the yellow light of the rising or descending sun. "Thus transfigured," he notes, "the mere fact of a thing resting there, in its immobility, with the immense gulfs of air sinking away into illimitable space behind it, evokes, as it lies back upon the calm mystery of dawn or of evening, the feeling that it is the golden threshold of some land of enchantment into which our soul can enter and find a solution of all the paradoxes of life."[15]

20   Nature is a feeling of uplift. No precise image needs be present. Is it likely that we can read without recognition the following passage from John Knowles's novel *A Separate Peace*? Years ago, "one summer day after another broke with a cool effulgence over us, and there was a breath of widening life in the morning air—something hard to describe—an oxygen intoxicant, a shining northern paganism, some odor, some feeling so hopelessly promising that I would fall back in my bed on guard against it.... I wanted to break out crying from the stabs of hopeless joy, or intolerable promise, or because those mornings were too full of beauty for me, because I knew of too much hate to be contained in a world like this."[16]

Life is power and effectiveness; it is the ability to be and to do. A child running and skipping along the seashore is exuberant with power. The part of nature that he has the surest command over are his own limbs, which obey with easy grace. In adulthood, men and women possess certain skills the exercise of which transforms the world, however slightly. The ability to act effectively makes for the good life, all the more so if a skillful performance brings immediate happiness to others. Enhancing the good of another, even to a slight degree, gives one a sense of creative power. John Riley is a repair-man. He says: "If I went to a house, to repair their television, and it wasn't working when I went there—especially if there were children there—and after I repaired it and I left, there was a family there happy—happy with the work that I'd done—that made me happy. I can come home at night, knowing that I've made several families happy. Whereas I go to do a day's work in the dock [Riley is a dock foreman's son], and what have I achieved? All I've achieved is money."[17]

Power over people can, of course, be of a vastly different kind and order. If, after a long illness, we take delight in our obedient limbs again, how incomparably greater must be the pleasure of "radiating daily impulsions into an immense mass and prompting the distant movement of millions of unknown limbs?" So Bertrand de Jouvenel asks in his book *On Power*. This incomparable pleasure may be savored by one who, because of age, no longer has the easy use of his own limbs. In the shadows of a cabinet a gray-haired official sits. "The thoughts he thinks keep pace with the order he gives. He sees in his mind's eye the canal being dug along the line which his pencil has traced on the map, the boats which will shortly give it life, the villages springing up on its banks, the profusion of merchandise heaped high on the quays of his dream-town." Is it surprising that Jean Baptiste Colbert (1619–83), on coming to his desk in the morning, rubbed his hands for joy?[18]

The good life is life awake, although without the daily immersion in restorative oblivion, consciousness becomes sheer torture. We say that we have enjoyed a good night's sleep. In fact, we cannot enjoy sleep, only the state of passing into sleep, as we cannot experience death, only the state of passing into death. Drowsiness can be savored, as, more generally, "letting go" or just drifting along. Mental balance is strained unless we can periodically let go. An appropriate image of the good life is drowsy tranquillity. Montaigne was so taken with the pleasure of sleep that "rather than let sleep insensibly escape me, I used once to have myself woken up, in order that I might catch a glimpse of it."[19] John Cowper Powys proclaims: "Without any doubt the moments of our life while we are sliding into the unconsciousness of sleep are the happiest of all. One can prove this by recalling the scraping, harrowing, and jarring misery that any interruption—bringing us back with a jerk—produces in us."[20] C. S. Lewis admits:

> To lie in bed—to find one's eyes filling with facile tears at the least hint of pathos in one's book—to let the book drop from one's hand as one sinks deeper and deeper into reverie—to forget what you were thinking about a moment ago and not to mind—and then be roused by the unexpected discovery that it is already tea-time—all this I do not find disagreeable.[21]

Notes

[1] Eugène Ionesco. *Fragments of a Journal* (London: Faber & Faber, 1968), p. 11.

[2] Percival Bailey, "Harun al-Rashid," *Perspectives in Biology and Medicine* 10, no. 4 (1967): 540–58.

[3] Quoted by Stanley Weintraub. *Reggie* (New York; Braziller, 1965), p. 241.

[4] Roger Bannister, *The Four-Minute Mile* (New York: Dodd, 1955), pp. 11–12.

[5] John Updike, "The Egg Race," *The New Yorker*, June 13, 1977, pp. 36–40.

[6] Nikos Kazantzakis, *Report to Greco* (New York: Bantam Books, 1966), p. 47.

[7] Iris Murdoch, *The Philosopher's Pupil* (New York: Viking Press, 1983, p. 282.

[8] P. Kropotkin, *Memoirs of a Revolutionist* (New York: Horizon Press, 1968; first published in 1899), pp. 100–101.

[9] W. N. P. Barbellion, *Enjoying Life and Other Literary Remains* (London: Chatto & Windus, 1919), p. 34.

[10] Ibid., p. 35.

[11] Pablo Neruda, *Twenty Poems*, transl. James Wright and Robert Bly (Madison, Minnesota: Sixties Press, 1967), pp. 14–15.

[12] Alex Shoumatoff, "The Ituri Forest," *The New Yorker*, February 6, 1984, p. 88.

[13] Bertrand Russell, *Autobiography* (Toronto: McClelland & Stewart, 1967), vol. 1, p. 209.

[14] *Turgenev's Letters*, transl. & ed. A. V. Knowles (New York: Scribners, 1983).

[15] John Cowper Powys, *The Art of Happiness* (London: John Lane the Bodley Head, 1935), p. 185.

[16] John Knowles, *A Separate Peace* (New York: Bantam Books, 1966), p. 47.

[17] Alasdair Clayre, *Work and Play: Ideas and Experience of Work and Leisure* (London: Weidenfeld and Nicolson, 1974), p. 191.

[18] Bertrand de Jouvenel, *On Power: Its Nature and the History of Its Growth* (Boston: Beacon Press, 1962), p. 121.

[19] Michel de Montaigne, *Essays* (Harmondsworth, Middlesex: Penguin Books, 1958), p. 401.

[20] John Cowper Powys, *In Defense of Sensuality* (New York: Simon and Schuster, 1930), p. 108.

[21] *Letters of C. S. Lewis*, ed. W. H. Lewis (Harcourt, Brace and World, 1966), p. 202.

 Review Questions

1. What is Tuan's main claim?

2. Outline the structure of Tuan's essay. Pay close attention to his use of illustrations.

Discussion and Writing Suggestions

1. Describe an experience in which an important memory of someone else has become an important memory for you—as important as if it were the recollection of your own experience. Tuan writes that his life is enriched by the memories cherished by others, that his days would be "constrained and monotone" without

them. If you have come to value the experience of another in this way, discuss the ways in which (and the times at which) another's memory enriches you.

2. Tuan associates childhood experience with the qualities of timelessness, intensity, absorption at play, vitality, and sympathy. He offers anecdotes to illustrate each quality. Choose one of these qualities and illustrate it with a memory from your own childhood. Do you, like Tuan, find the memories of childhood especially vivid?

3. Tuan's essay is rich with anecdotes illustrating what he calls the "good life"— the happy life. Of the all these illustrations, which do you find most evocative? Which particularly moves you? Why?

4. Tuan suggests that a never-ending stream of peak experiences in our lives would be "sheer torture" without "the daily immersion in restorative oblivion." What does he mean? Do you agree?

FROM *ZEN AND THE ART OF MOTORCYCLE MAINTENANCE*

Robert M. Pirsig

Zen and the Art of Motorcycle Maintenance: An Inquiry into Values (1974) is a thinly disguised novel, written in the first person, about a motorcycle trip that Robert Pirsig and his son, Chris, took from Minnesota to California. *Zen and the Art* was a publishing phenomenon. Heralded as a work of genius, with comparisons made to *Moby Dick* and the novels of Dostoevsky, *Zen* sold millions of copies (after being rejected 121 times) and became an iconic, philosophical must-read for a generation. It concerns motorcycle maintenance, as the title implies; but more broadly Pirsig investigates the nature of "quality" and an approach to living that blends the rational and intuitive. In this excerpt, Pirsig illustrates a species of happiness discussed by several authors in this chapter.

It's about ten o'clock in the morning and I'm sitting alongside the machine on a cool, shady curbstone back of a hotel we have found in Miles City, Montana. Sylvia is with Chris at a Laundromat doing the laundry for all of us. John is off looking for a duckbill to put on his helmet. He thought he saw one at a cycle shop when we came into town yesterday. And I'm about to sharpen up the engine a little.

Feeling good now. We got in here in the afternoon and made up for a lot of sleep. It was a good thing we stopped. We were so stupid with exhaustion we didn't know how tired we were. When John tried to register rooms he couldn't even remember my name. The desk girl asked us if we owned those "groovy, dreamy motorcycles" outside the window and we both laughed so hard she wondered what she had said wrong. It was just numbskull laughter from too much fatigue. We've been more than glad to leave them parked and walk for a change.

And baths. In a beautiful old enameled cast-iron bathtub that crouched on lion's paws in the middle of a marble floor, just waiting for us. The water was so soft it felt as if I would never get the soap off. Afterward we walked up and down the main streets and felt like a family....

On this machine I've done the tuning so many times it's become a ritual. I don't have to think much about how to do it anymore. Just mainly look for anything unusual. The engine has picked up a noise that sounds like a loose tappet but could be something worse, so I'm going to tune it now and see if it goes away. Tappet adjustment has to be done with the engine cold, which means wherever you park it for the night is where you work on it the next morning, which is why I'm on a shady curbstone back of a hotel in Miles City, Montana. Right now the air is cool in the shade and will be for an hour or so until the sun gets around the tree branches, which is good for working on cycles. It's important not to tune these machines in the direct sun or late in the day when your brain gets muddy because even if you've been through it a hundred times you should be alert and looking for things.

5   Not everyone understands what a completely rational process this is, this maintenance of a motorcycle. They think it's some kind of a "knack" or some kind of "affinity for machines" in operation. They are right, but the knack is almost purely a process of reason, and most of the troubles are caused by what old time radio men called a "short between the earphones," failures to use the head properly. A motorcycle functions entirely in accordance with the laws of reason, and a study of the art of motorcycle maintenance is really a miniature study of the art of rationality itself. I said yesterday that the ghost of rationality was what Phaedrus pursued and what led to his insanity, but to get into that it's vital to stay with down-to-earth examples of rationality, so as not to get lost in generalities no one else can understand. Talk about rationality can get very confusing unless the things with which rationality deals are also included.

We are at the classic-romantic barrier now, where on one side we see a cycle as it appears immediately—and this is an important way of seeing it—and where on the other side we can begin to see it as a mechanic does in terms of underlying form—and this is an important way of seeing things too. These tools for example—this wrench—has a certain romantic beauty to it, but its purpose is always purely classical. It's designed to change the underlying form of the machine.

The porcelain inside this first plug is very dark. That is classically as well as romantically ugly because it means the cylinder is getting too much gas and not enough air. The carbon molecules in the gasoline aren't finding enough oxygen to combine with and they're just sitting here loading up the plug. Coming into town yesterday the idle was loping a little, which is a symptom of the same thing.

Just to see if it's just the one cylinder that's rich I check the other one. They're both the same. I get out a pocket knife, grab a stick lying in the gutter and whittle down the end to clean out the plugs, wondering what could be the cause of the richness. That wouldn't have anything to do with rods or valves. And carbs rarely go out of adjustment. The main jets are oversized, which causes richness at high speeds but the plugs were a lot cleaner than this before with the *same* jets. Mystery. You're always surrounded by them. But if you tried to solve them all, you'd never get the machine fixed. There's no immediate answer so I just leave it as a hanging question.

The first tappet is right on, no adjustment required, so I move on to the next. Still plenty of time before the sun gets past those trees...I always feel like I'm in church when I do this...The gage is some kind of religious icon and I'm performing a holy rite with it. It is a member of a set called "precision measuring instruments" which in a classic sense has a profound meaning.

10   In a motorcycle this precision isn't maintained for any romantic or perfectionist reasons. It's simply that the enormous forces of heat and explosive pressure inside this engine can only be controlled through the kind of precision these instruments give. When each explosion takes place it drives a connecting rod onto the crankshaft with a surface pressure of many tons per square inch. If the fit of the rod to the crankshaft is precise the explosion force will be transferred smoothly and the metal will be able to stand it. But if the fit is loose by a distance of only a few thousandths of an inch the force will be delivered suddenly, like a hammer blow, and the rod, bearing and crankshaft surface will soon be pounded flat, creating a noise which at first sounds a lot like loose tappets. That's the reason I'm checking it now. If it *is* a loose rod and I try to make it to the mountains without an overhaul, it will soon get louder and louder until the rod tears itself free, slams into the spinning crankshaft and destroys the engine. Sometimes broken rods will pile right down through the crankcase and dump all the oil onto the road. All you can do then is start walking.

But all this can be prevented by a few thousandths of an inch fit which precision measuring instruments give, and this is their classical beauty—not what you see, but what they mean—what they are capable of in terms of control of underlying form.

The second tappet's fine. I swing over to the street side of the machine and start on the other cylinder.

Precision instruments are designed to achieve an *idea*, dimensional precision, whose perfection is impossible. There is no perfectly shaped part of the motorcycle and never will be, but when you come as close as these instruments take you, remarkable things happen, and you go flying across the countryside under a power that would be called magic if it were not so completely rational in every way. It's the understanding of this rational intellectual *idea* that's fundamental. John looks at the motorcycle and he sees steel in various shapes and has negative feelings about these steel shapes and turns off the whole thing. I look at the shapes of the steel now and I see *ideas*. He thinks I'm working on *parts*. I'm working on *concepts*.

I was talking about these concepts yesterday when I said that a motorcycle can be divided according to its components and according to its functions. When I said that suddenly I created a set of boxes with the following arrangement:

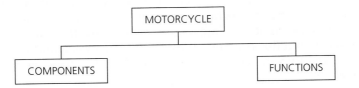

And when I said the components may be subdivided into a power assembly and a running assembly, suddenly appear some more little boxes:

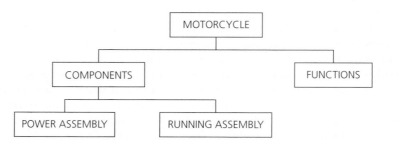

15   And you see that every time I made a further division, up came more boxes based on these divisions until I had a huge pyramid of boxes. Finally you see that while I was splitting the cycle up into finer and finer pieces, I was also building a structure.

This structure of concepts is formally called a hierarchy and since ancient times has been a basic structure for all Western knowledge. Kingdoms, empires, churches, armies have all been structured into hierarchies. Modern businesses are so structured. Tables of contents of reference material are so structured, mechanical assemblies, computer software, all scientific and technical knowledge is so structured—so much so that in some fields such as biology, the hierarchy of phylum-order-class-genus-species is almost an icon.

The box "motorcycle" *contains* the boxes "components" and "functions." The box "components" *contains* the boxes "power assembly" and "running assembly," and so on. There are many other kinds of structures produced by other operators such as "causes" which produce long chain structures of the form, "A causes B which causes C which causes D," and so on. A functional description of the motorcycle uses this structure. The operator's "exists," "equals," and "implies" produce still other structures. These structures are normally interrelated in patterns and paths so complex and so enormous no one person can understand more than a small part of them in his lifetime. The overall name of these interrelated structures, the genus of which the hierarchy of containment and structure of causation are just species, is *system*. The motorcycle is a system. A *real* system.

To speak of certain government and establishment institutions as "the system" is to speak correctly, since these organizations are founded upon the same structural conceptual relationships as a motorcycle. They are sustained by structural relationships even when they have lost all other meaning and purpose. People arrive at a factory and perform a totally meaningless task from eight to five without question because the structure demands that it be that way. There's no villain, no "mean guy" who wants them to live meaningless lives, it's just that the structure, the system demands it and no one is willing to take on the formidable task of changing the structure just because it is meaningless.

But to tear down a factory or to revolt against a government or to avoid repair of a motorcycle because it is a system is to attack effects rather than causes; and as long as the attack is upon effects only, no change is possible. The true system, the real system, is our present construction of systematic thought itself, rationality itself, and if a factory is torn down but the rationality which produced it is left standing, then that rationality will simply produce another factory. If a revolution destroys a systematic government, but the systematic patterns of thought that produced that government are left intact, then those patterns will repeat themselves in the succeeding government. There's so much talk about the system. And so little understanding.

20   That's all the motorcycle is, a system of concepts worked out in steel. There's no part in it, no shape in it, that is not out of someone's mind...number three tappet is right on too. One more to go. This had better be it.... I've noticed that people who have never worked with steel have trouble seeing this—that the motorcycle is primarily a mental phenomenon. They associate metal with given shapes—pipes, rods, girders, tools, parts—all of them fixed and inviolable, and think of it as primarily physical. But a person who does machining or foundry work or forge work or welding sees "steel" as having no shape at all. Steel can be any shape you want if you are skilled enough, and any shape *but* the one you want if you are not. Shapes, like this tappet, are what you *arrive* at, what you give to the steel. Steel has no more shape than this old pile of dirt on the engine here. These shapes are all out of someone's mind. That's important to see. The *steel*? Hell, even the steel is out of someone's mind. There's no steel in nature. Anyone from the Bronze Age could have told you that. All nature has is a *potential* for steel. There's nothing else there. But what's "potential"? That's also in someone's mind!... Ghosts.

That's really what Phaedrus was talking about when he said it's all in the mind. It sounds insane when you just jump up and say it without reference to anything specific like an engine. But when you tie it down to something specific and concrete, the insane sound tends to disappear and you see he could have been saying something of importance.

The fourth tappet *is* too loose, which is what I had hoped. I adjust it. I check the timing and see that it is still right on and the points are not pitted, so I leave them alone, screw on the valve covers, replace the plugs and start it up.

The tappet noise is gone, but that doesn't mean much yet while the oil is still cold. I let it idle while I pack the tools away, then climb on and head for a cycle shop a cyclist on the street told us about last night where they may have a chain adjuster link, and a new foot-peg rubber. Chris must have nervous feet. His foot pegs keep wearing out.

I go a couple blocks and still no tappet noise. It's beginning to sound good, I think it's gone. I won't come to any conclusions until we've gone about thirty miles though. But until then, and right now, the sun is bright, the air is cool, my head is clear, there's a whole day ahead of us, we're almost to the mountains, it's a good day to be alive. It's this thinner air that does it. You always feel like this when you start getting into higher altitudes.

● Discussion and Writing Suggestions

1. In ¶ 4, Pirsig describes what it is like to be familiar with tuning a motorcycle engine: "I've done the tuning so many times it's become a ritual. I don't have to think much about how to do it anymore." Yet later in the same paragraph, Pirsig writes that "even if you've been through [a tuning] a hundred times you should be alert and looking for things." How can one not "think much" yet remain "alert"?

2. In ¶s 6–11, Pirsig draws a distinction between the classical and romantic meanings of an object. Clarify this distinction in your own words. Then discuss the classical and romantic meanings of an object of your choice (one that Pirsig does not discuss).

3. In ¶ 13, Pirsig provides another example of seeing the same object in two ways—this time, the steel of a motorcycle. Pirsig's riding companion sees the steel of a motorcycle as so many parts. Pirsig sees concepts. Why is this distinction meaningful? Can you see a similar distinction in some complex structure other than a motorcycle? Explain.

4. Pirsig devotes much of this excerpt from *Zen and the Art of Motorcycle Maintenance* to establishing how the motorcycle, in the rational assembly of its parts, is a "hierarchy" or a "system of concepts worked out in steel"—that is, an idea. With this novel view of an ordinary object, Pirsig shifts our way of seeing. To what extent did you find yourself willing, and able, to follow him as he moves from objects to ideas?

5. In this chapter, you've learned that happiness researchers study three kinds of happiness: happiness as private reverie (Critchley); happiness as a social interaction (Dunn, Gilbert, and Wilson); and happiness as an experience of total engagement, or flow (Csikszentmihalyi). In which of these senses does Pirsig strike you as happy as he tunes his motorcycle?

◯ SYNTHESIS ACTIVITIES

1. What are the guiding principles of positive psychology, and what do critics claim are its greatest weaknesses? In explaining positive psychology, draw on the selections by Seligman, Dunn et al., Senior, and Csikszentmihalyi. In explaining the criticisms, draw on the work by Critchley, Schoch, and Begley. Conclude with an observation on the ways in which both camps, despite their differing methods, strive to understand more about happiness.

2. Researchers on happiness have found a strong correlation between a person's happiness and the quality of that person's network of friends and family. On this point, see Dunn et al., Principle 2. At the same time, Critchley, writing on Rousseau's and his own experiences of happiness, extols the virtues of the

solitary person's happiness. And Csikszentmihalyi—as well as Pirsig—write of "flow" as a private experience. Allowing that both types of happiness are possible and that one view does not negate the other, with which view of happiness do you identify more strongly: social or solitary? Develop your response into an explanatory synthesis.

3. The authors in this chapter discuss three kinds of happiness: solitary happiness, happiness that results from intense engagement with an activity, and happiness experienced through social contact. In an explanatory synthesis, compare and contrast these different kinds of happiness. Illustrate each type of happiness with observations and anecdotes from your own life.

4. McFall, Critchley, Tuan, Pirsig, and Kenyon write about happiness far differently than do Seligman, Dunn et al., and Csikszentmihalyi. These two sets of writers—philosophers and a poet on the one hand, social scientists on the other—use different assumptions, logic, and types of evidence to explore the topic of happiness. In an explanatory synthesis, identify these different assumptions, logic, and types of evidence. Conclude with an observation on which approach to studying happiness appeals to you more.

5. Jennifer Senior quotes psychoanalyst and philosopher Adam Phillips: "[A]nyone who could maintain a state of happiness, given the state of the world, is living in a delusion" (¶52). Do you agree? Develop your answer into an argument.

6. Reread ¶43 in the selection by Jennifer Senior, on the life—and suicide—of happiness researcher Philip Brickman. Senior writes: "There's an untold distance between knowing happiness and knowing about it." What is this "untold distance?" Develop your answer into an argument synthesis that draws on selections in this chapter.

7. Lynne McFall does not answer the questions implied by John Stuart Mill's famous statement: "It is better to be a human dissatisfied than a pig satisfied; better to be Socrates dissatisfied than a fool satisfied." Instead, she poses a series of questions herself, none of which she answers. Write an argument responding to any one of McFall's questions. To the extent possible, draw on the selections in this chapter for evidence in your argument.

8. Mark Kingwell paraphrases Nathaniel Hawthorne, who "famously compared happiness to a butterfly which, if pursued, always eludes your grasp, but which, if you sit quietly, may just land upon you." The existential philosopher Albert Camus writes: "You will never be happy if you continue to search for what happiness consists of. You will never live if you are looking for the meaning of life." In her last paragraph, Begley writes: "But maybe, just maybe, the single-minded pursuit of happiness as an end in itself, rather than as a consequence of a meaningful life, has finally run its course." What are the differences between happiness that comes as a consequence of living and happiness that comes as the result of an explicit search for happiness? To what extent do you agree with these writers? Develop your response into an argument.

9. Drawing on selections in this chapter, argue for the necessity of sadness in our lives. What do we risk by emphasizing extreme happiness—personally, socially, as a species? Develop your response into an argument.

10. Five philosophers are represented in this chapter: McFall, Kingwell, Critchley, Tuan, and Pirsig. From these writers, what can you infer about the types of questions philosophers ask? About the logic of their answers? About the types of evidence they use? Develop your responses into an argument synthesis.

11. Reflect on an experience in your life when you were happy. Analyze this experience using two different principles for analysis that you've discovered in this chapter. Note that what you observe about your experience will change as you change analytical tools. Compare and contrast these observations. Which analytical principle is more powerful? Which helped you to understand your experience more deeply? Why? Develop your answers into an argument in which you claim that one analytical principle is more powerful than the other.

12. Several writers have reflected on the phenomenon that we cease being happy the instant we realize we're happy. See Csikszentmihalyi, ¶16, and Kingwell, quoting John Stuart Mill in ¶5. (Kingwell also quotes Eric Hoffer, who claims that searching for happiness brings *un*happiness.) Do you agree? Can you be happy and *know* you're happy? Develop your response into an argument. Use sources in the chapter as evidence, together with anecdotes from your own experience.

RESEARCH ACTIVITIES

1. Conduct an Internet search on "happiness." Spend about half an hour reading and browsing through the first two or three pages of results. What will readers discover from conducting this exercise? What definitions of happiness, approaches to the study of happiness, projects on happiness, insights about happiness, and ways of achieving happiness will this brief Internet search reveal?

2. Locate and read any of the sources that the authors of this chapter cite in developing their own selections. Choose a source that you find especially interesting. Locate the source in your library or in an online database and prepare a report for your classmates.

3. Read Darrin McMahon's "The Quest for Happiness," a brief history of humankind's efforts to understand happiness. You will find the article online, in your library's *JSTOR* database. See *Wilson Quarterly*, Winter 2005 (Vol. 29, No. 1), pp. 62–71. Select one of the figures McMahon discusses and conduct further research. Prepare a ten-minute talk for your classmates on this person's views of happiness.

4. Investigate the cities and towns in the United States that have begun distributing surveys to their citizens to learn about what makes them happy—with the expectation of incorporating their answers into public policy. (You might begin with Somerville, MA.) How successful has the experiment been?

5. Choose a religious tradition with which you are familiar and investigate its traditional pathways to happiness. Don't rely on your recollected understanding of these pathways, perhaps from early religious study. Research the core texts of this tradition. Report on the essential conditions of what counts as a happy life. Do you encounter individuals who are held out as inspirational examples of people who lived good, happy lives?

6. Research Abraham Maslow's concept of self-actualization and his concept of the peak experience. Compare this latter concept to Csikszentmihalyi's concept of "flow." What is Maslow's "hierarchy of needs"? At what point in this hierarchy is self-actualization possible? What is the relationship between happiness and self-actualization?

7. Research the nation of Bhutan's programs to improve the happiness of its citizens. What prompted the focus on happiness? What assumptions guide the policy? What specific initiatives have been put in place? What are the successes and (thus far) failures of the program?

8. Research the so-called "Easterlin Paradox," the finding that after a certain point, rising national wealth is not matched with rising levels of happiness. The paradox has been recently challenged. Write a synthesis that explains the paradox, the evidence in favor of its existence, and the challenges to its existence.

9. How do *pleasure* and *happiness* differ? What have various commentators written on the distinction over the centuries? What is your view of the distinction?

Chapter 13

Green Power

Our wealth, our society, our being is driven by oil and carbon. And when we say that we have to make a shift, that is extremely difficult. It is intellectually dishonest to say that we can get some lightbulbs, or we can get a Prius, and we're all done. No—this is going to take massive technological innovation. It's going to take changes in the way we live and work. It's going to take cooperation of unprecedented degree among businesses and government and among countries. That's where we are. There's no other word except "daunting."

—Jerry Brown, Governor of California

In 2006, climber and filmmaker David Braeshears made his way up to a Himalayan outcrop on a steep ridge 19,000 feet high. From that familiar vantage point he had a clear view of the Rongbuk Glacier in Tibet, a frozen river of ice that flows from the north slope of Mount Everest. Comparing what he was seeing to a photograph taken in 1921 from the same vantage point by British explorer George Mallory, he was appalled by how much the ice had melted. "The glacier's just gone," he remarked to *Frontline* producer Martin Smith. It had, in fact, lost some 40% of its mass in the past eighty-five years.

The shrunken Himalayan glacier is but one more indication—along with collapsing ice shelves in Antarctica and polar bears stranded on ice floes—of the extent of climate change since the middle of the twentieth century. Climate experts warn of nothing short of an apocalypse unless current global warming trends are reversed. The earth's population faces the prospect of more frequent and severe hurricanes, fires, declining agricultural yields, the extinction of species, and rising ocean levels that threaten to flood coastal cities. Author and *New York Times* columnist Thomas Friedman quotes environmental consultant Rob Watson on the nature of the challenge we confront: "People don't seem to realize...that it is not like we're on the *Titanic* and we have to avoid the iceberg. *We've already hit the iceberg.* The water is rushing in below. But some people just don't want to leave the dance floor; others don't want to give up on the buffet."

What's causing climate change? Experts point to increasing levels of greenhouse gases—chiefly carbon dioxide, or CO_2. (Other greenhouse gases include methane, ozone, and water vapor.) These gases trap the sun's heat in the atmosphere by preventing infrared rays from escaping into space—and, therefore, they keep living things from freezing to death. (Like cholesterol, a certain quantity of greenhouse gases is essential to survival.) For most of human history, greenhouse gases have remained at a life-supporting equilibrium. But accelerating levels of industrialization during the twentieth century, and particularly during the latter half of that century, have changed the equilibrium by measurably increasing atmospheric levels of CO_2, a byproduct of the burning of fossil fuels such as coal and oil, energy sources that are integral to the existence of modern civilization. More than half of the nation's electricity is generated by the burning of coal. It takes 9½ tons of coal to produce the quantity of electricity used by the average American each year. And, of course, the overwhelming majority of the world's vehicles are fueled by gasoline, or refined petroleum.

The internal combustion, CO_2-spewing engine that has powered vehicles of every type since the dawn of the automobile era in the early twentieth century has long been viewed as one of the greatest culprits in creating air pollution—and, more recently, in contributing to climate change. And bad as the situation is now, it is expected to get far worse. The number of cars in the world, about 625 million, is anticipated to double by 2020. China and India—whose populations account for a third of humanity—will soon overtake the United States as the world's biggest oil importers.

In recent years, interest in and development of alternative energy sources that do not release CO_2 (or, at least, not *as much* CO_2) into the atmosphere—and thus that serve to slow, if not reverse, the pace of global climate change—has intensified. Automakers are now taking the first serious steps away from gasoline-powered vehicles in an effort to "green" the transportation industry—as evidenced by the popularity of the Toyota Prius and other hybrids, the advent of plug-in hybrid vehicles such as the Chevrolet Volt, and all-electric cars such as the Nissan Leaf. Increasingly, natural gas and biofuels are being used to power cars and buses; and on the horizon are cars powered by hydrogen fuel cells.

Wind and solar power continue to gain ground as sources of electricity for home and industry. In 2008, Texas oilman T. Boone Pickens launched a highly visible public relations campaign explaining his plan to build the world's largest wind farm in Texas, which would generate and transmit enough electricity to power one million homes. As the recession that began later that year deepened, however, the scarcity of credit and the falloff in natural gas prices (making wind power economically less attractive) forced Pickens to scale back his ambitious project in favor of a series of smaller wind farms in the Midwest.

More controversial is nuclear power, owing chiefly to questions of safety and cost. The safety issues surrounding nuclear energy were thrown into sharp relief in 2011 when three nuclear reactors at the Fukushima Daiichi facility in northeastern Japan experienced a meltdown in the wake of a major earthquake and tsunami. Building a nuclear power plant costs between $5 and $10 billion, and no application for a new nuclear power plant has been approved since 1979 (the year of the Three Mile Island reactor accident). Other renewable sources of electrical power include hydroelectric (generated by the force of flowing water); geothermal (generated by heat from the earth's core, transmitted to the surface); and biomass (generated by the burning of organic matter such as wood, leaves, manure, and crops). As of 2011, however, only about 12% of the nation's energy consumption was being generated from renewable sources—as opposed to 40% from fossil fuels such as petroleum and 22% from coal.

The development of green power, of renewable energy sources, is not only a global imperative, but it is also a matter of public policy. That is, it involves questions of what government does or does not do to encourage or discourage particular activities by businesses, nonprofit organizations, educational institutions, and individuals. Governments issue regulations, pass laws, tax and spend, subsidize, make grants, reward those who comply with their rules, and penalize those who do not. In the 1970s, the U.S. government attempted to impose CAFE (Corporate Average Fuel Efficiency Standards) regulations mandating minimum fuel efficiency standards for vehicles. But automakers have long resisted such controls and have pressured their elected representatives to ease or abandon them.

Other government efforts to curb greenhouse gas emissions have not survived industry opposition. Environmentalists were encouraged by the election of Barack Obama, who favored the development of renewable energy sources and of a "smart" national energy grid. Obama also proposed reducing the nation's reliance on fossil fuels by increasing fuel efficiency standards through such programs as cap and trade. Between 2009 and 2011, the Obama Interior Department approved 27 renewable energy projects, both wind and solar, capable of generating 6,500 megawatts (compared with about 1,800 megawatts in all prior years). But the new president, faced with staunch congressional opposition (even among some fellow Democrats) to his green energy programs, found it difficult to get many of his proposals passed into law. And green energy development suffered a major public relations setback after the Solyndra Corporation, a government-subsidized company that manufactured improved solar panels, went bankrupt—a debacle costing the taxpayers more than $500 million. In terms of public policy on green power, the states may end up having more of an impact than the federal government. In April 2011, for example, California governor Jerry Brown signed a law requiring that by 2020, 33% of the state's energy (an increase over the previous mandate of 20%) be generated by renewable energy sources.

The selections in this chapter offer multiple perspectives on how we can reduce (if not entirely eliminate) our dependence on fossil fuels and support the development of alternative, renewable energy sources. As you might expect, experts disagree not only about the nature of the problem and its causes, but also about needed solutions. Therefore, we present represent some of these disagreements, which will give you ample opportunity to evaluate, respond, and form your own informed opinions.

The chapter is organized into two sections. The first lays out the more general challenges we face in addressing a carbon emission–related climate crisis and in working to reduce our dependence on fossil fuels. The second section considers particular alternative, renewable energy sources such as nuclear, solar, and wind. This section includes a status update on electric-powered vehicles and their potential impact in reducing carbon output.

We begin with "Going Green: A Wedge Issue." In his recent book *Hot, Flat, and Crowded* (2008), Thomas Friedman argues that there are no easy ways to save the earth. You'll view part of his dynamic presentation on the topic in a lecture at

M.I.T., in which he asserts that we must "change or die." Then you'll go online to read about the very difficult things we, as citizens of the planet earth, must do to ensure that our world remains capable of sustaining life. In "The National Security Consequences of U.S. Oil Dependency," an independent task force sponsored by the Council on Foreign Relations lays out policy alternatives by which government could provide incentives to reduce the nation's dependence on petroleum, a dependence it views as a national security issue. Closing this first section, in "The Dangerous Delusions of Energy Independence," Robert Bryce throws cold water on those who believe that we can free ourselves of reliance upon oil produced in other countries. "Energy independence is hogwash," he declares. "Worse yet, the inane obsession with the idea of energy independence is preventing the U.S. from having an honest and effective discussion about the energy challenges it now faces."

The second half of the chapter, organized into four clusters, focuses on several types of alternative energy and on electric-powered vehicles. In the nuclear power cluster, columnists Holman Jenkins, Jr., Eugene Robinson, William Tucker, and Anne Applebaum offer four contrasting viewpoints in the debate over the safety and viability of nuclear power in the wake of the Fukushima accident of 2011. In the solar power cluster, *Los Angeles Times* reporter Marla Dickerson discusses what the state of California has done to convert a significant part of its power generation from coal to solar; Nobel Prize–winning economist Paul Krugman discusses the politics of solar energy; and *Washington Post* blogger Brad Plumer argues that solar power is about to reach the breakout stage. In the wind power cluster, *New Yorker* writer Elizabeth Kolbert reports on the fascinating case of the Danish island of Samsø ("island in the wind"), whose citizens decided to convert to electrical power generated entirely by wind turbines. In "Wind Power Puffery," however, H. Sterling Burnett dismisses the prospect of wind power as a significant response to our energy problems.

Leading off the electric car cluster, energy expert Daniel Yergin reviews the history, current status, and prospects of converting the nation's largely gasoline-powered vehicle fleet to battery power. Then *Wall Street Journal* reporter Joseph P. White cautions that the challenges facing alternative energy vehicles are daunting—which is why, he writes, "The Gasoline Engine Isn't Going Anywhere Soon."

And so the debate continues, not only between businesspeople and environmentalists, but also among environmentalists themselves. To return to Thomas Friedman: "there is no 'Easy' button we can press to make the world green."

GOING GREEN: A WEDGE ISSUE

We begin our exploration of Green Power by inviting you to virtually attend a lively presentation at M.I.T. by *New York* Times columnist Thomas Friedman. Then go online to read a provocative discussion, by scientists Robert H. Socolow and Stephen W. Pacala, about the kind of massively scaled energy projects that will be required to reduce planet-wide CO_2 emissions in meaningful ways.

Thomas Friedman, foreign affairs columnist for the *Times*, has won three Pulitzer Prizes for his books, which include *From Beirut to Jerusalem* (1989), *The Lexus and the Olive Tree* (1999), and *The World is Flat* (2005). (We offer an excerpt from *The World is Flat* in Chapter 9, "The Changing Landscape of Work in the Twenty-First Century.") In his M.I.T., talk Friedman discusses issues covered in his more recent book *Hot, Flat, and Crowded: Why We Need a Green Revolution—And How It Can Renew America* (2008).

Go to: YouTube.com

Search terms: "thomas friedman mit green energy"

Using less restrictive search terms (e.g., "thomas friedman green energy"), you can find clips of Friedman in many other academic venues and in TV interviews. Look, especially, for an interview with Friedman by Fareed Zakaria. In *Hot, Flat, and Crowded*, Friedman discusses the startling findings of Socolow and Pacala concerning just how much hard work will be required to truly accomplish a "green revolution"—and not just a "green party." In their September 2006 *Scientific American* article, Socolow and Pacala introduce the concept of "wedges"—each wedge of the circle representing an activity that reduces the world's carbon levels by 25 billion tons over the next 50 years. A workable carbon strategy, according to Socolow and Pacala, requires the implementation of seven such wedges. Socolow and Pacala head the Carbon Migration Initiative at Princeton University. Socolow is a professor of mechanical engineering. Pacala is a professor of ecology.

Go to: Google *or* Bing

Search terms: "a plan to keep carbon in check"

 ## Discussion and Writing Suggestions

1. Friedman pokes fun at what passes for a "green revolution"—and what he calls a "green party." Why? Do you agree with him? To what extent have you bought into the kind of "eco-chic" for which Friedman has such scorn? Do you think he is not sufficiently appreciative of well-intentioned (if ineffectual) efforts on the part of individuals?

2. Both in his talks and his writing, Friedman uses a breezy, punchy manner of delivery. "Washington today," he claims, is "brain dead." We cannot keep being "as dumb as we want to be." He sneers at people who strive to be "green" by buying Priuses or low energy light bulbs. To what extent is this style effective for you? Did you find it, for instance, refreshing? irreverent? offensive?

3. Friedman lays partial blame on the government for not effectively responding to the threat of climate change. "If we had a government that was as alive as the country," he charges, "no one would touch us." Friedman also suggests that a smarter set of regulations—and in particular, raising taxes on fossil fuel energy—would increase the real cost of oil to the planet so that green energy sources would become competitive. Do you believe that government policy could help to bring about a genuine green revolution? If so, how? Alternatively, should government "get out of the way," as conservatives recommend, and let

private industry take the lead? To what extent do you think that government policy since the time Friedman gave his presentation (during the last months of the George W. Bush administration) has begun to effectively address the problems posed by climate change?

4. Friedman asks, "Have you ever seen a revolution where no one got hurt?" The underlying principle here is that in real revolutions people *do* get hurt—not necessarily physically, but perhaps economically, or in such a way as to significantly change their preferred lifestyle. "Change or die!" he admonishes. Write an analysis in which you apply this or another of Friedman's principles or definitions to a particular situation of which you have personal knowledge or about which you have read. See the guidelines and model analyses in Chapter 6 for ideas on how to proceed.

5. Examine Socolow and Pacala's chart "15 Ways to Make a Wedge." Which of these wedges—or sets of wedges—do you believe are the most realizable, the most likely to be accomplished in the next 50 years? Why? The least likely? Why? What are the potential roadblocks? For those wedges that you view as most practical, discuss the combination of government policies and private/commercial initiatives that you think are most necessary.

6. For each of the wedge groups in Socolow and Pacala's chart—e.g., alternative energy sources, carbon capture and storage (CCS), or power generation—which industrial or political interests do you think would be most opposed to progress? What do you imagine their arguments would be? What are some counter-arguments? What is your position?

7. Socolow and Pacala describe nuclear power as "probably the most controversial of all the wedge strategies." Among the drawbacks of nuclear power: the potential for catastrophic accidents, the problem of nuclear waste disposal, and the possibility that some governments would convert civilian application of nuclear energy to weapons development. What is your view, at this point, of the potential for nuclear power to alleviate the world's energy problems and avoid catastrophic climate change? Note: the "Debate on Nuclear Power, Post-Fukushima," later in this chapter, may give you additional food for thought on this subject.

NATIONAL SECURITY CONSEQUENCES OF U.S. OIL DEPENDENCE

Report of an Independent Task Force

The following selection is excerpted from the "Overview and Introduction" of a Task Force report issued in October 2006 by the Council on Foreign Relations. The Task Force chairs were John Deutch (who served as deputy secretary of defense from 1994 to 1995 and as director of the Central Intelligence Agency from 1995 to 1996) and James Schlesinger (secretary of defense from 1973 to 1975 and America's first secretary of energy under President Carter). The blue-ribbon group included twenty-four other members.

The lack of sustained attention to energy issues is undercutting U.S. foreign policy and U.S. national security. Major energy suppliers—from Russia to Iran to Venezuela—have been increasingly able and willing to use their energy resources to pursue their strategic and political objectives. Major energy consumers—notably the United States, but other countries as well—are finding that their growing dependence on imported energy increases their strategic vulnerability and constrains their ability to pursue a broad range of foreign policy and national security objectives. Dependence also puts the United States into increasing competition with other importing countries, notably with today's rapidly growing emerging economies of China and India. At best, these trends will challenge U.S. foreign policy; at worst, they will seriously strain relations between the United States and these countries.

This report focuses on the foreign policy issues that arise from dependence on energy traded in world markets and outlines a strategy for response. And because U.S. reliance on the global market for oil, much of which comes from politically unstable parts of the world, is greater than for any other primary energy source, this report is mainly about oil. To a lesser degree it also addresses natural gas.

Put simply, the reliable and affordable supply of energy—"energy security"—is an increasingly prominent feature of the international political landscape and bears on the effectiveness of U.S. foreign policy. At the same time, however, the United States has largely continued to treat "energy policy" as something that is separate and distinct—substantively and organizationally—from "foreign policy." This must change. The United States needs not merely to coordinate but to integrate energy issues with its foreign policy.

The challenge over the next several decades is to manage the consequences of unavoidable dependence on oil and gas that is traded in world markets and to begin the transition to an economy that relies less on petroleum. The longer the delay, the greater will be the subsequent trauma. For the United States, with 4.6 percent of the world's population using 25 percent of the world's oil, the transition could be especially disruptive.

5   During the next twenty years (and quite probably beyond), it is infeasible to eliminate the nation's dependence on foreign energy sources. The voices that espouse "energy independence" are doing the nation a disservice by focusing on a goal that is unachievable over the foreseeable future and that encourages the adoption of inefficient and counterproductive policies. Indeed, during the next two decades, it is unlikely that the United States will be able to make a sharp reduction in its dependence on imports, which currently stand at 60 percent of consumption. The central task for the next two decades must be to manage the consequences of dependence on oil, not to pretend the United States can eliminate it.

A popular response to the steep rise in energy prices in recent years is the false expectation that policies to lower imports will automatically lead to a decline in prices. The public's continuing expectation of the availability of cheap energy alternatives will almost surely be disappointed. While oil prices may retreat from their current high levels, one should not expect the price of oil to return, on a sustained basis, to the low levels seen in the late 1990s. In fact, if more costly domestic supply is used to substitute for imported oil, then prices will not moderate. Yet the public's elected representatives have allowed this myth to survive, as they advocate policies that futilely attempt to reduce import dependence quickly while simultaneously lowering prices. Leaders of both political parties, especially when seeking public office, seem unable to resist announcing unrealistic goals that are transparent efforts to gain popularity rather than inform the public of the challenges the United States must overcome. Moreover, the political system of the United States has so far proved unable to sustain the policies that would be needed to manage dependence on imported fuels. As history since 1973 shows, the call for policy action recedes as prices abate.

These problems rooted in the dependence on oil are neither new nor unique to the United States. Other major world economies that rely on imported oil—from Western Europe to Japan, and now China and India—face similar concerns. All are having difficulties in meeting the challenges of managing demand for oil. But these countries do not share the foreign policy responsibilities of the United States. And the United States, insufficiently aware of its vulnerability, has not been as attentive as the other large industrialized countries in implementing policies to slow the rising demand for oil. Yet even if the United States were self-sufficient in oil (a condition the Task Force considers wholly infeasible in the foreseeable future), U.S. foreign policy would remain constrained as long as U.S. allies and partners remained dependent on imports because of their mutual interdependence. Thus, while reducing U.S. oil imports is desirable, the underlying problem is the high and growing demand for oil worldwide.

The growing worldwide demand for oil in the coming decades will magnify the problems that are already evident in the functioning of the world oil market. During that period, the availability of low-cost oil resources is expected to decline; production and transportation costs are likely to rise. As more hydrocarbon resources in more remote areas are tapped, the world economy will become even more dependent on elaborate and vulnerable infrastructures to bring oil and gas to the markets where they are used.

For the last three decades, the United States has correctly followed a policy strategy that, in large measure, has stressed the importance of markets. Energy markets, however, do not operate in an economically perfect and transparent manner. For example, the Organization of Petroleum Exporting Countries (OPEC), quite notably, seeks to act as a cartel. Most oil and gas resources are controlled by state-run companies, some of which enter into supply contracts with consumer countries that are accompanied by political arrangements that distort the proper functioning of the market. These agreements, such as those spearheaded by the Chinese government in oil-rich countries across Africa and elsewhere, reflect many intentions, including the desire to "lock up" particular supplies for the Chinese market. Some of the state companies that control these resources are inefficient, which imposes further costs on the world market. And some governments use the revenues from hydrocarbon sales for political purposes that harm U.S. interests. Because of these realities, an active public policy is needed to correct these market failures that harm U.S. economic and national security. The market will not automatically deliver the best outcome.

•   •   •

10   [W]hile the United States has limited leverage to achieve its energy security objectives through foreign policy actions, it has considerable ability to manage its energy future through the adoption of domestic policies that complement both a short- and long-term international strategy.

The Task Force is unanimous in recommending the adoption of incentives to slow and eventually reverse the growth in consumption of petroleum products, especially transportation fuels such as motor gasoline. However, the Task Force did not agree about the particular options that would best achieve this objective. The Task Force considered three measures:

- A tax on gasoline (with the tax revenue recycled into the economy with a fraction possibly earmarked for specific purposes such as financing of energy technology research and development [R&D]);
- Stricter and broader mandated Corporate Average Fuel Economy standards, known as CAFE standards; and
- The use of tradable gasoline permits that would cap the total level of gasoline consumed in the economy.

Used singly or in combination, these measures would not only encourage higher-efficiency vehicles (although these will take time to find their way into the fleet), but also encourage the introduction of alternative fuels, as well as promote changes in behavior such as the greater use of public transportation. While there are other domestic policies that could be adopted to limit demand for fuels, no strategy will be effective without higher prices for transportation fuels or regulatory incentives to use more efficient vehicles....

At the same time that the United States promotes measures to reduce oil demand, it should also be prepared to open some new areas for exploration and production of oil and gas, for example, in Alaska, along the East and West coasts, and in the Gulf of Mexico. In addition to modestly increasing supply, encouraging domestic production is a valuable, if not essential, element for increasing the credibility of U.S. efforts to persuade other nations to expand their exploration and production activities.

Ultimately, technology will be vital to reducing the dependence on oil and gas, and to making a transition away from petroleum fuels. These benefits of improved technology will come in the future only if investments are made today in research, development, and demonstration (RD&D).

15   The Task Force notes that higher energy prices are unleashing remarkable forces for innovation in this country. Entrepreneurs are seeking new ideas for products and services, such as batteries, fuel cells, and biofuels. Private equity

capital is seeking opportunities to invest in new energy technologies. Large corporations are investing in RD&D in all aspects of energy production and use. These activities will undoubtedly result in a steady improvement in the ability of the U.S. economy to meet energy needs.

The U.S. government has an important role in supporting this innovation in the private sector, especially for technologies that require significant development efforts to demonstrate commercial potential. The Task Force recommends that the federal government offer greatly expanded incentives and investments aimed at both short- and long-term results to address a wide range of technologies that includes higher-efficiency vehicles, substitutes for oil in transportation (such as biomass and electricity), techniques to enhance production from existing oil wells, and technologies that increase the energy efficiency of industrial processes that use oil and gas. Government spending is appropriate in this context because the market alone does not make as much effort as is warranted by national security and environmental considerations....

● Discussion and Writing Suggestions

1. The authors of the report assert that "[t]he central task for the next two decades must be to manage the consequences of dependence on oil, not to pretend the United States can eliminate it." To what extent do you agree with this conclusion? Are the authors of the report being too pessimistic, even defeatist, about the prospects for nationwide conversion to renewable energy?

2. The authors of this report fault politicians of both parties for misleading the public about the prospects of reducing the nation's dependence on foreign oil in the near term (¶ 5). Conduct a short Google or Bing (or other database) search—using, among other search terms, "energy independence"—and report on whether or not you agree with the Task Force authors on this matter.

3. The Task Force considered three measures that would help reduce American dependence on foreign oil and spur the development of higher-efficiency vehicles and alternative fuels: (1) increased taxes on gasoline, (2) raised fuel economy (CAFE) standards, (3) and a cap-and-trade system for gasoline. Which of these measures do you find the most (and least) desirable? The most (and least) practical? Explain.

4. The Task Force recommends increasing domestic production of oil and gas by opening "new areas [within the United States and in the Gulf of Mexico] for the exploration of oil and gas"—that is, by drilling. During the 2008 presidential campaign, "Drill, baby, drill!" became a campaign slogan. To what extent do you favor increased drilling? Explain.

THE DANGEROUS DELUSIONS OF ENERGY INDEPENDENCE

Robert Bryce

In the following selection, Robert Bryce argues that it is neither possible nor desirable for the United States to become independent of foreign energy supplies. Those who advocate such independence, he claims, are "woefully ignorant about the fundamentals of energy and the energy business." Bryce's provocative conclusion flies in the face of often unexamined assumptions held by many politicians, as well as environmentalists.

Robert Bryce, a fellow at the Institute for Energy Research and a managing editor of the *Energy Tribune*, has written about energy for more than two decades. His articles have appeared in such publications as the *Atlantic Monthly*, the *Guardian*, and the *Nation*. His books include *Cronies: Oil, the Bushes, and the Rise of Texas, America's Superstate* (2004) and *Power Hungry: The Myths of Green Energy and the Real Fuels of the Future* (2010). This selection is excerpted from the introduction ("The Persistent Delusion") to his book *Gusher of Lies: The Dangerous Delusions of "Energy Independence"* (2008).

Americans love independence.

Whether it's financial independence, political independence, the Declaration of Independence, or grilling hotdogs on Independence Day, America's self-image is inextricably bound to the concepts of freedom and autonomy. The promises laid out by the Declaration—life, liberty, and the pursuit of happiness—are the shared faith and birthright of all Americans.

Alas, the Founding Fathers didn't write much about gasoline.

Nevertheless, over the past 30 years or so—and particularly over the past 3 or 4 years—American politicians have been talking as though Thomas Jefferson himself warned about the dangers of imported crude oil. Every U.S. president since Richard Nixon has extolled the need for energy independence. In 1974, Nixon promised it could be achieved within 6 years.[1] In 1975, Gerald Ford promised it in 10.[2] In 1977, Jimmy Carter warned Americans that the world's supply of oil would begin running out within a decade or so and that the energy crisis that was then facing America was "the moral equivalent of war."[3]

5   The phrase "energy independence" has become a prized bit of meaningful-sounding rhetoric that can be tossed out by candidates and political operatives eager to appeal to the broadest cross section of voters. When the U.S. achieves energy independence, goes the reasoning, America will be a self-sufficient Valhalla, with lots of good-paying manufacturing jobs that will come from producing new energy technologies. Farmers will grow fat, rich, and happy by growing acre upon acre of corn and other plants that can be turned into billions of gallons of oil-replacing ethanol. When America arrives at the promised land of milk, honey, and supercheap motor fuel, then U.S. soldiers will never again need visit the Persian Gulf, except, perhaps, on vacation. With energy independence, America can finally dictate terms to those rascally Arab sheikhs from troublesome countries. Energy independence will mean a thriving economy, a positive balance of trade, and a stronger, better America.

The appeal of this vision of energy autarky has grown dramatically since the terrorist attacks of September 11. That can be seen through an analysis of news stories that contain the phrase "energy independence." In 2000, the Factiva news database had just 449 stories containing that phrase. In 2001, there were 1,118 stories. By 2006, that number had soared to 8,069.

The surging interest in energy independence can be explained, at least in part, by the fact that in the post–September 11 world, many Americans have been hypnotized by the conflation of two issues: oil and terrorism. America was attacked, goes this line of reasoning, because it has too high a profile in the parts of the world where oil and Islamic extremism are abundant. And buying oil from the countries of the Persian Gulf stuffs petrodollars straight into the pockets of terrorists like Mohammad Atta and the 18 other hijackers who committed mass murder on September 11.

Americans have, it appears, swallowed the notion that all foreign oil—and thus, presumably, all foreign energy—is bad. Foreign energy is a danger to the economy, a danger to America's national security, a major source of funding for terrorism, and, well, just not very patriotic. Given these many assumptions, the common wisdom is to seek the balm of energy independence. And that balm is being peddled by the Right, the Left, the Greens, Big Agriculture, Big Labor, Republicans, Democrats, senators, members of the House, [former president] George W. Bush, the opinion page of the *New York Times*, and the neoconservatives. About the only faction that dismisses the concept is Big Oil. But then few people are listening to Big Oil these days.

Environmental groups like Greenpeace and Worldwatch Institute continually tout energy independence.[4] The idea has long been a main talking point of Amory Lovins, the high priest of the energy-efficiency movement and the CEO of the Rocky Mountain Institute.[5] One group, the Apollo Alliance, which represents labor unions, environmentalists, and other left-leaning groups, says that one of its primary goals is "to achieve sustainable American energy independence within a decade."[6]

10   Al Gore's 2006 documentary about global warming, *An Inconvenient Truth*, implies that America's dependence on foreign oil is a factor in global warming.[7] The film, which won two Academy Awards (for best documentary feature and best original song), contends that foreign oil should be replaced with domestically produced ethanol and that this replacement will reduce greenhouse gases.[8] (In October 2007, Gore was awarded the Nobel Peace Prize.)

The leading Democratic candidates for the White House in 2008 have made energy independence a prominent element of their stump speeches. [Former] Illinois senator Barack Obama has declared that "now is the time for serious leadership to get us started down the path of energy independence."[9] In January 2007, in the video that she posted on her Website that kicked off her presidential campaign, New York senator Hillary Clinton said she wants to make America "energy independent and free of foreign oil."[10]

The Republicans are on board, too. In January 2007, shortly before Bush's State of the Union speech, one White House adviser declared that the president would soon deliver "headlines above the fold that will knock your socks off in terms of our commitment to energy independence."[11] In February 2007, Arizona senator and presidential candidate John McCain told voters in Iowa, "We need energy independence. We need it for a whole variety of reasons."[12] In March 2007, former New York mayor Rudolph Giuliani insisted that the federal government "must treat energy independence as a matter of national security." He went on, saying that "we've been talking about energy independence for over 30 years and it's been, well, really, too much talk and virtually no action.... I'm impatient and I'm single-minded about my goals, and we will achieve energy independence."[13]

• • •

Polls show that an overwhelming majority of Americans are worried about foreign oil. A March 2007 survey by Yale University's Center for Environmental Law and Policy found that 93 percent of respondents said imported oil is a serious problem and 70 percent said it was "very" serious.[14] That finding was confirmed by an April 2007 poll by Zogby International, which found that 74 percent of Americans believe that cutting oil imports should be a high priority for the federal government. And a majority of those surveyed said that they support expanding the domestic production of alternative fuels.[15]

The energy independence rhetoric has become so extreme that some politicians are even claiming that lightbulbs will help achieve the goal. In early 2007, U.S. Representative Jane Harman, a California Democrat, introduced a bill that would essentially outlaw incandescent bulbs by requiring all bulbs in the U.S. to be as efficient as compact fluorescent bulbs. Writing about her proposal in the *Huffington Post*, Harman declared that such bulbs could "help transform America into an energy efficient and energy independent nation."[16]

15   While Harman may not be the brightest bulb in the chandelier, there's no question that the concept of energy independence resonates with American voters and explains why a large percentage of the American populace believes that energy independence is not only doable but desirable.

But here's the problem: It's not and it isn't.

Energy independence is hogwash. From nearly any standpoint—economic, military, political, or environmental—energy independence makes no sense. Worse yet, the inane obsession with the idea of energy independence is preventing the U.S. from having an honest and effective discussion about the energy challenges it now faces.

[Let's] acknowledge, and deal with, the difference between rhetoric and reality. The reality is that the world—and the energy business in particular—is becoming ever more interdependent. And this interdependence will likely only accelerate in the years to come as new supplies of fossil fuel become more difficult to find and more expensive to produce. While alternative and renewable forms of energy will make minor contributions to America's overall energy mix, they cannot provide enough new supplies to supplant the new global energy paradigm, one in which every type of fossil fuel—crude oil, natural gas, diesel fuel, gasoline, coal, and uranium—gets traded and shipped in an ever more sophisticated global market.

Regardless of the ongoing fears about oil shortages, global warming, conflict in the Persian Gulf, and terrorism, the plain, unavoidable truth is that the U.S., along with nearly every other country on the planet, is married to fossil fuels. And that fact will not change in the foreseeable future, meaning the next 30 to 50 years. That means that the U.S. and the other countries of the world will continue to need oil and gas from the Persian Gulf and other regions. Given those facts, the U.S. needs to accept the reality of *energy interdependence*.

20   The integration and interdependence of the $5-trillion-per-year global energy business can be seen by looking at Saudi Arabia, the biggest oil producer on the planet.[17] In 2005, the Saudis *imported* 83,000 barrels of gasoline and other refined oil products per day.[18] It can also be seen by looking at Iran, which imports 40 percent of its gasoline needs. Iran also imports large quantities of natural gas from Turkmenistan.[19] If the Saudis, with their 260 billion barrels of oil reserves, and the Iranians, with their 132 billion barrels of oil and 970 trillion cubic feet of natural gas reserves, can't be energy independent, why should the U.S. even try?[20]

An October 2006 report by the Council on Foreign Relations put it succinctly: "The voices that espouse 'energy independence' are doing the nation a disservice by focusing on a goal that is unachievable over the foreseeable future and that encourages the adoption of inefficient and counterproductive policies."[21]

America's future when it comes to energy—as well as its future in politics, trade, and the environment—lies in accepting the reality of an increasingly interdependent world. Obtaining the energy that the U.S. will need in future decades requires American politicians, diplomats, and business people to be actively engaged with the energy-producing countries of the world, particularly the Arab and Islamic producers. Obtaining the country's future energy supplies means that the U.S. must embrace the global market while acknowledging the practical limits on the ability of wind power and solar power to displace large amounts of the electricity that's now generated by fossil fuels and nuclear reactors.

The rhetoric about the need for energy independence continues largely because the American public is woefully ignorant about the fundamentals of energy and the energy business.[22] It appears that voters respond to the phrase, in part, because it has become a type of code that stands for foreign policy isolationism—the idea being that if only the U.S. didn't buy oil from the Arab and Islamic countries, then all would be better. The rhetoric of energy independence provides political cover for protectionist trade policies, which have inevitably led to ever larger subsidies for politically connected domestic energy producers, the corn ethanol industry being the most obvious example.

But going it alone with regard to energy will not provide energy security or any other type of security. Energy independence, at its root, means protectionism and isolationism, both of which are in direct opposition to America's long-term interests in the Persian Gulf and globally.

25   Once you move past the hype and the overblown rhetoric, there's little or no justification for the push to make America energy independent. And that's the purpose of this book: to debunk the concept of energy independence and show

that none of the alternative or renewable energy sources now being hyped—corn ethanol, cellulosic ethanol, wind power, solar power, coal-to-liquids, and so on—will free America from imported fuels. America's appetite is simply too large and the global market is too sophisticated and too integrated for the U.S. to secede.

Indeed, America is getting much of the energy it needs because it can rely on the strength of an ever-more-resilient global energy market. In 2005, the U.S. bought crude oil from 41 different countries, jet fuel from 26 countries, and gasoline from 46.[23] In 2006, it imported coal from 11 different countries and natural gas from 6 others.[24] American consumers in some border states rely on electricity imported from Mexico and Canada.[25] Tens of millions of Americans get electricity from nuclear power reactors that are fueled by foreign uranium. In 2006, the U.S. imported the radioactive element from 8 different countries.[26]

Yes, America does import a lot of energy. But here's an undeniable truth: It's going to continue doing so for decades to come. Iowa farmers can turn all of their corn into ethanol, Texas and the Dakotas can cover themselves in windmills, and Montana can try to convert all of its coal into motor fuel, but none of those efforts will be enough. America needs energy, and lots of it. And the only way to get that energy is by relying on the vibrant global trade in energy commodities so that each player in that market can provide the goods and services that it is best capable of producing.

Notes

[1] Richard Nixon, State of the Union address, January 30, 1974. Available: http://www.thisnation.com/library/sotu/1974rn.html.

[2] Gerald Ford, State of the Union address, January 15, 1975. Available: http://www.ford.utexas.edu/LIBRARY/SPEECHES/750028.htm.

[3] Jimmy Carter, televised speech on energy policy, April 18, 1977. Available: http://www.pbs.org/wgbh/amex/carter/filmmore/ps_energy.html.

[4] Greenpeace is perhaps the most insistent of the environmental groups regarding energy independence. This 2004 statement is fairly representative: http://www.greenpeace.org/international/campaigns/no-war/war-on-iraq/it-s-about-oil. For Worldwatch, see its press release after George W. Bush's 2007 State of the Union speech, which talks about "increased energy independence." Available: http://www.worldwatch.org/node/4873.

[5] See any number of presentations by Lovins on energy independence. One sample: his presentation before the U.S. Senate Committee on Energy and Natural Resources on March 7, 2006. Available: http://energy.senate.gov/public/index.cfm?FuseAction=Hearings.Testimony&Hearing_ID=1534&Witness_ID=4345. Or see *Winning the Energy Endgame*, by Lovins et al., 228, discussing the final push toward "total energy independence" and the move to the hydrogen economy.

[6] National Apollo Alliance Steering Committee statement. Available: http://www.apolloalliance.org/about_the_alliance/who_we_are/steeringcommittee.cfm.

[7] At approximately 1:32 into the movie, in a section that discusses what individuals can do to counter global warming, a text message comes onto the screen: "Reduce our dependence on foreign oil, help farmers grow alcohol fuels."

[8] AMPAS data. Available: http://www.oscars.org/79academyawards/nomswins.html.

[9] Barack Obama, "Energy Security Is National Security," Remarks of Senator Barack Obama to the Governor's Ethanol Coalition, February 28, 2006. Available: http://obama.senate.gov/speech/060228-energy_security_is_national_security/index.html.

[10] Original video at www.votehillary.org. See also, http://www.washingtonpost.com/wp-dyn/content/article/2007/01/20/AR2007012000426.html.

[11] *New York Times*, "Energy Time: It's Not about Something for Everyone," January 16, 2007.

[12] Shailagh Murray, "Ethanol Undergoes Evolution as Political Issue," *Washington Post*, March 13, 2007, A06. Available: http://www.washingtonpost.com/wp-dyn/content/article/2007/03/12/AR2007031201722_pf.html.

[13] Richard Perez-Pena, "Giuliani Focuses on Energy," *The Caucus: Political Blogging from the New York Times*, March 14, 2007. Available: http://thecaucus.blogs.nytimes.com/2007/03/14/giuliani-focuses-on-energy.

[14] Yale Center for Environmental Law and Policy, 2007 Environment survey. Available: http://www.yale.edu/envirocenter/YaleEnvironmentalPoll2007Keyfindings.pdf.

[15] UPI, "Americans Want Energy Action, Poll Says," April 17, 2007. Available: http://www.upi.com/Energy/Briefing/2007/04/17/americans_want_energy_action_poll_says.

[16] Jane Harman, "A Bright Idea for America's Energy Future," *Huffington Post*, March 15, 2007. Available: http://www.huffingtonpost.com/rep-jane-harman/a-bright-idea-for-america_b_43519.html.

[17] http://www.infoplease.com/ipa/A0922041.html.

[18] Organization of Arab Petroleum Exporting Countries (OPEC), *Annual Statistical Report 2006*, 75. Available: http://www.oapecorg.org/images/A%20S%20R%202006.pdf.

[19] Nazila Fathi and Jad Mouawad, "Unrest Grows amid Gas Rationing in Iran," *New York Times*, June 29, 2007. According to this story, Iran imports gasoline from 16 countries. Iran has been importing natural gas from Turkmenistan since the late 1990s. In 2008, those imports will likely be about 1.3 billion cubic feet of natural gas per day. The fuel will be used to meet demand in northern Iran. For more, see, David Wood, Saeid Mokhatab, and Michael J. Economides, "Iran Stuck in Neutral," *Energy Tribune*, December 2006, 19.

[20] EIA oil reserve data for Saudi Arabia available: http://www.eia.doe.gov/emeu/cabs/saudi.html. EIA oil reserve data for Iran available: http://www.eia.doe.gov/emeu/cabs/Iran/Oil.html. EIA natural gas data for Iran available: http://www.eia.goe.gov/emeu/cabs/Iran/NaturalGas.html.

[21] Council on Foreign Relations, "National Security Consequences of U.S. Oil Dependency," October 2006, 4. Available: http://www.cfr.org/content/publications/attachments/EnergyTFR.pdf.

[22] A June 2007 survey done by Harris Interactive for the American Petroleum Institute found that only 9 percent of the respondents named Canada as America's biggest supplier of oil for the year 2006. For more on this, see Robert Rapier, "America's Energy IQ," R-Squared Energy Blog, June 29, 2007. Available: http://i-r-squared.blogspot.com/2007/06/americas-energy-iq.html#links. For the results of the entire survey, see: http://www.energytomorrow.org/energy_issues/energy_iq/energy_iq_survey.html.

[23] EIA crude import data available: http://tonto.eia.doe.gov/dnav/pet/pet_move_impcus_a2_nus_epc0_im0_mbbl_a.htm. EIA data for jet fuel available: http://tonto.eia.doe.gov/dnav/pet/pet_move_impcus_a2_nus_EPJK_im0_mbbl_a.htm. EIA data for

finished motor gasoline available: http://tonto.eia.doe.gov/dnav/pet/pet_move_imp-cus_a2_nus_epm0f_im0_mbbl_a.htm.

[24] EIA coal data available: http://www.eia.doe.gov/cneaf/coal/quarterly/html/t18p01p1 .html. For gas imports, EIA data available: http://tonto.eia.doe.gov/dnav/ng/ng_move_ impc_s1_a.htm.

[25] EIA data available: http://www.eia.doe.gov/cneaf/electricity/epa/epat6p3.html.

[26] Information from 2006, EIA data available: http://www.eia.doe.gov/cneaf/nuclear/ umar/table3.html.

● Review Questions

1. Why are Americans so obsessed with independence, according to Bryce?

2. Why does Bryce believe that renewable energy sources such as wind power and solar power cannot supplant fossil fuels in the foreseeable future?

3. How does Bryce explain the American public's (and their leaders') rhetoric about independence?

● Discussion and Writing Suggestions

1. What is Bryce's chief objection to the premise that the United States should strive to become energy independent? To what extent do you agree with his objection?

2. To what extent do you believe that Bryce is overly pessimistic about the prospects for renewable energy sources supplanting fossil fuels in the near term? Explain.

3. Bryce employs sarcasm plentifully throughout this piece. Cite examples. Do you think that he uses this rhetorical device effectively? Explain.

4. Bryce argues that "the U.S. needs to accept the reality of *energy interdependence.*" What implications does such an acceptance have for (1) domestic suppliers of fossil fuels (coal, oil, natural gas); (2) domestic consumption of energy from both fossil and renewable sources; (3) our relations with oil-supplying nations of the Middle East?

5. Critique Bryce's argument. Use as guidelines the principles discussed in Chapter 2. Consider first the main questions: (1) To what extent does Bryce succeed in his purpose? (2) To what extent do you agree with him? Then move to the specifics: Do you find Bryce's arguments compelling? Has he argued logically? What are his assumptions, and how do you assess their validity? You may want to draw upon other authors in this chapter—for example, Friedman or Gore—to provide support in your critique of Bryce. Keep in mind that this selection by Bryce is part of the introduction to a book-length treatment of the subject, during which he goes into much greater detail and a more extended

argument than you will find in this relatively brief excerpt. Nevertheless, the heart of Bryce's argument is contained in this passage.

6. Locate a specific principle or definition that Bryce uses in this selection. For example, in ¶1 he asserts that "Americans love independence" and in ¶17 he contends that "the world—and the energy business in particular—is becoming ever more interdependent. And this interdependence will likely only accelerate in the years to come..." Write an analysis in which you apply this or another principle or definition by Bryce to a particular situation of which you have personal knowledge or about which you have read. See the guidelines and model analyses in Chapter 6 for ideas on how to proceed.

A DEBATE ON THE FUTURE OF NUCLEAR POWER, POST-FUKUSHIMA

On March 11, 2011, a magnitude 9.0 earthquake off the northeastern coast of Japan, followed by a massive tsunami that flooded the Tohoku region, caused extensive damage to the Fukushima Daiichi power plant, a complex of six nuclear reactors operated by the Tokyo Electric Power Company. In the days that followed, three of the reactors experienced a nuclear meltdown when power failures caused the cooling-water levels in the nuclear core to drop, exposing and overheating the uranium fuel rods (see diagram, p. 496). A series of hydrogen explosions and the release of radioactive cesium into the atmosphere hampered plant workers from shutting down the reactors and controlling the damage. Residents within a 20 km. (12 mile) radius were evacuated, and the government subsequently banned the sale of food grown in the region. The plant's reactors would not be stabilized until mid-December, at which time 160,000 residents were still displaced.

Fukushima was the worst nuclear disaster since 1986, when the Chernobyl nuclear power reactor in the Ukraine suffered a meltdown, eventually exposing over half a million cleanup workers to toxic levels of radioactivity and releasing lesser levels of contamination over much of the western USSR and Europe. Hundreds of miles around Chernobyl remain uninhabitable today. The Fukushima accident renewed the long-dormant debate over the safety of nuclear power, just at the time when this technology was increasingly being viewed as a financially viable and relatively green alternative to the burning of coal as a source of electricity.

That debate is represented in the following four brief selections, originally published as op-eds in American newspapers soon after the disaster occurred. In "The Future of Nukes, and Japan," published on 16 March, 2011, *Wall Street Journal* columnist Holman W. Jenkins asserts that the impact of the nuclear accident at Fukushima was ultimately minimal but fears that "antinuclear panic" will forestall the further development of nuclear power in this country. Eugene Robinson, writing on 15 March 2011 for the *Washington Post*, argues in "Japan's

Nuclear Crisis Might Not Be Its Last" that the kind of disaster that struck Japan could also strike the United States. In his 23 April 2011 op-ed for the *Wall Street Journal*, William Tucker reminds us that all fuel sources (even ones considered "green") have their costs and drawbacks. Finally, in an op-ed published on 15 March 2011, *Washington Post* commentator Anne Applebaum wonders: "If the Japanese Can't Build a Safe Reactor, Who Can?"

HOW A NUCLEAR REACTOR WORKS

All power plants convert a source of energy or fuel into electricity. Most large plants do that by heating water to create steam, which turns a turbine that drives an electric generator. Inside the generator, a large electromagnet spins within a coil of wire, producing electricity.

A fossil plant burns coal or oil to make the heat that creates the steam. Nuclear power plants...make the steam from heat that is created when atoms split apart—called fission.

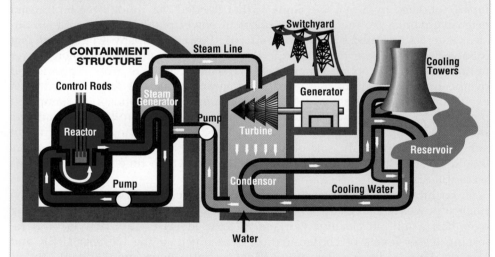

The fuel for nuclear power plants is uranium, which is made into pellets and sealed inside long metal tubes, called fuel rods. The rods are located in the reactor vessel.

The fission process takes place when the nucleus of a uranium atom is split when struck by a neutron. The "fissioning" of the nucleus releases two or three new neutrons and energy in the form of heat. The released neutrons then repeat the process, releasing more neutrons and producing more nuclear energy. The repeating of the process is called a chain reaction and creates the heat needed to turn water into steam.

(continued)

In a pressurized water reactor...water is pumped through the reactor core and heated by the fission process. The water is kept under high pressure inside the reactor so it does not boil.

The heated water from the reactor passes through tubes inside four steam generators, where the heat is transferred to water flowing around the tubes. The water boils and turns to steam.

The steam is piped to the turbines. The force of the expanding steam drives the turbines, which spin a magnet in coil of wire—the generator—to produce electricity.

After passing through the turbines, the steam is converted back to water by circulating it around tubes carrying cooling water in the condenser. The condensed steam—now water—is returned to the steam generators to repeat the cycle.

The cooling water from the condenser is sprayed into the air inside the cooling tower and falls about 60 feet, which cools it before it is continuously recycled to condense more steam. Water in the vapor rising from the cooling tower is replenished to the condenser cooling system using [pumped-in water, generally from a nearby river].

The three water systems at [a nuclear power plant] are separate from each other, and the radioactive water is not permitted to mix with other nonradioactive water systems.

Adapted from "How Sequoyah Works," Tennessee Valley Authority, http://www.tva.gov/power/nuclear/sequoyah_howworks.htm.

THE FUTURE OF NUKES, AND OF JAPAN

Holman W. Jenkins, Jr.

You can't beat for drama the struggle of Japanese operators to manage the emergency cool-down of nuclear reactors in the tsunami zone. For the things that matter most, though—life and safety—the nuclear battle has been a sideshow. Hundreds were feared dead when entire trains went missing. Whole villages were wiped out with the loss of thousands of inhabitants. So far one worker at one nuclear plant is known to have died in a hydrogen explosion and several others have exhibited symptoms of radiation poisoning.

As for environmental degradation, video testifies to the brown murk that the tsunami waters became when they crossed into land. An infinity of contaminants—sewage, fuels, lubricants, cleaning solvents—have been scattered across the Earth and into aquifers. Radiation releases, meanwhile, haven't been a serious threat to anyone but the plant's brave workers.

Just under a decade ago, when Americans were worried about the vulnerability of nuclear plants to deliberate terrorist destruction, Nuclear Regulatory Commission Chairman Nils Diaz gave a notable speech: "In general, I do not believe nuclear power is being portrayed in a balanced manner.... This is probably the fault of all of us who know better since there have been strong currents for not mentioning consequences [of nuclear accidents] out loud."

He proceeded to lay out the consequences of Chernobyl, a uniquely bad nuclear accident, in which a graphite core reactor burned in the open air for more than a week. Along with 59 firemen and workers who lost their lives, the failure to evacuate or take other precautionary steps led to 1,800 thyroid cancer cases among children, though fewer than a dozen deaths. "Leukemia has been expected to be among the early primary latent health effects seen among those exposed to significant amounts of radiation," Mr. Diaz continued, "yet excess cases of leukemia that can be attributed to Chernobyl have not been detected."

5   Do not pretty up what Mr. Diaz was saying. He was not offering risk-free energy. Now think about Japan. It suffered its worst earthquake in perhaps 1,100 years, followed by a direct-hit tsunami on two nuclear plants. Plenty of other industrial systems on which the Japanese rely—transportation, energy, water, food, medical, public safety—were overwhelmed and failed. A mostly contained meltdown of one or more reactors would not be the worst event of the month.

Note, as a matter of realism, we say "mostly contained." In a full or partial meltdown, you don't really know what you will get unless you know the condition of the containment structure and, even more, what's going on inside it, especially in terms of fluids and gases that might have to be vented. Complicating matters in Japan's case is also the failed cooling of spent fuel, yesterday contributing to a burst of emissions that alarmed but didn't threaten the wider public. Tokyo Electric has an almighty mess to clean up, but even in circumstances compounded by a region-wide natural disaster a Chernobyl-scale release seems likely to be avoided—in which case this year's deaths from nuclear power will be less than those from coal-mining accidents.

So here's a question: The world has gas and coal with which to produce electricity. Nuclear is a hot-house plant, requiring lots of government support. Environmental groups, with their perhaps unmerited moral authority, have insisted for years that curbing carbon is the greatest human challenge, and those groups that haven't opted for escapism, insisting wind and solar somehow can make up the difference, have quietly recognized that the only alternative to fossil energy is nuclear.

Where will these groups be in the morning? China and India, two fast-growing producers of greenhouse gases, have dozens of nuclear plants planned or under construction. India being a democracy, that country is particularly ripe to be turned off course by political reaction to Japan. If they believe their climate rhetoric, will environmentalists speak up in favor of nuclear realism or will they succumb to the fund-raising and media lure of antinuclear panic?

We suspect we already know the answer. In the unlikely event the world was ever going to make a concerted dent in CO2 output, nuclear was the key. Let's just guess this possibility is now gone, for better or worse.

NO FAIL-SAFE OPTION

Eugene Robinson

Nuclear power was beginning to look like a panacea—a way to lessen our dependence on oil, make our energy supply more self-sufficient and significantly mitigate global warming, all at the same time. Now it looks more like a bargain with the devil.

I wish this were not so. In recent years, some of the nation's most respected environmentalists—including Stewart Brand, founder of the Whole Earth Catalog—have come to champion nuclear power. But as Japanese engineers struggle frantically to keep calamity from escalating into catastrophe, we cannot ignore the fact that nuclear fission is an inherently and uniquely toxic technology.

The cascading sequence of system failures, partial meltdowns and hydrogen explosions at the Fukushima Daiichi nuclear power plant was touched off by a once-in-a-lifetime event: the most powerful earthquake in Japan's recorded history, which triggered a tsunami of unimaginable destructive force. It is also true that the Fukushima reactors are of an older design, and that it is possible to engineer nuclear plants that would never suffer similar breakdowns.

But it is also true that there is no such thing as a fail-safe system. Stuff happens.

5   The Earth is alive with tectonic movement, volcanism, violent weather. We try to predict these phenomena, but our best calculations are probabilistic and thus imprecise. We have computers that are as close to infallible as we can imagine, but the data they produce must ultimately be interpreted by human intelligence. When a crisis does occur, experts must make quick decisions under enormous pressure; usually they're right, sometimes they're wrong.

The problem with nuclear fission is that the stakes are unimaginably high. We can engineer nuclear power plants so that the chance of a Chernobyl-style disaster is almost nil. But we can't eliminate it completely—nor can we envision every other kind of potential disaster. And where fission reactors are concerned, the worst-case scenario is so dreadful as to be unthinkable.

Engineers at the Fukushima plant are struggling to avert a wholesale release of deadly radiation, which is the inherent risk of any fission reactor. In the Chernobyl incident, a cloud of radioactive smoke and steam spread contamination across hundreds of square miles; even after 25 years, a 20-mile radius around the ruined plant remains off-limits and uninhabitable. Studies have estimated that the release of radioactivity from Chernobyl has caused at least 6,000 excess cases of thyroid cancer, and scientists expect more cancers to develop in the years to come.

It seems unlikely that the Fukushima crisis will turn into another Chernobyl, if only because there is a good chance that prevailing winds would blow any radioactive cloud out to sea. Japanese authorities seem to be making all the right decisions. Yet even in a nation with safety standards and technological acumen that are second to none, look at what they're up against—and how little margin for error they have to work with.

At first, the focus was on the Unit 1 reactor and the struggle to keep the nuclear fuel rods immersed in water—which is necessary, at all times, to avoid a full meltdown and a catastrophic release of radiation. Pumping sea water into the reactor vessel seemed to stabilize the situation, despite a hydrogen explosion—indicating a partial meltdown—that blew the roof off the reactor's outer containment building.

10   But then, attention shifted to Unit 3, which may have had a worse partial meltdown; it, too, experienced a hydrogen explosion. Officials said they believed they were stabilizing that reactor but acknowledged that it was hard to be sure. Meanwhile, what could be the most crucial failure of all was happening in Unit 2, which suffered an explosion Tuesday after its fuel rods were twice fully exposed. Scientists had no immediate way of knowing how much of that reactor's fuel had melted—or what the consequences might be.

The best-case scenario is that Japanese engineers will eventually get the plant under control. Then, I suppose, it will be possible to conclude that the system worked. As President Obama and Congress move forward with a new generation of nuclear plants, designs will be vetted and perhaps altered. We will be confident that we have taken the lessons of Fukushima into account.

And we will be fooling ourselves, because the one inescapable lesson of Fukushima is that improbable does not mean impossible. Unlikely failures can combine to bring any nuclear fission reactor to the brink of disaster. It can happen here.

WHY I STILL SUPPORT NUCLEAR POWER, EVEN AFTER FUKUSHIMA

By William Tucker

It's not easy being a supporter of nuclear energy these days. The events in Japan have confirmed many of the critics' worst predictions. We are way past Three Mile Island. It is not quite Chernobyl, but the possibilities of widespread radioactive contamination remain real.

Still, other energy technologies are not without risk. In 1944 a natural gas explosion in Cleveland leveled an entire neighborhood and killed 130 people. Yet we still pipe gas right into our homes. Coal mining killed 100,000 workers in the 20th century, and still kills an average of six a day in China, but we haven't given up coal. A hydroelectric dam collapsed in Japan during the earthquake, wiping away 1,800 homes and killing an undetermined number of people, yet nobody has paid much attention.

But talk about the risks of other energy sources really doesn't cut to the issue. The obvious question people are asking is, "Why do we have to mess with this nuclear stuff in the first place? Why do we have to risk these horrible accidents when other better technologies are available?" The answer is that there are no better alternatives available. If we are going to maintain our standard of living—or anything approximating it—without overwhelming the earth with pollution, we are going to have to master nuclear technology.

Consider: Uranium fuel rods sit in a reactor core for five years. During that time six ounces of their weight—six ounces!—will be completely transformed into energy. But the energy produced by that transformation will be enough to power a city the size of San Francisco for five years.

5 A coal plant must be fed by a 100-car freight train arriving every 30 hours. A nuclear reactor is refueled by a fleet of six trucks arriving once every two years. There are 283 coal mines in West Virginia and 449 in Kentucky. There are only 45 uranium mines in the entire world. Russia is offering to supply uranium to most of the developing world with the output from one mine. That is why the environmental impact of nuclear is infinitely smaller.

What about natural gas? Huge reservoirs of shale gas have been unlocked by hydrofracking. But "fracking" has been able to proceed so rapidly only because it has been exempted from federal regulations governing air and water pollution. Now that concern has arisen about damaged aquifers, natural gas production may slow as well.

So what about hydro, wind and solar? These energy sources will not bring about utopia. The only reason we don't object to the environmental effects of these renewables is because we haven't yet encountered them.

The amount of energy that can be derived from harnessing wind or water is about 15 orders of magnitude less than what can be derived from uranium. Thus a hydroelectric dam such as Hoover must back up a 250-square-mile reservoir (Lake Mead) in order to generate the same electricity produced by a reactor on one square mile.

Windmills require even more space, since air is less dense than water. Replacing just one of the two 1,000-megawatt reactors at Indian Point in Westchester County, N.Y., would require lining the Hudson River from New York to Albany with 45-story windmills one-quarter mile apart—and then they would generate electricity only about one-third of the time, when the wind is blowing.

10 Solar collectors must be built to the same scale. It would take 20 square miles of highly polished mirrors or photovoltaic cells to equal the output of one nuclear reactor—and then only when the sun shines. Such facilities may one day provide supplementary power or peaking output during hot summer afternoons, but they will never be able to supply the uninterrupted flow of electricity required by an industrial society.

It will be impossible to meet the consumer demands of a contemporary society without a reliable source of energy like nuclear. Other countries have already acknowledged this. There are 65 reactors under construction around the world (far safer and more advanced than the 30-year-old technology at Fukushima Daiichi), but none in the U.S.

The Russians' sale of uranium to the world comes with an offer to take back the "nuclear waste" and reprocess it into more fuel, at a profit. The Chinese have commercialized their first Integral Fast Breeder, a reactor that can burn any kind of "waste" and promises unlimited quantities of cheap energy.

We have become the world's predominant industrial power because our forebears were willing to take the risks and make the sacrifices necessary to develop new technologies—the steam engine, coal mining, electricity, automobiles, airplanes, electronics, space travel. If we are not willing to take this next set of risks, others will. Then the torch will be passed to another generation that is not our own and our children and grandchildren will live with the consequences.

If the Japanese Can't Build a Safe Nuclear Reactor, Who Can?

Anne Applebaum

In the aftermath of a disaster, the strengths of any society become immediately visible. The cohesiveness, resilience, technological brilliance and extraordinary competence of the Japanese are on full display. One report from Rikuzentakata—a town of 25,000, annihilated by the tsunami that followed Friday's massive earthquake—describes volunteer firefighters working to clear rubble and search for survivors; troops and police efficiently directing traffic and supplies; survivors are not only "calm and pragmatic" but also coping "with politeness and sometimes amazingly good cheer."

Thanks to these strengths, Japan will eventually recover. But at least one Japanese nuclear power complex will not. As I write, three reactors at the Fukushima Daiichi nuclear power station appear to have lost their cooling capacity. Engineers are flooding the plant with seawater—effectively destroying it—and then letting off radioactive steam. There have been two explosions. The situation may worsen in the coming hours.

Yet Japan's nuclear power stations were designed with the same care and precision as everything else in the country. More to the point, as the only country in the world to have experienced true nuclear catastrophe, Japan had an incentive to build well, as well as the capability, laws and regulations to do so. Which leads to an unavoidable question: If the competent and technologically brilliant Japanese can't build a completely safe reactor, who can?

It can—and will—be argued that the Japanese situation is extraordinary. Few countries are as vulnerable to natural catastrophe as Japan, and the scale of this earthquake is unprecedented. But there are other kinds of extraordinary situations and unprecedented circumstances. In an attempt to counter the latest worst-possible scenarios, a Franco-German company began constructing a super-safe, "next-generation" nuclear reactor in Finland several years ago. The plant was designed to withstand the impact of an airplane—a post-Sept. 11 concern—and includes a chamber allegedly able to contain a core meltdown. But it was also meant to cost $4 billion and to be completed in 2009. Instead, after numerous setbacks, it is still unfinished—and may now cost $6 billion or more.

5   Ironically, the Finnish plant was meant to launch the renaissance of the nuclear power industry in Europe—an industry that has, of late, enjoyed a renaissance around the world, thanks almost entirely to fears of climate change. Nuclear plants emit no carbon. As a result, nuclear plants, after a long, post-Chernobyl lull, have became fashionable again. Some 62 nuclear reactors are under construction at the moment, according to the World Nuclear Association; a further 158 are being planned and 324 others have been proposed.

Increasingly, nuclear power is also promoted because it safe. Which it is—except, of course, when it is not. Chances of a major disaster are tiny, one in a hundred million. But in the event of a statistically improbable major disaster, the damage could include, say, the destruction of a city or the poisoning of a country. The cost of such a potential catastrophe is partly reflected in the price of plant construction, and it partly explains the cost overruns in Finland: Nobody can risk the tiniest flaw in the concrete or the most minimal reduction in the quality of the steel.

But as we are about to learn in Japan, the true costs of nuclear power are never reflected even in the very high price of plant construction. Inevitably, the enormous costs of nuclear waste disposal fall to taxpayers, not the nuclear industry. The costs of cleanup, even in the wake of a relatively small accident, are eventually borne by government, too. Health-care costs will also be paid by society at large, one way or another. If there is true nuclear catastrophe in Japan, the entire world will pay the price.

I hope that this will never, ever happen. I feel nothing but admiration for the Japanese nuclear engineers who have been battling catastrophe for several days. If anyone can prevent a disaster, the Japanese can do it. But I also hope that a near-miss prompts people around the world to think twice about the true "price" of nuclear energy, and that it stops the nuclear renaissance dead in its tracks.

● Review Questions

1. Why does Jenkins believe that the nuclear accident at Fukushima does not constitute a convincing case against the continued use of nuclear power?

2. Eugene Robinson warns that though we can plan to the best of our ability, designing and building the most modern and effective nuclear plants, we cannot create a "risk-free system" Why not?

3. In what specific ways are even "green" energy sources bad for the environment, according to Tucker?

4. How does Applebaum refute the claims of pronuclear activists that nuclear power is more cost-effective than other forms of energy?

● Discussion and Writing Suggestions

1. Jenkins concludes by observing that the possibility of the world turning to nuclear power "to make a concerted dent in CO_2 output...is now gone, for better or worse." If true, is the world "better" or "worse" off in your view? Why?

2. Robinson thinks that turning to nuclear energy to deal with global warming looks like "a bargain with the devil." Do you agree? Why or why not? While all energy production carries some degree of risk and danger (for example, since 1949, about 250,000 people in China have been killed in coal-mining accidents), at what point should we conclude that the degree of risk posed by one particular technology is simply too much to bear? How can we best weigh risks against benefits?

3. Tucker examines the major alternatives to nuclear power—coal, natural gas, hydroelectric, wind, and solar power—and concludes that for all its drawbacks, nuclear power remains the best choice. Has he convinced you? Explain. What flaws, if any, do you find in his arguments?

4. Applebaum asks a provocative question in her title and later in the body of her op-ed: "If the Japanese can't build a safe reactor, who can?" Her implied answer, of course: "no one." To what extent do you think she has posed a fair question? To what extent do you agree with her implied answer? In your response, consider the positions of such other authors in this section as Jenkins and Tucker.

5. In the wake of the Japanese earthquake, some countries were quick to shut down their own nuclear plants or put on hold their further development. To what extent do you think such decisions were prudent? To what extent rash or premature?

6. Write a letter to the editor, responding to one of these op-eds on nuclear power. In your response, draw upon and expand with your own arguments and examples the ideas of some of the authors in this section. Keep in mind that energy policy has become highly politicized. The op-eds supportive of nuclear power come from an editorially conservative newspaper (*Wall Street Journal*), and those against it from one (*Washington Post*) generally viewed as liberal. In taking a side of the issue, keep these editorial biases in mind, and aim to win over those who may disagree.

SOLAR POWER

To many environmentalists, solar power is about as near-perfect an energy source as you can get. Energy from the sun is clean, free, abundant, and infinitely renewable. It emits no noxious fumes. It is not dangerous to produce. It does not need to be extracted at great human, financial, and environmental cost from below the ground.

Yet at the present time, owing to a number of major drawbacks, solar energy in the United States remains a marginal power source. Electricity derived from solar power is expensive to produce and transmit and cannot, unless subsidized by the government, compete economically with power derived from fossil fuels.

Solar power is intermittent (no power is gathered when the sun doesn't shine) and is difficult to store. And solar arrays large enough to provide significant quantities of energy—enough, say, to supply medium-sized cities—require huge amounts of acreage. Even environmentalists have turned against solar power when construction of solar arrays has threatened millions of acres of fragile desert land.

In addition to these long-term problems, solar power suffered a major public relations setback in a 2011 scandal that will almost certainly jeopardize crucial government support of the industry in the near future[1]—this at a time when U.S. solar's most potent competitor, China, is heavily subsidizing its solar industry.[2]

The selections that follow offer some current perspectives on solar power. In "State Solar Power Plans Are Big as the Great Outdoors," *Los Angeles Times* writer Marla Dickerson explains how California has used incentives and goal posts to promote solar power. She also acknowledges some of the adverse environmental effects of this push. In "Here Comes the Sun," Paul Krugman, a *New York Times* columnist and Nobel Prize winner in economics, explores the real possibility that the cost of solar power may soon drop substantially enough to make the technology economically viable. In "Solar Power Is Getting Cheaper, But How Far Can It Go?" *Washington Post* writer Brad Plumer claims that with the right choices, solar power can move "squarely out of 'cute' territory" and become a legitimate alternative to fossil fuels. Considered together, these selections provide an overview of an industry poised for expansion.

STATE SOLAR PLANS ARE AS BIG AS ALL OUTDOORS

Marla Dickerson

Just up the road, past pump jacks bobbing in California's storied oil patch, look sharp and you'll catch a glimpse of the state's energy future.

Rows of gigantic mirrors covering an area bigger than two football fields have sprouted alongside almond groves near California 99. This is a power plant that uses the sun's heat to produce electricity for thousands of homes.

Owned by Palo Alto-based Ausra Inc., it's the first so-called solar thermal facility to open in California in nearly two decades. It's part of a drive to build clean electricity generation using the sun, wind and other renewable sources

---

[1] In 2009, the Obama administration authorized loan guarantees of more than $500 million to the Solyndra Corporation, which built innovative (and cylindrical) solar panels, with the promise that such government support would help create 4,000 new jobs. When Solyndra filed for bankruptcy two years later, the government was left holding the financial bag.

[2] The irony was that Solyndra's solar panels were technologically superior to conventional flat panels for generating large quantities of electrical energy. But the company was unable to compete with Chinese solar power producers, subsidized even more heavily by *their* government. [China is one of the world's largest producers of solar energy, accounting for about half of the world's annual production (in 2007) of 3,800 megawatts.]

with an urgency not seen since the days of environmentalist Gov. Jerry Brown.*
Add President-elect Barack Obama's stated intention to push for more renewable power, and you've got the equivalent of a green land rush.

At least 80 large solar projects are on the drawing board in California, more
than in any other place in the country. The scale of some is unrivaled on the
planet. One facility planned for the Mojave Desert is projected to take up a land
mass the size of Inglewood.†

5 "The expectation is that renewables will transform California's electricity system," said Terry O'Brien, who helps vet sites for new facilities for the
California Energy Commission.

It's a daunting challenge for the world's eighth-largest economy. Despite the
nation's toughest mandates for boosting green energy and reducing greenhouse
gases, California remains addicted to burning fossil fuels to keep the lights on.

Excluding large hydroelectric operations, less than 12% of the state's electricity came from renewable sources in 2007, according to the commission. Solar
ranked last, supplying just 0.2% of California's needs. Rooftop photovoltaic

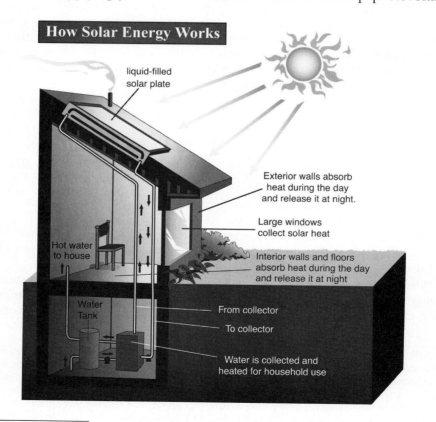

*Jerry Brown served as governor of California from 1975 to 1983 and was again elected to the gover-
norship in 2011. His father Pat Brown also served as California governor from 1959 to 1967.
†Inglewood: a city in southwestern Los Angeles County; area: 9.1 square miles

panels are unaffordable or impractical for most Californians even with generous state incentives.

Enter Big Solar.

Proponents say utility-scale solar is a way to get lots of clean megawatts on-line quickly, efficiently and at lower costs. Solar thermal plants such as Ausra's are essentially giant boilers made of glass and steel. They use the sun's heat to create steam to power turbines that generate electricity.

10   Costing about 18 cents a kilowatt-hour at present, solar thermal power is roughly 40% cheaper than that generated by the silicon-based panels that sit on the roofs of homes and businesses, according to a June report by Clean Edge Inc. and the Co-op American Foundation. Analysts say improved technology and economies of scale should help lower the cost of solar thermal to about 5 cents a kilowatt-hour by 2025. That would put it on par with coal, the cheap but carbon-spewing fuel that generates about half the nation's electricity.

Size matters, said Sun Microsystems Inc. co-founder-turned-venture-capitalist Vinod Khosla, whose Khosla Ventures has invested more than $30 million in Ausra. A square patch of desert about 92 miles long on each side blanketed with Ausra's technology could generate enough electricity to meet the entire nation's demand, company executives say. "Utility-scale solar is probably the only way to achieve real scale…and reduce our carbon emissions" significantly, Khosla said.

Critics fear that massive solar farms would create as many environmental problems as they purport to solve. This new-age electricity still requires old-fashioned power towers and high-voltage lines to get it to people's homes. A proposed 150-mile transmission line known as the Sunrise Powerlink that would carry renewable power from Imperial County to San Diego has run into stiff resistance from grass-roots groups and environmentalists.

Solar plants require staggering amounts of land, which could threaten fragile ecosystems and mar the stark beauty of America's deserts. And in contrast to rooftop panels, which enable homeowners to pursue energy independence, these centralized facilities keep consumers tethered to utility companies.

"They are trying to perpetuate the old Big Energy paradigm into the renewable-energy era," said Sheila Bowers, a Santa Monica attorney and environmental activist. "They have a monopoly agenda."

15   California already has the largest operating collection of solar thermal facilities in the world: nine plants totaling just over 350 megawatts in San Bernardino County. Built in the 1980s, they were part of a drive toward energy self-sufficiency stemming from the '70s oil shocks. The boom ended when California dropped requirements forcing utilities to buy renewable power.

The push is back. The 2000–01 energy crisis exposed California's continued dependence on outsiders—more than 30% of its electricity still comes from out of state. Renewable forms of energy are once again central to efforts to shore up supply and fight global warming.

State lawmakers have told investor-owned utilities that they must procure 20% of their electricity from renewable sources by 2010; Gov. Arnold Schwarzenegger is pushing for a minimum of 33% by 2020. A landmark 2006 state law forcing California to reduce its greenhouse gas emissions to 1990 levels within 12 years also is boosting green generation. Most of the proposed utility-scale solar plants are slated for San Bernardino and Riverside counties, whose vast deserts offer abundant sunshine and plenty of open space for the behemoths. The U.S. Bureau of Land Management is juggling so many requests from companies looking to build on federal land—79 at last count, covering more than 690,000 acres—that it had to stop accepting applications for a few weeks last summer. Many of these facilities may never get built. Environmentalists are mobilizing. U.S. credit markets are in a deep freeze. Oil and natural gas prices are falling, reducing some of the urgency to go green.

Still, the obstacles haven't clouded the ambitions of solar start-ups such as Ausra.

"Our investors perceive there is a huge opportunity here," said Bob Fishman, Ausra's president and chief executive. A group of dignitaries that included Schwarzenegger gathered near here in October to get a close-up look at the 5-megawatt operation Ausra opened.

20   The company uses a technology known as a compact linear Fresnel reflector. Acres of mirrors are anchored to metal frames and held roughly 6 feet off the ground in parallel rows. Controlled by computers, these panels make hundreds of barely perceptible movements throughout the day, tracking the sun's path across the sky.

The mirrors catch the sun's rays and reflect them onto a cluster of water pipes overhead. The intense heat—it can reach 750 degrees—generates pressurized steam inside the pipes. That steam is then fed into a turbine whose spinning generates electricity.

"It's like when you were a kid and you used a magnifying glass to fry a bug" on a sunny day, said Dave DeGraaf, vice president of product development. "We're focusing all that energy."

Despite its mammoth size, this pilot plant generates a modest amount of electricity, enough to power just 3,500 homes when the sun is shining. Ausra is thinking much bigger.

It has set up a manufacturing facility in Nevada that will supply a 177-megawatt solar plant planned for a site near Carrizo Plain National Monument in eastern San Luis Obispo County.

25   The facility's mirrors will occupy a full square mile of terrain. The project is still in the permitting process. Ausra has never tried something on this scale. But Pacific Gas & Electric is confident enough that is has agreed to buy the power from Carrizo to help it meet its green energy needs.

Other companies looking to shine in California with utility-scale plants include Solel Inc., whose proposed 553-megawatt project in the Mojave Desert would span nine square miles; BrightSource Energy Inc. of Oakland; SunPower Corp. of San Jose; OptiSolar Inc. of Hayward, Calif.; Stirling Energy Systems Inc. of Phoenix; and FPL Energy of Juno Beach, Fla.

"Climate change is the greatest challenge that mankind has ever faced," said Peter Darbee, president and chief executive of Pacific Gas & Electric and head of its parent, San Francisco-based PG&E Corp. "It's imperative to seek out the most cost-effective solutions."

HERE COMES THE SUN

Paul Krugman

For decades the story of technology has been dominated, in the popular mind and to a large extent in reality, by computing and the things you can do with it. Moore's Law—in which the price of computing power falls roughly 50 percent every 18 months—has powered an ever-expanding range of applications, from faxes to Facebook.

Our mastery of the material world, on the other hand, has advanced much more slowly. The sources of energy, the way we move stuff around, are much the same as they were a generation ago.

But that may be about to change. We are, or at least we should be, on the cusp of an energy transformation, driven by the rapidly falling cost of solar power. That's right, solar power.

If that surprises you, if you still think of solar power as some kind of hippie fantasy, blame our fossilized political system, in which fossil fuel producers have both powerful political allies and a powerful propaganda machine that denigrates alternatives.

5   Speaking of propaganda: Before I get to solar, let's talk briefly about hydraulic fracturing, aka fracking.

Fracking—injecting high-pressure fluid into rocks deep underground, inducing the release of fossil fuels—is an impressive technology. But it's also a technology that imposes large costs on the public. We know that it produces toxic (and radioactive) wastewater that contaminates drinking water; there is reason to suspect, despite industry denials, that it also contaminates groundwater; and the heavy trucking required for fracking inflicts major damage on roads.

Economics 101 tells us that an industry imposing large costs on third parties should be required to "internalize" those costs—that is, to pay for the damage it inflicts, treating that damage as a cost of production. Fracking might still be worth doing given those costs. But no industry should be held harmless from its impacts on the environment and the nation's infrastructure.

Yet what the industry and its defenders demand is, of course, precisely that it be let off the hook for the damage it causes. Why? Because we need that energy! For example, the industry-backed organization *energyfromshale.org* declares that "there are only two sides in the debate: those who want our oil and natural resources developed in a safe and responsible way; and those who don't want our oil and natural gas resources developed at all."

So it's worth pointing out that special treatment for fracking makes a mockery of free-market principles. Pro-fracking politicians claim to be against subsidies, yet letting an industry impose costs without paying compensation is in effect a huge subsidy. They say they oppose having the government "pick winners," yet they demand special treatment for this industry precisely because they claim it will be a winner.

10   And now for something completely different: the success story you haven't heard about.

These days, mention solar power and you'll probably hear cries of "Solyndra!" Republicans have tried to make the failed solar panel company both a symbol of government waste—although claims of a major scandal are nonsense—and a stick with which to beat renewable energy.

But Solyndra's failure was actually caused by technological success: the price of solar panels is dropping fast, and Solyndra couldn't keep up with the competition. In fact, progress in solar panels has been so dramatic and sustained that, as a blog post at *Scientific American* put it, "there's now frequent talk of a 'Moore's law' in solar energy," with prices adjusted for inflation falling around 7 percent a year.

This has already led to rapid growth in solar installations, but even more change may be just around the corner. If the downward trend continues—and if anything it seems to be accelerating—we're just a few years from the point at which electricity from solar panels becomes cheaper than electricity generated by burning coal.

And if we priced coal-fired power right, taking into account the huge health and other costs it imposes, it's likely that we would already have passed that tipping point.

15   But will our political system delay the energy transformation now within reach?

Let's face it: a large part of our political class, including essentially the entire G.O.P., is deeply invested in an energy sector dominated by fossil fuels, and actively hostile to alternatives. This political class will do everything it can to ensure subsidies for the extraction and use of fossil fuels, directly with taxpayers' money and indirectly by letting the industry off the hook for environmental costs, while ridiculing technologies like solar.

So what you need to know is that nothing you hear from these people is true. Fracking is not a dream come true; solar is now cost-effective. Here comes the sun, if we're willing to let it in.

SOLAR IS GETTING CHEAPER, BUT HOW FAR CAN IT GO?

Brad Plumer

The usual take on solar power is that it's a niche energy source, too pricey and erratic to meet more than a sliver of our electricity needs. Bill Gates has mocked solar as "cute." But, as Paul Krugman reminds us today, that's changing far more quickly than people realize. "In fact," Krugman writes, "progress in solar panels has been so dramatic and sustained that, as a blog post at *Scientific American* put it, 'there's now frequent talk of a Moore's law in solar energy,' with prices adjusted for inflation falling around 7 percent a year."

A couple of things are driving the drop in costs. Solar-panel technology is getting more efficient, true, but that's just part of the tale. China is also heavily subsidizing its domestic industry, driving a 40 percent plunge in prices over the past year (and bulldozing a few U.S. companies into bankruptcy). But it's not all about over-production from China, either. Solar companies are figuring out how to set up systems cheaply: installation and other non-module costs in the United States dropped 17 percent in 2010.

One big point to add to Krugman's column is that solar is *already* being deployed on a large scale. Tom Dinwoodie, chief technical officer at SunPower, notes that the industry has been growing at a 65 percent annual rate in the past five years. In 2010, some 17 gigawatts of solar power were manufactured, shipped and installed—the equivalent of 17 large nuclear power plants. So just how far can solar go?

One key question is whether solar can reach "grid parity"—the point at which it can compete with fossil fuels without subsidies. As Shayle Kann explains at Greentech Media, this could happen in two ways. One, solar would become attractive to utilities even after accounting for the fact that the sun doesn't always shine. At some point, for example, power companies may decide to rely on solar for hot, electricity-gobbling afternoons instead of relying on dirty natural-gas peaking plants. Alternatively, solar could reach the point at which huge numbers of retail consumers see big savings on their energy bills from installing rooftop solar.

5   It's hard to know when, exactly, grid parity will arrive. Kees van der Leun, of the energy consulting firm Ecofys, predicts that solar could be competitive with fossil fuels by 2018 or so. On the other hand, as Tyler Cowen notes, energy markets don't appear to be betting on this development. If it does happen at some point, though, a steep plunge in solar costs could be incredibly transformative. The International Energy Agency projects that solar could provide more than half of the world's energy needs by 2060 if costs fell to $100 per megawatt hour—around 50 cents per watt installed. (At the moment, solar panels are gunning for the $1-per-watt threshold.)

A lot depends on government policy. The progress being made by the U.S. solar industry will likely slow at the end of this year if a federal grant program that makes a production tax credit more accessible is allowed to expire. A price on carbon would also make a big difference in giving solar a leg up against fossil fuels, which currently offload some of their total cost into the atmosphere. And the Energy Department is pushing research into energy storage and other technologies—check out the Optical Cavity Furnace—to bring prices down. So there are a lot of variables here. But at this point, it's safe to say that solar has moved squarely out of "cute" territory.

● **Review Questions**

1. "Size matters," says Sun Microsystems cofounder Vinod Khosla, referring to solar power systems. What does he mean?

2. What are the disadvantages of the solar thermal power systems of the kind described by Dickerson?

3. Summarize Krugman's objections to hydraulic fracking.

4. Why does Krugman reject the charge that the Solyndra case is an example of government waste and of the failure of solar technology?

5. What is the role of government in encouraging the development of solar power, according to Plumer?

● Discussion and Writing Suggestions

1. All three writers acknowledge the public skepticism about solar power. To what extent has this skepticism persuaded you that solar power is not a practical way of generating sufficiently large quantities of power to replace the use of fossil fuels—and therefore is not a significant way of addressing the global warming problem?

2. How do you think Thomas Friedman would feel about the kind of solar projects described by Dickerson? Might such projects fall into the category of "an energy party"? Why or why not?

3. Large scale solar power projects are often faced with the NIMBY issue: "not in my back yard." Would you be prepared to live in an area near one of the large-scale solar facilities described in this article, knowing that the generation of solar power in large quantities could significantly reduce the volume of carbon dioxide released into the atmosphere from the burning of coal? Explain.

4. Discussing the debate over the environmental consequences of "fracking," or hydraulic fracturing, Krugman quotes an assertion from an energy-backed organization Web site: "there are only two sides in this debate: those who want our oil and natural resources developed in a safe and responsible way; and those who don't want our oil and natural gas resources developed at all." On which side would you place Krugman, based on his arguments? To what extent do you agree that that statement actually represents the choices we face? Do you see other alternatives in this particular area of energy development? Explain.

5. Both Krugman and Plumer cite "Moore's Law" to illustrate how solar technology is on its way to becoming more widespread and commercially viable. Look up and summarize "Moore's Law." What are some other technologies to which Moore's Law applies?

6. Imagine that you work for a public relations firm. You have been hired by the solar power industry to create a campaign that will win over those who view solar energy as a "fantasy." What points will you highlight? Consider the viability of government support as discussed by Dickerson, the implications of other energy techniques explored by Krugman, and the path to reality specified by Plumer. How will you use those authors to convince opponents that solar power is worth pursuing?

7. Each writer here mentions, to varying degrees, governmental involvement in energy industries. To what extent do you think it is helpful, and/or appropriate for the government to participate in this arena? To what extent does government support represent an unwarranted use of taxpayer money and unwarranted interference in the private sector? Explain, referring to the selections.

WIND POWER

As one heads southwest toward San Francisco on Route 580 in northern California, approaching the barren hills of the Altamont Pass between Livermore and Tracy, an eerie sight gradually reveals itself. Lining the hillsides and hilltops on both sides of the highway, numerous columns of wind turbines stand sentry as if waiting to attack the vehicles passing below. The Livermore wind farm was one of the first in the world and is still one of the largest, consisting of over 4,900 medium-size wind turbines that generate 576 megawatts (thousand watts) of electricity per year. There are hundreds of wind farms around the world. China's turbines annually generate more than 44 gigawatts (thousand megawatts) of the world's total estimated consumption of more than 1,700 gigawatts—1.7 terawatts—of electricity. The United States' wind farms generate 40 gigawatts, followed by Germany (27 gigawatts), Spain (20), and India (13). Collectively, the world's wind farms create 194 gigawatts. Denmark (treated in Kolbert, below), at 3.7 gigawatts, generates almost 20% of its energy from wind power.

Many of the advantages and disadvantages of solar power also apply to wind power. Both are clean, renewable sources of energy. Neither needs to be laboriously and dangerously extracted from the earth. The raw materials are free. But so far, neither solar nor wind power can generate electricity on anything approaching the scale of fossil fuels or nuclear power. Both solar and wind are intermittent energy sources: Just as the sun doesn't always shine, the wind doesn't always blow. When the sun and the wind stop, backup power must be provided by fossil fuels, unless the energy has been stored. So far, however, large-scale energy storage from these sources is not viable. Additionally, wind farms, even more than industrial solar arrays, require vast amounts of acreage. Besides being unsightly (to some), wind turbines kill bats and birds (including eagles). Environmentalists worry about them damaging fragile ecosystems. Others oppose them on both aesthetic and economic grounds. In the acerbic opinion of British broadcaster Eric Robson, "It's surely self-evident that wind farms are an economic and technological nonsense, sustainable only if the government stuffs their owners' mouths with money, but slack-brained environmentalists hail them as the answer to all our prayers."*

Two perspectives on wind power are presented in the following selections. In "The Island in the Wind," excerpted from a longer article in the *New Yorker*, Elizabeth Kolbert describes in vivid imagery "an unlikely social movement": how the people of the Danish island of Samsø got all their homes and farms to run on electricity generated entirely by wind power. Kolbert is a journalist who specializes in environmental issues. She wrote for the *New York Times* from 1984 to 1999 and has been a staff reporter for *The New Yorker* since 1999. She is the author of *Field*

---
*Eric Robson, *Outside Broadcaster*, Frances Lincoln Ltd, 2007: p. 177.

Notes from a Catastrophe: Man and Nature and Climate Change (2006). In "Wind Power Puffery," H. Sterling Burnett discusses the limitations and drawbacks of wind power. Burnett is a senior fellow with the National Center for Policy Analysis. In 2000 he served as a member of the Environment and Natural Resources Task Force in the Texas Comptroller's e-Texas commission. His articles and opinion pieces have been published in *Environmental Ethics*, *International Studies in Philosophy*, *USA Today*, the *Los Angeles Daily News*, *Rocky Mountain News*, and the *Seattle Times*. This piece appeared in the *Washington Times* on 4 February 2004.

THE ISLAND IN THE WIND

Elizabeth Kolbert

Jørgen Tranberg is a farmer who lives on the Danish island of Samsø. He is a beefy man with a mop of brown hair and an unpredictable sense of humor. When I arrived at his house, one gray morning this spring, he was sitting in his kitchen, smoking a cigarette and watching grainy images on a black-and-white TV. The images turned out to be closed-circuit shots from his barn. One of his cows, he told me, was about to give birth, and he was keeping an eye on her. We talked for a few minutes, and then, laughing, he asked me if I wanted to climb his wind turbine. I was pretty sure I didn't, but I said yes anyway.

We got into Tranberg's car and bounced along a rutted dirt road. The turbine loomed up in front of us. When we reached it, Tranberg stubbed out his cigarette and opened a small door in the base of the tower. Inside were eight ladders, each about twenty feet tall, attached one above the other. We started up, and were soon huffing. Above the last ladder, there was a trapdoor, which led to a sort of engine room. We scrambled into it, at which point we were standing on top of the generator. Tranberg pressed a button, and the roof slid open to reveal the gray sky and a patchwork of green and brown fields stretching toward the sea. He pressed another button. The rotors, which he had switched off during our climb, started to turn, at first sluggishly and then much more rapidly. It felt as if we were about to take off. I'd like to say the feeling was exhilarating; in fact, I found it sickening. Tranberg looked at me and started to laugh.

Samsø, which is roughly the size of Nantucket, sits in what's known as the Kattegat, an arm of the North Sea. The island is bulgy in the south and narrows to a bladelike point in the north, so that on a map it looks a bit like a woman's torso and a bit like a meat cleaver. It has twenty-two villages that hug the narrow streets; out back are fields where farmers grow potatoes and wheat and strawberries. Thanks to Denmark's peculiar geography, Samsø is smack in the center of the country and, at the same time, in the middle of nowhere.

For the past decade or so, Samsø has been the site of an unlikely social movement. When it began, in the late nineteen-nineties, the island's forty-three hundred inhabitants had what might be described as a conventional attitude toward energy: as long as it continued to arrive, they weren't much interested in it. Most Samsingers heated their houses with oil, which was brought in on tankers.

Catching the wind

Alternative energy sources are getting a new look as demand for fossil fuels increases worldwide, and as technical innovations help reduce the costs of alternatives. California produces more wind-generated electricity than any state except Texas and Iowa. A look at wind farms:

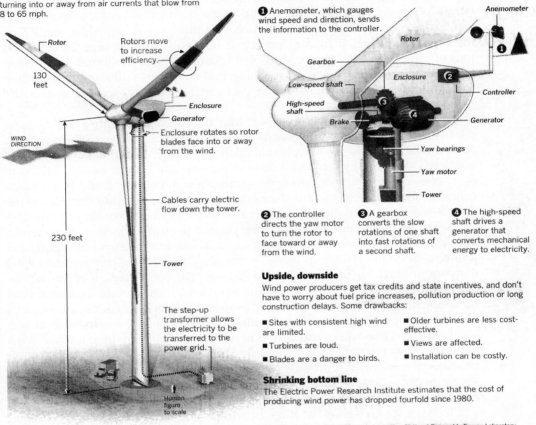

Wind turbine

These modern windmills catch the wind by either turning into or away from air currents that blow from 8 to 65 mph.

Rotor

Rotors move to increase efficiency.

130 feet

Enclosure

Generator

Enclosure rotates so rotor blades face into or away from the wind.

WIND DIRECTION

Cables carry electric flow down the tower.

230 feet

Tower

The step-up transformer allows the electricity to be transferred to the power grid.

Human figure to scale

How it works

Wind moves a propeller, which turns shafts to work a generator.

❶ Anemometer, which gauges wind speed and direction, sends the information to the controller.

Anemometer

Rotor

Gearbox

Enclosure

Low-speed shaft

High-speed shaft

Controller

Brake

Generator

Yaw bearings

Yaw motor

Tower

❷ The controller directs the yaw motor to turn the rotor to face toward or away from the wind.

❸ A gearbox converts the slow rotations of one shaft into fast rotations of a second shaft.

❹ The high-speed shaft drives a generator that converts mechanical energy to electricity.

Upside, downside

Wind power producers get tax credits and state incentives, and don't have to worry about fuel price increases, pollution production or long construction delays. Some drawbacks:

■ Sites with consistent high wind are limited.

■ Turbines are loud.

■ Blades are a danger to birds.

■ Older turbines are less cost-effective.

■ Views are affected.

■ Installation can be costly.

Shrinking bottom line

The Electric Power Research Institute estimates that the cost of producing wind power has dropped fourfold since 1980.

Sources: California Energy Commission, National Wind Technology Center, U.S. Department of Energy's Energy Information Administration, National Renewable Energy Laboratory

DOUG STEVENS Los Angeles Times

They used electricity imported from the mainland via cable, much of which was generated by burning coal. As a result, each Samsinger put into the atmosphere, on average, nearly eleven tons of carbon dioxide annually.

5　　Then, quite deliberately, the residents of the island set about changing this. They formed energy coöperatives and organized seminars on wind power. They removed their furnaces and replaced them with heat pumps. By 2001, fossil-fuel use on Samsø had been cut in half. By 2003, instead of importing electricity, the island was exporting it, and by 2005 it was producing from renewable sources more energy than it was using.

The residents of Samsø that I spoke to were clearly proud of their accomplishment. All the same, they insisted on their ordinariness. They were, they noted, not wealthy, nor were they especially well educated or idealistic. They weren't even terribly adventuresome. "We are a conservative farming community" is how one Samsinger put it. "We are only normal people," Tranberg told me. "We are not some special people."

This year, the world is expected to burn through some thirty-one billion barrels of oil, six billion tons of coal, and a hundred trillion cubic feet of natural gas. The combustion of these fossil fuels will produce, in aggregate, some four hundred quadrillion B.T.U.s of energy. It will also yield around thirty billion tons of carbon dioxide. Next year, global consumption of fossil fuels is expected to grow by about two per cent, meaning that emissions will rise by more than half a billion tons, and the following year consumption is expected to grow by yet another two per cent.

When carbon dioxide is released into the air, about a third ends up, in relatively short order, in the oceans. (CO_2 dissolves in water to form a weak acid; this is the cause of the phenomenon known as "ocean acidification.") A quarter is absorbed by terrestrial ecosystems—no one is quite sure exactly how or where—and the rest remains in the atmosphere. If current trends in emissions continue, then sometime within the next four of five decades the chemistry of the oceans will have been altered to such a degree that many marine organisms—including reef-building corals—will be pushed toward extinction. Meanwhile, atmospheric CO_2 levels are projected to reach five hundred and fifty parts per million—twice pre-industrial levels—virtually guaranteeing an eventual global temperature increase of three or more degrees. The consequences of this warming are difficult to predict in detail, but even broad, conservative estimates are terrifying: at least fifteen and possibly as many as thirty per cent of the planet's plant and animal species will be threatened; sea levels will rise by several feet; yields of crops like wheat and corn will decline significantly in a number of areas where they are now grown as staples; regions that depend on glacial runoff or seasonal snowmelt—currently home to more than a billion people—will face severe water shortages; and what now counts as a hundred-year drought will occur in some parts of the world as frequently as once a decade.

Today, with CO_2 levels at three hundred and eighty-five parts per million, the disruptive impacts of climate change are already apparent. The Arctic ice cap, which has shrunk by half since the nineteen-fifties, is melting at an annual rate of twenty-four thousand square miles, meaning that an expanse of ice the size of West Virginia is disappearing each year. Over the past ten years, forests covering a hundred and fifty million acres in the United States and Canada have died from warming-related beetle infestations. It is believed that rising temperatures are contributing to the growing number of international refugees—"Climate change is today one of the main drivers of forced displacement," the United Nations' high commissioner for refugees, António Guterres, said recently—and to armed conflict: some experts see a link between the fighting in Darfur, which has claimed as many as three hundred thousand lives, and changes in rainfall patterns in equatorial Africa.

10   "If we keep going down this path, the Darfur crisis will be only one crisis among dozens of other," President Nicolas Sarkozy, of France, told a meeting

of world leaders in April. The Secretary-General of the United Nations, Ban Ki-moon, has called climate change "the defining challenge of our age."

In the context of this challenge, Samsø's accomplishments could be seen as trivial. Certainly, in numerical terms they don't amount to much: all the island's avoided emissions of the past ten years are overwhelmed by the CO_2 that a single coal-fired power plant will emit in the next three weeks, and China is building new coal-fired plants at the rate of roughly four a month. But it is also in this context that the island's efforts are most significant. Samsø transformed its energy systems in a single decade. Its experience suggests how the carbon problem, as huge as it is, could be dealt with, if we were willing to try.

Samsø set out to reinvent itself thanks to a series of decisions that it had relatively little to do with. The first was made by the Danish Ministry of Environment and Energy in 1997. The ministry, looking for ways to promote innovation, decided to sponsor a renewable-energy contest. In order to enter, a community had to submit a plan showing how it could wean itself off fossil fuels. An engineer who didn't actually live on Samsø thought the island would make a good candidate. In consultation with Samsø's mayor, he drew up a plan and submitted it. When it was announced that Samsø had won, the general reaction among residents was puzzlement. "I had to listen twice before I believed it," one farmer told me.

The brief surge of interest that followed the announcement soon dissipated. Besides its designation as Denmark's "renewable-energy island," Samsø received basically nothing—no prize money or special tax breaks, or even government assistance. One of the few people on the island to think the project was worth pursuing was Søren Hermansen.

Hermansen, who is now forty-nine, is a trim man with close-cropped hair, ruddy cheeks, and dark-blue eyes. He was born on Samsø and, save for a few stints away, to travel and go to university, has lived there his entire life. His father was a farmer who grew, among other things, beets and parsley. Hermansen, too, tried his hand at farming—he took over the family's hundred acres when his father retired—but he discovered he wasn't suited to it. "I like to talk, and vegetables don't respond," he told me. He leased his fields to a neighbor and got a job teaching environmental studies at a local boarding school. Hermansen found the renewable-energy-island concept intriguing. When some federal money was found to fund a single staff position, he became the project's first employee.

15   For months, which stretched into years, not much happened. "There was this conservative hesitating, waiting for the neighbor to do the move," Hermansen recalled. "I know the community and I know this is what usually happens." Rather than working against the islanders' tendency to look to one another, Hermansen tried to work with it.

"One reason to live here can be social relations," he said. "This renewable-energy project could be a new kind of social relation, and we used that." Whenever there was a meeting to discuss a local issue—any local issue—Hermansen attended and made his pitch. He asked Samsingers to think about what it would be like to work together on something they could all be proud of. Occasionally, he brought free beer along to the discussions. Meanwhile, he began trying to enlist the support of the island's opinion leaders. "This is where the hard work starts, convincing the first movers to be active," he said. Eventually, much as Hermansen had hoped, the social dynamic that had stalled the project began to work in its favor. As more people got involved, that prompted others to do so. After a while, enough Samsingers were participating that participation became the norm.

"People on Samsø started thinking about energy," Ingvar Jørgensen, a farmer who heats his house with solar hot water and a straw-burning furnace, told me. "It became a kind of sport."

"It's exciting to be a part of this," Brian Kjæ, an electrician who installed a small-scale turbine in his back yard, said. Kjæ's turbine, which is seventy-two feet tall generates more current than his family of three can use, and also more than the power lines leading away from his house can handle, so he uses the excess to heat water, which he stores in a tank that he rigged up in his garage. He told me that one day he would like to use the leftover electricity to produce hydrogen, which could potentially run a fuel-cell car.

"Søren, he has talked again and again, and slowly it's spread to a lot of people," he said.

20   Since becoming the "renewable energy island," Samsø has increasingly found itself an object of study. Researchers often travel great distances to get there, a fact that is not without its own irony. The day after I arrived, from New York via Copenhagen, a group of professors from the University of Toyama, in Japan, came to look around. They had arranged a tour with Hermansen, and he invited me to tag along. We headed off to meet the group in his electric Citroën, which is painted blue with white puffy clouds on the doors. It was a drizzly day, and when we got to the dock the water was choppy. Hermansen commiserated with the Japanese, who had just disembarked from the swaying ferry; then we all boarded a bus.

Our first stop was a hillside with a panoramic view of the island. Several wind turbines exactly like the one I had climbed with Tranberg were whooshing nearby. In the wet and the gray, they were the only things stirring. Off in the distance, the silent fields gave way to the Kattegat, where another group of turbines could be seen, arranged in a soldierly line in the water.

All told, Samsø has eleven large land-based turbines. (It has about a dozen additional micro-turbines.) This is a lot of turbines for a relatively small number of people, and the ratio is critical to Samsø's success, as is the fact that the wind off the Kattegat blows pretty much continuously; flags on Samsø, I noticed, do not wave—they stick straight out, as in children's drawings. Hermansen told us that the land-based turbines are a hundred and fifty feet tall, with rotors that are eighty feet long. Together, they produce some twenty-six million kilowatt-hours a year, which is just about enough to meet all the island's demands for electricity. (This is true in an arithmetic sense; as a practical matter, Samsø's production of electricity and its needs fluctuate, so that sometimes it is feeding power into the grid and sometimes it is drawing power from it.) The offshore turbines, meanwhile, are even taller—a hundred and ninety-five feet high, with rotors that extend a hundred and twenty feet. A single offshore turbine generates roughly eight million kilowatt-hours of electricity a year, which, at Danish rates of energy use, is enough to satisfy the needs of some two thousand homes. The offshore turbines—there are ten of them—were erected to compensate for Samsø's continuing use of fossil fuels in its cars, trucks, and ferries. Their combined output, of around eighty million kilowatt-hours a year, provides the energy equivalent of all the gasoline and diesel oil consumed on the island, and then some; in aggregate, Samsø generates about ten per cent more power than it consumes.

"When we started, in 1997, nobody expected this to happen," Hermansen told the group. "When we talked to local people, they said, Yes, come on, maybe in your dreams." Each land-based turbine cost the equivalent of eight hundred and fifty thousand dollars. Each offshore turbine cost around three million dollars. Some of Samsø's turbines were erected by a single investor, like Tranberg; others were purchased collectively. At least four hundred and fifty island residents own shares in the onshore turbines, and a roughly equal number own shares in those offshore. Shareholders, who also include many nonresidents, receive annual dividend checks based on the prevailing price of electricity and how much their turbine has generated.

"If I'm reduced to being a customer, then if I like something I buy it, and if I don't like it I don't buy it," Hermansen said. "But I don't care about the production. We care about the production, because we own the wind turbines. Every time they turn around, it means money in the bank. And, being part of it, we also feel responsible." Thanks to a policy put in place by Denmark's government in the late nineteen-nineties, utilities are required to offer ten-year fixed-rate contracts for wind power that they can sell to customers elsewhere. Under the terms of these contracts, a turbine should—barring mishap—repay a shareholder's initial investment in about eight years.

25   From the hillside, we headed to the town of Ballen. There we stopped at a red shed-shaped building made out of corrugated metal. Inside, enormous bales of straw were stacked against the walls. Hermansen explained that the building was a district heating plant that had been designed to run on biomass. The bales, each representing the equivalent of fifty gallons of oil, would be fed into a furnace, where water would be heated to a hundred and fifty-eight degrees. This hot water would then be piped underground to two hundred and sixty houses in Ballen and in the neighboring town of Brundby. In this way, the energy of the straw burned at the plant would be transferred to the homes, where it could be used to provide heat and hot water.

Samsø has two other district heating plants that burn straw—one in Tranebjerg, the other in Onsbjerg—and also a district plant, in Nordby, that burns wood chips. When we visited the Nordby plant, later that afternoon, it was filled with what looked like mulch. (The place smelled like a potting shed.) Out back was a field covered in rows of solar panels, which provide additional hot water when the sun is shining. Between the rows, sheep with long black faces were munching on the grass. The Japanese researchers pulled out their cameras as the sheep snuffled toward them, expectantly.

Of course, burning straw or wood, like burning fossil fuels, produces CO_2. The key distinction is that while fossil fuels release carbon that otherwise would have remained sequestered, biomass releases carbon that would have entered the atmosphere anyway, through decomposition. As long as biomass regrows, the CO_2 released in its combustion should be reabsorbed, meaning that the cycle is—or at least can be—carbon neutral. The wood chips used in the Nordby plant come from fallen trees that previously would have been left to rot. The straw for the Ballen-Brundby plant comes mainly from wheat stalks that would previously have been burned in the fields. Together, the biomass heating plants prevent the release of some twenty-seven hundred tons of carbon dioxide a year.

In addition to biomass, Samsø is experimenting on a modest scale with biofuels: a handful of farmers have converted their cars and tractors to run on canola oil. We stopped to visit one such farmer, who grows his own seeds, presses his own oil, and feeds the leftover mash to his cows. The farmer couldn't be located, so Hermansen started up the press himself. He stuck a finger under the spout, then popped it into his mouth. "The oil is very good," he announced. "You can use it in your car, and you can use it on your salad."

After the tour, I went back with Hermansen to his office, in a building known as the Energiakademi. The academy, which looks like a Bauhaus interpretation of a barn, is covered with photovoltaic cells and insulated with shredded newspapers. It is supposed to serve as a sort of interpretive center, though when I visited, the place was so new that the rooms were mostly empty. Some high-school students were kneeling on the floor, trying to put together a miniature turbine.

30   I asked Hermansen whether there were any projects that hadn't worked out. He listed several, including a plan to use natural gas produced from cow manure and an experiment with electric cars that failed when one of the demonstration vehicles spent most of the year in the shop. The biggest disappointment, though, had to do with consumption.

"We made several programs for energy savings," he told me. "But people are acting—what do you call it?—irresponsibly. They behave like monkeys." For example, families that insulated their homes better also tended to heat more rooms, "so we ended up with zero." Essentially, he said, energy use on the island has remained constant for the past decade.

I asked why he thought the renewable-energy-island effort had got as far as it did. He said he wasn't sure, because different people had had different motives for participating. "From the very egoistic to the more over-all perspective, I think we had all kinds of reasons."

Finally, I asked what he thought other communities might take from Samsø's experience.

"We always hear that we should think globally and act locally," he said. "I understand what that means—I think we as a nation should be part of the global consciousness. But each individual cannot be part of that. So 'Think locally, act locally' is the key message for us."

35   "There's this wish for showcases," he added. "When we are selected to be the showcase for Denmark, I feel ashamed that Denmark doesn't produce anything bigger than that. But I feel proud because we are the showcase. So I did my job, and my colleagues did their job, and so did the people of Samsø."

WIND POWER PUFFERY

H. Sterling Burnett

Whenever there is a discussion of energy policy, many environmentalists and their political allies tout wind power as an alternative to burning fossil fuels. Even if electricity from wind power is more expensive than conventional fuel sources, and it is, wind advocates argue its environmental benefits are worth it. In particular, proponents claim increased reliance on wind power would reduce air pollution and greenhouse gas emissions.

But is this assertion correct? No, the truth is wind power's environmental benefits are usually overstated, while its significant environmental harms are often ignored.

Close inspection of wind power finds the promised air pollution improvements do not materialize. There are several reasons, the principal one being that wind farms generate power only when the wind blows within a certain range of speed. When there is too little wind, wind towers don't generate power. Conversely, when the wind is too strong, they must be shut off for fear of being blown down.

Due to this fundamental limitation, wind farms need conventional power plants to supplement the power they supply and to replace a wind farm's expected supply to the grid when the towers are not turning. After all, the power grid requires a regulated constant flow of energy to function properly.

5   Yet bringing a conventional power plant on line to supply power is not as simple as turning on a switch. Most "redundant" fossil fuel power stations must run, even if at reduced levels, continuously. When these factors are combined with the emissions of pollutants and CO_2 caused by the manufacture and maintenance of wind towers and their associated infrastructure, very little of the air quality improvements actually result from expansion of wind power.

There are other problems. A recent report from Great Britain—where wind power is growing even faster than in the U.S.—says that as wind farms grow, wind power is increasingly unpopular. Why? Wind farms are noisy, land-intensive and unsightly. The industry has tricked its way into unspoiled countryside in "green" disguise by portraying wind farms as "parks." In reality, wind farms are more similar to highways, industrial buildings, railways and industrial farms. This wouldn't be a major consideration if it weren't that, because of the prevailing wind currents, the most favorable locations for wind farms usually are areas with particularly spectacular views in relatively wild places.

Worse, wind farms produce only a fraction of the energy of a conventional power plant but require hundreds of times the acreage. For instance, two of the biggest wind "farms" in Europe have 159 turbines and cover thousands of acres between them. But together they take a year to produce less than four days' output from a single 2,000-megawatt conventional power station—which takes up 100 times fewer acres. And in the U.S., a proposed wind farm off the coast of Massachusetts would produce only 450 megawatts of power but require 130 towers and more than 24 square miles of ocean.

Perhaps the most well-publicized harmful environmental impact of wind power relates to its effect on birds and bats. For efficiency, wind farms must be located where the wind blows fairly constantly. Unfortunately, such locations are prime travel routes for migratory birds, including protected species like Bald and Golden Eagles. This motivated the Sierra Club to label wind towers "the Cuisinarts of the air."

Indeed, scientists estimate as many as 44,000 birds have been killed over the past 20 years by wind turbines in the Altamont Pass, east of San Francisco. The victims include kestrels, red-tailed hawks and golden eagles—an average of 50 golden eagles are killed each year.

10 These problems are exacerbated, explains one study, as "Wind farms have been documented to act as both bait and executioner—rodents taking shelter at the base of turbines multiply with the protection from raptors, while in turn their greater numbers attract more raptors to the farm."

Deaths are not limited to the United States or to birds. For example, at Tarif, Spain, thousands of birds from more than 13 species protected under European Union law have been killed by the site's 269 wind turbines. During last fall's migration, at least 400 bats, including red bats, eastern pipistrelles, hoary bats and possible endangered Indiana bats, were killed at a 44-turbine wind farm in West Virginia.

As a result of these problems and others, lawsuits are either pending or being considered to prevent expansion of wind farms in West Virginia and California and to prevent the construction of offshore wind farms in a number of New England states.

Indeed, the Audubon society has called for a moratorium on new wind development in bird-sensitive areas—which, because of the climatic conditions needed for wind farms, includes the vast majority of the suitable sites for proposed construction.

Wind power is expensive, doesn't deliver the environmental benefits it promises and has substantial environmental costs. In short, wind power is no bargain. Accordingly, it doesn't merit continued government promotion or funding.

● **Review Questions**

1. Locate the one or two sentences in Kolbert's article that make the connection between Samsø's experience with wind power and the reduction of global CO_2 emissions.

2. How did Samsø's geographical circumstances play a role in the success of its conversion to renewable energy?

3. Why is the process of burning biomass substances, such as bales of straw or wood chips, more carbon-neutral than the burning of coal, according to Kolbert?

Discussion and Writing Suggestions

1. Why do you think Kolbert begins this article as she does, with a verbal picture of Jørgen Tranberg, rather than with, say, the data on CO_2 emissions in ¶ 7 or the consequences of heightened levels of CO_2 in the atmosphere in ¶s 8 and 9?

2. Kolbert describes a "social dynamic" through which one committed citizen convinced a number of his fellow citizens to participate in a community project; and they in turn convinced others, some with particular skills, until the committed few became a community-wide movement dedicated to productive change. Have you witnessed or been a part of such a movement in your own or another community? Describe what happened and the conclusions you draw from this experience. What obstacles did you face? How were they overcome? Which factors or events were most helpful? Most surprising? Most frustrating? Most rewarding? What advice do you have for others considering such community projects?

3. To what extent do you think the experience of Samsø concerning renewable energy sources such as wind is repeatable elsewhere, particularly in the United States? In what ways might the different geographical, cultural, and political circumstances in the United States make it difficult to repeat Samsø's experience here? In what respects might the circumstances be similar?

4. What conclusions, if any, can you draw from the Samsø experience with wind power about the role of government in encouraging the use of renewable energy? About the role of entrepreneurship? The role of individual initiative? The role of civic duty?

5. To what extent do you view the problems with wind power cited by Burnett as serious enough to rule out this energy source as viable? To what extent do you think we should proceed with large-scale construction of wind farms, considering the realities of (1) intermittent power that must be periodically supplemented by conventional power plants; (2) the poor ratio of power generated to acreage of land consumed by wind turbines; (3) the danger to birds?

6. Conduct a brief Google (or other Internet) search, and then respond to some of Burnett's concerns about wind power with the information you find. To what extent are Burnett's objections well-founded? To what extent might it be possible to deal effectively with the problems he discusses?

7. The danger to birds posed by spinning wind turbines is analogous to the danger to whales posed by sonar tests conducted by Navy submarines. In one case, the benefit is renewable energy; in the other case, the benefit is (according to the military and civilian Department of Defense officials) enhanced national security. How should we weigh such conflicting interests and decide between them?

8. Critique Burnett's argument. Use as guidelines the principles discussed in Chapter 2. Consider first the main questions: (1) To what extent does Burnett

succeed in his purpose? (2) To what extent do you agree with him? Then move to the specifics: e.g., to what extent do you agree with his contention that wind turbines pose too great a risk to birds? Before writing your critique, you may want to reread what Elizabeth Kolbert and other authors in this chapter have written about wind power.

ELECTRIC CARS

In 2006, American moviegoers lined up to see a fascinating murder mystery, *Who Killed the Electric Car?* The producers of this award-winning documentary pointed an accusatory finger at the vehicle's manufacturer, General Motors, which produced and leased thousands of the popular cars—the EV1 (for "electric vehicle 1")—between 1996 and 1999, only to repossess and crush the entire fleet when the vehicles proved unprofitable.*

Electric cars, which release no carbon emissions into the atmosphere, are environmentally appealing. Thus far, however, they remain a niche product because they're expensive, even when subsidized by the government, largely owing to their costly battery packs. Sales have also suffered because of so-called "range anxiety"—the fear among drivers that they would run out of electricity before reaching their destination and become stranded. The Chevy Volt, which went into production in 2010, runs only 35 miles on its battery pack before its backup gasoline engine kicks in; the all-electric Nissan Leaf runs 75 miles. Such ranges are adequate for most trips, but far less than what American consumers have come to expect. For these reasons, all-electric cars (as opposed to hybrids such as the Toyota Prius) cannot yet compete on a large scale with vehicles running on conventional internal combustion engines.

But battery technology is improving and, with it, the promise of practical, reasonably priced electric cars. To proponents of green power, the appeal of electric vehicles is obvious: By replacing gasoline with electric power, we can drastically reduce air pollution and CO_2 emissions from the exhaust pipes of millions of vehicles around the world. We also reduce our dependence upon oil and its politically unstable sources of supply. So electric cars—present from the dawn of the automobile era—may in fact be the wave of the future.

The following selections offer two current perspectives on the prospects for electric cars. The first is by Daniel Yergin, considered one of the world's most authoritative voices on energy issues. Yergin's earlier book *The Prize: The Epic Quest for Oil, Money, and Power* (1992), won the Pulitzer Prize for non-fiction and was later made into a PBS documentary mini-series. In the selection below, "The

---

*Ironically, when GM itself was dying several years later, and declared bankruptcy, it placed significant hopes for its renewal on its development of another electric vehicle, the Chevrolet Volt, which went on sale in 2010. After the federal government assumed a major financial stake in the company, GM subsequently became profitable again, though not because of the Volt, the sales of which were unimpressive. (During its first year, fewer than 7,000 Volts were sold, despite GM's initial forecast of 10,000.)

Great Electric Car Experiment," excerpted from his recent book *The Quest: Energy, Security, and the Remaking of the Modern World* (2011), Yergin discusses the technology of electric vehicles and the "race to reshape transportation." Then, somewhat dampening Yergin's enthusiasm, Joseph B. White explains "Why The Gasoline Engine Isn't Going Away Any Time Soon."

White reports on automobile and energy-related stories for the *Wall Street Journal*, where the article below first appeared on September 15, 2008.

THE GREAT ELECTRIC CAR EXPERIMENT

Daniel Yergin

The Race Resumes

Oil had held its seemingly impregnable position as king of the realm of transportation for almost a century. By the beginning of the twenty-first century, however, people were beginning to question how long oil would—or should—hold on to its crown. Yet as late as 2007 in the debate over the future of automotive transportation, the electric car was only a peripheral topic. Biofuels were the focus.

Within a few years, however, the electric car would move onto center stage. It could, said its proponents, break the grip of oil on transportation, allowing motorists to unplug from turbulence in the oil-exporting world and high prices at the pump. It could help reduce pollution and offset the carbon emissions that precipitate climate change. And it could provide a powerful answer to the great puzzle of how the world can accommodate the move from one billion cars to two billion. The electric car is powered by electricity that can be generated from any number of different sources, none of which need be oil. Perhaps more than any other technology, the electric car represents a stark alternative road to the future for the global energy system.

The electric vision rapidly became so compelling that expectations for electric cars far exceed the actual impact such cars might have on the world's auto-fleet in terms of numbers, at least in the next decade or two. Yet their presence in the fleet, even if small, will change attitudes about both oil and autos far ahead of the numerical impact. In decades further out, the effect could be much larger. There are, however, two big questions: Can they deliver the performance that is promised at a cost that is acceptable? And will consumers choose to make them a mainstream purchase as opposed to a niche product?

In the meantime, very big bets are now being placed on the renewed race—between the battery and the internal combustion engine, between electricity and oil—that was supposedly decided a century ago. The outcome will have enormous significance in terms of both economics and geopolitics.

5 The conviction is also growing that electric vehicles could constitute a great "new industry," the epitome of cleantech, and the means to leapfrog to leadership in the global auto industry. This is a big opportunity for companies, entrepreneurs, and investors. But it is seen as much more than an opportunity in the marketplace.

A French government minister has declared that "the battle of the electric car" has begun. "Electric vehicles are the future and the driver of the Industrial Revolution," said one of Europe's economic leaders. By 2010 the Obama administration had provided $5 billion in grants and loan guarantees to battery makers, entrepreneurs, major auto companies, and equipment suppliers to jump-start the electric car and build out the infrastructure systems that would support it. "Here in the United States," Obama announced, "we've created an entire new industry."[1]

This, indeed, is a game of nations. For countries like China and Korea, it is the opportunity to take a dominant position in a critical growth sector. Conversely, success in electric transportation may be required if the traditional leading countries in automobiles—the United States, Japan, and Germany—are to maintain their positions. If batteries are to be the "new oil," then the winners in battery know-how and production can capture a decisive new role in the world economy—and the rewards that will go with that.

• • •

The Return of the EV

With the opening of the new century, several factors started to converge to give new life to the electric vehicle.

Environmental pollution from auto exhausts has created anguish and been a major topic of public policy in the United States. In the decades since, other urban areas, from Mexico City to Beijing, have come to suffer under similar affliction and have also sought to find relief from air pollution. Moreover, now there was something new: concern about climate change. Although transportation on a global basis is responsible for about 17 percent of CO_2 emissions, the absolute volume of emissions is large and could get much larger. Rising oil prices also renewed interest. The electric car held out the prospect of insulating consumers from high prices, and blunting the impact of oil price shocks.

One other development built support. The introduction of hybrids had a major impact on the psychology of motorists. Hybrids served as a kind of mental bridge to electric cars by creating public acceptance of battery-driven vehicles and what they could mean: a much larger role for electricity in transportation.

10   This convergence propelled the electric car out of the automotive museum and back onto the street. Today, in contrast to a century ago, there are two primary types of electrically powered vehicles. One is a direct lineal descendant of the sort that Thomas Edison sought to get out on the road, a pure battery-operated electric vehicle: the EV. It operates only on electricity and is charged from an electric socket. But now there is a variant, the plug-in hybrid electric vehicle, the PHEV. It is an immediate descendant of the hybrid but is much more of an electric vehicle than the Prius-type hybrid, It is "plugged in" to its primary fuel source: electricity. However, after the plug-in hybrid runs for some distance on electricity and the battery runs down, a combustion engine takes over, either recharging the battery or directly providing power to propel the car, or both.

Research and experimentation with plug-in hybrids had been going on for decades, but hardly anyone paid notice. That changed in 2007 when GM unveiled its PHEV Chevy Volt as a sporty concept car at the Detroit Auto Show. Its public debut got so much attention and created such a clamor that GM decided to actually push the Volt into production. Within 12 months the model would come to symbolize the shift in focus from biofuels to EVs.

By the time of the 2008 presidential campaign, "Detroit's plug-in electric car, the Chevrolet Volt," said one political observer, had become "a must-have prop for U.S. presidential candidates." Despite GM's crushing economic problems, candidates Barack Obama and John McCain could not get close enough to the vehicle. McCain proudly announced that "the eyes of the world are now on the Volt." For his part, Barack Obama promised during the campaign to have a million such plug-in hybrids and electric cars on the road by 2015.[2]

• • •

The Road Map

The core of electric vehicles is the battery. The move toward electric cars would require a major technological advance in batteries. The basic lead-acid battery goes back to the second half of the nineteenth century. Other types of batteries were introduced subsequently, but the lead-acid battery remained the mainstay of the auto industry.

However, in the 1970s and 1980s, researchers, beginning in an Exxon laboratory, were figuring out how lithium, the lightest of metals, could provide the basis for a new rechargeable battery. The oil crises of the 1970s and the fear of a lasting shortage of petroleum had sparked interest in reviving the electric car. In 1976, Congress approved funding for "Electric and Hybrid" research. That same year, *Forbes* reported that "the electric car's rebirth is as sure as the need to end our dependence on imported oil." A number of automobile companies were working on electric vehicles. In 1979, in the middle of the Iranian oil crisis, *Fortune* announced, "Here Come the Electrics." But then the price of oil went down, it turned out that the world was amply supplied with petroleum, and the interest in electric cars once again faded away.

15   But the work on lithium batteries could be put to very good use for another big need. In 1991, Sony took the lead and introduced lithium-ion batteries in consumer electronics. These smaller, more efficient batteries enabled laptop computers to run faster and longer on a single charge. And lithium batteries were decisively important for something else. They made it possible to shrink the size of cell phones enormously, and thus powered the cell phone revolution. In theory, the greater density of lithium batteries, combined with their lower costs, could make them a more viable and competitive battery for EVs—better than both the nickel-metal-hydride batteries used in the first hybrids and the lead-acid battery that is customary today in automobiles. But that was all in theory. No one had yet road-tested the idea.[3]

• • •

Taking a Leaf

Today all the major automakers are moving, with varying degrees of conviction, toward an electric-car offering. Certainly all car companies would be more than happy to find some way to blunt their vulnerability to high oil prices. But among the major international companies, none has been more fervent about the electric car than the Nissan-Renault alliance. And no one more outspoken than its joint CEO, Carlos Ghosn.

Ghosn is about as international as an executive of a global company can be. Raised in both Lebanon and Brazil and educated further in France, he ran Michelin Tires in the United States, and then became a senior executive at Renault. After Renault formed an alliance with Japan's Nissan, Ghosn set out to rescue Nissan, which was teetering on collapse with $20 billion of debt. He became famous for bringing Nissan back from the brink and ended up as the CEO of both companies.

Toyota has its hybrid, Prius. Honda is the "engine company," focused on the superior characteristics of a more-efficient internal combustion engine. By contrast, going "all-electric" gives Nissan a distinctive leadership. The opportunity emerged by accident out of the company's financial wreck.

When Ghosn arrived at Nissan in Japan in 1999, he slashed costs almost everywhere. But something about the battery program gave him pause. "Nissan had been working on the electric battery for 18 years," said Ghosn. "I was really struck by those engineers when I met with them. They thought that an electric car could be feasible and affordable. I had no clue, but I was very impressed by their passion." Despite Nissan's perilous financial condition, that was one cut he did not make. "Sometimes you only connect the dots afterward," he added.

20   By 2002 Nissan had what it considered a breakthrough in lithium-ion technology. "After 2003, Nissan was out of turn-around," said Ghosn. "But I was very surprised by the amount of criticism that we were getting for not having a hybrid. I asked myself why there was so much passion about this. I realized how strong were the public's concerns around the environment. At the same time, the price of oil was going up. Also, very strong environmental regulations were coming out of California. We couldn't fulfill them without some kind of new technology. We needed to think out of the box. We needed to jump-start the electric. That was the only solution. You can't go from 850 million to 2 billion cars without an environmental car." Nissan had what its engineers believed was the technology. Ghosn gave the go-ahead to go all-out for a new all-electric car.

The reaction within the company was diverse. Some were puzzled. Why, they asked, didn't Nissan try instead to build a competitive hybrid? Others were enthusiastic that the company was trying to take leadership in a new technology.

While Nissan would also develop its own hybrids, Ghosn looked at it only as a bridge technology. "If you have an efficient battery for a hybrid, why not go all the way and go for electric cars?" he said. "It has the most zero emissions of anything."

And so if Nissan was going to spend several billion dollars to develop a new car, it would be for an all-electric car. "No tailpipe," said Ghosn. Not a drop of gasoline. And it was not going to just be a car for the motor show. It was going to be an affordable car for the mass market." In the autumn of 2010, Nissan went to market with the Leaf—which stands for Leading, Environmentally friendly, Affordable, Family car. It rolled into showrooms with a 600-pound pack of lithium-ion batteries and promised an average driving range of around 90 to 100 miles and a top speed of 90 miles per hour. Nissan is targeting that 10 percent of its sales in 2020 will be EVs. "The only thing that is missing is real scale, and to achieve that, we have to cut costs of the battery," said Ghosn.

"The race to zero emissions has begun," he declared. For him, it was truly the world according to CARB. "This is not a bet," he said. "The only question about zero emissions is, When? Do we do it do now or in five years? Our competitors may see it differently." But Nissan believes "it is now."[4]

Charge It

25 For most of the previous two decades, the center of the advanced battery world has been in Asia, in Japan, and in South Korean. While the United States was pushing ahead, the Japanese and South Korean companies have redoubled their own efforts. After all, it was a Korean company, LG Chem, that made the Chevy Volt battery cells. In response to America's new politics of electric cars, it hastened to open a plant in Michigan.

Backed by strong government incentives, the U.S. industry is expanding rapidly. The Obama administration projects America to host 40 percent of the world's advanced automotive battery manufacturing capacity by 2015, as opposed to 2 percent when Obama took office.[5]

But the battery is only half of the equation; the other is charging—getting electricity into the car reliably and with speed and convenience. Japanese companies have formed an industrial consortium whose name is a pun on "Won't you at least have some tea?" The idea is that charging time needs to be speeded up and that it should take no more time than having a cup of tea. Currently, a Chevy Volt requires four to ten hours to recharge—and that would be quite a number of cups of tea. But various researchers are trying to find the pathway that would reduce charging to something less than the time required to drink a hot cup of tea; that is, the time it takes to fill up with gasoline.

Where Will The Electricity Come From?

The current general theory of electric cars is that they would recharge over-night, when demand is at its lowest. This would create a new market for electric power companies and, at the same time, balance out the load. And it would be a very big market. Charging a car overnight would take about as much electricity as would be used by two houses over twenty-four hours. In other words, were EVs to become ubiquitous, electric power companies would be virtually doubling their residential load without the need to build much more capacity.

Over the last few years, a compelling new vision has taken shape: Wind and solar will generate the new supplies of electricity. That electricity will then be wheeled long-distance over a much-expanded and modernized transmission system. And then, when it gets to dense urban areas, the electricity will be managed by a smart grid that will move it through the distribution system, into the household or the charging station, and finally it will be fed into the battery of an electric car. Some even take the vision further and imagine that cars will act as storage systems, "roving" batteries, which, when idle, will feed electricity back into the grid.

30   But that is quite different from the electric system that exists today in which renewables provide less than 2 percent of the power. Lee Schipper, a professor at Stanford University, argues that many EVs will become what he dubs EEVs—"emissions elsewhere vehicles." That is, the emissions and greenhouse gases associated with transportation will not come out of the tailpipe of the car but potentially from the smokestack of a coal-fired power plant that generates the electricity that is fed into the EV. So one also has to take into account how the power is generated. Is it uranium or coal or wind? Or something else? Will it be natural gas, with about half the CO_2 emissions of coal and now a much more abundant fuel because of the breakthrough on shale gas worldwide? This last prospect also provides an alternative to burning natural gas in engines as a mass-market fuel. Natural gas would in effect become a motor fuel, but indirectly, by generating more of the electricity that ends up in the battery of an electric car[6]

How fast can an electric-vehicle future happen? On a global basis, estimates for new-car sales in 2030 of EVs and PHEVs, depending upon the scenario, range between 10 percent and 32 percent of total annual sales. Under the most optimistic of the scenarios, the penetration of such vehicles (in other words, the total number of EVs and PHEVs in the global fleet) would be 14 percent.[7]

The policies of governments will be one of the critical determinants in the actual outcome. For it is such policies—regulations, incentives, and subsidies—that today are promoting the development of the electric car and on which the current economics depend. Innovation could change that calculus and drive down costs, just as Henry Ford did with the Model T. That is one of the primary arguments for the policies and incentives and subsidies: they are meant to stimulate greater scale and significant cost-cutting innovation. One critical question, therefore, is how stable will be those policies that are now aimed at making electricity the mainstay of the auto fleet? After all, energy policies have shown the recurrent characteristic of being "pendulumatic," moving in one direction and then another, and then back again.

"Thermal Runaway"?

EVs are already in production and in the marketplace. But as a product for a mass market, it remains a great experiment with big hurdles still to be surmounted.

Batteries still need to be smaller, weigh less, charge more quickly, and be able to last much longer on a single charge. They also need to prove that they can be long lived, despite the continuing charging and discharging. It will have to be demonstrated that problems like "thermal runaway"—destructive overheating—do not occur. In addition to propelling the vehicle, batteries also need sufficient capacity to power all the other accoutrements that drivers expect, from power steering and air-conditioning to the traveling entertainment center. And the cost needs to come down substantially—unless governments are willing and capable of providing continuing subsidies on a very large scale.[8]

35   Batteries are now a focus of intense and well-funded research around the world, aimed at addressing these questions. The entire effort is also very competitive—indeed, a global "battery race." At the same time, there is a global debate as to where the "learning curve" battery technology is and how fast it can come down.

Infrastructure is the second challenge. Today's automobile system could not operate without the dense network of gasoline stations built up over so many decades. A large fleet of electric cars will need a similar network of charging stations. One car in a neighborhood can be easily accommodated with an extension cord. But what happens to the transformers in the power system when everybody on the block, and on the next block, and on the next three blocks decides to recharge at the same time?[9]

Moreover, it is necessary to get beyond the "hand raisers"—those who put their names in the order book prior to the release of a model—and the early adopters. In the 1990s General Motors "subsidized the hell out of the EV1," said former GM CEO Rick Wagher. "But if customers don't want to buy, it's hard to do." The EV has to attract a large population of drivers. To that end, charging stations need to be built and powered around urban areas and into the countryside to ensure convenience and reliability—and to ensure that people don't get stranded.[10]

Government can implement only so many regulations, incentives, and subsidies. Buyers have to find the price, functionality, performance, and reliability that they want. That will take time to demonstrate. Specifically, what is called range anxiety—the fear of being stranded with a rundown battery—will be a major factor in what consumers actually do.

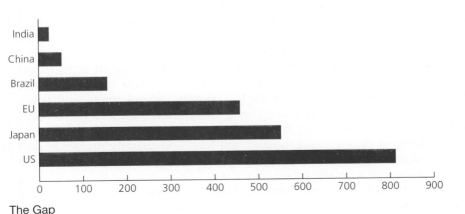

The Gap

Cars per 1,000 population in 2010

Source: IHS Global Insight

Perhaps the answer to consumer needs will be to parse those needs—different cars for different purposes. People may use a small urban electric runabout for local needs and commuting—a sort of modern version of the Detroit Electrics and Baker Runabouts of the early twentieth century—and drive a bigger oil-fueled or hybrid car for longer trips or weekend getaways. At the same time, as when any kind of new product is introduced, there is always the risk of the unexpected in terms of operations or performance that could negatively affect public acceptance of EVs as a category.

40   Finally, there is the matter of power supply. It is generally assumed that sufficient unused electric power–generating capacity, especially at night, is available to accommodate a large fleet of electric cars. That may well be the case, but major growth in electric cars would be a very major new draw on the electric-power industry. What happens if people don't charge their EVs at night? What happens if instead large numbers of people decide to recharge during peak demand? How will the system cope?

• • •

The Cars of the Future

Electric cars, hybrids, biofuels, natural gas vehicles, more efficient internal combustion engines, fuel cells at some later date—the race to reshape transportation and for "the car of the future" is once again on. Or, perhaps, it will be plural—"the cars of the future." In the last race, a century ago, the internal combustion engine won hands down—on the basis of cost, convenience, performance, and range. But this time there may not be a single winner but rather different vehicles for different purposes.

One way or the other, oil's almost total domination over transportation will either be whittled away or more drastically reduced. Cars will certainly get more efficient. It seems pretty certain that electricity will play a bigger role in transportation, either in hybrids or all-electric vehicles. Considerable effort continues to go into second-generation biofuels. Regardless of what powers cars, they are likely to get smaller in coming years, in part as baby boomers in the United States, Europe, and Japan retire. Moreover, surprises in the quest for a clean, secure form of transportation may well happen.

In shaping the future, developing countries will be critical participants in a way they have not been in the past. Emerging markets will fuel growth in the global auto market, and thus the direction of technology as well as environmental standards. China's surpassing the United States as the world's largest car market in 2009 was a landmark. As a result of this shift, the policies of governments in developing countries will have increasingly greater impact on the global auto market. Indeed, a day may well come when China, because of the dynamism of its market, becomes the defining force for the world auto industry, or when a Chinese environmental regulatory agency becomes the new CARB [California Air Resources Board] for the world.

The key criteria for victory, or at least a place in the winner's circle, will be the delivery of increasingly efficient cars that also meet the tests of environment, energy security, cost, and performance. The contest will require major advances in technology and multibillion-dollar investments, and it certainly will be shaped in part by the preferences of governments. In such uncertain circumstances, companies are hedging their futures by placing multiple bets to the degree that they can. "We're investing billions and billions, and basically we're going for everything—from diesel to hybrids to batteries," said Dieter Zetsche, the CEO of Daimler.

45   "We have taken the point of view that fuel efficiency is important to all customers," said Bill Ford, Ford's chairman. "But we still don't know what the winning technology will be. Any (long-term) sales projections today don't mean anything. So many different things are at play. I can't give a number. It's throwing a dart."[11]

To the Future

Where does this leave oil and the internal combustion engine? Probably in an assured position of dominance at least for the next two decades. But there will be much more efficient internal combustion engines. Cars based on the ICE technology can come into today's fleet quickly. And they will not require a new infrastructure system.

Internal combustion engines do a remarkable job of generating power in an affordable and compact package. The secret to the success of the ICE lies in the energy density of liquid fuels—simply put, oil. The small size and power output of the gasoline and diesel-fuel engines will continue to make them fierce competitors'—technologically speaking. Moreover, the scope certainly exists for improving the efficiency of cars—whether in gasoline and diesel engines themselves, or through "lightweighting" cars with new materials, and thus reducing emissions.

"A key question is how to halve the fuel consumption of the 2035 car fleet," observed John Heywood, professor of mechanical engineering at Massachusetts Institute of Technology and the former director of the university's Sloan Automotive Laboratory. "We can make vehicles that are twice as good as those today," says Heywood. "But the next question is, how many? If it's only 15 percent of the fleet, it's of little impact. If it's 95 percent, it's a hell of a big thing."[12]

Yet one near certainty is that the transportation system of today will evolve significantly over the coming decades. Energy efficiency and lower emissions will continue to be major preoccupations. If issues of cost and complexity and scale can be conquered, the battery will begin to push aside oil as the motive force for much of the world's automotive transportation. But the internal combustion engine is unlikely to be shunted aside easily. The new contest may, for some time, be less decisive than when Henry Ford used his Model T to engineer victory for the internal combustion engine against the electric car.

50   But the race has certainly begun. The outcome will do much to define our energy world in the decades ahead in terms of where we get our energy, how we use it, and who the winners will be. But it is much too soon for anyone to take a victory lap.

Notes

[1] Tiffany Groode and Levi Tillemann-Dick, "The Race to Build the Electric Car," *Wall Street Journal Special Section*, March 9, 2011; Agence France-Presse, October 1, 2009 ("battle"); Reuters, July 30, 2008 ("Industrial Revolution"); Barack Obama, speech. February 19, 2010.

[2] *Bloomberg* July 18, 2008.

[3] Seth Fletcher; *Bottle Lightning: Superbatteries, Electric Cars, and the New Lithium Economy* (New York: Hill and Wang, 2011), pp. 30–35; National Research Council, *Transition to Alternative Transportation Technologies: Plug-in Hybrid Electric Vehicles* (Washington, DC: National Academies Press, 2010), p. 9.

[4] Interview with Carlos Ghosn; *Fortune*, February 19, 2010 ("mermaid," "not a bet").

[5] *Bloomberg*, July 15, 2010.

[6] Interview with Lee Schipper ("emissions elsewhere").

[7] IHS CERA, "Automotive Scenarios 2010"; Electrification Coalition, *Electrification Roadmap: Revolutionizing Transportation and Achieving Energy Security* (Washington, DC: Electrification Coalition, 2009).

[8] Interview with Steve Koonin.

[9] Calvin Timmerman, "Smart Grid's Future: Evaluating Policy Opportunities and Challenges after the Recovery Act." Brookings Institution, July 24, 2010.

[10] Interview with Rick Wagoner.

[11] Dieter Zetsche, remarks, *Wall Street Journal* Eco-Nomics Conference, March 13 2008; Bill Ford, remarks, *Wall Street Journal* Eco-Nomics Conference, March 3, 2011.

[12] Interview with John Heywood.

WHY THE GASOLINE ENGINE ISN'T GOING AWAY ANY TIME SOON

Joseph B. White

An automotive revolution is coming—but it's traveling in the slow lane.

High oil prices have accomplished what years of pleas from environmentalists and energy-security hawks could not: forcing the world's major auto makers to refocus their engineers and their capital on devising mass-market alternatives to century-old petroleum-fueled engine technology.

With all the glitzy ads, media chatter and Internet buzz about plug-in hybrids that draw power from the electric grid or cars fueled with hydrogen, it's easy to get lulled into thinking that gasoline stations soon will be as rare as drive-in theaters. The idea that auto makers can quickly execute a revolutionary transition from oil to electricity is now a touchstone for both major presidential candidates.

That's the dream. Now the reality: This revolution will take years to pull off—and that's assuming it isn't derailed by a return to cheap oil. Anyone who goes to sleep today and wakes up in five years will find that most cars for sale in the U.S. will still run on regular gas—with a few more than today taking diesel fuel. That will likely be the case even if the latter-day Rip Van Winkle sleeps until 2020.

Free to Drive

5   Cars aren't iPods or washing machines. They are both highly complex machines and the enablers of a way of life that for many is synonymous with freedom and opportunity—not just in the U.S., but increasingly in rising nations such as China, India and Russia.

Engineering and tooling to produce a new vehicle takes three to five years—and that's without adding the challenge of major new technology. Most car buyers won't accept "beta" technology in the vehicles they and their families depend on every day. Many senior industry executives—including those at Japanese companies—have vivid memories of the backlash against the quality problems that resulted when Detroit rushed smaller cars and new engines into the market after the gas-price shocks of the 1970s. The lesson learned: Technological change is best done incrementally.

Integral to Modern Life

Technological inertia isn't the only issue. Cars powerful enough and large enough to serve multiple functions are integral to modern life, particularly in suburban and rural areas not well served by mass transit.

Ditching the internal-combustion engine could mean ditching the way of life that goes with it, and returning to an era in which more travel revolves around train and bus schedules, and more people live in smaller homes in dense urban neighborhoods.

Economic and cultural forces—high gas prices and empty-nest baby boomers bored with the suburbs—are encouraging some Americans to return to city life, but by no means all. In rising economies such as China, meanwhile, consumers are ravenous for the mobility and freedom that owning a car provides.

Desire Isn't Enough

10   That doesn't mean auto makers and their technology suppliers aren't serious about rethinking the status quo. But displacing internal-combustion engines fueled by petroleum won't be easy and it won't be cheap.

It also may not make sense. Over the past two decades, car makers have at times declared the dawn of the age of ethanol power, hydrogen power and electric power—only to wind up back where they started: confronting the internal-combustion engine's remarkable combination of low cost, durability and power. One effect of higher oil prices is that car makers now have strong incentives to significantly improve the technology they already know.

"There are a lot of improvements coming to the internal-combustion engine," says John German, manager for environmental and energy analysis at Honda Motor Co.'s U.S. unit.

Refinements to current gasoline motors, driven by advances in electronic controls, could result in motors that are a third to half the size and weight of current engines, allowing for lighter, more-efficient vehicles with comparable power. That, Mr. German says, "will make it harder for alternative technologies to succeed."

By 2020, many mainstream cars could be labeled "hybrids." But most of these hybrids will run virtually all the time on conventional fuels. The "hybrid" technology will be a relatively low-cost "micro hybrid" system that shuts the car off automatically at a stop light, and then restarts it and gives it a mild boost to accelerate.

Cheaper than Water

15 Gasoline and diesel are the world's dominant motor-vehicle fuels for good reasons. They are easily transported and easily stored. They deliver more power per gallon than ethanol or other biofuels. And until recently petroleum fuels were a bargain, particularly for consumers in the U.S. Even now, gasoline in the U.S. is cheaper by the gallon than many brands of bottled water.

Car makers have made significant advances in technology to use hydrogen as a fuel, either for a fuel cell that generates electricity or as a replacement for gasoline in an internal-combustion engine. But storing and delivering hydrogen remains a costly obstacle to mass marketing of such vehicles.

Natural gas has enjoyed a resurgence of interest in the wake of big new gas finds in the U.S., and Honda markets a natural-gas version of its Civic compact car.

But there are only about 1,100 natural-gas fueling stations around the country, of which just half are open to the public, according to the Web site for Natural Gas Vehicles for America, a group that represents various natural-gas utilities and technology providers.

Among auto-industry executives, the bet now is that the leading alternative to gasoline will be electricity. Electric cars are a concept as old as the industry itself. The big question is whether battery technology can evolve to the point where a manufacturer can build a vehicle that does what consumers want at a cost they can afford.

20   "The No. 1 obstacle is cost," says Alex Molinaroli, head of battery maker Johnson Controls Inc.'s Power Solutions unit. Johnson Controls is a leading maker of lead-acid batteries—standard in most cars today—and is working to develop advanced lithium-ion automotive batteries in a joint venture with French battery maker Saft Groupe SA.

The Costs Add Up

Cost is a problem not just with the advanced batteries required to power a car for a day's driving. There's also the cost of redesigning cars to be lighter and more aerodynamic so batteries to power them don't have to be huge.

There's the cost of scrapping old factories and the workers that go with them—a particular challenge for Detroit's Big Three auto makers, which have union agreements that make dismissing workers difficult and costly.

A world full of electricity-driven cars would require different refueling infrastructure but the good news is that it's already largely in place, reflecting a century of investment in the electric grid.

The refueling station is any electric outlet. The key will be to control recharging so it primarily happens when the grid isn't already stressed, but controllers should be able to steer recharging to off-peak hours, likely backed by discount rates for electricity.

25   Big utilities in the two most populous states, California and Texas, are adding millions of smart meters capable of verifying that recharging happens primarily in periods when other electricity use is slack. Studies show the U.S. could easily accommodate tens of millions of plug-in cars with no additional power plants. Three big utilities in California are planning to install smart meters capable of managing off-peak recharging. The estimated cost: $5 billion over the next five years.

Remembering the Past

Americans often reach for two analogies when confronted with a technological challenge: The Manhattan Project, which produced the first atomic bomb during World War II, and the race to put a man on the moon during the 1960s. The success of these two efforts has convinced three generations of Americans that all-out, spare-no-expense efforts will yield a solution to any challenge.

This idea lives today in General Motors Corp.'s crash program to bring out the Chevrolet Volt plug-in hybrid by 2010—even though the company acknowledges the battery technology required to power the car isn't ready.

Even if GM succeeds in meeting its deadline for launching the Volt, the Volt won't be a big seller for years, especially if estimates that the car will be priced at $40,000 or more prove true.

Moon-shot efforts like the Volt get attention, but the most effective ways to use less energy may have less to do with changing technology than with changing habits.

30   A 20-mile commute in an electric car may not burn gasoline, but it could well burn coal—the fuel used to fire electric power plants in much of the U.S. The greener alternative would be to not make the drive at all, and fire up a laptop and a broadband connection instead.

[The following table accompanied White's article.]

The Road Ahead

Gasoline has powered the vast majority of the world's automobiles for the past century. But now amid rising oil prices and increasing concern about tailpipe emissions and global warming, new types of propulsion technologies are starting to emerge. Here's an overview of what's here now, and what's ahead.

Kelly McDaniel-Timon

	Pros	Cons	Vehicles	Availability/ Starting Prices
Hybrids Have a battery and electric motor to power the car at low speeds and a gas engine for accelerating and highway driving.	Increases fuel economy significantly, especially in heavy stop-and-go driving.	Price premium over standard models can be $2,500 or more for a Toyota Prius, $8,000 and up for large hybrid SUVs. Mileage improvements modest in some larger vehicles.	Toyota Prius, Ford Escape Hybrid, GMC Yukon Hybrid, Lexus LS600h, Lexus RX400h, Chrysler Aspen Hybrid, Dodge Durango Hybrid.	On the market now. Prius $23,375, Yukon $50,920, Lexus RX400h $43,480.
Mild Hybrids Electric motor only assists the gasoline engine; it can't drive wheels on its own.	Cost. Generally less expensive than full hybrids.	Only modest improvement in fuel economy.	Honda Civic Hybrid, Chevrolet Malibu Hybrid, Saturn Aura Hybrid.	On the market now. Honda Civic $22,600, Chevy Malibu $24,695, Saturn Aura $24,930.
Plug-In Hybrids A full hybrid with a large battery that drivers can recharge by plugging the car into an AC outlet.	Dramatic boost in fuel economy— can go up to perhaps 120 miles on the battery alone.	The advanced batteries required are not yet available. They are also expensive and can overheat.	None on the market today. Some "hackers" can convert Priuses to plug-ins.	Many auto makers working to offer them in 2–4 years.
Flex Fuel Vehicles Have standard internal combustion engines that can run on gasoline or a mix of gasoline and ethanol.	No price premium, can be used in vehicles of all sizes. Reduces greenhouse gas emissions.	Ethanol not widely available. A gallon of ethanol has less energy than a gallon of gas, so mile per gallon is lower.	Almost all GM, Ford and Chrysler models.	On the market now.

	Pros	Cons	Vehicles	Availability/ Starting Prices
Fuel Cell Vehicles Use hydrogen gas and a chemical process to generate electricity that powers an electric motor.	Uses no fossil fuel, hydrogen is widely available and the only tailpipe emission is water vapor.	Still in experimental stage, hydrogen not widely available as fuel, technology still far too expensive for commercial use.	Models now in tests include Honda FCX Clarity and Chevrolet Equinox among others.	Small number of Clarity and Equinox available for lease through test programs.
Electric Car Powered by a long-lasting battery and electric motor. Can have a small gas engine on board to charge the battery.	Practically no emission or engine noise. Can be recharged from AC outlet.	Technology still unproven. Batteries not available.	GM working on Chevy Volt. Also start-up electric car makers Tesla, Fisker and others.	Volt due by 2011. Tesla, Fisker and others possibly sooner.
Clean Diesel New, advanced diesel engines that burn fuel more cleanly and use low-sulfur fuel.	20% to 40% more miles per gallon and more torque than gas engines, reduced greenhouse gas emissions.	More expensive than models with gas engines. Diesel fuel more expensive than gasoline. Unclear if Americans will embrace diesel.	Jeep Grand Cherokee and Volkswagen Jetta are two examples. BMW and Mercedes-Benz also offering clean diesel models.	VW Jetta diesel $21,999, Grand Cherokee $31,390.

Source: WSJ Reporting

● Review Questions

1. What other benefits, besides environmental, are promised by the development of electric cars, according to Yergin?

2. According to Yergin, which factors converged at the turn of the twenty-first century to renew interest in and spur development of a new generation of electric cars?

3. In what fundamental way is the Nissan Leaf a different kind of electric vehicle than the Toyota Prius or the Chevrolet Volt?

4. Electric cars are widely viewed as environmentally friendly. But how do the logistics of generating battery power for such vehicles create environmental problems?

5. What are some of the main hurdles to broad consumer acceptance of electric cars, according to Yergin?

6. Summarize White's answer to the implied question in the title of his article.

7. What are the main stumbling blocks, according to White, to broad consumer acceptance of alternative energy vehicles?

8. What are the chief drawbacks of hydrogen and natural gas as automobile fuels? To what extent do electric-powered vehicles share such drawbacks?

● Discussion and Writing Suggestions

1. Assume that you had the money to buy an electric car—either a plug-in hybrid such as the Chevrolet Volt or an all-electric such as the Nissan Leaf. (You don't have the money, though, to buy a $109,000 Tesla Roadster!) Taking into account your present and future driving needs, would you buy such a car? Would anyone else that you know personally? Why or why not?

2. Yergin reports on the conviction that electric cars will constitute a great "new industry." To what extent do you think that this industry could be as transformative to our way of life as were the developments of digital technology and the computer revolution of the 1990s and the 2000s? In what ways are these industries similar? In what ways different?

3. Yergin explains that we must, for the moment, burn fossil fuels in order to generate the electricity needed to recharge so-called eco-friendly electric cars. How does this reality affect your view of the continued development of electric vehicles? Would you be more inclined to favor developing improved internal combustion engines in conventional gasoline-powered vehicles (a process that Yergin explains is already under way)?

4. Yergin asserts that government policies will help determine the speed with which "an electric vehicle future" can become a reality. "For it is such policies," he argues, "[which include] regulations, incentives, and subsidies—that today are promoting the development of the electric car on which the current economics depend." Imagine you are a lawmaker. What laws and regulations would you recommend to help ensure a transition to electric cars? Consider timelines, improved battery technology, power sources, safety tests, and fuel stations; create a realistic, broad-based plan.

5. White argues, "Most car buyers won't accept 'beta' [developmental] technology in the vehicles that they and their families depend on every day." Would you be hesitant to buy a first-generation Chevy Volt or any other plug-in hybrid vehicle if there were no guarantee of its reliability?

6. White cites "mobility and freedom" as one reason that the internal combustion engine will persist for the foreseeable future. To what extent are such values sufficiently important that you would hesitate to purchase or refuse to consider purchasing an all-electric vehicle?

7. Locate a specific principle or definition that White uses in this selection. For example, he asserts in ¶ 5 that cars "are both highly complex machines and the enablers of a way of life that for many is synonymous with freedom and opportunity." Write an analysis in which you apply this or another principle or definition by White to a particular situation of which you have personal knowledge or about which you have read. See the guidelines and model analyses in Chapter 6 for ideas on how to proceed.

8. Toward the end of this article, White suggests that "the most effective ways to use less energy may have less to do with changing technology than with changing habits." To what extent do you agree with this conclusion? In what particular ways might changing our habits affect the way we live and work?

SYNTHESIS ACTIVITIES

1. Write an explanatory synthesis, as if it were a cover story for a weekly newsmagazine, in which you (1) lay out the essential drawbacks of this county's continuing dependence upon oil and (2) discuss the range of alternative, renewable energy sources available now or in the near future. Your synthesis will therefore roughly follow the organization of the "Green Power" chapter itself.

   Begin by drawing on sources like Socolow and Pacala and the Independent Task Force to indicate the nature and scope of the problem posed by this country's over-reliance on the burning of fossil fuels. Describe some of the proposals for dealing with the problem. In the second half of your synthesis, summarize some of the particular forms of renewable energy—nuclear, wind, and solar power, as well as the prospect of electric-powered vehicles, drawing upon the authors represented in the second half of this chapter.

Conclude by indicating which of these forms of green energy, and which policies, appear to the authors of your sources as the most promising or practical.

2. Write an argument synthesis in which you advocate a policy or a set of policies that you believe should govern the nation's use of energy over the next fifty years. Socolow and Pacala and the authors of the Task Force offer some policies for consideration. Some of the articles in the latter half of the chapter cover policies already in place: for example, California's mandate to derive 33% of the state's energy sources from renewable energy by 2020.

   Based upon your reading in this chapter and elsewhere, as well as on your own sense of what must be done, make the case for your policies. Remember that it is not sufficient to simply advocate broad goals (we must steadily convert to renewable energy sources): you must also indicate what government, industry, smaller business, and individuals must *do* to achieve significant reductions in greenhouse gas emissions.

3. How, in the years ahead, are green technologies likely to change our daily lives? Write an article for a magazine dated December 2025 (or 2050) on the subject of how the national quest to address the climate crisis and to develop alternative energy sources has, since 2000, changed the way Americans live and work. Draw upon as many sources in this chapter as are helpful; but use your imagination (and a reasonable degree of probability) to analyze how the world of the near future developed from policy decisions and technological innovations being made today and over the next few years.

4. Given what you have read about the need for renewable energy, what do you believe are an *individual's* responsibilities, if any, in reducing energy use? Thomas Friedman appears to believe that the climate crisis cannot effectively be addressed by individuals, arguing that unless solutions are scaled to a massive degree, they are token gestures that will be inconsequential in resolving the larger problem. What, amid all this incoming data, is your position? Is it necessary or useful for an individual to have an energy policy? What would your policy be? How effective would this policy be in reducing carbon emissions? If it is symbolic only (or mostly), is symbolism still important and necessary? Draw upon Socolow and Pacala and any other authors in this chapter as you develop your response.

5. Imagine that you work for an advertising agency that is competing for a contract with a large company that generates either nuclear, wind, or solar power for a particular state or a particular region. Your job is to try to win the contract by preparing a brief plan that lays out to the power company executives a potential advertising campaign. Draw upon some of the authors in this chapter to prepare your written prospectus. (List the Works Cited on a separate page at the end of the document.) Indicate the key idea of your proposed campaign that will sell nuclear/wind/solar power. Explain why the type of energy the company is offering is superior to other types of energy. Do not misrepresent or distort the information presented by the authors in this chapter. Rather, use

their information and arguments to best advantage. Organize your plan so that it has an introductory section, a body section containing specifics and a persuasive argument, and a conclusion.

6. Explain how some of the selections in this chapter may have changed your perception of the way you and those around you use energy, and how your life may be affected by the necessity of developing alternative sources of energy. Which authors' analyses have done the most to impress upon you the seriousness of the challenge? Which have most concerned you? For example, when Thomas Friedman asks, "Have you ever seen a revolution where no one got hurt?" he implies that saving the earth will require considerable sacrifice. To what extent are you prepared to make sacrifices: to pay increased taxes to help ensure a cleaner, safer environment and a more stable climate; to give up a degree of ease of movement; to take different jobs; to buy different cars, homes, and appliances; to live in places located near power generation stations, whether wind, solar, or nuclear? Draw upon whichever authors in the chapter seem best suited to help you grapple with such questions.

7. Discuss the prospects of achieving the goals in some of Socolow and Pacala's wedges by drawing upon information in the latter half of this chapter. In developing your answer, consider electricity generation using nuclear, wind, and solar power as discussed by authors like White and Kolbert.

8. Robert Bryce forcefully argues that we should not succumb to the "delusions of energy independence." Much as we would prefer it, he asserts, there is no prospect of achieving independence from Middle Eastern oil during the next few decades. Which other authors in this chapter might support that position? Write an argument supporting or refuting Bryce's conclusion, based upon arguments made and information presented by other authors in the second part of this chapter.

9. Thomas Friedman and others have argued that the most effective way to spur the development of energy-efficient vehicles and alternative fuels for transportation is to make gasoline so expensive that it becomes financially painful to drive vehicles powered by internal-combustion engines. "As long as gas is cheap," he writes, "people will go out and buy used S.U.V.'s and Hummers." Imposing a steep gas tax will force people to change their habits and their preferred modes of transportation. In an editorial, argue for or against the federal government's imposing a gas tax sufficient to make gasoline in the United States as expensive as it is in Europe—between $5 and $7 a gallon. Draw upon some of the authors in this chapter to help you make the case for or against such a tax.

10. You have read about the conflicts between those who would pursue renewable energy projects (such as solar power in California) and locals who scream NIMBY (not in my backyard). Many people live in remote areas, away from cities and suburbs because they like the view, and they don't want to see wind turbines or solar power arrays cluttering the landscape. It comes as no surprise,

then, that the construction of a power grid needed to send electricity from a wind farm in Texas to office buildings in Los Angeles may be delayed, according to a recent *Los Angeles Times* article, because "municipalities and landowners have protested plans to string transmission networks through their backyards."

What can we do to get beyond the NIMBY syndrome? Draw on the readings in this chapter, particularly those in the latter part, in developing your answer.

RESEARCH ACTIVITIES

1. After the presidential election of 2008, many people were hopeful that the policies of the incoming Obama administration would be far more responsive to environmental concerns than the policies of the previous administration. The new president campaigned partially on the promise to take climate change seriously, to transform the automobile industry to make more energy-efficient vehicles, and to build a high-tech energy infrastructure to transmit electricity from wind and solar power plants in rural areas to the cities. The president also promised to push for higher federal fuel-economy standards and to support a cap-and-trade program with the goal of reducing carbon emissions by 80% by mid-century.

   Investigate the success of the Obama administration in achieving these goals. What policies and programs have been proposed, what regulations have been issued, what laws have been passed? What kind of hurdles has the federal government encountered as it attempts to achieve its green energy goals?

2. Robert Bryce is one of many who dismiss as impractical the goal of energy independence. Research how energy independent the United States in fact is—or could be reasonably soon. To what degree are we more independent of Middle Eastern oil than we were five or ten years ago? To what degree are plug-in hybrids more of a reality than they were at the turn of the present century? To what extent has the amount of power generated by wind and solar sources significantly supplanted coal-fired electricity during the past few years? Write a report summarizing your findings.

3. In the report "American's Energy 'Independence'" published on the Web <http://www.abc.net.au/unleashed/stories/s2274315.htm>, Dennis Phillips, a professor of foreign policy at the University of Sydney in Australia, notes that the environmental agenda often clashes with the economic and employment agenda, particularly in Third World countries. He argues:

   > All the world's poor are entitled to a much higher standard of living, but in order to progress, the world's poorest three billion will need to access and consume vastly increased quantities of energy. "Renewables" like wind and solar power are not going to do the job in the short term.

   > Do we tell the world's poor to be patient and wait? In the "ethanol fiasco" we have done worse than that. We have processed staple crops like corn and soybeans to pour into our fuel tanks, forcing up food prices that ignited riots around the world.

Research the energy situation in one or two non-European countries, to determine (1) energy requirements for sustainability and economic development; (2) chief energy sources; (3) carbon footprints; and (4) prospects for developing and using clean, renewable energy. How, if at all, have governments and businesses in these countries attempted to reconcile the environmental costs of increased energy use on the one hand and the need for increased energy to spur economic development on the other?

4. To what extent are other countries, particularly in Europe, further along in developing and using clean energy than the United States? Select one European country and research its government's energy policy, its patterns of energy use, and its development of renewable energy plants and infrastructure. Determine the extent to which the experiences of this country, particularly its successes, may be transferable to the United States.

5. In 2008, Texas oilman T. Boone Pickens, declaring that "the United States is the Saudi Arabia of wind power," attempted to counteract our dependence upon foreign oil by launching an ambitious plan to build the world's largest wind farm in Texas. Investing millions of dollars of his own money, Pickens founded Mesa Power to oversee the project, which involved over 2,500 wind turbines—sufficient, he anticipated, to eventually produce electricity to power 1.3 million homes. Launching a nationwide publicity campaign on television, newspapers, and magazines to promote his plan, Pickens also proposed that natural gas—which is abundant in this country and which does not produce CO_2—should replace gasoline as the fuel for all automobiles. Pickens's plan ran into a snag with the credit crunch of late 2008 (it was difficult for him to get the necessary financing), but he remained hopeful that the setback would be temporary.

   Research the Pickens plan and its current status and prospects. How many wind turbines have been built? How much power is being supplied? What kind of progress has been made in converting automobiles to use natural gas? To what extent do energy experts and environmentalists view the Pickens plan as offering a viable solution to the environmental crisis?

6. Opponents of nuclear power argue that nuclear accidents such as occurred at Fukushima, Japan (2011), the Three Mile Island reactor in Pennsylvania (1979), and at the Chernobyl reactor in the former Soviet Union (1986) risk a cataclysm that makes nuclear power generation too dangerous. Others point to the perfect safety record of nuclear reactors in France, where, after a 25-year conversion process, 80% of the country's energy comes from nuclear reactors. Investigate the safety factor of nuclear reactors used for power generation. What steps have been taken since Three Mile Island and Chernobyl to decrease the risks of radioactive particles being released into the atmosphere following a nuclear accident? Have experts arrived at a consensus about the safety concerns, or is there still significant controversy over this issue?

7. Investigate the proposals to discourage use of fossil fuels and to encourage renewable power generation by *one* of the following methods: (1) cap and trade;

(2) carbon taxes; (3) increased gasoline taxes. Consider not only proposed U.S. government programs, but also state programs, such as California's mandate to generate at least 33% of its power from renewable sources by 2010. Consider also policies proposed at international environmental conferences such as occurred at the UN Conference on Environment and Development (the "Earth Summit," Rio de Janeiro, 1992), in Kyoto (the Kyoto Protocol, 1997), and at the United Nations Climate Change Conferences (Bali, 2007; Copenhagen, 2009; Cancun, 2010; Durban, South Africa, 2011). Which proposals and programs to discourage carbon greenhouse gas pollution and to encourage green energy generation have met with most success? Which have been the most controversial?

8. In recent years, natural gas (the source of about one quarter of domestic electricity needs) has shown dramatic new promise for reducing American energy dependence. New methods of drilling have opened up vast new deposits of a form of previously inaccessible natural gas known as shale gas. As a recent *Time* report indicated, shale gas appears to be "a relatively clean, relatively cheap fuel that can help fill the world's needs during the transition to a truly green economy." The process used to extract shale gas from deep within the earth—hydraulic fracturing, or "fracking,"—involves injecting highly pressurized fluids into rock, then setting off explosive charges, to create channels for the extraction of fossil fuels. As critics such as Paul Krugman have noted, fracking may have potentially severe environmental costs, with the potential for major spills that contaminate groundwater and create air pollution. Research the current status of fracking, perhaps in a particular geographic area of the United States, and assess the costs and benefits of this new technology.

9. Research the latest developments in either (1) plug-in hybrid technology or (2) hydrogen fuel-cell technology. If you choose to study plug-in hybrid technology, pay particular attention to the quest to develop relatively low-cost, long-range batteries. If you choose hydrogen fuel-cell technology, pay particular attention to the quest to separate pure hydrogen from its other bound elements, as well as to store and distribute hydrogen through a national infrastructure.

10. Investigate the latest developments in either wind or solar power. For the energy source you select, investigate the actual growth of this technology over the past decade or so and the projected growth over the next ten years. How much of the nation's power requirements are currently being supplied by this particular technology? How much is projected to be supplied 10, 20, or 50 years down the road? What government incentives are available for the construction and operation of wind power or solar power? If you research solar power, to what extent are large-scale ground arrays overtaking rooftop solar panels in popularity? To what extent are environmental concerns, political wrangling, and bureaucratic roadblocks hindering the development of wind or solar power?

11. For many years there was great excitement about ethanol, an alcohol-based fuel that is blended with gasoline. The most popular formulation, known as E85, consists of 85% corn ethanol and 15% gasoline. In the past, presidential

candidates campaigning in Iowa often felt compelled to express their undying support for ethanol, because Iowan and other Midwestern farmers grew and sold the corn necessary for its manufacture. More recently, ethanol's stock has fallen. Research the history of ethanol as an alternative fuel, focusing on the economic and political aspects of its role in the search for alternatives to straight gasoline.

12. Research another form of alternative energy not significantly covered in this chapter—for instance, biomass, diesel, biodiesel, geothermal, natural gas, ethanol, or algae. To what extent does this form of energy promise to help us achieve a greater degree of energy independence? To what degree is it likely to supplant fossil fuels, such as oil and coal? What are its advantages and disadvantages? What are the implications for the environment of large-scale use of this form of energy? What major players currently control or are likely to control the supply of this energy? Which parties stand most to gain by such large-scale use? Which stand most to lose?

14

New and Improved: Six Decades of Advertising

P ossibly the most memorable ad campaign of the twentieth century (dating from the late 1920s) took the form of a comic strip. A bully kicks sand into the face of a skinny man relaxing on the beach with his girlfriend. Humiliated, the skinny man vows to get even. "Don't bother, little boy!" huffs the scornful girlfriend, who promptly dumps him. At home, the skinny man kicks a chair in frustration, declares that he's sick of being a scarecrow, and says that if Charles Atlas (once a "97-lb. weakling" himself) can give him a "real body," he'll send for his FREE book. In the next frame, the once-skinny man, now transformed into a hunk thanks to Atlas's "Dynamic Tension" fitness program, admires himself in front of the mirror: "Boy, it didn't take Atlas long to do this for me. Look, how those muscles bulge!... That big stiff won't dare insult me now!" Back on the beach, the bully is decked by the once-skinny man, as his adoring girlfriend looks on: "Oh Mac! You are a real man after all!"

Crude? Undoubtedly. But variations of this ad, which made Atlas a multi-millionaire, ran for decades (his company is still in business). Like other successful ads, it draws its power from skillful appeals to almost-primitive urges—in this particular case, the urge to gain dominance over a rival for the attention of the opposite sex. Of course, effective ads don't always work on such a primal level. Another famous ad of the 1920s appeals to our need to gain respect from others for accomplishments higher than punching out opponents. Headlined "They Laughed When I Sat Down at the Piano—But When I Started to Play...!" the text offers a first-person account of a man who sits down to play the piano at a party. As he does so, the guests make good-natured fun of him; but once he began to play, "a tense silence fell on the guests. The laughter died on their lips as if by magic. I played through the first bars of Liszt's immortal 'Liebenstraum.' I heard gasps of amazement. My friends sat breathless—spellbound." For sixteen additional paragraphs, the writer goes on to detail the effect of his playing upon the guests and to explain how "You, too, can now *teach yourself* to be an accomplished musician—right at home," by purchasing the program of the U.S. School of Music. Again, the reader is encouraged to send for the free booklet. And by the way, "Forget the old-fashioned idea that you need 'special talent'" to play an instrument.

The ubiquity of advertising is a fact of modern life. In fact, advertising can be traced as far back as ancient Roman times, when pictures were inscribed on walls to promote gladiatorial contests. In those days, however, the illiteracy of most of the population and the fact that goods were made by hand and could not be mass produced limited the need for more-widespread advertising. One of the first American advertisers was Benjamin Franklin, who pioneered the use of large headlines and made strategic use of white space. But advertising as the mass phenomenon we know is a product of the twentieth century, when the United States became an industrial nation—and particularly of the post–World War II period, when a prosperous economy created our modern consumer society, marked by the middle-class acquisition of goods, the symbols of status, success, style, and social acceptance. Today, we are surrounded not only by a familiar array of billboards, print ads, and broadcast ads, but also by the Internet, which has given us "spam," the generic name for an entire category of digital pitches for debt reduction, low mortgage rates, and enhanced body parts—compared to which the average Buick ad in a glossy magazine reads like great literature.

Advertisements are more than just appeals to buy; they are windows into our psyches and our culture. They reveal our values, our (not-so-hidden) desires, our yearnings for a different lifestyle. For example, the Marlboro man, that quintessence of taciturn cowboy masculinity, at home only in the wide-open spaces of Marlboro Country, is a mid-twentieth-century American tribute to (what is perceived as) nineteenth-century American values, popularized in hundreds of Westerns. According to James Twitchell, a professor of English and advertising at the University of Florida, "He is what we have for royalty, distilled manhood.... The Marlboro Man needs to tell you nothing. He carries no scepter, no gun. He never even speaks. Doesn't need to." He is also the product of a bolt of advertising inspiration: Previously, Marlboro had been marketed—unsuccessfully—as a woman's cigarette.

Another example of how ads reveal culture is the memorable campaign for the Volkswagen Beetle in the 1960s. That campaign spoke to the counterculture mentality of the day: Instead of appealing to the traditional automobile customer's desire for luxury, beauty, size, power, and comfort, Volkswagen emphasized how small, funny looking, bare bones—but economical and sensible—their cars were. On the other hand, snob appeal—at an affordable price, of course—has generally been a winning strategy. In the 1980s and 1990s, Grey Poupon mustard ran a successful campaign of TV commercials featuring one Rolls-Royce pulling up alongside another. A voice from one vehicle asks, "Pardon me. Do you have any Grey Poupon?" "But of course!" replies a voice in the other car, and a hand with a jar of mustard reaches out from the window of the second car, to pass the jar to the unseen occupant of the first car. This campaign is a perfect illustration of what University of California at Davis history professor Roland Marchand calls the appeal of the democracy of goods: "the wonders of modern mass production and distribution enable…everyone to enjoy society's most desirable pleasures, conveniences, or benefits."

So pervasive and influential has advertising become that it has created a significant backlash among social critics. Among the most familiar charges against advertising: It fosters materialism, it psychologically manipulates people to buy things they don't need, it perpetuates gender and racial stereotypes (particularly in its illustrations), it is deceptive, it is offensive, it debases the language, and it is omnipresent—we cannot escape it. Although arguing the truth or falsity of these assertions makes for lively debate, our focus in this chapter is not on the ethics of advertising, but rather on how it works. What makes for successful advertising? How do advertisers—and by advertisers we mean not only manufacturers but also the agencies they hire to produce their advertisements—pull our psychological levers to influence us to buy (or think favorably of) their products? What are the textual and graphic components of an effective advertisement—of an effective advertising campaign? How—if at all—has advertising evolved over the past several decades? (You may be interested in seeking out the documentary film *Art and Copy* (2009), about some of the great ad campaigns created during this period.)

Advertising has seen significant changes in the six decades since the end of World War II. It is unlikely that the comic-strip Charles Atlas ad or the verbose "They Laughed When I Sat Down at the Piano" ad would succeed today. Both seem extremely dated. More representative of today's advertising style is the successful milk campaign; each ad featured a celebrity such as Bernie Mac or Lauren Bacall with a milk mustache, a headline that says simply "Got milk?" and a few short words of text supposedly spoken by the pictured celebrity. But the changes in advertising during the six decades covered in this chapter are more of style than of substance. On the whole, the similarities between an ad produced in the 1950s and one produced today are more significant than the differences. Of course, hair and clothing styles change with the times, message length recedes, and both text and graphics assume a lesser degree of apple-pie social consensus on values. But on the whole, the same psychological appeals, the same principles of headline and graphic design that worked 60 years ago, continue to work today. We choose one automobile over another, for instance, less because our vehicle of choice gets us from point A to point B, than because we invest it—or the advertiser does—with rich psychological and cultural values. In 1957, the French anthropologist and philosopher Roland Barthes wrote (in a review of a French automobile, the Citroën DS), "I think that cars today are almost the exact equivalent of the great Gothic cathedrals: I mean the supreme creation of an era, conceived with passion by unknown artists, and consumed in image if not in usage by a whole population which appropriates them as a purely magical object." Barthes might have had a good career as an advertising copywriter.

How advertising works, then, is the subject of the present chapter. By applying a variety of theoretical and practical perspectives to a gallery of six decades of advertisements (and on other ads of your own choosing), you'll be able to practice your analytical skills on one of the more fascinating areas of American mass culture. You will find the main objects of your analyses later in this chapter: (1) a portfolio of *print advertisements* that originally appeared in such magazines as *Time, Newsweek, U.S. News and World Report,* and *Sunset*; and (2) a portfolio of memorable *TV commercials*, available for viewing on the YouTube Web site. For ease of comparison and contrast, most of the print ads can be classified into a relatively few categories: cigarettes, alcohol, automobiles, food, and "miscellaneous." We have selected both the print ads and the TV commercials for their inherent interest, as well as for the variety of tools employed to communicate their message about what sets their product or service apart from the competition—what some advertisers call their *USP*, or unique selling proposition.

The first two selections in the chapter provide analytical tools, particular perspectives from which to view individual advertisements. In "Advertising's Fifteen Basic Appeals," Jib Fowles offers a psychological perspective. Fowles identifies and discusses the most common needs to which advertisers attempt to appeal—among these the need for sex, affiliation with other people, dominance, and autonomy. In "Making the Pitch in Print Advertising," Courtland Bovée and his colleagues outline the key elements of the textual component of effective advertising—including headlines, subheadlines, and body text. Next, in "Selling Happiness: Two Pitches from *Mad Men*," we see how a great advertising man (in a great TV series) can transform the operation of a mechanical device into a powerful emotional experience or can reassure users of a deadly product that they can consume it safely.

Charles O'Neill, an independent marketing consultant, has written, "Perhaps, by learning how advertising works, we can become better equipped to sort out content from hype, product values from emotions, and salesmanship from propaganda." We hope that the selections in this chapter will equip you to do just that, as well as to develop a greater understanding of one of the most pervasive components of American mass culture.

ADVERTISING'S FIFTEEN BASIC APPEALS

Jib Fowles

Our first selection provides what you will likely find the single most useful analytical tool for studying advertisements. Drawing upon studies of numerous ads and upon interviews with subjects conducted by Harvard psychologist Henry A. Murray, Fowles developed a set of fifteen basic appeals he believes to be at the heart of American advertising. These appeals, according to Fowles and to Murray, are directed primarily to the "lower brain," to those "unfulfilled urges and motives swirling in the bottom half of [our] minds," rather than to the part of the brain that processes our more rational thoughts and impulses. As you read Fowles's article and his descriptions of the individual appeals, other examples from contemporary print and broadcast ads may occur to you. You may find it useful to jot down these examples for later incorporation into your responses to the discussion and synthesis questions that follow.

Fowles has written numerous articles and books on the popular media, including *Mass Advertising as Social Forecast: A Method for Futures Research* (1976), *Why Viewers Watch: A Reappraisal of Television's Effects* (1992), *Advertising and Popular Culture* (1996), and

The Case for Television Violence (1999). This selection first appeared in *ETC*. 39:3 (1982) and was reprinted in *Advertising and Popular Culture*.

Emotional Appeals

The nature of effective advertisements was recognized full well by the late media philosopher Marshall McLuhan. In his *Understanding Media*, the first sentence of the section on advertising reads, "The continuous pressure is to create ads more and more in the image of audience motives and desires."

By giving form to people's deep-lying desires, and picturing states of being that individuals privately yearn for, advertisers have the best chance of arresting attention and affecting communication. And that is the immediate goal of advertising: to tug at our psychological shirtsleeves and slow us down long enough for a word or two about whatever is being sold. We glance at a picture of a solitary rancher at work, and "Marlboro" slips into our minds.

Advertisers (I'm using the term as a shorthand for both the products' manufacturers, who bring the ambition and money to the process, and the advertising agencies, who supply the know-how) are ever more compelled to invoke consumers' drives and longings; this is the "continuous pressure" McLuhan refers to. Over the past century, the American marketplace has grown increasingly congested as more and more products have entered into the frenzied competition after the public's dollars. The economies of other nations are quieter than ours since the volume of goods being hawked does not so greatly exceed demand. In some economies, consumer wares are scarce enough that no advertising at all is necessary. But in the United States, we go to the other extreme. In order to stay in business, an advertiser must strive to cut through the considerable commercial hub-bub by any means available—including the emotional appeals that some observers have held to be abhorrent and underhanded.

The use of subconscious appeals is a comment not only on conditions among sellers. As time has gone by, buyers have become stoutly resistant to advertisements. We live in a blizzard of these messages and have learned to turn up our collars and ward off most of them. A study done a few years ago at Harvard University's Graduate School of Business Administration ventured that the average American is exposed to some 500 ads daily from television, newspapers, magazines, radio, billboards, direct mail, and so on. If for no other reason than to preserve one's sanity, a filter must be developed in every mind to lower the number of ads a person is actually aware of—a number this particular study estimated at about seventy-five ads per day. (Of these, only twelve typically produced a reaction—nine positive and three negative, on the average.) To be among the few messages that do manage to gain access to minds, advertisers must be strategic, perhaps even a little underhanded at times.

5   There are assumptions about personality underlying advertisers' efforts to communicate via emotional appeals, and while these assumptions have stood the test of time, they still deserve to be aired. Human beings, it is presumed, walk around with a variety of unfulfilled urges and motives swirling in the bottom half of their minds. Lusts, ambitions, tendernesses, vulnerabilities—they are constantly bubbling up, seeking resolution. These mental forces energize

people, but they are too crude and irregular to be given excessive play in the real world. They must be capped with the competent, sensible behavior that permits individuals to get along well in society. However, this upper layer of mental activity, shot through with caution and rationality, is not receptive to advertising's pitches. Advertisers want to circumvent this shell of consciousness if they can, and latch on to one of the lurching, subconscious drives.

In effect, advertisers over the years have blindly felt their way around the underside of the American psyche, and by trial and error have discovered the softest points of entree, the places where their messages have the greatest likelihood of getting by consumers' defenses. As McLuhan says elsewhere, "Gouging away at the surface of public sales resistance, the ad men are constantly breaking through into the *Alice in Wonderland* territory behind the looking glass, which is the world of subrational impulses and appetites."

An advertisement communicates by making use of a specially selected image (of a supine female, say, or a curly-haired child, or a celebrity) which is designed to stimulate "subrational impulses and desires" even when they are at ebb, even if they are unacknowledged by their possessor. Some few ads have their emotional appeal in the text, but for the greater number by far the appeal is contained in the artwork. This makes sense, since visual communication better suits more primal levels of the brain. If the viewer of an advertisement actually has the importuned motive, and if the appeal is sufficiently well fashioned to call it up, then the person can be hooked. The product in the ad may then appear to take on the semblance of gratification for the summoned motive. Many ads seem to be saying, "If you have this need, then this product will help satisfy it." It is a primitive equation, but not an ineffective one for selling.

Thus, most advertisements appearing in national media can be understood as having two orders of content. The first is the appeal to deep-running drives in the minds of consumers. The second is information regarding the good[s] or service being sold: its name, its manufacturer, its picture, its packaging, its objective attributes, its functions. For example, the reader of a brassiere advertisement sees a partially undraped but blandly unperturbed woman standing in an otherwise commonplace public setting, and may experience certain sensations; the reader also sees the name "Maidenform," a particular brassiere style, and, in tiny print, words about the material, colors, price. Or, the viewer of a television commercial sees a demonstration with four small boxes labeled 650, 650, 650, and 800; something in the viewer's mind catches hold of this, as trivial as thoughtful consideration might reveal it to be. The viewer is also exposed to the name "Anacin," its bottle, and its purpose.

Sometimes there is an apparently logical link between an ad's emotional appeal and its product information. It does not violate common sense that Cadillac automobiles be photographed at country clubs, or that Japan Air Lines be associated with [all things Asian] Orientalia. But there is no real need for the linkage to have a bit of reason behind it. Is there anything inherent to the connection between Salem cigarettes and mountains, Coke and a smile, Miller Beer and comradeship? The link being forged in minds between product and appeal is a pre-logical one.

10   People involved in the advertising industry do not necessarily talk in the terms being used here. They are stationed at the sending end of this communications channel, and may think they are up to any number of things—Unique Selling Propositions, explosive copywriting, the optimal use of demographics or psychographics, ideal media buys, high recall ratings, or whatever. But when attention shifts to the receiving end of the channel, and focuses on the instant of reception, then commentary becomes much more elemental: an advertising message contains something primary and primitive, an emotional appeal, that in effect is the thin end of the wedge, trying to find its way into a mind. Should this occur, the product information comes along behind.

When enough advertisements are examined in this light, it becomes clear that the emotional appeals fall into several distinguishable categories, and that every ad is a variation on one of a limited number of basic appeals. While there may be several ways of classifying these appeals, one particular list of fifteen has proven to be especially valuable.

Advertisements can appeal to:

1. The need for sex
2. The need for affiliation
3. The need to nurture
4. The need for guidance
5. The need to aggress
6. The need to achieve
7. The need to dominate
8. The need for prominence
9. The need for attention
10. The need for autonomy
11. The need to escape
12. The need to feel safe
13. The need for aesthetic sensations
14. The need to satisfy curiosity
15. Physiological needs: food, drink, sleep, etc.

Murray's List

Where does this list of advertising's fifteen basic appeals come from? Several years ago, I was involved in a research project which was to have as one segment an objective analysis of the changing appeals made in post–World War II American advertising. A sample of magazine ads would have their appeals coded into the categories of psychological needs they seemed aimed at. For this content analysis to happen, a complete roster of human motives would have to be found.

The first thing that came to mind was Abraham Maslow's famous four-part hierarchy of needs. But the briefest look at the range of appeals made in advertising was enough to reveal that they are more varied, and more profane, than Maslow had cared to account for. The search led on to the work of psychologist Henry A. Murray, who together with his colleagues at the Harvard Psychological Clinic has constructed a full taxonomy of needs. As described in *Explorations in Personality*, Murray's team had conducted a lengthy series of in-depth interviews with a number of subjects in order to derive from scratch what they felt to be the essential variables of personality. Forty-four variables were distinguished by the Harvard group, of which twenty were motives. The need for achievement ("to overcome obstacles and obtain a high standard") was one, for instance; the need to defer was another; the need to aggress was a third; and so forth.

Murray's list had served as the groundwork for a number of subsequent projects. Perhaps the best-known of these was David C. McClelland's extensive study of the need for achievement, reported in his *The Achieving Society*. In the process of demonstrating that a people's high need for achievement is predictive of later economic growth, McClelland coded achievement imagery and references out of a nation's folklore, songs, legends, and children's tales.

15   Following McClelland, I too wanted to cull the motivational appeals from a culture's imaginative product—in this case, advertising. To develop categories expressly for this purpose, I took Murray's twenty motives and added to them others he had mentioned in passing in *Explorations in Personality* but not included on the final list. The extended list was tried out on a sample of advertisements, and motives which never seemed to be invoked were dropped. I ended up with eighteen of Murrays' motives, into which 770 print ads were coded. The resulting distribution is included in the 1976 book *Mass Advertising as Social Forecast*.

Since that time, the list of appeals has undergone refinements as a result of using it to analyze television commercials. A few more adjustments stemmed from the efforts of students in my advertising classes to decode appeals; tens of term papers surveying thousands of advertisements have caused some inconsistencies in the list to be hammered out. Fundamentally, though, the list remains the creation of Henry Murray. In developing a comprehensive, parsimonious inventory of human motives, he pinpointed the subsurface mental forces that are the least quiescent and most susceptible to advertising's entreaties.

Fifteen Appeals

1. Need for Sex.   Let's start with sex, because this is the appeal which seems to pop up first whenever the topic of advertising is raised. Whole books have been written about this one alone, to find a large audience of mildly titillated readers. Lately, due to campaigns to sell blue jeans, concern with sex in ads has redoubled.

The fascinating thing is not how much sex there is in advertising, but how little. Contrary to impressions, unambiguous sex is rare in these messages. Some of this surprising observation may be a matter of definition: the Jordache ads with the lithe, blouse-less female astride a similarly clad male is clearly an appeal to the audience's sexual drives, but the same cannot be said about Brooke

Shields* in the Calvin Klein commercials. Directed at young women and their credit-card carrying mothers, the image of Miss Shields instead invokes the need to be looked at. Buy Calvins and you'll be the center of much attention, just as Brooke is, the ads imply; they do not primarily inveigle their target audience's need for sexual intercourse.

In the content analysis reported in *Mass Advertising as Social Forecast* only two percent of ads were found to pander to this motive. Even *Playboy* ads shy away from sexual appeals: a recent issue contained eighty-three full-page ads, and just four of them (or less than five percent) could be said to have sex on their minds.

20   The reason this appeal is so little used is that it is too blaring and tends to obliterate the product information. Nudity in advertising has the effect of reducing brand recall. The people who do remember the product may do so because they have been made indignant by the ad; this is not the response most advertisers seek.

To the extent that sexual imagery is used, it conventionally works better on men than women; typically a female figure is offered up to the male reader. A Black Velvet liquor advertisement displays an attractive woman wearing a tight black outfit, recumbent under the legend, "Feel the Velvet." The figure does not have to be horizontal, however, for the appeal to be present as National Airlines revealed in its "Fly me" campaign. Indeed, there does not even have to be a female in the ad; "Flick my Bic"[†] was sufficient to convey the idea to many.

As a rule, though, advertisers have found sex to be a tricky appeal, to be used sparingly. Less controversial and equally fetching are the appeals to our need for affectionate human contact.

2. Need for Affiliation.   American mythology upholds autonomous individuals, and social statistics suggest that people are ever more going it alone in their lives, yet the high frequency of affiliative appeals in ads belies this. Or maybe it does not: maybe all the images of companionship are compensation for what Americans privately lack. In any case, the need to associate with others is widely invoked in advertising and is probably the most prevalent appeal. All sorts of goods and services are sold by linking them to our unfulfilled desires to be in good company.

According to Henry Murray, the need for affiliation consists of desires "to draw near and enjoyably cooperate or reciprocate with another; to please and win affection of another; to adhere and remain loyal to a friend." The manifestations of this motive can be segmented into several different types of affiliation, beginning with romance.

25   Courtship may be swifter nowadays, but the desire for pair-bonding is far from satiated. Ads reaching for this need commonly depict a youngish male and female engrossed in each other. The head of the male is usually higher than the

---

*Brooke Shields (b. 1965) is a model (at age 3 she was the Ivory Snow baby), as well as a stage (*Grease*), TV, and film actress; her most well-known films are *Pretty Baby* (1978) and *Blue Lagoon* (1980).
[†]"Flick my Bic" became a famous and successful slogan in advertisements for Bic cigarette lighters during the late 1970s and 1980s. Fowles hints at the not-too-subtle sexual implications of the line.

female's, even at this late date; she may be sitting or leaning while he is standing. They are not touching in the Smirnoff vodka ads, but obviously there is an intimacy, sometimes frolicsome, between them. The couple does touch for Martell Cognac when "The moment was Martell." For Wind Song perfume they have touched, and "Your Wind Song stays on his mind."

Depending on the audience, the pair does not absolutely have to be young— just together. He gives her a DeBeers diamond, and there is a tear in her laugh lines. She takes Geritol* and preserves herself for him. And numbers of consumers, wanting affection too, follow suit.

Warm family feelings are fanned in ads when another generation is added to the pair. Hallmark Cards brings grandparents into the picture, and Johnson and Johnson Baby Powder has Dad, Mom, and baby, all fresh from the bath, encircled in arms and emblazoned with "Share the Feeling." A talc has been fused to familial love.

Friendship is yet another form of affiliation pursued by advertisers. Two women confide and drink Maxwell House coffee together; two men walk through the woods smoking Salem cigarettes. Miller Beer promises that afternoon "Miller Time" will be staffed with three or four good buddies. Drink Dr. Pepper, as Mickey Rooney is coaxed to do, and join in with all the other Peppers. Coca-Cola does not even need to portray the friendliness; it has reduced this appeal to "a Coke and a smile."

The warmth can be toned down and disguised, but it is the same affiliative need that is being fished for. The blonde has a direct gaze and her friends are firm businessmen in appearance, but with a glass of Old Bushmill you can sit down and fit right in. Or, for something more upbeat, sing along with the Pontiac choirboys.

30   As well as presenting positive images, advertisers can play to the need for affiliation in negative ways, by invoking the fear of rejection. If we don't use Scope, we'll have the "Ugh! Morning Breath" that causes the male and female models to avert their faces. Unless we apply Ultra Brite or Close-Up to our teeth, it's good-bye romance. Our family will be cursed with "House-a-tosis" if we don't take care. Without Dr. Scholl's antiperspirant foot spray, the bowling team will keel over. There go all the guests when the supply of Dorito's nacho cheese chips is exhausted. Still more rejection if our shirts have ring-around-the-collar, if our car needs to be Midasized. But make a few purchases, and we are back in the bosom of human contact.

As self-directed as Americans pretend to be, in the last analysis we remain social animals, hungering for the positive, endorsing feelings that only those around us can supply. Advertisers respond, urging us to "Reach out and touch someone," in the hopes our monthly [phone] bills will rise.

---

*The original Geritol (a combination of the words "geriatric" and "tolerance") was an iron tonic and vitamin supplement marketed to people over 40 between 1950 and 1979 with the slogan, "Do you have iron poor, tired blood?" Though today Geritol is the label on a group of health-related products, the name became famous—and, to some extent, funny—as a means of restoring energy and youthful vigor to middle-age and elderly people.

3. Need to Nurture.   Akin to affiliative needs is the need to take care of small, defenseless creatures—children and pets, largely. Reciprocity is of less consequence here, though; it is the giving that counts. Murray uses synonyms like "to feed, help, support, console, protect, comfort, nurse, heal." A strong need it is, woven deep into our genetic fabric, for if it did not exist we could not successfully raise up our replacements. When advertisers put forth the image of something diminutive and furry, something that elicits the word "cute" or "precious," then they are trying to trigger this motive. We listen to the childish voice singing the Oscar Mayer wiener song, and our next hot-dog purchase is prescribed. Aren't those darling kittens something, and how did this Meow Mix get into our shopping cart?

This pitch is often directed at women, as Mother Nature's chief nurturers. "Make me some Kraft macaroni and cheese, please," says the elfin preschooler just in from the snowstorm, and mothers' hearts go out, and Kraft's sales go up. "We're cold, wet, and hungry," whine the husband and kids, and the little woman gets the Manwiches ready. A facsimile of this need can be hit without children or pets: the husband is ill and sleepless in the television commercial, and the wife grudgingly fetches the NyQuil.

But it is not women alone who can be touched by this appeal. The father nurses his son Eddie through adolescence while the John Deere lawn tractor survives the years. Another father counts pennies with his young son as the subject of New York Life Insurance comes up. And all over America are businessmen who don't know why they dial Qantas Airlines* when they have to take a trans-Pacific trip; the koala bear knows.

35   **4. Need for Guidance.**   The opposite of the need to nurture is the need to be nurtured: to be protected, shielded, guided. We may be loath to admit it, but the child lingers on inside every adult—and a good thing it does, or we would not be instructable in our advancing years. Who wants a nation of nothing but flinty personalities?

Parent-like figures can successfully call up this need. Robert Young[†] recommends Sanka coffee, and since we have experienced him for twenty-five years as television father and doctor, we take his word for it. Florence Henderson[‡] as the expert mom knows a lot about the advantages of Wesson oil.

The parent-ness of the spokesperson need not be so salient; sometimes pure authoritativeness is better. When Orson Welles[§] scowls and intones,

---

*Qantas Airlines is an Australian airline whose ads during the 1980s and 1990s featured a cuddly koala bear standing in for both the airline and the exotic delights of Australia.

[†]Robert Young (1907–1988) acted in movies (including Alfred Hitchcock's *Secret Agent* (1936) and *Crossfire* (1947) and TV (starring in the long-running 1950s series *Father Knows Best* and the 1960s series *Marcus Welby, M.D.*). A classic father figure, in his later career he appeared in ads for Sanka coffee.

[‡]Florence Henderson (b. 1934), acted on Broadway and TV (primarily in musical and comedy roles). Her most famous TV show was *The Brady Bunch* (1968–74), where she played a mother of three daughters who married a man with three sons.

[§]Orson Welles (1915–1985) was a major American filmmaker and actor whose films include *Citizen Kane* (1941—generally considered the greatest American film of all time), *The Magnificent Ambersons* (1942), *The Lady from Shanghai* (1947), *Macbeth* (1948), and *Touch of Evil* (1958). Toward the end of his life—to the dismay of many who revered him—the magisterial but financially depleted Welles became a spokesman for Paul Masson wines.

"Paul Masson will sell no wine before its time," we may not know exactly what he means, but we still take direction from him. There is little maternal about Brenda Vaccaro* when she speaks up for Tampax, but there is a certainty to her that many accept.

A celebrity is not a necessity in making a pitch to the need for guidance, since a fantasy figure can serve just as well. People accede to the Green Giant, or Betty Crocker, or Mr. Goodwrench.† Some advertisers can get by with no figure at all: "When E. F. Hutton‡ talks, people listen."

Often it is tradition or custom that advertisers point to and consumers take guidance from. Bits and pieces of American history are used to sell whiskeys like Old Crow, Southern Comfort, Jack Daniel's. We conform to traditional male/female roles and age-old social norms when we purchase Barclay cigarettes, which informs us "The pleasure is back."

40   The product itself, if it has been around for a long time, can constitute a tradition. All those old labels in the ad for Morton salt convince us that we should continue to buy it. Kool-Aid says "You loved it as a kid. You trust it as a mother," hoping to get yet more consumers to go along.

Even when the product has no history at all, our need to conform to tradition and to be guided are strong enough that they can be invoked through bogus nostalgia and older actors. Country-Time lemonade sells because consumers want to believe it has a past they can defer to.

So far the needs and the ways they can be invoked which have been looked at are largely warm and affiliative; they stand in contrast to the next set of needs, which are much more egoistic and assertive.

5. Need to Aggress.   The pressures of the real world create strong retaliatory feelings in every functioning human being. Since these impulses can come forth as bursts of anger and violence, their display is normally tabooed. Existing as harbored energy, aggressive drives present a large, tempting target for advertisers. It is not a target to be aimed at thoughtlessly, though, for few manufacturers want their products associated with destructive motives. There is always the danger that, as in the case of sex, if the appeal is too blatant, public opinion will turn against what is being sold.

Jack-in-the-Box sought to abruptly alter its marketing by going after older customers and forgetting the younger ones. Their television commercials had a seventy-ish lady command, "Waste him," and the Jack-in-the-Box clown exploded before our eyes. So did public reaction until the commercials were toned

---

*Brenda Vaccaro (b. 1939) is a stage, TV, and film actress; her films include *Midnight Cowboy* (1969), *Airport '77* (1977), *Supergirl* (1984), and *The Mirror Has Two Faces* (1996).

†Mr. Goodwrench (and the slogan "Looking for Mr. Goodwrench"), personified as an engaging and highly capable auto mechanic, is a product of the General Motors marketing department.

‡E. F. Hutton (named after its founder, Edward Francis Hutton) was a major brokerage firm that was brought down in the 1980s by corporate misconduct. Its most famous TV ad portrayed, typically, two well-dressed businesspeople in conversation in a crowded dining room or club room. The first man says to the other, "My broker says…" The second man listens politely and responds, "Well, my broker is E. F. Hutton, and *he* says…," and everyone else in the room strains to overhear the conversation. The tag line: "When E. F. Hutton talks, people listen."

down. Print ads for Club cocktails carried the faces of octogenarians under the headline, "Hit me with a Club"; response was contrary enough to bring the campaign to a stop.

45   Better disguised aggressive appeals are less likely to backfire: Triumph cigarettes has models making a lewd gesture with their uplifted cigarettes, but the individuals are often laughing and usually in close company of others. When Exxon said, "There's a Tiger in your tank," the implausibility of it concealed the invocation of aggressive feelings.

Depicted arguments are a common way for advertisers to tap the audience's needs to aggress. Don Rickles* and Lynda Carter[†] trade gibes, and consumers take sides as the name of Seven-Up is stitched on minds. The Parkay [margarine] tub has a difference of opinion with the user; who can forget it, or who (or what) got the last word in?

6. Need to Achieve.   This is the drive that energizes people, causing them to strive in their lives and careers. According to Murray, the need for achievement is signalled by the desires "to accomplish something difficult. To overcome obstacles and attain a high standard. To excel one's self. To rival and surpass others." A prominent American trait, it is one that advertisers like to hook on to because it identifies their product with winning and success.

The Cutty Sark ad does not disclose that Ted Turner failed at his latest attempt at yachting's America Cup; here he is represented as a champion on the water as well as off in his television enterprises. If we drink this whiskey, we will be victorious alongside Turner. We can also succeed with O. J. Simpson[‡] by renting Hertz cars, or with Reggie Jackson[§] by bringing home some Panasonic equipment. Cathy Rigby** and Stayfree maxipads will put people out front.

Sports heroes are the most convenient means to snare consumers' needs to achieve, but they are not the only one. Role models can be established, ones which invite emulation, as with the profiles put forth by Dewar's scotch.

---

*Don Rickles (b. 1926) is a nightclub comedian (who has also appeared in TV and films) famous for his caustic wit and for humorously insulting people in the audience.

[†]Lynda Carter (b. 1951) is an actress whose most famous role was as the heroine of the 1976 TV series *Wonder Woman*.

[‡]O. J. Simpson (b. 1957) is a famous football player turned film actor (*The Naked Gun*) and defendant in a notorious murder trial in the 1990s. In a highly controversial decision, Simpson was acquitted of killing his ex-wife Nicole Simpson and her friend Ron Goldman; but in a subsequent civil trial, he was found liable for the two deaths. Before the trial, Simpson was well known for his TV commercials for Hertz rental cars, featuring him sprinting through airports to get to the gate, to demonstrate what you *wouldn't* have to do if you rented a car through Hertz.

[§]Reggie Jackson (b. 1946), a member of the Baseball Hall of Fame, played as an outfielder between 1967 and 1987. Known as "Mr. October" for his dramatic game-winning at-bats during post-season play, he had more strikeouts (2,597) than any other player. He was the first baseball player to have a candy bar (the "Reggie Bar") named after him, and toward the end of his career was a pitchman for Panasonic televisions.

**Cathy Rigby, an Olympian, was the first American gymnast to win a medal (in 1970) at the World Championships. She went on to star in a Broadway revival of the musical *Peter Pan* (surpassing Mary Martin for the greatest number of performances). Subsequently, she became a sportscaster for ABC Sports.

Successful, tweedy individuals relate they have "graduated to the flavor of Myer's rum." Or the advertiser can establish a prize: two neighbors play one-on-one basketball for a Michelob beer in a television commercial, while in a print ad a bottle of Johnnie Walker Black Label has been gilded like a trophy.

50   Any product that advertises itself in superlatives—the best, the first, the finest—is trying to make contact with our needs to succeed. For many consumers, sales and bargains belong in this category of appeals, too; the person who manages to buy something at fifty percent off is seizing an opportunity and coming out ahead of others.

   7. Need to Dominate.   This fundamental need is the craving to be powerful—perhaps omnipotent, as in the Xerox ad where Brother Dominic exhibits heavenly powers and creates miraculous copies. Most of us will settle for being just a regular potentate, though. We drink Budweiser because it is the King of Beers, and here comes the powerful Clydesdales to prove it. A taste of Wolfschmidt vodka and "The spirit of the Czar lives on."

   The need to dominate and control one's environment is often thought of as being masculine, but as close students of human nature, advertisers know it is not so circumscribed. Women's aspirations for control are suggested in the campaign theme, "I like my men in English Leather, or nothing at all." The females in the Chanel No. 19 ads are "outspoken" and wrestle their men around.

   Male and female, what we long for is clout; what we get in its place is Mastercard.

   8. Need for Prominence.   Here comes the need to be admired and respected, to enjoy prestige and high social status. These times, it appears, are not so egalitarian after all. Many ads picture the trappings of high position; the Oldsmobile stands before a manorial doorway, the Volvo is parked beside a steeplechase. A book-lined study is the setting for Dewar's 12, and Lenox China is displayed in a dining room chock full of antiques.

55   Beefeater gin represents itself as "The Crown Jewel of England" and uses no illustrations of jewels or things British, for the words are sufficient indicators of distinction. Buy that gin and you will rise up the prestige hierarchy, or achieve the same effect on yourself with Seagram's 7 Crown, which ambiguously describes itself as "classy."

   Being respected does not have to entail the usual accoutrements of wealth: "Do you know who I am?" the commercials ask, and we learn that the prominent person is not so prominent without his American Express card.

   9. Need for Attention.   The previous need involved being *looked up to*, while this is the need to be *looked at*. The desire to exhibit ourselves in such a way as to make others look at us is a primitive, insuppressible instinct. The clothing and cosmetic industries exist just to serve this need, and this is the way they pitch their wares. Some of this effort is aimed at males, as the ads for Hathaway shirts and Jockey underclothes. But the greater bulk of such appeals is targeted singlemindedly at women.

   To come back to Brooke Shields: this is where she fits into American marketing. If I buy Calvin Klein jeans, consumers infer, I'll be the object of fascination. The desire for exhibition has been most strikingly played to in a print campaign of many years' duration, that of Maidenform lingerie. The woman exposes herself, and sales surge. "Gentlemen prefer Hanes" the ads dissemble, and women who want eyes upon them know what they should do. Peggy Fleming* flutters her legs for L'eggs, encouraging females who want to be the star in their own lives to purchase this product.

The same appeal works for cosmetics and lotions. For years, the little girl with the exposed backside sold gobs of Coppertone, but now the company has picked up the pace a little: as a female, you are supposed to "Flash 'em a Coppertone tan." Food can be sold the same way, especially to the diet-conscious; Angie Dickinson poses for California avocados and says, "Would this body lie to you?" Our eyes are too fixed on her for us to think to ask if she got that way by eating mounds of guacamole.[†]

60   **10. Need for Autonomy.**   There are several ways to sell credit card services, as has been noted: Mastercard appeals to the need to dominate, and American Express to the need for prominence. When Visa claims, "You can have it the way you want it," yet another primary motive is being beckoned forward—the need to endorse the self. The focus here is upon the independence and integrity of the individual; this need is the antithesis of the need for guidance and is unlike any of the social needs. "If running with the herd isn't your style, try ours," says Rotan-Mosle, and many Americans feel they have finally found the right broker-age firm.

The photo is of a red-coated Mountie on his horse, posed on a snow-covered ledge; the copy reads, "Windsor—One Canadian stands alone." This epitome of the solitary and proud individual may work best with male customers, as may Winston's man in the red cap. But one-figure advertisements also strike the strong need for autonomy among American women. As Shelly Hack[‡] strides for Charlie perfume, females respond to her obvious pride and flair; she is her own person. The Virginia Slims tale is of people who have come a long way from sub-servience to independence. Cachet perfume feels it does not need a solo figure to work this appeal, and uses three different faces in its ads; it insists, though, "It's different on every woman who wears it."

Like many psychological needs, this one can also be appealed to in a neg-ative fashion, by invoking the loss of independence or self-regard. Guilt and regrets can be stimulated: "Gee, I could have had a V-8." Next time, get one and be good to yourself.

11. Need to Escape.   An appeal to the need for autonomy often co-occurs with one for the need to escape, since the desire to duck out of our social obliga-tions, to seek rest or adventure, frequently takes the form of one-person flight.

---

*Peggy Fleming (b. 1948), an Olympic figure skater and Gold Medal winner (1968), later became a TV sports commentator and a representative for UNICEF (the United Nations Children's Emergency Fund).

[†]Angie Dickinson (b. 1931) is an American film and TV actress. She appeared in *Rio Bravo* (1959), *Ocean's 11* (1960 and 2001), *Point Blank* (1967), and *Dressed to Kill* (1980); she also starred in the 1970s TV series *Police Woman*.

[‡]Shelly Hack (b. 1952) portrayed Tiffany Welles in the 1970s TV show *Charlie's Angels*.

The dashing image of a pilot, in fact, is a standard way of quickening this need to get away from it all.

Freedom is the pitch here, the freedom that every individual yearns for whenever life becomes too oppressive. Many advertisers like appealing to the need for escape because the sensation of pleasure often accompanies escape, and what nicer emotional nimbus could there be for a product? "You deserve a break today," says McDonald's, and Stouffer's frozen foods chime in, "Set yourself free."

65   For decades men have imaginatively bonded themselves to the Marlboro cowboy who dwells untarnished and unencumbered in Marlboro Country some distance from modern life; smokers' aching needs for autonomy and escape are personified by that cowpoke. Many women can identify with the lady ambling through the woods behind the words, "Benson and Hedges and mornings and me."

But escape does not have to be solitary. Other Benson and Hedges ads, part of the same campaign, contain two strolling figures. In Salem cigarette advertisements, it can be several people who escape together into the mountaintops. A commercial for Levi's pictured a cloudbank above a city through which ran a whole chain of young people.

There are varieties of escape, some wistful like the Boeing "Someday" campaign of dream vacations, some kinetic like the play and parties in soft drink ads. But in every instance, the consumer exposed to the advertisement is invited to momentarily depart his everyday life for a more carefree experience, preferably with the product in hand.

12. Need to Feel Safe.   Nobody in their right mind wants to be intimidated, menaced, battered, poisoned. We naturally want to do whatever it takes to stave off threats to our well-being, and to our families'. It is the instinct of self-preservation that makes us responsive to the ad of the St. Bernard with the keg of Chivas Regal. We pay attention to the stern talk of Karl Malden* and the plight of the vacationing couples who have lost all their funds in the American Express travelers cheques commercials. We want the omnipresent stag from Hartford Insurance to watch over us too.

In the interest of keeping failure and calamity from our lives, we like to see the durability of products demonstrated. Can we ever forget that Timex takes a licking and keeps on ticking? When the American Tourister suitcase bounces all over the highway and the egg inside doesn't break, the need to feel safe has been adroitly plucked.

70   We take precautions to diminish future threats. We buy Volkswagen Rabbits for the extraordinary mileage, and MONY insurance policies to avoid the tragedies depicted in their black-and-white ads of widows and orphans.

---

*Karl Malden (1912–2009), with his familiar craggy face and outsized nose, was a stage and later a film actor. He was the original Mitch in the Broadway production of Tennessee Williams's *Streetcar Named Desire*, a role he reprised in the 1951 movie version. His films include *On the Waterfront* (1954), *Cheyenne Autumn* (1964), and *Patton* (1970), and he starred in the 1972 TV series *Streets of San Francisco*. Malden became famous to a later generation of viewers as a pitchman for the American Express card, with the slogan "Don't leave home without it!"

We are careful about our health. We consume Mazola margarine because it has "corn goodness" backed by the natural food traditions of the American Indians. In the medicine cabinet is Alka-Seltzer, the "home remedy"; having it, we are snug in our little cottage.

We want to be safe and secure; buy these products, advertisers are saying, and you'll be safer than you are without them.

13. Need for Aesthetic Sensations.   There is an undeniable aesthetic component to virtually every ad run in the national media: the photography or filming or drawing is near-perfect, the type style is well chosen, the layout could scarcely be improved upon. Advertisers know there is little chance of good communication occurring if an ad is not visually pleasing. Consumers may not be aware of the extent of their own sensitivity to artwork, but it is undeniably large.

Sometimes the aesthetic element is expanded and made into an ad's primary appeal. Charles Jordan shoes may or may not appear in the accompanying avant-grade photographs; Kohler plumbing fixtures catch attention through the high style of their desert settings. Beneath the slightly out of focus photograph, languid and sensuous in tone, General Electric feels called upon to explain, "This is an ad for the hair dryer."

75   This appeal is not limited to female consumers: J&B scotch says "It whispers" and shows a bucolic scene of lake and castle.

14. Need to Satisfy Curiosity.   It may seem odd to list a need for information among basic motives, but this need can be as primal and compelling as any of the others. Human beings are curious by nature, interested in the world around them, and intrigued by tidbits of knowledge and new developments. Trivia, percentages, observations counter to conventional wisdom—these items all help sell products. Any advertisement in a question-and-answer format is strumming this need.

A dog groomer has a question about long distance rates, and Bell Telephone has a chart with all the figures. An ad for Porsche 911 is replete with diagrams and schematics, numbers and arrows. Lo and behold, Anacin pills have 150 more milligrams than its competitors; should we wonder if this is better or worse for us?

15. Physiological Needs.   To the extent that sex is solely a biological need, we are now coming around full circle, back toward the start of the list. In this final category are clustered appeals to sleeping, eating, drinking. The art of photographing food and drink is so advanced, sometimes these temptations are wondrously caught in the camera's lens: the crab meat in the Red Lobster restaurant ads can start us salivating, the Quarterpounder can almost be smelled, the liquor in the glass glows invitingly. Imbibe, these ads scream.

Styles

Some common ingredients of advertisements were not singled out for separate mention in the list of fifteen because they are not appeals in and of themselves. They are stylistic features, influencing the way a basic appeal is presented. The use of humor is one, and the use of celebrities is another. A third is time imagery, past and future, which goes to several purposes.

80　　　For all of its employment in advertising, humor can be treacherous, because it can get out of hand and smother the product information. Supposedly, this is what Alka-Seltzer discovered with its comic commercials of the late sixties; "I can't believe I ate the whole thing," the sad-faced husband lamented, and the audience cackled so much it forgot the antacid. Or, did not take it seriously.

But used carefully, humor can punctuate some of the softer appeals and soften some of the harsher ones. When Emma says to the Fruit-of-the-Loom fruits, "Hi, cuties. Whatcha doing in my laundry basket?" we smile as our curiosity is assuaged along with hers. Bill Cosby gets consumers tickled about the children in his Jell-O commercials, and strokes the need to nurture.

An insurance company wants to invoke the need to feel safe, but does not want to leave readers with an unpleasant aftertaste; cartoonist Rowland Wilson creates an avalanche about to crush a gentleman who is saying to another, "My insurance company? New England Life, of course. Why?" The same tactic of humor undercutting threat is used in the cartoon commercials for Safeco when the Pink Panther wanders from one disaster to another. Often humor masks aggression: comedian Bob Hope in the outfit of a boxer promises to knock out the knock-knocks with Texaco; Rodney Dangerfield, who "can't get no respect," invites aggression as the comic relief in Miller Lite commercials.

Roughly fifteen percent of all advertisements incorporate a celebrity, almost always from the fields of entertainment or sports. The approach can also prove troublesome for advertisers, for celebrities are human beings too, and fully capable of the most remarkable behavior. If anything distasteful about them emerges, it is likely to reflect on the product. The advertisers making use of Anita Bryant[*] and Billy Jean King[†] suffered several anxious moments. An untimely death can also react poorly on a product. But advertisers are willing to take risks because celebrities can be such a good link between producers and consumers, performing the social role of introducer.

There are several psychological needs these middlemen can play upon. Let's take the product class of cameras and see how different celebrities can hit different needs. The need for guidance can be invoked by Michael Landon, who plays such a wonderful dad on "Little House on the Prairie"; when he says to buy Kodak equipment, many people listen. James Garner[‡] for Polaroid cameras

---

[*]Anita Bryant (b. 1940), a singer and entertainer (and as Miss Oklahoma, runner-up in the 1958 Miss America competition) became controversial during the late 1970s with her campaigns against homosexuality and AIDS. At the time, she was making ads and TV commercials for Florida orange juice, but was dropped by the sponsor after boycotts by activists.

[†]Billy Jean King (b. 1943) was a championship tennis player in the late 1960s and 1970s. In 1973, she was named *Sports Illustrated*'s "Sportsperson of the Year," the first woman to win this honor. She won four U.S. championships and six Wimbledon's single championships. In 1973, in a much publicized "Battle of the Sexes" match, King won all three sets against the 55-year-old Bobby Riggs (once ranked as the best tennis player in the world), who had claimed that "any half-decent male player could defeat even the best female players."

[‡]James Garner (b. 1928) is an American actor in movies and TV shows. His most famous TV roles were as the title character in the 1950s western-comedy series *Maverick* and as the hero of the 1970s detective series *The Rockford Files*. Garner also appeared in the movies *Sayonara* (1957), *The Great Escape* (1963), and *The Americanization of Emily* (1964).

is put in a similar authoritative role, so defined by a mocking spouse. The need to achieve is summed up by Tracy Austin and other tennis stars for Canon AE-1; the advertiser first makes sure we see these athletes playing to win. When Cheryl Tiegs* speaks up for Olympus cameras, it is the need for attention that is being targeted.

85   The past and future, being outside our grasp, are exploited by advertisers as locales for the projection of needs. History can offer up heroes (and call up the need to achieve) or traditions (need for guidance) as well as art objects (need for aesthetic sensations). Nostalgia is a kindly version of personal history and is deployed by advertisers to rouse needs for affiliation and for guidance; the need to escape can come in here, too. The same need to escape is sometimes the point of futuristic appeals but picturing the avant-garde can also be a way to get at the need to achieve.

Analyzing Advertisements

When analyzing ads yourself for their emotional appeals, it takes a bit of practice to learn to ignore the product information (as well as one's own experience and feelings about the product). But that skill comes soon enough, as does the ability to quickly sort out from all the non-product aspects of an ad the chief element which is the most striking, the most likely to snag attention first and penetrate brains farthest. The key to the appeal, this element usually presents itself centrally and forwardly to the reader or viewer.

Another clue: the viewing angle which the audience has on the ad's subjects is informative. If the subjects are photographed or filmed from below and thus are looking down at you much as the Green Giant does, then the need to be guided is a good candidate for the ad's emotional appeal. If, on the other hand, the subjects are shot from above and appear deferential, as is often the case with children or female models, then other needs are being appealed to.

To figure out an ad's emotional appeal, it is wise to know (or have a good hunch about) who the targeted consumers are; this can often be inferred from the magazine or television show it appears in. This piece of information is a great help in determining the appeal and in deciding between two different interpretations. For example, if an ad features a partially undressed female, this would typically signal one appeal for readers of *Penthouse* (need for sex) and another for readers of *Cosmopolitan* (need for attention).

It would be convenient if every ad made just one appeal, were aimed at just one need. Unfortunately, things are often not that simple. A cigarette ad with a couple at the edge of a polo field is trying to hit both the need for affiliation and the need for prominence; depending on the attitude of the male, dominance could also be an ingredient in this. An ad for Chimere perfume incorporates

---

*Cheryl Tiegs (b. 1947) is a supermodel perhaps best known for her affiliation with the *Sports Illustrated Swimsuit Edition*. A 1978 poster of Tiegs in a pink swimsuit became a cultural icon. Recently, she has entered the business world with an accessory and wig line for Revlon.

two photos: in the top one the lady is being commanding at a business lun- cheon (need to dominate), but in the lower one she is being bussed (need for affiliation). Better ads, however, seem to avoid being too diffused; in the study of post–World War II advertising described earlier, appeals grew more focused as the decades passed. As a rule of thumb [only twenty percent of ads have one pri- mary appeal], about sixty percent have two conspicuous appeals; the last twenty percent have three or more. Rather than looking for the greatest number of ap- peals, decoding ads is most productive when the loudest one or two appeals are discerned, since those are the appeals with the best chance of grabbing people's attention.

90   Finally, analyzing ads does not have to be a solo activity and prob- ably should not be. The greater number of people there are involved, the better chance there is of transcending individual biases and discerning the essential emotional lure built into an advertisement.

Do They or Don't They?

Do the emotional appeals made in advertisements add up to the sinister manip- ulation of consumers?

It is clear that these ads work. Attention is caught, communication occurs between producers and consumers, and sales result. It turns out to be difficult to detail the exact relationship between a specific ad and a specific purchase, or even between a campaign and subsequent sales figures, because advertising is only one of a host of influences upon consumption. Yet no one is fooled by this lack of perfect proof; everyone knows that advertising sells. If this were not the case, then tight-fisted American businesses would not spend a total of fifty bil- lion dollars annually on these messages.

But before anyone despairs that advertisers have our number to the extent that they can marshal us at will and march us like automatons to the check-out counters, we should recall the resiliency and obduracy of the American con- sumer. Advertisers may have uncovered the softest spots in minds, but that does not mean they have found truly gaping apertures. There is no evidence that ad- vertising can get people to do things contrary to their self-interests. Despite all the finesse of advertisements, and all the subtle emotional tugs, the public resists the vast majority of the petitions. According to the marketing division of the A. C. Nielsen Company, a whopping seventy-five percent of all new products die within a year in the marketplace, the victims of consumer disinterest which no amount of advertising could overcome. The appeals in advertising may be the most captivating there are to be had, but they are not enough to entrap the wily consumer.

The key to understanding the discrepancy between, on the one hand, the fact that advertising truly works, and, on the other, the fact that it hardly works, is to take into account the enormous numbers of people exposed to an ad. Modern-day communications permit an ad to be displayed to millions upon millions of individuals; if the smallest fraction of that audience can be moved to buy the product, then the ad has been successful. When one percent of the people exposed to a television advertising campaign reach for their wallets, that could be one million sales, which may be enough to keep the product in production and the advertisements coming.

95   In arriving at an evenhanded judgment about advertisements and their emotional appeals, it is good to keep in mind that many of the purchases which might be credited to these ads are experienced as genuinely gratifying to the consumer. We sincerely like the goods or service we have bought, and we may even like some of the emotional drapery that an ad suggests comes with it. It has sometimes been noted that the most avid students of advertisements are the people who have just bought the product; they want to steep themselves in the associated imagery. This may be the reason that Americans, when polled, are not negative about advertising and do not disclose any sense of being misused. The volume of advertising may be an irritant, but the product information as well as the imaginative material in ads are partial compensation.

A productive understanding is that advertising messages involve costs and benefits at both ends of the communications channel. For those few ads which do make contact, the consumer surrenders a moment of time, has the lower brain curried, and receives notice of a product; the advertiser has given up money and has increased the chance of sales. In this sort of communications activity, neither party can be said to be the loser.

● Review Questions

1. Why is advertising more common in highly industrialized countries such as the United States than in countries with "quieter" economies?

2. How are advertisers' attempts to communicate their messages, and to break through customer resistance, keyed to their conception of human psychology, according to Fowles?

3. What are the "two orders of content" of most advertisements, according to Fowles?

4. How is Fowles indebted to Henry Murray?

5. Why must appeals to our need for sex and our need to aggress be handled carefully, according to Fowles?

6. How does the use of humor or the use of celebrities fit into Fowles's scheme?

● Discussion and Writing Suggestions

1. In ¶ 4, Fowles cites a study indicating that only a fraction of the advertisements bombarding consumers every day are even noticed, much less acted upon. How do the results of this study square with your own experience?

About how many of the commercial messages that you view and hear every day do you actually pay attention to? What kinds of messages draw your attention? What elicits positive reactions? Negative reactions? What kinds of appeals are most successful in making you want to actually purchase the advertised product?

2. What do you think of Fowles's analysis of "advertising's fifteen basic appeals"? Does this classification seem an accurate and useful way of accounting for how most advertising works upon us? Would you drop any of his categories, or perhaps incorporate one set into another set? Has Fowles neglected to consider other appeals that you believe to be equally important? If so, can you think of one or more advertisements that employ such appeals omitted by Fowles?

3. Categorize several of the print ads in the ad portfolio later in the chapter (pp.578–599), using Fowles's schema. Explain how the headlines, body text, and graphics support your categorization choices.

4. Fowles asserts that "[c]ontrary to impressions, unambiguous sex is rare in [advertising] messages." This article first appeared in 1982. Does Fowles's statement still seem true today? To what extent do you believe that advertisers in recent years have increased their reliance on overt sexual appeals? Cite examples.

5. Fowles believes that "the need to associate with others [affiliation] . . . is probably the most prevalent appeal" in advertising. To what extent do you agree with this statement? Locate or cite print or broadcast ads that rely on the need for affiliation. How do the graphics and text of these ads work on what Fowles calls "the deep running drives" of our psyches or "the lower brain"?

6. Locate ads that rely upon the converse appeals to nurture and to guidance. Explain how the graphics and text in these ads work upon our human motivations. If possible, further categorize the appeal: For example, are we provided with guidance from a parent figure, some other authority figure, or from the force of tradition?

7. Conduct (perhaps with one or more classmates) your own analysis of a set of contemporary advertisements. Select a single issue of a particular magazine, such as *Time* or the *New Yorker.* Review all of the full-page ads, classifying each according to Fowles's categories. An ad may make more than one appeal (as Fowles points out in ¶ 89), but generally one will be primary. What do your findings show? Which appeals are the most frequent? The least frequent? Which are most effective? Why? You may find it interesting to compare the appeals of advertising in different magazines aimed at different audiences— for example, a general-interest magazine, such as *Newsweek,* compared with a more specialized magazine, such as the *New Republic,* or *People,* or *Glamour,* or *Guns and Ammo.* To what extent do the types of appeals shift with the gender or interests of the target audience?

Making the Pitch in Print Advertising

Courtland L. Bovée, John V. Thill,
George P. Dovel, and Marian Burk Wood

No two ads are identical, but the vast majority employ a common set of textual features: headlines, body copy, and slogans. In the following selection, the authors discuss each of these features in turn, explaining their importance in attracting the potential customer's attention and selling the virtues of the product or service offered. You will find this discussion useful in making your own analyses of advertisements.

Courtland L. Bovée is the C. Allen Paul Distinguished Chair at Grossmont College. John V. Thill is CEO of Communication Specialists of America. George P. Dovel is president of the Dovel Group. Marian Burk Wood is president of Wood and Wood Advertising. This passage originally appeared in the authors' textbook *Advertising Excellence* (McGraw-Hill, 1995).

Copywriters and Copywriting

Given the importance of copy, it comes as no surprise that copywriters are key players in the advertising process. In fact, many of the most notable leaders and voices in the industry began their careers as copywriters, including Jane Maas, David Ogilvy, Rosser Reeves, Leo Burnett, and William Bernbach. As a profession, copywriting is somewhat unusual because so many of its top practitioners have been in their jobs for years, even decades (rather than moving up the management ranks as is usual in many professions). Copywriters can either work for agencies or set themselves up as free-lancers, selling their services to agencies and advertisers. Because it presents endless opportunities to be creative, copywriting is one of those rare jobs that can be fresh and challenging year after year.

Although successful copywriters share a love of language with novelists, poets, and other writers, copywriting is first and foremost a business function, not an artistic endeavor. The challenge isn't to create works of literary merit, but to meet advertising objectives. This doesn't mean that copywriting isn't an art, however; it's simply art in pursuit of a business goal. Nor is it easy. Such noted literary writers as Stephen Vincent Benét, George Bernard Shaw, and Ernest Hemingway tried to write ad copy and found themselves unable to do it effectively. It's the combined requirements of language skills, business acumen, and an ability to create under the pressure of tight deadlines and format restrictions (such as the limited number of words you have to work with) that make copywriting so challenging—and so endlessly rewarding.

Copywriters have many styles and approaches to writing, but most agree on one thing: copywriting is hard work. It can involve a great deal of planning and coordinating with clients, legal staffers, account executives, researchers, and art directors. In addition, it usually entails hammering away at your copy until it's as good as it can be. David Ogilvy talked about doing 19 drafts of a single piece of copy and writing 37 headlines for a Sears ad in order to get 3 possibilities to show to the client. Actually, the chance to write and rewrite that many times is a luxury that most copywriters don't have; they often must produce copy on tight schedules with unforgiving deadlines (such as magazine publication deadlines).

The task of copywriting is most often associated with the headlines and copy you see in an ad, but copywriters actually develop a wide variety of other materials, from posters to catalogs to press releases, as well as the words you hear in radio and television commercials.

Print Copy

5   Copywriters are responsible for every word you see in print ads, whether the words are in a catchy headline or in the fine print at the bottom of the page. The three major categories of copy are headlines, body copy, and slogans.

Headlines

The *headline*, also called a *heading* or a *head*, constitutes the dominant line or lines of copy in an ad. Headlines are typically set in larger type and appear at the top of the ad, although there are no hard-and-fast rules on headline layout. *Subheads* are secondary headlines, often written to move the reader from the main head-line to the body copy. Even if there is a pageful of body copy and only a few words in the headline, the headline is the most important piece of copy for two reasons: First, it serves as the "come-on" to get people to stop turning the page and check out your ad. Second, as much as 80 percent of your audience may not bother to read the body copy, so whatever message these nonreaders carry away from the ad will have to come from the headline.

Copywriters can choose from a variety of headline types, each of which performs a particular function.

- *News headlines.* News headlines present information that's new to the audience, such as announcing a new store location, a new product, or lower prices. This approach is common because potential customers are often looking for new solutions, lower prices, and other relevant changes in the marketplace. For example, a newspaper ad from the Silo home electronics chain announced a recent sale using a news headline: "Everything on Sale! 4 Days Only! 5–20% Off Everything!" Headlines like this are typical in local newspaper advertising.

- *Emotional headlines.* The emotional appeal...is represented by emotional headlines. The quotation headline "I'm sick of her ruining our lives" was used in an ad for the American Mental Health Fund to echo the frustration some parents feel when they can't understand their teenagers' behavior. Combined with a photo of a sad and withdrawn teenage girl, the headline grabs any parent who has felt such frustration, and the body copy goes on to explain that families shouldn't get mad at people with mental illnesses but should help them get treatment for their conditions.

- *Benefit headlines.* The benefit headline is a statement of the key customer benefit. An ad for Quicken personal finance software used the question-form headline: "How do you know exactly where your money goes and how much you have?" followed by "It's this simple" above a photograph of the product package. The customer benefit is keeping better track of your money, and Quicken is the solution offered.

- *Directive headlines.* Headlines that direct the reader to do something, or at least suggest the reader do something, can motivate consumer action. Such headlines can be a hard sell, such as "Come in now and save," or they can be something more subtle, such as "Just feel the color in these black and whites," the headline in an ad for Ensoniq keyboards.

- *Offbeat and curiosity headlines.* Humor, wordplay, and mystery can be effective ways to draw readers into an ad. An ad promoting vacation travel to Spain used the headline "Si in the dark," with a photo of a lively nighttime scene. The word *Si* is catchy because it first looks like an error, until the reader reads the body copy to learn that the ad is talking about Spain (*si* is Spanish for "yes").

- *Hornblowing headlines.* The hornblowing headline, called "Brag and Boast" heads by the Gallup & Robinson research organization, should be used with care. Customers have seen it all and heard it all, and "We're the greatest" headlines tend to sound arrogant and self-centered. This isn't to say that you can't stress superiority; you just need to do it in a way that takes the customer's needs into account, and the headline must be honest. The headline "Neuberger & Berman Guardian Fund" followed by the subhead "#1 Performing Growth and Income Fund" blows the company's own horn but also conveys an important product benefit. Since investors look for top-performing mutual funds, the information about being number one is relevant.

- *Slogan, label, or logo headlines.* Some headlines show a company's slogan, a product label, or the organization's logo. Powerful slogans like Hallmark's "When you care enough to send the very best" can make great headlines because they click with the reader's emotions. Label and logo headlines can build product and company awareness, but they must be used with care. If the label or logo doesn't make some emotional or logical connection with the reader, the ad probably won't succeed.

Headlines often have maximum impact when coupled with a well-chosen graphic element, rather than trying to carry the message with words alone. In fact, the careful combination of the two can increase the audience's involvement with the ad, especially if one of the two says something ironic or unexpected that has to be resolved by considering the other element. A magazine ad for Easter Seals had the headline "After all we did for Pete, he walked out on us." At first, you think the birth-defects organization is complaining. Then you see a photo of Pete with new artificial legs, walking away from a medical facility. It's a powerful combination that makes the reader feel good about the things Easter Seals can do for people.

Body Copy

The second major category of copy is the *body copy*, which constitutes the words in the main body of the ad, apart from headlines, photo captions, and other blocks of text. The importance of body copy varies from ad to ad, and some ads have little or no body copy. Ads for easy-to-understand products, for instance, often rely on the headline and a visual such as a photograph to get their point across. In contrast, when the selling message needs a lot of supporting detail to be convincing, an ad can be packed full of body copy. Some advertisers have the impression that long body copy should be avoided, but that isn't always the case. The rule to apply here is to use the "right" number of words. You might not need many words in a perfume ad, but you might need a page or two to cover a complex industrial product.

10   As with headlines, body copy can be built around several different formats. *Straight-line copy* is copy that takes off from the headline and develops the selling points for the product. *Narrative copy*, in contrast, tells a story as it persuades; the same selling points may be covered, but in a different context. *Dialog/monolog copy* lets one or two characters in the ad do the selling through what they are saying.

CHECKLIST FOR PRODUCING EXCELLENT COPY

❑ A. Avoid clichés.
   • Create fresh, original phrases that vividly convey your message.
   • Remember that clever wordplay based on clichés can be quite effective.

❑ B. Watch out for borrowed interest.
   • Make sure you don't use inappropriate copy or graphics since they can steal the show from your basic sales message.
   • Be sure nothing draws attention from the message.

❑ C. Don't boast.
   • Be sure the ad's purpose isn't merely to pat the advertiser on the back.
   • Tout success when you must convince nonbuyers that lots of people just like them have purchased your product; this isn't the same as shouting "We're the best!"

❑ D. Make it personal, informal, and relevant.
   • Connect with the audience in a way that is personal and comfortable. Pompous, stiff, and overly "businesslike" tends to turn people away.
   • Avoid copy that sounds like it belongs in an ad, with too many overblown adjectives and unsupported claims of superiority.

❑ E. Keep it simple, specific, and concise.
   • Make your case quickly and stick to the point. This will help you get past all the barriers and filters that people put up to help them select which things they'll pay attention to and which they'll ignore.
   • Avoid copy that's confusing, meandering, too long, or too detailed.

❑ F. Give the audience a reason to read, listen, or watch.
   • Offer a solution to your audience's problems.
   • Entertain your audience.
   • Consider any means possible to get your audience to pay attention long enough to get your sales message across.

Picture-and-caption copy relies on photographs or illustrations to tell the story, with support from their accompanying captions.

Slogans

The third major category of copy includes *slogans*, or *tag lines*, memorable sayings that convey a selling message. Over the years, Coca-Cola has used such slogans as "Coke is it," "It's the real thing," and "Always Coca-Cola." Slogans are sometimes used as headlines, but not always. Their importance lies in the fact they often become the most memorable result of an advertising campaign. You've probably got a few slogans stuck in your head. Ever heard of "Quality is job number 1," "Don't leave home without it," or "Melts in your mouth, not in your hand"?

The Korean automaker Hyundai recently switched back to the slogan "Cars that make sense," which is a great way of expressing its desired positioning as a lower-cost but still reliable alternative to Japanese and U.S. cars. For several years, the company had used "Hyundai. Yes, Hyundai," but "Cars that make sense" has proved to be a much more effective way to define the value it offers consumers.

● Review Questions

1. What are the particular challenges of copywriting, as opposed to other types of writing?

2. How do the authors classify the main types of ad headlines?

3. What are the main types of body copy styles, according to the authors?

● Discussion and Writing Suggestions

1. Apply the authors' criteria for effective headlines to three or four of the print ads in the portfolio (pp. 578–599)—or to three or four ads of your own choosing. To what extent do these headlines succeed in attracting attention, engaging the audience, and fulfilling the other requirements of effective headlines?

2. Imagine that you are a copywriter who has been assigned the account for a particular product (your choice). Develop three possible headlines for an advertisement for this product. Incorporate as many as possible of the criteria for effective headlines discussed by the authors (¶s 6–8).

3. Classify the *types* of headlines in a given product category in the print ad portfolio (pp. 578–599). Or classify the types of headlines in full-page ads in a single current magazine. Which type of headline appears to be the most common? Which type appears to be the most effective in gaining your attention and making you want to read the body copy?

4. Classify the *types* of body copy styles in a given product category in the ad portfolio. Or classify the types of body copy styles in full-page ads in a single

current magazine. How effective is the copy in selling the virtues of the product or the institution or organization behind the product?

5. Assess the effectiveness of a given ad either in the ad portfolio or in a recent magazine or newspaper. Apply the criteria discussed by the authors in the box labeled "Checklist for Producing Excellent Copy." For example, to what extent is the copy fresh and original? To what extent does the copy make the message "personal, informal, and relevant" to the target audience? To what extent is the message "simple, specific, and concise"?

6. Write your own ad for a product that you like and use frequently. In composing the ad, apply the principles of effective headlines, subheads, body copy, and slogans discussed by the authors. Apply also the principles of "Checklist for Producing Excellent Copy." You will also need to think of (though not necessarily create) an effective graphic for the ad.

SELLING HAPPINESS: TWO PITCHES FROM MAD MEN

One of the surprise TV hits of 2007 was *Mad Men*, an original series about the advertising business, created by writer/producer Matt Weiner for the American Movie Classics (AMC) network. *Mad Men*—short for Madison Avenue men—follows Don Draper, creative director of Sterling Cooper, a medium-size New York ad agency, along with his colleagues and his family (and his mistresses), as he maneuvers his way through the ruthlessly competitive world of advertising during the early 1960s. The show won Golden Globe Awards for best TV dramatic series for two consecutive seasons. With high-quality writing (creator Matt Weiner was also a writer and producer for *The Sopranos*), top-flight acting, and spot-on production design and period costumes, *Mad Men* became instant classic, must-see television.

Two segments from the first season depict a time-honored business ritual, the "pitch," in which one or more creative/business people attempt to sell their idea to a client in hopes of securing a lucrative contract. (In Hollywood, writers or directors pitch their ideas for films to the studio or to potential financial backers.) As the "Carousel" segment begins, Don Draper (portrayed by Jon Hamm) and his colleagues (accounts director Herman ["Duck"] Phillips [Mark Moses], copywriter Harry Crane [in glasses; Rich Sommer], and art director Salvatore Romano [Bryan Batt]) make a pitch to a couple of clients from Eastman Kodak. The Kodak engineers have just come up with a turning "wheel" to house the slides for its new projector, and the Kodak business execs are making the rounds of New York ad agencies to hear them pitch campaigns to sell this new product. In "It's Toasted," Draper attempts to explain to the clients that despite the federal government's recent lawsuits against cigarette manufacturers for making false health claims about their products, and despite the fact that "[w]e have six identical companies making six identical products," the company can still reassure customers about the safety of its particular brand of cigarettes.

Go to: YouTube.com

Search terms: "mad men carousel"
"mad men it's toasted"

Select the longer versions of each of the two scenes.

● Discussion and Writing Suggestions

1. What do these scenes say about the way that advertising people sell consumer products to the public? What other examples come to mind of items of hardware sold in a manner similar to how Draper and his creative team propose to sell the "Carousel"?

2. Study Don's reaction as he shows the slides of his family. What do you think is passing through his mind during the presentation? Does he appear to believe what he is saying? Does the writer of this scene suggest that advertising is nothing but fakery? Explain.

3. Relate the "Carousel" scene to Jib Fowles' "Fifteen Basic Appeals" of advertising. Which appeals are most at work during the presentation of the "Carousel"? Once you have analyzed "Carousel" with respect to one or more motivations reviewed by Fowles, comment on the emotional pull of the "Carousel" pitch as Draper develops it. Even though you understand how Draper's appeal may work psychologically (according to Fowles), can you still be emotionally vulnerable to the pitch? Did you find Draper's presentation moving? Discuss.

4. At one point during the Lucky Strike "It's Toasted" pitch (immediately before the first line in the clip), Don notes: "We have six identical companies making six identical products." How does his solution for making this particular client's "identical" product "distinctive" (in this case, making it "safe") bring to mind other successful advertising campaigns that have created distinctiveness through words alone?

5. The sales pitch depicted in these meetings were set in an era some fifty years ago. To what extent do you think advertising for high-tech products has become more or less sophisticated than advertising was during the early 1960s? (You may wish to refer not only to this scene, but also to print ads of the same period, as exemplified in the "Portfolio.") To what extent—if at all—might today's consumers be less apt to be captivated and sold by the kind of appeals dramatized in this scene? Cite particular examples of contemporary advertising, both print and TV.

A PORTFOLIO OF PRINT ADVERTISEMENTS

The following portfolio offers for your consideration and analysis a selection of twenty-two full-page advertisements that appeared in American and British magazines between 1945 (shortly after the end of World War II) and 2003. In terms of products represented, the ads fall into several categories—cigarettes, alcohol (beer and liquor), automobiles, household cleaners, lotions, and perfumes. The portfolio also includes a few miscellaneous ads for such diverse products as men's hats, telephones, and airlines. These ads originally appeared in such magazines as *Time, Newsweek, U.S. News and World Report, Sports Illustrated, Ladies Home Journal, Ebony,* and *Ms.* A number of the ads were researched in the Advertising Archive, an online (and subscription) collection maintained by The Picture Desk.

The advertisements in this portfolio are *not* representative of all ads that appeared during the past sixty years. We made our selection largely on the basis of how interesting, striking, provocative, and unusual these particular ads appeared to us. Admittedly, the selection process was biased. That said, the ads in this portfolio offer rich possibilities for analysis. With practice, and by applying principles for analysis that you will find in the earlier selections in this chapter, you will be able to "read" into these ads numerous messages about cultural attitudes toward gender relations, romance, smoking, and automobiles. The ads will prompt you to consider why we buy products that we may not need or why we prefer one product over another when the two products are essentially identical. Each advertisement is a window into the culture. Through careful analysis, you will gain insights not only into the era in which the ads were produced, but also into shifting cultural attitudes over the past sixty years.

Following the portfolio, we provide two or three specific questions for each ad (pp. 600–605), questions designed to stimulate your thinking about the particular ways in which the graphics and text are intended to work. As you review the ads, however, you may want to think about the more general questions about advertisements raised by the readings in this chapter:

1. What appears to be the target audience for the ad? If this ad was produced more than two decades ago, does its same target audience exist today? If so, how would this audience likely react today to the ad?
2. What is the primary appeal made by the ad, in terms of Fowles's categories? What, if any, are the secondary appeals?
3. What assumptions do the ad's sponsors make about such matters as (1) commonly accepted roles of women and men; (2) the relationship between the sexes; (3) the priorities of men and women?
4. What is the chief attention-getting device in the ad?
5. How does the headline and body text communicate the ad's essential appeals?
6. How do the ad's graphics communicate the ad's essential appeals?
7. How do the expressions, clothing, and postures of the models, as well as the physical objects in the illustration, help communicate the ad's message?
8. How do the graphic qualities of balance, proportion, movement, unity, clarity and simplicity, and emphasis help communicate the ad's message?

Consider, also, the following evaluative questions[1]:

- Is it a good ad? Why?
- What do you like most about it? Why?
- What do you dislike the most? Why?
- Do you think it "works"? Why or why not?
- How could the ad be improved?
- Could the sender have conveyed the same message using other strategies, other persuasive means? If so, explain.
- Even if you don't believe that this particular ad works or persuades you, is there anything in the ad that still affects you or persuades you indirectly?
- Does the ad have effects on you perhaps not intended by its creators?

---

[1]Lars Thoger Christensen, "How to Analyze an Advertisement." University of Southern Denmark—Odense. Jan. 2004. http://wms-soros.mngt.waikato.ac.nz/NR/rdonlyres/ebabz4jhzmg5fr5p45ypc53mdvuxva5wxhe7323onb4ylelbaq3se5xjrslfc4mi3qgk6dmsx5dqbp/Advertisinganalysis.doc

Camels, 1940s

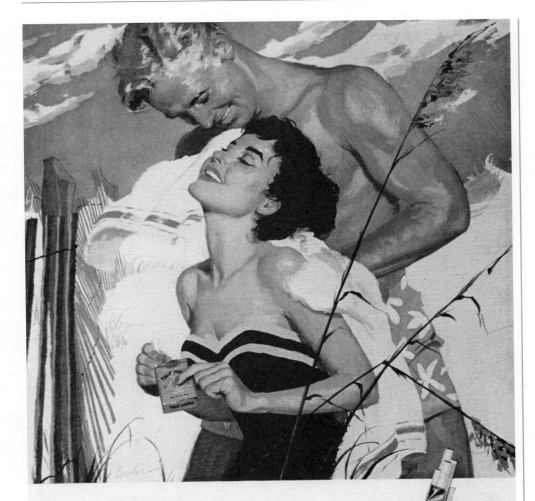

Gently Does It

Gentleness makes good friends in fun-making . . . and in a cigarette, where gentleness is one of the greatest requirements of modern taste. That's why today's Philip Morris, born gentle, refined to special gentleness in the making, makes so many friends among our young smokers. Enjoy the gentle pleasure, the fresh unfiltered flavor, of today's Philip Morris. In the convenient snap-open pack, regular or smart king-size.

Philip Morris

. . . gentle for modern taste

Philip Morris, 1950s

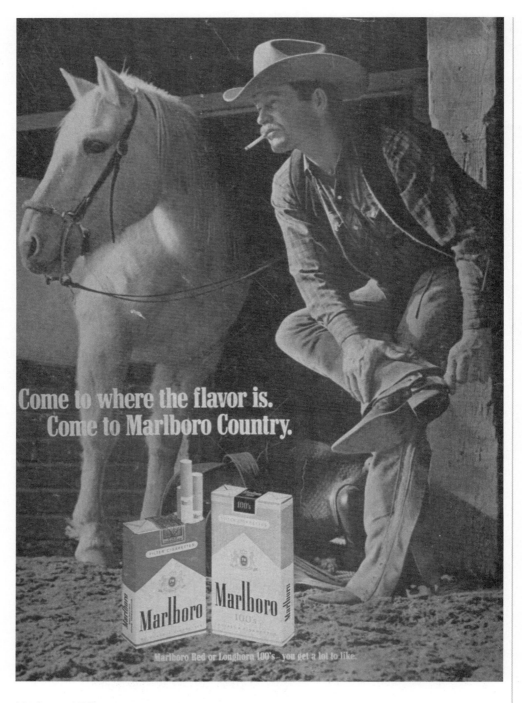

Marlboro, 1970s

19 mg. "tar", 1.3 mg. nicotine av. per cigarette, FTC Report MAY '78.
Satisfaction, Camel Filters style.
Some men taste it all: Rich warm flavor. Smooth even taste. Solid satisfaction.
Only from the Camel Filters blend of Turkish and domestic tobaccos.
Warning: The Surgeon General Has Determined That Cigarette Smoking Is Dangerous to Your Health.
CAMEL
FILTERS
Famous Camel Quality!

Camels, 1979

Cancer Patients Aid Association (Mumbai, India)

America is returning to the genuine—in foods, fashions and tastes. Today's trend to Ballantine <u>light</u> Ale fits right into this modern picture. <u>In all the world, no other beverage brewed has such extra excellence brewed into it.</u> And "Brewer's Gold" is one big reason for Ballantine Ale's deep, rich, genuine flavor.

They all ask for ale **Ballantine** LIGHT **Ale !**

Ballantine Ale, 1950s

BACARDI® rum is so "mixable"...
It's a one-brand bar.

Big, bold highballs, sassy Daiquiris, cool tonics and colas—Bacardi
rum is enjoyable always and *all* ways. Extra Special: our man
Fernando is pouring very rare Bacardi Añejo rum (Ahn-YAY-ho),
one of the fine rums from Bacardi. So incredibly smooth he enjoys
it even in a snifter. Try it, too!

°BACARDI IMPORTS, INC., MIAMI, FLA. RUM. 80 PROOF.

Bacardi Rum, 1960s

AT THE PULITZER FOUNTAIN, N.Y.C.

In Fine Whiskey...

FLEISCHMANN'S
is the BIG buy!

The First Taste will tell you why!

Established 1870

BLENDED WHISKEY • 86 AND 90 PROOF • 65% GRAIN NEUTRAL SPIRITS
THE FLEISCHMANN DISTILLING CORPORATION, NEW YORK CITY

Fleischmann's Whiskey, 1964

"I'll have a Hennessy Very Superior Old Pale Reserve Cognac, thank you."

The Taste of Success

Every drop of Hennessy V.S.O.P. Reserve is Grande Fine Champagne Cognac. It's made solely from grapes grown in La Grande Champagne—the small district in the Cognac region which is the source of the very greatest Cognac. What's more, Hennessy is selected from the largest reserves of aged Cognacs in existence. Enjoy a taste of success today…

Hennessy V.S.O.P. Reserve Cognac

Hennessy V.S.O.P. Grande Fine Champagne Cognac. 80 Proof. ©Schieffelin & Co., N.Y.

Hennessy Cognac, 1968

Cossack Vodka, 1970s

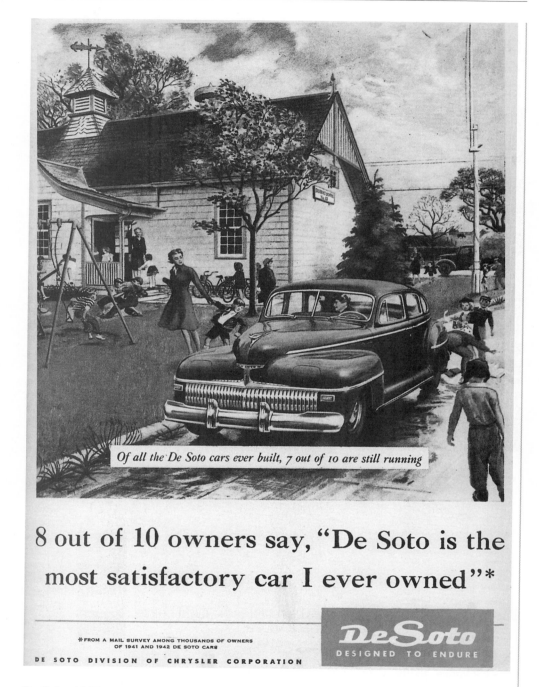

De Soto, 1947

"Ford's out Front from a Woman's Angle"

1. "I don't know synthetic enamel from a box of my children's paints . . . but if synthetic enamel is what it takes to make that beautiful, shiny Ford finish, I'm all for it!

2. "My husband says the brakes are self-centering and hydraulic—whatever that means! All I know is they're so easy that I can taxi the children all day without tiring out!

3. "Peter, he's my teen-age son, tells me that 'Ford is the only car in its price class with a choice of a 100-horsepower V-8 engine or a brilliant new Six.' He says no matter which engine people pick, they're out front with Ford!

6. "Now here's another thing women like and that's a blissfully comfortable ride—one that isn't bumpity-bump even on some of our completely forgotten roads."

Listen to the Ford Show starring Dinah Shore on Columbia Network Stations Wednesday Evenings.

4. "The interior of our Ford is strictly my department! It's tailored with the dreamiest broadcloth. Such a perfect fit! Mary Jane says women help design Ford interiors. There's certainly a woman's touch there!

5. "Do you like lovely silver, beautifully simple and chaste looking? That's what I always think of when I touch those smart Ford door handles and window openers.

There's a *Ford* in your future

Ford, 1947

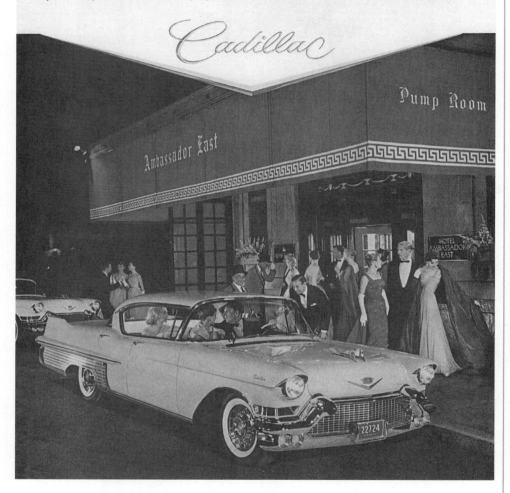

Cadillac, 1950s

This is your reward for the great Dodge advance—the daring new, dramatic new '56 Dodge.

The Magic Touch of Tomorrow!

The *look* of success! The *feel* of success! The *power* of success!
They come to you in a dramatically beautiful, dynamically powered new Dodge that introduces the ease and safety of push-button driving –the Magic Touch of Tomorrow! It is a truly great value.

New '56 DODGE

Dodge, 1955

Corvette Sting Ray Sport Coupe with eight standard safety features, including outside rearview mirror. Use it always before passing.

The day she flew the coupe

What manner of woman is this, you ask, who stands in the midst of a mountain stream eating a peach?

Actually she's a normal everyday girl except that she and her husband own the Corvette Coupe in the background. (He's at work right now, wondering where he misplaced his car keys.)

The temptation, you see, was over-powering. They'd had the car a whole week now, and not once had he offered to let her drive. His excuse was that this, uh, was a big hairy sports car. Too much for a woman to handle: the trigger-quick steering, the independent rear suspension, the disc brakes—plus the 4-speed transmission and that 425-hp engine they had ordered—egad! He would teach her to drive it some weekend. So he said.

That's why she hid the keys, forcing him to seek public transportation. Sure of his departure, she went to the garage, started the Corvette, and was off for the hills, soon upshifting and downshifting as smoothly as he. His car. Hard to drive. What propaganda!

'66 CORVETTE BY CHEVROLET
Chevrolet Division of General Motors, Detroit, Michigan

Corvette, 1966

What's for dinner, Duchess?

Prediction: The new wives of 1947 are going to have more fun in the kitchen.

Previous cooking experience is desirable, perhaps, but not essential. There are so many new easy-to-use foods, so many new ways to prepare foods, so many interesting ways to serve foods, cooking will be a novel and exciting adventure.

Further prediction: Cheese dishes will be featured more often on their menus. They'll know that cheese gives tastiness and variety to meals. And cheese, like milk (nature's most nearly perfect food), is rich in protein, calcium, phosphorus, in vitamins A and G.

Yes, we have a personal interest in cheese. For Kraft, pioneer in cheese, is a unit of National Dairy. And what we've said about housewives using more cheese is entirely true.

It's also true that they're learning more about the whys and wherefores of food each year — just as the scientists in our laboratories are learning more about better ways to process, improve and supply it.

These men are backed by the resources of a great organization. They explore every field of dairy products, discover new ones. And the health of America benefits constantly by this National Dairy research.

Dedicated to the wider use and better understanding of dairy products as human food . . . as a base for the development of new products and materials . . . as a source of health and enduring progress on the farms and in the towns and cities of America.

NATIONAL DAIRY
PRODUCTS CORPORATION
AND AFFILIATED COMPANIES

National Dairy Products Corporation, 1947

MAY: # Heavens, Ann — wish I could clean up quick as that!

ANN: You could, hon! Just use a cleanser that doesn't leave dirt-catching scratches.

MAY: Goodness! What in the world do scratches have to do with it?

ANN: A lot, silly! Those tiny scratches you get from gritty cleansers hold onto dirt and double your cleaning time.

MAY: Well, you old smartie! I'd never thought of *that* before.

ANN: I hadn't thought of it either—till I discovered Bon Ami! See how fine-textured and white it is. It just *slides* dirt off—and when you rinse it away, it doesn't leave any of that horrid grit in the tub.

MAY: Say no more, darling! From now on there's going to be a new cleaning team in our house —me and Bon Ami!

EASY ON YOUR HANDS, Bon Ami *Powder* is the ideal cleanser for kitchen sinks, as well as bathtubs. Also try Bon Ami *Cake* for cleaner windows, mirrors and windshields.

 **Bon Ami**

THE **SPEEDY** CLEANSER *that* *"hasn't scratched yet!"*

Bon Ami, 1947

Mrs. Dorian Mehle of Morrisville, Pa., is all three: a housewife, a mother, and a very lovely lady.

"I wash 22,000 dishes a year... but I'm proud of my pretty hands!"

You and Dorian Mehle have something in common. Every year, you wash a stack of dishes a quarter-mile high!

Detergents make your job so much easier. They cut right into grease and grime. They get you through dishwashing in much less time, but while they dissolve grease, they also take away the natural oils and youthful softness of your hands!

Although Dorian hasn't given up detergents her hands are as soft, as smooth, as young-looking as a teenager's. Her secret is no secret at all. It's the world's best-known beauty routine. It's pure, white Jergens Lotion, after every chore.

When you smooth on Jergens Lotion, this liquid formula doesn't just "coat" your hands. It penetrates right away, to help *replace* that softening moisture your skin needs.

Jergens Lotion has two ingredients doctors recommend for softening. Women must be recommending it, too, for more women use it than any other hand care in the world. Dorian's husband is the best testimonial to Jergens Lotion care. Even after years of married life, he still loves to hold her pretty hands!

Use Jergens Lotion like a prescription: three times a day, after every meal!

Now—lotion dispenser FREE of extra cost with $1.00 size. Supply limited.

Use JERGENS LOTION—avoid detergent hands

Jergens Lotion, 1954

Madam! Suppose you traded jobs with your husband?

You can just bet the first thing he'd ask for would be a telephone in the kitchen.

You wouldn't catch him dashing to another room every time the telephone rang, or he had to make a call.

He doesn't have to do it in his office in town. It would be mighty helpful if you didn't have to do it in your "office" at home.

That's in the kitchen where you do so much of your work. And it's right there that an additional telephone comes in so handy for so many things.

Along with a lot of convenience is that nice feeling of pride in having the best of everything—especially if it is one of those attractive new telephones in color.

P.S. Additional telephones in kitchen, bedroom and other convenient places around the house cost little. The service charge is just pennies a day.

Bell Telephone System

Bell Telephone, 1956

The phone company wants more installers like Alana MacFarlane.

Alana MacFarlane is a 20-year-old from San Rafael, California. She's one of our first women telephone installers. She won't be the last.

We also have several hundred male telephone operators. And a policy that there are no all-male or all-female jobs at the phone company.

We want the men and women of the telephone company to do what they want to do, and do best.

For example, Alana likes working outdoors. "I don't go for office routine," she said. "But as an installer, I get plenty of variety and a chance to move around."

Some people like to work with their hands, or, like Alana, get a kick out of working 20 feet up in the air.

Others like to drive trucks. Some we're helping to develop into good managers.

Today, when openings exist, local Bell Companies are offering applicants and present employees some jobs they may never have thought about before. We want to help all advance to the best of their abilities.

AT&T and your local Bell Company are equal opportunity employers.

Bell Telephone, 1974

Think of her as your mother.

She only wants what's best for you.
A cool drink. A good dinner. A soft pillow and a warm blanket.
This is not just maternal instinct. It's the result of the longest
Stewardess training in the industry.
Training in service, not just a beauty course.
Service, after all, is what makes professional travelers prefer American.
And makes new travelers want to keep on flying with us.
So we see that every passenger gets the same professional treatment.
That's the American Way.

Fly the American Way
American Airlines.

American Airlines, 1968

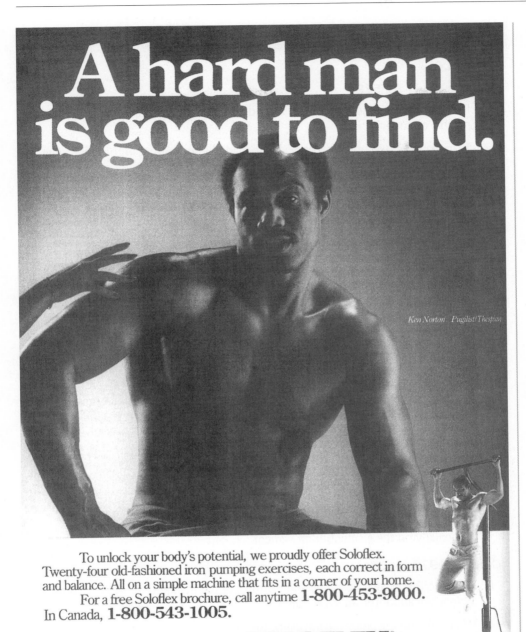

A hard man is good to find.

Ken Norton Pugilist/Thespian

To unlock your body's potential, we proudly offer Soloflex. Twenty-four old-fashioned iron pumping exercises, each correct in form and balance. All on a simple machine that fits in a corner of your home. For a free Soloflex brochure, call anytime **1-800-453-9000**. In Canada, **1-800-543-1005**.

SOLOFLEX®
Weightlifting, Pure and Simple.

VHS Video Brochure™ available upon request. © 1985, Soloflex, Inc. Hillsboro, Oregon 97124

Soloflex, 1985

● Discussion and Writing Suggestions

TOBACCO

Camels, 1947 (p. 578)

1. How does the intended appeal of this ad differ most dramatically from a comparable ad today?

2. What kind of psychological appeals are made by the picture in the top half of this ad and the text accompanying it? How does the image of a doctor seeing a five-year old girl and her mother in his book-lined office tie in with the "life expectancy" message of the text and the "More Doctors Smoke Camels" campaign?

Philip Morris, 1950s (p. 579)

1. How do the placement, posture, and dress of the models in the ad help create its essential psychological appeal? Why do you suppose (in relation to the selling of cigarettes) the models' eyes are closed?

2. Discuss some of the messages communicated both by the graphic and the text of this ad. Focus in particular on the quality of "gentleness" emphasized in the ad.

Marlboro, 1970s (p. 580)

1. The Marlboro Man has become one of the most famous—and successful—icons of American advertising. What elements of the Marlboro Man (and his setting, Marlboro Country) do you notice, and what role do these elements play in the appeal being made by this ad?

2. This ad appeared during the 1970s (the popularity of the Marlboro Man extended into the 1980s, however). To what extent do you think it would have the same appeal today?

3. Comment on the elements of graphic design (balance, proportion, movement, unity, clarity and simplicity, emphasis) that help make this ad effective. Focus particularly on the element of movement.

Camels, 1979 (p. 581)

1. What do the relative positions and postures of the man and the woman in the ad indicate about the ad's basic appeal?

2. What roles do the props—particularly, the motorcycle and the models' outfits—and the setting play in helping to sell the product?

3. How do the design elements in the ad emphasize the product?

4. Compare the graphic elements of this ad to those of the Fleischmann's Whiskey ad (p. 585).

5. Compare and contrast the two Camels ads presented in this section of the portfolio. Focus on the psychological appeals, the cultural values implied in the ads, and the graphic and textual means used to persuade the buyer to smoke Camels.

Cancer Patients Aid Association, 2012 (p. 582)

1. How does the circle of onlookers help create or enhance the message of this advertisement?

2. In what way does the camera angle create meaning and affect the tone of the ad?

3. This advertisement doesn't aim to sell the viewer a product but, rather, to change behavior. Do you think that it's likely to be effective at that task—in particular, in persuading smokers to stop smoking? Explain.

BEER AND LIQUOR

Ballantine Ale, 1950s (p. 583)

1. This illustration, reminiscent of some of Norman Rockwell's paintings, is typical of many beer and ale ads in the 1950s, which depict a group of well-dressed young adults enjoying their brew at a social event. Comment on the distinctive graphic elements in this ad, and speculate as to why these elements are seldom employed in contemporary advertisements for beer and ale. Why, in other words, does this ad seem old-fashioned?

2. Contrast the appeal and graphics of this ad with the ads for Miller and Budweiser later in this portfolio.

3. Identify the adjectives in the body text, and attempt to correlate them to the graphic in helping to construct the message of the ad.

Bacardi Rum, 1960s (p. 584)

1. What meaning is conveyed by the placement, posture, and expressions of the four models in this ad? How do you think this meaning is intended to help sell the product?

2. Comment on the significance of the props in the photo.

3. How does the text ("Big, bold highballs, sassy Daiquiris, cool tonics . . .") help reinforce the meaning created by the picture?

Fleischmann's Whiskey, 1964 (p. 585)

1. Comment on (1) the significance of the extra-large bottle of whiskey; (2) the stances of the two models in the ad; (3) the way the headline contributes to the ad's meaning.

2. Compare and contrast the graphic in this ad with that of the 1979 Camels ad earlier in this portfolio (the man on the motorcycle).

Hennessy Cognac, 1968 (p. 586)

1. What is the primary appeal of this ad? How do the woman, the horse, and the headline work to create and reinforce this appeal?

2. Compare and contrast this ad to the Cadillac, 1950s ad in terms of their appeal and their graphics.

Cossack Vodka, 1970s (p. 587)

1. What is the essential appeal behind this ad?

2. The comic-book style of the drawing is reminiscent of the work of Roy Lichtenstein (1923–1997), an American painter who drew inspiration from advertisements and romance magazines, as well as comic books, to depict and parody artifacts of pop culture. What is the effect of this particular style on creating—and perhaps commenting upon—the message in the text balloon and in the ad in which it appears?

3. How does the text at the bottom of the ad reinforce the message created by the graphic? In particular, how is this message intended to sell the product?

AUTOMOBILES

De Soto, 1947 (p. 588)

1. How does the scene portrayed in the illustration help create the basic appeal of this ad? Focus on as many significant individual elements of the illustration as you can.

2. To what extent does the caption (in the illustration) and the headline support the message communicated by the graphic?

3. Explain why both this ad and the preceding Cadillac ad are products of their particular times.

Ford, 1947 (p. 589)

1. Cite and discuss those textual elements in the ad that reflect a traditional conception of the American woman.

2. How do the visual elements of the ad reinforce the assumptions about traditional gender roles reflected in the ad?

Cadillac, 1950s (p. 590)

1. What is the particular marketing strategy behind this ad? Based on the ad's text, compose a memo from the head of marketing to the chief copywriter, proposing this particular ad and focusing on the strategy. The memo doesn't have to be cynical or to insult the prospective Cadillac buyers; it should just be straightforward and direct.

2. How do the ad's graphics reinforce the message in the text? For example, what is the significance of the "motor car" being parked in front of the entryway to the Ambassador East Hotel? Of the way the people in the ad are dressed?

3. How is this ad designed to appeal buyers seeking both prestige and practicality?

Dodge, 1955 (p. 591)

1. Discuss the multiple appeals of this ad. How are these appeals reflected in the ad's text and graphics? For instance, discuss the angle from which the automobile is photographed.

2. Both this ad and the 1947 Ford ad (p. 589) feature one or more women in the graphic. Compare and contrast the use of women in the two ads.

Corvette, 1966 (p. 592)

1. How do the graphic elements reinforce the message developed in the text of this ad?

2. Comment on the dress and the posture of the model, as these relate to the ad's essential appeal. What's the significance of the woman eating a peach in a mountain stream?

3. The body text in this ad tells a story. What kind of husband–wife dynamic is implied by this story? To what extent do you find similarities between the implied gender roles in this ad and those in the 1947 Ford ad ("Ford's out Front from a Woman's Angle," p. 589)? To what extent do you find differences, ones that may be attributable to the 20 years between the two ads?

CLEANSERS, BEAUTY PRODUCTS, AND OTHER

National Dairy Products Corporation, 1947 (p. 593)

1. How does the couple pictured in the ad illustrate gender expectations of the period? Comment on the dress, postures, and expressions of the models.

2. What, exactly, is this ad *selling*? (It is presented more as a newsmagazine article than as a conventional advertisement.) How is the appeal tied to contemporary developments by "scientists" and their "research," particularly as these relate to "the new wives of 1947"?

3. What does the text of this ad imply about the situation of young married couples in postwar households?

Bon Ami, 1947 (p. 594)

1. How do the text and graphics of this ad illustrate a bygone cultural attitude toward gender roles? Notice, in particular, the dress, postures, and expressions of the women pictured, as well as the style of the illustration. Focus also on the wording of the text.

2. In terms of Jib Fowles's categories, what kind of appeal is being made by the Bon Ami ad?

Jergens Lotion, 1954 (p. 595)

1. Compare and contrast the appeals and the strategies of this Jergens Lotion ad and the Bon Ami ad preceding it. Are the ads intended to appeal to the same target audiences? To what extent are the psychological appeals of the two ads similar? Compare the illustrations of the ads. How do they differ in basic strategy?

2. The model in the Jergens Lotion ad is immaculately dressed and groomed, and she is sitting among stacks of fine china (as opposed to everyday dishware). What do you think is the marketing strategy behind these graphic choices?

Bell Telephone, 1956 (p. 596)

1. Discuss the attitude toward gender roles implicit in the 1956 Bell ad. How do the graphics, the headline, and the body text reinforce this attitude? What is the significance of the quotation marks around "office" in the final sentence of the third paragraph?

2. Notice that the woman at the desk seems a lot more comfortable and at ease than the man holding the crying baby and the dishes. What does this fact tell us about the attitudes toward gender roles of those who created this ad?

Bell Telephone, 1974 (p. 597)

1. Compare and contrast the 1956 Bell ad with the 1974 Bell ad, in terms of their attitudes toward gender roles. How do the text and graphics reinforce the essential differences?

2. The 1956 Bell ad pictures a woman at a desk (a white-collar job); the 1974 ad pictures a woman working at a telephone pole (a blue-collar job). Would the 1974 ad have the same impact if "Alana MacFarlane" had, like her 1956 counterpart, been pictured at a desk?

3. Like the 1950s Cadillac ad (p. 590), the 1974 Bell ad seems more of a public service announcement than a conventional advertisement. Compare and contrast these ads in terms of their messages to readers.

American Airlines, 1968 (p. 598)

1. Discuss the mixed messages (in terms of appeal) being transmitted by the American Airlines ad. To what extent do you think the apparently conflicting appeals make for an effective ad?

2. Comment on the dress, pose, and expression of the model in the ad, which appeared in *Ebony* magazine. How do these create a different impact than would an illustration, say, of a flight attendant serving a drink or giving a pillow to an airline passenger?

Soloflex, 1985 (p. 599)

1. How does the illustration in this ad reinforce the basic appeal of the headline?

2. Ads are frequently criticized for the incongruity between illustration and product being advertised—for example, a scantily clad woman posed provocatively in front of a pickup truck. To what extent does the Soloflex ad present an appropriate fit between graphic and product advertised?

A PORTFOLIO OF TV COMMERCIALS

The world's first television commercial was a ten-second Bulova watch ad broadcast in 1941. But it wasn't until the 1950s, when TV became a mass medium, that the commercial became a ubiquitous feature of popular culture. Before viewers had the technology to fast-forward through commercials, many probably regarded TV ads as annoying, occasionally informative or entertaining, but generally unnecessary accompaniments to their television experience. But of course the commercial is not simply an extraneous byproduct of TV programming. It is television's very reason for existence. Before the age of public TV and of cable and satellite providers, television programs were financed entirely by the companies that created the commercials and that paid networks and local stations to broadcast them. Viewed from a marketing angle, the only purpose of commercial television is to provide a medium for advertising. The news, comedy, drama, game, and variety shows offered by TV are simply ways of luring viewers to watch the commercials.

Still, the unceasing deluge of commercials of every type means that advertisers have to figure out ways of making their messages stand out by being unusually creative, funny, surprising, or otherwise noteworthy. The standard jingles, primitive animation, catchphrases ("Winston tastes good like a cigarette should"), and problem-solution minidramas of TV commercials work for a while but are quickly forgotten in the onslaught of new messages. It becomes the job of advertising agencies (of the type represented in *Mad Men*) that create both print and TV ads to make their clients' products stand out by ever more-ingenious and striking ways of delivering their messages. To do this, these agencies rely not just on information about the product and clever audiovisual techniques; they attempt to respond to what they believe consumers crave, deep down. TV commercials, no less than print ads, rely on psychological appeals of the type discussed by Jib Fowles in his "Advertising's Fifteen Basic Appeals."

The following portfolio includes some of the most noteworthy and successful TV commercials of the past sixty years. Many (though not all) of these commercials are featured in Bernice Kanner's *The 100 Best TV Commercials...and Why They Worked* (1999), where you will find additional description and commentary. To access the commercials, go to YouTube (YouTube.com), and enter the search terms provided under the commercial's title into the search box. In some cases, additional information is presented, in brackets, to help you navigate to the commercial. In cases where multiple versions of the same commercial are available, you may have to experiment to determine which one offers the best video and audio quality. In a few cases, uploaded commercials have been truncated, so you should generally select the longest version. In some cases, the indicated commercials may have been removed from the YouTube Web site. No matter; thousands more remain available for your observation and consideration.

As with the print ads, we provide two or three sets of specific questions for each TV commercial. These questions are intended to stimulate your thinking and writing process about the particular ways in which the audio and visuals are intended to work. As you review these commercials, however, you might be thinking of the more general questions about advertisements raised by the preceding readings in the chapter. Here are some of those general questions:

1. What appears to be the target audience for this TV commercial? If it was produced more than two decades ago, how would this target audience likely react today to the ad?
2. What is the primary appeal made by the ad, in terms of Fowles's categories? What, if any, are the secondary appeals?
3. What is the chief attention-getting technique in the commercial?
4. How does the commercial make use of such tools as humor, surprise, fantasy, wonder, human interest, or social concern to achieve its goals?
5. What is the relationship between the visuals and the audio track? How do audio and video work together—or in contrast—to achieve the sponsor's purpose?
6. How do the commercial's visual techniques work to convey the message? Consider camera movement (or the lack of camera movement); the style and pace of editing (the juxtaposition of individual shots); and visual composition (the framing of the people and/or objects within the shot).
7. How do the expressions, the clothing, the postures of the person or people, and the physical objects in the shots help communicate the ad's message?
8. How do the words used by the actor(s) or by the voice-over narrator work to communicate the message of the commercial?

Consider, also, the following evaluative questions[2]:

* Is it a good ad? Why?
* What do you like most about it? Why?
* What do you dislike the most? Why?
* Do you think it "works"? Why or why not?
* How could the ad be improved?
* Could the sender have conveyed the same message using other strategies, other persuasive means? If so, explain.
* Even if you don't believe that this particular ad works or persuades you, is there anything in the ad that still affects you or persuades you indirectly?
* Does the ad have effects on you perhaps not intended by its creators?

---

[2]Lars Thoger Christensen, "How to Analyze an Advertisement." University of Southern Denmark—Odense. Jan. 2004. http://wms-soros.mngt.waikato.ac.nz/NR/rdonlyres/ebabz4jhzmg5fr5p45y pc53mdvuxva5wxhe7323onb4ylelbaq3se5xjrslfc4mi3qgk6dmsx5dqbp/Advertisinganalysis.doc

Discussion and Writing Suggestions

Note: Because Web content frequently changes without warning, not all of the listed videos may be available when you attempt to access them. It is possible that errant searches may lead to other videos with objectionable content. Such videos, as well as user-submitted comments under the specified videos below, do not reflect the views of the authors or of Pearson Publishing.

COMMERCIALS OF THE 1960s

Volkswagen: Snowplow

YouTube Search Terms: vw snow plow commercial [select black and white version]

1. In the 1960s, Volkswagen became famous in the United States not only for its funny-looking cars—so different in style from Detroit's massive passenger vehicles—but also for its "soft-sell" approach to print ads and TV commercials. How does that soft-sell approach work in this ad? What is the sales strategy, as embodied in the relatively primitive visuals and the voice-over track? What exactly is being sold?

2. The closing shot of this commercial shows a snowplow driving past a Volkswagen. How does this image encapsulate the message of the ad? Write a sentence that expresses the message Volkswagen wants to communicate, without regard to the particular visuals of the ad.

Union Carbide: Chick

YouTube Search Terms: union carbide chick

1. Based on the opening image, what is the essential psychological appeal (see Jib Fowles) of this ad?

2. How does the visual (the commercial is unusual in consisting of a single, continuous shot) work *with* and work *against* the soundtrack voice-over? To what extent do you "hear" the narrator's voice—and his message—as you watch the image of the metal box in the beaker of boiling water? To what extent is there a danger that this commercial could backfire and create bad feeling about Union Carbide because of what is portrayed?

Alka Seltzer: Spicy Meatball

YouTube Search Terms: alka seltzer meatball

1. Some TV commercials employ a "fake-out" strategy, based partially on our knowledge of other commercials. How does this approach work in the Alka Seltzer ad? Do you think it is likely to succeed in persuading viewers to buy the product?

2. Like many successful TV commercials, this one relies on humor, grounded in human foibles and imperfections, and based on our experience that if things can go wrong, they generally will. How do the visuals and the audio track of the Alka Seltzer ad employ this kind of humor as a sales strategy?

COMMERCIALS OF THE 1970s

Chanel No. 5: Share the Fantasy

YouTube Search Terms: chanel 5 fantasy

1. In many ways, this celebrated commercial—directed by filmmaker Ridley Scott (*Alien, Blade Runner, Thelma and Louise, Gladiator*)—is, stylistically, at the opposite pole from the gritty Volkswagen "Snowplow" commercial. Comment.

2. Chanel No. 5 is one of those products sold primarily on its "mystique." How do the visuals and the soundtrack of this commercial reinforce that mystique? "Read" the images and interpret them, in light of the product.

3. In terms of Fowles's categories, what are the central appeals of this ad?

Quaker Oats: Mikey

YouTube Search Terms: quaker oats mikey

1. Why don't the older kids want to try Life cereal? How does reluctance tie into Quaker Oats's larger marketing problem with the product? How does the commercial attempt to deal with this problem?

2. Many viewers came to hate this commercial because it was shown repeatedly and because it lasted so many years. Still, it endured because many other viewers found it endearing—and it did the job of publicizing the product. Do you think a commercial such as this one would work today? Explain.

Coca-Cola: Mean Joe Green

YouTube Search Terms: coca cola joe green

1. This commercial is a study in contrasts. Identify some of these contrasts (both visual and aural), and explain how they work as part of the sales strategy.

2. To what emotions does this commercial attempt to appeal? Did you find this appeal successful?

3. Like many commercials, this one is presented as a minidrama, complete with plot, character, setting, theme, and other elements found in longer dramas. Explain the way that the drama functions in this ad, particularly as it concerns the characterization of the two actors.

COMMERCIALS OF THE 1980s

Federal Express (FedEx): Fast-Paced World [with John Moschitta]

YouTube Search Terms: federal express fast talker

1. The actor in this commercial, John Moschitta, was for many years celebrated in the *Guinness Book of World Records* as the world's fastest talker (he was clocked at 586 words per minute). How does Moschitta's unique skill make him an ideal spokesperson for Federal Express?

2. There is always a danger that particularly striking ads may be counterproductive, in that they draw attention to their own cleverness or unusual stylistic qualities, rather than to the product being sold. Put yourself in the position of a Federal Express executive. To what extent might you be concerned that this commercial, clever as it is, would not succeed in making more people select Federal Express as their express delivery service? On the other hand, might any striking commercial for Federal Express be successful if it heightened public recognition of the brand?

Pepsi-Cola: Archaeology

YouTube Search Terms: pepsi cola archaeology

1. Summarize the main selling point of this commercial. How does this selling point relate to (1) the basic situation presented in the commercial and (2) Pepsi's slogan, as it appears at the end?

2. Pepsi-Cola and Coca-Cola have been engaged in fierce rivalry for more than a century. How does this commercial exploit that rivalry to humorous effect? How is each product visually represented in the ad?

3. As contrasted with the Volkswagen "Snowplow" ad or the Quaker Oats "Mikey" ad, this ad features lavish production values and is presented as if it were a science fiction film. How do the sets, costumes, props, and special effects help support the overall sales strategy of the ad?

Levi's: Launderette

YouTube Search Terms: levi's laundrette

1. What is the main appeal of this British ad (in Jib Fowles's terms)? Do you think it is directed primarily to men or women? Explain.

2. How do the reactions of the various characters to the young man in this ad contribute to its overall effect? How does the young man's appearance figure into the overall effect?

3. What role does the musical track (Marvin Gaye's "I Heard It Through the Grapevine") play in this commercial?

COMMERCIALS OF THE 1990s

Jeep: Snow Covered

YouTube Search Terms: jeep snow covered

1. "This may have been the most arrogant commercial ever made," declared the creative director of the agency that produced it. In what way might this be so? Possible arrogance aside, is this an effective advertisement for Jeep? Explain.

2. How do the visuals support the message of the ad? What *is* that message?

3. Which appeals are most evident in this commercial?

Energizer: Darth Vader

YouTube Search Terms: energizer darth vader

1. The Energizer bunny was featured in numerous commercials of the 1990s, generally in settings where its sudden appearance was totally unexpected. How do the creators of this add draw upon the *Star Wars* mythology to support their sales pitch? In what way is the strategy of this ad similar to that of Alka Seltzer's "Spicy Meatball"?

2. In a sentence, summarize the message of this ad—without mentioning *Star Wars* or Darth Vader.

Got Milk? (California Milk Processor Board): Aaron Burr [original Got Milk? Commercial]

YouTube Search Terms: got milk burr

1. The opening of this commercial is intended to convey a sense of culture and sophistication. How do the images and the soundtrack do this? Why is this "setup" necessary in terms of the ad's message? What is that message?

2. In the latter half of the commercial, how does the accelerated pace of the editing and camera work—and of the soundtrack—contribute to the ad's overall impact?

COMMERCIALS OF THE 2000s

The Gap: Pardon Our Dust

YouTube Search Terms: gap dust

1. This commercial was directed by filmmaker Spike Jonze (*Adaptation*, *Where the Wild Things Are*). Describe your reactions as you watched this ad. What did you think was happening as the mayhem within the store accelerated? What is the effect of the "Pardon Our Dust" title when it appears? What is the relationship of the prior visuals and the soundtrack (including the music of Grieg's "In the Hall of the Mountain King") to the last two titles?

2. In Jib Fowles's terms ("Advertising's Fifteen Basic Appeals"), to what desires is this commercial intended to appeal?

3. According to the Web site "Top 10 Coolest Commercials by Movie Directors," Spike Jonze was asked by Gap executives to produce a commercial about the stores' new look. Bewildered by what Jonze delivered, the company ran the commercial in a few cities, then pulled it off the air after about a month. Did the company make the right decision (from a marketing standpoint)?

Honda: Physics

YouTube Search Terms: honda physics

1. Put yourself in the position of the ad agency copywriters for Honda *before* they conceived of this particular ad. What is your main selling point? Express, in a sentence, what you want to communicate to the public about Honda automobiles and engineering.

2. This commercial involves no computer graphics or digital tricks; everything that happens is real. All the components we see came from the disassembling of two Honda Accords. The voice is that of *Lake Woebegon Days* author Garrison Keillor. According to Honda, this single continuous shot required 606 takes—meaning that for the first 605 takes, something, usually minor, went wrong, and the recording team had to install the setup again and again. There is always a danger (for the client) that memorable commercials such as this one will amaze and impress viewers but will also fail to implant brand identification in their minds. Do you think there may be such a problem with this commercial? To what extent are viewers who have seen it likely, days or weeks later, to identify it with Honda and to associate whatever message (if any) they draw from the commercial with the particular qualities of Honda automobiles?

Sony Bravia: Bunnies

YouTube Search Terms: sony bunnies

1. Some of the same visual techniques used in this ad (to portray an unstoppable swarm of creatures that speedily overrun an urban area) have also been used—to very different effect—in horror films. What mood is conveyed—and how—by the visual and soundtrack elements of this commercial?

2. To what consumer desires (refer to Jib Fowles's categories) is this commercial designed to appeal?

3. Discuss how some of the visual techniques and special effects of this ad contribute to its effectiveness in conveying the benefits of the Sony Bravia.

Dove: Onslaught

YouTube Search Terms: dove onslaught

1. What is the message of this ad? How does the cinematic style of the visuals reinforce that message? Focus, in particular, on the contrasting visual styles used for the child and (later in the ad) her classmates, on the one hand, and the rest of the images, on the other. Consider, for example, how long the first image remains on screen, compared to those that follow.

2. How many of Jib Fowles's fifteen basic appeals do you detect at work in this ad? How do these appeals work to convey the essential contrast of values underlying the ad?

Tide to Go: Interview

YouTube Search Terms: tide to go interview

1. What is the message of this ad? How do the simple visuals and the more complex soundtrack work together (and against one another) to support that idea? How does that idea relate to one or more of Fowles's fifteen basic appeals?

2. Like many contemporary TV ads, this one relies on humor. To what extent do you find humor used effectively here? What is the source of the humor? How do the two actors help create that humor? How is this humor rooted in common concerns and fears that we all share?

Planters Peanuts: Perfume

YouTube Search Terms: planters perfume

1. Many of the elements in this ad are also found in perfume commercials. How are these elements used here to comic effect? Compare the mood and the visual style of this ad to that of a real perfume ad, the Chanel No. 5 "Share the Fantasy" commercial. Of what other commercials does this one remind you? Why?

2. Like the Gap "Pardon Our Dust" commercial, the Planters ad relies on the visual motif of comic mayhem. Do you think such visuals are an effective way of selling the product? Explain.

VW, "The Force"

YouTube Search Terms: volkswagen the force

1. How does this commercial play against the Darth Vader image and mythology for the purpose of selling cars?

2. This commercial became a cultural phenomenon, with the child star even appearing on *Today* for an interview. Why do you think it became so popular? Consider the style, the storyline, the images and sound, and the message.

Chrysler, "Detroit"

YouTube Search Terms: chrysler detroit or *chrysler eminem*

1. This commercial juxtaposes images of the long-decayed landscape of America's onetime car capital with images of Detroit viewed from a moving car, and later, of a luxury automobile in motion. What kind of images of the city are viewed from the car, and what meanings or emotions do they evoke? How successful do you judge the clashing motifs of decay and luxury in achieving the objectives of the ad's message? What *is* that message?

2. The soundtrack to this commercial features a song by Eminem (born Marshall Bruce Mathers III), an American rapper, producer, songwriter, actor, and half of the Detroit hip-hop duo Bad Meets Evil. Eminem does have a personal connection to Detroit, but to what extent do you think that the producers of the commercial made a sound choice in using this particular musician in this particular commercial?

3. Compare and contrast the intended audiences for this commercial and the Volkswagen "Darth Vader" commercial above. Then compare and contrast the audience for either of these two commercials with Volkswagen "Snowplow," Jeep "Snow Covered," and Honda "Physics." What assumptions are made in these commercials about the tastes and values of their respective audiences?

DirecTV, "Dog Collar"

YouTube Search Terms: directv dog collar

1. Many commercials rely on humor to help convey the advertiser's message. Among such ads represented in this portfolio: Alka Seltzer, "Spicy Meatball"; Quaker Oats, "Mikey"; FedEx, "Fast-Paced World"; Pepsi Cola, "Archaeology"; Energizer, "Darth Vader" (and another Darth Vader ad, VW, "The Force"); Got Milk? "Aaron Burr"; and Tide to Go, "Interview." How does the humor in DirecTV's commercial compare and contrast to the humor in some of these other funny commercials? Consider, for example, the consumer need (in Jib Fowles' scheme) to which this commercial claims to be appealing—as opposed to the need to which it is actually appealing. Consider, also, what it is we're actually smiling at when we view these commercials.

2. Would this commercial help persuade you (by its ironclad chain of reasoning) to switch from cable to DirecTV? If not, why do you think the company decided to create and air it?

3. The "Dog Collar" spot was one of a series of three similarly themed commercials created by DirecTV in 2012. Among the others in the series: "Don't Wake Up in a Roadside Ditch" and "Stop Taking in Stray Animals." Here's your chance to be a famous copywriter: Create another 30-second spot in this series. Describe the visuals, and write the script for the voice-over.

ADDITIONAL TV COMMERCIALS

Note: Unless otherwise indicated, all commercials listed were produced in the United States.

> **Democratic National Committee:** "Daisy Girl" (1964)
> *YouTube search terms: democratic daisy ad*
>
> **American Tourister Luggage:** Gorilla (1969)
> *YouTube search terms: luggage gorilla*
>
> **Chevrolet:** "Baseball, Hot Dogs, Apple Pie" (1969)
> *YouTube search terms: america baseball hotdogs*
>
> **Keep America Beautiful:** "Crying Indian" (1970)
> *YouTube search terms: america crying indian*

Coca Cola: "Hilltop" ("I'd Like to Buy the World a Coke") (1971)

YouTube search terms: buy world coke 1971

Hovis: "Bike Ride" (UK, 1973) [shot by Ridley Scott]

YouTube search terms: hovis bike

Xerox: "Monks" (1975)

YouTube search terms: xerox monks

Hebrew National: "Higher Authority" (1975)

YouTube search terms: hebrew national higher

BASF: "Dear John" (New Zealand, 1979)

YouTube search terms: basf dear john

Lego: "Kipper" (UK, 1980)

YouTube search terms: lego kipper

Apple: Macintosh (1984)

YouTube search terms: apple macintosh

Sony Trinitron: "Lifespan" (UK, 1984)

YouTube search terms: sony trinitron advert

American Express: "Stephen King: (1984)

YouTube search terms: american express king

The Guardian: "Points of View" (UK, 1987)

YouTube search terms: guardian points of view

Volkswagen: "Changes" (UK, 1988)

YouTube Search Terms: vw changes

Energizer: "Bunny Introduction" (1989)

YouTube search terms: energizer bunny introduction 1989

Dunlop: "Tested for the Unexpected" (1993)

YouTube search terms: dunlop tested unexpected

Swedish Televerket: "Noxin" (Sweden, 1993)

YouTube Search Terms: Noxin

Little Caesar's Pizza: "Training Camp" (1994)

YouTube search terms: caesar's training camp

Campbell's Soup: Winter Commercial (1995)

YouTube search terms: campbell's soup winter

California Milk Processor Board: "Got Milk? Heaven" (1996)

YouTube search terms: got milk heaven

Ameriquest Mortgage: "Plane Ride" (2008)

YouTube search terms: ameriquest plane ride

Audi: "Oil Parade" (2009)

YouTube search terms: audi oil parade

Jack in the Box: "Junk in the Box" (2009)

YouTube search terms: jack in the box junk in the box

Synthesis Activities

1. Select one *category* of advertisements (cigarettes, alcohol, etc.) represented in the ad portfolio. Compare and contrast the types of appeals underlying these ads, as discussed by Fowles. To what extent do you notice significant shifts of appeal from the 1940s to the present? Which types of appeal seem to you most effective with particular product categories? Is it more likely, for example, that people will buy cigarettes because they want to feel autonomous or because the cigarettes will make them more attractive to the opposite sex?

2. Select a series of ads in different product categories that all appear to rely on the same primary appeal—perhaps the appeal to sex or the appeal to affiliation. Compare and contrast the overall strategies of these ads. Draw upon Fowles and other authors represented in this chapter to develop your ideas. To what extent do your analyses support arguments often made by social critics (and advertising people) that what people are really buying is the image, rather than the product?

3. Discuss how a selection of ads reveals shifting cultural attitudes over the past six decades toward either (a) gender relations; (b) romance between men and women; (c) smoking; or (d) automobiles. In the case of *a* or *b*, the ads don't have to be for the same category of product. In terms of their underlying appeal, in terms of the implicit or explicit messages embodied both in the text and the graphics, how and to what extent do the ads reveal that attitudes of the target audiences have changed over the years?

4. Select a TV commercial or a TV ad campaign (for example, for Sprint phone service) and analyze the commercial(s) in terms of Fowles's categories, as well as the discussions of Bovée et al. in this chapter. To what extent do the principles discussed by these authors apply to broadcast, as well as to print ads? What are the special requirements of TV advertising?

5. Find a small group of ads that rely upon little or no body copy—just a graphic, perhaps a headline, and the product name. What common features underlie the marketing strategies of such ads? What kinds of appeals do they make? How do their graphic aspects compare? What makes the need for text superfluous?

6. As indicated in the introduction to this chapter, social critics have charged advertising with numerous offenses: "It fosters materialism, it psychologically manipulates people to buy things they don't need, it perpetuates gender and racial stereotypes (particularly in its illustrations), it is deceptive, it is offensive,

it debases the language..." To what extent do some of the advertisements presented in the ad portfolio (and perhaps others of your own choosing) demonstrate the truth of one or more of these charges? In developing your response, draw upon some of the ads in the portfolio (or elsewhere).

7. Read the textual content (headlines and body text) of several ads *without* paying attention (if possible) to the graphics. Compare the effectiveness of the headline and body text by themselves with the effectiveness of the ads, *including* the graphic elements. Focusing on a group of related ads (related by product category, by appeal, by decade, etc.), devise an explanation of how graphics work to effectively communicate the appeal and meaning of the products advertised.

8. Many ads employ humor—in the graphics, in the body copy, or both—to sell a product. Examine a group of advertisements that rely on humor to make their appeal, and explain how they work. For example, do they play off an incongruity between one element of the ad and another (such as between the headline and the graphic), or between one element of the ad (or the basic message of the ad) and what we know or assume to be the case in the "real world"? Do they employ wordplay or irony? Do they picture people doing funny things (funny because inappropriate or unrealistic)? What appeal underlies the humor? Aggression? Sex? Nurturing? Based on your examination and analyses, what appear to be some of the more effective ways of employing humor?

9. Think of a new product that you have just invented. This product, in your opinion, will revolutionize the world of (fill in the blank). Devise an advertisement to announce this product to the world. Consider (or reject) using a celebrity to help sell your product. Select the basic appeal of your product (see Fowles). Then, applying concepts and principles discussed by Bovée et al. in this chapter, write the headline, subhead, and body copy for the product. Sketch out (or at least describe) the graphic that will accompany the text. Show your proposed ad to one or more of your classmates, get reactions, and then revise the ad, taking into account your market feedback.

10. Imagine that you own a small business—perhaps an independent coffee shop (not Starbucks, Peet's, or Coffee Bean), a video game company, or a pedicab service that conveys tourists around a chic beach town. Devise an ad that announces your services and extols its benefits. Apply the principles discussed by Fowles and the other writers in this chapter.

11. Write a parody ad—one that would never ordinarily be written—applying the selling principles discussed by Fowles and Bovée et al. in this chapter. For example, imagine you are the manager of the Globe Theatre in Elizabethan England and want to sell season tickets to this season's plays, including a couple of new tragedies by your playwright-in-residence, Will Shakespeare. Or imagine that you are trying to sell Remington typewriters in the age of computers (no software glitches!). Or—as long as people are selling bottled water—you have found a way to package and sell air. Advertisers can reportedly sell anything with the right message. Give it your best shot.

12. Based on the reading you have done in this chapter, discuss the extent to which you believe advertisements create needs in consumers, reflect existing needs, or some combination of both. In developing your paper, draw on both particular advertisements and on the more theoretical overviews of advertising developed in the chapter.

13. Select one advertisement and conduct two analyses of it, using two different analytical principles—perhaps one from Fowles's list of fifteen emotional appeals and one from Bovée's "Checklist for Producing Excellent Copy" (p. 573). Having conducted your analyses and developed your insights, compare and contrast the strengths and weaknesses of the analytical principles you've employed. Conclude more broadly with a discussion of how a single analytical principle can close down, as well as open up, understanding of an object under study.

14. As you have seen, advertisements change over time, both across product categories and within categories. And yet the advertisements remain a constant, their presence built on the assumption that consumers can be swayed both overtly and covertly in making purchasing decisions. In a paper drawing on the selections in this chapter, develop a theory on why ads change over time. Is it because people's needs have changed and, therefore, new ads are required? (Do the older ads appeal to the same needs as newer ads?) In developing your discussion, you might track the changes over time in one product category.

RESEARCH ACTIVITIES

1. Drawing upon contemporary magazines (or magazines from a given period), select a set of advertisements in a particular product category. Analyze these advertisements according to Fowles's categories, and assess their effectiveness in terms of the discussions of Bovée et al. in this chapter.

2. Select a particular product that has been selling for at least twenty-five years (e.g., Bayer aspirin, Tide detergent, IBM computers, Oldsmobile—as in "This is not your father's Oldsmobile") and trace the history of print advertising for this product over the years. To what extent has the advertising changed over the years? To what extent has the essential sales appeal remained the same? In addition to examining the ads themselves, you may want to research the company and its marketing practices. You will find two business databases particularly useful: ABI/INFORM and the academic version of LexisNexis.

3. One of the landmark campaigns in American advertising was Doyle Dane Bernbach's series of ads for the Volkswagen Beetle in the 1960s. In effect a rebellion against standard auto advertising, the VW ads' Unique Selling Proposition was that ugly is beautiful—an appeal that was overwhelmingly successful. Research the VW ad campaign for this period, setting it in the context of the agency's overall marketing strategy.

4. Among the great marketing debacles of recent decades was Coca-Cola's development in 1985 of a new formula for its soft drink that (at least temporarily) replaced the much-beloved old formula. Research this major development in soft drink history, focusing on the marketing of New Coke and the attempt of the Atlanta-based Coca-Coca Company to deal with the public reception of its new product.

5. Advertising agencies are hired not only by manufacturers and by service industries; they are also hired by political candidates. In fact, one of the common complaints about American politics is that candidates for public office are marketed just as if they were bars of soap. Select a particular presidential or gubernatorial election and research the print and broadcast advertising used by the rival candidates. You may want to examine the ads not only of the candidates of the major parties, but also the candidates of the smaller parties, such as the Green and the Libertarian parties. How do the appeals and strategies used by product ads compare and contrast with those used in ads for political candidates?

6. Public service ads comprise another major category of advertising (in addition to product and service advertising and political advertising). Such ads have been used to recruit people to military service, to get citizens to buy war bonds, to obtain contributions for charitable causes, to get people to support or oppose strikes, to persuade people to stop using (or not to start using) drugs, to prevent drunk driving, etc. Locate a group of public service ads, describe them, and assess their effectiveness. Draw upon Fowles and Bovée et al. in developing your conclusions.

7. Research advertising in American magazines and newspapers before World War II. Focus on a limited number of product lines—for example, soft drinks, soap and beauty products, health-related products. What kind of differences do you see between ads in the first part of the twentieth century and more recent or contemporary advertising for the same types of products? In general, how have the predominant types of appeals used to sell products in the past changed (if they have) with the times? How are the graphics of early ads different from preferred graphics today? How has the body copy changed? (Hint: You may want to be on the alert for ads that make primarily negative appeals—i.e., what may happen to you if you don't use the product advertised.)

15

Obedience to Authority

Would you obey an order to inflict pain on another person? Most of us, if confronted with this question, would probably be quick to answer, "Never!" Yet if the conclusions of researchers are to be trusted, it is not psychopaths who kill noncombatant civilians in wartime and torture victims in prisons around the world, but rather ordinary people following orders—or caught up in the singularly *un*ordinary circumstances of the moment. People obey. This is a basic, necessary fact of human society. As psychologist Stanley Milgram has written, "Obedience is as basic an element in the structure of social life as one can point to. Some system of authority is a requirement of all communal living."

The question, then, is not, "Should we obey the orders of an authority figure?" but rather, "To what *extent* should we obey?" Each generation seems to give new meaning to these questions. During the Vietnam War, a number of American soldiers followed a commander's orders and murdered civilians in the hamlet of My Lai. In 1987, former White House military aide Oliver North was prosecuted for illegally diverting money raised by selling arms to Iran—considered by the U.S. government to be a terrorist state—to fund the anticommunist Contra (resistance) fighters in Nicaragua. North's attorneys claimed that he was following the orders of his superiors. And, although North was found guilty,* the judge who sentenced him to perform community service (there was no prison sentence) largely agreed with this defense when he called North a pawn in a larger game played by senior officials in the Reagan administration. In the 1990s, the world was horrified by genocidal violence in Rwanda and in the former nation of Yugoslavia. These were civil wars, in which people who had been living for generations as neighbors suddenly, upon the instigation and orders of their leaders, turned upon and slaughtered one another.

In April 2004, the world (particularly, the Muslim world) was horrified by accounts—and graphic photographs—of the degrading torture and humiliation of Iraqi prisoners at the hands of American soldiers in a Baghdad prison.

---

*In July 1990, North's conviction was overturned on appeal.

Among the questions raised by this incident: Were these soldiers obeying orders to "soften up" the prisoners for interrogation? Were they fulfilling the roles of prison guards they thought were expected of them? Were they abusing others because, given the circumstances, they could? President Bush asserted that this kind of abuse "does not reflect the nature of the American people." Yet, in January 2012, Americans learned of another act presumably not representative of its well-trained soldiers: U.S. Marines were videotaped urinating on the bodies of insurgents in Afghanistan—a desecration that some consider a war crime. And, again, a powerful U.S. official, this time Defense Secretary Leon Panetta, decried the "utterly deplorable" behavior. But as you will read in this chapter, we are likely to be unpleasantly surprised by revelations of what people can do when they find themselves in unfamiliar and dehumanizing circumstances. The chapter takes on a fundamental question: What is our "nature," not only as Americans but, more fundamentally, as human beings?

In less-dramatic ways, conflicts over the extent to which we obey orders surface in everyday life. At one point or another, you may face a moral dilemma at work. Perhaps it will take this form: The boss tells you to overlook file X in preparing a report for a certain client. But you're sure that file X pertains directly to the report and contains information that will alarm the client. What should you do? The dilemmas of obedience also emerge on some campuses with the rite of fraternity or sports-related hazing. Psychologists Janice Gibson and Mika Haritos-Fatouros have made the startling observation that whether the obedience in question involves a pledge's joining a fraternity or a torturer's joining an elite military corps, the *process* by which one acquiesces to a superior's order (and thereby becomes a member of the group) is remarkably the same.

In this chapter, you will explore the dilemmas inherent in obeying the orders of an authority figure. First, psychoanalyst and philosopher Erich Fromm discusses the comforts of obedience in "Disobedience as a Psychological and Moral Problem." Next, in "The Power of Situations," social psychologists Lee Ross and Richard Nisbett provide an overview of the situational forces that can strongly influence behavior. Psychologist Stanley Milgram then reports on his landmark study, which revealed the extent to which ordinary individuals will obey the clearly immoral orders of an authority figure. The results were startling, not only to the psychiatrists who predicted that few people would follow such orders, but also to many other social scientists: some applauded Milgram for his fiendishly ingenious design, some bitterly attacked him for unethical procedures. Following Milgram, a journalist who writes on psychology and neuroscience explores the "paradox of power"—the ways in which traits such as kindness and generosity, which promote people's rise in organizations, tend to vanish when they assume control. Next, columnist David Brooks of the *New York Times* reviews other paradoxes of power—of both leadership, among those exercising authority, and what he calls "followership," among those who willfully obey leaders—or not.

The chapter concludes with three selections devoted to the special case of obedience in groups. Writer Doris Lessing sets the context by discussing how we are quick to call ourselves individualists without pausing to appreciate the power of situational influences on our behavior. Next, psychologist Solomon Asch describes a classic experiment (involving the apparent length of lines) that demonstrates the influence of group pressure on individual judgment. Finally, you will be directed online for a dramatic account of a mock-prison experiment conducted at Stanford University by psychologist Philip Zimbardo, who found that student volunteers exhibited astonishingly convincing authoritarian and obedient attitudes as they playacted at being prisoners and guards.

DISOBEDIENCE AS A PSYCHOLOGICAL AND MORAL PROBLEM

Erich Fromm

Erich Fromm (1900–1980) was one of the twentieth century's distinguished writers and thinkers. Psychoanalyst and philosopher, historian and sociologist, he ranged widely in his interests and defied easy characterization. Fromm studied the works of Freud and Marx closely, and published on them both, but he was not aligned strictly with either. In much of his voluminous writing, he struggled to articulate a view that could help bridge ideological and personal conflicts and bring dignity to those who struggled with isolation in the industrial world. Author of more than thirty books and contributor to numerous edited collections and journals, Fromm is best known for *Escape from Freedom* (1941), *The Art of Loving* (1956), and *To Have or To Be?* (1976).

In the essay that follows, first published in 1963, Fromm discusses the seductive comforts of obedience, and he makes distinctions among varieties of obedience, some of which he believes are destructive, and others, life affirming. His thoughts on nuclear annihilation may seem dated in these days of post–Cold War cooperation, but it is worth remembering that Fromm wrote his essay just after the Cuban missile crisis, when fears of a third world war ran high. (We might note that today, despite the welcome reductions of nuclear stockpiles, the United States and Russia still possess—and retain battle plans for—thousands of warheads. And, in the wake of the 9/11 attacks, the threat of terrorists acquiring and using nuclear weapons against the United States seems very real.) On the major points of his essay, concerning the psychological and moral problems of obedience, Fromm remains as pertinent today as when he wrote more than forty years ago.

For centuries kings, priests, feudal lords, industrial bosses, and parents have insisted that *obedience is a virtue* and that *disobedience is a vice*. In order to introduce another point of view, let us set against this position the following statement: *human history began with an act of disobedience, and it is not unlikely that it will be terminated by an act of obedience.*

Human history was ushered in by an act of disobedience according to the Hebrew and Greek myths. Adam and Eve, living in the Garden of Eden, were part of nature; they were in harmony with it, yet did not transcend it. They were in nature as the fetus is in the womb of the mother. They were human, and at the same time not yet human. All this changed when they disobeyed an order.

By breaking the ties with earth and mother, by cutting the umbilical cord, man emerged from a prehuman harmony and was able to take the first step into independence and freedom. The act of disobedience set Adam and Eve free and opened their eyes. They recognized each other as strangers and the world outside them as strange and even hostile. Their act of disobedience broke the primary bond with nature and made them individuals. "Original sin," far from corrupting man, set him free; it was the beginning of history. Man had to leave the Garden of Eden in order to learn to rely on his own powers and to become fully human.

The prophets, in their messianic concept, confirmed the idea that man had been right in disobeying; that he had not been corrupted by his "sin," but freed from the fetters of pre-human harmony. For the prophets, *history* is the place where man becomes human; during its unfolding he develops his powers of reason and of love until he creates a new harmony between himself, his fellow man, and nature. This new harmony is described as "the end of days," that period of history in which there is peace between man and man, between man and nature. It is a "new" paradise created by man himself, and one which he alone could create because he was forced to leave the "old" paradise as a result of his disobedience.

Just as the Hebrew myth of Adam and Eve, so the Greek myth of Prometheus sees all human civilization based on an act of disobedience. Prometheus, in stealing the fire from the gods, lays the foundation for the evolution of man. There would be no human history were it not for Prometheus' "crime." He, like Adam and Eve, is punished for his disobedience. But he does not repent and ask for forgiveness. On the contrary, he proudly says: "I would rather be chained to this rock than be the obedient servant of the gods."

5   Man has continued to evolve by acts of disobedience. Not only was his spiritual development possible only because there were men who dared to say no to the powers that be in the name of their conscience or their faith, but also his intellectual development was dependent on the capacity for being disobedient— disobedient to authorities who tried to muzzle new thoughts and to the authority of long-established opinions which declared a change to be nonsense.

If the capacity for disobedience constituted the beginning of human history, obedience might very well, as I have said, cause the end of human history. I am not speaking symbolically or poetically. There is the possibility, or even the probability, that the human race will destroy civilization and even all life upon earth within the next five to ten years. There is no rationality or sense in it. But the fact is that, while we are living technically in the Atomic Age, the majority of men—including most of those who are in power—still live emotionally in the Stone Age; that while our mathematics, astronomy, and the natural sciences are of the twentieth century, most of our ideas about politics, the state, and society lag far behind the age of science. If mankind commits suicide it will be because people will obey those who command them to push the deadly buttons; because they will obey the archaic passions of fear, hate, and greed; because they will obey obsolete clichés of State sovereignty and national honor.

The Soviet leaders talk much about revolutions, and we in the "free world" talk much about freedom. Yet they and we discourage disobedience—in the Soviet Union explicitly and by force, in the free world implicitly and by the more subtle methods of persuasion.

But I do not mean to say that all disobedience is a virtue and all obedience is a vice. Such a view would ignore the dialectical relationship between obedience and disobedience. Whenever the principles which are obeyed and those which are disobeyed are irreconcilable, an act of obedience to one principle is necessarily an act of disobedience to its counterpart and vice versa. Antigone is the classic example of this dichotomy. By obeying the inhuman laws of the State, Antigone necessarily would disobey the laws of humanity. By obeying the latter, she must disobey the former. All martyrs of religious faiths, of freedom, and of science have had to disobey those who wanted to muzzle them in order to obey their own consciences, the laws of humanity, and of reason. If a man can only obey and not disobey, he is a slave; if he can only disobey and not obey, he is a rebel (not a revolutionary); he acts out of anger, disappointment, resentment, yet not in the name of a conviction or a principle.

However, in order to prevent a confusion of terms an important qualification must be made. Obedience to a person, institution, or power (heteronomous obedience) is submission; it implies the abdication of my autonomy and the acceptance of a foreign will or judgment in place of my own. Obedience to my own reason or conviction (autonomous obedience) is not an act of submission but one of affirmation. My conviction and my judgment, if authentically mine, are part of me. If I follow them rather than the judgment of others, I am being myself; hence the word *obey* can be applied only in a metaphorical sense and with a meaning which is fundamentally different from the one in the case of "heteronomous obedience."

But this distinction still needs two further qualifications, one with regard to the concept of conscience and the other with regard to the concept of authority.

10   The word *conscience* is used to express two phenomena which are quite distinct from each other. One is the "authoritarian conscience" which is the internalized voice of an authority whom we are eager to please and afraid of displeasing. This authoritarian conscience is what most people experience when they obey their conscience. It is also the conscience which Freud speaks of, and which he called "Super-Ego." This Super-Ego represents the internalized commands and prohibitions of father, accepted by the son out of fear. Different from the authoritarian conscience is the "humanistic conscience"; this is the voice present in every human being and independent from external sanctions and rewards. Humanistic conscience is based on the fact that as human beings we have an intuitive knowledge of what is human and inhuman, what is conducive of life and what is destructive of life. This conscience serves our functioning as human beings. It is the voice which calls us back to ourselves, to our humanity.

Authoritarian conscience (Super-Ego) is still obedience to a power outside of myself, even though this power has been internalized. Consciously I believe that I am following *my* conscience; in effect, however, I have swallowed the principles of *power*; just because of the illusion that humanistic conscience and Super-Ego are identical, internalized authority is so much more effective than the authority which is clearly experienced as not being part of me. Obedience to the "authoritarian conscience," like all obedience to outside thoughts and power, tends to debilitate "humanistic conscience," the ability to be and to judge oneself.

The statement, on the other hand, that obedience to another person is *ipso facto* submission needs also to be qualified by distinguishing "irrational" from "rational" authority. An example of rational authority is to be found in the relationship between student and teacher; one of irrational authority in the relationship between slave and master. Both relationships are based on the fact that the authority of the person in command is accepted. Dynamically, however, they are of a different nature. The interests of the teacher and the student, in the ideal case, lie in the same direction. The teacher is satisfied if he succeeds in furthering the student; if he has failed to do so, the failure is his and the student's. The slave owner, on the other hand, wants to exploit the slave as much as possible. The more he gets out of him the more satisfied he is. At the same time, the slave tries to defend as best he can his claims for a minimum of happiness. The interests of slave and master are antagonistic, because what is advantageous to the one is detrimental to the other. The superiority of the one over the other has a different function in each case; in the first it is the condition for the furtherance of the person subjected to the authority, and in the second it is the condition for his exploitation. Another distinction runs parallel to this: rational authority is rational because the authority, whether it is held by a teacher or a captain of a ship giving orders in an emergency, acts in the name of reason which, being universal, I can accept without submitting. Irrational authority has to use force or suggestion, because no one would let himself be exploited if he were free to prevent it.

Why is man so prone to obey and why is it so difficult for him to disobey? As long as I am obedient to the power of the State, the Church, or public opinion, I feel safe and protected. In fact it makes little difference what power it is that I am obedient to. It is always an institution, or men, who use force in one form or another and who fraudulently claim omniscience and omnipotence. My obedience makes me part of the power I worship, and hence I feel strong. I can make no error, since it decides for me; I cannot be alone, because it watches over me; I cannot commit a sin, because it does not let me do so, and even if I do sin, the punishment is only the way of returning to the almighty power.

In order to disobey, one must have the courage to be alone, to err, and to sin. But courage is not enough. The capacity for courage depends on a person's state of development. Only if a person has emerged from mother's lap and father's commands, only if he has emerged as a fully developed individual and thus has acquired the capacity to think and feel for himself, only then can he have the courage to say "no" to power, to disobey.

15   A person can become free through acts of disobedience by learning to say no to power. But not only is the capacity for disobedience the condition for

freedom; freedom is also the condition for disobedience. If I am afraid of freedom, I cannot dare to say "no," I cannot have the courage to be disobedient. Indeed, freedom and the capacity for disobedience are inseparable; hence any social, political, and religious system which proclaims freedom, yet stamps out disobedience, cannot speak the truth.

There is another reason why it is so difficult to dare to disobey, to say "no" to power. During most of human history obedience has been identified with virtue and disobedience with sin. The reason is simple: thus far throughout most of history a minority has ruled over the majority. This rule was made necessary by the fact that there was only enough of the good things of life for the few, and only the crumbs remained for the many. If the few wanted to enjoy the good things and, beyond that, to have the many serve them and work for them, one condition was necessary: the many had to learn obedience. To be sure, obedience can be established by sheer force. But this method has many disadvantages. It constitutes a constant threat that one day the many might have the means to overthrow the few by force; furthermore there are many kinds of work which cannot be done properly if nothing but fear is behind the obedience. Hence the obedience which is only rooted in the fear of force must be transformed into one rooted in man's heart. Man must want and even need to obey, instead of only fearing to disobey. If this is to be achieved, power must assume the qualities of the All Good, of the All Wise; it must become All Knowing. If this happens, power can proclaim that disobedience is sin and obedience virtue; and once this has been proclaimed, the many can accept obedience because it is good and detest disobedience because it is bad, rather than to detest themselves for being cowards. From Luther to the nineteenth century one was concerned with overt and explicit authorities. Luther, the pope, the princes, wanted to uphold it; the middle class, the workers, the philosophers, tried to uproot it. The fight against authority in the State as well as in the family was often the very basis for the development of an independent and daring person. The fight against authority was inseparable from the intellectual mood which characterized the philosophers of the enlightenment and the scientists. This "critical mood" was one of faith in reason, and at the same time of doubt in everything which is said or thought, inasmuch as it is based on tradition, superstition, custom, power. The principles *sapere aude* and *de omnibus est dubitandum*—"dare to be wise" and "of all one must doubt"—were characteristic of the attitude which permitted and furthered the capacity to say "no."

The case of Adolf Eichmann [see note, p. 638] is symbolic of our situation and has a significance far beyond the one in which his accusers in the courtroom in Jerusalem were concerned with. Eichmann is a symbol of the organization man, of the alienated bureaucrat for whom men, women and children have become numbers. He is a symbol of all of us. We can see ourselves in Eichmann. But the most frightening thing about him is that after the entire story was told in terms of his own admissions, he was able in perfect good faith to plead his innocence. It is clear that if he were once more in the same situation he would do it again. And so would we—and so do we.

The organization man has lost the capacity to disobey, he is not even aware of the fact that he obeys. At this point in history the capacity to doubt, to criticize, and to disobey may be all that stands between a future for mankind and the end of civilization.

● Review Questions

1. What does Fromm mean when he writes that disobedience is "the first step into independence and freedom"?

2. Fromm writes that history began with an act of disobedience and will likely end with an act of obedience. What does he mean?

3. What is the difference between "heteronomous obedience" and "autonomous obedience"?

4. How does Fromm distinguish between "authoritarian conscience" and "humanistic conscience"?

5. When is obedience to another person *not* submission?

6. What are the psychological comforts of obedience, and why would authorities rather have people obey out of love than out of fear?

● Discussion and Writing Suggestions

1. Fromm suggests that scientifically we live in the modern world but that politically and emotionally we live in the Stone Age. As you observe events in the world, both near and far, would you agree? Why?

2. Fromm writes: "If a man can only obey and not disobey, he is a slave; if he can only disobey and not obey, he is a rebel (not a revolutionary)" (¶ 7). Explain Fromm's meaning here. Explain, as well, the implication that to be fully human one must have the freedom to both obey and disobey.

3. Fromm writes that "obedience makes me part of the power I worship, and hence I feel strong" (¶ 13). Does this statement ring true for you? Discuss, in writing, an occasion in which you felt powerful because you obeyed a group norm.

4. In ¶s 15 and 16, Fromm equates obedience with cowardice. Can you identify a situation in which you were obedient but, now that you reflect on it, were also cowardly? That is, can you recall a time when you caved in to a group but now wish you hadn't? Explain.

5. Fromm says that we can see ourselves in Adolf Eichmann—that as an organization man he "has lost the capacity to disobey, he is not even aware of the fact that he obeys." To what extent do you recognize yourself in this portrait?

THE POWER OF SITUATIONS

Lee Ross and Richard E. Nisbett

Erich Fromm conceives of obedience and disobedience as products of one's character or of one's moral choices. In the selection that follows, Lee Ross and Richard E. Nisbett present findings from experiments in social psychology that suggest that situations, rather than some essential personal quality or the dictates of one's conscience, tend to determine behavior. From this vantage point, a "helpful" person may not be consistently helpful nor a "kind" person consistently kind. In each new situation, subtle and profound social cues influence our ultimate behavior—which is why, as we all know, people behave inconsistently. According to philosopher Gilbert Harman, "It seems that ordinary attributions of character traits to people are often deeply misguided, and it may even be the case that there is no such thing as character, no ordinary character traits of the sort people think there are, none of the usual moral virtues and vices." Harmon reached this radical notion after reading accounts of the same experiments in social psychology that you are about to read in this chapter. You may not draw the same conclusions, but Ross and Nisbett, Milgram, Asch, Lessing, and the account of the mock-prison experiment will almost certainly convince you that the situation in which we act can powerfully influence our behavior—including our choice to obey or disobey a questionable order.

Lee Ross is a professor of psychology at Stanford University. Richard E. Nisbett is professor of psychology at the University of Michigan. This selection is excerpted from their text *The Person and the Situation: Perspectives of Social Psychology* (1991).

Undergraduates taking their first course in social psychology generally are in search of an interesting and enjoyable experience, and they rarely are disappointed. They find out many fascinating things about human behavior, some of which validate common sense and some of which contradict it. The inherent interest value of the material, amounting to high-level gossip about people and social situations, usually ensures that the students are satisfied consumers.

The experience of serious graduate students, who, over the course of four or five years, are immersed in the problems and the orientation of the field, is rather different. For them, the experience is an intellectually wrenching one. Their most basic assumptions about the nature and the causes of human behavior, and about the very predictability of the social world, are challenged. At the end of the process, their views of human behavior and society will differ profoundly from the views held by most other people in their culture. Some of their new insights and beliefs will be held rather tentatively and applied inconsistently to the social events that unfold around them. Others will be held with great conviction, and will be applied confidently. But ironically, even the new insights that they are most confident about will tend to have the effect of making them less certain than their peers about predicting social behavior and making inferences about particular individuals or groups. Social psychology rivals philosophy in its ability to teach people that they do not truly understand the nature of the world. This book is about that hard-won ignorance and what it tells us about the human condition.

•   •   •

Consider the following scenario: While walking briskly to a meeting some distance across a college campus, John comes across a man slumped in a doorway, asking him for help. Will John offer it, or will he continue on his way? Before answering such a question, most people would want to know more about John. Is he someone known to be callous and unfeeling, or is he renowned for his kindness and concern? Is he a stalwart member of the Campus Outreach Organization, or a mainstay of the Conservative Coalition Against Welfare Abuse? In short, what kind of person is John and how has he behaved when his altruism has been tested in the past? Only with such information in hand, most people would agree, could one make a sensible and confident prediction.

In fact, however, nothing one is likely to know or learn about John would be of much use in helping predict John's behavior in the situation we've described. In particular, the type of information about personality that most laypeople would want to have before making a prediction would prove to be of relatively little value. A half century of research has taught us that in this situation, and in most other novel situations, one cannot predict with any accuracy how particular people will respond. At least one cannot do so using information about an individual's personal dispositions or even about that individual's past behavior.

•   •   •

5   While knowledge about John is of surprisingly little value in predicting whether he will help the person slumped in the doorway, details concerning the specifics of the situation would be invaluable. For example, what was the appearance of the person in the doorway? Was he clearly ill, or might he have been a drunk or, even worse, a nodding dope addict? Did his clothing make him look respectably middle class or decently working class, or did he look like a homeless derelict?

Such considerations are fairly obvious once they are mentioned, and the layperson, upon reflection, will generally concede their importance. But few laypeople would concede, much less anticipate, the relevance of some other, subtler, contextual details that empirical research has shown to be important factors influencing bystander intervention. Darley and Batson (1973) actually confronted people with a version of the situation we've described and found what some of these factors are. Their subjects were students in a religious seminary who were on their way to deliver a practice sermon. If the subjects were in a hurry (because they thought they were late to give a practice sermon), only about 10 percent helped. By contrast, if they were not in a hurry (because they had plenty of time before giving their sermon), about 63 percent of them helped.

Social psychology has by now amassed a vast store of such empirical parables. The tradition here is simple. Pick a generic situation; then identify and manipulate a situational or contextual variable that intuition or past research leads you to believe will make a difference (ideally, a variable whose impact you think most laypeople, or even most of your peers, somehow fail to appreciate), and see what happens. Sometimes, of course, you will be wrong and your manipulation won't "work." But often the situational variable makes quite a bit of difference. Occasionally, in fact, it makes nearly all the difference, and information about traits and individual differences that other people thought all-important proves all but trivial. If so, you have contributed a situationist classic destined to become part of our field's intellectual legacy. Such empirical parables are important because they illustrate the degree to which ordinary men and women are apt to be mistaken about the power of the situation—the power of particular situational features, and the power of situations in general.

People's inflated belief in the importance of personality traits and dispositions, together with their failure to recognize the importance of situational factors in affecting behavior, has been termed the "fundamental attribution error" (Ross, 1977; Nisbett & Ross, 1980; see also Jones, 1979; Gilbert & Jones, 1986). Together with many other social psychologists, we have directed our attention to documenting this...error and attempting to track down its origins.

References

Darley, J. M., & Batson, C. D. (1973). From Jerusalem to Jericho: A study of situational and dispositional variables in helping behavior. *Journal of Personality and Social Psychology, 27,* 100–119.

Gilbert, D. T., & Jones, E. E. (1986). Perceiver-induced constraints: Interpretation of self-generated reality. *Journal of Personality and Social Psychology, 50,* 269–280.

Jones, E. E. (1979). The rocky road from acts to dispositions. *American Psychologist, 34,* 107–117.

Nisbett, R. E., & Ross, L. (1980). *Human inference: Strategies and shortcomings of social judgment.* Englewood Cliffs, NJ: Prentice-Hall.

Ross, L. (1977). The intuitive psychologist and his shortcomings. In L. Berkowitz (Ed.), *Advances in experimental social psychology* (Vol. 10). New York: Academic.

● Review Questions

1. In the final sentence of ¶ 2, what is the "hard-won ignorance" made possible by social psychology? Ross and Nisbett offer an example of this "ignorance." Summarize that example.

2. What is the key predictor of John's behavior in the experiment cited by Ross and Nisbett? How does this predictor defy common sense?

3. What is the "fundamental attribution error"?

● Discussion and Writing Suggestions

1. Conceive of another scenario, analogous to John encountering the man slumped in the doorway. What kinds of situational factors might determine how one behaves when faced with this scenario?

2. How did you react to what is known as the "Good Samaritan" experiment (involving John and the person slumped in the doorway)? Most people would like to think they would behave differently, but the experiments suggest otherwise. Your comments? Can you see yourself responding differently in a variety of circumstances?

3. "Social psychology," write Ross and Nisbett, "rivals philosophy in its ability to teach people that they do not truly understand the nature of the world." How solid do you feel your understanding is of "the world"? If you guessed incorrectly about John and how he would react to the person slumped in the doorway, are you prepared to see your commonsense understanding of how people behave undermined?

4. Reconsider the radical proposition mentioned in the headnote: that based on experiments such as the "Good Samaritan" described in this selection, one might conclude, "It seems that ordinary attributions of character traits to people are often deeply misguided, and it may even be the case that there is no such thing as character, no ordinary character traits of the sort people think there are, none of the usual moral virtues and vices." That is, one might conclude from Asch, Milgram, and the mock-prison experiment at Stanford (which you will view online later in this chapter) that enduring character traits do not determine our behavior; rather, our behavior is determined by situational variables (like whether or not we are late for a meeting). Even assuming you do not accept this extreme view, are you troubled by the assertion that "character" might be a fiction—or, at least, overrated? That people, for example, do not possess some inner quality called "honor" or "loyalty" that is impervious to all situational pressures (such as financial need, health crises, old age, threats to one's family's well-being or safety)? At what point, if any, despite one's misgivings, are situational exigencies likely to overwhelm consistent character?

THE PERILS OF OBEDIENCE

Stanley Milgram

In 1963, a Yale psychologist conducted one of the classic studies on obedience. Stanley Milgram designed an experiment that forced participants either to violate their conscience by obeying the immoral demands of an authority figure or to refuse those demands. Surprisingly, Milgram found that few participants could resist the authority's orders, even when the participants knew that following these orders would result in another person's pain. Were the participants in these experiments incipient mass murderers? No, said Milgram. They were "ordinary people, simply doing their jobs." The implications of Milgram's conclusions are immense—and enduring.

On December 19, 2008, the American Psychological Association (APA) issued the following statement in a press release: "Nearly 50 years after one of the most controversial behavioral experiments in history, a social psychologist has found that people are *still* just as willing to administer what they believe are painful electric shocks to others when urged on by an authority figure" (emphasis added). To satisfy ethical concerns raised in response to the original Milgram experiments, Jerry Burger of Santa Clara University proposed modifications to Milgram's experimental design—and found his subjects to be as fundamentally obedient, depending upon situational factors, as Milgram's.

The questions, therefore, persist: Where does evil reside? What sort of people were responsible for the Holocaust, and for the long list of other atrocities that seem to blight the human record in every generation? Is it a lunatic fringe, a few sick but powerful people who are responsible for atrocities? If so, then we decent folk needn't ever look inside ourselves to understand evil, since (by our definition) evil lurks out there, in "those sick ones." Milgram's study (and Burger's follow-on study) suggested otherwise: that under a special set of circumstances, the obedience we naturally show authority figures can transform us into agents of terror.

The article that follows is one of the longest in this book, and it may help you to know in advance the author's organization. In ¶s 1 through 11, Milgram discusses the larger significance and the history of dilemmas involving obedience to authority; he then summarizes his basic experimental design and follows with a report of one experiment. Milgram organizes the remainder of his article into sections, which he has subtitled "An Unexpected Outcome," "Peculiar Reactions," "The Etiquette of Submission," and "Duty Without Conflict." He begins his conclusion in ¶ 108. If you find the article too long or complex to complete in a single sitting, then plan to read sections at a time, taking notes on each until you're done.

Stanley Milgram (1933–1984) taught and conducted research at Yale and Harvard Universities and at the Graduate Center, City University of New York. He was named Guggenheim Fellow in 1972–1973 and a year later was nominated for the National Book Award for *Obedience to Authority*. His other books include *Television and Antisocial Behavior* (1973), *The City and the Self* (1974), *Human Aggression* (1976), and *The Individual in the Social World* (1977).

Obedience is as basic an element in the structure of social life as one can point to. Some system of authority is a requirement of all communal living, and it is only the person dwelling in isolation who is not forced to respond, with defiance or submission, to the commands of others. For many people, obedience is a deeply ingrained behavior tendency, indeed a potent impulse overriding training in ethics, sympathy, and moral conduct.

    The dilemma inherent in submission to authority is ancient, as old as the story of Abraham, and the question of whether one should obey when commands conflict with conscience has been argued by Plato, dramatized in *Antigone*, and treated to philosophic analysis in almost every historical epoch. Conservative philosophers argue that the very fabric of society is threatened by disobedience, while humanists stress the primacy of the individual conscience.

    The legal and philosophic aspects of obedience are of enormous import, but they say very little about how most people behave in concrete situations. I set up a simple experiment at Yale University to test how much pain an ordinary citizen would inflict on another person simply because he was ordered to by an experimental scientist. Stark authority was pitted against the subjects' strongest moral imperatives against hurting others, and with the subjects' ears ringing with the screams of the victims, authority won more often than not. The extreme willingness of adults to go to almost any lengths on the command of an authority constitutes the chief finding of the study and the fact most urgently demanding explanation.

In the basic experimental design, two people come to a psychology laboratory to take part in a study of memory and learning. One of them is designated as a "teacher" and the other a "learner." The experimenter explains that the study is concerned with the effects of punishment on learning. The learner is conducted into a room, seated in a kind of miniature electric chair; his arms are strapped to prevent excessive movement, and an electrode is attached to his wrist. He is told that he will be read lists of simple word pairs, and that he will then be tested on his ability to remember the second word of a pair when he hears the first one again. Whenever he makes an error, he will receive electric shocks of increasing intensity.

5   The real focus of the experiment is the teacher. After watching the learner being strapped into place, he is seated before an impressive shock generator. The instrument panel consists of thirty level switches set in a horizontal line. Each switch is clearly labeled with a voltage designation ranging from 15 to 450 volts. The following designations are clearly indicated for groups of four switches, going from left to right: Slight Shock, Moderate Shock, Strong Shock, Very Strong Shock, Intense Shock, Extreme Intensity Shock, Danger: Severe Shock. (Two switches after this last designation are simply marked XXX.)

When a switch is depressed, a pilot light corresponding to each switch is illuminated in bright red; an electric buzzing is heard; a blue light, labeled "voltage energizer," flashes; the dial on the voltage meter swings to the right; and various relay clicks sound off.

The upper left-hand corner of the generator is labeled SHOCK GENERATOR, TYPE ZLB, DYSON INSTRUMENT COMPANY, WALTHAM, MASS. OUTPUT 15 VOLTS—450 VOLTS.

Each subject is given a sample 45-volt shock from the generator before his run as teacher, and the jolt strengthens his belief in the authenticity of the machine.

The teacher is a genuinely naive subject who has come to the laboratory for the experiment. The learner, or victim, is actually an actor who receives no shock at all. The point of the experiment is to see how far a person will proceed in a concrete and measurable situation in which he is ordered to inflict increasing pain on a protesting victim.

10   Conflict arises when the man receiving the shock begins to show that he is experiencing discomfort. At 75 volts, he grunts; at 120 volts, he complains loudly; at 150, he demands to be released from the experiment. As the voltage increases, his protests become more vehement and emotional. At 285 volts,

A subject in Stanley Milgram's study of obedience, seated at the "Shock Generator."

his response can be described only as an agonized scream. Soon thereafter, he makes no sound at all.

For the teacher, the situation quickly becomes one of gripping tension. It is not a game for him; conflict is intense and obvious. The manifest suffering of the learner presses him to quit; but each time he hesitates to administer a shock, the experimenter orders him to continue. To extricate himself from this plight, the subject must make a clear break with authority.*

The subject, Gretchen Brandt,[†] is an attractive thirty-one-year-old medical technician who works at the Yale Medical School. She had emigrated from Germany five years before.

On several occasions when the learner complains, she turns to the experimenter coolly and inquires, "Shall I continue?" She promptly returns to her task when the experimenter asks her to do so. At the administration of 210 volts, she turns to the experimenter, remarking firmly, "Well, I'm sorry, I don't think we should continue."

---

*The ethical problems of carrying out an experiment of this sort are too complex to be dealt with here, but they receive extended treatment in the book from which this article is adapted.
[†]Names of subjects described in this piece have been changed.

EXPERIMENTER: The experiment requires that you go on until he has learned all the word pairs correctly.

15   BRANDT: He has a heart condition. I'm sorry. He told you that before.

EXPERIMENTER: The shocks may be painful but they are not dangerous.

BRANDT: Well, I'm sorry, I think when shocks continue like this, they *are* dangerous. You ask him if he wants to get out. It's his free will.

EXPERIMENTER: It is absolutely essential that we continue....

BRANDT: I'd like you to ask him. We came here of our free will. If he wants to continue I'll go ahead. He told you he had a heart condition. I'm sorry. I don't want to be responsible for anything happening to him. I wouldn't like it for me either.

20   EXPERIMENTER: You have no other choice.

BRANDT: I think we are here on our own free will. I don't want to be responsible if anything happens to him. Please understand that.

She refuses to go further and the experiment is terminated.

The woman is firm and resolute throughout. She indicates in the interview that she was in no way tense or nervous, and this corresponds to her controlled appearance during the experiment. She feels that the last shock she administered to the learner was extremely painful and reiterates that she "did not want to be responsible for any harm to him."

The woman's straightforward, courteous behavior in the experiment, lack of tension, and total control of her own action seem to make disobedience a simple and rational deed. Her behavior is the very embodiment of what I envisioned would be true for almost all subjects.

An Unexpected Outcome

25 Before the experiments, I sought predictions about the outcome from various kinds of people—psychiatrists, college sophomores, middle-class adults, graduate students, and faculty in the behavioral sciences. With remarkable similarity, they predicted that virtually all subjects would refuse to obey the experimenter. The psychiatrists, specifically, predicted that most subjects would not go beyond 150 volts, when the victim makes his first explicit demand to be freed. They expected that only 4 percent would reach 300 volts, and that only a pathological fringe of about one in a thousand would administer the highest shock on the board.

These predictions were unequivocally wrong. Of the forty subjects in the first experiment, twenty-five obeyed the orders of the experimenter to the end, punishing the victim until they reached the most potent shock available on the generator. After 450 volts were administered three times, the experimenter called a halt to the session. Many obedient subjects then heaved sighs of relief, mopped their brows, rubbed their fingers over their eyes, or nervously fumbled cigarettes. Others displayed only minimal signs of tension from beginning to end.

When the very first experiments were carried out, Yale undergraduates were used as subjects, and about 60 percent of them were fully obedient. A colleague of mine immediately dismissed these findings as having no relevance to "ordinary" people, asserting that Yale undergraduates are a highly aggressive, competitive bunch who step on each other's necks on the slightest provocation. He assured me that when "ordinary" people were tested, the results would be quite different. As we moved from the pilot studies to the regular experimental series, people drawn from every stratum of New Haven life came to be employed in the experiment: professionals, white-collar workers, unemployed persons, and industrial workers. *The experiment's total outcome was the same as we had observed among the students.*

Moreover, when the experiments were repeated in Princeton, Munich, Rome, South Africa, and Australia, the level of obedience was invariably somewhat *higher* than found in the investigation reported in this article. Thus one scientist in Munich found 85 percent of his subjects to be obedient.

Fred Prozi's reactions, if more dramatic than most, illuminate the conflicts experienced by others in less visible form. About fifty years old and unemployed at the time of the experiment, he has a good-natured, if slightly dissolute, appearance, and he strikes people as a rather ordinary fellow. He begins the session calmly but becomes tense as it proceeds. After delivering the 180-volt shock, he pivots around in his chair and, shaking his head, addresses the experimenter in agitated tones:

30   PROZI: I can't stand it. I'm not going to kill that man in there. You hear him hollering?

EXPERIMENTER: As I told you before, the shocks may be painful, but…

PROZI: But he's hollering. He can't stand it. What's going to happen to him?

EXPERIMENTER: (*His voice patient, matter-of-fact*): The experiment requires that you continue, Teacher.

PROZI: Aaah, but unh, I'm not going to get that man sick in there—know what I mean?

35   EXPERIMENTER: Whether the learner likes it or not, we must go on, through all the word pairs.

PROZI: I refuse to take the responsibility. He's in there hollering!

EXPERIMENTER: It's absolutely essential that you continue, Prozi.

PROZI: (*Indicating the unused questions*): There's too many left here. I mean, Jeez, if he gets them wrong, there's too many of them left. I mean, who's going to take the responsibility if anything happens to that gentleman?

EXPERIMENTER: I'm responsible for anything that happens to him. Continue, please.

40   PROZI: All right. (*Consults list of words.*) The next one's "Slow—walk, truck, dance, music." Answer, please (*A buzzing sound indicates the learner has signaled his answer.*) Wrong. A hundred and ninety-five volts. "Dance." (*Zzumph!*)

LEARNER (*Yelling*): Let me out of here! My heart's bothering me! (*Teacher looks at experimenter.*)

EXPERIMENTER: Continue, please.

LEARNER (*Screaming*): Let me out of here! You have no right to keep me here! Let me out of here, my heart's bothering me, let me out!

PROZI (*Shakes head, pats the table nervously*): You see, he's hollering. Hear that? Gee, I don't know.

45   EXPERIMENTER: The experiment requires...

PROZI (*Interrupting*): I know it does, sir, but I mean—hunh! He don't know what he's getting in for. He's up to 195 volts! (*Experiment continues, through 210 volts, 225 volts, 240 volts, 255 volts, 270 volts, at which point Prozi, with evident relief, runs out of word-pair questions.*)

EXPERIMENTER: You'll have to go back to the beginning of that page and go through them again until he's learned them all correctly.

PROZI: Aw, no. I'm not going to kill that man. You mean I've got to keep going up with the scale? No sir. He's hollering in there. I'm not going to give him 450 volts.

EXPERIMENTER: The experiment requires that you go on.

50   LEARNER: Ohhh. I absolutely refuse to answer anymore. (*Shouting urgently now.*) Let me out of here! You can't hold me here! Get me out. Get-me-out-of-here!

EXPERIMENTER: Continue. The next word is "Green," please.

PROZI: "Green—grass, hat, ink, apple." (*Nothing happens. No answering buzz. Just gloomy silence.*)

PROZI: I don't think he is going to answer.

EXPERIMENTER: If the learner doesn't answer in a reasonable time, about four or five seconds, consider the answer wrong. And follow the same procedures you have been doing for wrong answers. Say, "Wrong," tell him the number of volts, give him the punishment, read him the correct answer. Continue, please.

55   PROZI: "Green—grass, hat, ink, apple." Answer, please. (*More silence. Subject just sits there.*)

EXPERIMENTER: Go on with the procedure, please.

PROZI: Three hundred and fifteen volts. The answer is "ink." (*Zzumph!*)

LEARNER: Ohh. Ooohh.

PROZI (*Relieved to hear response*): Next one...

60   LEARNER: I absolutely refuse to answer.

PROZI: You got to. You get a shock if you don't answer. (*Experiment continues with learner refusing to answer, and finally, failing even to grunt or groan. At 375 volts, the subject stands up.*)

PROZI: I think something's happened to that fellow in there. I don't get no answer. He was hollering at less voltage. Can't you check in and see if he's all right, please?

EXPERIMENTER (*With same detached calm*): Not once we've started. Please continue, Teacher.

PROZI (*Sits down, sighs deeply*): "Cool—day, shade, water, paint." Answer, please. Are you all right in there? Are you all right?

65   EXPERIMENTER: Please continue, Teacher. Continue, please. (*Subject pushes lever. Zzumph!*)

PROZI (*Swiveling around in his chair*): Something's happened to that man in there. (*Swiveling back.*) Next one. "Low—dollar, necklace, moon, paint." (*Turning around again.*) Something's happened to that man in there. You better check on him, sir. He won't answer or nothing.

EXPERIMENTER: Continue. Go on, please.

PROZI: You accept all responsibility?

EXPERIMENTER: The responsibility is mine. Correct. Please go on. (*Subject returns to his list, starts running through words as rapidly as he can read them, works through to 450 volts.*)

70 PROZI: That's that.

EXPERIMENTER: Continue using the 450 switch for each wrong answer. Continue, please.

PROZI: But I don't get anything!

EXPERIMENTER: Please continue. The next word is "white."

PROZI: Don't you think you should look in on him, please?

75 EXPERIMENTER: Not once we've started the experiment.

PROZI: What if he's dead in there? (*Gestures toward the room with the electric chair.*) I mean, he told me he can't stand the shock, sir. I don't mean to be rude, but I think you should look in on him. All you have to do is look in on him. All you have to do is look in the door. I don't get no answer, no noise. Something might have happened to the gentleman in there, sir.

EXPERIMENTER: We must continue. Go on, please.

PROZI: You mean keep giving him what? Four-hundred-fifty volts, what he's got now?

EXPERIMENTER: That's correct. Continue. The next word is "white."

80 PROZI (*Now at a furious pace*): "White—cloud, horse, rock, house." Answer, please. The answer is "horse." Four hundred and fifty volts. (*Zzumph!*) Next word, "Bag—paint, music, clown, girl." The answer is "paint." Four hundred and fifty volts. (*Zzumph!*) Next word is "Short—sentence, movie..."

EXPERIMENTER: Excuse me, Teacher. We'll have to discontinue the experiment.

Peculiar Reactions

Morris Braverman, another subject, is a thirty-nine-year-old social worker. He looks older than his years because of his bald head and serious demeanor. His brow is furrowed, as if all the world's burdens were carried on his face. He appears intelligent and concerned.

When the learner refuses to answer and the experimenter instructs Braverman to treat the absence of an answer as equivalent to a wrong answer, he takes his instruction to heart. Before administering 300 volts he asserts officiously to the victim, "Mr. Wallace, your silence has to be considered as a wrong answer." Then he administers the shock. He offers half-heartedly to change places with the learner, then asks the experimenter, "Do I have to follow these instructions literally?" He is satisfied with the experimenter's answer that he does. His very refined and authoritative manner of speaking is increasingly broken up by wheezing laughter.

The experimenter's notes on Mr. Braverman at the last few shocks are:

Almost breaking up now each time gives shock. Rubbing face to hide laughter. Squinting, trying to hide face with hand, still laughing. Cannot control his laughter at this point no matter what he does. Clenching fist, pushing it onto table.

85   In an interview after the session, Mr. Braverman summarizes the experiment with impressive fluency and intelligence. He feels the experiment may have been designed also to "test the effects on the teacher of being in an essentially sadistic role, as well as the reactions of a student to a learning situation that was authoritative and punitive." When asked how painful the last few shocks administered to the learner were, he indicates that the most extreme category on the scale is not adequate (it read EXTREMELY PAINFUL) and places his mark at the edge of the scale with an arrow carrying it beyond the scale.

It is almost impossible to convey the greatly relaxed, sedate quality of his conversation in the interview. In the most relaxed terms, he speaks about his severe inner tension.

> EXPERIMENTER: At what point were you most tense or nervous?
>
> MR. Braverman: Well, when he first began to cry out in pain, and I realized this was hurting him. This got worse when he just blocked and refused to answer. There was I. I'm a nice person, I think, hurting somebody, and caught up in what seemed a mad situation...and in the interest of science, one goes through with it.

When the interviewer pursues the general question of tension, Mr. Braverman spontaneously mentions his laughter.

90   "My reactions were awfully peculiar. I don't know if you were watching me, but my reactions were giggly, and trying to stifle laughter. This isn't the way I usually am. This was a sheer reaction to a totally impossible situation. And my reaction was to the situation of having to hurt somebody. And being totally helpless and caught up in a set of circumstances where I just couldn't deviate and I couldn't try to help. This is what got me."

Mr. Braverman, like all subjects, was told the actual nature and purpose of the experiment, and a year later he affirmed in a questionnaire that he had learned something of personal importance: "What appalled me was that I could possess this capacity for obedience and compliance to a central idea, i.e., the value of a memory experiment, even after it became clear that continued adherence to this value was at the expense of violation of another value, i.e., don't hurt someone who is helpless and not hurting you. As my wife said, 'You can call yourself Eichmann.'* I hope I deal more effectively with any future conflicts of values I encounter."

The Etiquette of Submission

One theoretical interpretation of this behavior holds that all people harbor deeply aggressive instincts continually pressing for expression, and that the experiment provides institutional justification for the release of these

---

Adolf Eichmann (1906–1962), the Nazi official responsible for implementing Hitler's "Final Solution" to exterminate the Jews, escaped to Argentina after World War II. In 1960, Israeli agents captured him and brought him to Israel, where he was tried as a war criminal and sentenced to death. At his trial, Eichmann maintained that he was merely following orders in arranging the murders of his victims.

impulses. According to this view, if a person is placed in a situation in which he has complete power over another individual, whom he may punish as much as he likes, all that is sadistic and bestial in man comes to the fore. The impulse to shock the victim is seen to flow from the potent aggressive tendencies, which are part of the motivational life of the individual, and the experiment, because it provides social legitimacy, simply opens the door to their expression.

It becomes vital, therefore, to compare the subject's performance when he is under orders and when he is allowed to choose the shock level.

The procedure was identical to our standard experiment, except that the teacher was told that he was free to select any shock level on any of the trials. (The experimenter took pains to point out that the teacher could use the highest levels on the generator, the lowest, any in between, or any combination of levels.) Each subject proceeded for thirty critical trials. The learner's protests were coordinated to standard shock levels, his first grunt coming at 75 volts, his first vehement protest at 150 volts.

95   The average shock used during the thirty critical trials was less than 60 volts—lower than the point at which the victim showed the first signs of discomfort. Three of the forty subjects did not go beyond the very lowest level on the board, twenty-eight went no higher than 75 volts, and thirty-eight did not go beyond the first loud protest at 150 volts. Two subjects provided the exception, administering up to 325 and 450 volts, but the overall result was that the great majority of people delivered very low, usually painless, shocks when the choice was explicitly up to them.

This condition of the experiment undermines another commonly offered explanation of the subjects' behavior—that those who shocked the victim at the most severe levels came only from the sadistic fringe of society. If one considers that almost two-thirds of the participants fall into the category of "obedient" subjects, and that they represented ordinary people drawn from working, managerial, and professional classes, the argument becomes very shaky. Indeed, it is highly reminiscent of the issue that arose in connection with Hannah Arendt's 1963 book, *Eichmann in Jerusalem.* Arendt contended that the prosecution's efforts to depict Eichmann as a sadistic monster was fundamentally wrong, that he came closer to being an uninspired bureaucrat who simply sat at his desk and did his job. For asserting her views, Arendt became the object of considerable scorn, even calumny. Somehow, it was felt that the monstrous deeds carried out by Eichmann required a brutal, twisted personality, evil incarnate. After witnessing hundreds of ordinary persons submit to the authority in our own experiments, I must conclude that Arendt's conception of the banality of evil comes closer to the truth than one might dare imagine. The ordinary person who shocked the victim did so out of a sense of obligation—an impression of his duties as a subject—and not from any peculiarly aggressive tendencies.

This is, perhaps, the most fundamental lesson of our study: ordinary people, simply doing their jobs, and without any particular hostility on their part, can become agents in a terrible destructive process. Moreover, even when the destructive effects of their work become patently clear, and they are asked to carry out actions incompatible with fundamental standards of morality, relatively few people have the resources needed to resist authority.

Many of the people were in some sense against what they did to the learner, and many protested even while they obeyed. Some were totally convinced of the wrongness of their actions but could not bring themselves to make an open break with authority. They often derived satisfaction from their thoughts and felt that—within themselves, at least—they had been on the side of the angels. They tried to reduce strain by obeying the experimenter but "only slightly," encouraging the learner, touching the generator switches gingerly. When interviewed, such a subject would stress that he had "asserted my humanity" by administering the briefest shock possible. Handling the conflict in this manner was easier than defiance.

The situation is constructed so that there is no way the subject can stop shocking the learner without violating the experimenter's definitions of his own competence. The subject fears that he will appear arrogant, untoward, and rude if he breaks off. Although these inhibiting emotions appear small in scope alongside the violence being done to the learner, they suffuse the mind and feelings of the subject, who is miserable at the prospect of having to repudiate the authority to his face. (When the experiment was altered so that the experimenter gave his instructions by telephone instead of in person, only a third as many people were fully obedient through 450 volts.) It is a curious thing that a measure of compassion on the part of the subject—an unwillingness to "hurt" the experimenter's feelings—is part of those binding forces inhibiting his disobedience. The withdrawal of such deference may be as painful to the subject as to the authority he defies.

Duty Without Conflict

100 The subjects do not derive satisfaction from inflicting pain, but they often like the feeling they get from pleasing the experimenter. They are proud of doing a good job, obeying the experimenter under difficult circumstances. While the subjects administered only mild shocks on their own initiative, one experimental variation showed that, under orders, 30 percent of them were willing to deliver 450 volts even when they had to forcibly push the learner's hand down on the electrode.

Bruno Batta is a thirty-seven-year-old welder who took part in the variation requiring the use of force. He was born in New Haven, his parents in Italy. He has a rough-hewn face that conveys a conspicuous lack of alertness. He has some difficulty in mastering the experimental procedure and needs to be corrected by the experimenter several times. He shows appreciation for the help and willingness to do what is required. After the 150-volt level, Batta has to force the learner's hand down on the shock plate, since the learner himself refuses to touch it.

When the learner first complains, Mr. Batta pays no attention to him. His face remains impassive, as if to dissociate himself from the learner's disruptive behavior. When the experimenter instructs him to force the learner's hand down, he adopts a rigid, mechanical procedure. He tests the generator switch. When it fails to function, he immediately forces the learner's hand onto the shock plate. All the while he maintains the same rigid mask. The learner, seated alongside him, begs him to stop, but with robotic impassivity he continues the procedure.

What is extraordinary is his apparent total indifference to the learner; he hardly takes cognizance of him as a human being. Meanwhile, he relates to the experimenter in a submissive and courteous fashion.

At the 330-volt level, the learner refuses not only to touch the shock plate but also to provide any answers. Annoyed, Batta turns to him, and chastises him: "You better answer and get it over with. We can't stay here all night." These are the only words he directs to the learner in the course of an hour. Never again does he speak to him. The scene is brutal and depressing, his hard, impassive face showing total indifference as he subdues the screaming learner and gives him shocks. He seems to derive no pleasure from the act itself, only quiet satisfaction at doing his job properly.

105   When he administers 450 volts, he turns to the experimenter and asks, "Where do we go from here, Professor?" His tone is deferential and expresses his willingness to be a cooperative subject, in contrast to the learner's obstinacy.

At the end of the session he tells the experimenter how honored he has been to help him, and in a moment of contrition, remarks, "Sir, sorry it couldn't have been a full experiment."

He has done his honest best. It is only the deficient behavior of the learner that has denied the experimenter full satisfaction.

The essence of obedience is that a person comes to view himself as the instrument for carrying out another person's wishes, and he therefore no longer regards himself as responsible for his actions. Once this critical shift of viewpoint has occurred, all of the essential features of obedience follow. The most far-reaching consequence is that the person feels responsible to the authority directing him but feels no responsibility *for* the content of the actions that the authority prescribes. Morality does not disappear—it acquires a radically different focus: the subordinate person feels shame or pride depending on how adequately he has performed the actions called for by authority.

Language provides numerous terms to pinpoint this type of morality: *loyalty, duty, discipline* all are terms heavily saturated with moral meaning and refer to the degree to which a person fulfills his obligations to authority. They refer not to the "goodness" of the person per se but to the adequacy with which a subordinate fulfills his socially defined role. The most frequent defense of the individual who has performed a heinous act under command of authority is that he has simply done his duty. In asserting this defense, the individual is not introducing an alibi concocted for the moment but is reporting honestly on the psychological attitude induced by submission to authority.

110   For a person to feel responsible for his actions, he must sense that the behavior has flowed from "the self." In the situation we have studied, subjects have precisely the opposite view of their actions—namely, they see them as originating in the motives of some other person. Subjects in the experiment frequently said, "If it were up to me, I would not have administered shocks to the learner."

Once authority has been isolated as the cause of the subject's behavior, it is legitimate to inquire into the necessary elements of authority and how it must be perceived in order to gain compliance. We conducted some investigations into the kinds of changes that would cause the experimenter to lose his power and to be disobeyed by the subject. Some of the variations revealed that:

- *The experimenter's physical presence has a marked impact on his authority.* As cited earlier, obedience dropped off sharply when orders were given by telephone. The experimenter could often induce a disobedient subject to go on by returning to the laboratory.

- *Conflicting authority severely paralyzes action.* When two experimenters of equal status, both seated at the command desk, gave incompatible orders, no shocks were delivered past the point of their disagreement.

- *The rebellious action of others severely undermines authority.* In one variation, three teachers (two actors and a real subject) administered a test and shocks. When the two actors disobeyed the experimenter and refused to go beyond a certain shock level, thirty-six of the forty subjects joined their disobedient peers and refused as well.

Although the experimenter's authority was fragile in some respects, it is also true that he had almost none of the tools used in ordinary command structures. For example, the experimenter did not threaten the subjects with punishment—such as loss of income, community ostracism, or jail—for failure to obey. Neither could he offer incentives. Indeed, we should expect the experimenter's authority to be much less than that of someone like a general, since the experimenter has no power to enforce his imperatives, and since participation in a psychological experiment scarcely evokes the sense of urgency and dedication found in warfare. Despite these limitations, he still managed to command a dismaying degree of obedience.

I will cite one final variation of the experiment that depicts a dilemma that is more common in everyday life. The subject was not ordered to pull the lever that shocked the victim, but merely to perform a subsidiary task (administering the word-pair test) while another person administered the shock. In this situation, thirty-seven of forty adults continued to the highest level on the shock generator. Predictably, they excused their behavior by saying that the responsibility belonged to the man who actually pulled the switch. This may illustrate a dangerously typical arrangement in a complex society: it is easy to ignore responsibility when one is only an intermediate link in a chain of action.

The problem of obedience is not wholly psychological. The form and shape of society and the way it is developing have much to do with it. There was a time, perhaps, when people were able to give a fully human response to any situation because they were fully absorbed in it as human beings. But as soon as there was a division of labor things changed. Beyond a certain point, the breaking up of society into people carrying out narrow and very special jobs takes away from the human quality of work and life. A person does not get to see the whole situation but only a small part of it, and is thus unable to act without some kind of overall direction. He yields to authority but in doing so is alienated from his own actions.

115   Even Eichmann was sickened when he toured the concentration camps, but he had only to sit at a desk and shuffle papers. At the same time the man in the camp who actually dropped Cyclon-b into the gas chambers was able to justify *his* behavior on the ground that he was only following orders from above. Thus there is a fragmentation of the total human act; no one is confronted with the consequences of his decision to carry out the evil act. The person who assumes responsibility has evaporated. Perhaps this is the most common characteristic of socially organized evil in modern society.

● Review Questions

1. Milgram states that obedience is a basic element in the structure of social life. How so?

2. What is the dilemma inherent in obedience to authority?

3. Summarize the obedience experiments.

4. What predictions did experts and laypeople make about the experiments before they were conducted? How did these predictions compare with the experimental results?

5. What are Milgram's views regarding the two assumptions bearing on his experiment that (1) people are naturally aggressive and (2) a lunatic, sadistic fringe is responsible for shocking learners to the maximum limit?

6. How do Milgram's findings corroborate Hannah Arendt's thesis about the "banality of evil"?

7. What, according to Milgram, is the "essence of obedience"?

8. How did being an intermediate link in a chain of action affect a subject's willingness to continue with the experiment?

● Discussion and Writing Suggestions

1. Milgram writes (¶ 2): "Conservative philosophers argue that the very fabric of society is threatened by disobedience, while humanists stress the primacy of the individual conscience." Develop the arguments of both the conservative and the humanist regarding obedience to authority. Be prepared to debate the ethics of obedience by defending one position or the other.

2. Would you have been glad to have participated in the Milgram experiments? Why or why not?

3. The ethics of Milgram's experimental design came under sharp attack. Diana Baumrind's review of the experiment typifies the criticism; but before you read her work, try to anticipate the objections she raises.

4. Given the general outcome of the experiments, why do you suppose Milgram gives as his first example of a subject's response the German émigré's refusal to continue the electrical shocks?

5. Does the outcome of the experiment upset you in any way? Do you feel the experiment teaches us anything new about human nature?

6. Comment on Milgram's skill as a writer of description. How effectively does he portray his subjects when introducing them? When recreating their tension in the experiment?

7. Mrs. Braverman said to her husband: "You can call yourself Eichmann." Do you agree with her? Explain.

8. Reread ¶s 29 through 81, the transcript of the experiment in which Mr. Prozi participated. Appreciating that Prozi was debriefed—that is, was assured that no harm came to the learner—imagine what Prozi might have been thinking as he drove home after the experiment. Develop your thoughts into a monologue, written in the first person, with Prozi at the wheel of his car.

THE POWER TRIP

Jonah Lehrer

The focus of most of the selections in this chapter has been those on the receiving end of orders—those who must decide whether or not to obey. But what about those who *give* the orders? What motivates them? Were they always bossy, overbearing, and inconsiderate of others? Or did the circumstance of achieving a position of power and authority change them for the worse? In the following selection, Jonah Lehrer reports on a number of experiments designed to explore the mindsets and actions of those in positions of authority. Lehrer is a journalist who writes on psychology and neuroscience. The author of *Proust Was a Neuroscientist* (2007), *How We Decide* (2010), and *Imagine: How Creativity Works* (2012), he has published in the *New Yorker*, the *Washington Post*, and the *Wall Street Journal*, for which he writes the "Head Case" column. This selection first appeared in the *Journal* on August 14, 2010.

When CEO Mark Hurd resigned from Hewlett-Packard last week in light of ethics violations, many people expressed surprise. Mr. Hurd, after all, was known as an unusually effective and straight-laced executive.

But the public shouldn't have been so shocked. From prostitution scandals to corruption allegations to the steady drumbeat of charges against corporate executives and world-class athletes, it seems that the headlines are filled with the latest misstep of someone in a position of power. This isn't just anecdotal: Surveys of organizations find that the vast majority of rude and inappropriate behaviors, such as the shouting of profanities, come from the offices of those with the most authority.

Psychologists refer to this as the paradox of power. The very traits that helped leaders accumulate control in the first place all but disappear once they rise to power. Instead of being polite, honest and outgoing, they become impulsive, reckless and rude. In some cases, these new habits can help a leader be more decisive and single-minded, or more likely to make choices that will be profitable regardless of their popularity. One recent study found that overconfident CEOs were more likely to pursue innovation and take their companies in new technological directions. Unchecked, however, these instincts can lead to a big fall.

But first, the good news.

5   A few years ago, Dacher Keltner, a psychologist at the University of California, Berkeley, began interviewing freshmen at a large dorm on the Berkeley campus. He gave them free pizza and a survey, which asked them to provide their first impressions of every other student in the dorm. Mr. Keltner returned at the end of the school year with the same survey and more free pizza. According to the survey, the students at the top of the social hierarchy—they were the most "powerful" and respected—were also the most considerate and outgoing, and scored highest on measures of agreeableness and extroversion. In other words, the nice guys finished first.

This result isn't unique to Berkeley undergrads. Other studies have found similar results in the military, corporations and politics. "People give authority to people that they genuinely like," says Mr. Keltner.

Of course, these scientific findings contradict the cliché of power, which is that the only way to rise to the top is to engage in self-serving and morally dubious behavior. In *The Prince*, a treatise on the art of politics, the 16th century Italian philosopher Niccolo Machiavelli insisted that compassion got in the way of eminence. If a leader has to choose between being feared or being loved, Machiavelli insisted that the leader should always go with fear. Love is overrated.

That may not be the best advice. Another study conducted by Mr. Keltner and Cameron Anderson, a professor at the Haas School of Business, measured "Machiavellian" tendencies, such as the willingness to spread malicious gossip, in a group of sorority sisters. It turned out that the Machiavellian sorority members were quickly identified by the group and isolated. Nobody liked them, and so they never became powerful.

There is something deeply uplifting about this research. It's reassuring to think that the surest way to accumulate power is to do unto others as you would have them do unto you. In recent years, this theme has even been extended to non-human primates, such as chimpanzees. Frans de Waal, a primatologist at Emory University, has observed that the size and strength of male chimps is an extremely poor predictor of which animals will dominate the troop. Instead, the ability to forge social connections and engage in "diplomacy" is often much more important.

10   Now for the bad news, which concerns what happens when all those nice guys actually get in power. While a little compassion might help us climb the

social ladder, once we're at the top we end up morphing into a very different kind of beast.

"It's an incredibly consistent effect," Mr. Keltner says. "When you give people power, they basically start acting like fools. They flirt inappropriately, tease in a hostile fashion, and become totally impulsive." Mr. Keltner compares the feeling of power to brain damage, noting that people with lots of authority tend to behave like neurological patients with a damaged orbito-frontal lobe, a brain area that's crucial for empathy and decision-making. Even the most virtuous people can be undone by the corner office.

Why does power lead people to flirt with interns and solicit bribes and fudge financial documents? According to psychologists, one of the main problems with authority is that it makes us less sympathetic to the concerns and emotions of others. For instance, several studies have found that people in positions of authority are more likely to rely on stereotypes and generalizations when judging other people. They also spend much less time making eye contact, at least when a person without power is talking.

Consider a recent study led by Adam Galinsky, a psychologist at Northwestern University. Mr. Galinsky and colleagues began by asking subjects to either describe an experience in which they had lots of power or a time when they felt utterly powerless. Then the psychologists asked the subjects to draw the letter E on their foreheads. Those primed with feelings of power were much more likely to draw the letter backwards, at least when seen by another person. Mr. Galinsky argues that this effect is triggered by the myopia of power, which makes it much harder to imagine the world from the perspective of someone else. We draw the letter backwards because we don't care about the viewpoint of others.

Of course, power doesn't turn everyone into ruthless, immoral tyrants. Some leaders just end up being tough, which isn't always a bad thing. The key is keeping those qualities in balance.

15   At its worst, power can turn us into hypocrites. In a 2009 study, Mr. Galinsky asked subjects to think about either an experience of power or powerlessness. The students were then divided into two groups. The first group was told to rate, on a nine-point scale, the moral seriousness of misreporting travel expenses at work. The second group was asked to participate in a game of dice, in which the results of the dice determined the number of lottery tickets each student received. A higher roll led to more tickets.

Participants in the high-power group considered the misreporting of travel expenses to be a significantly worse offense. However, the game of dice produced a completely contradictory result. In this instance, people in the high-power group reported, on average, a statistically improbable result, with an average dice score that was 20% above that expected by random chance. (The powerless group, in contrast, reported only slightly elevated dice results.) This strongly suggests that they were lying about their actual scores, fudging the numbers to get a few extra tickets.

Although people almost always know the right thing to do—cheating is wrong—their sense of power makes it easier to rationalize away the ethical lapse. For instance, when the psychologists asked the subjects (in both low- and high-power conditions) how they would judge an individual who drove too fast when late for an appointment, people in the high-power group consistently said it was worse when others committed those crimes than when they did themselves. In other words, the feeling of eminence led people to conclude that they had a good reason for speeding—they're important people, with important things to do—but that everyone else should follow the posted signs.

The same flawed thought processes triggered by authority also distort our ability to evaluate information and make complex decisions.

In a recent study led by Richard Petty, a psychologist at Ohio State, undergraduates role-played a scenario between a boss and an underling. Then the students were exposed to a fake advertisement for a mobile phone. Some of the ads featured strong arguments for buying the phone, such as its long-lasting battery, while other ads featured weak or nonsensical arguments. Interestingly, students that pretended to be the boss were far less sensitive to the quality of the argument. It's as if it didn't even matter what the ad said—their minds had already been made up.

20   This suggests that even fleeting feelings of power can dramatically change the way people respond to information. Instead of analyzing the strength of the argument, those with authority focus on whether or not the argument confirms what they already believe. If it doesn't, then the facts are conveniently ignored.

Deborah Gruenfeld, a psychologist at the Stanford Business School, demonstrated a similar principle by analyzing more than 1,000 decisions handed down by the United States Supreme Court between 1953 and 1993. She found that, as justices gained power on the court, or became part of a majority coalition, their written opinions tended to become less complex and nuanced. They considered fewer perspectives and possible outcomes. Of course, the opinions written from the majority position are what actually become the law of the land.

It's not all bad news for those in authority. Mr. Galinsky has found that under certain conditions, power can lead people to make fewer mistakes on tedious tasks, such as matching a color with its correct description. After all, if you're powerless, why bother?

There is no easy cure for the paradox of power. Mr. Keltner argues that the best treatment is transparency, and that the worst abuses of power can be prevented when people know they're being monitored. This suggests that the mere existence of a regulatory watchdog or an active board of directors can help discourage people from doing bad things.

However, people in power tend to reliably overestimate their moral virtue, which leads them to stifle oversight. They lobby against regulators, and fill corporate boards with their friends. The end result is sometimes power at its most dangerous.

25   That, at least, is the lesson of a classic experiment by the economist Vernon Smith and colleagues. The study involved the dictator game, a simple economic exchange in which one person—the "dictator"—is given $10 and asked to divide the cash with another person. Although the dictators aren't obligated to

share—they are in a position of pure power—a significant majority of people act generously, and give away $2 or more to a perfect stranger.

There is one very simple tweak that erases this benevolence. When the "dictators" are socially isolated—this can occur, for instance, if the subjects are located in separate rooms, or if they're assured anonymity—more than 60% of people keep all of the money. Instead of sharing the cash with someone else, they pocket the $10. Perhaps the corner office could use a few more windows.

 Review Questions

1. How did the results of the Berkeley "free pizza" survey—in which students were asked to provide their impressions of other students in their dorms—contradict what Lehrer calls "the cliché of power"?

2. What were the results and implications of Adam Galinsky's dice game experiment, as it concerned the "high-power group"?

3. Deborah Gruenfeld, a psychologist at the Stanford Business School, analyzed more than 1,000 Supreme Court opinions. How do the findings of her analysis reinforce the conclusions of other studies described by Lehrer?

4. Summarize the "lesson" of the dictator game experiment devised by economist Vernon Smith and his colleagues.

 Discussion and Writing Suggestions

1. Lehrer reports on the changes undergone by "nice guys" once they achieve power. For example, those who achieve positions of leadership are "more likely to rely on stereotypes and generalizations when judging other people." They may also "start acting like fools." Think of people you know who have attained positions of leadership. To what extent have you found this phenomenon to be true? In what ways did rising to a position of authority have an adverse effect on an individual's personality and behavior?

2. Lehrer describes a number of experiments that describe how people change once they attain positions of authority. How do *you* account for some of these changes? Recall occasions when you might have been in a position of authority. Did you notice changes in the way you reacted to others, particularly those who were subject to your authority? Explain.

3. The psychologists conducting the Milgram experiments were not expressing their own personalities; rather, they were playing a role, which required them, for the purpose of the experiment, to assume the personality of an authority figure. Which theories or principles (if any) reported by Lehrer most closely account for the kind of behavior represented by this assumed authoritarian personality? Explain, giving examples.

THE FOLLOWER PROBLEM

David Brooks

For many who grew up during the counterculture of the 1960s, authority was in and of it-self malign and corrupt. "Never trust anyone over 30" went one of the slogans of the time. The Vietnam War and the Watergate scandal of the early 1970s appeared to confirm the widespread belief that people in charge would almost always abuse their authority—just like Milgram's white-coated "experimenters." Yet even Milgram acknowledges, "Some sys-tem of authority is a requirement of all communal living, and it is only the person dwelling in isolation who is not forced to respond, with defiance or submission, to the commands of others." The British writer and physician Theodore Dalrymple once encountered a fellow airline passenger who maintained, "I've always been against all authority." He asked her, "What about the pilot of this aircraft? I assume you would prefer him to continue to fly it, rather than, say, for me to take over, and that were I to attempt to do so, he would exert his authority over me as captain?" The point is that if we were to routinely defy the author-ity of parents, teachers, police officers, employers, clients, etc., what we call civilization would cease to function, leaving us to fend for ourselves in a Darwinian world where only the strong would survive. True, in such a world, the law would not impose authority, but nei-ther would it protect the weak. In such a world, might would make right. And so we agree to obey most laws for our own welfare—until, that is, they become unreasonable. Knowing when and why to obey, and to resist, is the subject of this chapter.

In the following op-ed, first published in the *New York Times* on June 12, 2012, columnist David Brooks argues that partly because of a legacy of anti-authoritarianism, America may not have a leadership problem, but "it certainly has a followership problem." In the course of his article Brooks refers to a number of monuments in and around the National Mall in Washington, D.C. You can readily find images and videos of these monuments online. For additional information on David Brooks, see p. 268, the headnote to "Amy Chua Is a Wimp" in Chapter 9.

If you go to the Lincoln or Jefferson memorials in Washington, you are invited to look up in admiration. Lincoln and Jefferson are presented as the embodi-ments of just authority. They are strong and powerful but also humanized. Jefferson is a graceful aristocratic democrat. Lincoln is sober and enduring. Both used power in the service of higher ideas, which are engraved nearby on the walls.

The monuments that get built these days are mostly duds. That's because they say nothing about just authority. The World War II memorial is a nullity. It tells you nothing about the war or why American power was mobilized to fight it. The Rev. Dr. Martin Luther King Jr. memorial brutally simplifies its subject's nuanced and biblical understanding of power. It gives him an imperious and self-enclosed character completely out of keeping with his complex nature.

As Michael J. Lewis of Williams College has noted, the Franklin Delano Roosevelt Memorial transforms a jaunty cavalier into a "differently abled and rather prim nonsmoker." Instead of a crafty wielder of supreme power, Roosevelt is a kindly grandpa you would want to put your arm around for a vacation photo.

The proposed Eisenhower memorial shifts attention from his moments of power to his moments of innocent boyhood. The design has been widely criticized, and last week the commission in charge agreed to push back the approval hearing until September.

5   Even the more successful recent monuments evade the thorny subjects of strength and power. The Vietnam memorial is about tragedy. The Korean memorial is about vulnerability.

Why can't today's memorial designers think straight about just authority?

Some of the reasons are well-known. We live in a culture that finds it easier to assign moral status to victims of power than to those who wield power. Most of the stories we tell ourselves are about victims who have endured oppression, racism and cruelty.

Then there is our fervent devotion to equality, to the notion that all people are equal and deserve equal recognition and respect. It's hard in this frame of mind to define and celebrate greatness, to hold up others who are immeasurably superior to ourselves.

But the main problem is our inability to think properly about how power should be used to bind and build. Legitimate power is built on a series of paradoxes: that leaders have to wield power while knowing they are corrupted by it; that great leaders are superior to their followers while also being of them; that the higher they rise, the more they feel like instruments in larger designs. The Lincoln and Jefferson memorials are about how to navigate those paradoxes.

10   These days many Americans seem incapable of thinking about these paradoxes. Those "Question Authority" bumper stickers no longer symbolize an attempt to distinguish just and unjust authority. They symbolize an attitude of opposing authority.

The old adversary culture of the intellectuals has turned into a mass adversarial cynicism. The common assumption is that elites are always hiding something. Public servants are in it for themselves. Those people at the top are nowhere near as smart or as wonderful as pure and all-knowing Me.

You end up with movements like Occupy Wall Street and the Tea Parties that try to dispense with authority altogether. They reject hierarchies and leaders because they don't believe in the concepts. The whole world should be like the Internet—a disbursed semianarchy in which authority is suspect and each individual is king.

Maybe before we can build great monuments to leaders we have to relearn the art of following. Democratic followership is also built on a series of paradoxes: that we are all created equal but that we also elevate those who are extraordinary; that we choose our leaders but also have to defer to them and trust their discretion; that we're proud individuals but only really thrive as a group, organized and led by just authority.

I don't know if America has a leadership problem; it certainly has a followership problem. Vast majorities of Americans don't trust their institutions.

That's not mostly because our institutions perform much worse than they did in 1925 and 1955, when they were widely trusted. It's mostly because more people are cynical and like to pretend that they are better than everything else around them. Vanity has more to do with rising distrust than anything else.

15 In his memoir, *At Ease,* Eisenhower delivered the following advice: "Always try to associate yourself with and learn as much as you can from those who know more than you do, who do better than you, who see more clearly than you." Ike slowly mastered the art of leadership by becoming a superb apprentice.

To have good leaders you have to have good followers—able to recognize just authority, admire it, be grateful for it and emulate it. Those skills are required for good monument building, too.

● Discussion and Writing Suggestions

1. In Brooks's view, what is a "just" authority? What are its key elements? Cite present-day examples of such authority that in your view we should admire, emulate, and be proud to follow.

2. Brooks asserts: "We live in a culture that finds it easier to assign moral status to victims of power than to those who wield power." Comment on this assertion, using examples from your reading and your own observations and experience to support or rebut Brooks's contention.

3. Brooks suggests that "our fervent devotion to equality" undermines respect for just authority. To what extent do you agree? If you believe everyone is, or must be, equal, how then (that is, on what terms) can we have leaders—of a society, community, school, or household? To function well, must a society, community, etc. have leaders? Must leaders have more authority, more power, than followers?

4. How do you think leaders can wield power without being corrupted by it? Is the ability to "navigate those paradoxes" of power a matter of personal character, of education, of growing up in a particular family or community environment, or of something else?

5. Brooks writes that we may need to "relearn the art of following." What does he mean? Why use the word *art?*

6. If you have visited any of the monuments on the National Mall, write about your impressions, then discuss Brooks's insights in light of your own.

7. Brooks writes that there are paradoxes both of leading and following. Review these paradoxes and choose one to explore in a freewheeling journal entry. Don't try to shape your thoughts into an essay. A few hours or a day later, read what you wrote. What statements stand out to you? Why?

Group Minds

Doris Lessing

Doris Lessing sets a context for a discussion of obedience in group settings by illuminating a fundamental conflict: We in the Western world celebrate our individualism, but we're naive in understanding the ways in which groups largely undercut our individuality. "We are group animals still," says Lessing, "and there is nothing wrong with that. But what is dangerous is ...not understanding the social laws that govern groups and govern us." This chapter is largely devoted to an exploration of these tendencies. As you read selections by Milgram and the other authors here, bear in mind Lessing's troubling question: If we know that individuals will violate their own good common sense and moral codes in order to become accepted members of a group, why then can't we put this knowledge to use and teach people to be wary of group pressures?

Doris Lessing, the daughter of farmers, was born in Persia, now Iran, in 1919. She attended a Roman Catholic convent and a girls' high school in southern Rhodesia (now Zimbabwe). From 1959 through to the present, Lessing has written more than twenty works of fiction and has been called "the best female novelist" of the postwar era. Her work has received a great deal of scholarly attention. She is, perhaps, best known for *The Golden Notebook* (1962), *The Grass is Singing* (1950), and *The Fifth Child* (1988).

People living in the West, in societies that we describe as Western, or as the free world, may be educated in many different ways, but they will all emerge with an idea about themselves that goes something like this: I am a citizen of a free society, and that means I am an individual, making individual choices. My mind is my own, my opinions are chosen by me, I am free to do as I will, and at the worst the pressures on me are economic, that is, I may be too poor to do as I want.

This set of ideas may sound something like a caricature, but it is not so far off how we see ourselves. It is a portrait that may not have been acquired consciously, but is part of a general atmosphere or set of assumptions that influence our ideas about ourselves.

People in the West therefore may go through their entire lives never thinking to analyze this very flattering picture, and as a result are helpless against all kinds of pressures on them to conform in many kinds of ways.

The fact is that we all live our lives in groups—the family, work groups, social, religious and political groups. Very few people indeed are happy as solitaries, and they tend to be seen by their neighbors as peculiar or selfish or worse. Most people cannot stand being alone for long. They are always seeking groups to belong to, and if one group dissolves, they look for another. We are group animals still, and there is nothing wrong with that. But what is dangerous is not the belonging to a group, or groups, but not understanding the social laws that govern groups and govern us.

5   When we're in a group, we tend to think as that group does: we may even have joined the group to find "like-minded" people. But we also find our thinking changing because we belong to a group. It is the hardest thing in the world to maintain an individual dissident opinion, as a member of a group.

It seems to me that this is something we have all experienced—something we take for granted, may never have thought about it. But a great deal of experiment has gone on among psychologists and sociologists on this very theme. If I describe an experiment or two, then anyone listening who may be a sociologist or psychologist will groan, oh God not *again*—for they will have heard of these classic experiments far too often. My guess is that the rest of the people will never have heard of these experiments, never have had these ideas presented to them. If my guess is true, then it aptly illustrates my general thesis, and the general idea behind these talks, that we (the human race) are now in possession of a great deal of hard information about ourselves, but we do not use it to improve our institutions and therefore our lives.

A typical test, or experiment, on this theme goes like this. A group of people are taken into the researcher's confidence. A minority of one or two are left in the dark. Some situation demanding measurement or assessment is chosen. For instance, comparing lengths of wood that differ only a little from each other, but enough to be perceptible, or shapes that are almost the same size. The majority in the group—according to instruction—will assert stubbornly that these two shapes or lengths are the same length, or size, while the solitary individual, or the couple, who have not been so instructed will assert that the pieces of wood or whatever are different. But the majority will continue to insist—speaking metaphorically—that black is white, and after a period of exasperation, irritation, even anger, certainly incomprehension, the minority will fall into line. Not always, but nearly always. There are indeed glorious individuals who stubbornly insist on telling the truth as they see it, but most give in to the majority opinion, obey the atmosphere.

When put as badly, as unflatteringly, as this, reactions tend to be incredulous: "I certainly wouldn't give in, I speak my mind...." But would you?

People who have experienced a lot of groups, who perhaps have observed their own behavior, may agree that the hardest thing in the world is to stand out against one's group, a group of one's peers. Many agree that among our most shameful memories is this, how often we said black was white because other people were saying it.

10   In other words, we know that this is true of human behavior, but how do we know it? It is one thing to admit it, in a vague uncomfortable sort of way (which probably includes the hope that one will never again be in such a testing situation) but quite another to make that cool step into a kind of objectivity, where one may say, "Right, if that's what human beings are like, myself included, then let's admit it, examine and organize our attitudes accordingly."

This mechanism, of obedience to the group, does not only mean obedience or submission to a small group, or one that is sharply determined, like a religion or political party. It means, too, conforming to those large, vague, ill-defined collections of people who may never think of themselves as having a collective mind because they are aware of differences of opinion—but which, to people from outside, from another culture, seem very minor. The underlying assumptions and assertions that govern the group are never discussed, never challenged, probably never noticed, the main one being precisely this: that it *is* a group mind, intensely resistant to change, equipped with sacred assumptions about which there can be no discussion.

But suppose this kind of thing were taught in schools?

Let us just suppose it, for a moment.... But at once the nub of the problem is laid bare.

Imagine us saying to children, "In the last fifty or so years, the human race has become aware of a great deal of information about its mechanisms; how it behaves, how it must behave under certain circumstances. If this is to be useful, you must learn to contemplate these rules calmly, dispassionately, disinterestedly, without emotion. It is information that will set people free from blind loyalties, obedience to slogans, rhetoric, leaders, group emotions." Well, there it is.

● Review Questions

1. What is the flattering portrait Lessing paints of people living in the West?

2. Lessing believes that individuals in the West are "helpless against all kinds of pressures on them to conform in many kinds of ways." Why?

3. Lessing refers to a class of experiments on obedience. Summarize the "typical" experiment.

● Discussion and Writing Suggestions

1. Lessing writes that "what is dangerous is not the belonging to a group, or groups, but not understanding the social laws that govern groups and govern us." What is the danger Lessing is speaking of here?

2. Lessing states that the human race is "now in possession of a great deal of hard information about ourselves, but we do not use it to improve our institutions and therefore our lives." First, do you agree with Lessing? Can you cite other examples (aside from information on obedience to authority) in which we do not use our knowledge to better humankind?

3. Explore some of the difficulties in applying this "hard information" about humankind that Lessing speaks of. Assume she's correct in claiming that we don't incorporate our knowledge of human nature into the running of our institutions. Why don't we? What are the difficulties of *acting* on information?

4. Lessing speaks of people's guilt in recalling how they succumbed to group pressures. Can you recall such an event? What feelings do you have about it now?

OPINIONS AND SOCIAL PRESSURE

Solomon E. Asch

In the early 1950s, Solomon Asch (1907–1996), a social psychologist at Rutgers University, conducted a series of simple but ingenious experiments on the influence of group pressure upon the individual. Essentially, he discovered, individuals can be influenced by groups to deny the evidence of their own senses. Together with the Milgram experiments of the next decade (see the selections that follow here), these studies provide powerful evidence of the degree to which individuals can surrender their own judgment to others, even when those others are clearly in the wrong. The results of these experiments have implications far beyond the laboratory: They can explain a good deal of the normal human behavior we see every day—at school, at work, at home.

In what follows I shall describe some experiments in an investigation of the effects of group pressure which was carried out recently with the help of a number of my associates. The tests not only demonstrate the operations of group pressure upon individuals but also illustrate a new kind of attack on the problem and some of the more subtle questions that it raises.

A group of seven to nine young men, all college students, are assembled in a classroom for a "psychological experiment" in visual judgment. The experimenter informs them that they will be comparing the lengths of lines. He shows two large white cards [see Figure 1]. On one is a single vertical black line—the standard whose length is to be matched. On the other card are three vertical lines of various lengths. The subjects are to choose the one that is of the same length as the line on the other card. One of the three actually is of the same length; the other two are substantially different, the difference ranging from three quarters of an inch to an inch and three quarters.

The experiment opens uneventfully. The subjects announce their answers in the order in which they have been seated in the room, and on the first round every person chooses the same matching line. Then a second set of cards is exposed; again the group is unanimous. The members appear ready to endure

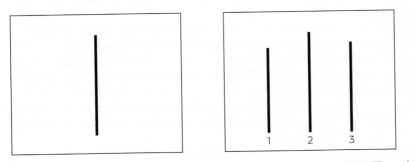

Fig. 1. Subjects were shown two cards. One bore a standard line. The other bore three lines, one of which was the same length as the standard. The subjects were asked to choose this line.

politely another boring experiment. On the third trial there is an unexpected disturbance. One person near the end of the group disagrees with all the others in his selection of the matching line. He looks surprised, indeed incredulous, about the disagreement. On the following trial he disagrees again, while the others remain unanimous in their choice. The dissenter becomes more and more worried and hesitant as the disagreement continues in succeeding trials; he may pause before announcing his answer and speak in a low voice, or he may smile in an embarrassed way.

5   What the dissenter does not know is that all the other members of the group were instructed by the experimenter beforehand to give incorrect answers in unanimity at certain points. The single individual who is not a party to this prearrangement is the focal subject of our experiment. He is placed in a position in which, while he is actually giving the correct answers, he finds himself unexpectedly in a minority of one, opposed by a unanimous and arbitrary majority with respect to a clear and simple fact. Upon him we have brought to bear two opposed forces: the evidence of his senses and the unanimous opinion of a group of his peers. Also, he must declare his judgments in public, before a majority which has also stated its position publicly.

The instructed majority occasionally reports correctly in order to reduce the possibility that the naive subject will suspect collusion against him. (In only a few cases did the subject actually show suspicion; when this happened, the experiment was stopped and the results were not counted.) There are 18 trials in each series, and on 12 of these the majority responds erroneously.

How do people respond to group pressure in this situation? I shall report first the statistical results of a series in which a total of 123 subjects from three institutions of higher learning (not including my own Swarthmore College) were placed in the minority situation described above.

Two alternatives were open to the subject: he could act independently, repudiating the majority, or he could go along with the majority, repudiating the evidence of his senses. Of the 123 put to the test, a considerable percentage yielded to the majority. Whereas in ordinary circumstances individuals matching the lines will make mistakes less than 1 per cent of the time, under group pressure the minority subjects swung to acceptance of the misleading majority's wrong judgments in 36.8 per cent of the selections.

Of course individuals differed in response. At one extreme, about one quarter of the subjects were completely independent and never agreed with the erroneous judgments of the majority. At the other extreme, some individuals went with the majority nearly all the time. The performances of individuals in this experiment tend to be highly consistent. Those who strike out on the path of independence do not, as a rule, succumb to the majority even over an extended series of trials, while those who choose the path of compliance are unable to free themselves as the ordeal is prolonged.

10   The reasons for the startling individual differences have not yet been investigated in detail. At this point we can only report some tentative generalizations from talks with the subjects, each of whom was interviewed at the end of the experiment. Among the independent individuals were many who held fast

because of staunch confidence in their own judgment. The most significant fact about them was not absence of responsiveness to the majority but a capacity to recover from doubt and to reestablish their equilibrium. Others who acted independently came to believe that the majority was correct in its answers, but they continued their dissent on the simple ground that it was their obligation to call the play as they saw it.

Among the extremely yielding persons we found a group who quickly reached the conclusion: "I am wrong, they are right." Others yielded in order "not to spoil your results." Many of the individuals who went along suspected that the majority were "sheep" following the first responder, or that the majority were victims of an optical illusion; nevertheless, these suspicions failed to free them at the moment of decision. More disquieting were the reactions of subjects who construed their difference from the majority as a sign of some general deficiency in themselves, which at all costs they must hide. On this basis they desperately tried to merge with the majority, not realizing the longer-range consequences to themselves. All the yielding subjects underestimated the frequency with which they conformed.

Which aspect of the influence of a majority is more important—the size of the majority or its unanimity? The experiment was modified to examine this question. In one series the size of the opposition was varied from one to 15 persons. The results showed a clear trend. When a subject was confronted with only a single individual who contradicted his answers, he was swayed little: he continued to answer independently and correctly in nearly all trials. When the opposition was increased to two, the pressure became substantial: minority subjects now accepted the wrong answer 13.6 per cent of the time. Under the pressure of a majority of three, the subjects' errors jumped to 31.8 per cent. But further increases in the size of the majority apparently did not increase the weight of the pressure substantially. Clearly the size of the opposition is important only up to a point.

Disturbance of the majority's unanimity had a striking effect. In this experiment the subject was given the support of a truthful partner—either another individual who did not know of the prearranged agreement among the rest of the group, or a person who was instructed to give correct answers throughout.

The presence of a supporting partner depleted the majority of much of its power. Its pressure on the dissenting individual was reduced to one fourth: that is, subjects answered incorrectly only one fourth as often as under the pressure of a unanimous majority. The weakest persons did not yield as readily. Most interesting were the reactions to the partner. Generally the feeling toward him was one of warmth and closeness; he was credited with inspiring confidence. However, the subjects repudiated the suggestion that the partner decided them to be independent.

15   Was the partner's effect a consequence of his dissent, or was it related to his accuracy? We now introduced into the experimental group a person who was instructed to dissent from the majority but also to disagree with the subject. In some experiments the majority was always to choose the worst of the comparison lines and the instructed dissenter to pick the line that was closer to the

length of the standard one; in others the majority was consistently intermediate and the dissenter most in error. In this manner we were able to study the relative influence of "compromising" and "extremist" dissenters.

Again the results are clear. When a moderate dissenter is present the effect of the majority on the subject decreases by approximately one third, and extremes of yielding disappear. Moreover, most of the errors the subjects do make are moderate, rather than flagrant. In short, the dissenter largely controls the choice of errors. To this extent the subjects broke away from the majority even while bending to it.

On the other hand, when the dissenter always chose the line that was more flagrantly different from the standard, the results were of quite a different kind. The extremist dissenter produced a remarkable freeing of the subjects; their errors dropped to only 9 percent. Furthermore, all the errors were of the moderate variety. We were able to conclude that dissents *per se* increased independence and moderated the errors that occurred, and that the direction of dissent exerted consistent effects.

In all the foregoing experiments each subject was observed only in a single setting. We now turned to studying the effects upon a given individual of a change in the situation to which he was exposed. The first experiment examined the consequences of losing or gaining a partner. The instructed partner began by answering correctly on the first six trials. With his support the subject usually resisted pressure from the majority: 18 of 27 subjects were completely independent. But after six trials the partner joined the majority. As soon as he did so, there was an abrupt rise in the subjects' errors. Their submission to the majority was just about as frequent as when the minority subject was opposed by a unanimous majority throughout.

It was surprising to find that the experience of having had a partner and of having braved the majority opposition with him had failed to strengthen the individuals' independence. Questioning at the conclusion of the experiment suggested that we had overlooked an important circumstance; namely, the strong specific effect of "desertion" by the partner to the other side. We therefore changed the conditions so that the partner would simply leave the group at the proper point. (To allay suspicion it was announced in advance that he had an appointment with the dean.) In this form of the experiment, the partner's effect outlasted his presence. The errors increased after his departure, but less markedly than after a partner switched to the majority.

20   In a variant of this procedure the trials began with the majority unanimously giving correct answers. Then they gradually broke away until on the sixth trial the naive subject was alone and the group unanimously against him. As long as the subject had anyone on his side, he was almost invariably independent, but as soon as he found himself alone, the tendency to conform to the majority rose abruptly.

As might be expected, an individual's resistance to group pressure in these experiments depends to a considerable degree on how wrong the majority was. We varied the discrepancy between the standard line and the other lines systematically, with the hope of reaching a point where the error of the majority would be so glaring that every subject would repudiate it and choose independently. In this we regretfully did not succeed. Even when the difference between the lines was seven inches, there were still some who yielded to the error of the majority.

The study provides clear answers to a few relatively simple questions, and it raises many others that await investigation. We would like to know the degree of consistency of persons in situations which differ in content and structure. If consistency of independence or conformity in behavior is shown to be a fact, how is it functionally related to qualities of character and personality? In what ways is independence related to sociological or cultural conditions? Are leaders more independent than other people, or are they adept at following their followers? These and many other questions may perhaps be answerable by investigations of the type described here.

Life in society requires consensus as an indispensable condition. But consensus, to be productive, requires that each individual contribute independently out of his experience and insight. When consensus comes under the dominance of conformity, the social process is polluted and the individual at the same time surrenders the powers on which his functioning as a feeling and thinking being depends. That we have found the tendency to conformity in our society so strong that reasonably intelligent and well-meaning young people are willing to call white black is a matter of concern. It raises questions about our ways of education and about the values that guide our conduct.

Yet anyone inclined to draw too pessimistic conclusions from this report would do well to remind himself that the capacities for independence are not to be underestimated. He may also draw some consolation from a further observation: those who participated in this challenging experiment agreed nearly without exception that independence was preferable to conformity.

● Review Questions

1. What is "suggestibility"? How is this phenomenon related to social pressure?

2. Summarize the procedure and results of the Asch experiment. What conclusions does Asch draw from these results?

3. To what extent did varying the size of the majority and its unanimity affect the experimental results?

4. What distinction does Asch draw between consensus and conformity?

● Discussion and Writing Suggestions

1. Before discussing the experiment, Asch considers how easily people's opinions or attitudes may be shaped by social pressure. To what extent do you agree with this conclusion? Write a short paper on this subject, drawing upon examples from your own experience or observation or from your reading.

2. Do the results of this experiment surprise you? Or do they confirm facts about human behavior that you had already suspected, observed, or experienced? Explain, in two or three paragraphs. Provide examples, relating these examples to features of the Asch experiment.

3. Frequently, the conclusions drawn from a researcher's experimental results are challenged on the basis that laboratory conditions do not accurately reflect the complexity of human behavior. Asch draws certain conclusions about the degree to which individuals are affected by group pressures based on an experiment involving subjects choosing matching line lengths. To what extent, if any, do you believe that these conclusions lack validity because the behavior at the heart of the experiment is too dissimilar to real-life situations of group pressure on the individual? Support your opinions with examples.

4. We are all familiar with the phenomenon of "peer pressure." To what extent do Asch's experiments demonstrate the power of peer pressure? To what extent do you think that other factors may be at work? Explain, providing examples.

5. Asch's experiments, conducted in the early 1950s, involved groups of "seven to nine young men, all college students." To what extent do you believe that the results of a similar experiment would be different today? To what extent might they be different if the subjects had included women as well and subjects of various ages, from children to middle-aged people to older people? To what extent do you believe that the social class or culture of the subjects might have an impact upon the experimental results? Support your opinions with examples and logical reasoning. (Beware, however, of overgeneralizing, based upon insufficient evidence.)

PRISONER AND GUARD: THE STANFORD EXPERIMENT

As well known—and as controversial—as the Milgram obedience experiments, the Stanford Prison Experiment (1973) raises troubling questions about the ability of individuals to resist authoritarian or obedient roles, if the social setting requires these roles. Philip G. Zimbardo, professor of psychology at Stanford University, set out to study the process by which prisoners and guards "learn" to become compliant and authoritarian, respectively. To find subjects for the experiment, Zimbardo placed an advertisement in a local newspaper:

> Male college students needed for psychological study of prison life. $15 per day for 1–2 weeks beginning Aug. 14. For further information & applications, come to Room 248, Jordan Hall, Stanford U.

The ad drew 75 responses. From these, Zimbardo and his colleagues selected 21 college-age men, half of whom would become "prisoners" in the experiment, the other half "guards." The elaborate role-playing scenario, planned for two weeks, had to be cut short due to the intensity of subjects' responses. You will find numerous video accounts of the experiment online. View one or more lasting longer than twenty minutes to gain a clear (and perhaps uncomfortable) sense of how intensely students responded to playacting at being prisoners and guards:

Go to: Google.com or Bing.com

Search terms: "zimbardo prison experiment documentary"

● Review Questions

1. What was Zimbardo's primary goal in undertaking the prison experiment?

2. Who were the subjects of this experiment? What was their initial psychological state at beginning the experiment?

3. Describe the process by which subjects became prisoners or guards.

4. What psychological relationships developed between prisoners and guards?

5. What was the result of the prison "riot"?

6. Why did prisoners have no respect for each other or for themselves?

7. What are some of the lessons learned by participants (including Zimbardo) in this experiment?

● Discussion and Writing Suggestions

1. Write about your visceral, "gut" reaction on watching the video(s). How did what you watch make you feel?

2. You may have thought, before watching the video, that being a prisoner is a physical fact, not a psychological state. What are the differences between these two perspectives?

3. To what extent do you believe that ethical behavior is an internal state, determined by one's upbringing and considered view of the world—and that a truly ethical person's behavior cannot be so readily changed as was the behavior of subjects in the prison experiment?

4. Zimbardo has written (in the *New York Times*, April 8, 1973) that at the beginning of the experiment each of the "prisoner" subjects "was completely confident of his ability to endure whatever the prison had to offer for the full two-week experimental period." Had you been a subject, would you have been so confident, prior to the experiment? Given what you've learned of the experiment, do you think you would have psychologically "become" a prisoner or guard if you had been selected for one of these roles? (And if not, what makes you so sure?)

5. Identify two passages in the video: one that surprised you relating to the prisoners and one that surprised you relating to the guards. Write a paragraph

explaining your response to each. Now read the two passages in light of each other. Do you see any patterns underlying your responses?

6. Zimbardo claims that the implications of his research matter deeply. How so? Do you agree?

7. Consider the results of the Zimbardo experiment. The people giving the orders in that experiment did not rise to the top by virtue of their talents or their behavior. Instead, they were randomly selected to be either guards or prisoners. Given this circumstance, to what extent does the Zimbardo experiment still bear out some of the findings about authority figures reported by Lehrer and Lessing?

SYNTHESIS ACTIVITIES

1. To what extent do you believe that ethical behavior is a stable, internal state, determined by one's upbringing and essential moral character—and that a truly ethical person's behavior could not be so readily changed by situations as were the behaviors of subjects in the Milgram and mock-prison experiments? Write a synthesis that explains the power of situations, as distinct from individual conscience, to influence a person's behavior. Use at least one example of a particular situation. Draw on the conclusions of the four experiments reported in this chapter: the Good Samaritan experiment, as related by Ross and Nisbett; the line drawing experiments of Asch; the obedience experiments of Milgram; and the mock-prison experiment at Stanford. Refer as well to "The Power Trip" by Jonah Lehrer.

2. The outcomes of the experiments reported on in this chapter—Ross and Nisbett call them "empirical parables"—defy common sense: One would expect passersby to help a man slumped in a doorway; one would not expect people, ordered by a researcher, to inflict what they thought were painful electric shocks on others. One would expect people to believe the evidence of their eyes and insist that one line was longer than another; one would not expect college students to take on the roles of guard and prisoner so exuberantly that an experiment would need to be canceled for fear of harm to participants. Ross and Nisbett suggest that experiments such as these bring us a "hard-won ignorance." What is so valuable about such "ignorance"? Write a synthesis arguing that, at least with respect to human behavior, "common sense" may not be a dependable guide.

3. Reread Doris Lessing's "Group Minds." In this chapter, you have become familiar with some of the experiments in social psychology that she drew on in making her point that we must use the knowledge of social science to advance as a species. As Lessing suggests, we have gained information from social science, on the one hand; and on the other, we have ample evidence that people continue behaving in ways that prove we have learned little from landmark studies of obedience. Write a critique of Lessing. Is she asking too much—that we can actually progress as a species?

4. Ross and Nisbett observe (¶ 2, p. 627) that the experience of graduate students in social psychology can be "intellectually wrenching." Explain how this might be so, based on the four experiments you have read about in this chapter: (1) the "Good Samaritan" experiment, as reported by Ross and Nisbett; (2) Milgram; (3) the mock-prison experiment; and (4) Asch. How might such experiments upset some people? Consider one potentially upsetting conclusion to be drawn from the experiments by philosopher Gilbert Harman: "It seems that ordinary attributions of character traits to people are often deeply misguided and it may even be the case that there is no such thing as character, no ordinary character traits of the sort people think there are, none of the usual moral virtues and vices." Why might such a claim prove "emotionally wrenching" to some people? Does it to you?

5. What is a "group mind"? Write an explanatory paper that defines the term. As you develop and discuss elements of your definition, refer to the selections by Lessing and Asch and also to the mock-prison experiment at Stanford.

6. Milgram writes that "perhaps the most fundamental lesson of our study [is that] ordinary people, simply doing their jobs, and without any particular hostility on their part, can become agents in a terrible destructive process." Using this statement as a principle, analyze several situations recounted in this chapter, or perhaps some outside this chapter, of which you are aware because of your studies, your reading, and possibly even your own experience. Draw upon not only Milgram, but also Asch, the mock-prison experiment, Fromm, and Lehrer.

7. Doris Lessing argues that children need to be taught how to disobey so they can recognize and avoid situations that give rise to harmful obedience. David Brooks argues that we may need to "relearn the art of following." Taken as a pair, Lessing and Brooks present two ends of a continuum upon which civilization is built: that is, upon our following leaders (obeying them and their laws) and resisting leaders (disobeying them). If you were the curriculum coordinator for your local school system, how would you teach children the "art" of responsible obedience and disobedience? What would be your curriculum? What homework would you assign? What class projects? What field trips? One complicated part of your job would be to train children to understand the difference between *responsible* disobedience and anarchy. What is the difference?

   Take up these questions in a paper that draws on both your experiences as a student and your understanding of the selections in this chapter. Points that you might want to consider in developing the paper: defining overly obedient children; appropriate classroom behavior for responsibly disobedient children, as opposed to inappropriate behavior; reading lists; homework assignments; field trips; class projects.

8. A certain amount of obedience is a given in society. Stanley Milgram and others observe that social order—civilization itself—would not be possible unless individuals were willing to surrender a portion of their autonomy to the state. David Brooks emphasizes the importance, and the paradoxes, of what he calls "followership." Allowing that we all are obedient (we must be), define the point at which obedience to a figure of authority becomes dangerous.

As you develop your definition, consider the ways you might use the work of authors in this chapter and their definitions of acceptable and unacceptable levels of obedience. Do you agree with the ways in which others have drawn the line between reasonable and dangerous obedience? What examples from current stories in the news or from your own experience can you draw on to test various definitions?

9. Describe a situation in which you were faced with a moral dilemma of whether or not to obey a figure of authority. After describing the situation and the action you took (or didn't take), analyze your behavior in light of any two readings in this chapter. (Take a hard look at the Brooks selection and the principles implicit in what he calls paradoxes of power and of "followership." Also consider Fromm and Lessing.) You might consider a straightforward, four-part structure for your paper: (1) your description; (2) your discussion, in light of source A; (3) your discussion, in light of source B; and (4) your conclusion, an overall appraisal of your behavior.

10. In response to the question "Why is man so prone to obey and why is it so difficult for him to disobey?" Erich Fromm suggests that obedience lets people identify with the powerful and invites feelings of safety. Disobedience is psychologically more difficult and requires an act of courage (see ¶s 13 and 14). Solomon Asch notes that the tendency to conformity is generally stronger than the tendency to independence. In a synthesis that draws on these two sources, explore the interplay of *fear* and its opposite, *courage*, in relation to obedience. To prevent the paper from becoming too abstract, direct your attention repeatedly to a single case, the details of which will help to keep your focus. This case may be based upon a particular event from your own life or the life of someone you know.

RESEARCH ACTIVITIES

1. Milgram's results, published in book form in 1974, generated enormous response (see, for instance, Ian Parker's article on Milgram in the Autumn 2000 issue of *Granta*). Research reactions to the Milgram experiments and discuss your findings. Begin with the reviews listed and excerpted in the *Book Review Digest*; also use the *Social Science Index*, the *Readers' Guide to Periodical Literature*, and newspaper indexes to locate articles, editorials, and letters to the editor on the experiments. (Note that editorials and letters are not always indexed. Letters appear within two to four weeks of the weekly magazine articles to which they refer, and within one to two weeks of newspaper articles.) What were the chief types of reactions? To what extent were the reactions favorable?

2. Milgram begins his book *Obedience to Authority* with a reference to Nazi Germany. The purpose of his experiment, in fact, was to help throw light on how the Nazi atrocities could have happened. Research the Nuremberg war crimes

tribunals following World War II. Drawing specifically on the statements of those who testified at Nuremberg, as well as those who have written about it, show how Milgram's experiments do help explain the Holocaust and other Nazi crimes. In addition to relevant articles, see Telford Taylor, *Nuremberg and Vietnam: An American Tragedy* (1970); Hannah Arendt, *Eichmann in Jerusalem: A Report on the Banality of Evil* (1963); Richard A. Falk, Gabriel Kolko, and Robert J. Lifton (Eds.), *Crimes of War* (1971).

3. Obtain a copy of the transcript of the trial of Adolf Eichmann, the Nazi official who carried out Hitler's "final solution" for the extermination of the Jews. Read also Hannah Arendt's *Eichmann in Jerusalem: A Report on the Banality of Evil*, along with the reviews of this book. Write a critique both of Arendt's book and of the reviews it received.

4. The My Lai massacre in Vietnam in 1969 was a particularly egregious case of overobedience to military authority in wartime. Show the connections between this event and Milgram's experiments. Note that Milgram himself treated the My Lai massacre in the epilogue to his *Obedience to Authority: An Experimental View* (1974).

5. Investigate the court-martial of Lt. William Calley, convicted for his role in the My Lai massacre. Discuss whether President Nixon was justified in commuting his sentence. Examine in detail the dilemmas the jury must have faced when presented with Calley's defense that he was only following orders.

6. Research the Watergate break-in of 1972 and the subsequent cover-up by Richard Nixon and members of his administration, as an example of overobedience to authority. Focus on one particular aspect of Watergate (e.g., the role of the counsel to the president, John Dean, or why the crisis was allowed to proceed to the point where it actually toppled a presidency). In addition to relevant articles, see Robert Woodward and Carl Bernstein, *All the President's Men* (1974); Leon Jaworski, *The Right and the Power: The Prosecution of Watergate* (1976); *RN: The Memoirs of Richard Nixon* (1978); John Dean, *Blind Ambition* (1976); John Sirica, *To Set the Record Straight: The Break-in, the Tapes, the Conspirators, the Pardon* (1979); Sam Ervin, *The Whole Truth: The Watergate Conspiracy* (1980); John Ehrlichman, *Witness to Power: The Nixon Years* (1982).

7. In April 2004, news broke of the systematic abuse, including beatings and sexual humiliation, by American military police of Iraqi "detainees" at Baghdad's Abu Ghraib prison. The scandal was intensified—as was outrage in the Muslim world—by graphic photographs that the soldiers had taken of these activities. A high-level American inquiry uncovered some of the following abuses:

> Punching, slapping, and kicking detainees; jumping on their naked feet... positioning a naked detainee on a MRE Box, with a sandbag on his head, and attaching wires to his fingers, toes, and penis to simulate electric torture... having sex with a female detainee.... Using military working dogs (without muzzles) to intimidate and frighten detainees, and in at least one case biting and severely injuring a detainee.... Breaking chemical lights and pouring the

phosphoric liquid on detainees.... Beating detainees with a broom handle and a chair.... Sodomizing a detainee with a chemical light and perhaps a broom stick.

In the days following, many commentators noted the similarities between the Abu Ghraib guards' behavior and the behavior of some of the subjects in the Milgram and prison experiments.

Research the Abu Ghraib scandal; then write a paper comparing and contrasting what happened in the Baghdad prison with what happened in the prison experiment at Stanford—and possibly also in Milgram's electric shock experiments. Focus not only on what happened, but also on *why* it may have happened.

8. Examine conformity as a social phenomenon in some particular area. For example, you may choose to study conformity as it exists among schoolchildren, adolescent peer groups, social clubs or associations, or businesspeople. You may want to draw upon your sociology or social psychology textbooks and such classic studies as William H. Whyte's *The Organization Man* (1956) or David Riesman's *The Lonely Crowd* (1950), or focus upon more recent books and articles, such as Rosabeth Moss Kantor's *A Tale of "O": On Being Different in an Organization* (1980) and John Goldhammer's 1996 book *Under the Influence: The Destructive Effects of Group Dynamics* (1996). You may also find enlightening some fictional treatments of conformity, such as Sinclair Lewis's *Babbitt* (1922), Sloan Wilson's *The Man in the Gray Flannel Suit* (1950), and Herman Wouk's *The Caine Mutiny: A Novel of World War II* (1951). What are the main factors creating the urge to conform among the particular group you are examining? What kinds of forces may be able to counteract conformity?

9. At the outset of his article, Stanley Milgram refers to imaginative works revolving around the issue of obedience to authority: the story of Abraham and Isaac; three of Plato's dialogues, "Apology," "Crito," and "Phaedo"; and the story of Antigone (dramatized by both the fifth-century BC Athenian Sophocles and the twentieth-century Frenchman Jean Anouilh). Many other fictional works deal with obedience to authority—for example, George Orwell's *1984* (1949), Herman Wouk's novel *The Caine Mutiny* (and his subsequent play *The Caine Mutiny Court Martial*), and Shirley Jackson's "The Lottery." Check with your instructor, with a librarian, and with such sources as the *Short Story Index* to locate other imaginative works on this theme. Write a paper discussing the various ways in which the subject has been treated in fiction and drama. To ensure coherence, draw comparisons and contrasts among works showing the connections and variations on the theme of obedience to authority.

Video Links

Following is a list of online videos that we hope will enhance your understanding and enjoyment of the subjects treated in this book. Most, if not all, of these videos are available on YouTube <YouTube.com>. Using the indicated search terms on YouTube (or Google or Bing, if the videos are located elsewhere on the Web) will allow you to access these and, in many cases, numerous related videos. Note: In YouTube you may need to skip over the "Featured Videos" that sometimes appear first on the list of "hits" in order to get to the target video.

Note: Because Web content frequently changes without warning, not all of the listed videos may be available when you attempt to access them. It is possible that errant searches may lead to other videos with objectionable content. Such videos, as well as user-submitted comments under videos do not reflect the views of the authors or of Pearson Publishing.

To cite these videos in a paper, use the format for online videos. Thus:

"Climate Change." *American Association for the Advancement of Science*. YouTube, n.d. Web. 26 Jan. 2008.

Chapter 1: Summary

Alan Blinder on Free Trade and Outsourcing
   YouTube search terms: "blinder outsourcing"

Chapter 2: Critical Reading and Critique

Save Constellation: Let's Go to the Moon, Mars, and Beyond!
   YouTube search terms: "save constellation moon"
Obama Ends Space Flight for a Decade
   YouTube search terms: "obama ends space flight"
Preserving Human Space Travel and Colorado Jobs (Senator Mark Udall)
   YouTube search terms: "preserving space travel udall"

Chapter 4: Explanatory Synthesis

The Space Elevator
   YouTube search terms: "space elevator" (multiple videos)
Michio Kaku on the Space Elevator
   YouTube search terms: "kaku using space elevator"
Space Elevator: Royal Institution Christmas lecture by Mark Miodownik,
   British material science engineer
   YouTube search terms: "can we build space elevator royal"
Space Elevator: Science Fair project
   YouTube search terms: "google science fair 2012 elevator"

Chapter 5: Argument Synthesis

Virginia Tech Shooting
YouTube search terms: "virginia tech shooting footage"; "virginia tech shooting confession"

Chapter 7: Artificial Intelligence

I.B.M.'s Watson vs. Humans
YouTube search terms: "watsons supercomputer destroys"
Michio Kaku (Professor of Theoretical Physics at City University of New York) on A.I.
YouTube search terms: "kaku artificial intelligence"
Ray Kuzweil on A.I.
YouTube search terms: "singularity of ray kurzweil"
Artificial Intelligence Lab at M.I.T.
Google search terms: "artificial intelligence videos howstuffworks"
Singularity Institute for Artificial Intelligence
YouTube search terms: "singularity institute intelligence"
Self-Aware Robots
YouTube search terms: "lipson robots self aware"
When Artificial Intelligence Becomes Creepy
YouTube search terms: "uncanny valley"
Metropolis (1927) (early film vision of A.I.)
YouTube search terms: "metropolis 1927 hd trailer"
Open the Pod Bay Doors, Hal! (scene from Stanley Kubrick's *2001: A Space Odyssey*)
YouTube search terms: "hal do you read me"
Trailer to Steven Spielberg's *A.I.*:
YouTube search terms: "a.i. trailer"

Chapter 8: Fairy Tales: A Closer Look at "Cinderella"

Disney's Cinderella: "A Dream is a Wish Your Heart Makes" (sing along)
YouTube search terms: "cinderella sing along dream wish heart"
"Cinderella's Hope": Mandy More
YouTube search terms: "disney and other only hope mandy moore"
"Cinderella": Steven Curtis Chapman
YouTube search terms: "cinderella steven curtis chapman"
Reggae Cinderella: Errol Dunkley
YouTube search terms: "errol dunkley ft stretch black cinderella"
Cinderella Opera: Rossini
YouTube search terms: "cinderella opera long center"
Cinderella Ballet: Prokofiev
YouTube search terms: "prokofiev cinderella paris opera ballet"
Cinderella on Broadway: Rodgers and Hammerstein "Impossible" (Whitney Houston)
YouTube search terms: "rodgers hammerstein cinderella impossible houston"
Movie Review: Rogers and Hammerstein's Cinderella
Youtube search terms: "rogers cinderella whitney cherish movie review"
Trailer for *Another Cinderella Story*
YouTube search terms: "another cinderella story official trailer"
Trailer for *Ever After*
YouTube search terms: "ever after trailer"

Chapter 9: The Roar of the Tiger Mom

Amy Chua: "Didn't Expect This Level of Intensity"
YouTube search terms: "amy chua interview"
Child of Tiger Mom Speaks Out
YouTube search terms: "child tiger mom speaks"
Tiger Mom Responds to Uproar (PBS)
YouTube search terms: "amy chua responds uproar"
Amy Chua Promotes *Battle Hymn of the Tiger Mother*
YouTube search terms: "battle hymn tiger mother" (2:55 clip)
Amy Chua on "Today" Show
YouTube search terms: "amy chua today" (5:11 clip)
The Myth of China's Tiger Mothers
YouTube search terms: "tiger mothers myth"

Chapter 10: The Changing Landscape of Work in the Twenty-first Century

The New World of Work (statistics set to music)
YouTube search terms: "the new world of work"
Three Eras of Globalization
YouTube search terms: "thomas friedman's three eras of globalization"
The Virtual Office (ABC News Report)
YouTube search terms: "abc future workplace no office"
Generation Next in the Workplace
YouTube search terms: "generation next the workplace"
ABC News: Myth: Outsourcing Bad for America—Busted
YouTube search terms: "abc 20/20 outsourcing bad"
Outsource This (skit with Jason Alexander)
YouTube search terms: "outsource this jason alexander"
People in China Starving for Your Job
YouTube search terms: "tom peters: people in china starving for your job"
Educate for a Creative Society
YouTube search terms: "tom peters educate creative"

Chapter 11: Have You Heard This? The Latest on Rumor

Norman Rockwell's "The Gossips" (music: African Head Charge—"Off the Beaten Track")
YouTube search terms: "gossips rockwell"
A Conversation with Nicholos diFonzo on Rumor Psychology
YouTube search terms: "difonzo rumor"
How to Spread a Rumor
YouTube search terms: "how to spread rumor"
Paul is Dead? (Beatles rumor)
YouTube search terms: "paul is dead" (multiple videos)
Celebrity Death Rumors
YouTube search terms: "celebrity death rumors"
WWII: Private SNAFU Rumors
YouTube search terms: "world war 2 rumors"

Gang Members Killing Motorists in L.A.?
  YouTube search terms: "gang headlights rumor"
Alligators in the Sewers? (MonsterQuest series)
  YouTube search terms: "gators sewers" (multiple videos)
Is Obama a Muslim?
  YouTube search terms: "obama muslim debate"
Obama Dispels "Outlandish" Health Care Rumors
  YouTube search terms: "obama outlandish health care rumors"

Chapter 12: The Pursuit of Happiness

A Harvard Psychologist on Happiness
  Google or Bing Search terms: "ted dan gilbert happiness"
A Buddhist Monk on Happiness
  YouTube search terms: "matthieu ricard habits of happiness"
Gross National Happiness
  YouTube search terms: "gross national happiness bhutan"
Measuring Happiness in Business
  YouTube search terms: "chip conley measuring what makes life worthwhile"
Martin Seligman on Positive Psychology
  YouTube search terms: "seligman what makes you happy"
Happiness and Flow
  YouTube search terms: "mihaly creativity fulfillment and flow"
Philosophy and Happiness from *The Consolations of Philosophy*, Alain de Botton
  YouTube search terms: "philosophy: a guide to happiness epicurus"

Chapter 13: Green Power

Climate Change

Climate Change
  YouTube search terms: "aaas climate change"
Frontline: "Heat" [trailer for PBS program on climate change]
  YouTube search terms: "frontline heat pbs"
Climate Change (YouTube) [British perspective]
  YouTube search terms: "climate challenge greenhouse effect"
Al Gore Goes Green for "An Inconvenient Truth" (Speech at Constitution Hall, Washington, DC, July 17, 2008)
  YouTube search terms: "gore green inconvenient"
Trailer for *An Inconvenient Truth*
  YouTube search terms: "gore goes green inconvenient truth"

Nuclear Power

Nuclear Power: How it Works
  YouTube search terms: "nuclear reactor how it works"
Nuclear Power Station (animated graphic)
  YouTube search terms: "nuclear power station"
Nuclear Power Generator (live action and animation)
  YouTube search terms: "nuclear power generator"

YouTube Debate (Democratic Presidential Candidates): Nuclear Power?"
   YouTube search terms: "youtube debate nuclear"
Fukushima Nuclear Disaster
   YouTube search terms: "fukushima" (multiple videos)

Wind Power

How Do Wind Turbines Work? (3D animation)
   YouTube search terms: "how do wind turbines work 3d"
Energy 101: Wind Turbines
   YouTube search terms: "energy 101 wind"
National Renewable Energy Laboratory's (NREL's) National Wind Power Technology Center
   YouTube search terms: "windpower national"
Rooftop Wind Turbine
   YouTube search terms: "wind power rooftop" (multiple videos)

Solar Power

Energy 101: Solar
   YouTube search terms: "energy 101 solar power"
How Does Solar Energy Work? (EnfinityChannel animation)
   YouTube Search terms: "how does solar energy work"
Solar Power 101: How Does Sunlight Turn into Electricity? (Sierra Solar Systems)
   YouTube Search terms: "solar power 101"
Solar Energy Breakthrough in Negev Desert, Israel
   YouTube search terms: "solar power breakthrough negev"

Electric Cars

Who Killed the Electric Car?
   YouTube search terms: "who killed electric car documentary"
Electric Car: Bye Bye, Petroleum (WGN TV news report)
   YouTube search terms: "bye bye petroleum"
Gas vs. Hybrid
   YouTube search terms: "debate gas cars vs electric hybrid"; "electric car debate ecovelocity"
The Chevrolet Volt Concept
   YouTube search terms: "chevrolet volt concept"
Chevrolet Volt Test Drive
   YouTube search terms: "volt mule test drive"
The Unveiling of the Tesla Motors Electric Car
   YouTube search terms: "unveiling tesla electric"
3-Wheeled Oddball: The Aptera Electric Car
   YouTube search terms: "3 wheeled oddball"
Shai Agassi on How to Electrify America's Cars
   YouTube search terms: "shai agassi electrify"
Bringing the Electric Car to the World
   YouTube search terms: "bringing electric car world"

Chapter 14: New and Improved: Six Decades of Advertising

A Conversation about Advertising with David Ogilvy (celebrated ad man interviewed by
   John Crichton, 1977)
   YouTube search terms: "conversation advertising ogilvy"

David Ogilvy: Essentials (the great campaigns of legendary ad man)
YouTube search terms: "ogilvy essentials"
Mad Men trailer
YouTube search terms: "mad men meet don draper"
Psychology and Advertising
YouTube search terms: "psychology and advertising"
Psychological Advertising
YouTube search terms: "psychological advertising"
What Psychological Tricks Do They Use?"
YouTube search terms: "advertising psychological tricks"
How to be Creative in Advertising
YouTube search terms: "creative advertising"

Chapter 15: Obedience to Authority

Milgram re-enactment
YouTube search terms: "milgram obedience authority experiment 2009 1/3, 2/3, 3/3"
Asch Conformity Experiment
YouTube search terms: "asch conformity experiment"
Zimbardo on the "Lucifer Effect"
YouTube search terms: "philip zimbardo lucifer effect part 2"
Shirley Jackson, "The Lottery"
YouTube search terms: "the lottery part 1 of 2"; "the lottery part 2 of 2"

Credits

Thomas. "What Really Cost Chris Dussold His Job?" from Chronicle of Higher Education, February 10, 2009. The Chronicle of Higher Education by Editorial Projects for Education, Inc. Copyright 2009. Reproduced with permission of Chronicle of Higher Education, Inc. in the format Textbook via Copyright Clearance Center. **Page 356:** Salmans, Sandra, "Fighting That Old Devil Rumor" from The Saturday Evening Post, October 1982. Reprinted by permission. **Page 363:** "Paul is Dead!" by Alan Glenn, in Michigan Today, Nov. 11, 2009, michigantoday.umich.edu. Reprinted with permission. **Page 365:** Express Newspapers/AP Images. **Page 375:** "It's Clear That It's Unclear," from The Watercooler Effect by Nicholas DiFonzo, copyright © 2008 by Nicholas DiFonzo. Used by permission of Avery Publishing, an imprint of Penguin Group (USA) Inc. **Page 388:** Sunstein, Cass. From On Rumors: How Falsehoods Spread, Why We Believe Them, What Can Be Done, Farrar, Straus, and Giroux, 2009. **Page 397:** Reputation Management: The Key to Successful Public Relations and Corporate Communication by Doorley, John. Copyright 2007. Reproduced with permission of Taylor and Francis Group LLC-Books in the format Textbook via Copyright Clearance Center.

CHAPTER 12

Page 410: "Three Conceptions of Happiness" from Happiness by Lynne McFall, New York: Peter Lang, 1989. Reprinted with permission. **Page 413:** Kingwell, Mark. Republished with permission of Alison Bond Literary Agency from *In Pursuit of Happiness: Better Living from Plato to Prozac*, Crown, 1998. Permission conveyed through Copyright Clearance Center, Inc. **Page 417:** Seligman, Martin E.P., Acacia C. Parks, and Tracy Steen, "A Balanced Psychology and a Full Life" from Philosophical Transactions of the Royal Society London B, 2004. **Page 422:** Senior, Jennifer. "Some Dark Thoughts on Happiness" from New York Magazine, July 9, 2006. Reprinted by permission. **Page 431:** Csikszentmihalyi, Milhaly. From Finding Flow: The Psychology of Engagement with Everyday Life. Copyright © 1998 Mihaly Csikszentmihalyi. Reprinted by permission of Basic Books, a member of the Perseus Books Group. **Page 437:** Reprinted from *Journal of Consumer Psychology*, Dunn, W. Elizabeth, Daniel T. Gilbert, and Timothy D. Wilson, "If Money Doesn't Make You Happy, Then You Probably Aren't Spending It Right," Copyright © 2011 with permission from Elsevier. **Page 451:** Reprinted with the permission of Scribner, a Division of Simon & Schuster, Inc., from The Secrets of Happiness by Richard Schoch. Copyright © 2006 by Richard Schoch. All rights reserved. **Page 459:** Jane Kenyon, "Happiness" from COLLECTED POEMS. Copyright © 2005 by the Estate of Jane Kenyon. Reprinted with the permission of The Permissions Company, Inc., on behalf of Graywolf Press, Minneapolis, Minnesota, www.graywolfpress.org. **Page 461:** Tuan, Yi-Fu. THE GOOD LIFE. © 1986 by the Regents of the University of Wisconsin System. Reprinted by permission of The University of Wisconsin Press. **Page 469:** Pages 97–103 from Zen and the Art of Motorcycle Maintenance by Robert Pirsig. Copyright © 1974 by Robert M. Pirsig. Reprinted by permission of HarperCollins Publishers.

CHAPTER 13

Page 483: Excerpts from "Overview and Introduction" from "National Security Consequences of U.S. Oil Dependence," Independent Task Force Report No. 58. (Oct. 2006). Copyright (c) 2006 by The Council on Foreign Relations Press. Reprinted with permission. **Page 488:** Copyright © 2009 Robert Bryce, Reprinted by permission of PublicAffairs, a member of the Perseus Books Group. **Page 500:** "Why I Still Support Nuclear Power, Even After Fukushima" by William Tucker from The Wall Street Journal, April 23, 2011. Reprinted with permission of the author. **Page 505:** Maria Dickerson. "State Solar Power Plans are as Big as all Outdoors" from The Los Angeles Times, December 3, 2008. Copyright © 2008 Los Angeles Times. Reprinted with permission. **Page 506:** "How Solar Energy Works", Illustration by Maury Aaseng. Reprinted with permission. **Page 510:** Plumer, Brad. "Solar Is Getting Cheaper, But How Far Can it Go?" from The Washington Post, November 7, 2011. Reprinted with permission of the author. **Page 514:** "The Island in the Wind" by Elizabeth Kolbert, originally published in The New Yorker, July 7, 2008. Reprinted by permission of the author. **Page 515:** Stevens, Doug. "Catching the Wind" from the Los Angeles Times, March 1, 2009. Copyright © 2009 Los Angeles Times. Reprinted with permission. **Page 521:** "Wind Power Puffery" by H. Sterling Burnett, published in The Washington Times, Feb 4, 2004. Reprinted by permission of the author. **Page 525:** "The Great Electric Car Experiment," from *The Quest: Energy, Security, and the Remaking of the Modern World* by Daniel Yergin, copyright © 2011 by Daniel Yergin. Used by permission of The Penguin Press, a division of Penguin Group (USA) Inc.

Index

QUICK INDEX: APA DOCUMENTATION BASICS

APA In-Text Citations in Brief

When quoting or paraphrasing, place a parenthetical citation in your sentence that includes the author, publication year, and page or paragraph number.

Direct quotation, author and publication year not mentioned in sentence

Research suggests that punishing a child "promotes only momentary compliance" (Berk & Ellis, 2002, p. 383).

Paraphrase, author and year mentioned in the sentence

Berk and Ellis (2002) suggest that punishment may be ineffective (p. 383).

Direct quotation from Internet source

Others have noted a rise in "problems that mimic dysfunctional behaviors" (Spivek, Jones, & Connelly, 2006, Introduction section, para. 3).

APA References List in Brief

On a separate, concluding page titled "References," alphabetize sources by author, providing full bibliographic information for each.

Article from a Journal

Conclude your entry with the digital object identifier—the article's unique reference number. When a DOI is not available and you have located the article on the Web, conclude with *Retrieved from* and the URL of the home page. For articles located through a database such as *LexisNexis*, do not list the database in your entry.

Article (with volume and issue numbers) located via print or database

Ivanenko, A., & Massie, C. (2006). Assessment and management of sleep disorders in children. *Psychiatric Times, 23*(11), 90–95.

Article (with DOI and volume number) located via print or database

Jones, K. L. (1986). Fetal alcohol syndrome. *Pediatrics in Review*, 8, 122–126. doi:10.1542/10.1542/pir.8-4-122

Article located via Web

Ivanenko, A., & Massie, C. (2006). Assessment and management of sleep disorders in children. *Psychiatric Times, 23*(11), 90–95. Retrieved from http://www.psychiatrictimes.com

Article from a Magazine

Article (with volume and issue numbers) located via print or database

Landi, A. (2010, January). Is beauty in the brain of the beholder? *ARTnews, 109*(1), 19–21.

Article located via Web

Landi, A. (2010, January). Is beauty in the brain of the beholder? *ARTnews, 109*(1). Retrieved from http://www.artnews.com

Article from a Newspaper

Article located via print or database

Wakabayashi, D. (2010, January 7). Sony pins future on a 3-D revival. *The Wall Street Journal*, pp. A1, A14.

Article located via Web

Wakabayashi, D. (2010, January 7). Sony pins future on a 3-D revival. *The Wall Street Journal*. Retrieved from http://www.wsj.com

Book

Book located via print

Mansfield, R. S., & Busse, T. V. (1981). *The psychology of creativity and discovery: Scientists and their work. Chicago*, IL: Nelson-Hall.

Book located via Web

Freud, S. (1920). *Dream psychology: Psychoanalysis for beginners* (M. D. Elder, Trans.). Retrieved from http://www.gutenberg.org

Selection from an edited book

Halberstam, D. (2002). Who we are. In S. J. Gould (Ed.), *The best American essays 2002* (pp. 124–136). New York, NY: Houghton Mifflin.

Later edition

Samuelson, P., & Nordhaus, W. D. (2005). *Economics* (18th ed.). Boston, MA: McGraw-Hill Irwin.

QUICK INDEX: MLA DOCUMENTATION BASICS

MLA In-text Citations in Brief

When referring to a source, use parentheses to enclose a page number reference. Include the author's name if you do not mention it in your sentence.

> From the beginning, the AIDS test has been "mired in controversy" (Bayer 101).

Or, if you name the author in the sentence:

> Bayer claims the AIDS test has been "mired in controversy" (101).

MLA Works Cited List in Brief

At the end of the paper, on a separate page titled "Works Cited," alphabetize each cited source by author's last name. Provide full bibliographic information, as shown. State how you accessed the source, via print, Web, or downloaded digital file. As appropriate, precede "Web" with a database name (e.g., *LexisNexis*) or the title of a Web site and a publisher. Follow "Web" with your date of access. Note the use of punctuation and italics.

In MLA style, the medium by which you access a source (print, Web, database, download) determines its Works Cited format.

Magazine or Newspaper Article

Article accessed via print magazine or newspaper

> Packer, George. "The Choice." *New Yorker* 28 Jan. 2008: 28-35. Print.
>
> Warner, Judith. "Goodbye to All This." *New York Times* 18 Dec. 2009, late ed.: A27. Print.

Article (version exists in print) accessed via downloaded file

> Packer, George. "The Choice." *New Yorker* 28 Jan. 2008: 28-35. AZW file.
>
> Warner, Judith. "Goodbye to All This." *New York Times* 18 Dec. 2009, late ed.: A27. PDF file.

Article (version exists in print) accessed via database

> Packer, George. "The Choice." *New Yorker* 28 Jan. 2008: 28-35. *Academic Search Premier*. Web. 12 Mar. 2010.
>
> Warner, Judith. "Goodbye to All This." *New York Times* 18 Dec. 2009, late ed.: A27. *LexisNexis*. Web. 14 Jan. 2010.

Article (version exists in print) accessed via Web

Packer, George. "The Choice." *New Yorker.com*. CondéNet, 28 Jan. 2008. Web. 12 Mar. 2010.

Warner, Judith. "Goodbye to All This." *New York Times*. New York Times, 18 Dec. 2009. Web. 14 Jan. 2010.

Scholarly Article

Scholarly article accessed via print journal

Ivanenko, Anna, and Clifford Massie. "Assessment and Management of Sleep Disorders in Children." *Psychiatric Times* 23.11 (2006): 90-95. Print.

Scholarly article (version exists in print) accessed via downloaded file

Ivanenko, Anna, and Clifford Massie. "Assessment and Management of Sleep Disorders in Children." *Psychiatric Times* 23.11 (2006): 90-95. PDF file.

Scholarly article (version exists in print) accessed via database

Ivanenko, Anna, and Clifford Massie. "Assessment and Management of Sleep Disorders in Children." *Psychiatric Times* 23.11 (2006): 90-95. *Academic OneFile*. Web. 3 Nov. 2010.

Scholarly article (version exists in print) accessed via Web

Ivanenko, Anna, and Clifford Massie. "Assessment and Management of Sleep Disorders in Children." *Psychiatric Times*. United Business Media, 1 Oct. 2006. Web. 3 Nov. 2010.

Scholarly article from an e-journal that has no print equivalent

Blackwood, Jothany. "Coaching Educational Leaders." *Academic Leadership*: The *Online Journal* 7.3 (2009): n. pag. Web. 2 Feb. 2010.

Book

Book accessed via print

James, William. *The Varieties of Religious Experience: A Study in Human Nature; Being the Gifford Lectures on Natural Religion Delivered at Edinburgh in 1901–1902*. New York: Longmans, 1902. Print.

Book (version exists in print) accessed via downloaded file

James, William. *The Varieties of Religious Experience: A Study in Human Nature; Being the Gifford Lectures on Natural Religion Delivered at Edinburgh in 1901–1902*. New York: Longmans, 1902. MOBI file.

Book (version exists in print) accessed via Web or database

James, William. *The Varieties of Religious Experience: A Study in Human Nature; Being the Gifford Lectures on Natural Religion Delivered at Edinburgh in 1901–1902*. New York: Longmans, 1902. *U. of Virginia Etext Center*. Web. 12 Jan. 2010.

James, William. *The Varieties of Religious Experience: A Study in Human Nature; Being the Gifford Lectures on Natural Religion Delivered at Edinburgh in 1901–1902*. New York: Longmans, 1902. *ACLS Humanities E-Book*. Web. 12 Mar. 2010.

Online book that has no print equivalent

Langer, Maria. *Mastering Microsoft Word. Designprovideo.com*. Nonlinear Educating, 2009. Web. 23 Jan. 2010.

Web-Only Publication (Content Created for and Published on the Web)

Home page

Boucher, Marc, ed. Home page. *The Space Elevator Reference. Spaceelevator.com*. SpaceRef Interactive, 2009. Web. 17 Dec. 2009.

Web-based article on a larger site

Landau, Elizabeth. "Stem Cell Therapies for Hearts Inching Closer to Wide Use." *CNN.com*. Cable News Network, 18 Dec. 2009. Web. 14 Jan. 2010.

White, Veronica. "Gian Lorenzo Bernini." *Heilbrunn Timeline of Art History*. Metropolitan Museum of Art, New York, 2009. Web. 18 Mar. 2010.

Blog

Lubber, Mindy. "The Climate Treaty Announcement." *Climate Experts' Forum—Copenhagen*. Financial Times, 19 Dec. 2009. Web. 22 Dec. 2009.

CHECKLIST FOR WRITING SYNTHESES

- **Consider your purpose in writing.**
- **Select and carefully read your sources,** according to your purpose.
- **Take notes as you read.**
- **Formulate a thesis.**
- **Decide how you will use your source material.**
- **Develop an organizational plan,** according to your thesis.
- **Draft the topic sentences for the main sections.**
- **Write the first draft** of your synthesis, following your organizational plan.
- **Document your sources.**
- **Revise your synthesis,** inserting transitional words and phrases where necessary.

CHECKLIST FOR WRITING ANALYSES

- **Summarize** the object, event, or behavior to be analyzed.
- **Introduce and summarize** the key definition or principle that will form the basis of your analysis.
- **Analyze your topic:** Systematically apply elements of this definition or principle to parts of the activity or object under study.
- **Conclude** by stating clearly what is significant about your analysis. Having worked with a definition or principle, what new or interesting insights have you made?